CORE STATUTES ON
PROPERTY LAW 2016–17

The *palgrave core statutes* series:

Core EU Legislation	Rhona Smith & Paul Drury
Core Statutes on Commercial & Consumer Law	Graham Stephenson
Core Statutes on Company Law	Cowan Ervine
Core Statutes on Contract, Tort & Restitution	Graham Stephenson
Core Statutes on Criminal Justice & Sentencing	Martin Wasik
Core Statutes on Criminal Law	Kate Cook, Mark James & Richard Lee
Core Statutes on Employment Law	Dominique Lauterburg
Core Statutes on Evidence	Christina McAlhone
Core Statutes on Family Law	Frances Burton
Core Statutes on Intellectual Property	Margaret Dowie-Whybrow
Core Statutes on Property Law	Peter Luther & Alan Moran
Core Statutes on Public Law & Civil Liberties	Rhona Smith, Eimear Spain & Richard Glancey
Core Documents on International Law	Karen Hulme
Core Documents on European/International Human Rights	Rhona Smith

CORE STATUTES ON PROPERTY LAW 2016–17

Peter Luther & Alan Moran

 macmillan education   palgrave

First published 2016 by
PALGRAVE

Palgrave in the UK is an imprint of Macmillan Publishers Limited, registered in England, company number 785998, of 4 Crinan Street, London, N1 9XW.

Palgrave Macmillan in the US is a division of St Martin's Press LLC, 175 Fifth Avenue, New York, NY 10010.

Palgrave is a global imprint of the above companies and is represented throughout the world.

Palgrave® and Macmillan® are registered trademarks in the United States, the United Kingdom, Europe and other countries.

ISBN 978–1–137–60666–2

This book is printed on paper suitable for recycling and made from fully managed and sustained forest sources. Logging, pulping and manufacturing processes are expected to conform to the environmental regulations of the country of origin.

A catalogue record for this book is available from the British Library.

A catalog record for this book is available from the Library of Congress.

Printed and bound in the UK by The Lavenham Press Ltd, Suffolk.

MIX
Paper from
responsible sources
FSC
www.fsc.org FSC® C010693

PREFACE

In this twelfth edition of *Core Statutes on Property Law*, we continue the aim of previous editions of providing essential up-to-date statutory material, with no comments or annotations, for students of property law. This edition contains the same list of statutes as its predecessor, but we have updated the text to take account of statutory amendments which have come into force during the past year, principally as a consequence of the Enterprise and Regulatory Reform Act 2013, the Deregulation Act 2015, and the Small Business, Enterprise and Employment Act 2015.

We have always been very grateful for the many helpful suggestions for improvement we have received from teachers and students of property law, and we hope that they will continue to let us have their views. Once again, we would like to thank the staff at Palgrave for their continuing help and support.

We have tried to state the law as at 1 June 2016.

Peter Luther
Alan Moran

CONTENTS

Preface v

Prescription Act 1832 1
Wills Act 1837.. 3
Wills (Soldiers and Sailors) Act 1918 9
Law of Property Act 1922 9
Trustee Act 1925 11
Law of Property Act 1925.. 30
Land Registration Act 1925 99
Administration of Estates Act 1925 100
Landlord and Tenant Act 1927............................... 116
Leasehold Property (Repairs) Act 1938 118
Intestates' Estates Act 1952 120
Landlord and Tenant Act 1954............................... 122
Variation of Trusts Act 1958 137
Perpetuities and Accumulations Act 1964............... 138
Law of Property (Joint Tenants) Act 1964 142
Wills Act 1968.. 143
Law of Property Act 1969....................................... 143
Administration of Justice Act 1970 145
Matrimonial Proceedings and Property Act 1970 146
Powers of Attorney Act 1971................................. 146
Land Charges Act 1972... 147
Administration of Justice Act 1973 154
Matrimonial Causes Act 1973 155
Inheritance (Provision for Family and Dependants) Act 1975 158
Protection from Eviction Act 1977 173
Criminal Law Act 1977... 175
Limitation Act 1980 176
Senior Courts Act 1981 185
Forfeiture Act 1982.. 189
Administration of Justice Act 1982 190
Landlord and Tenant Act 1985................................ 191
Insolvency Act 1986.. 194
Landlord and Tenant Act 1988................................ 199
Law of Property (Miscellaneous Provisions) Act 1989........ 201
Access to Neighbouring Land Act 1992................... 203
Landlord and Tenant (Covenants) Act 1995............. 208
Treasure Act 1996... 221
Family Law Act 1996 224
Trusts of Land and Appointment of Trustees Act 1996 235
Human Rights Act 1998... 244
Trustee Delegation Act 1999 245
Contracts (Rights of Third Parties) Act 1999 246
Trustee Act 2000 247
Land Registration Act 2002 256
Commonhold and Leasehold Reform Act 2002......... 302
Civil Partnership Act 2004 319
Tribunals, Courts and Enforcement Act 2007 320
Perpetuities and Accumulations Act 2009................ 324

Equality Act 2010 328
Mortgage Repossessions (Protection of Tenants etc.) Act 2010 328
Charities Act 2011 329

Index 333

ALPHABETICAL LIST OF CONTENTS

Access to Neighbouring Land Act 1992. 203
Administration of Estates Act 1925 100
Administration of Justice Act 1970 145
Administration of Justice Act 1973 154
Administration of Justice Act 1982 190
Charities Act 2011 329
Civil Partnership Act 2004 319
Commonhold and Leasehold Reform Act 2002. 302
Contracts (Rights of Third Parties) Act 1999 246
Criminal Law Act 1977. 175
Equality Act 2010. 328
Family Law Act 1996 224
Forfeiture Act 1982. 189
Human Rights Act 1998. 244
Inheritance (Provision for Family and Dependants) Act 1975 158
Insolvency Act 1986. 194
Intestates' Estates Act 1952 120
Land Charges Act 1972 147
Land Registration Act 1925 99
Land Registration Act 2002 256
Landlord and Tenant Act 1927. 116
Landlord and Tenant Act 1954. 122
Landlord and Tenant Act 1985. 191
Landlord and Tenant Act 1988. 199
Landlord and Tenant (Covenants) Act 1995. 208
Law of Property Act 1922 9
Law of Property Act 1925. 30
Law of Property Act 1969. 143
Law of Property (Joint Tenants) Act 1964 142
Law of Property (Miscellaneous Provisions) Act 1989. 201
Leasehold Property (Repairs) Act 1938 118
Limitation Act 1980 176
Matrimonial Causes Act 1973 155
Matrimonial Proceedings and Property Act 1970 146
Mortgage Repossessions (Protection of Tenants etc.) Act 2010. 328
Perpetuities and Accumulations Act 1964. 138
Perpetuities and Accumulations Act 2009. 324
Powers of Attorney Act 1971. 146
Prescription Act 1832 1
Protection from Eviction Act 1977 173
Senior Courts Act 1981 185
Treasure Act 1996. 221
Tribunals, Courts and Enforcement Act 2007 320
Trustee Act 1925 11
Trustee Act 2000 247
Trustee Delegation Act 1999 245
Trusts of Land and Appointment of Trustees Act 1996 235
Variation of Trusts Act 1958 137
Wills Act 1837. 3
Wills Act 1968. 143
Wills (Soldiers and Sailors) Act 1918 9

PRESCRIPTION ACT 1832
(1832, c. 71)

1. **Claims to right of common and other profits à prendre, not to be defeated after thirty years enjoyment by merely showing the commencement; after sixty years enjoyment the right to be absolute, unless had by consent or agreement**

   No claim which may be lawfully made at the common law, by custom, prescription, or grant, to any right of common or other profit or benefit to be taken and enjoyed from or upon any land of our sovereign lord the King, or any land being parcel of the duchy of Lancaster or of the duchy of Cornwall, or of any ecclesiastical or lay person, or body corporate, except such matters and things as are herein specially provided for, and except tithes, rent, and services, shall, where such right, profit, or benefit shall have been actually taken and enjoyed by any person claiming right thereto without interruption for the full period of thirty years, be defeated or destroyed by showing only that such right, profit, or benefit was first taken or enjoyed at any time prior to such period of thirty years, but nevertheless such claim may be defeated in any other way by which the same is now liable to be defeated; and when such right, profit, or benefit shall have been so taken and enjoyed as aforesaid for the full period of sixty years, the right thereto shall be deemed absolute and indefeasible, unless it shall appear that the same was taken and enjoyed by some consent or agreement expressly made or given for that purpose by deed or writing.

2. **In claims of right of way or other easement the periods to be twenty years and forty years**

   No claim which may be lawfully made at the common law, by custom, prescription, or grant, to any way or other easement, or to any watercourse, or the use of any water, to be enjoyed or derived upon, over, or from any land or water of our said lord the King, or being parcel of the duchy of Lancaster or of the duchy of Cornwall, or being the property of any ecclesiastical or lay person, or body corporate, when such way or other matter as herein last before mentioned shall have been actually enjoyed by any person claiming right thereto without interruption for the full period of twenty years, shall be defeated or destroyed by showing only that such way or other matter was first enjoyed at any time prior to such period of twenty years, but nevertheless such claim may be defeated in any other way by which the same is now liable to be defeated; and where such way or other matter as herein last before mentioned shall have been so enjoyed as aforesaid for the full period of forty years, the right thereto shall be deemed absolute and indefeasible, unless it shall appear that the same was enjoyed by some consent or agreement expressly given or made for that purpose by deed or writing.

3. **Claim to the use of light enjoyed for 20 years**

   When the access and use of light to and for any dwelling house, workshop, or other building shall have been actually enjoyed therewith for the full period of twenty years without interruption, the right thereto shall be deemed absolute and indefeasible, any local usage or custom to the contrary notwithstanding, unless it shall appear that the same was enjoyed by some consent or agreement expressly made or given for that purpose by deed or writing.

4. **Before mentioned periods to be deemed those next before suits**

   Each of the respective periods of years hereinbefore mentioned shall be deemed and taken to be the period next before some suit or action wherein the claim or matter to which such period may relate shall have been or shall be brought into question and that no act or other matter shall be deemed to be an interruption, within the meaning of this statute, unless the same shall have been or shall be submitted to or acquiesced in for one year after the party interrupted shall have had or shall have notice thereof, and of the person making or authorizing the same to be made.

5. **In actions on the case, the claimant may allege his right generally, as at present. In pleas to trespass and certain other pleadings, the period mentioned in this Act may be alleged. Exceptions, etc. to be replied to specially**

   In all actions upon the case and other pleadings, wherein the party claiming may now by law allege his right generally, without averring the existence of such right from time immemorial, such general allegation shall still be deemed sufficient, and if the same shall be denied all and every the matters in this Act mentioned and provided, which shall be applicable to the case, shall be admissible in evidence to sustain or rebut such allegation; and that in all pleadings to actions of trespass, and in all other pleadings wherein before the passing of this Act it would have been necessary to allege the right to have existed from time immemorial, it shall be sufficient to allege the enjoyment thereof as of right by the occupiers of the tenement in respect whereof the same is claimed for and during such of the periods mentioned in this Act as may be applicable to the case, and without claiming in the name or right of the owner of the fee, as is now usually done; and if the other party shall intend to rely on any proviso, exception, incapacity, disability, contract, agreement, or other matter herein-before mentioned, or on any cause or matter of fact or of law not inconsistent with the simple fact of enjoyment, the same shall be specially alleged and set forth in answer to the allegation of the party claiming, and shall not be received in evidence on any general traverse or denial of such allegation.

6.   Presumption to be allowed in claims herein provided for

In the several cases mentioned in and provided for by this Act, no presumption shall be allowed or made in favour or support of any claim, upon proof of the exercise or enjoyment of the right or matter claimed for any less period of time or number of years than for such period or number mentioned in this Act as may be applicable to the case and to the nature of the claim.

7.   Proviso for infants, etc.

Provided also, that the time during which any person otherwise capable of resisting any claim to any of the matters before mentioned shall have been or shall be an infant, idiot, non compos mentis, feme covert, or tenant for life, or during which any action or suit shall have been pending, and which shall have been diligently prosecuted, until abated by the death of any party or parties thereto, shall be excluded in the computation of the periods herein-before mentioned, except only in cases where the right or claim is hereby declared to be absolute and indefeasible.

8.   What time to be excluded in computing the term of forty years appointed by this Act

Provided always, that when any land or water upon, over, or from which any such way or other convenient watercourse or use of water shall have been or shall be enjoyed or derived hath been or shall be held under or by virtue of any term of life, or any term of years exceeding three years from the granting thereof, the time of the enjoyment of any such way or other matter as herein last before mentioned, during the continuance of such terms, shall be excluded in the computation of the said period of forty years, in case the claim shall within three years next after the end or sooner determination of such term be resisted by any person entitled to any reversion expectant on the determination thereof.

8A.   Exclusion of time because of mediation in certain cross-border disputes

(1) In this section—
    (a) 'Mediation Directive' means Directive 2008/52/EC of the European Parliament and of the Council of 21 May 2008 on certain aspects of mediation in civil and commercial matters;
    (b) 'mediation' has the meaning given by article 3(a) of the Mediation Directive;
    (c) 'mediator' has the meaning given by article 3(b) of the Mediation Directive;
    (d) 'relevant dispute' means a dispute to which article 8(1) of the Mediation Directive applies (certain cross-border disputes).

(2) Where a period is prescribed by this Act in relation to the subject of the whole or part of a relevant dispute, any time after the start of a mediation in relation to the relevant dispute is to be excluded in the computation of that period, but only if—
    (a) the time when the period must end by virtue of section 4 falls before the mediation ends or less than eight weeks after it ends, or
    (b) a further mediation in relation to the relevant dispute starts less than eight weeks after the previous mediation ends, and the time when the period must end by virtue of section 4 falls before the further mediation ends or less than eight weeks after it ends.

(3) Any time excluded under subsection (2) is also to be excluded in the computation of the second period of three years mentioned in section 8 (period within which claim is resisted).

(4) For the purposes of this section, a mediation starts on the date of the agreement to mediate that is entered into by the parties and the mediator.

(5) For the purposes of this section, a mediation ends on the date of the first of these to occur—
    (a) the parties reach an agreement in resolution of the relevant dispute;
    (b) a party completes the notification of the other parties that it has withdrawn from the mediation;
    (c) a party to whom a qualifying request is made fails to give a response reaching the other parties within 14 days of the request;
    (d) the parties, after being notified that the mediator's appointment has ended (by death, resignation or otherwise), fail to agree within 14 days to seek to appoint a replacement mediator;
    (e) the mediation otherwise comes to an end pursuant to the terms of the agreement to mediate.

(6) For the purpose of subsection (5), a qualifying request is a request by a party that another (A) confirm to all parties that A is continuing with the mediation.

(7) In the case of any relevant dispute, references in this section to a mediation are references to the mediation so far as it relates to that dispute, and references to a party are to be read accordingly.

WILLS ACT 1837
1837 (7 Will. 4 and 1 Vict. c. 26)

1. Meaning of certain words in this Act

... the words and expressions herein-after mentioned, which in their ordinary signification have a more confined or a different meaning, shall in this Act, except where the nature of the provisions or the context of the Act shall exclude such construction, be interpreted as follows; (that is to say,) the word 'will' shall extend to a testament, and to a codicil, and to an appointment by will or by writing in the nature of a will in exercise of a power, and also to an appointment by will of a guardian of a child, and also to an appointment by will of a representative under section 4 of the Human Tissue Act 2004 or section 8 of the Human Transplantation (Wales) Act 2013, and to any other testamentary disposition; and the words 'real estate' shall extend to manors, advowsons, messuages, lands, tithes, rents, and hereditaments, whether corporeal, incorporeal, or personal, and to any estate, right, or interest (other than a chattel interest) therein; and the words 'personal estate' shall extend to leasehold estates and other chattels real, and also to monies, shares of government and other funds, securities for money (not being real estates), debts, choses in action, rights, credits, goods, and all other property whatsoever which by law devolves upon the executor or administrator, and to any share or interest therein; and every word importing the singular number only shall extend and be applied to several persons or things as well as one person or thing; and every word importing the masculine gender only shall extend and be applied to a female as well as a male.

3. All property may be disposed of by will

It shall be lawful for every person to devise, bequeath, or dispose of, by his will executed in manner herein-after required, all real estate and all personal estate which he shall be entitled to, either at law or in equity, at the time of his death, and which, if not so devised, bequeathed, or disposed of, would devolve upon his executor or administrator; and the power hereby given shall extend to all contingent, executory or other future interests in any real or personal estate, whether the testator may or may not be ascertained as the person or one of the persons in whom the same respectively may become vested, and whether he may be entitled thereto under the instrument by which the same respectively were created, or under any disposition thereof by deed or will; and also to all rights of entry for conditions broken, and other rights of entry; and also to such of the same estates, interests, and rights respectively, and other real and personal estate, as the testator may be entitled to at the time of his death, notwithstanding that he may become entitled to the same subsequently to the execution of his will.

7. No will of a person under age valid

No will made by any person under the age of eighteen years shall be valid.

9. **Signing and attestation of wills**

No will shall be valid unless—

(a) it is in writing, and signed by the testator, or by some other person in his presence and by his direction; and

(b) it appears that the testator intended by his signature to give effect to the will; and

(c) the signature is made or acknowledged by the testator in the presence of two or more witnesses present at the same time; and

(d) each witness either—

    (i) attests and signs the will; or

    (ii) acknowledges his signature, in the presence of the testator (but not necessarily in the presence of any other witness), but no form of attestation shall be necessary.

10. **Appointments by will to be executed like other wills, and to be valid, although other required solemnities are not observed**

No appointment made by will, in exercise of any power, shall be valid, unless the same be executed in manner herein-before required; and every will executed in manner herein-before required shall, so far as respects the execution and attestation thereof, be a valid execution of a power of appointment by will, notwithstanding it shall have been expressly required that a will made in exercise of such power should be executed with some additional or other form of execution or solemnity.

11. **Soldiers and mariners wills excepted**

Provided always, that any soldier being in actual military service, or any mariner or seaman being at sea, may dispose of his personal estate as he might have done before the making of this Act.

13. **Publication of will not requisite**

Every will executed in manner herein-before required shall be valid without any other publication thereof.

14. **Will not to be void on account of incompetency of attesting witness**

If any person who shall attest the execution of a will shall at the time of the execution thereof or at any time afterwards be incompetent to be admitted a witness to prove the execution thereof, such will shall not on that account be invalid.

15. **Gifts to an attesting witness to be void**

If any person shall attest the execution of any will to whom or to whose wife or husband any beneficial devise, legacy, estate, interest, gift, or appointment, of or affecting any real or personal estate (other than and except charges and directions for the payment of any debt or debts), shall be thereby given or made, such devise, legacy, estate, interest, gift; or appointment shall, so far only as concerns such person attesting the execution of such will, or the wife or husband of such person, or any person claiming under such person or wife or husband, be utterly null and void, and such person so attesting shall be admitted as a witness to prove the execution of such will, or to prove the validity or invalidity thereof, notwithstanding such devise, legacy, estate, interest, gift, or appointment mentioned in such will.

16. **Creditor attesting a will charging estate with debts shall be admitted a witness**

In case by any will any real or personal estate shall be charged with any debt or debts, and any creditor, or the wife or husband or civil partner of any creditor, whose debt is so charged, shall attest the execution of such will, such creditor notwithstanding such charge shall be admitted a witness to prove the execution of such will, or to prove the validity or invalidity thereof.

17. **Executor shall be admitted a witness**

No person shall, on account of his being an executor of a will, be incompetent to be admitted a witness to prove the execution of such will, or a witness to prove the validity or invalidity thereof.

18. **Wills to be revoked by marriage, except in certain cases**

(1) Subject to subsections (2) to (5) below, a will shall be revoked by the testator's marriage.

(2)   A disposition in a will in exercise of a power of appointment shall take effect notwithstanding the testator's subsequent marriage unless the property so appointed would in default of appointment pass to his personal representatives.

(3)   Where it appears from a will that at the time it was made the testator was expecting to be married to a particular person and that he intended that the will should not be revoked by the marriage, the will shall not be revoked by his marriage to that person.

(4)   Where it appears from a will that at the time it was made the testator was expecting to be married to a particular person and that he intended that a disposition in the will should not be revoked by his marriage to that person,—

   (a)   that disposition shall take effect notwithstanding the marriage; and

   (b)   any other disposition in the will shall take effect also, unless it appears from the will that the testator intended the disposition to be revoked by the marriage.

(5)   Nothing in this section applies in the case of a marriage which results from—

   (a)   the conversion of a civil partnership into a marriage under section 9 of the Marriage (Same Sex Couples) Act 2013 and regulations made under that section; or

   (b)   the changing of a civil partnership formed under Part (3) of the Civil Partnership Act 2004 into a marriage under—

      (i)   the Marriage (Scotland) Act 1977;

      (ii)   the Marriage and Civil Partnership (Scotland) Act 2014; or

      (iii)   any order made under section 104 of the Scotland Act 1988 in consequence of the Marriage and Civil Partnership (Scotland) Act 2014.

18A. Effect of dissolution or annulment of marriage on wills

(1)   Where, after a testator has made a will, a decree of a court of civil jurisdiction in England and Wales dissolves or annuls his marriages or his marriage is dissolved or annulled and the divorce or annulment is entitled to recognition in England and Wales by virtue of Part II of the Family Law Act 1986,—

   (a)   provisions of the will appointing executors or trustees or conferring a power of appointment, if they appoint or confer the power on the former spouse, shall take effect as If the former spouse had died on the date on which the marriage is dissolved or annulled, and

   (b)   any property which, or an interest in which, is devised or bequeathed to the former spouse shall pass as if the former spouse had died on that date,

   except in so far as a contrary intention appears by the will.

(2)   Subsection (1)(b) above is without prejudice to any right of the former spouse to apply for financial provision under the Inheritance (Provision for Family and Dependants) Act 1975.

18B Will to be revoked by civil partnership

(1)   Subject to subsections (2) to (6), a will is revoked by the formation of a civil partnership between the testator and another person.

(2)   A disposition in a will in exercise of a power of appointment takes effect despite the formation of a subsequent civil partnership between the testator and another person unless the property so appointed would in default of appointment pass to the testator's personal representatives.

(3)   If it appears from a will—

   (a)   that at the time it was made the testator was expecting to form a civil partnership with a particular person, and

   (b)   that he intended that the will should not be revoked by the formation of the civil partnership, the will is not revoked by its formation.

(4)   Subsections (5) and (6) apply if it appears from a will—

   (a)   that at the time it was made the testator was expecting to form a civil partnership with a particular person, and

   (b)   that he intended that a disposition in the will should not be revoked by the formation of the civil partnership.

(5)   The disposition takes effect despite the formation of the civil partnership.

(6)   Any other disposition in the will also takes effect, unless it appears from the will that the testator intended the disposition to be revoked by the formation of the civil partnership.

18C. Effect of dissolution or annulment of civil partnership on wills

(1) This section applies if, after a testator has made a will—
  (a) a court of civil jurisdiction in England and Wales dissolves his civil partnership or makes a nullity order in respect of it, or
  (b) his civil partnership is dissolved or annulled and the dissolution or annulment is entitled to recognition in England and Wales by virtue of Chapter 3 of Part 5 of the Civil Partnership Act 2004.

(2) Except in so far as a contrary intention appears by the will—
  (a) provisions of the will appointing executors or trustees or conferring a power of appointment, if they appoint or confer the power on the former civil partner, take effect as if the former civil partner had died on the date on which the civil partnership is dissolved or annulled, and
  (b) any property which, or an interest in which, is devised or bequeathed to the former civil partner shall pass as if the former civil partner had died on that date.

(3) Subsection (2)(b) does not affect any right of the former civil partner to apply for financial provision under the Inheritance (Provision for Family and Dependants) Act 1975.

18D. Effect on subsisting will of conversion of civil partnership into marriage

(1) The conversion of a civil partnership into a marriage does not—
  (a) revoke any will made by a party to the civil partnership before the conversion; or
  (b) affect any disposition in such a will.

(2) The conversion of a civil partnership into a marriage does not affect any previous application of section 18B(2) to (6) to—
  (a) a will made by a party to the civil partnership before the conversion; or
  (b) a disposition in such a will.

(3) Subsections (1) and (2) are subject to subsection (4).

(4) Any reference in a will to a civil partnership or civil partners (howsoever expressed) is to be read in relation to any civil partnership that has been converted into a marriage, or civil partners who have converted their civil partnership into a marriage, as referring to that marriage or married couple, as appropriate.

(5) Subsection (4) is subject to any contrary intention appearing from the will.

(6) In this section 'conversion' means—
  (a) the conversion of a civil partnership into a marriage under section 9 of the Marriage (Same Sex Couples) Act 2013 and regulations made under that section;
  (b) the changing of a civil partnership formed under Part 3 of the Civil Partnership Act 2004 into a marriage under—
    (i) the Marriage (Scotland) Act 1977;
    (ii) the Marriage and Civil Partnership (Scotland) Act 2014; or
    (iii) any order made under section 104 of the Scotland Act 1998 in consequence of the Marriage and Civil Partnership (Scotland) Act 2014, and
  'converted' is to be read accordingly.

20. No will to be revoked but by another will or codicil, or by a writing executed like a will, or by destruction

No will or codicil, or any part thereof, shall be revoked otherwise than as aforesaid, or by another will or codicil executed in manner herein-before required, or by some writing declaring an intention to revoke the same, and executed in the manner in which a will is herein-before required to be executed, or by the burning, tearing, or otherwise destroying the same by the testator, or by some person in his presence and by his direction, with the intention of revoking the same.

21. No alteration in a will shall have any effect unless executed as a will

No obliteration, interlineation, or other alteration made in any will after the execution thereof shall be valid or have any effect, except so far as the words or effect of the will before such alteration shall not be apparent, unless such alteration shall be executed in like manner as herein-before is required for the execution of the will; but the will, with such alteration as part thereof, shall be deemed to be duly executed if the signature of the testator and the subscription of the witnesses be made in the margin or on some other part of the will opposite or near to such alteration, or at the foot or end of or opposite to a memorandum referring to such alteration, and written at the end or some other part of the will.

22. No revoked will shall be revived otherwise than by re-execution or a codicil, &c

No will or codicil, or any part thereof, which shall be in any manner revoked, shall be revived otherwise than by the re-execution thereof or by a codicil executed in manner herein-before required and showing an intention to revive the same; and when any will or codicil which shall be partly revoked, and afterwards wholly revoked, shall be revived, such revival shall not extend to so much thereof as shall have been revoked before the revocation of the whole thereof, unless an intention to the contrary shall be shown.

23. Subsequent conveyance or other act not to prevent operation of will

No conveyance or other act made or done subsequently to the execution of a will of or relating to any real or personal estate therein comprised, except an act by which such will shall be revoked as aforesaid, shall prevent the operation of the will with respect to such estate or interest in such real or personal estate as the testator shall have power to dispose of by will at the time of his death.

24. A will shall be construed to speak from the death of the testator

Every will shall be construed, with reference to the real estate and personal estate comprised in it, to speak and take effect as if it had been executed immediately before the death of the testator, unless a contrary intention shall appear by the will.

25. Residuary devises shall include estates comprised in lapsed and void devises

Unless a contrary intention shall appear by the will, such real estate or interest therein as shall be comprised or intended to be comprised in any devise in such will contained, which shall fail or be void by reason of the death of the devisee in the lifetime of the testator, or by reason of such devise being contrary to law or otherwise incapable of taking effect shall be included in the residuary devise (if any) contained in such will.

26. A general devise of the testator's lands shall include copyhold and leasehold as well as freehold lands, in the absence of a contrary intention

A devise of the land of the testator, or of the land of the testator in any place or in the occupation of any person mentioned in his will, or otherwise described in a general manner, and any other general devise which would describe a leasehold estate if the testator had no freehold estate which could be described by it, shall be construed to include the leasehold estates of the testator, or his leasehold estates, or any of them, to which such description shall extend, as the case may be, as well as freehold estates, unless a contrary intention shall appear by the will.

27. A general gift of realty or personalty shall include property over which the testator has a general power of appointment

A general devise of the real estate of the testator, or of the real estate of the testator in any place or in the occupation of any person mentioned in his will, or otherwise described in a general manner, shall be construed to include any real estate, or any real estate to which such description shall extend (as the case may be), which he may have power to appoint in any manner he may think proper, and shall operate as an execution of such power, unless a contrary intention shall appear by the will; and in like manner a bequest of the personal estate of the testator, or any bequest of personal property described in a general manner, shall be construed to include any personal estate, or any personal estate to which such description shall extend (as the case may be), which he may have power to appoint in any manner he may think proper, and shall operate as an execution of such power, unless a contrary intention shall appear by the will.

28. A devise of real estate without any words of limitation shall pass the fee, &c

Where any real estate shall be devised to any person without any words of limitation, such devise shall be construed to pass the fee simple, or other the whole estate or interest which the testator had power to dispose of by will in such real estate, unless a contrary intention shall appear by the will.

29. **The words 'die without issue,' or 'die without leaving issue,' &c shall mean a want or failure of issue in the lifetime or at the death of the person, except in certain cases**

In any devise or bequest of real or personal estate the words 'die without issue' or 'die without leaving issue', or 'have no issue,' or any other words which may import either a want or failure of issue of any person in his lifetime or at the time of his death, or an indefinite failure of his issue, shall be construed to mean a want or failure of issue in the lifetime or at the time of the death of such person, and not an indefinite failure of his issue, unless a contrary intention shall appear by the will, by reason of such person having a prior estate tail, or of a preceding gift, being, without any implication arising from such words, a limitation of an estate tail to such person or issue, or otherwise: Provided, that this Act shall not extend to cases where such words as aforesaid import if no issue described in a preceding gift shall be born, or if there shall be no issue who shall live to attain the age or otherwise answer the description required for obtaining a vested estate by a preceding gift to such issue.

30. **Devise of realty to trustees or executors shall pass the fee, &c, except in certain cases**

Where any real estate (other than or not being a presentation to a church) shall be devised to any trustee or executor, such devise shall be construed to pass the fee simple or other the whole estate or interest which the testator had power to dispose of by will in such real estate, unless a definite term of years, absolute or determinable, or an estate of freehold, shall thereby be given to him expressly or by implication.

31. **Trustees under an unlimited devise, where the trust may endure beyond the life of a person beneficially entitled for life, shall take the fee, &c**

Where any real estate shall be devised to a trustee, without any express limitation of the estate to be taken by such trustee, and the beneficial interest in such real estate, or in the surplus rents and profits thereof, shall not be given to any person for life, or such beneficial interest shall be given to any person for life, but the purposes of the trust may continue beyond the life of such person, such devise shall be construed to vest in such trustee the fee simple, or other the whole legal estate which the testator had power to dispose of by will in such real estate, and not an estate determinable when the purposes of the trust shall be satisfied.

33. **Gifts to children or other issue who leave issue living at the testator's death shall not lapse**

(1) Where—
  (a) a will contains a devise or bequest to a child or remoter descendant of the testator; and
  (b) the intended beneficiary dies before the testator, leaving issue; and
  (c) issue of the intended beneficiary are living at the testator's death, then, unless a contrary intention appears by the will, the devise or bequest shall take effect as a devise or bequest to the issue living at the testator's death.

(2) Where—
  (a) a will contains a devise or bequest to a class of persons consisting of children or remoter descendants of the testator; and
  (b) a member of the class dies before the testator, leaving issue; and
  (c) issue of that member are living at the testator's death, then, unless a contrary intention appears by the will, the devise or bequest shall take effect as if the class included the issue of its deceased member living at the testator's death.

(3) Issue shall take under this section through all degrees, according to their stock, in equal shares if more than one, any gift or share which their parent would have taken and so that (subject to section 33A) no issue shall take whose parent is living at the testator's death and so capable of taking.

(4) For the purposes of this section—
  (a) the illegitimacy of any person is to be disregarded; and
  (b) a person conceived before the testator's death and born living thereafter is to be taken to have been living at the testator's death.

33A. **Disclaimer or forfeiture of gift**

(1) This section applies where a will contains a devise or bequest to a person who—
  (a) disclaims it, or
  (b) has been precluded by the forfeiture rule from acquiring it.

(2) The person is, unless a contrary intention appears by the will, to be treated for the purposes of this Act as having died immediately before the testator.

(3) But in a case within subsection (1)(b), subsection (2) does not affect the power conferred by section 2 of the Forfeiture Act 1982 (power of court to modify the forfeiture rule).

(4) In this section 'forfeiture rule' has the same meaning as in the Forfeiture Act 1982.

WILLS (SOLDIERS AND SAILORS) ACT 1918
(1918, c. 58)

1.   Explanation of s 11 of Wills Act 1837

In order to remove doubts as to the construction of the Wills Act 1837, it is hereby declared and enacted that section eleven of that Act authorises and always has authorised any soldier being in actual military service, or any mariner or seaman being at sea, to dispose of his personal estate as he might have done before the passing of that Act, though under the age of eighteen years.

2.   Extension of s 11 of Wills Act 1837

Section eleven of the Wills Act 1837, shall extend to any member of His Majesty's naval or marine forces not only when he is at sea but also when he is so circumstanced that if he were a soldier he would be in actual military service within the meaning of that section.

3.   Validity of testamentary dispositions of real property made by soldiers and sailors

(1) A testamentary disposition of any real estate in England or Ireland made by a person to whom section eleven of the Wills Act 1837, applies, and who dies after the passing of this Act, shall, notwithstanding that the person making the disposition was at the time of making it under eighteen years of age or that the disposition has not been made in such manner or form as was at the passing of this Act required by law, be valid in any case where the person making the disposition was of such age and the disposition has been made in such manner and form that if the disposition had been a disposition of personal estate made by such a person domiciled in England or Ireland it would have been valid.

(2) ...

4.   Power to appoint testamentary guardians

Where any person dies after the passing of this Act having made a will which is, or which, if it had been a disposition of property, would have been rendered valid by section eleven of the Wills Act 1837, any appointment contained in that will of any person as guardian of the infant children of the testator shall be of full force and effect.

5.   Short title and interpretation

(1) This Act may be cited as the Wills (Soldiers and Sailors) Act 1918.

(2) For the purposes of section eleven of the Wills Act 1837, and this Act the expression 'soldier' includes a member of the Air Force, and references in this Act to the said section eleven include a reference to that section as explained and extended by this Act.

LAW OF PROPERTY ACT 1922
(1922, c. 16)

PART VII
PROVISIONS RESPECTING LEASEHOLDS CONVERSION OF
PERPETUALLY RENEWABLE LEASEHOLDS INTO LONG TERMS

145.   Conversion of perpetually renewable leaseholds

For the purpose of converting perpetually renewable leases and underleases (not being an interest in perpetually renewable copyhold land enfranchised by Part V of this Act, but including a perpetually renewable underlease derived out of an interest in perpetually renewable copyhold land) into long terms, for preventing the creation of perpetually renewable leasehold interests and for providing for the interests of the persons affected, the provisions contained in the Fifteenth Schedule to this Act shall have effect.

SCHEDULE 15
PROVISIONS RELATING TO PERPETUALLY RENEWABLE LEASES AND UNDERLEASES

Conversion of perpetually renewable leases into long terms

1.   (1)   Land comprised in a perpetually renewable lease which was subsisting at the commencement of this Act shall, by virtue of this Act, vest in the person who at such commencement was entitled to such lease, for a term of two thousand years, to be calculated from the date at which the existing term or interest commenced, at the rent and subject to the lessees' covenants and conditions (if any) which under the lease would have been payable or enforceable during the subsistence of such term or interest.

     (2)   The rent, covenants and conditions (if any) shall (subject to the express provisions of this Act to the contrary) be payable and enforceable during the subsistence of the term created by this Act; and that term shall take effect in substitution for the term or interest created by the lease, and be subject to the like power of re-entry (if any) and other provisions which affected the term or interest created by the lease, but without any right of renewal.

Conversion of perpetually renewable underleases into long terms

2.   (1)   Land comprised in any underlease, which at the commencement of this Act was perpetually renewable and was derived out of a head term affected by this Act, shall, by virtue of this Act, vest in the person who at such commencement was entitled to the subterm or interest for a term of two thousand years less one day, to be calculated from the date at which the head term created by this Act commenced, at the rent and subject to the underlessee's covenants and conditions (if any) which under the underlease would have been payable or enforceable during the subsistence of such subterm or interest.

     (2)   The rent, covenants and conditions (if any) shall (subject to the express provisions of this Act to the contrary) be payable and enforceable during the subsistence of the subterm created by this Act; and that subterm shall take effect in substitution for the subterm or interest created by the underlease, and be subject to the like power of re-entry (if any) and other provisions which affected the subterm or interest created by the underlease, but without any right of renewal.

     (3)   The foregoing provisions of this section shall also apply to any perpetually renewable subterm or interest which, at the commencement of this Act, was derived out of any other subterm or interest, but so that in every case the subterm created by this Act shall be one day less in duration than the derivative term created by this Act, out of which it takes effect.

Dispositions purporting to create perpetually renewable leaseholds

5.   (1)   A grant, after the commencement of this Act, of a term, subterm, or other leasehold interest with a covenant or obligation for perpetual renewal, which would have been valid if this Part of this Act had not been passed, shall (subject to the express provisions of this Act) take effect as a demise for a term of two thousand years or in the case of a subdemise for a term less in duration by one day than the term out of which it is derived, to commence from the date fixed for the commencement of the term, subterm, or other interest, and in every case free from any obligation for renewal or for payment of any fines, fees, costs, or other money in respect of renewal.

     (2)   Sub-paragraph (3) applies where a grant—
           (a)   relates to commonhold land, and
           (b)   would take effect by virtue of sub-paragraph (1) as a demise for a term of two thousand years or a subdemise for a fixed term.

     (3)   The grant shall be treated as if it purported to be a grant of the term referred to in sub-paragraph (2)(b) (and sections 17 and 18 of the Commonhold and Leasehold Reform Act 2002 (residential and non-residential leases) shall apply accordingly).

TRUSTEE ACT 1925
(1925, c. 19)

PART II
GENERAL POWERS OF TRUSTEES AND PERSONAL REPRESENTATIVES

General Powers

12.   Power of trustees for sale to sell by auction, etc.

(1)   Where a trustee has a duty or power to sell property, he may sell or concur with any other person in selling all or any part of the property, either subject to prior charges or not, and either together or in lots, by public auction or by private contract, subject to any such conditions respecting title or evidence of title or other matter as the Trustee thinks fit, with power to vary any contract for sale, and to buy in at any auction, or to rescind any contract for sale and to re-sell, without being answerable for any loss.

(2)   A duty or power to sell or dispose of land includes a duty or power to sell or dispose of part thereof, whether the division is horizontal, vertical, or made in any other way.

(3)   This section does not enable an express power to sell settled land to be exercised where the power is not vested in the tenant for life or statutory owner.

13.   Power to sell subject to depreciatory conditions

(1)   No sale made by a trustee shall be impeached by any beneficiary upon the ground that any of the conditions subject to which the sale was made have been unnecessarily depreciatory, unless it also appears that the consideration for the sale was thereby rendered inadequate.

(2)   No sale made by a trustee shall, after the execution of the conveyance, be impeached as against the purchaser upon the ground that any of the conditions subject to which the sale was made may have been unnecessarily depreciatory, unless it appears that the purchaser was acting in collusion with the trustee at the time when the contract for sale was made.

(3)   No purchaser, upon any sale made by a trustee, shall be at liberty to make any objection against the title upon any of the grounds aforesaid.

(4)   This section applies to sales made before or after the commencement of this Act.

14.   Power of trustees to give receipts

(1)   The receipt in writing of a trustee for any money, securities, investments or other personal property or effects payable, transferable, or deliverable to him under any trust or power shall be a sufficient discharge to the person paying, transferring, or delivering the same and shall effectually exonerate him from seeing to the application or being answerable for any loss or misapplication thereof.

(2)   This section does not, except where the trustee is a trust corporation, enable a sole trustee to give a valid receipt for—

(a)   proceeds of sale or other capital money arising under a trust of land;

(b)   capital money arising under the Settled Land Act, 1925.

(3)   This section applies notwithstanding anything to the contrary in the instrument, if any, creating the trust.

15.   Power to compound liabilities

A personal representative, or two or more trustees acting together, or, subject to the restrictions imposed in regard to receipts by a sole trustee not being a trust corporation, a sole acting trustee where by the instrument, if any, creating the trust, or by statute, a sole trustee is authorised to execute the trusts and powers reposed in him, may, if and as he or they think fit—

(a)   accept any property, real or personal, before the time at which it is made transferable or payable; or

(b)   sever and apportion any blended trust funds or property; or

(c)   pay or allow any debt or claim on any evidence that he or they think sufficient; or

(d)   accept any composition or any security, real or personal, for any debt or for any property, real or personal claimed; or

(e) allow any time of payment of any debt; or

(f) compromise, compound, abandon, submit to arbitration, or otherwise settle any debt, account, claim, or thing whatever relating to the testator's or intestate's estate or to the trust;

and for any of those purposes may enter into, give, execute, and do such agreements, instruments of composition or arrangement, releases, and other things as to him or them seem expedient, without being responsible for any loss occasioned by any act or thing so done by him or them if he has or they have discharged the duty of care set out in section 1(1) of the Trustee Act 2000.

16. Power to raise money by sale, mortgage, etc.

(1) Where trustees are authorised by the instrument, if any, creating the trustor by law to pay or apply capital money subject to the trust for any purpose or in any manner, they shall have and shall be deemed always to have had power to raise the money required by sale, conversion, calling in, or mortgage of all or any part of the trust property for the time being in possession.

(2) This section applies notwithstanding anything to the contrary contained in the instrument, if any, creating the trust, but does not apply to trustees of property held for charitable purposes, or to trustees of a settlement for the purposes of the Settled Land Act, 1925, not being also the statutory owners.

17. Protection to purchasers and mortgagees dealing with trustees

No purchaser or mortgagee, paying or advancing money on a sale or mortgage purporting to be made under any trust or power vested in trustees, shall be concerned to see that such money is wanted, or that no more than is wanted is raised, or otherwise as to the application thereof.

18. Devolution of powers or trusts

(1) Where a power or trust is given to or imposed on two or more trustees jointly, the same may be exercised or performed by the survivors or survivor of them for the time being.

(2) Until the appointment of new trustees, the personal representatives or representative for the time being of a sole trustee, or, where there were two or more trustees of the last surviving or continuing trustee, shall be capable of exercising or performing any power or trust which was given to, or capable of being exercised by, the sole or last surviving or continuing trustee, or other the trustees or trustee for the time being of the trust.

(3) This section takes effect subject to the restrictions imposed in regard to receipts by a sole trustee, not being a trust corporation.

(4) In this section 'personal representative' does not include an executor who has renounced or has not proved.

19. Power to insure

(1) A trustee may—

   (a) insure any property which is subject to the trust against risks of loss or damage due to any event, and

   (b) pay the premiums out of the trust funds.

(2) In the case of property held on a bare trust, the power to insure is subject to any direction given by the beneficiary or each of the beneficiaries—

   (a) that any property specified in the direction is not to be insured;

   (b) that any property specified in the direction is not to be insured except on such conditions as may be so specified.

(3) Property is held on a bare trust if it is held on trust for—

   (a) a beneficiary who is of full age and capacity and absolutely entitled to the property subject to the trust, or

   (b) beneficiaries each of whom is of full age and capacity and who (taken together) are absolutely entitled to the property subject to the trust.

(4) If a direction under subsection (2) of this section is given, the power to insure, so far as it is subject to the direction, ceases to be a delegable function for the purposes of section 11 of the Trustee Act 2000 (power to employ agents).

(5) In this section 'trust funds' means any income or capital funds of the trust.

20. **Application of insurance money where policy kept up under any trust, power or obligation**

(1)   Money receivable by trustees or any beneficiary under a policy of insurance against the loss or damage of any property subject to a trust or to a settlement within the meaning of the Settled Land Act, 1925, shall, where the policy has been kept up under any trust in that behalf or under any power statutory or otherwise, or in performance of any covenant or of any obligation statutory or otherwise, or by a tenant for life impeachable for waste, be capital money for the purposes of the trust or settlement, as the case may be.

(2)   If any such money is receivable by any person, other than the trustees of the trust or settlement, that person shall use his best endeavours to recover and receive the money, and shall pay the net residue thereof, after discharging any costs of recovering and receiving it, to the trustees of the trust or settlement, or, if there are no trustees capable of giving a discharge therefor, into court.

(3)   Any such money—

   (a)   if it was receivable in respect of settled land within the meaning of the Settled Land Act, 1925, or any building or works thereon, shall be deemed to be capital money arising under that Act from the settled land, and shall be invested or applied by the trustees, or, if in court, under the direction of the court, accordingly;

   (b)   if it was receivable in respect of personal chattels settled as heirlooms within the meaning of the Settled Land Act, 1925, shall be deemed to be capital money arising under that Act, and shall be applicable by the trustees, or, if in court, under the direction of the court, in like manner as provided by that Act with respect to money arising by a sale of chattels settled as heirlooms as aforesaid;

   (c)   if it was receivable in respect of land subject to a trust of land or personal property held on trust for sale, shall be held upon the trusts and subject to the powers and provisions applicable to money arising by a sale under such trust;

   (d)   in any other case, shall be held upon trusts corresponding as nearly as may be with the trusts affecting the property in respect of which it was payable.

(4)   Such money, or any part thereof, may also be applied by the trustees, or, if in court, under the direction of the court, in rebuilding, reinstating, replacing, or repairing the property lost or damaged, but any such application by the trustees shall be subject to the consent of any person whose consent is required by the instrument, if any, creating the trust to the investment of money subject to the trust, and, in the case of money which is deemed to be capital money arising under the Settled Land Act, 1925, be subject to the provisions of that Act with respect to the application of capital money by the trustees of the settlement.

(5)   Nothing contained in this section prejudices or affects the right of any person to require any such money or any part thereof to be applied in rebuilding, reinstating, or repairing the property lost or damaged, or the rights of any mortgagee, lessor, or lessee, whether under any statute or otherwise.

(6)   This section applies to policies effected either before or after the commencement of this Act, but only to money received after such commencement.

22. **Reversionary interests, valuations and audit**

(1)   Where trust property includes any share or interest in property not vested in the trustees, or the proceeds of the sale of any such property, or any other thing in action, the trustees on the same falling into possession, or becoming payable or transferable may—

   (a)   agree or ascertain the amount or value thereof or any part thereof in such manner as they may think fit;

   (b)   accept in or towards satisfaction thereof, at the market or current value, or upon any valuation or estimate of value which they may think fit, any authorised investments;

   (c)   allow any deductions for duties, costs, charges and expenses which they may think proper or reasonable;

   (d)   execute any release in respect of the premises so as effectually to discharge all accountable parties from all liability in respect of any matters coming within the scope of such release;

without being responsible in any such case for any loss occasioned by any act or thing so done by them if they have discharged the duty of care set out in section 1(1) of the Trustee Act 2000.

(2)   The trustees shall not be under any obligation and shall not be chargeable with any breach of trust by reason of any omission—

(a)   to place any distringas notice or apply for any stop or other like order upon any securities or other property out of or on which such share or interest or other thing in action as aforesaid is derived, payable or charged; or

(b)   to take any proceedings on account of any act, default, or neglect on the part of the persons in whom such securities or other property or any of them or any part thereof are for the time being, or had at any time been, vested; unless and until required in writing so to do by some person, or the guardian of some person, beneficially interested under the trust, and unless also due provision is made to their satisfaction for payment of the costs of any proceedings required to be taken:

Provided that nothing in this subsection shall relieve the trustees of the obligation to get in and obtain payment or transfer of such share or interest or other thing in action on the same falling into possession.

(3)   Trustees may, for the purpose of giving effect to the trust, or any of the provisions of the instrument, if any, creating the trust or of any statute, from time to time (by duly qualified agents) ascertain and fix the value of any trust property in such manner as they think proper, and any valuation so made shall be binding upon all persons interested under the trust if the trustees have discharged the duty of care set out in section 1(1) of the Trustee Act 2000.

(4)   Trustees may, in their absolute discretion, from time to time, but not more than once in every three years unless the nature of the trust or any special dealings with the trust property make a more frequent exercise of the right reasonable, cause the accounts of the trust property to be examined or audited by an independent accountant, and shall, for that purpose, produce such vouchers and give such information to him as he may require; and the costs of such examination or audit, including the fee of the auditor, shall be paid out of the capital or income of the trust property, or partly in one way and partly in the other, as the trustees, in their absolute discretion, think fit, but, in default of any direction by the trustees to the contrary in any special case, costs attributable to capital shall be borne by capital and those attributable to income by income.

24.   Power to concur with others

Where an undivided share in any property is subject to a trust, or forms part of the estate of a testator or intestate, the trustees or personal representatives may (without prejudice to the trust affecting the entirety of the land and the powers of the trustees in reference thereto) execute or exercise any duty or power vested in them in relation to such share in conjunction with the persons entitled to or having power in that behalf over the other share or shares, and notwithstanding that any one or more of the trustees or personal representatives may be entitled to or interested in any such other share, either in his or their own right or in a fiduciary capacity.

25.   Delegation of trustee's functions by power of attorney

(1)   Notwithstanding any rule of law or equity to the contrary, a trustee may, by power of attorney, delegate the execution or exercise of all or any of the trusts, powers and discretions vested in him as trustee either alone or jointly with any other person or persons.

(2)   A delegation under this section—

(a)   commences as provided by the instrument creating the power or, if the instrument makes no provision as to the commencement of the delegation, with the date of the execution of the instrument by the donor; and

(b)   continues for a period of twelve months or any shorter period provided by the instrument creating the power.

(3)   The persons who may be donees of a power of attorney under this section include a trust corporation.

(4)   Before or within seven days after giving a power of attorney under this section the donor shall give written notice of it (specifying the date on which the power comes into operation and its duration, the donee of the power, the reason why the power is given and, where some only are delegated, the trusts, powers and discretions delegated) to—

(a)   each person (other than himself), if any, who under any instrument creating the trust has power (whether alone or jointly) to appoint a new trustee; and

(b)   each of the other trustees, if any;

but failure to comply with this subsection shall not, in favour of a person dealing with the donee of the power, invalidate any act done or instrument executed by the donee.

(5)   A power of attorney given under this section by a single donor—

in the form set out in subsection (6) of this section; or

    (a)   in a form to the like effect but expressed to be made under this subsection,

    (b)   shall operate to delegate to the person identified in the form as the single donee of the power the execution and exercise of all the trusts, powers and discretions vested in the donor as trustee (either alone or jointly with any other person or persons) under the single trust so identified.

(6)   The form referred to in subsection (5) of this section is as follows—

'THIS GENERAL TRUSTEE POWER OF ATTORNEY is made on *date* by *name* of *one donor* of *address of donor* as trustee of *name or details of one trust*.

I appoint *name of one donee* of *address of donee* to be my attorney *if desired, the date on which the delegation commences or the period for which it continues (or both)* in accordance with section 25(5) of the Trustee Act 1925. *To be executed as a deed*'.

(7)   The donor of a power of attorney given under this section shall be liable for the acts or defaults of the donee in the same manner as if they were the acts or defaults of the donor.

(8)   For the purpose of executing or exercising the trusts or powers delegated to him, the donee may exercise any of the powers conferred on the donor as trustee by statute or by the instrument creating the trust, including power, for the purpose of the transfer of any inscribed stock, himself to delegate to an attorney power to transfer, but not including the power of delegation conferred by this section.

(9)   The fact that it appears from any power of attorney given under this section, or from any evidence required for the purposes of any such power of attorney or otherwise, that in dealing with any stock the donee of the power is acting in the execution of a trust shall not be deemed for any purpose to affect any person in whose books the stock is inscribed or registered with any notice of the trust.

(10) This section applies to a personal representative, tenant for life and statutory owner as it applies to a trustee except that subsection (4) shall apply as if it required the notice there mentioned to be given—

    (a)   in the case of a personal representative, to each of the other personal representatives, if any, except any executor who has renounced probate;

    (b)   in the case of a tenant for life, to the trustees of the settlement and to each person, if any, who together with the person giving the notice constitutes the tenant for life; and

    (c)   in the case of a statutory owner, to each of the persons, if any, who together with the person giving the notice constitute the statutory owner and, in the case of a statutory owner by virtue of section 23(1)(a) of the Settled Land Act 1925, to the trustees of the settlement.

Indemnities

26.   Protection against liability in respect of rents and covenants

(1)   Where a personal representative or trustee liable as such for—

    (a)   any rent, covenant, or agreement reserved by or contained in any lease; or

    (b)   any rent, covenant or agreement payable under or contained in any grant made in consideration of a rentcharge; or

    (c)   any indemnity given in respect of any rent, covenant or agreement referred to in either of the foregoing paragraphs;

satisfies all liabilities under the lease or grant which may have accrued and been claimed up to the date of the conveyance hereinafter mentioned, and, where necessary, sets apart a sufficient fund to answer any future claim that may be made in respect of any fixed and ascertained sum which the lessee or grantee agreed to lay out on the property demised or granted, although the period for laying out the same may not have arrived, then and in any such case the personal representative or trustee may convey the property demised or granted to a purchaser, legatee, devisee, or other person entitled to call for a conveyance thereof and thereafter—

        (i)   he may distribute the residuary real and personal estate of the deceased testator or intestate, or, as the case may be, the trust estate (other than the fund, if any, set apart as aforesaid) to or amongst the persons entitled thereto, without appropriating any part, or any further part, as the case may be, of the estate of the deceased or of the trust estate to meet any future liability under the said lease or grant;

    (ii)   notwithstanding such distribution, he shall not be personally liable in respect of any subsequent claim under the said lease or grant.

(1A) Where a personal representative or trustee has as such entered into, or may as such be required to enter into, an authorised guarantee agreement with respect to any lease comprised in the estate of a deceased testator or intestate or a trust estate (and, in a case where he has entered into such an agreement, he has satisfied all liabilities under it which may have accrued and been claimed up to the date of distribution)—

    (a)   he may distribute the residuary real and personal estate of the deceased testator or intestate, or the trust estate, to or amongst the persons entitled thereto—

        (i)   without appropriating any part of the estate of the deceased, or the trust estate, to meet any future liability (or, as the case may be, any liability) under any such agreement, and

        (ii)   notwithstanding any potential liability of his to enter into any such agreement; and

    (b)   notwithstanding such distribution, he shall not be personally liable in respect of any subsequent claim (or, as the case may be, any claim) under any such agreement.

In this subsection 'authorised guarantee agreement' has the same meaning as in the Landlord and Tenant (Covenants) Act 1995.

(2)   This section operates without prejudice to the right of the lessor or grantor, or the persons deriving title under the lessor or grantor, to follow the assets of the deceased or the trust property into the hands of the persons amongst whom the same may have been respectively distributed, and applies notwithstanding anything to the contrary in the will or other instrument, if any, creating the trust.

(3)   In this section 'lease' includes an underlease and an agreement for a lease or underlease and any instrument giving any such indemnity as aforesaid or varying the liabilities under the lease; 'grant' applies to a grant whether the rent is created by limitation, grant, reservation or otherwise, and includes an agreement for a grant and any instrument giving any such indemnity as aforesaid or varying the liabilities under the grant; 'lessee' and 'grantee' include persons respectively deriving title under them.

27.   Protection by means of advertisements

(1)   With a view to the conveyance to or distribution among the persons entitled to any real or personal property, the trustees of a settlement, trustees of land, trustees for sale of personal property or personal representatives may give notice by advertisement in the Gazette, and in a newspaper circulating in the district in which the land is situated and such other like notices, including notices elsewhere than in England and Wales, as would, in any special case, have been directed by a court of competent jurisdiction in an action for administration, of their intention to make such conveyance or distribution as aforesaid, and requiring any person interested to send to the trustees or personal representatives within the time, not being less than two months, fixed in the notice or, where more than one notice is given, in the last of the notices, particulars of his claim in respect of the property or any part thereof to which the notice relates.

(2)   At the expiration of the time fixed by the notice the trustees or personal representatives may convey or distribute the property or any part thereof to which the notice relates, to or among the persons entitled thereto, having regard only to the claims, whether formal or not, of which the trustees or personal representatives then had notice and shall not, as respects the property so conveyed or distributed, be liable to any person of whose claim the trustees or personal representatives have not had notice at the time of conveyance or distribution; but nothing in this section—

    (a)   prejudices the right of any person to follow the property, or any property representing the same, into the hands of any person, other than a purchaser, who may have received it; or

    (b)   frees the trustees or personal representatives from any obligation to make searches or obtain official certificates of search similar to those which an intending purchaser would be advised to make or obtain.

(3)   This section applies notwithstanding anything to the contrary in the will or other instrument, if any, creating the trust.

28.　Protection in regard to notice

A trustee or personal representative acting for the purposes of more than one trust or estate shall not, in the absence of fraud, be affected by notice of any instrument, matter, fact or thing in relation to any particular trust or estate if he has obtained notice thereof merely by reason of his acting or having acted for the purposes of another trust or estate.

Maintenance, Advancement and Protective Trusts

31.　Power to apply income for maintenance and to accumulate surplus income during a minority

(1)　Where any property is held by trustees in trust for any person for any interest whatsoever, whether vested or contingent, then, subject to any prior interests or charges affecting that property—

    (i)　during the infancy of any such person, if his interest so long continues, the trustees may, at their sole discretion, pay to his parent or guardian, if any, or otherwise apply for or towards his maintenance, education, or benefit, the whole or such part, if any, of the income of that property as the trustees may think fit, whether or not there is—

        (a)　any other fund applicable to the same purpose: or

        (b)　any person bound by law to provide for his maintenance or education; and

    (ii)　if such person on attaining the age of eighteen years has not a vested interest in such income, the trustees shall thenceforth pay the income of that property and of any accretion thereto under subsection (2) of this section to him, until he either attains a vested interest therein or dies, or until failure of his interest.

(2)　During the infancy of any such person, if his interest so long continues, the trustees shall accumulate all the residue of that income by investing it, and any profits from so investing it from time to time in authorised investments, and shall hold those accumulations as follows:—

    (i)　If any such person—

        (a)　attains the age of eighteen years, or marries under that age or forms a civil partnership under that age, and his interest in such income during his infancy, or until his marriage or his formation of a civil partnership, is a vested interest or;

        (b)　on attaining the age of eighteen years or on marriage, or formation of a civil partnership, under that age becomes entitled to the property from which such income arose in fee simple, absolute or determinable, or absolutely, or for an entailed interest;

the trustees shall hold the accumulations in trust for such person absolutely, but without prejudice to any provision with respect thereto contained in any settlement by him made under any statutory powers during his infancy, and so that the receipt of such person after marriage or formation of a civil partnership, and though still an infant shall be a good discharge; and

    (ii)　In any other case the trustees shall, notwithstanding that such person had a vested interest in such income, hold the accumulations as an accretion to the capital of the property from which such accumulations arose, and as one fund with such capital for all purposes, and so that, if such property is settled land, such accumulations shall be held upon the same trusts as if the same were capital money arising therefrom;

but the trustees may, at any time during the infancy of such person if his interest so long continues, apply those accumulations, or any part thereof, as if they were income arising in the then current year.

(3)　This section applies in the case of a contingent interest only if the limitation or trust carries the intermediate income of the property, but it applies to a future or contingent legacy by the parent of, or a person standing in loco parentis to, the legatee, if and for such period as, under the general law, the legacy carries interest for the maintenance of the legatee, and in any such case as last aforesaid the rate of interest shall (if the income available is sufficient, and subject to any rules of court to the contrary) be five pounds per centum per annum.

(4) This section applies to a vested annuity in like manner as if the annuity were the income of property held by trustees in trust to pay the income thereof to the annuitant for the same period for which the annuity is payable, save that in any case accumulations made during the infancy of the annuitant shall be held in trust for the annuitant or his personal representatives absolutely.

(5) This section does not apply where the instrument, if any, under which the interest arises came into operation before the commencement of this Act.

32. Power of advancement

(1) Trustees may at any time or times pay or apply any capital money subject to a trust, or transfer or apply any other property forming part of the capital of the trust property, for the advancement or benefit, in such manner as they may, in their absolute discretion, think fit, of any person entitled to the capital of the trust property or of any share thereof, whether absolutely or contingently on his attaining any specified age or on the occurrence of any other event, or subject to a gift over on his death under any specified age or on the occurrence of any other event, and whether in possession or in remainder or reversion, and such payment, transfer or application may be made notwithstanding that the interest of such person is liable to be defeated by the exercise of a power of appointment or revocation, or to be diminished by the increase of the class to which he belongs:

Provided that—

(a) property (including any money) so paid, transferred or applied for the advancement or benefit of any person must not, altogether, represent more than the presumptive or vested share or interest of that person in the trust property; and

(b) if that person is or becomes absolutely and indefeasibly entitled to a share in the trust property the money or other property so paid, transferred or applied shall be brought into account as part of such share; and

(c) no such payment, transfer or application shall be made so as to prejudice any person entitled to any prior life or other interest, whether vested or contingent, in the money or other property paid, transferred or applied unless such person is in existence and of full age and consents in writing to such payment, transfer or application.

(1A) In exercise of the foregoing power trustees may pay, transfer or apply money or other property on the basis (express or implied) that it shall be treated as a proportionate part of the capital out of which it was paid, transferred or applied, for the purpose of bringing it into account in accordance with proviso (b) to subsection (1) of this section.

(2) This section does not apply to capital money arising under the Settled Land Act 1925.

(3) This section does not apply to trusts constituted or created before the commencement of this Act.

33. Protective trusts

(1) Where any income, including an annuity or other periodical income payment, is directed to be held on protective trusts for the benefit of any person (in this section called 'the principal beneficiary') for the period of his life or for any less period, then, during that period (in this section called the 'trust period') the said income shall, without prejudice to any prior interest, be held on the following trusts, namely:—

(i) Upon trust for the principal beneficiary during the trust period or until he, whether before or after the termination of any prior interest, does or attempts to do or suffers any act or thing, or until any event happens, other than an advance under any statutory or express power, whereby, if the said income were payable during the trust period to the principal beneficiary absolutely during that period, he would be deprived of the right to receive the same or any part thereof, in any of which cases, as well as on the termination of the trust period, whichever first happens, this trust of the said income shall fail or determine;

(ii) If the trust aforesaid fails or determines during the subsistence of the trust period, then, during the residue of that period, the said income shall be held upon trust for the application thereof for the maintenance or support, or otherwise for the benefit, of all or any one or more exclusively of the other or others of the following persons (that is to say)—

(a) the principal beneficiary and his or her spouse or civil partner, if any, and his or her children or more remote issue, if any; or

(b)   if there is no spouse or civil partner or issue of the principal beneficiary in existence, the principal beneficiary and the persons who would, if he were actually dead, be entitled to the trust property or the income thereof or to the annuity fund, if any, or arrears of the annuity, as the case may be;

as the trustees in their absolute discretion, without being liable to account for the exercise of such discretion, think fit.

(2)   This section does not apply to trusts coming into operation before the commencement of this Act, and has effect subject to any variation of the implied trusts aforesaid contained in the instrument creating the trust.

(3)   Nothing in this section operates to validate any trust which would, if contained in the instrument creating the trust, be liable to be set aside.

(4)   In relation to the dispositions mentioned in section 19(1) of the Family Law Reform Act 1987, this section shall have effect as if any reference (however expressed) to any relationship between two persons were construed in accordance with section 1 of that Act.

PART III
APPOINTMENT AND DISCHARGE OF TRUSTEES

34.   Limitation of the number of trustees

(1)   Where, at the commencement of this Act, there are more than four trustees of a settlement of land, or more than four trustees holding land on trust for sale, no new trustees shall (except where as a result of the appointment the number is reduced to four or less) be capable of being appointed until the number is reduced to less than four, and thereafter the number shall not be increased beyond four.

(2)   In the case of settlements and dispositions creating trusts of land made or coming into operation after the commencement of this Act—

(a)   the number of trustees thereof shall not in any case exceed four, and where more than four persons are named as such trustees, the four first named (who are able and willing to act) shall alone be the trustees, and the other persons named shall not be trustees unless appointed on the occurrence of a vacancy;

(b)   the number of the trustees shall not be increased beyond four.

(3)   This section only applies to settlements and dispositions of land, and the restrictions imposed on the number of trustees do not apply—

(a)   in the case of land vested in trustees for charitable, ecclesiastical, or public purposes; or

(b)   where the net proceeds of the sale of the land are held for like purposes; or

(c)   to the trustees of a term of years absolute limited by a settlement on trusts for raising money, or of a like term created under the statutory remedies relating to annual sums charged on land.

35.   Appointments of trustees of settlements and trustees of land

(1)   Appointments of new trustees of land and of new trustees of any trust of the proceeds of sale of the land shall, subject to any order of the court, be effected by separate instruments, but in such manner as to secure that the same persons become trustees of land and trustees of the trust of the proceeds of sale.

(2)   Where new trustees of a settlement are appointed, a memorandum of the names and addresses of the persons who are for the time being the trustees thereof for the purposes of the Settled Land Act, 1925, shall be endorsed on or annexed to the last or only principal vesting instrument by or on behalf of the trustees of the settlement, and such vesting instrument shall, for that purpose, be produced by the person having the possession thereof to the trustees of the settlement when so required.

(3)   Where new trustees of land are appointed, a memorandum of the persons who are for the time being the trustees of the land shall be endorsed on or annexed to the conveyance by which the land was vested in trustees of land; and that conveyance shall be produced to the persons who are for the time being the trustees of the land by the person in possession of it in order for that to be done when the trustees require its production.

(4)   This section applies only to settlements and dispositions of land.

36.   Power of appointing new or additional trustees

(1) Where a trustee, either original or substituted, and whether appointed by a court or otherwise, is dead, or remains out of the United Kingdom for more than twelve months, or desires to be discharged from all or any of the trusts or powers reposed in or conferred on him, or refuses or is unfit to act therein, or is incapable of acting therein, or is an infant, then, subject to the restrictions imposed by this Act on the number of trustees, —

    (a)   the person or persons nominated for the purpose of appointing new trustees by the instrument, if any, creating the trust; or

    (b)   if there is no such person, or no such person able and willing to act, then the surviving or continuing trustees or trustee for the time being, or the personal representatives of the last surviving or continuing trustee;

may, by writing, appoint one or more other persons (whether or not being the persons exercising the power) to be a trustee or trustees in the place of the trustee so deceased remaining out of the United Kingdom, desiring to be discharged, refusing, or being unfit or being incapable, or being an infant, as aforesaid.

(2) Where a trustee has been removed under a power contained in the instrument creating the trust, a new trustee or new trustees may be appointed in the place of the trustee who is removed, as if he were dead, or, in the case of a corporation, as if the corporation desired to be discharged from the trust, and the provisions of this section shall apply accordingly, but subject to the restrictions imposed by this Act on the number of trustees.

(3) Where a corporation being a trustee is or has been dissolved, either before or after the commencement of this Act, then, for the purposes of this section and of any enactment replaced thereby, the corporation shall be deemed to be and to have been from the date of the dissolution incapable of acting in the trusts or powers reposed in or conferred on the corporation.

(4) The power of appointment given by subsection (1) of this section or any similar previous enactment to the personal representatives of last surviving or continuing trustee shall be and shall be deemed always to have been exercisable by the executors for the time being (whether original or by representation) of such surviving or continuing trustee who have proved the will of their testator or by the administrators for the time being of such trustee without the concurrence of any executor who has renounced or has not proved.

(5) But a sole or last surviving executor intending to renounce, or all the executors where they all intend to renounce, shall have and shall be deemed always to have had power, at any time before renouncing probate, to exercise the power of appointment given by this section, or by any similar previous enactment, if willing to act for that purpose and without thereby accepting the office of executor.

(6) Where, in the case of any trust, there are not more than three trustees—

    (a)   the person or persons nominated for the purpose of appointing new trustees by the instrument, if any, creating the trust; or

    (b)   if there is no such person, or no such person able and willing to act, then the trustee or trustees for the time being;

may, by writing, appoint another person or other persons to be an additional trustee or additional trustees, but it shall not be obligatory to appoint any additional trustee, unless the instrument, if any, creating the trust, or any statutory enactment provides to the contrary, nor shall the number of trustees be increased beyond four by virtue of any such appointment.

(6A) A person who is either—

    (a)   both a trustee and attorney for the other trustee (if one other), or for both of the other trustees (if two others), under a registered power; or

    (b)   attorney under a registered power for the trustee (if one) or for both or each of the trustees (if two or three),

may, if subsection (6B) of this section is satisfied in relation to him, make an appointment under subsection (6)(b) of this section on behalf of the trustee or trustees.

(6B) This subsection is satisfied in relation to an attorney under a registered power for one or more trustees if (as attorney under the power)—

    (a)   he intends to exercise any function of the trustee or trustees by virtue of section 1(1) of the Trustee Delegation Act 1999; or

    (b)   he intends to exercise any function of the trustee or trustees in relation to any land, capital proceeds of a conveyance of land or income from land by virtue of its delegation to him under section 25 of this Act or the instrument (if any) creating the trust.

(6C) In subsections (6A) and (6B) of this section 'registered power' means an enduring power of attorney or lasting power of attorney registered under the Mental Capacity Act 2005.

(6D) Subsection (6A) of this section—

  (a)   applies only if and so far as a contrary intention is not expressed in the instrument creating the power of attorney (or, where more than one, any of them) or the instrument (if any) creating the trust; and

  (b)   has effect subject to the terms of those instruments.

(7)   Every new trustee appointed under this section as well before as after all the trust property becomes by law, or by assurance, or otherwise, vested in him, shall have the same powers, authorities, and discretions, and may in all respects act as if he had been originally appointed a trustee by the instrument, if any, creating the trust.

(8)   The provisions of this section relating to a trustee who is dead include the case of a person nominated trustee in a will but dying before the testator, and those relative to a continuing trustee include a refusing or retiring trustee, if willing to act in the execution of the provisions of this section.

(9)   Where a trustee lacks capacity to exercise his functions as trustee and is also entitled in possession to some beneficial interest in the trust property, no appointment of a new trustee in his place shall be made by virtue of paragraph (b) of subsection (1) of this section unless leave to make the appointment has been given by the Court of Protection.

37.   Supplemental provisions as to appointment of trustees

(1)   On the appointment of a trustee for the whole or any part of trust property—

  (a)   the number of trustees may, subject to the restrictions imposed by this Act on the number of trustees, be increased; and

  (b)   a separate set of trustees, not exceeding four, may be appointed for any part of the trust property held on trusts distinct from those relating to any other part or parts of the trust property, notwithstanding that no new trustees or trustee are or is to be appointed for other parts of the trust property, and any existing trustee may be appointed or remain one of such separate set of trustees, or, if only one trustee was originally appointed, then, save as hereinafter provided, one separate trustee may be so appointed; and

  (c)   it shall not be obligatory, save as hereinafter provided, to appoint more than one new trustee where only one trustee was originally appointed, or to fill up the original number of trustees where more than two trustees were originally appointed, but, except where only one trustee was originally appointed, and a sole trustee when appointed will be able to give valid receipts for all capital money, a trustee shall not be discharged from his trust unless there will be either a trust corporation or at least two persons to act as trustees to perform the trust; and

  (d)   any assurance or thing requisite for vesting the trust property, or any part thereof, in a sole trustee, or jointly in the persons who are the trustees, shall be executed or done.

(2)   Nothing in this Act shall authorise the appointment of a sole trustee, not being a trust corporation, where the trustee, when appointed, would not be able to give valid receipts for all capital money arising under the trust.

38.   Evidence as to a vacancy in a trust

(1)   A statement, contained in any instrument coming into operation after the commencement of this Act by which a new trustee is appointed for any purpose connected with land, to the effect that a trustee has remained out of the United Kingdom for more than twelve months or refuses or is unfit to act, or is incapable of acting, or that he is not entitled to a beneficial interest in the trust property in possession, shall, in favour of a purchaser of a legal estate, be conclusive evidence of the matter stated.

(2)   In favour of such purchaser any appointment of a new trustee depending on that statement, and any vesting declaration, express or implied, consequent on the appointment, shall be valid.

39.   Retirement of trustee without a new appointment

(1)   Where a trustee is desirous of being discharged from the trust, and after this discharge there will be either a trust corporation or at least two persons to act as trustees to perform the trust, then, if such trustee as aforesaid by deed declares that he is desirous

of being discharged from the trust, and if his co-trustees and such other person, if any, as is empowered to appoint trustees, by deed consent to the discharge of the trustee, and to the vesting in the co-trustees alone of the trust property, the trustee desirous of being discharged shall be deemed to have retired from the trust, and shall, by the deed, be discharged therefrom under this Act, without any new trustee being appointed in his place.

(2) Any assurance or thing requisite for vesting the trust property in the continuing trustees alone shall be executed or done.

40. Vesting of trust property in new or continuing trustees

(1) Where by a deed a new trustee is appointed to perform any trust, then—

    (a) if the deed contains a declaration by the appointor to the effect that any estate or interest in any land subject to the trust, or in any chattel so subject, or the right to recover or receive any debt or other thing in action so subject, shall vest in the persons who by virtue of the deed become or are the trustees for performing the trust, the deed shall operate, without any conveyance or assignment, to vest in those persons as joint tenants and for the purposes of the trust the estate interest or right to which the declaration relates; and

    (b) if the deed is made after the commencement of this Act and does not contain such a declaration, the deed shall, subject to any express provision to the contrary therein contained, operate as if it had contained such a declaration by the appointor extending to all the estates interests and rights with respect to which a declaration could have been made.

(2) Where by a deed a retiring trustee is discharged under section 39 of this Act or section 19 of the Trusts of Land and Appointment of Trustees Act 1996 without a new trustee being appointed, then—

    (a) if the deed contains such a declaration as aforesaid by the retiring and continuing trustees, and by the other person, if any, empowered to appoint trustees, the deed shall, without any conveyance or assignment, operate to vest in the continuing trustees alone, as joint tenants, and for the purposes of the trust, the estate, interest, or right to which the declaration relates; and

    (b) if the deed is made after the commencement of this Act and does not contain such a declaration, the deed shall, subject to any express provision to the contrary therein contained, operate as if it had contained such a declaration by such persons as aforesaid extending to all the estates, interests and rights with respect to which a declaration could have been made.

(3) An express vesting declaration, whether made before or after the commencement of this Act, shall, notwithstanding that the estate, interest or right to be vested is not expressly referred to, and provided that the other statutory requirements were or are complied with, operate and be deemed always to have operated (but without prejudice to any express provision to the contrary contained in the deed of appointment or discharge) to vest in the persons respectively referred to in subsections (1) and (2) of this section, as the case may require, such estates, interests and rights as are capable of being and ought to be vested in those persons.

(4) This section does not extend—

    (a) to land conveyed by way of mortgage for securing money subject to the trust, except land conveyed on trust for securing debentures or debenture stock;

    (b) to land held under a lease which contains any covenant, condition or agreement against assignment or disposing of the land without licence or consent, unless, prior to the execution of the deed containing expressly or impliedly the vesting declaration, the requisite licence or consent has been obtained, or unless, by virtue of any statute or rule of law, the vesting declaration, express or implied, would not operate as a breach of covenant or give rise to a forfeiture;

    (c) to any share, stock, annuity or property which is only transferable in books kept by a company or other body, or in manner directed by or under an Act of Parliament.

In this subsection 'lease' includes an underlease and an agreement for a lease or underlease.

(5) For purposes of registration of the deed in any registry, the person or persons making the declaration expressly or impliedly, shall be deemed the conveying party or parties, and the conveyance shall be deemed to be made by him or them under a power conferred by this Act.

(6) This section applies to deeds of appointment or discharge executed on or after the first day of January, eighteen hundred and eighty-two.

PART IV
POWERS OF THE COURT

Appointment of new Trustees

41. Power of court to appoint new trustees

(1) The court may, whenever it is expedient to appoint a new trustee or new trustees, and it is found inexpedient difficult or impracticable so to do without the assistance of the court, make an order appointing a new trustee or new trustees either in substitution for or in addition to any existing trustees, or although there is no existing trustee.

In particular and without prejudice to the generality of the foregoing provision, the court may make an order appointing a new trustee in substitution for a trustee who lacks capacity to exercise his functions as trustee, or is a bankrupt, or is a corporation which is in liquidation or has been dissolved.

(2) ...

(3) An order under this section, and any consequential vesting order or conveyance, shall not operate further or otherwise as a discharge to any former or continuing trustee than an appointment of new trustees under any power for that purpose contained in any instrument would have operated.

(4) Nothing in this section gives power to appoint an executor or administrator.

42. Power to authorise remuneration

Where the court appoints a corporation, other than the Public Trustee, to be a trustee either solely or jointly with another person, the court may authorise the corporation to charge such remuneration for its services as trustee as the court may think fit.

43. Powers of new trustee appointed by the court

Every trustee appointed by a court of competent jurisdiction shall, as well before as after the trust property becomes by law, or by assurance, or otherwise, vested in him, have the same powers, authorities, and discretions, and may in all respects act as if he had been originally appointed a trustee by the instrument, if any, creating the trust.

Vesting Orders

44. Vesting orders of land

In any of the following cases, namely:—

(i) Where the court appoints or has appointed a trustee, or where a trustee has been appointed out of court under any statutory or express power;

(ii) Where a trustee entitled to or possessed of any land or interest therein, whether by way of mortgage or otherwise, or entitled to a contingent right therein, either solely or jointly with any other person—

(a) is under disability; or

(b) is out of the jurisdiction of the High Court; or

(c) cannot be found, or, being a corporation, has been dissolved.

(iii) Where it is uncertain who was the survivor of two or more trustees jointly entitled to or possessed of any interest in land;

(iv) Where it is uncertain whether the last trustee known to have been entitled to or possessed of any interest in land is living or dead;

(v) Where there is no personal representative of a deceased trustee who was entitled to or possessed of any interest in land, or where it is uncertain who is the personal representative of a deceased trustee who was entitled to or possessed of any interest in land;

(vi) Where a trustee jointly or solely entitled to or possessed of any interest in land, or entitled to a contingent right therein, has been required, by or on behalf of a person entitled to require a conveyance of the land or interest or a release of the right, to convey the land or interest or to release the right, and has wilfully refused or neglected to convey the land or interest or release the right for twenty-eight days after the date of the requirement;

(vii) Where land or any interest therein is vested in a trustee whether by way of mortgage or otherwise, and it appears to the court to be expedient;

the court may make an order (in this Act called a vesting order) vesting the land or interest therein in any such person in any such manner and for any such estate or interest as the court may direct, or releasing or disposing of the contingent right to such person as the court may direct:

Provided that—

(a)   Where the order is consequential on the appointment of a trustee the land or interest therein shall be vested for such estate as the court may direct in the persons who on the appointment are the trustees; and

(b)   Where the order relates to a trustee entitled or formerly entitled jointly with another person, and such trustee is under disability or out of the jurisdiction of the High Court or cannot be found, or being a corporation has been dissolved, the land interest or right shall be vested in such other person who remains entitled, either alone or with any other person the court may appoint.

45.   Orders as to contingent rights of unborn persons

Where any interest in land is subject to a contingent right in an unborn person or class of unborn persons who, on coming into existence would, in respect thereof, become entitled to or possessed of that interest on any trust, the court may make an order releasing the land or interest therein from the contingent right, or may make an order vesting in any person the estate or interest to or of which the unborn person or class of unborn persons would, on coming into existence, be entitled or possessed in the land.

46.   Vesting order in place of conveyance by infant mortgagee

Where any person entitled to or possessed of any interest in land, or entitled to a contingent right in land, by way of security for money, is an infant, the court may make an order vesting or releasing or disposing of the interest in the land or the right in like manner as in the case of a trustee under disability.

47.   Vesting order consequential on order for sale or mortgage of land

Where any court gives a judgment or makes an order directing the sale or mortgage of any land, every person who is entitled to or possessed of any interest in the land, or entitled to a contingent right therein, and is a party to the action or proceeding in which the judgment or order is given or made or is otherwise bound by the judgment or order, shall be deemed to be so entitled or possessed, as the case may be, as a trustee for the purpose of this Act, and the court may, if it thinks expedient, make an order vesting the land or any part thereof for such estate or interest as that court thinks fit in the purchaser or mortgagee or in any other person:

Provided that, in the case of a legal mortgage, the estate to be vested in the mortgagee shall be a term of years absolute.

48.   Vesting order consequential on judgment for specific performance, etc.

Where a judgment is given for the specific performance of a contract concerning any interest in land, or for sale or exchange of any interest in land, or generally where any judgment is given for the conveyance of any interest in land either in cases arising out of the doctrine of election or otherwise, the court may declare—

(a)   that any of the parties to the action are trustees of any interest in the land or any part thereof within the meaning of this Act; or

(b)   that the interests of unborn persons who might claim under any party to the action, or under the will or voluntary settlement of any deceased person who was during his lifetime a party to the contract or transaction concerning which the judgment is given, are the interests of persons who, on coming into existence, would be trustees within the meaning of this Act;

and thereupon the court may make a vesting order relating to the rights of those persons, born and unborn, as if they had been trustees.

49.   Effect of vesting order

A vesting order under any of the foregoing provisions shall in the case of a vesting order consequential on the appointment of a trustee, have the same effect—

(a) as if the persons who before the appointment were the trustees, if any, had duly executed all proper conveyances of the land for such estate or interest as the court directs; or

(b) if there is no such person, or no such person of full capacity, as if such person had existed and been of full capacity and had duly executed all proper conveyances of the land for such estate or interest as the court directs;

and shall in every other case have the same effect as if the trustee or other person or description or class of persons to whose rights or supposed rights the said provisions respectively relate had been an ascertained and existing person of full capacity, and had executed a conveyance or release to the effect intended by the order.

50. Power to appoint person to convey

In all cases where a vesting order can be made under any of the foregoing provisions, the court may, if it is more convenient, appoint a person to convey the land or any interest therein or release the contingent right, and a conveyance or release by that person in conformity with the order shall have the same effect as an order under the appropriate provision.

51. Vesting orders as to stock and things in action

(1) In any of the following cases, namely:—

    (i) Where the court appoints or has appointed a trustee, or where a trustee has been appointed out of court under any statutory or express power;

    (ii) Where a trustee entitled, whether by way of mortgage or otherwise, alone or jointly with another person to stock or to a thing in action—

        (a) is under disability; or

        (b) is out of the jurisdiction of the High Court; or

        (c) cannot be found, or, being a corporation, has been dissolved; or

        (d) neglects or refuses to transfer stock or receive the dividends or income thereof, or to sue for or recover a thing in action, according to the direction of the person absolutely entitled thereto for twenty-eight days next after a request in writing has been made to him by the person so entitled; or

        (e) neglects or refuses to transfer stock or receive the dividends or income thereof, or to sue for or recover a thing in action for twenty-eight days next after an order of the court for that purpose has been served on him;

    (iii) Where it is uncertain whether a trustee entitled alone or jointly with another person to stock or to a thing in action is alive or dead;

    (iv) Where stock is standing in the name of a deceased person whose personal representative is under disability;

    (v) Where stock or a thing in action is vested in a trustee whether by way of mortgage or otherwise and it appears to the court to be expedient;

the court may make an order vesting the right to transfer or call for a transfer of stock, or to receive the dividends or income thereof, or to sue for or recover the thing in action, in any such person as the court may appoint:

    Provided that—

        (a) Where the order is consequential on the appointment of a trustee, the right shall be vested in the persons who, on the appointment, are the trustees; and

        (b) Where the person whose right is dealt with by the order was entitled jointly with another person, the right shall be vested in that last-mentioned person either alone or jointly with any other person whom the court may appoint.

(2) In all cases where a vesting order can be made under this section, the court may, if it is more convenient, appoint some proper person to make or join in making the transfer:

    Provided that the person appointed to make or join in making a transfer of stock shall be some proper officer of the bank, or the company or society whose stock is to be transferred.

(3) The person in whom the right to transfer or call for the transfer of any stock is vested by an order of the court under this Act, may transfer the stock to himself or any other person, according to the order, and the Registrar of Government Stock and any company shall obey every order under this section according to its tenor.

(4) After notice in writing of an order under this section it shall not be lawful for the Registrar of Government Stock or any company to transfer any stock to which the order relates or to pay any dividends thereon except in accordance with the order.

(5)   The court may make declarations and give directions concerning the manner in which the right to transfer any stock or thing in action vested under the provisions of this Act is to be exercised.

(6)   The provisions of this Act as to vesting orders shall apply to shares in ships registered under the Merchant Shipping Act 1995 as if they were stock.

52.   Vesting orders of charity property

The powers conferred by this Act as to vesting orders may be exercised for vesting any interest in land, stock, or thing in action in any trustee of a charity or society over which the court would have jurisdiction upon action duly instituted, whether the appointment of the trustee was made by instrument under a power or by the court under its general or statutory jurisdiction.

53.   Vesting orders in relation to infant's beneficial interests

Where an infant is beneficially entitled to any property the court may, with a view to the application of the capital or income thereof for the maintenance, education, or benefit of the infant, make an order—

(a)   appointing a person to convey such property; or

(b)   in the case of stock, or a thing in action, vesting in any person the right to transfer or call for a transfer of such stock, or to receive the dividends or income thereof, or to sue for and recover such thing in action, upon such terms as the court may think fit.

54.   Jurisdiction in regard to mental patients

(1)   Subject to subsection (2), the Court of Protection may not make an order, or give a direction or authority, in relation to a person who lacks capacity to exercise his functions as trustee, if the High Court may make an order to that effect under this Act.

(2)   Where a person lacks capacity to exercise his functions as a trustee and a deputy is appointed for him by the Court of Protection or an application for the appointment of a deputy has been made but not determined, then, except as respects a trust which is subject to an order for administration made by the High Court, the Court of Protection shall have concurrent jurisdiction with the High Court in relation to—

(a)   mortgaged property of which the person concerned has become a trustee merely by reason of the mortgage having been paid off;

(b)   matters consequent on the making of provision by the Court of Protection for the exercise of a power of appointing trustees or retiring from a trust;

(c)   matters consequent on the making of provision by the Court of Protection for the carrying out of any contract entered into by the person concerned;

(d)   property to some interest in which the person concerned is beneficially entitled but which, or some interest in which, is held by the person concerned under an express, implied or constructive trust.

(2A) Rules may be made in accordance with Part 1 of Schedule 1 to the Constitutional Reform Act 2005 with respect to the exercise of the jurisdiction referred to in subsection (2).

55.   Orders made upon certain allegations to be conclusive evidence

Where a vesting order is made as to any land under this Act or under sections 15 to 20 of the Mental Capacity Act 2005 or any corresponding provisions having effect in Northern Ireland, founded on an allegation of any of the following matters namely—

(a)   that a trustee or mortgagee lacks capacity in relation to the matter in question; or

(b)   that a trustee or mortgagee or the personal representative of or other person deriving title under a trustee or mortgagee is out of the jurisdiction of the High Court or cannot be found, or being a corporation has been dissolved; or

(c)   that it is uncertain which of two or more trustees, or which of two or more persons interested in a mortgage, was the survivor, or

(d)   that it is uncertain whether the last trustee or the personal representative of or other person deriving title under a trustee or mortgagee, or the last surviving person interested in a mortgage is living or dead; or

(e)   that any trustee or mortgagee has died intestate without leaving a person beneficially interested under the intestacy or has died and it is not known who is his personal representative or the person interested;

the fact that the order has been so made shall be conclusive evidence of the matter so alleged in any court upon any question as to the validity of the order; but this section does not prevent the court from directing a reconveyance or surrender or the payment of costs occasioned by any such order if improperly obtained.

Jurisdiction to make other Orders

57. Power of court to authorise dealings with trust property

(1) Where in the management or administration of any property vested in trustees, any sale, lease, mortgage, surrender, release, or other disposition, or any purchase, investment, acquisition, expenditure or other transaction, is in the opinion of the court expedient, but the same cannot be effected by reason of the absence of any power for that purpose vested in the trustees by the trust instrument, if any, or by law, the court may by order confer upon the trustees, either generally or in any particular instance, the necessary power for the purpose, on such terms, and subject to such provisions and conditions, if any, as the court may think fit and may direct in what manner any money authorised to be expended, and the costs of any transaction, are to be paid or borne as between capital and income.

(2) The court may, from time to time, rescind or vary any order made under this section, or may make any new or further order.

(3) An application to the court under this section may be made by the trustees, or by any of them, or by any person beneficially interested under the trust.

(4) This section does not apply to trustees of a settlement for the purposes of the Settled Land Act, 1925.

58. Persons entitled to apply for orders

(1) An order under this Act for the appointment of a new trustee or concerning any interest in land, stock, or thing in action subject to a trust, may be made on the application of any person beneficially interested in the land, stock, or thing in action, whether under disability or not, or on the application of any person duly appointed trustee thereof.

(2) An order under this Act concerning any interest in land, stock, or thing in action subject to a mortgage may be made on the application of any person beneficially interested in the equity of redemption, whether under disability or not, or of any person interested in the money secured by the mortgage.

59. Power to give judgment in absence of a trustee

Where in any action the court is satisfied that diligent search has been made for any person who, in the character of trustee, is made a defendant in any action, to serve him with a process of the court, and that he cannot be found, the court may hear and determine the action and give judgment therein against that person in his character of a trustee as if he had been duly served, or had entered an appearance in the action, and had also appeared by his counsel and solicitor at the hearing, but without prejudice to any interest he may have in the matters in question in the action in any other character.

60. Power to charge costs on trust estate

The court may order the costs and expenses of and incident to any application for an order appointing a new trustee, or for a vesting order, or of and incident to any such order, or any transfer in pursuance thereof, to be raised and paid out of the property in respect whereof the same is made, or out of the income thereof, or to be borne and paid in such manner and by such persons as to the court may seem just.

61. Power to relieve trustee from personal liability

If it appears to the court that a trustee, whether appointed by the court or otherwise, is or may be personally liable for any breach of trust, whether the transaction alleged to be a breach of trust occurred before or after the commencement of this Act, but has acted honestly and reasonably, and ought fairly to be excused for the breach of trust and for omitting to obtain the directions of the court in the matter in which he committed such breach, then the court may relieve him either wholly or partly from personal liability for the same.

62. Power to make beneficiary indemnify for breach of trust

(1) Where a trustee commits a breach of trust at the instigation or request or with the consent in writing of a beneficiary, the court may, if it thinks fit, make such order as to the court seems just, for impounding all or any part of the interest of the beneficiary in the trust estate by way of indemnity to the trustee or persons claiming through him.

(2) This section applies to breaches of trust committed as well before as after the commencement of this Act.

Payment into Court

63. Payment into court by trustees
(1) Trustees, or the majority of trustees, having in their hands or under their control money or securities belonging to a trust, may pay the same into court;
(2) The receipt or certificate of the proper officer shall be a sufficient discharge to trustees for the money or securities so paid into court.
(3) Where money or securities are vested in any persons as trustees, and the majority are desirous of paying the same into court, but the concurrence of the other or others cannot be obtained, the court may order the payment into court to be made by the majority without the concurrence of the other or others.
(4) Where any such money or securities are deposited with any banker, broker, or other depositary, the court may order payment or delivery of the money or securities to the majority of the trustees for the purpose of payment into court.
(5) Every transfer payment and delivery made in pursuance of any such order shall be valid and take effect as if the same had been made on the authority or by the act of all the persons entitled to the money and securities so transferred, paid, or delivered.

PART V
GENERAL PROVISIONS

64. Application of Act to Settled Land Act Trustees
(1) All the powers and provisions contained in this Act with reference to the appointment of new trustees, and the discharge and retirement of trustees, apply to and include trustees for the purposes of the Settled Land Act, 1925, and trustees for the purpose of the management of land during a minority, whether such trustees are appointed by the court or by the settlement, or under provisions contained in any instrument.
(2) Where, either before or after the commencement of this Act, trustees of a settlement have been appointed by the court for the purposes of the Settled Land Acts, 1882 to 1890, or of the Settled Land Act, 1925, then, after the commencement of this Act—
   (a) the person or persons nominated for the purpose of appointing new trustees by the instrument, if any, creating the settlement, though no trustees for the purposes of the said Acts were thereby appointed; or
   (b) if there is no such person, or no such person able and willing to act, the surviving or continuing trustees or trustee for the time being for the purposes of the said Acts, or the personal representatives of the last surviving or continuing trustee for those purposes,
   shall have the powers conferred by this Act to appoint new or additional trustees of the settlement for the purposes of the said Acts.
(3) Appointments of new trustees for the purposes of the said Acts made or expressed to be made before the commencement of this Act by the trustees or trustee or personal representatives referred to in paragraph (b) of the last preceding subsection or by the persons referred to in paragraph (a) of that subsection are, without prejudice to any order of the court made before such commencement, hereby confirmed.

66. Indemnity to banks, etc.
This Act, and every order purporting to be made under this Act, shall be a complete indemnity to the Bank of England, the Registrar of Government Stock, any previous Registrar of Government Stock, and to all persons for any acts done pursuant thereto, and it shall not be necessary for the Bank, the Registrar of Government Stock, any previous Registrar of Government Stock or for any person to inquire concerning the propriety of the order, or whether the court by which the order was made had jurisdiction to make it.

67. Jurisdiction of the 'court'
(1) In this Act 'the court' means the High Court, or the county court, where those courts respectively have jurisdiction.
(2) The procedure under this Act in the county court shall be in accordance with the Acts and rules regulating the procedure of those courts.

68.   Definitions

(1)   In this Act, unless the context otherwise requires, the following expressions have the meanings hereby assigned to them respectively, that is to say: —

(1)   'Authorised investments' mean investments authorised by the instrument, if any, creating the trust for the investment of money subject to the trust, or by law;

(2)   'Contingent right' as applied to land includes a contingent or executory interest, a possibility coupled with an interest, whether the object of the gift or limitation of the interest, or possibility is or is not ascertained, also a right of entry, whether immediate or future, and whether vested or contingent;

(3)   'Convey' and 'conveyance' as applied to any person include the execution by that person of every necessary or suitable assurance (including an assent) for conveying, assigning, appointing, surrendering, or otherwise transferring or disposing of land whereof he is seised or possessed, or wherein he is entitled to a contingent right, either for his whole estate or for any less estate, together with the performance of all formalities required by law for the validity of the conveyance; 'sale' includes an exchange;

(4)   'Gazette' means the London Gazette;

(5)   'Instrument' includes Act of Parliament;

(6)   'Land' includes land of any tenure, and mines and minerals, whether or not severed from the surface, buildings or parts of buildings, whether the division is horizontal, vertical or made in any other way, and other corporeal hereditaments; also a manor, an advowson, and a rent and other incorporeal hereditaments, and an easement, right, privilege, or benefit in, over, or derived from land; and in this definition 'mines and minerals' include any strata or seam of minerals or substances in or under any land, and powers of working and getting the same; and 'hereditaments' mean real property which under an intestacy occurring before the commencement of this Act might have devolved on an heir;

(7)   'Mortgage' and 'mortgagee' include a charge or chargee by way of legal mortgage, and relate to every estate and interest regarded in equity as merely a security for money, and every person deriving title under the original mortgagee;

(8)   ...

(9)   Personal representative' means the executor, original or by representation, or administrator for the time being of a deceased person;

(10)   'Possession' includes receipt of rents and profits or the right to receive the same, if any; 'income' includes rents and profits; and 'possessed' applies to receipt of income of and to any vested estate less than a life interest in possession or in expectancy in any land;

(11)   'Property' includes real and personal property, and any estate share and interest in any property, real or personal, and any debt, and any thing in action, and any other right or interest, whether in possession or not;

(12)   'Rights' include estates and interests;

(13)   'Securities' include stocks, funds, and shares; and 'securities payable to bearer' include securities transferable by delivery or by delivery and endorsement;

(14)   'Stock' includes fully paid up shares, and so far as relates to vesting orders made by the court under this Act, includes any fund, annuity, or security transferable in books kept by any company or society, or by instrument of transfer either alone or accompanied by other formalities, and any share of interest therein;

(15)   'Tenant for life,' 'statutory owner,' 'settled land,' 'settlement,' 'trust instrument,' 'trustees of the settlement', 'term of years absolute' and 'vesting instrument' have the same meanings as in the Settled Land Act, 1925, and 'entailed interest' has the same meaning as in the Law of Property Act, 1925;

(16)   'Transfer' in relation to stock or securities, includes the performance and execution of every deed, power of attorney, act, and thing on the part of the transferor to effect and complete the title in the transferee;

(17)   'Trust' does not include the duties incident to an estate conveyed by way of mortgage, but with this exception the expressions 'trust' and 'trustee' extend to implied and constructive trusts, and to cases where the trustee has a beneficial interest in the trust property, and to the duties incident to the office of a personal representative, and 'trustee' where the context admits, includes a personal representative, and 'new trustee' includes an additional trustee;

(18)   'Trust corporation' means the Public Trustee or a corporation either appointed by the court in any particular case to be a trustee, or entitled by rules made under subsection (3) of section four of the Public Trustee Act, 1906, to act as custodian trustee;

(19)   'Trust for sale' in relation to land means an immediate trust for sale, whether or not exercisable at the request or with the consent of any person;

(20)   'United Kingdom' means Great Britain and Northern Ireland.

(2)   Any reference in this Act to paying money or securities into court shall be construed as referring to paying the money or transferring or depositing the securities into or in the Senior Courts or into or in any other court that has jurisdiction, and any reference in this Act to payment of money or securities into court shall be construed—

     (a)   with reference to an order of the High Court, as referring to payment of the money or transfer or deposit of the securities into or in the Senior Courts; and

     (b)   with reference to an order of any other court, as referring to payment of the money or transfer or deposit of the securities into or in that court.

(3)   Any reference in this Act to a person who lacks capacity in relation to a matter is to a person—

     (a)   who lacks capacity within the meaning of the Mental Capacity Act 2005 in relation to that matter, or

     (b)   in respect of whom the powers conferred by section 48 of that Act are exercisable and have been exercised in relation to that matter.

69.   Application of Act

(1)   This Act, except where otherwise expressly provided, applies to trusts including, so far as this Act applies thereto, executorships and administratorships constituted or created either before or after the commencement of this Act.

(2)   The powers conferred by this Act on trustees are in addition to the powers conferred by the instrument, if any, creating the trust, but those powers, unless otherwise stated, apply if and so far only as a contrary intention is not expressed in the instrument, if any, creating the trust, and have effect subject to the terms of that instrument.

70.   Enactments repealed

… without prejudice to the provisions of section thirty-eight of the Interpretation Act, 1889:

     (a)   Nothing in this repeal shall affect any vesting order or appointment made or other thing done under any enactment so repealed, and any order or appointment so made may be revoked or varied in like manner as if it had been made under this Act;

     (b)   References in any document to any enactment repealed by this Act shall be construed as references to this Act or to the corresponding enactment in this Act.

LAW OF PROPERTY ACT 1925
(1925, c. 20)

Note. References to the Land Charges Act, 1925 should be read as references to the Land Charges Act, 1972.

PART I

GENERAL PRINCIPLES AS TO LEGAL ESTATES, EQUITABLE INTERESTS AND POWERS

1.   Legal estates and equitable interests

(1)   The only estates in land which are capable of subsisting or of being conveyed or created at law are—

     (a)   An estate in fee simple absolute in possession;

     (b)   A term of years absolute.

(2)   The only interests or charges in or over land which are capable of subsisting or of being conveyed or created at law are—

     (a)   An easement, right, or privilege in or over land for an interest equivalent to an estate in fee simple absolute in possession or a term of years absolute;

     (b)   A rentcharge in possession issuing out of or charged on land being either perpetual or for a term of years absolute;

(c)   A charge by way of legal mortgage;

(d)   ... and any other similar charge on land which is not created by an instrument;

(e)   Rights of entry exercisable over or in respect of a legal term of years absolute, or annexed, for any purpose, to a legal rentcharge.

(3) All other estates, interests, and charges in or over land take effect as equitable interests.

(4) The estates, interests, and charges which under this section are authorised to subsist or to be conveyed or created at law are (when subsisting or conveyed or created at law) in this Act referred to as 'legal estates', and have the same incidents as legal estates subsisting at the commencement of this Act; and the owner of a legal estate is referred to as an 'estate owner' and his legal estate is referred to as his estate.

(5) A legal estate may subsist concurrently with or subject to any other legal estate in the same land in like manner as it could have done before the commencement of this Act.

(6) A legal estate is not capable of subsisting or of being created in an undivided share in land or of being held by an infant.

(7) Every power of appointment over, or power to convey or charge land or any interest therein, whether created by a statute or other instrument or implied by law, and whether created before or after the commencement of this Act (not being a power vested in a legal mortgagee or an estate owner in right of his estate and exercisable by him or by another person in his name and on his behalf), operates only in equity.

(8) Estates, interests, and charges in or over land which are not legal estates are in this Act referred to as 'equitable interests,' and powers which by this Act are to operate in equity only are in this Act referred to as 'equitable powers.'

(9) The provisions in any statute or other instrument requiring land to be conveyed to uses shall take effect as directions that the land shall (subject to creating or reserving thereout any legal estate authorised by this Act which may be required) be conveyed to a person of full age upon the requisite trusts.

(10) The repeal of the Statute of Uses (as amended) does not affect the operation thereof in regard to dealings taking effect before the commencement of this Act.

2.   Conveyances overreaching certain equitable interests and powers

(1) A conveyance to a purchaser of a legal estate in land shall overreach any equitable interest or power affecting that estate, whether or not he has notice thereof, if—

(i)   the conveyance is made under the powers conferred by the Settled Land Act 1925, or any additional powers conferred by a settlement, and the equitable interest or power is capable of being overreached thereby, and the statutory requirements respecting the payment of capital money arising under the settlement are complied with;

(ii)   the conveyance is made by trustees of land and the equitable interest or power is at the date of the conveyance capable of being overreached by such trustees under the provisions of subsection (2) of this section or independently of that subsection, and the requirements of section 27 of this Act respecting the payment of capital money arising on such a conveyance are complied with;

(iii) the conveyance is made by a mortgagee or personal representative in the exercise of his paramount powers, and the equitable interest or power is capable of being overreached by such conveyance, and any capital money arising from the transaction is paid to the mortgagee or personal representative;

(iv)   the conveyance is made under an order of the court and the equitable interest or power is bound by such order, and any capital money arising from the transaction is paid into, or in accordance with the order of, the court.

(1A) An equitable interest in land subject to a trust of land which remains in, or is to revert to, the settlor shall (subject to any contrary intention) be overreached by the conveyance if it would be so overreached were it an interest under the trust.

(2) Where the legal estate affected is subject to a trust of land, then if at the date of a conveyance made after the commencement of this Act by the trustees, the trustees (whether original or substituted) are either—

(a)   two or more individuals approved or appointed by the court or the successors in office of the individuals so approved or appointed; or

(b)   a trust corporation,

any equitable interest or power having priority to the trust shall, notwithstanding any stipulation to the contrary, be overreached by the conveyance, and shall, according to its priority, take effect as if created or arising by means of a primary trust affecting the proceeds of sale and the income of the land until sale.

(3)   The following equitable interests and powers are excepted from the operation of subsection (2) of this section, namely—

    (i)   Any equitable interest protected by a deposit of documents relating to the legal estate affected;

    (ii)   The benefit of any covenant or agreement restrictive of the user of land;

    (iii)   Any easement, liberty, or privilege over or affecting land and being merely an equitable interest (in this Act referred to as an 'equitable easement');

    (iv)   The benefit of any contract (in this Act referred to as an 'estate contract') to convey or create a legal estate, including a contract conferring either expressly or by statutory implication a valid option to purchase, a right of preemption, or any other like right;

    (v)   Any equitable interest protected by registration under the Land Charges Act, 1925, other than—

        (a)   an annuity within the meaning of Part II of that Act;

        (b)   a limited owner's charge or a general equitable charge within the meaning of that Act.

(4)   Subject to the protection afforded by this section to the purchaser of a legal estate, nothing contained in this section shall deprive a person entitled to an equitable charge of any of his rights or remedies for enforcing the same.

(5)   So far as regards the following interests, created before the commencement of this Act (which accordingly are not within the provisions of the Land Charges Act, 1925), namely—

    (a)   the benefit of any covenant or agreement restrictive of the user of the land;

    (b)   any equitable easement;

    (c)   the interest under a puisne mortgage within the meaning of the Land Charges Act, 1925, unless and until acquired under a transfer made after the commencement of this Act;

    (d)   the benefit of an estate contract, unless and until the same is acquired under a conveyance made after the commencement of this Act;

a purchaser of a legal estate shall only take subject thereto if he has notice thereof, and the same are not overreached under the provisions contained or in the manner referred to in this section.

3.   Manner of giving effect to equitable interests and powers

(1)   All equitable interests and powers in or over land shall be enforceable against the estate owner of the legal estate affected in manner following (that is to say):—

    (a)   Where the legal estate affected is settled land, the tenant for life or statutory owner shall be bound to give effect to the equitable interests and powers in manner provided by the Settled Land Act, 1925;

    (b)   ...

    (c)   In any other case, the estate owner shall be bound to give effect to the equitable interests and powers affecting his estate of which he has notice according to their respective priorities. This provision does not affect the priority or powers of a legal mortgagee, or the powers of personal representatives for purposes of administration.

(2)   ...

(3)   Where, by reason of an equitable right of entry taking effect, or for any other reason, a person becomes entitled to require a legal estate to be vested in him, then and in any such case the estate owner whose estate is affected shall be bound to convey or create such legal estate as the case may require.

(4)   If any question arises whether any and what legal estate ought to be transferred or created as aforesaid, any person interested may apply to the court for directions in the manner provided by this Act.

(5)   If the owners refuse or neglect for one month after demand to transfer or create any such legal estate, or if by reason of their being out of the United Kingdom or being unable to be found, or by reason of the dissolution of a corporation, or for any other reason, the court is satisfied that the transaction cannot otherwise be effected, or cannot be effected without undue delay or expense, the court may, on the application of any person

interested, make a vesting order transferring or creating a legal estate in the manner provided by this Act.

(6) This section does not affect a purchaser of a legal estate taking free from an equitable interest or power.

(7) The county court has jurisdiction under this section where the land which is to be dealt with in the court does not exceed £30,000 in capital value... .

4. Creation and disposition of equitable interests

(1) Interests in land validly created or arising after the commencement of this Act, which are not capable of subsisting as legal estates, shall take effect as equitable interests, and, save as otherwise expressly provided by statute, interests in land which under the Statute of Uses or otherwise could before the commencement of this Act have been created as legal interests, shall be capable of being created as equitable interests:

Provided that, after the commencement of this Act (and save as hereinafter expressly enacted), an equitable interest in land shall only be capable of being validly created in any case in which an equivalent equitable interest in property real or personal could have been validly created before such commencement.

(2) All rights and interests in land may be disposed of, including—

(a) a contingent, executory or future equitable interest in any land, or a possibility coupled with an interest in any land, whether or not the object of the gift or limitation of such interest or possibility be ascertained;

(b) a right of entry, into or upon land whether immediate or future, and whether vested or contingent.

(3) All rights of entry affecting a legal estate which are exercisable on condition broken or for any other reason may, after the commencement of this Act, be made exercisable by any person and the persons deriving title under him.

5. Satisfied terms, whether created out of freehold or leasehold land to cease

(1) Where the purposes of a term of years created or limited at any time out of freehold land, become satisfied either before or after the commencement of this Act (whether or not that term either by express declaration or by construction of law becomes attendant upon the freehold reversion) it shall merge in the reversion expectant thereon and shall cease accordingly.

(2) Where the purposes of a term of years created or limited, at any time, out of leasehold land, become satisfied after the commencement of this Act, that term shall merge in the reversion expectant thereon and shall cease accordingly.

(3) Where the purposes are satisfied only as respects part of the land comprised in a term, this section shall have effect as if a separate term had been created in regard to that part of the land.

6. Saving of lessors' and lessees' covenants

(1) Nothing in this Part of this Act affects prejudicially the right to enforce any lessor's or lessee's covenants, agreements or conditions (including a valid option to purchase or right of preemption over the reversion), contained in any such instrument as is in this section mentioned, the benefit or burden of which runs with the reversion or the term.

(2) This section applies where the covenant, agreement or condition is contained in any instrument—

(a) creating a term of years absolute, or

(b) varying the rights of the lessor or lessee under the instrument creating the term.

7. Saving of certain legal estates and statutory powers

(1) A fee simple which, by virtue of the Lands Clauses Acts, or any similar statute, is liable to be divested, is for the purposes of this Act a fee simple absolute, and remains liable to be divested as if this Act had not been passed, and a fee simple subject to a legal or equitable right of entry or re-entry is for the purposes of this Act a fee simple absolute.

(2) A fee simple vested in a corporation which is liable to determine by reason of the dissolution of the corporation is, for the purposes of this Act, a fee simple absolute.

(3) The provisions of—

(a) ...

(b) ...

(c)   any other statutes conferring special facilities or prescribing special modes (whether by way of registered memorial or otherwise) for disposing of or acquiring land, or providing for the vesting (by conveyance or otherwise) of the land in trustees or any person, or the holder for the time being of an office or any corporation sole or aggregate (including the Crown);
shall remain in full force.
...

(4)   Where any such power for disposing of or creating a legal state is exercisable by a person who is not the estate owner, the power shall, when practicable, be exercised in the name and on behalf of the estate owner.

8.   Saving of certain legal powers to lease

(1)   All leases or tenancies at a rent for a term of years absolute authorised to be granted by a mortgagor or mortgagee or by the Settled Land Act, 1925, or any other statute (whether or not extended by any instrument) may be granted in the name and on behalf of the estate owner by the person empowered to grant the same, whether being an estate owner or not, with the same effect and priority as if this Part of this Act had not been passed; but this section does not (except as respects the usual qualified covenant for quiet enjoyment) authorise any person granting a lease in the name of an estate owner to impose any personal liability on him.

(2)   Where a rentcharge is held for a legal estate, the owner thereof may under the statutory power or under any corresponding power, create a legal term of years absolute for securing or compelling payment of the same; but in other cases terms created under any such power shall, unless and until the estate owner of the land charged gives legal effect to the transaction, take effect only as equitable interests.

9.   Vesting orders and dispositions of legal estates operating as conveyances by an estate owner

(1)   Every such order, declaration, or conveyance as is hereinafter mentioned, namely—
      (a)   every vesting order made by any court or other competent authority;
      (b)   every vesting declaration (express or implied) under any statutory power;
      (c)   every vesting instrument made by the trustees of a settlement or other persons under the provisions of the Settled Land Act, 1925;
      (d)   every conveyance by a person appointed for the purpose under an order of the court or authorised under any statutory power to convey in the name or on behalf of an estate owner;
      (e)   every conveyance made under any power reserved or conferred by this Act,
which is made or executed for the purpose of vesting, conveying, or creating a legal estate, shall operate to convey or create the legal estate disposed of in like manner as if the same had been a conveyance executed by the estate owner of the legal estate to which the order, declaration, vesting instrument, or conveyance relates.

(2)   Where the order, declaration, or conveyance is made in favour of a purchaser, the provisions of this Act relating to a conveyance of a legal estate to a purchaser shall apply thereto.

(3)   The provisions of the Trustee Act, 1925, relating to vesting orders and orders appointing a person to convey shall apply to all vesting orders authorised to be made by this Part of this Act.

10.   Title to be shown to legal estates

(1)   Where title is shown to a legal estate in land, it shall be deemed not necessary or proper to include in the abstract of title an instrument relating only to interests or powers which will be overreached by the conveyance of the estate to which title is being shown; but nothing in this Part of this Act affects the liability of any person to disclose an equitable interest or power which will not be so overreached, or to furnish an abstract of any instrument creating or affecting the same.

(2)   A solicitor delivering an abstract framed in accordance with this Part of this Act shall not incur any liability on account of an omission to include therein an instrument which, under this section, is to be deemed not necessary or proper to be included, nor shall any liability be implied by reason of the inclusion of any such instrument.

12.   Limitation and Prescription Acts

Nothing in this Part of this Act affects the operation of any statute, or of the general law for the limitation of actions or proceedings relating to land or with reference to the acquisition of easements or rights over or in respect of land.

13.   Effect of possession of documents

This Act shall not prejudicially affect the right or interest of any person arising out of or consequent on the possession by him of any documents relating to a legal estate in land, nor affect any question arising out of or consequent upon any omission to obtain or any other absence of possession by any person of any documents relating to a legal estate in land.

14.   Interests of persons in possession

This Part of this Act shall not prejudicially affect the interest of any person in possession or in actual occupation of land to which he may be entitled in right of such possession or occupation.

15.   Presumption that parties are of full age

The persons expressed to be parties to any conveyance shall, until the contrary is proved, be presumed to be of full age at the date thereof.

Infants and Lunatics

20.   Infants not to be appointed trustees

The appointment of an infant to be a trustee in relation to any settlement or trust shall be void, but without prejudice to the power to appoint a new trustee to fill the vacancy.

21.   Receipts by married infants

A married infant shall have power to give valid receipts for all income (including statutory accumulations of income made during the minority) to which the infant may be entitled in like manner as if the infant were of full age.

22.   Conveyances on behalf of persons suffering from mental disorder and as to land held by them in trust

(1)   Where a legal estate in land (whether settled or not) is vested, either solely or jointly with any other person or persons, in a person lacking capacity (within the meaning of the Mental Capacity Act 2005) to convey or create a legal estate, a deputy appointed for him by the Court of Protection or (if no deputy is appointed for him) any person authorised in that behalf shall, under an order of the Court of Protection, or of the court, or under any statutory power, make or concur in making all requisite dispositions for conveying or creating a legal estate in his name and on his behalf.

(2)   If land subject to a trust of land is vested, either solely or jointly with any other person or persons, in a person who lacks capacity (within the meaning of that Act) to exercise his functions as trustee, a new trustee shall be appointed in the place of that person, or he shall be otherwise discharged from the trust, before the legal estate is dealt with by the trustees.

(3)   Subsection (2) of this section does not prevent a legal estate being dealt with without the appointment of a new trustee, or the discharge of the incapable trustee, at a time when the donee of an enduring power of attorney or lasting power of attorney (within the meaning of the 2005 Act) is entitled to act for the trustee who lacks capacity in relation to the dealing.

Trusts of land

24.   Appointment of trustees of land

(1)   The persons having power to appoint new trustees of land shall be bound to appoint the same persons (if any) who are for the time being trustees of any trust of the proceeds of sale of the land.

(2)   A purchaser shall not be concerned to see that subsection (1) of this section has been complied with.

(3)   This section applies whether the trust of land and the trust of proceeds of sale are created, or arise, before or after the commencement of this Act.

27. Purchaser not to be concerned with the trusts of the proceeds of sale which are to be paid to two or more trustees or to a trust corporation

(1) A purchaser of a legal estate from trustees of land shall not be concerned with the trusts affecting the land, the net income of the land or the proceeds of sale of the land whether or not those trusts are declared by the same instrument as that by which the trust of land is created.

(2) Notwithstanding anything to the contrary in the instrument (if any) creating a trust of land or in any trust affecting the net proceeds of sale of the land if it is sold, the proceeds of sale or other capital money shall not be paid to or applied by the direction of fewer than two persons as trustees, except where the trustee is a trust corporation, but this subsection does not affect the right of a sole personal representative as such to give valid receipts for, or direct the application of, proceeds of sale or other capital money, nor, except where capital money arises on the transaction, render it necessary to have more than one trustee.

31. Trust of mortgaged property where right of redemption is barred

(1) Where any property, vested in trustees by way of security, becomes, by virtue of the statutes of limitation, or of an order for foreclosure or otherwise, discharged from the right of redemption, it shall be held by them in trust—

(a) to apply the income from the property in the same manner as interest paid on the mortgage debt would have been applicable; and

(b) if the property is sold, to apply the net proceeds of sale, after payment of costs and expenses, in the same manner as repayment of the mortgage debt would have been applicable.

(2) Subsection (1) of this section operates without prejudice to any rule of law relating to the apportionment of capital and income between tenant for life and remainderman.

(3) ...

(4) Where—

(a) the mortgage money is capital money for the purposes of the Settled Land Act 1925;

(b) land other than any forming the whole or part of the property mentioned in subsection (1) of this section is, or is deemed to be, subject to the settlement; and

(c) the tenant for life or statutory owner requires the trustees to execute with respect to land forming the whole or part of that property a vesting deed such as would have been required in relation to the land if it had been acquired and purchased with capital money,

the trustees shall execute such a vesting deed.

(5) This section applies whether the right of redemption was discharged before or after the first day of January, nineteen hundred and twelve, but has effect without prejudice to any dealings or arrangements made before that date.

33. Application of Part I to personal representatives

The provisions of this Part of this Act relating to trustees of land apply to personal representatives holding land in trust, but without prejudice to their rights and powers for purposes of administration.

Undivided Shares and Joint Ownership

34. Effect of future dispositions to tenants in common

(1) An undivided share in land shall not be capable of being created except as provided by the Settled Land Act, 1925, or as hereinafter mentioned.

(2) Where, after the commencement of this Act, land is expressed to be conveyed to any persons in undivided shares and those persons are of full age, the conveyance shall (notwithstanding anything to the contrary in this Act) operate as if the land had been expressed to be conveyed to the grantees, or, if there are more than four grantees, to the four first named in the conveyance, as joint tenants in trust for the persons interested in the land:

Provided that, where the conveyance is made by way of mortgage the land shall vest in the grantees or such four of them as aforesaid for a term of years absolute (as provided by this Act) as joint tenants subject to cesser on redemption in like manner as if the mortgage money had belonged to them on a joint account, but without prejudice to the beneficial interests in the mortgage money and interest.

(3)   A devise bequest or testamentary appointment, coming into operation after the commencement of this Act, of land to two or more persons in undivided shares shall operate as a devise bequest or appointment of the land to the personal representatives of the testator, and (but without prejudice to the rights and powers of the personal representatives for purposes of administration) in trust for the persons interested in the land.

(3A) In subsections (2) and (3) of this section references to the persons interested in the land include persons interested as trustees or personal representatives (as well as persons beneficially interested).

36.   Joint tenancies

(1)   Where a legal estate (not being settled land) is beneficially limited to or held in trust for any persons as joint tenants, the same shall be held in trust in like manner as if the persons beneficially entitled were tenants in common, but not so as to sever their joint tenancy in equity.

(2)   No severance of a joint tenancy of a legal estate, so as to create a tenancy in common in land, shall be permissible, whether by operation of law or otherwise, but this subsection does not affect the right of a joint tenant to release his interest to the other joint tenants, or the right to sever a joint tenancy in an equitable interest whether or not the legal estate is vested in the joint tenants:

Provided that, where a legal estate (not being settled land) is vested in joint tenants beneficially, and any tenant desires to sever the joint tenancy in equity, he shall give to the other joint tenants a notice in writing of such desire or do such other acts or things as would, in the case of personal estate, have been effectual to sever the tenancy in equity, and thereupon the land shall be held in trust on terms which would have been requisite for giving effect to the beneficial interests if there had been an actual severance.

Nothing in this Act affects the right of a survivor of joint tenants, who is solely and beneficially interested, to deal with his legal estate as if it were not held in trust.

(3)   Without prejudice to the right of a joint tenant to release his interest to the other joint tenants no severance of a mortgage term or trust estate, so as to create a tenancy in common, shall be permissible.

37.   Rights of husband and wife

A husband and wife shall, for all purposes of acquisition of any interest in property, under a disposition made or coming into operation after the commencement of this Act, be treated as two persons.

38.   Party structures

(1)   Where under a disposition or other arrangement which, if a holding in undivided shares had been permissible, would have created a tenancy in common, a wall or other structure is or is expressed to be made a party wall or structure, that structure shall be and remain severed vertically as between the respective owners, and the owner of each part shall have such rights to support and user over the rest of the structure as may be requisite for conferring rights corresponding to those which would have subsisted if a valid tenancy in common had been created.

(2)   Any person interested may, in case of dispute, apply to the court for an order declaring the rights and interests under this section of the persons interested in any such party structure, and the court may make such order as it thinks fit.

Transitional Provisions

39.   Transitional provisions in First Schedule

For the purpose of effecting the transition from the law existing prior to the commencement of the Law of Property Act, 1922, to the law enacted by that Act (as amended), the provisions set out in the First Schedule to this Act shall have effect—

(1)   for converting existing legal estates, interests and charges not capable under the said Act of taking effect as legal interests into equitable interests;

(2)   for discharging, getting in or vesting outstanding legal estates;

(3)   for making provision with respect to legal estates vested in infants;

(4)   for subjecting land held in undivided shares to trusts;

(5)   for dealing with party structures and open spaces held in common;

(6)   ...

(7)   for converting existing freehold mortgages into mortgages by demise;

(8)   for converting existing leasehold mortgages into mortgages by sub-demise.

PART II
CONTRACTS, CONVEYANCES AND OTHER INSTRUMENTS

Contracts

41. Stipulations not of the essence of a contract

Stipulations in a contract, as to time or otherwise, which according to rules of equity are not deemed to be or to have become of the essence of the contract, are also construed and have effect at law in accordance with the same rules.

42. Provisions as to contracts

(1) A stipulation that a purchaser of a legal estate in land shall accept a title made with the concurrence of any person entitled to an equitable interest shall be void, if a title can be made discharged from the equitable interest without such concurrence—
   (a)   under a trust of land; or
   (b)   under this Act, or the Settled Land Act, 1925, or any other statute.

(2) A stipulation that a purchaser of a legal estate in land shall pay or contribute towards the costs of or incidental to—
   (a)   obtaining a vesting order, or the appointment of trustees of a settlement, or the appointment of trustees of land; or
   (b)   the preparation stamping or execution of a conveyance in trust, or of a vesting instrument for bringing into force the provisions of the Settled Land Act, 1925; shall be void.

(3) A stipulation contained in any contract for the sale or exchange of land made after the commencement of this Act, to the effect that an outstanding legal estate is to be traced or got in by or at the expense of a purchaser or that no objection is to be taken on account of an outstanding legal estate, shall be void.

(4) If the subject matter of any contract for the sale or exchange of land—
   (i)   is a mortgage term and the vendor has power to convey the fee simple in the land, or, in the case of a mortgage of a term of years absolute, the leasehold reversion affected by the mortgage, the contract shall be deemed to extend to the fee simple in the land or such leasehold reversion;
   (ii)   is an equitable interest capable of subsisting as a legal estate, and the vendor has power to vest such legal estate in himself or in the purchaser or to require the same to be so vested, the contract shall be deemed to extend to such legal estate;
   (iii) is an entailed interest in possession and the vendor has power to vest in himself or in the purchaser the fee simple in the land, (or, if the entailed interest is an interest in a term of years absolute, such term,) or to require the same to be so vested, the contract shall be deemed to extend to the fee simple in the land or the term of years absolute.

(5) This section does not affect the right of a mortgagee of leasehold land to sell his mortgage term only if he is unable to convey or vest the leasehold reversion expectant thereon.

(6) ...

(7) Where a purchaser has power to acquire land compulsorily, and a contract, whether by virtue of a notice to treat or otherwise, is subsisting under which title can be made without payment of the compensation money into court, title shall be made in that way unless the purchaser, to avoid expense or delay or for any special reason, considers it expedient that the money should be paid into court.

(8) A vendor shall not have any power to rescind a contract by reason only of the enforcement of any right under this section.

(9) This section only applies in favour of a purchaser for money or money's worth.

43. Rights protected by registration

(1) Where a purchaser of a legal estate is entitled to acquire the same discharged from an equitable interest which is protected by registration as a pending action, annuity, writ, order or land charge, and which will not be overreached by the conveyance to him, he may notwithstanding any stipulation to the contrary, require—
   (a)   that the registration shall be cancelled; or
   (b)   that the person entitled to the equitable interest shall concur in the conveyance; and in either case free of expense to the purchaser.

    (2)   Where the registration cannot be cancelled or the person entitled to the equitable interest refuses to concur in the conveyance, this section does not affect the right of any person to rescind the contract.

44. Statutory commencements of title

    (1)   After the commencement of this Act fifteen years shall be substituted for forty years as the period of commencement of title which a purchaser of land may require; nevertheless earlier title than fifteen years may be required in cases similar to those in which earlier title than forty years might immediately before the commencement of this Act be required.

    (2)   Under a contract to grant or assign a term of years, whether derived or to be derived out of freehold or leasehold land, the intended lessee or assign shall not be entitled to call for the title to the freehold.

    (3)   Under a contract to sell and assign a term of years derived out of a leasehold interest in land, the intended assign shall not have the right to call for the title to the leasehold reversion.

    (4)   On a contract to grant a lease for a term of years to be derived out of a leasehold interest, with a leasehold reversion, the intended lessee shall not have the right to call for the title to that reversion.

    (4A) Subsections (2) and (4) of this section do not apply to a contract to grant a term of years if the grant will be an event within section 4(1) of the Land Registration Act 2002 (events which trigger first registration of title).

    (5)   Where by reason of any of subsections (2) to (4) of this section, an intending lessee or assign is not entitled to call for the title to the freehold or to a leasehold reversion, as the case may be, he shall not, where the contract is made after the commencement of this Act, be deemed to be affected with notice of any matter or thing of which, if he had contracted that such title should be furnished, he might have had notice.

    (6)   Where land of copyhold or customary tenure has been converted into freehold by enfranchisement, then, under a contract to sell and convey the freehold, the purchaser shall not have the right to call for the title to make the enfranchisement.

    (7)   Where the manorial incidents formerly affecting any land have been extinguished, then, under a contract to sell and convey the freehold, the purchaser shall not have the right to call for the title of the person entering into any compensation agreement or giving a receipt for the compensation money to enter into such agreement or to give such receipt, and shall not be deemed to be affected with notice of any matter or thing of which, if he had contracted that such title should be furnished, he might have had notice.

    (8)   A purchaser shall not be deemed to be or ever to have been affected with notice of any matter or thing of which, if he had investigated the title or made enquiries in regard to matters prior to the period of commencement of title fixed by this Act, or by any other statute, or by any rule of law, he might have had notice, unless he actually makes such investigation or enquiries.

    (9)   Where a lease whether made before or after the commencement of this Act, is made under a power contained in a settlement, will, Act of Parliament, or other instrument, any preliminary contract for or relating to the lease shall not, for the purpose of the deduction of title to an intended assign, form part of the title, or evidence of the title, to the lease.

    (10) This section, save where otherwise expressly provided, applies to contracts for sale whether made before or after the commencement of this Act, and applies to contracts for exchange in like manner as to contracts for sale, save that it applies only to contracts for exchange made after such commencement.

    (11) This section applies only if and so far as a contrary intention is not expressed in the contract.

    (12) Nothing in this section applies in relation to registered land or to a term of years to be derived out of registered land.

45. Other statutory conditions of sale

    (1)   A purchaser of any property shall not—

        (a)   require the production, or any abstract or copy, of any deed, will, or other document, dated or made before the time prescribed by law, or stipulated, for the commencement of the title, even though the same creates a power subsequently exercised by an instrument abstracted in the abstract furnished to the purchaser; or

(b)　require any information, or make any requisition, objection, or inquiry, with respect to any such deed, will, or document, or the title prior to that time, notwithstanding that any such deed, will, or other document, or that prior title, is recited, agreed to be produced, or noticed;

and he shall assume, unless the contrary appears, that the recitals, contained in the abstracted instruments, of any deed, will, or other document, forming part of that prior title, are correct, and give all the material contents of the deed, will, or other document so recited, and that every document so recited was duly executed by all necessary parties, and perfected, if and as required, by fine, recovery, acknowledgment, inrolment, or otherwise:

Provided that this subsection shall not deprive a purchaser of the right to require the production, or an abstract or copy of—

(i)　any power of attorney under which any abstracted document is executed; or

(ii)　any document creating or disposing of an interest, power or obligation which is not shown to have ceased or expired, and subject to which any part of the property is disposed of by an abstracted document; or

(iii)　any document creating any limitation or trust by reference to which any part of the property is disposed of by an abstracted document.

(2)　Where land sold is held by lease (other than an under-lease), the purchaser shall assume, unless the contrary appears, that the lease was duly granted; and, on production of the receipt for the last payment due for rent under the lease before the date of actual completion of the purchase, he shall assume, unless the contrary appears, that all the covenants and provisions of the lease have been duly performed and observed up to the date of actual completion of the purchase.

(3)　Where land sold is held by under-lease, the purchaser shall assume, unless the contrary appears, that the under-lease and every superior lease were duly granted; and, on production of the receipt for the last payment due for rent under the under-lease before the date of actual completion of the purchase, he shall assume, unless the contrary appears, that all the covenants and provisions of the under-lease have been duly performed and observed up to the date of actual completion of the purchase, and further that all rent due under every superior lease, and all the covenants and provisions of every superior lease, have been paid and duly performed and observed up to that date.

(4)　On a sale of any property, the following expenses shall be borne by the purchaser where he requires them to be incurred for the purpose of verifying the abstract or any other purpose, that is to say—

(a)　the expenses of the production and inspection of all Acts of Parliament, inclosure awards, records, proceedings of courts, court rolls, deeds, wills, probates, letters of administration, and other documents, not in the possession of the vendor or his mortgagee or trustee, and the expenses of all journeys incidental to such production or inspection; and

(b)　the expenses of searching for, procuring, making, verifying, and producing all certificates, declarations, evidences, and information not in the possession of the vendor or his mortgagee or trustee, and all attested, stamped, office, or other copies or abstracts of, or extracts from, any Acts of Parliament or other documents aforesaid, not in the possession of the vendor or his mortgagee or trustee,

and where the vendor or his mortgagee or trustee retains possession of any document, the expenses of making any copy thereof, attested or unattested, which a purchaser requires to be delivered to him, shall be borne by that purchaser.

(5)　On a sale of any property in lots, a purchaser of two or more lots, held wholly or partly under the same title, shall not have a right to more than one abstract of the common title, except at his own expense.

(6)　Recitals, statements, and descriptions of facts, matters, and parties contained in deeds, instruments, Acts of Parliament, or statutory declarations, twenty years old at the date of the contract, shall, unless and except so far as they may be proved to be inaccurate, be taken to be sufficient evidence of the truth of such facts, matters, and descriptions.

(7)　The inability of a vendor to furnish a purchaser with an acknowledgment of his right to production and delivery of copies of documents of title or with a legal covenant to produce and furnish copies of documents of title shall not be an objection to title in case the purchaser will, on the completion of the contract, have an equitable right to the production of such documents.

(8) Such acknowledgments of the right of production or covenants for production and such undertakings or covenants for safe custody of documents as the purchaser can and does require shall be furnished or made at his expense, and the vendor shall bear the expense of perusal and execution on behalf of and by himself, and on behalf of and by necessary parties other than the purchaser.

(9) A vendor shall be entitled to retain documents of title where—

    (a)   he retains any part of the land to which the documents relate; or

    (b)   the document consists of a trust instrument or other instrument creating a trust which is still subsisting, or an instrument relating to the appointment or discharge of a trustee of a subsisting trust.

(10) This section applies to contracts for sale made before or after the commencement of this Act, and applies to contracts for exchange in like manner as to contracts for sale, except that it applies only to contracts for exchange made after such commencement:

    Provided that this section shall apply subject to any stipulation or contrary intention expressed in the contract.

(11) Nothing in this section shall be construed as binding a purchaser to complete his purchase in any case where, on a contract made independently of this section, and containing stipulations similar to the provisions of this section, or any of them, specific performance of the contract would not be enforced against him by the court.

46. Forms of contracts and conditions of sale

The Lord Chancellor may from time to time prescribe and publish forms of contracts and conditions of sale of land, and the forms so prescribed shall, subject to any modification, or any stipulation or intention to the contrary, expressed in the correspondence, apply to contracts by correspondence, and may, but only by express reference thereto, be made to apply to any other cases for which the forms are made available.

47. Application of insurance money on completion of a sale or exchange

(1) Where after the date of any contract for sale or exchange of property, money becomes payable under any policy of insurance maintained by the vendor in respect of any damage to or destruction of property included in the contract, the money shall, on completion of the contract, be held or receivable by the vendor on behalf of the purchaser and paid by the vendor to the purchaser on completion of the sale or exchange, or so soon thereafter as the same shall be received by the vendor.

(2) This section applies only to contracts made after the commencement of this Act, and has effect subject to—

    (a)   any stipulation to the contrary contained in the contract,

    (b)   any requisite consents of the insurers,

    (c)   the payment by the purchaser of the proportionate part of the premium from the date of the contract.

(3) This section applies to a sale or exchange by an order of the court, as if—

    (a)   for references to the 'vendor' there were substituted references to the 'person bound by the order';

    (b)   for the reference to the completion of the contract there were substituted a reference to the payment of the purchase or equality money (if any) into court;

    (c)   for the reference to the date of the contract there were substituted a reference to the time when the contract becomes binding.

48. Stipulations preventing a purchaser, lessee, or underlessee from employing his own solicitor to be void

(1) Any stipulation made on the sale of any interest in land after the commencement of this Act to the effect that the conveyance to, or the registration of the title of, the purchaser shall be prepared or carried out at the expense of the purchaser by a solicitor appointed by or acting for the vendor, and any stipulation which might restrict a purchaser in the selection of a solicitor to act on his behalf in relation to any interest in land agreed to be purchased, shall be void; and, if a sale is effected by demise or subdemise, then, for the purposes of this subsection, the instrument required for giving effect to the transaction shall be deemed to be a conveyance:

Provided that nothing in this subsection shall affect any right reserved to a vendor to furnish a form of conveyance to a purchaser from which the draft can be prepared, or to charge a reasonable fee therefor, or, where a perpetual rentcharge is to be reserved as the only consideration in money or money's worth, the right of a vendor to stipulate that the draft conveyance is to be prepared by his solicitor at the expense of the purchaser.

(2) Any covenant or stipulation contained in, or entered into with reference to any lease or underlease made before or after the commencement of this Act—

(a) whereby the right of preparing, at the expense of a purchaser, any conveyance of the estate or interest of the lessee or underlessee in the demised premises or in any part thereof, or of otherwise carrying out, at the expense of the purchaser, any dealing with such estate or interest, is expressed to be reserved to or vested in the lessor or underlessor or his solicitor; or

(b) which in any way restricts the right of the purchaser to have such conveyance carried out on his behalf by a solicitor appointed by him;

shall be void:

Provided that, where any covenant or stipulation is rendered void by this subsection, there shall be implied in lieu thereof a covenant or stipulation that the lessee or underlessee shall register with the lessor or his solicitor within six months from the date thereof, or as soon after the expiration of that period as may be practicable, all conveyances and devolutions (including probates or letters of administration) affecting the lease or underlease and pay a fee of one guinea in respect of each registration, and the power of entry (if any) on breach of any covenant contained in the lease or underlease shall apply and extend to the breach of any covenant so to be implied.

(3) Save where a sale is effected by demise or sub-demise, this section does not affect the law relating to the preparation of a lease or underlease or the draft thereof.

(4) In this section 'lease' and 'underlease' include any agreement therefor or other tenancy, and 'lessee' and 'underlessee' and 'lessor' and 'underlessor' have corresponding meanings.

49. Applications to the court by vendor and purchaser

(1) A vendor or purchaser of any interest in land, or their representatives respectively, may apply in a summary way to the court, in respect of any requisitions or objections, or any claim for compensation, or any other question arising out of or connected with the contract (not being a question affecting the existence or validity of the contract), and the court may make such order upon the application as to the court may appear just, and may order how and by whom all or any of the costs of and incident to the application are to be borne and paid.

(2) Where the court refuses to grant specific performance of a contract, or in any action for the return of a deposit, the court may, if it thinks fit, order the repayment of any deposit.

(3) This section applies to a contract for the sale or exchange of any interest in land.

(4) The county court has jurisdiction under this section where land which is to be dealt with in the court does not exceed £30,000 in capital value.

50. Discharge of incumbrances by the court on sales or exchanges

(1) Where land subject to any incumbrance, whether immediately realisable or payable or not, is sold or exchanged by the court, or out of court, the court may, if it thinks fit, on the application of any party to the sale or exchange, direct or allow payment into court of such sum as is hereinafter mentioned, that is to say—

(a) in the case of an annual sum charged on the land, or of a capital sum charged on a determinable interest in the land, the sum to be paid into court shall be of such amount as, when invested in Government securities, the court considers will be sufficient, by means of the dividends thereof, to keep down or otherwise provide for that charge; and

(b) in any other case of capital money charged on the land, the sum to be paid into court shall be of an amount sufficient to meet the incumbrance and any interest due thereon;

but in either case there shall also be paid into court such additional amount as the court considers will be sufficient to meet the contingency of further costs, expenses and interest, and any other contingency, except depreciation of investments, not exceeding one-tenth part of the original amount to be paid in, unless the court for special reason thinks fit to require a larger additional amount.

(2)   Thereupon, the court may, if it thinks fit, and either after or without any notice to the incumbrancer, as the court thinks fit, declare the land to be freed from the incumbrance, and make any order for conveyance, or vesting order, proper for giving effect to the sale or exchange, and give directions for the retention and investment of the money in court and for the payment or application of the income thereof.

(3)   The court may declare all other land, if any, affected by the incumbrance (besides the land sold or exchanged) to be freed from the incumbrance, and this power may be exercised either after or without notice to the incumbrancer, and notwithstanding that on a previous occasion an order, relating to the same incumbrance, has been made by the court which was confined to the land then sold or exchanged.

(4)   On any application under this section the court may, if it thinks fit, as respects any vendor or purchaser, dispense with the service of any notice which would otherwise be required to be served on the vendor or purchaser.

(5)   After notice served on the persons interested in or entitled to the money or fund in court, the court may direct payment or transfer thereof to the persons entitled to receive or give a discharge for the same, and generally may give directions respecting the application or distribution of the capital or income thereof.

(6)   This section applies to sales or exchanges whether made before or after the commencement of this Act, and to incumbrances whether created by statute or otherwise.

Conveyances and other Instruments

51.   Lands lie in grant only

(1)   All lands and all interests therein lie in grant and are incapable of being conveyed by livery or livery and seisin, or by feoffment, or by bargain and sale; and a conveyance of an interest in land may operate to pass the possession or right to possession thereof, without actual entry, but subject to all prior rights thereto.

(2)   The use of the word grant is not necessary to convey land or to create any interest therein.

52.   Conveyances to be by deed

(1)   All conveyances of land or of any interest therein are void for the purpose of conveying or creating a legal estate unless made by deed.

(2)   This section does not apply to—

(a)   assents by a personal representative;

(b)   disclaimers made in accordance with sections 178 to 180 or sections 315 to 319 of the Insolvency Act 1986 or not required to be evidenced in writing;

(c)   surrenders by operation of law, including surrenders which may, by law, be effected without writing;

(d)   leases or tenancies or other assurances not required by law to be made in writing;

(da) flexible tenancies;

(db) assured tenancies of dwelling-houses in England that are granted by private registered providers of social housing and are not long tenancies or shared ownership leases;

(e)   receipts other than those falling within section 115 below;

(f)   vesting orders of the court or other competent authority;

(g)   conveyances taking effect by operation of law.

(3)   In this section—

'assured tenancy' has the same meaning as in Part 1 of the Housing Act 1988;

'dwelling-house' has the same meaning as in Part 1 of the Housing Act 1988;

'flexible tenancy' has the meaning given by section 107A of the Housing Act 1985;

'long tenancy' means a tenancy granted for a term certain of more than 21 years, whether or not it is (or may become) terminable before the end of that term by notice given by the tenant or by re-entry or forfeiture;

'shared ownership lease' means a lease of a dwelling-house—

(a)   granted on payment of a premium calculated by reference to a percentage of the value of the dwellinghouse or of the cost of providing it, or

(b)   under which the lessee (or the lessee's personal representatives) will or may be entitled to a sum calculated by reference, directly or indirectly, to the value of the dwelling-house.

53.   Instruments required to be in writing
(1)   Subject to the provision hereinafter contained with respect to the creation of interests in land by parol—
    (a)   no interest in land can be created or disposed of except by writing signed by the person creating or conveying the same, or by his agent thereunto lawfully authorised in writing, or by will, or by operation of law;
    (b)   a declaration of trust respecting any land or any interest therein must be manifested and proved by some writing signed by some person who is able to declare such trust or by his will;
    (c)   a disposition of an equitable interest or trust subsisting at the time of the disposition, must be in writing signed by the person disposing of the same, or by his agent thereunto lawfully authorised in writing or by will.
(2)   This section does not affect the creation or operation of resulting, implied or constructive trusts.

54.   Creation of interests in land by parol
(1)   All interests in land created by parol and not put in writing and signed by the persons so creating the same, or by their agents thereunto lawfully authorised in writing, have, notwithstanding any consideration having been given for the same, the force and effect of interests at will only.
(2)   Nothing in the foregoing provisions of this Part of this Act shall affect the creation by parol of leases taking effect in possession for a term not exceeding three years (whether or not the lessee is given power to extend the term) at the best rent which can be reasonably obtained without taking a fine.

55.   Savings in regard to last two sections
Nothing in the last two foregoing sections shall—
(a)   invalidate dispositions by will; or
(b)   affect any interest validly created before the commencement of this Act; or
(c)   affect the right to acquire an interest in land by virtue of taking possession; or
(d)   affect the operation of the law relating to part performance.

56.   Persons taking who are not parties and as to indentures
(1)   A person may take an immediate or other interest in land or other property, or the benefit of any condition, right of entry, covenant or agreement over or respecting land or other property, although he may not be named as a party to the conveyance or other instrument.
(2)   A deed between parties, to effect its objects, has the effect of an indenture though not indented or expressed to be an indenture.

57.   Description of deeds
Any deed, whether or not being an indenture, may be described (at the commencement thereof or otherwise) as a deed simply, or as a conveyance, deed of exchange, vesting deed, trust instrument, settlement, mortgage, charge, transfer of mortgage, appointment, lease or otherwise according to the nature of the transaction intended to be effected.

58.   Provisions as to supplemental instruments
Any instrument (whether executed before or after the commencement of this Act) expressed to be supplemental to a previous instrument, shall, as far as may be, be read and have effect as if the supplemental instrument contained a full recital of the previous instrument, but this section does not operate to give any right to an abstract or production of any such previous instrument, and a purchaser may accept the same evidence that the previous instrument does not affect the title as if it had merely been mentioned in the supplemental instrument.

59.   Conditions and certain covenants not implied
(1)   An exchange or other conveyance of land made by deed after the first day of October, eighteen hundred and forty-five, does not imply any condition in law.

(2)   The word 'give' or 'grant' does not in a deed made after the date last aforesaid, imply any covenant in law, save where otherwise provided by statute.

60.   Abolition of technicalities in regard to conveyances and deeds

(1)   A conveyance of freehold land to any person without words of limitation, or any equivalent expression, shall pass to the grantee the fee simple or other the whole interest which the grantor had power to convey in such land, unless a contrary intention appears in the conveyance.

(2)   A conveyance of freehold land to a corporation sole by his corporate designation without the word 'successors' shall pass to the corporation the fee simple or other the whole interest which the grantor had power to convey in such land, unless a contrary intention appears in the conveyance.

(3)   In a voluntary conveyance a resulting trust for the grantor shall not be implied merely by reason that the property is not expressed to be conveyed for the use or benefit of the grantee.

(4)   The foregoing provisions of this section apply only to conveyances and deeds executed after the commencement of this Act:

Provided that in a deed executed after the thirty-first day of December, eighteen hundred and eighty-one, it is sufficient—

(a)   In the limitation of an estate in fee simple, to use the words 'in fee simple,' without the word 'heirs';

...

61.   Construction of expressions used in deeds and other instruments

In all deeds, contracts, wills, orders and other instruments executed, made or coming into operation after the commencement of this Act, unless the context otherwise requires—

(a)   'Month' means calendar month;
(b)   'Person' includes a corporation;
(c)   The singular includes the plural and vice versa;
(d)   The masculine includes the feminine and vice versa.

62.   General words implied in conveyances

(1)   A conveyance of land shall be deemed to include and shall by virtue of this Act operate to convey, with the land, all buildings, erections, fixtures, commons, hedges, ditches, fences, ways, waters, water-courses, liberties, privileges, easements, rights, and advantages whatsoever, appertaining or reputed to appertain to the land, or any part thereof, or, at the time of conveyance, demised, occupied, or enjoyed with, or reputed or known as part or parcel of or appurtenant to the land or any part thereof.

(2)   A conveyance of land, having houses or other buildings thereon, shall be deemed to include and shall by virtue of this Act operate to convey, with the land, houses, or other buildings, all outhouses, erections, fixtures, cellars, areas, courts, courtyards, cisterns, sewers, gutters, drains, ways, passages, lights, water-courses, liberties, privileges, easements, rights, and advantages whatsoever, appertaining or reputed to appertain to the land, houses, or other buildings conveyed, or any of them, or any part thereof, or, at the time of conveyance, demised, occupied, or enjoyed with, or reputed or known as part or parcel of or appurtenant to, the land, houses, or other buildings conveyed, or any of them, or any part thereof.

(3)   A conveyance of a manor shall be deemed to include and shall by virtue of this Act operate to convey, with the manor, all pastures, feedings, wastes, warrens, commons, mines, minerals, quarries, furzes, trees, woods, underwoods, coppices, and the ground and soil thereof, fishings, fisheries, fowlings, courts leet, courts baron, and other courts, view of frankpledge and all that to view of frankpledge doth belong, mills, mulctures, customs, tolls, duties, reliefs, heriots, fines, sums of money, amerciaments, waifs, estrays, chief-rents, quitrents, rentscharge, rents seck, rents of assize, fee farm rents, services, royalties, jurisdictions, franchises, liberties, privileges, easements, profits, advantages, rights, emoluments, and hereditaments whatsoever, to the manor appertaining or reputed to appertain, or, at the time of conveyance, demised, occupied, or enjoyed with the same, or reputed or known as part, parcel, or member thereof.

For the purposes of this subsection the right to compensation for manorial incidents on the extinguishment thereof shall be deemed to be a right appertaining to the manor.

(4) This section applies only if and as far as a contrary intention is not expressed in the conveyance, and has effect subject to the terms of the conveyance and to the provisions therein contained.

(5) This section shall not be construed as giving to any person a better title to any property, right, or thing in this section mentioned than the title which the conveyance gives to him to the land or manor expressed to be conveyed, or as conveying to him any property, right, or thing in this section mentioned, further or otherwise than as the same could have been conveyed to him by the conveying parties.

(6) This section applies to conveyances made after the thirty-first day of December, eighteen hundred and eighty-one.

63. All estate clause implied

(1) Every conveyance is effectual to pass all the estate, right, title, interest, claim, and demand which the conveying parties respectively have, in, to, or on the property conveyed, or expressed or intended so to be, or which they respectively have power to convey in, to, or on the same.

(2) This section applies only if and as far as a contrary intention is not expressed in the conveyance, and has effect subject to the terms of the conveyance and to the provisions therein contained.

(3) This section applies to conveyances made after the thirty-first day of December, eighteen hundred and eighty-one.

64. Production and safe custody of documents

(1) Where a person retains possession of documents, and gives to another an acknowledgment in writing of the right of that other to production of those documents, and to delivery of copies thereof (in this section called an acknowledgment), that acknowledgment shall have effect as in this section provided.

(2) An acknowledgment shall bind the documents to which it relates in the possession or under the control of the person who retains them, and in the possession or under the control of every other person having possession or control thereof from time to time, but shall bind each individual possessor or person as long only as he has possession or control thereof; and every person so having possession or control from time to time shall be bound specifically to perform the obligations imposed under this section by an acknowledgment, unless prevented from so doing by fire or other inevitable accident.

(3) The obligations imposed under this section by an acknowledgment are to be performed from time to time at the request in writing of the person to whom an acknowledgment is given, or of any person, not being a lessee at a rent, having or claiming any estate, interest, or right through or under that person, or otherwise becoming through or under that person interested in or affected by the terms of any document to which the acknowledgment relates.

(4) The obligations imposed under this section by an acknowledgment are—

(i) An obligation to produce the documents or any of them at all reasonable times for the purpose of inspection, and of comparison with abstracts or copies thereof, by the person entitled to request production or by any person by him authorised in writing; and

(ii) An obligation to produce the documents or any of them at any trial, hearing, or examination in any court, or in the execution of any commission, or elsewhere in the United Kingdom, on any occasion on which production may properly be required, for proving or supporting the title or claim of the person entitled to request production, or for any other purpose relative to that title or claim; and

(iii) An obligation to deliver to the person entitled to request the same true copies or extracts, attested or unattested, of or from the documents or any of them.

(5) All costs and expenses of or incidental to the specific performance of any obligation imposed under this section by an acknowledgment shall be paid by the person requesting performance.

(6) An acknowledgment shall not confer any right to damages for loss or destruction of, or injury to, the documents to which it relates, from whatever cause arising.

(7)   Any person claiming to be entitled to the benefit of an acknowledgment may apply to the court for an order directing the production of the documents to which it relates, or any of them, or the delivery of copies of or extracts from those documents or any of them to him, or some person on his behalf; and the court may, if it thinks fit, order production, or production and delivery, accordingly, and may give directions respecting the time, place, terms, and mode of production or delivery, and may make such order as it thinks fit respecting the costs of the application, or any other matter connected with the application.

(8)   An acknowledgment shall by virtue of this Act satisfy any liability to give a covenant for production and delivery of copies of or extracts from documents.

(9)   Where a person retains possession of documents and gives to another an undertaking in writing for safe custody thereof, that undertaking shall impose on the person giving it, and on every person having possession or control of the documents from time to time, but on each individual possessor or person as long only as he has possession or control thereof, an obligation to keep the documents safe, whole, uncancelled, and undefaced, unless prevented from so doing by fire or other inevitable accident.

(10) Any person claiming to be entitled to the benefit of such an undertaking may apply to the court to assess damages for any loss or destruction of, or injury to, the documents or any of them, and the court may, if it thinks fit, direct an inquiry respecting the amount of damages, and order payment thereof by the person liable, and may make such order as it thinks fit respecting the costs of the application, or any other matter connected with the application.

(11) An undertaking for safe custody of documents shall by virtue of this Act satisfy any liability to give a covenant for safe custody of documents.

(12) The rights conferred by an acknowledgment or an undertaking under this section shall be in addition to all such other rights relative to the production, or inspection, or the obtaining of copies of documents, as are not, by virtue of this Act, satisfied by the giving of the acknowledgment or undertaking, and shall have effect subject to the terms of the acknowledgment or undertaking, and to any provisions therein contained.

(13) This section applies only if and as far as a contrary intention is not expressed in the acknowledgment or undertaking.

(14) This section applies to an acknowledgment or undertaking given, or a liability respecting documents incurred, after the thirty-first day of December, eighteen hundred and eighty-one.

65. Reservation of legal estates

(1)   A reservation of a legal estate shall operate at law without any execution of the conveyance by the grantee of the legal estate out of which the reservation is made, or any regrant by him, so as to create the legal estate reserved, and so as to vest the same in possession in the person (whether being the grantor or not) for whose benefit the reservation is made.

(2)   A conveyance of a legal estate expressed to be made subject to another legal estate not in existence immediately before the date of the conveyance, shall operate as a reservation, unless a contrary intention appears.

(3)   This section applies only to reservations made after the commencement of this Act.

66. Confirmation of past transactions

(1)   A deed containing a declaration by the estate owner that his estate shall go and devolve in such a manner as may be requisite for confirming any interests intended to affect his estate and capable under this Act of subsisting as legal estates which, at some prior date, were expressed to have been transferred or created, and any dealings therewith which would have been legal if those interests had been legally and validly transferred or created, shall, to the extent of the estate of the estate owner, but without prejudice to the restrictions imposed by this Act in the case of mortgages, operate to give legal effect to the interests so expressed to have been transferred or created and to the subsequent dealings aforesaid.

(2)   The powers conferred by this section may be exercised by a tenant for life or statutory owner, trustee of land or a personal representative (being in each case an estate owner) as well as by an absolute owner, but if exercised by any person, other than an absolute owner, only with the leave of the court.

(3) This section applies only to deeds containing such a declaration as aforesaid if executed after the commencement of this Act.

(4) The county court has jurisdiction under this section where the land which is to be dealt with in the court does not exceed £30,000 in capital value.

67. Receipt in deed sufficient

(1) A receipt for consideration money or securities in the body of a deed shall be a sufficient discharge for the same to the person paying or delivering the same, without any further receipt for the same being indorsed on the deed.

(2) This section applies to deeds executed after the thirty-first day of December, eighteen hundred and eighty-one.

68. Receipt in deed or indorsed evidence

(1) A receipt for consideration money or other consideration in the body of a deed or indorsed thereon shall, in favour of a subsequent purchaser, not having notice that the money or other consideration thereby acknowledged to be received was not in fact paid or given, wholly or in part, be sufficient evidence of the payment or giving of the whole amount thereof.

(2) This section applies to deeds executed after the thirty-first day of December, eighteen hundred and eighty-one.

69. Receipt in deed or indorsed authority for payment to solicitor

(1) Where a solicitor produces a deed, having in the body thereof or indorsed thereon a receipt for consideration money or other consideration, the deed being executed, or the indorsed receipt being signed, by the person entitled to give a receipt for that consideration, the deed shall be a sufficient authority to the person liable to pay or give the same for his paying or giving the same to the solicitor, without the solicitor producing any separate or other direction or authority in that behalf from the person who executed or signed the deed or receipt.

(2) This section applies whether the consideration was paid or given before or after the commencement of this Act.

70. Partial release of security from rentcharge

(1) A release from a rentcharge of part of the land charged therewith does not extinguish the whole rentcharge, but operates only to bar the right to recover any part of the rentcharge out of the land released, without prejudice to the rights of any persons interested in the land remaining unreleased, and not concurring in or confirming the release.

(2) This section applies to releases made after the twelfth day of August, eighteen hundred and fifty-nine.

71. Release of part of land affected from a judgment

(1) A release from a judgment (including any writ or order imposing a charge) or part of any land charged therewith does not affect the validity of the judgment as respects any land not specifically released.

(2) This section operates without prejudice to the rights of any persons interested in the property remaining unreleased and not concurring in or confirming the release.

(3) This section applies to releases made after the twelfth day of August, eighteen hundred and fifty-nine.

72. Conveyances by a person to himself, etc.

(1) In conveyances made after the twelfth day of August, eighteen hundred and fifty-nine, personal property, including chattels real, may be conveyed by a person to himself jointly with another person by the like means by which it might be conveyed by him to another person.

(2) In conveyances made after the thirty-first day of December, eighteen hundred and eighty- one, freehold land, or a thing in action, may be conveyed by a person to himself jointly with another person, by the like means by which it might be conveyed by him to another person; and may, in like manner, be conveyed by a husband to his wife, and by a wife to her husband, alone or jointly with another person.

(3)   After the commencement of this Act a person may convey land to or vest land in himself.

(4)   Two or more persons (whether or not being trustees or personal representatives) may convey, and shall be deemed always to have been capable of conveying, any property vested in them to any one or more of themselves in like manner as they could have conveyed such property to a third party; provided that if the persons in whose favour the conveyance is made are, by reason of any fiduciary relationship or otherwise, precluded from validly carrying out the transaction, the conveyance shall be liable to be set aside.

74.   Execution of instruments by or on behalf of corporations

(1)   In favour of a purchaser an instrument shall be deemed to have been duly executed by a corporation aggregate if a seal purporting to be the corporation's seal purports to be affixed to the instrument in the presence of and attested by—

(a)   two members of the board of directors, council or other governing body of the corporation, or

(b)   one such member and the clerk, secretary or other permanent officer of the corporation or his deputy.

(1A) Subsection (1) of this section applies in the case of an instrument purporting to have been executed by a corporation aggregate in the name or on behalf of another person whether or not that person is also a corporation aggregate.

(1B) For the purposes of subsection (1) of this section, a seal purports to be affixed in the presence of and attested by an officer of the corporation, in the case of an officer which is not an individual, if it is affixed in the presence of and attested by an individual authorised by the officer to attest on its behalf.

(2)   The board of directors, council or other governing body of a corporation aggregate may, by resolution or otherwise, appoint an agent either generally or in any particular case, to execute on behalf of the corporation any agreement or other instrument which is not a deed in relation to any matter within the powers of the corporation.

(3)   Where a person is authorised under a power of attorney or under any statutory or other power to convey any interest in property in the name or on behalf of a corporation sole or aggregate, he may as attorney execute the conveyance by signing the name of the corporation in the presence of at least one witness who attests the signature, and such execution shall take effect and be valid in like manner as if the corporation had executed the conveyance.

(4)   Where a corporation aggregate is authorised under a power of attorney or under any statutory or other power to convey any interest in property in the name or on behalf of any other person (including another corporation), an officer appointed for that purpose by the board of directors, council or other governing body of the corporation by resolution or otherwise, may execute the instrument by signing it in the name of such other person or, if the instrument is to be a deed, by so signing it in the presence of a witness who attests the signature; and where an instrument appears to be executed by an officer so appointed, then in favour of a purchaser the instrument shall be deemed to have been executed by an officer duly authorised.

(5)   The foregoing provisions of this section apply to transactions wherever effected, but only to deeds and instruments executed after the commencement of this Act, except that, in the case of powers or appointments of an agent or officer, they apply whether the power was conferred or the appointment was made before or after the commencement of this Act or by this Act.

(6)   Notwithstanding anything contained in this section, any mode of execution or attestation authorised by law or by practice or by the statute, charter, articles, deed of settlement or other instrument constituting the corporation or regulating the affairs thereof, shall (in addition to the modes authorised by this section) be as effectual as if this section had not been passed.

74A.   Execution of instrument as a deed

(1)   An instrument is validly executed by a corporation aggregate as a deed for the purposes of section 1(2)(b) of the Law of Property (Miscellaneous Provisions) Act 1989, if and only if—

(a)   it is duly executed by the corporation, and

(b)   it is delivered as a deed.

(2)   An instrument shall be presumed to be delivered for the purposes of subsection (1)(b) of this section upon its being executed, unless a contrary intention is proved.

75. Rights of purchaser as to execution

(1) On a sale, the purchaser shall not be entitled to require that the conveyance to him be executed in his presence, or in that of his solicitor, as such; but shall be entitled to have, at his own cost, the execution of the conveyance attested by some person appointed by him, who may, if he thinks fit, be his solicitor.

(2) This section applies to sales made after the thirty-first day of December, eighteen hundred and eighty-one.

Covenants

77. Implied covenants in conveyances subject to rents

(1) In addition to the covenants implied under Part I of the Law of Property (Miscellaneous Provisions) Act 1994, there shall in the several cases in this section mentioned, be deemed to be included and implied, a covenant to the effect in this section stated, by and with such persons as are hereinafter mentioned, that is to say:—

   (a) In a conveyance for valuable consideration, other than a mortgage, of the entirety of the land affected by a rentcharge, a covenant by the grantee or joint and several covenants by the grantees, if more than one, with the conveying parties and with each of them, if more than one, in the terms set out in Part VII of the Second Schedule to this Act. Where a rentcharge has been apportioned in respect of any land, with the consent of the owner of the rentcharge, the covenants in this paragraph shall be implied in the conveyance of that land in like manner as if the apportioned rentcharge were the rentcharge referred to, and the document creating the rentcharge related solely to that land:

   (b) In a conveyance for valuable consideration, other than a mortgage, of part of land affected by a rentcharge, subject to a part of that rentcharge which has been or is by that conveyance apportioned (but in either case without the consent of the owner of the rentcharge) in respect of the land conveyed:—

      (i) A covenant by the grantee of the land or joint and several covenants by the grantees, if more than one, with the conveying parties and with each of them, if more than one, in the terms set out in paragraph (i) of Part VIII of the Second Schedule to this Act;

      (ii) A covenant by a person who conveys or is expressed to convey as beneficial owner, or joint and several covenants by the persons who so convey or are expressed to so convey, if at the date of the conveyance any part of the land affected by such rentcharge is retained, with the grantees of the land and with each of them (if more than one) in the terms set out in paragraph (ii) of Part VIII of the Second Schedule to this Act:

(2) Where in a conveyance for valuable consideration, other than a mortgage, part of land affected by a rentcharge is, without the consent of the owner of the rentcharge, expressed to be conveyed subject to or charged with the entire rent, paragraph (B)(i) of subsection (1) of this section shall apply as if, in paragraph (i) of Part VII of the Second Schedule to this Act—

   (a) any reference to the apportioned rent were to the entire rent; and

   (b) the words '(other than the covenant to pay the entire rent)' were omitted.

(2A) Where in a conveyance for valuable consideration, other than a mortgage, part of land affected by a rentcharge is, without the consent of the owner of the rentcharge, expressed to be conveyed discharged or exonerated from the entire rent, paragraph (b) (ii) of subsection (1) of this section shall apply as if, in paragraph (ii) of Part VIII of the Second Schedule to this Act—

   (a) any reference to the balance of the rent were to the entire rent; and

   (b) the words ', other than the covenant to pay the entire rent,' were omitted.

(3) In this section 'conveyance' does not include a demise by way of lease at a rent.

(4) Any covenant which would be implied under this section by reason of a person conveying or being expressed to convey as beneficial owner may, by express reference to this section, be implied, with or without variation, in a conveyance, whether or not for valuable consideration, by a person who conveys or is expressed to convey as settlor, or as trustee, or as mortgagee, or as personal representative of a deceased person, or under an order of the court.

(5) The benefit of a covenant implied as aforesaid shall be annexed and incident to, and shall go with, the estate or interest of the implied covenantee, and shall be capable of

being enforced by every person in whom that estate or interest is, for the whole or any part thereof, from time to time vested.

(6) A covenant implied as aforesaid may be varied or extended by deed, and, as so varied or extended, shall, as far as may be, operate in the like manner, and with all the like incidents, effects and consequences, as if such variations or extensions were directed in this section to be implied.

(7) In particular any covenant implied under this section may be extended by providing that—
   (a) the land conveyed; or
   (b) the part of the land affected by the rentcharge which remains vested in the covenantor;
   shall, as the case may require, stand charged with the payment of all money which may become payable under the implied covenant.

(8) This section applies only to conveyances made after the commencement of this Act.

78. Benefit of covenants relating to land

(1) A covenant relating to any land of the covenantee shall be deemed to be made with the covenantee and his successors in title and the persons deriving title under him or them, and shall have effect as if such successors and other persons were expressed.

   For the purposes of this subsection in connexion with covenants restrictive of the user of land 'successors in title' shall be deemed to include the owners and occupiers for the time being of the land of the covenantee intended to be benefited.

(2) This section applies to covenants made after the commencement of this Act, but the repeal of section fifty-eight of the Conveyancing Act, 1881, does not affect the operation of covenants to which that section applied.

79. Burden of covenants relating to land

(1) A covenant relating to any land of a covenantor or capable of being bound by him, shall, unless a contrary intention is expressed, be deemed to be made by the covenantor on behalf of himself his successors in title and the persons deriving title under him or them, and, subject as aforesaid, shall have effect as if such successors and other persons were expressed.

   This subsection extends to a covenant to do some act relating to the land, notwithstanding that the subject-matter may not be in existence when the covenant is made.

(2) For the purposes of this section in connexion with covenants restrictive of the user of land 'successors in title' shall be deemed to include the owners and occupiers for the time being of such land.

(3) This section applies only to covenants made after the commencement of this Act.

80. Covenants binding land

(1) A covenant and a bond and an obligation or contract made under seal after 31st December 1881 but before the coming into force of section 1 of the Law of Property (Miscellaneous Provisions) Act 1989 or executed as a deed in accordance with that section after its coming into force binds the real estate as well as the personal estate of the person making the same if and so far as a contrary intention is not expressed in the covenant, bond, obligation, or contract.

   This subsection extends to a covenant implied by virtue of this Act.

(2) Every covenant running with the land, whether entered into before or after the commencement of this Act, shall take effect in accordance with any statutory enactment affecting the devolution of the land, and accordingly the benefit or burden of every such covenant shall vest in or bind the persons who by virtue of any such enactment or otherwise succeed to the title of the covenantee or the covenantor, as the case may be.

(3) The benefit of a covenant relating to land entered into after the commencement of this Act may be made to run with the land without the use of any technical expression if the covenant is of such a nature that the benefit could have been made to run with the land before the commencement of this Act.

(4) For the purposes of this section, a covenant runs with the land when the benefit or burden of it, whether at law or in equity, passes to the successors in title of the covenantee or the covenantor, as the case may be.

81.   Effect of covenant with two or more jointly

(1)   A covenant, and a contract under seal, and a bond or obligation under seal, made with two or more jointly, to pay money or to make a conveyance, or to do any other act, to them or for their benefit, shall be deemed to include, and shall, by virtue of this Act, imply, an obligation to do the act to, or for the benefit of, the survivor or survivors of them, and to, or for the benefit of, any other person to whom the right to sue on the covenant, contract, bond, or obligation devolves, and where made after the commencement of this Act shall be construed as being also made with each of them.

(2)   This section extends to a covenant implied by virtue of this Act.

(3)   This section applies only if and as far as a contrary intention is not expressed in the covenant, contract, bond, or obligation, and has effect subject to the covenant, contract, bond, or obligation, and to the provisions therein contained.

(4)   Except as otherwise expressly provided, this section applies to a covenant, contract, bond, or obligation made or implied after the thirty-first day of December, eighteen hundred and eighty-one.

(5)   In its application to instruments made after the coming into force of section 1 of the Law of Property (Miscellaneous Provisions) Act 1989 subsection (1) above shall have effect as if the words 'under seal, and a bond or obligation under seal,' there were substituted the words 'bond or obligation executed as a deed in accordance with section 1 of the Law of Property (Miscellaneous Provisions) Act 1989'.

82.   Covenants and agreements entered into by a person with himself and another or others

(1)   Any covenant, whether express or implied, or agreement entered into by a person with himself and one or more other persons shall be construed and be capable of being enforced in like manner as if the covenant or agreement had been entered into with the other person or persons alone.

(2)   This section applies to covenants or agreements entered into before or after the commencement of this Act, and to covenants implied by statute in the case of a person who conveys or is expressed to convey to himself and one or more other persons, but without prejudice to any order of the court made before such commencement.

83.   Construction of implied covenants

In the construction of a covenant or proviso, or other provision, implied in a deed or assent by virtue of this Act, words importing the singular or plural number, or the masculine gender, shall be read as also importing the plural or singular number, or as extending to females, as the case may require.

84.   Power to discharge or modify restrictive covenants affecting land

(1)   The Upper Tribunal shall (without prejudice to any concurrent jurisdiction of the court) have power from time to time, on the application of any person interested in any freehold land affected by any restriction arising under covenant or otherwise as to the user thereof or the building thereon, by order wholly or partially to discharge or modify any such restriction ... on being satisfied—

   (a)   that by reason of changes in the character of the property or the neighbourhood or other circumstances of the case which the Upper Tribunal may deem material, the restriction ought to be deemed obsolete, or

   (aa) that in a case falling within subsection (1A) below the continued existence thereof would impede some reasonable user of the land for public or private purposes ... or, as the case may be, would unless modified so impede such user; or

   (b)   that the persons of full age and capacity for the time being or from time to time entitled to the benefit of the restriction, whether in respect of estates in fee simple or any lesser estates or interests in the property to which the benefit of the restriction is annexed, have agreed, either expressly or by implication, by their acts or omissions, to the same being discharged or modified; or

   (c)   that the proposed discharge or modification will not injure the persons entitled to the benefit of the restriction:

   and an order discharging or modifying a restriction under this subsection may direct the applicant to pay to any person entitled to the benefit of the restriction such sum by way of consideration as the Tribunal may think it just to award under one, but not both, of the following heads, that is to say, either—

(i) a sum to make up for any loss or disadvantage suffered by that person in consequence of the discharge or modification; or

(ii) a sum to make up for any effect which the restriction had, at the time when it was imposed, in reducing the consideration then received for the land affected by it.

(1A) Subsection (1)(aa) above authorises the discharge or modification of a restriction by reference to its impeding some reasonable user of land in any case in which the Upper Tribunal is satisfied that the restriction, in impeding that user, either—

(a) does not secure to persons entitled to the benefit of it any practical benefits of substantial value or advantage to them; or

(b) is contrary to the public interest;

and that money will be an adequate compensation for the loss or disadvantage (if any) which any such person will suffer from the discharge or modification.

(1B) In determining whether a case is one falling within subsection (1A) above, and in determining whether (in any such case or otherwise) a restriction ought to be discharged or modified, the Upper Tribunal shall take into account the development plan and any declared or ascertainable pattern for the grant or refusal of planning permissions in the relevant areas, as well as the period at which and context in which the restriction was created or imposed and any other material circumstances.

(1C) It is hereby declared that the power conferred by this section to modify a restriction includes power to add such further provisions restricting the user of or the building on the land affected as appear to the Upper Tribunal to be reasonable in view of the relaxation of the existing provisions, and as may be accepted by the applicant; and the Upper Tribunal may accordingly refuse to modify a restriction without some such addition.

(2) The court shall have power on the application of any person interested—

(a) To declare whether or not in any particular case any freehold land is or would in any given event be affected by a restriction imposed by any instrument; or

(b) To declare what, upon the true construction of any instrument purporting to impose a restriction, is the nature and extent of the restriction thereby imposed and whether the same is or would in any given event be enforceable and if so by whom.

Neither subsections (7) and (11) of this section nor, unless the contrary is expressed, any later enactment providing for this section not to apply to any restrictions shall affect the operation of this subsection or the operation for purposes of this subsection of any other provisions of this section.

(3) The Upper Tribunal shall, before making any order under this section, direct such enquiries, if any, to be made of any government department or local authority, and such notices, if any, whether by way of advertisement or otherwise, to be given to such of the persons who appear to be entitled to the benefit of the restriction intended to be discharged, modified, or dealt with as, having regard to any enquiries notices or other proceedings previously made, given or taken, the Upper Tribunal may think fit.

(3A) On an application to the Upper Tribunal under this section the Upper Tribunal shall give any necessary directions as to the persons who are or are not to be admitted (as appearing to be entitled to the benefit of the restriction) to oppose the application, and no appeal shall lie against any such direction; but Tribunal Procedure Rules shall make provision whereby, in cases in which there arises on such an application (whether or not in connection with the admission of persons to oppose) any such question as is referred to in subsection (2)(a) or (b) of this section, the proceedings on the application can and, if the rules so provide, shall be suspended to enable the decision of the court to be obtained on that question by an application under that subsection, or otherwise, as may be provided by those rules or by rules of court.

(4) ...

(5) Any order made under this section shall be binding on all persons, whether ascertained or of full age or capacity or not, then entitled or thereafter capable of becoming entitled to the benefit of any restriction, which is thereby discharged, modified, or dealt with, and whether such persons are parties to the proceedings or have been served with notice or not.

(6) An order may be made under this section notwithstanding that any instrument which is alleged to impose the restriction intended to be discharged, modified, or dealt with, may not have been produced to the court or the Upper Tribunal, and the court or the Upper Tribunal may act on such evidence of that instrument as it may think sufficient.

(7) This section applies to restrictions whether subsisting at the commencement of this Act or imposed thereafter, but this section does not apply where the restriction was imposed on the occasion of a disposition made gratuitously or for a nominal consideration for public purposes.

(8) This section applies whether the land affected by the restrictions is registered or not.

(9) Where any proceedings by action or otherwise are taken to enforce a restrictive covenant, any person against whom the proceedings are taken, may in such proceedings apply to the court for an order giving leave to apply to the Upper Tribunal under this section, and staying the proceedings in the meantime.

(10) ...

(11) This section does not apply to restrictions imposed by the Commissioners of Works under any statutory power for the protection of any Royal Park or Garden or to restrictions of a like character imposed upon the occasion of any enfranchisement effected before the commencement of this Act in any manor vested in His Majesty in right of the Crown or the Duchy on Lancaster, nor subject to subsection (11A) below to restrictions created or imposed—

    (a) for Naval, Military or Air Force purposes,

    (b) for civil aviation purposes under the powers of the Air Navigation Act, 1920 or of section 19 or 23 of the Civil Aviation Act 1949 or of sections 30 or 41 of the Civil Aviation Act 1982.

(11A) Subsection (11) of this section—

    (a) shall exclude the application of this section to a restriction falling within subsection (11)(a), and not created or imposed in connection with the use of any land as an aerodrome, only so long as the restriction is enforceable by or on behalf of the Crown; and

    (b) shall exclude the application of this section to a restriction falling within subsection (11)(b), or created or imposed in connection with the use of any land as an aerodrome, only so long as the restriction is enforceable by or on behalf of the Crown or any public or international authority.

(12) Where a term of more than forty years is created in land (whether before or after the commencement of this Act) this section shall, after the expiration of twenty-five years of the term, apply to restrictions affecting such leasehold land in like manner as it would have applied had the land been freehold:

Provided that this subsection shall not apply to mining leases.

PART III

MORTGAGES, RENTCHARGES, AND POWERS OF ATTORNEY

85.   Mode of mortgaging freeholds

(1) A mortgage of an estate in fee simple shall only be capable of being effected at law either by a demise for a term of years absolute, subject to a provision for cesser on redemption, or by a charge by deed expressed to be by way of legal mortgage:

Provided that a first mortgagee shall have the same right to the possession of documents as if his security included the fee simple.

(2) Any purported conveyance of an estate in fee simple by way of mortgage made after the commencement of this Act shall (to the extent of the estate of the mortgagor) operate as a demise of the land to the mortgagee for a term of years absolute, without impeachment for waste, but subject to cesser on redemption, in manner following, namely:—

    (a) A first or only mortgagee shall take a term of three thousand years from the date of the mortgage:

    (b) A second or subsequent mortgagee shall take a term (commencing from the date of the mortgage) one day longer than the term vested in the first or other mortgagee whose security ranks immediately before that of such second or subsequent mortgagee: and, in this subsection, any such purported conveyance as aforesaid includes an absolute conveyance with a deed of defeasance and any other assurance which, but for this subsection, would operate in effect to vest the fee simple in a mortgagee subject to redemption.

(3) Subsection (2) does not apply to registered land, but, subject to that, this section applies whether or not the land is registered land and whether or not the mortgage is expressed to be made by way of trust for sale or otherwise.

(4) Without prejudice to the provisions of this Act respecting legal and equitable powers, every power to mortgage or to lend money on mortgage of an estate in fee simple shall be construed as a power to mortgage the estate for a term of years absolute, without impeachment for waste, or by a charge by way of legal mortgage or to lend on such security.

86. Mode of mortgaging leaseholds

(1) A mortgage of a term of years absolute shall only be capable of being effected at law either by a subdemise for a term of years absolute, less by one day at least than the term vested in the mortgagor, and subject to a provision for cesser on redemption, or by a charge by deed expressed to be by way of legal mortgage; and where a licence to subdemise by way of mortgage is required, such licence shall not be unreasonably refused:

Provided that a first mortgagee shall have the same right to the possession of documents as if his security had been effected by assignment.

(2) Any purported assignment of a term of years absolute by way of mortgage made after the commencement of this Act shall (to the extent of the estate of the mortgagor) operate as a subdemise of the leasehold land to the mortgagee for a term of years absolute, but subject to cesser on redemption, in manner following, namely:—

(a) The term to be taken by a first or only mortgagee shall be ten days less than the term expressed to be assigned:

(b) The term to be taken by a second or subsequent mortgagee shall be one day longer than the term vested in the first or other mortgagee whose security ranks immediately before that of the second or subsequent mortgagee, if the length of the last mentioned term permits, and in any case for a term less by one day at least than the term expressed to be assigned:

and, in this subsection, any such purported assignment as aforesaid includes an absolute assignment with a deed of defeasance and any other assurance which, but for this subsection, would operate in effect to vest the term of the mortgagor in a mortgagee subject to redemption.

(3) Subsection (2) does not apply to registered land, but, subject to that, this section applies whether or not the land is registered land and whether or not the mortgage is made by way of sub-mortgage of a term of years absolute, or is expressed to be by way of trust for sale or otherwise.

(4) Without prejudice to the provisions of this Act respecting legal and equitable powers, every power to mortgage for or to lend money on mortgage of a term of years absolute by way of assignment shall be construed as a power to mortgage the term by subdemise for a term of years absolute or by a charge by way of legal mortgage, or to lend on such security.

87. Charges by way of legal mortgage

(1) Where a legal mortgage of land is created by a charge by deed expressed to be by way of legal mortgage, the mortgagee shall have the same protection, powers and remedies (including the right to take proceedings to obtain possession from the occupiers and the persons in receipt of rents and profits, or any of them) as if—

(a) where the mortgage is a mortgage of an estate in fee simple, a mortgage term for three thousand years without impeachment of waste had been thereby created in favour of the mortgagee; and

(b) where the mortgage is a mortgage of a term of years absolute, a sub-term less by one day than the term vested in the mortgagor had been thereby created in favour of the mortgagee.

(2) Where an estate vested in a mortgagee immediately before the commencement of this Act has by virtue of this Act been converted into a term of years absolute or sub-term, the mortgagee may, by a declaration in writing to that effect signed by him, convert the

mortgage into a charge by way of legal mortgage, and in that case the mortgage term shall be extinguished in the inheritance or in the head term as the case may be, and the mortgagee shall have the same protection, powers and remedies (including the right to take proceedings to obtain possession from the occupiers and the persons in receipt of rents and profits or any of them) as if the mortgage term or sub-term had remained subsisting.

The power conferred by this subsection may be exercised by a mortgagee notwithstanding that he is a trustee or personal representative.

(3) Such declaration shall not affect the priority of the mortgagee or his right to retain possession of documents, nor affect his title to or right over any fixtures or chattels personal comprised in the mortgage.

(4) Subsection (1) of this section shall not be taken to be affected by section 23(1)(a) of the Land Registration Act 2002 (under which owner's powers in relation to a registered estate do not include power to mortgage by demise or sub-demise).

88. Realisation of freehold mortgages

(1) Where an estate in fee simple has been mortgaged by the creation of a term of years absolute limited thereout or by a charge by way of legal mortgage and the mortgagee sells under his statutory or express power of sale—

(a) the conveyance by him shall operate to vest in the purchaser the fee simple in the land conveyed subject to any legal mortgage having priority to the mortgage in right of which the sale is made and to any money thereby secured, and thereupon;

(b) the mortgage term or the charge by way of legal mortgage and any subsequent mortgage term or charges shall merge or be extinguished as respects the land conveyed; and such conveyance may, as respects the fee simple, be made in the name of the estate owner in whom it is vested.

(2) Where any such mortgagee obtains an order for foreclosure absolute, the order shall operate to vest the fee simple in him (subject to any legal mortgage having priority to the mortgage in right of which the foreclosure is obtained and to any money thereby secured), and thereupon the mortgage term, if any, shall thereby be merged in the fee simple, and any subsequent mortgage term or charge by way of legal mortgage bound by the order shall thereupon be extinguished.

(3) Where any such mortgagee acquires a title under the Limitation Acts, he, or the persons deriving title under him, may enlarge the mortgage term into a fee simple under the statutory power for that purpose discharged from any legal mortgage affected by the title so acquired, or in the case of a chargee by way of legal mortgage may by deed declare that the fee simple is vested in him discharged as aforesaid, and the same shall vest accordingly.

(4) Where the mortgage includes fixtures or chattels personal any statutory power of sale and any right to foreclose or take possession shall extend to the absolute or other interest therein affected by the charge.

(5) In the case of a sub-mortgage by subdemise of a long term (less a nominal period) itself limited out of an estate in fee simple, the foregoing provisions of this section shall operate as if the derivative term, if any, created by the sub-mortgage had been limited out of the fee simple, and so as to enlarge the principal term and extinguish the derivative term created by the sub-mortgage as aforesaid, and to enable the sub-mortgagee to convey the fee simple or acquire it by foreclosure, enlargement, or otherwise as aforesaid.

(6) This section applies to a mortgage whether created before or after the commencement of this Act, and to a mortgage term created by this Act, but does not operate to confer a better title to the fee simple than would have been acquired if the same had been conveyed by the mortgage (being a valid mortgage) and the restrictions imposed by this Act in regard to the effect and creation of mortgages were not in force, and all prior mortgages (if any) not being merely equitable charges had been created by demise or by charge by way of legal mortgage.

89. Realisation of leasehold mortgages

(1) Where a term of years absolute has been mortgaged by the creation of another term of years absolute limited thereout or by a charge by way of legal mortgage and the mortgagee sells under his statutory or express power of sale,—

(a) the conveyance by him shall operate to convey to the purchaser not only the mortgage term, if any, but also (unless expressly excepted with the leave of the court) the leasehold reversion affected by the mortgage, subject to any legal mortgage having priority to the mortgage in right of which the sale is made and to any money thereby secured, and thereupon

(b)   the mortgage term, or the charge by way of legal mortgage and any subsequent mortgage term or charge, shall merge in such leasehold reversion or be extinguished unless excepted as aforesaid;

and such conveyance may, as respects the leasehold reversion, be made in the name of the estate owner in whom it is vested.

Where a licence to assign is required on a sale by a mortgagee, such licence shall not be unreasonably refused.

(2)   Where any such mortgagee obtains an order for foreclosure absolute, the order shall, unless it otherwise provides, operate (without giving rise to a forfeiture for want of a licence to assign) to vest the leasehold reversion affected by the mortgage and any subsequent mortgage term in him, subject to any legal mortgage having priority to the mortgage in right of which the foreclosure is obtained and to any money thereby secured, and thereupon the mortgage term and any subsequent mortgage term or charge by way of legal mortgage bound by the order shall, subject to any express provision to the contrary contained in the order, merge in such leasehold reversion or be extinguished.

(3)   Where any such mortgagee acquires a title under the Limitation Acts, he, or the persons deriving title under him, may by deed declare that the leasehold reversion affected by the mortgage and any mortgage term affected by the title so acquired shall vest in him, free from any right of redemption which is barred, and the same shall (without giving rise to a forfeiture for want of a licence to assign) vest accordingly, and thereupon the mortgage term, if any, and any other mortgage term or charge by way of legal mortgage affected by the title so acquired shall, subject to any express provision to the contrary contained in the deed, merge in such leasehold reversion or be extinguished.

(4)   Where the mortgage includes fixtures or chattels personal, any statutory power of sale and any right to foreclose or take possession shall extend to the absolute or other interest therein affected by the charge.

(5)   In the case of a sub-mortgage by subdemise of a term (less a nominal period) itself limited out of a leasehold reversion, the foregoing provisions of this section shall operate as if the derivative term created by the sub-mortgage had been limited out of the leasehold reversion, and so as (subject as aforesaid) to merge the principal mortgage term therein as well as the derivative term created by the sub-mortgage and to enable the sub-mortgagee to convey the leasehold reversion or acquire it by foreclosure, vesting, or otherwise as aforesaid.

(6)   This section takes effect without prejudice to any incumbrance or trust affecting the leasehold reversion which has priority over the mortgage in right of which the sale, foreclosure, or title is made or acquired, and applies to a mortgage whether executed before or after the commencement of this Act, and to a mortgage term created by this Act, but does not apply where the mortgage term does not comprise the whole of the land included in the leasehold reversion unless the rent (if any) payable in respect of that reversion has been apportioned as respects the land affected, or the rent is of no money value or no rent is reserved, and unless the lessee's covenants and conditions (if any) have been apportioned, either expressly or by implication, as respects the land affected.

In this subsection references to an apportionment include an equitable apportionment made without the consent of the lessor.

(7)   The county court has jurisdiction under this section where the amount owing in respect of the mortgage or charge at the commencement of the proceedings does not exceed £30,000.

90.   Realisation of equitable charges by the court

(1)   Where an order for sale is made by the court in reference to an equitable mortgage on land (not secured by a legal term of years absolute or by a charge by way of legal mortgage) the court may, in favour of a purchaser, make a vesting order conveying the land or may appoint a person to convey the land or create and vest in the mortgagee a legal term of years absolute to enable him to carry out the sale, as the case may require, in like manner as if the mortgage had been created by deed by way of legal mortgage pursuant to this Act, but without prejudice to any incumbrance having priority to the equitable mortgage unless the incumbrancer consents to the sale.

(2)   This section applies to equitable mortgages made or arising before or after the commencement of this Act, but not to a mortgage which has been overreached under the powers conferred by this Act or otherwise.

(3)   The county court has jurisdiction under this section where the amount owing in respect of the mortgage or charge at the commencement of the proceedings does not exceed £30,000.

91.   Sale of mortgaged property in action for redemption or foreclosure

(1)   Any person entitled to redeem mortgaged property may have a judgment or order for sale instead of for redemption in an action brought by him either for redemption alone, or for sale alone, or for sale or redemption in the alternative.

(2)   In any action, whether for foreclosure, or for redemption, or for sale, or for the raising and payment in any manner of mortgage money, the court, on the request of the mortgagee, or of any person interested either in the mortgage money or in the right of redemption, and, notwithstanding that—

(a)   any other person dissents; or

(b)   the mortgagee or any person so interested does not appear in the action;

and without allowing any time for redemption or for payment of any mortgage money, may direct a sale of the mortgaged property, on such terms as it thinks fit, including the deposit in court of a reasonable sum fixed by the court to meet the expenses of sale and to secure performance of the terms.

(3)   But, in an action brought by a person interested in the right of redemption and seeking a sale, the court may, on the application of any defendant, direct the plaintiff to give such security for costs as the court thinks fit, and may give the conduct of the sale to any defendant, and may give such directions as it thinks fit respecting the costs of the defendants or any of them.

(4)   In any case within this section the court may, if it thinks fit, direct a sale without previously determining the priorities of incumbrancers.

(5)   This section applies to actions brought either before or after the commencement of this Act.

(6)   In this section 'mortgaged property' includes the estate or interest which a mortgagee would have had power to convey if the statutory power of sale were applicable.

(7)   For the purposes of this section the court may, in favour of a purchaser, make a vesting order conveying the mortgaged property, or appoint a person to do so, subject or not to any incumbrance, as the court may think fit; or, in the case of an equitable mortgage, may create and vest a mortgage term in the mortgagee to enable him to carry out the sale as if the mortgage had been made by deed by way of legal mortgage.

(8)   The county court has jurisdiction under this section where the amount owing in respect of the mortgage or charge at the commencement of the proceedings does not exceed £30,000.

92.   Power to authorise land and minerals to be dealt with separately

(1)   Where a mortgagee's power of sale in regard to land has become exercisable but does not extend to the purposes mentioned in this section, the court may, on his application, authorise him and the persons deriving title under him to dispose—

(a)   of the land, with an exception or reservation of all or any mines and minerals, and with or without rights and powers of or incidental to the working, getting or carrying away of minerals; or

(b)   of all or any mines and minerals, with or without the said rights or powers separately from the land;

and thenceforth the powers so conferred shall have effect as if the same were contained in the mortgage.

(2)   The county court has jurisdiction under this section where the amount owing in respect of the mortgage or charge at the commencement of the proceedings does not exceed £30,000.

93.   Restriction on consolidation of mortgages

(1)   A mortgagor seeking to redeem any one mortgage is entitled to do so without paying any money due under any separate mortgage made by him, or by any person through whom he claims, solely on property other than that comprised in the mortgage which he seeks to redeem.

This subsection applies only if and as far as a contrary intention is not expressed in the mortgage deeds or one of them.

(2) This section does not apply where all the mortgages were made before the first day of January, eighteen hundred and eight-two.

(3) Save as aforesaid, nothing in this Act, in reference to mortgages, affects any right of consolidation or renders inoperative a stipulation in relation to any mortgage made before or after the commencement of this Act reserving a right to consolidate.

94. Tacking and further advances

(1) After the commencement of this Act, a prior mortgagee shall have a right to make further advances to rank in priority to subsequent mortgages (whether legal or equitable) —

   (a) if an arrangement has been made to that effect with the subsequent mortgagees, or

   (b) if he had no notice of such subsequent mortgages at the time when the further advance was made by him; or

   (c) whether or not he had such notice as aforesaid, where the mortgage imposes an obligation on him to make such further advances.

This subsection applies whether or not the prior mortgage was made expressly for securing further advances.

(2) In relation to the making of further advances after the commencement of this Act a mortgagee shall not be deemed to have notice of a mortgage merely by reason that it was registered as a land charge if it was not so registered at the time when the original mortgage was created or when the last search (if any) by or on behalf of the mortgagee was made, whichever last happened.

This subsection only applies where the prior mortgage was made expressly for securing a current account or other further advances.

(3) Save in regard to the making of further advances as aforesaid, the right to tack is hereby abolished:

Provided that nothing in this Act shall affect any priority acquired before the commencement of this Act by tacking, or in respect of further advances made without notice of a subsequent incumbrance or by arrangement with the subsequent incumbrancer.

(4) This section applies to mortgages of land made before or after the commencement of this Act, but not to charges on registered land.

95. Obligation to transfer instead of re-conveying, and as to right to take possession

(1) Where a mortgagor is entitled to redeem, then subject to compliance with the terms on compliance with which he would be entitled to require a reconveyance or surrender, he shall be entitled to require the mortgagee, instead of re-conveying or surrendering, to assign the mortgage debt and convey the mortgaged property to any third person, as the mortgagor directs; and the mortgagee shall be bound to assign and convey accordingly.

(2) The rights conferred by this section belong to and are capable of being enforced by each incumbrancer, or by the mortgagor, notwithstanding any intermediate incumbrance; but a requisition of an incumbrancer prevails over a requisition of the mortgagor, and, as between incumbrancers, a requisition of a prior incumbrancer prevails over a requisition of a subsequent incumbrancer.

(3) The foregoing provisions of this section do not apply in the case of a mortgagee being or having been in possession.

(4) Nothing in this Act affects prejudicially the right of a mortgagee of land whether or not his charge is secured by a legal term of years absolute to take possession of the land, but the taking of possession by the mortgagee does not convert any legal estate of the mortgagor into an equitable interest.

(5) This section applies to mortgages made either before or after the commencement of this Act, and takes effect notwithstanding any stipulation to the contrary.

96. Regulations respecting inspection, production and delivery of documents, and priorities

(1) A mortgagor, as long as his right to redeem subsists, shall be entitled from time to time, at reasonable times, on his request, and at his own cost, and on payment of the mortgagee's costs and expenses in this behalf, to inspect and make copies or abstracts

of or extracts from the documents of title relating to the mortgaged property in the custody or power of the mortgagee.

This section applies to mortgages made after the thirty-first day of December, eighteen hundred and eighty-one, and takes effect notwithstanding any stipulation to the contrary.

(2) A mortgagee, whose mortgage is surrendered or otherwise extinguished, shall not be liable on account of delivering documents of title in his possession to the person not having the best right thereto, unless he has notice of the right or claim of a person having a better right, whether by virtue of a right to require a surrender or reconveyance or otherwise.

In this sub-section notice does not include notice implied by reason of registration under the Land Charges Act, 1925.

97. Priorities as between puisne mortgages

Every mortgage affecting a legal estate in land made after the commencement of this Act, whether legal or equitable (not being a mortgage protected by the deposit of documents relating to the legal estate affected) shall rank according to its date of registration as a land charge pursuant to the Land Charges Act, 1925.

This section does not apply to mortgages or charges to which the Land Charges Act 1972 does not apply by virtue of section 14(3) of that Act (which excludes certain land charges created by instruments necessitating registration under the Land Registration Act 2002), or to mortgages or charges of registered land.

98. Actions for possession by mortgagors

(1) A mortgagor for the time being entitled to the possession or receipt of the rents and profits of any land, as to which the mortgagee has not given notice of his intention to take possession or to enter into the receipt of the rents and profits thereof, may sue for such possession, or for the recovery of such rents or profits, or to prevent or recover damages in respect of any trespass or other wrong relative thereto, in his own name only, unless the cause of action arises upon a lease or other contract made by him jointly with any other person.

(2) This section does not prejudice the power of a mortgagor independently of this section to take proceedings in his own name only, either in right of any legal estate vested in him or otherwise.

(3) This section applies whether the mortgage was made before or after the commencement of this Act.

99. Leasing powers of mortgagor and mortgagee in possession

(1) A mortgagor of land while in possession shall, as against every incumbrancer, have power to make from time to time any such lease of the mortgaged land, or any part thereof, as is by this section authorised.

(2) A mortgagee of land while in possession shall, as against all prior incumbrancers, if any, and as against the mortgagor, have power to make from time to time any such lease as aforesaid.

(3) The leases which this section authorises are—

(i) agricultural or occupation leases for any term not exceeding twenty-one years, or, in the case of a mortgage made after the commencement of this Act, fifty years; and

(ii) building leases for any term not exceeding ninety-nine years, or, in the case of a mortgage made after the commencement of this Act, nine hundred and ninety-nine years.

(4) Every person making a lease under this section may execute and do all assurances and things necessary or proper in that behalf.

(5) Every such lease shall be made to take effect in possession not later than twelve months after its date.

(6) Every such lease shall reserve the best rent that can reasonably be obtained, regard being had to the circumstances of the case, but without any fine being taken.

(7) Every such lease shall contain a covenant by the lessee for payment of the rent, and condition of re-entry on the rent not being paid within a time therein specified not exceeding thirty days.

(8) A counterpart of every such lease shall be executed by the lessee and delivered to the lessor, of which execution and delivery the execution of the lease by the lessor shall, in favour of the lessee and all persons deriving title under him, be sufficient evidence.

(9)   Every such building lease shall be made in consideration of the lessee, or some person by whose direction the lease is granted, having erected, or agreeing to erect within not more than five years from the date of the lease, buildings, new or additional, or having improved or repaired buildings, or agreeing to improve or repair buildings within that time, or having executed, or agreeing to execute within that time, on the land leased, an improvement for or in connexion with building purposes.

(10)   In any such building lease a peppercorn rent, or a nominal or other rent less than the rent ultimately payable, may be made payable for the first five years, or any less part of the term.

(11)   In case of a lease by the mortgagor, he shall, within one month after making the lease, deliver to the mortgagee, or, where there are more than one, to the mortgagee first in priority, a counterpart of the lease duly executed by the lessee, but the lessee shall not be concerned to see that this provision is complied with.

(12)   A contract to make or accept a lease under this section may be enforced by or against every person on whom the lease if granted would be binding.

(13)   Subject to subsection 13A below this section applies only if and as far as a contrary intention is not expressed by the mortgagor and mortgagee in the mortgage deed, or otherwise in writing, and has effect subject to the terms of the mortgage deed or of any such writing and to the provisions therein contained.

(13A) Subsection 13 of this section—
   (a)   shall not enable the application of any provision of this section to be excluded or restricted in relation to any mortgage of agricultural land made after 1st March 1984 but before 1st September 1995; and
   (b)   shall not enable the power to grant a lease of any agricultural holding to which, by virtue of section 4 of the Agricultural Tenancies Act 1995, the Agricultural Holdings Act 1986 will apply, to be excluded or restricted in relation to any mortgage of agricultural land made on or after 1st September 1995.

(13B) In subsection (13A) of this section—
   'agricultural holding' has the same meaning as in the Agricultural Holdings Act 1986; and 'agricultural land' has the same meaning as in the Agricultural Act 1947.

(14)   The mortgagor and mortgagee may, by agreement in writing, whether or not contained in the mortgage deed, reserve to or confer on the mortgagor or the mortgagee, or both, any further or other powers of leasing or having reference to leasing; and any further or other powers so reserved or conferred shall be exercisable, as far as may be, as if they were conferred by this Act, and with all the like incidents, effects, and consequences:

   Provided that the powers so reserved or conferred shall not prejudicially affect the rights of any mortgagee interested under any other mortgage subsisting at the date of the agreement, unless that mortgagee joins in or adopts the agreement.

(15)   Nothing in this Act shall be construed to enable a mortgagor or mortgagee to make a lease for any longer term or on any other conditions than such as could have been granted or imposed by the mortgagor, with the concurrence of all the incumbrancers, if this Act and the enactments replaced by this section had not been passed:

   Provided that, in the case of a mortgage of leasehold land, a lease granted under this section shall reserve a reversion of not less than one day.

(16)   Subject as aforesaid, this section applies to any mortgage made after the thirty-first day of December, eighteen hundred and eighty-one, but the provisions thereof, or any of them, may, by agreement in writing made after that date between mortgagor and mortgagee, be applied to a mortgage made before that date, so nevertheless that any such agreement shall not prejudicially affect any right or interest of any mortgagee not joining in or adopting the agreement.

(17)   The provisions of this section referring to a lease shall be construed to extend and apply, as far as circumstances admit, to any letting, and to an agreement, whether in writing or not, for leasing or letting.

(18)   For the purposes of this section 'mortgagor' does not include an incumbrancer deriving title under the original mortgagor.

(19)   The powers of leasing conferred by this section shall, after a receiver of the income of the mortgaged property or any part thereof has been appointed by a mortgagee under his statutory power, and so long as the receiver acts, be exercisable by such mortgagee instead of by the mortgagor, as respects any land affected by the receivership, in like manner as if such mortgagee were in possession of the land, and the mortgagee may, by writing, delegate any of such powers to the receiver.

100. Powers of mortgagor and mortgagee in possession to accept surrenders of leases

(1) For the purpose only of enabling a lease authorised under the last preceding section, or under any agreement made pursuant to that section, or by the mortgage deed (in this section referred to as an authorised lease) to be granted, a mortgagor of land while in possession shall, as against every incumbrancer, have, by virtue of this Act, power to accept from time to time a surrender of any lease of the mortgaged land or any part thereof comprised in the lease, with or without an exception of or in respect of all or any of the mines and minerals therein, and, on a surrender of the lease so far as it comprises part only of the land or mines and minerals leased, the rent may be apportioned.

(2) For the same purpose, a mortgagee of land while in possession shall, as against all prior or other incumbrancers, if any, and as against the mortgagor, have, by virtue of this Act, power to accept from time to time any such surrender as aforesaid.

(3) On a surrender of part only of the land or mines and minerals leased, the original lease may be varied, provided that the lease when varied would have been valid as an authorised lease if granted by the person accepting the surrender; and, on a surrender and the making of a new or other lease, whether for the same or for any extended or other term, and whether subject or not to the same or to any other covenants, provisions, or conditions, the value of the lessee's interest in the lease surrendered may, subject to the provisions of this section, be taken into account in the determination of the amount of the rent to be reserved, and of the nature of the covenants, provisions and conditions to be inserted in the new or other lease.

(4) Where any consideration for the surrender, other than an agreement to accept an authorised lease, is given by or on behalf of the lessee to or on behalf of the person accepting the surrender, nothing in this section authorises a surrender to a mortgagor without the consent of the incumbrancers, or authorises a surrender to a second or subsequent incumbrancer without the consent of every prior incumbrancer.

(5) No surrender shall, by virtue of this section, be rendered valid unless:—

    (a) An authorised lease is granted of the whole of the land or mines and minerals comprised in the surrender to take effect in possession immediately or within one month after the date of the surrender; and

    (b) The term certain or other interest granted by the new lease is not less in duration than the unexpired term or interest which would have been subsisting under the original lease if that lease had not been surrendered; and

    (c) Where the whole of the land mines and minerals originally leased has been surrendered, the rent reserved by the new lease is not less than the rent which would have been payable under the original lease if it had not been surrendered; or where part only of the land or mines and minerals has been surrendered, the aggregate rents respectively remaining payable or reserved under the original lease and new lease are not less than the rent which would have been payable under the original lease if no partial surrender had been accepted.

(6) A contract to make or accept a surrender under this section may be enforced by or against every person on whom the surrender, if completed, would be binding.

(7) This section applies only if and as far as a contrary intention is not expressed by the mortgagor and mortgagee in the mortgage deed, or otherwise in writing, and shall have effect subject to the terms of the mortgage deed or of any such writing and to the provisions therein contained.

(8) This section applies to a mortgage made after the thirty-first day of December, nineteen hundred and eleven, but the provisions of this section, or any of them, may, by agreement in writing made after that date, between mortgagor and mortgagee, be applied to a mortgage made before that date, so nevertheless that any such agreement shall not prejudicially affect any right or interest of any mortgagee not joining in or adopting the agreement.

(9) The provisions of this section referring to a lease shall be construed to extend and apply, as far as circumstances admit, to any letting, and to an agreement, whether in writing or not, for leasing or letting.

(10) The mortgagor and mortgagee may, by agreement in writing, whether or not contained in the mortgage deed, reserve or confer on the mortgagor or mortgagee, or both, any further or other powers relating to the surrender of leases; and any further or other powers so conferred or reserved shall be exercisable, as far as may be, as if they were conferred by this Act, and with all the like incidents, effects and consequences:

Provided that the powers so reserved or conferred shall not prejudicially affect the rights of any mortgagee interested under any other mortgage subsisting at the date of the agreement, unless that mortgagee joins in or adopts the agreement.

(11) Nothing in this section operates to enable a mortgagor or mortgagee to accept a surrender which could not have been accepted by the mortgagor with the concurrence of all the incumbrancers if this Act and the enactments replaced by this section had not been passed.

(12) For the purposes of this section 'mortgagor' does not include an incumbrancer deriving title under the original mortgagor.

(13) The powers of accepting surrenders conferred by this section shall, after a receiver of the income of the mortgaged property or any part thereof has been appointed by the mortgagee, under the statutory power, and so long as the receiver acts, be exercisable by such mortgagee instead of by the mortgagor, as respects any land affected by the receivership, in like manner as if such mortgagee were in possession of the land; and the mortgagee may, by writing, delegate any of such powers to the receiver.

101. Powers incident to estate or interest of mortgagee

(1) A mortgagee, where the mortgage is made by deed, shall, by virtue of this Act, have the following powers, to the like extent as if they had been in terms conferred by the mortgage deed, but not further (namely):

(i) A power, when the mortgage money has become due, to sell, or to concur with any other person in selling, the mortgaged property, or any part thereof, either subject to prior charges or not, and either together or in lots, by public auction or by private contract, subject to such conditions respecting title, or evidence of title, or other matter, as the mortgagee thinks fit, with power to vary any contract for sale, and to buy in at an auction, or to rescind any contract for sale, and to re-sell, without being answerable for any loss occasioned thereby; and

(ii) A power, at any time after the date of the mortgage deed, to insure and keep insured against loss or damage by fire any building, or any effects or property of an insurable nature, whether affixed to the freehold or not, being or forming part of the property which or an estate or interest wherein is mortgaged, and the premiums paid for any such insurance shall be a charge on the mortgaged property or estate or interest, in addition to the mortgage money, and with the same priority, and with interest at the same rate, as the mortgage money; and

(iii) A power, when the mortgage money has become due, to appoint a receiver of the income of the mortgaged property, or any part thereof; or, if the mortgaged property consists of an interest in income, or of a rentcharge or an annual or other periodical sum, a receiver of that property or any part thereof; and

(iv) A power, while the mortgagee is in possession, to cut and sell timber and other trees ripe for cutting, and not planted or left standing for shelter or ornament, or to contract for any such cutting and sale, to be completed within any time not exceeding twelve months from the making of the contract.

(1A) Subsection (1)(i) is subject to section 21 of the Commonhold and Leasehold Reform Act 2002 (no disposition of part-units).

(2) Where the mortgage deed is executed after the thirty-first day of December, nineteen hundred and eleven, the power of sale aforesaid includes the following powers as incident thereto (namely):—

(i) A power to impose or reserve or make binding, as far as the law permits, by covenant, condition, or otherwise, on the unsold part of the mortgaged property or any part thereof, or on the purchaser and any property sold, any restriction or reservation with respect to building on or other user of land, or with respect to mines and minerals, or for the purpose of the more beneficial working thereof, or with respect to any other thing:

(II) A power to sell the mortgaged property, or any part thereof, or all or any mines and minerals apart from the surface:—

(a) With or without a grant or reservation of rights of way, rights of water, easements, rights, and privileges for or connected with building or other purposes in relation to the property remaining in mortgage or any part thereof, or to any property sold: and

(b)   With or without an exception or reservation of all or any of the mines and minerals in or under the mortgaged property, and with or without a grant or reservation of powers or working, wayleaves, or rights of way, rights of water and drainage and other powers, easements, rights, and privileges for or connected with mining purposes in relation to the property remaining unsold or any part thereof, or to any property sold: and

(c)   With or without covenants by the purchaser to expend money on the land sold.

(3)   The provisions of this Act relating to the foregoing powers, comprised either in this section, or in any other section regulating the exercise of those powers, may be varied or extended by the mortgage deed, and, as so varied or extended, shall, as far as may be, operate in the like manner and with all the like incidents, effects, and consequences, as if such variations or extensions were contained in this Act.

(4)   This section applies only if and as far as a contrary intention is not expressed in the mortgage deed, and has effect subject to the terms of the mortgage deed and to the provisions therein contained.

(5)   Save as otherwise provided, this section applies where the mortgage deed is executed after the thirty-first day of December, eighteen hundred and eighty-one.

(6)   The power of sale conferred by this section includes such power of selling the estate in fee simple or any leasehold reversion as is conferred by the provisions of this Act relating to the realisation of mortgages.

102.   Provision as to mortgages of undivided shares in land

(1)   A person who was before the commencement of this Act a mortgagee of an undivided share in land shall have the same power to sell his interest under the trust to which the land is subject, as, independently of this Act, he would have had in regard to the share in the land; and shall also have a right to require the trustees in whom the land is vested to account to him for the income attributable to that share or to appoint a receiver to receive the same from such trustees corresponding to the right which, independently of this Act, he would have had to take possession or to appoint a receiver of the rents and profits attributable to the same share.

(2)   The powers conferred by this section are exercisable by the persons deriving title under such mortgagee.

103.   Regulation of exercise of power of sale

A mortgagee shall not exercise the power of sale conferred by this Act unless and until—

(i)   Notice requiring payment of the mortgage money has been served on the mortgagor or one of two or more mortgagors, and default has been made in payment of the mortgage money, or of part thereof, for three months after such service; or

(ii)   Some interest under the mortgage is in arrear and unpaid for two months after becoming due; or

(iii) There has been a breach of some provision contained in the mortgage deed or in this Act, or in an enactment replaced by this Act, and on the part of the mortgagor, or of some person concurring in making the mortgage, to be observed or performed, other than and besides a covenant for payment of the mortgage money or interest thereon.

104.   Conveyance on sale

(1)   A mortgagee exercising the power of sale conferred by this Act shall have power, by deed, to convey the property sold, for such estate and interest therein as he is by this Act authorised to sell or convey or may be the subject of the mortgage, freed from all estates, interests, and rights to which the mortgage has priority, but subject to all estates, interests, and rights which have priority to the mortgage.

(2)   Where a conveyance is made in exercise of the power of sale conferred by this Act, or any enactment replaced by this Act, the title of the purchaser shall not be impeachable on the ground—

(a)   that no case had arisen to authorise the sale; or

(b)   that due notice was not given; or

(c)   where the mortgage is made after the commencement of this Act, that leave of the court, when so required, was not obtained; or

(d)   whether the mortgage was made before or after such commencement, that the power was otherwise improperly or irregularly exercised;

and a purchaser is not, either before or on conveyance, concerned to see or inquire whether a case has arisen to authorise the sale, or due notice has been given, or the power is otherwise properly and regularly exercised; but any person damnified by an unauthorised, or improper, or irregular exercise of the power shall have his remedy in damages against the person exercising the power.

(3) A conveyance on sale by a mortgagee, made after the commencement of this Act, shall be deemed to have been made in exercise of the power of sale conferred by this Act unless a contrary intention appears.

105. Application of proceeds of sale

The money which is received by the mortgagee, arising from the sale, after discharge of prior incumbrances to which the sale is not made subject, if any, or after payment into court under this Act of a sum to meet any prior incumbrance, shall be held by him in trust to be applied by him, first, in payment of all costs, charges, and expenses properly incurred by him as incident to the sale or any attempted sale, or otherwise; and secondly, in discharge of the mortgage money, interest, and costs, and other money, if any, due under the mortgage; and the residue of the money so received shall be paid to the person entitled to the mortgaged property, or authorised to give receipts for the proceeds of the sale thereof.

106. Provisions as to exercise of power of sale

(1) The power of sale conferred by this Act may be exercised by any person for the time being entitled to receive and give a discharge for the mortgage money.

(2) The power of sale conferred by this Act does not affect the right of foreclosure.

(3) The mortgagee shall not be answerable for any involuntary loss happening in or about the exercise or execution of the power of sale conferred by this Act, or of any trust connected therewith, or, where the mortgage is executed after the thirty-first day of December, nineteen hundred and eleven, of any power or provision contained in the mortgage deed.

(4) At any time after the power of sale conferred by this Act has become exercisable the person entitled to exercise the power may demand and recover from any person, other than a person having in the mortgaged property an estate, interest, or right in priority to the mortgage, all the deeds and documents relating to the property, or to the title thereto, which a purchaser under the power of sale would be entitled to demand and recover from him.

107. Mortgagee's receipts, discharges, etc.

(1) The receipt in writing of a mortgagee shall be a sufficient discharge for any money arising under the power of sale conferred by this Act, or for any money or securities comprised in his mortgage, or arising thereunder; and a person paying or transferring the same to the mortgagee shall not be concerned to inquire whether any money remains due under the mortgage.

(2) Money received by a mortgagee under his mortgage or from the proceeds of securities comprised in his mortgage shall be applied in like manner as in this Act directed respecting money received by him arising from a sale under the power of sale conferred by this Act, but with this variation, that the costs, charges, and expenses payable shall include the costs, charges, and expenses properly incurred of recovering and receiving the money or securities, and of conversion of securities into money, instead of those incident to sale.

108. Amount and application of insurance money

(1) The amount of an insurance effected by a mortgagee against loss or damage by fire under the power in that behalf conferred by this Act shall not exceed the amount specified in the mortgage deed, or, if no amount is therein specified, two third parts of the amount that would be required, in case of total destruction, to restore the property insured.

(2) An insurance shall not, under the power conferred by this Act, be effected by a mortgagee in any of the following cases (namely):

(i) Where there is a declaration in the mortgage deed that no insurance is required:

(ii) Where an insurance is kept up by or on behalf of the mortgagor in accordance with the mortgage deed:

(iii) Where the mortgage deed contains no stipulation respecting insurance, and an insurance is kept up by or on behalf of the mortgagor with the consent of the mortgagee to the amount to which the mortgagee is by this Act authorised to insure.

(3)   All money received on an insurance of mortgaged property against loss or damage by fire or otherwise effected under this Act, or any enactment replaced by this Act, or on an insurance for the maintenance of which the mortgagor is liable under the mortgage deed, shall, if the mortgagee so requires, be applied by the mortgagor in making good the loss or damage in respect of which the money is received.

(4)   Without prejudice to any obligation to the contrary imposed by law, or by special contract, a mortgagee may require that all money received on an insurance of mortgaged property against loss or damage by fire or otherwise effected under this Act, or any enactment replaced by this Act, or on an insurance for the maintenance of which the mortgagor is liable under the mortgage deed, be applied in or towards the discharge of the mortgage money.

109.   Appointment, powers, remuneration and duties of receiver

(1)   A mortgagee entitled to appoint a receiver under the power in that behalf conferred by this Act shall not appoint a receiver until he has become entitled to exercise the power of sale conferred by this Act, but may then, by writing under his hand, appoint such person as he thinks fit to be receiver.

(2)   A receiver appointed under the powers conferred by this Act, or any enactment replaced by this Act, shall be deemed to be the agent of the mortgagor; and the mortgagor shall be solely responsible for the receiver's acts or defaults unless the mortgage deed otherwise provides.

(3)   The receiver shall have power to demand and recover all the income of which he is appointed receiver, by action or under section 72(1) of the Tribunals, Courts and Enforcement Act 2007 (commercial rent arrears recovery), or otherwise, in the name either of the mortgagor or of the mortgagee, to the full extent of the estate or interest which the mortgagor could dispose of, and to give effectual receipts accordingly for the same, and to exercise any powers which may have been delegated to him by the mortgagee pursuant to this Act.

(4)   A person paying money to the receiver shall not be concerned to inquire whether any case has happened to authorise the receiver to act.

(5)   The receiver may be removed, and a new receiver may be appointed, from time to time by the mortgagee by writing under his hand.

(6)   The receiver shall be entitled to retain out of any money received by him, for his remuneration, and in satisfaction of all costs, charges, and expenses incurred by him as receiver, a commission at such rate, not exceeding five per centum on the gross amount of all money received, as is specified in his appointment, and if no rate is so specified, then at the rate of five per centum on that gross amount, or at such other rate as the court thinks fit to allow, on application made by him for that purpose.

(7)   The receiver shall, if so directed in writing by the mortgagee, insure to the extent, if any, to which the mortgagee might have insured and keep insured against loss or damage by fire, out of the money received by him, any building, effects, or property comprised in the mortgage, whether affixed to the freehold or not, being of an insurable nature.

(8)   Subject to the provisions of this Act as to the application of insurance money, the receiver shall apply all money received by him as follows, namely:

     (i)   In discharge of all rents, taxes, rates, and outgoings whatever affecting the mortgaged property; and

     (ii)   In keeping down all annual sums or other payments, and the interest on all principal sums, having priority to the mortgage in right whereof he is receiver; and

     (iii)   In payment of his commission, and of the premiums on fire, life, or other insurances, if any, properly payable under the mortgage deed or under this Act, and the cost of executing necessary or proper repairs directed in writing by the mortgagee; and

     (iv)   In payment of the interest accruing due in respect of any principal money due under the mortgage; and

     (v)   In or towards discharge of the principal money if so directed in writing by the mortgagee;

and shall pay the residue, if any, of the money received by him to the person who, but for the possession of the receiver, would have been entitled to receive the income of which he is appointed receiver, or who is otherwise entitled to the mortgaged property.

110. Effect of bankruptcy of the mortgagor on the power to sell or appoint a receiver

(1) Where the statutory or express power for a mortgagee either to sell or to appoint a receiver is made exercisable by reason of the mortgagor being adjudged a bankrupt, such power shall not be exercised only on account of the adjudication, without the leave of the court.

(2) This section applies only where the mortgage deed is executed after the commencement of this Act.

111. Effect of advance on joint account

(1) Where—

(a) in a mortgage, or an obligation for payment of money, or a transfer of a mortgage or of such an obligation, the sum, or any part of the sum, advanced or owing is expressed to be advanced by or owing to more persons than one out of money, or as money, belonging to them on a joint account; or

(b) a mortgage, or such an obligation, or such a transfer is made to more persons than one, jointly;

the mortgage money, or other money or money's worth, for the time being due to those persons on the mortgage or obligation, shall, as between them and the mortgagor or obligor, be deemed to be and remain money or money's worth belonging to those persons on a joint account; and the receipt in writing of the survivors or last survivor of them, or of the personal representative of the last survivor, shall be a complete discharge for all money or money's worth for the time being due, notwithstanding any notice to the payer of a severance of the joint account.

(2) This section applies if and so far as a contrary intention is not expressed in the mortgage, obligation, or transfer, and has effect subject to the terms of the mortgage, obligation, or transfer, and to the provisions therein contained.

(3) This section applies to any mortgage obligation or transfer made after the thirty-first day of December, eighteen hundred and eighty-one.

113. Notice of trusts affecting mortgage debts

(1) A person dealing in good faith with a mortgagee, or with the mortgagor if the mortgage has been discharged released or postponed as to the whole or any part of the mortgaged property, shall not be concerned with any trust at any time affecting the mortgage money or the income thereof, whether or not he has notice of the trust, and may assume unless the contrary is expressly stated in the instruments relating to the mortgage—

(a) that the mortgagees (if more than one) are or were entitled to the mortgage money on a joint account; and

(b) that the mortgagee has or had power to give valid receipts for the purchase money or mortgage money and the income thereof (including any arrears of interest) and to release or postpone the priority of the mortgage debt or any part thereof or to deal with the same or the mortgaged property or any part thereof;

without investigating the equitable title to the mortgage debt or the appointment or discharge of trustees in reference thereto.

(2) This section applies to mortgages made before or after the commencement of this Act, but only as respects dealings effected after such commencement.

(3) This section does not affect the liability of any person in whom the mortgage debt is vested for the purposes of any trust to give effect to that trust.

114. Transfers of mortgages

(1) A deed executed by a mortgagee purporting to transfer his mortgage or the benefit thereof shall, unless a contrary intention is therein expressed, and subject to any provisions therein contained, operate to transfer to the transferee—

(a) the right to demand, sue for, recover, and give receipts for, the mortgage money or the unpaid part thereof, and the interest then due, if any, and thenceforth to become due thereon; and

(b) the benefit of all securities for the same, and the benefit of and the right to sue on all covenants with the mortgagee, and the right to exercise all powers of the mortgagee; and

(c) all the estate and interest in the mortgaged property then vested in the mortgagee subject to redemption or cesser, but as to such estate and interest subject to the right of redemption then subsisting.

(2)   In this section 'transferee' includes his personal representatives and assigns.
...
(4)   This section applies, whether the mortgage transferred was made before or after the commencement of this Act, but applies only to transfers made after the commencement of this Act.
(5)   This section does not extend to a transfer of a bill of sale of chattels by way of security.

115. Reconveyances of mortgages by endorsed receipts

(1)   A receipt endorsed on, written at the foot of, or annexed to, a mortgage for all money thereby secured, which states the name of the person who pays the money and is executed by the chargee by way of legal mortgage or the person in whom the mortgaged property is vested and who is legally entitled to give a receipt for the mortgage money shall operate, without any reconveyance, surrender, or release—
   (a)   Where a mortgage takes effect by demise or subdemise, as a surrender of the term, so as to determine the term or merge the same in the reversion immediately expectant thereon;
   (b)   Where the mortgage does not take effect by demise or subdemise, as a reconveyance thereof to the extent of the interest which is the subject matter of the mortgage, to the person who immediately before the execution of the receipt was entitled to the equity of redemption;
   and in either case, as a discharge of the mortgaged property from all principal money and interest secured by, and from all claims under the mortgage, but without prejudice to any term or other interest which is paramount to the estate or interest of the mortgagee or other person in whom the mortgaged property was vested.
(2)   Provided that, where by the receipt the money appears to have been paid by a person who is not entitled to the immediate equity of redemption, the receipt shall operate as if the benefit of the mortgage had by deed been transferred to him; unless—
   (a)   it is otherwise expressly provided; or
   (b)   the mortgage is paid off out of capital money, or other money in the hands of a personal representative or trustee properly applicable for the discharge of the mortgage,
   and it is not expressly provided that the receipt is to operate as a transfer.
(3)   Nothing in this section confers on a mortgagor a right to keep alive a mortgage paid off by him, so as to affect prejudicially any subsequent incumbrancer; and where there is no right to keep the mortgage alive, the receipt does not operate as a transfer.
(4)   This section does not affect the right of any person to require a reassignment, surrender, release, or transfer to be executed in lieu of a receipt.
...
(6)   In a receipt given under this section the same covenants shall be implied as if the person who executes the receipt had by deed been expressed to convey the property as mortgagee, subject to any interest which is paramount to the mortgage.
(7)   Where the mortgage consists of a mortgage and a further charge or of more than one deed, it shall be sufficient for the purposes of this section, if the receipt refers either to all the deeds whereby the mortgage money is secured or to the aggregate amount of the mortgage money thereby secured and for the time being owing, and is endorsed on, written at the foot of, or annexed to, one of the mortgage deeds.
(8)   This section applies to the discharge of a charge by way of legal mortgage, and to the discharge of a mortgage, whether made by way of statutory mortgage or not, executed before or after the commencement of this Act, but only as respects discharges effected after such commencement.
(9)   The provisions of this section relating to the operation of a receipt shall (in substitution for the like statutory provisions relating to receipts given by or on behalf of a building society) apply to the discharge of a mortgage made to any such society, provided that the receipt is executed in the manner required by the statute relating to the society.
(10) This section does not apply to the discharge of a registered charge (within the meaning of the Land Registration Act 2002).
(11) In this section 'mortgaged property' means the property remaining subject to the mortgage at the date of the receipt.

116. Cesser of mortgage terms

Without prejudice to the right of a tenant for life or other person having only a limited interest in the equity of redemption to require a mortgage to be kept alive by transfer or otherwise, a mortgage term shall, when the money secured by the mortgage has been discharged, become a satisfied term and shall cease.

Rentcharges

121. Remedies for the recovery of annual sums charged on land

(1) Where a person is entitled to receive out of any land, or out of the income of any land, any annual sum, payable half-yearly or otherwise, whether charged on the land or on the income of the land, and whether by way of rentcharge of otherwise not being rent incident to a reversion, then, subject and without prejudice to all estates, interests, and rights having priority to the annual sum, the person entitled to receive the annual sum shall have such remedies for recovering and compelling payment thereof as are described in this section, as far as those remedies might have been conferred by the instrument under which the annual sum arises, but not further.

(2) ...

(3) If at any time the annual sum or any part thereof is unpaid for forty days next after the time appointed for any payment in respect thereof, then, although no legal demand has been made for payment thereof, the person entitled to receive the annual sum may enter into possession of and hold the land charged or any part thereof, and take the income thereof, until thereby or otherwise the annual sum and all arrears thereof due at the time of his entry, or afterwards becoming due during his continuance in possession, and all costs and expenses occasioned by nonpayment of the annual sum, are fully paid; and such possession when taken shall be without impeachment of waste.

(4) In the like case the person entitled to the annual sum, whether taking possession or not, may also by deed demise the land charged, or any part thereof, to a trustee for a term of years, with or without impeachment of waste, on trust, by all or any of the means hereinafter mentioned, or by any other reasonable means, to raise and pay the annual sum and all arrears thereof due or to become due, and all costs and expenses occasioned by nonpayment of the annual sum, or incurred in compelling or obtaining payment thereof, or otherwise relating thereto, including the costs of the preparation and execution of the deed of demise, and the costs of the execution of the trusts of that deed:

Provided that this subsection shall not authorise the creation of a legal term of years absolute after the commencement of this Act, save where the annual sum is a rentcharge held for a legal estate.

The surplus, if any, of the money raised, or of the income received, under the trusts of the deed shall be paid to the person for the time being entitled to the land therein comprised in reversion immediately expectant on the term thereby created.

The means by which such annual sum, arrears, costs, and expenses may be raised includes—

(a) the creation of a legal mortgage or a sale (effected by assignment or subdemise) of the term created in the land charged or any part thereof,

(b) the receipt of the income of the land comprised in the term.

(5) This section applies only if and as far as a contrary intention is not expressed in the instrument under which the annual sum arises, and has effect subject to the terms of that instrument and to the provisions therein contained.

122. Creation of rentcharges charged on another rentcharge and remedies for recovery thereof

(1) A rentcharge or other annual sum (not being rent incident to a reversion) payable half yearly or otherwise may be granted, reserved, charged or created out of or on another rentcharge or annual sum (not being rent incident to a reversion) charged on or payable out of land or on or out of the income of land, in like manner as the same could have been made to issue out of land.

(2) If at any time the annual sum so created or any part thereof is unpaid for twenty-one days next after the time appointed for any payment in respect thereof, the person entitled to receive the annual sum shall (without prejudice to any prior interest or charge) have power to appoint a receiver of the annual sum charged or any part thereof, and the

provisions of this Act relating to the appointment, powers, remuneration and duties of a receiver, shall apply in like manner as if such person were a mortgagee entitled to exercise the power of sale conferred by this Act, and the annual sum charged were the mortgaged property and the person entitled thereto were the mortgagor.

(3) The power to appoint a receiver conferred by this section shall (where the annual sum is charged on a rentcharge) take effect in substitution for the remedies conferred, in the case of annual sums charged on land, by the last preceding section, but subsection (6) of that section shall apply and have effect as if herein re-enacted and in terms made applicable to the powers conferred by this section.

(4) This section applies to annual sums expressed to be created before as well as after the commencement of this Act, and, but without prejudice to any order of the court made before the commencement of this Act, operates to confirm any annual sum which would have been validly created if this section had been in force.

PART IV
EQUITABLE INTERESTS AND THINGS IN ACTION

130. Entailed interests in real and personal property

(1)–(3) ...

(4) In default of and subject to the execution of a disentailing assurance or the exercise of the testamentary power conferred by this Act, an entailed interest (to the extent of the property affected) shall devolve as an equitable interest, from time to time, upon the persons who would have been successively entitled thereto as the heirs of the body (either generally or of a particular class) of the tenant in tail or other person, or as tenant by the curtesy, if the entailed interest had, before the commencement of this Act, been limited in respect of freehold land governed by the general law in force immediately before such commencement, and such law had remained unaffected.

(5) Where personal chattels are settled without reference to settled land on trusts creating entailed interests therein, the trustees, with the consent of the usufructuary for the time being if of full age, may sell the chattels or any of them, and the net proceeds of any such sale shall be held in trust for and shall go to the same persons successively, in the same manner and for the same interests, as the chattels sold would have been held and gone if they had not been sold, and the income of investments representing such proceeds of sale shall be applied accordingly.

(6) ...

(7) In this Act where the context so admits 'entailed interest' includes an estate tail (now made to take effect as an equitable interest) created before the commencement of this Act.

131. Abolition of the rule in Shelley's case

Where by any instrument coming into operation after the commencement of this Act an interest in any property is expressed to be given to the heir or heirs or issue or any particular heir or any class of the heirs or issue of any person in words which, but for this section (and paragraph 5 of Schedule 1 of the Trusts of Land and Appointment of Trustees Act 1996) would, under the rule of law known as the Rule in Shelley's case, have operated to give to that person an interest in fee simple or an entailed interest, such words shall operate in equity as words of purchase and not of limitation, and shall be construed and have effect accordingly, and in the case of an interest in any property expressed to be given to an heir or heirs or any particular heir or class of heirs, the same person or persons shall take as would in the case of freehold land have answered that description under the general law in force before the commencement of this Act.

132. As to heirs taking by purchase

(1) A limitation of real or personal property in favour of the heir, either general or special, of a deceased person which, if limited in respect of freehold land before the commencement of this Act, would have conferred on the heir an estate in the land by purchase, shall operate to confer a corresponding equitable interest in the property on the person who would, if the general law in force immediately before such commencement had remained unaffected, have answered the description of the heir, either general or special, of the deceased in respect of his freehold land, either at the death of the deceased or at the time named in the limitation, as the case may require.

(2) This section applies whether the deceased person dies before or after the commencement of this Act, but only applies to limitations or trusts created by an instrument coming into operation after such commencement.

134. Restriction on executory limitations

(1)   Where there is a person entitled to—

    (a)   an equitable interest in land for an estate in fee simple or for any less interest not being an entailed interest, or

    (b)   any interest in other property, not being an entailed interest,

with an executory limitation over on default or failure of all or any of his issue, whether within or at any specified period or time or not, that executory limitation shall be or become void and incapable of taking effect, if and as soon as there is living any issue who has attained the age of eighteen years of the class on default or failure whereof the limitation over was to take effect.

(2)   This section applies where the executory limitation is contained in an instrument coming into operation after the thirty-first day of December, eighteen hundred and eighty-two, save that, as regards instruments coming into operation before the commencement of this Act, it only applies to limitations of land for an estate in fee, or for a term of years absolute or determinable on life, or for a term of life.

135. Equitable waste

An equitable interest for life without impeachment of waste does not confer upon the tenant for life any right to commit waste of the description known as equitable waste, unless an intention to confer such right expressly appears by the instrument creating such equitable interest.

136. Legal assignments of things in action

(1)   Any absolute assignment by writing under the hand of the assignor (not purporting to be by way of charge only) of any debt or other legal thing in action, of which express notice in writing has been given to the debtor, trustee or other person from whom the assignor would have been entitled to claim such debt or thing in action, is effectual in law (subject to equities having priority over the right of the assignee) to pass and transfer from the date of such notice—

    (a)   the legal right to such debt or thing in action;

    (b)   all legal and other remedies for the same; and

    (c)   the power to give a good discharge for the same without the concurrence of the assignor:

Provided that, if the debtor, trustee or other person liable in respect of such debt or thing in action has notice—

    (a)   that the assignment is disputed by the assignor or any person claiming under him; or

    (b)   of any other opposing or conflicting claims to such debt or thing in action; he may, if he thinks fit, either call upon the persons making claim thereto to interplead concerning the same, or pay the debt or other thing in action into court under the provisions of the Trustee Act, 1925.

(2)   This section does not affect the provisions of the Policies of Assurance Act, 1867.

(3)   The county court has jurisdiction (including power to receive payments of money or securities into court) under the proviso to subsection (1) of this section where the amount or value of the debt or thing in action does not exceed £30,000.

137. Dealings with life interests, reversions and other equitable interests

(1)   The law applicable to dealings with equitable things in action which regulates the priority of competing interests therein, shall, as respects dealings with equitable interests in land, capital money, and securities representing capital money effected after the commencement of this Act, apply to and regulate the priority of competing interests therein.

    This subsection applies whether or not the money or securities are in court.

(2)   (i)   In the case of a dealing with an equitable interest in settled land, capital money or securities representing capital money, the persons to be served with notice of the dealing shall be the trustees of the settlement; and where the equitable interest is created by a derivative or subsidiary settlement, the persons to be served with notice shall be the trustees of that settlement.

    (ii)   In the case of a dealing with an equitable interest in land subject to a trust of land, or the proceeds of the sale of such land, the persons to be served with notice shall be the trustees.

(iii)   In any other case the person to be served with notice of a dealing with an equitable interest in land shall be the estate owner of the land affected.

The persons on whom notice is served pursuant to this subsection shall be affected thereby in the same manner as if they had been trustees of personal property out of which the equitable interest was created or arose.

This subsection does not apply where the money or securities are in court.

(3)   A notice, otherwise than in writing, given to, or received by, a trustee after the commencement of this Act as respects any dealing with an equitable interest in real or personal property, shall not affect the priority of competing claims of purchasers in that equitable interest.

(4)   Where, as respects any dealing with an equitable interest in real or personal property—
    (a)   the trustees are not persons to whom a valid notice of the dealing can be given; or
    (b)   there are no trustees to whom a notice can be given; or
    (c)   for any other reason a valid notice cannot be served, or cannot be served without unreasonable cost or delay;

a purchaser may at his own cost require that—
    (i)   a memorandum of the dealing be endorsed, written on or permanently annexed to the instrument creating the trust;
    (ii)   the instrument be produced to him by the person having the possession or custody thereof to prove that a sufficient memorandum has been placed thereon or annexed thereto.

Such memorandum shall, as respects priorities, operate in like manner as if notice in writing of the dealing had been given to trustees duly qualified to receive the notice at the time when the memorandum is placed on or annexed to the instrument creating the trust.

(5)   Where the property affected is settled land, the memorandum shall be placed on or annexed to the trust instrument and not the vesting instrument.

Where the property affected is land subject to a trust of land, the memorandum shall be placed on or annexed to the instrument whereby the equitable interest is created.

(6)   Where the trust is created by statute or by operation of law, or in any other case where there is no instrument whereby the trusts are declared, the instrument under which the equitable interest is acquired or which is evidence of the devolution thereof shall, for the purposes of this section, be deemed the instrument creating the trust.

In particular, where the trust arises by reason of an intestacy, the letters of administration or probate in force when the dealing was effected shall be deemed such instrument.

(7)   Nothing in this section affects any priority acquired before the commencement of this Act.

(8)   Where a notice in writing of a dealing with an equitable interest in real or personal property has been served on a trustee under this section, the trustees from time to time of the property affected shall be entitled to the custody of the notice, and the notice shall be delivered to them by any person who for the time being may have the custody thereof; and subject to the payment of costs, any person interested in the equitable interest may require production of the notice.

(9)   The liability of the estate owner of the legal estate affected to produce documents and furnish information to persons entitled to equitable interests therein shall correspond to the liability of a trustee for sale to produce documents and furnish information to persons entitled to equitable interests in the proceeds of sale of the land.

(10)   This section does not apply until a trust has been created, and in this section 'dealing' includes a disposition by operation of law.

138.   Power to nominate a trust corporation to receive notices

(1)   By any settlement or other instrument creating a trust, a trust corporation may be nominated to whom notices of dealings affecting real or personal property may be given, whether or not under the foregoing section, and in default of such nomination the trustees (if any) of the instrument, or the court on the application of any person interested, may make the nomination.

(2)   The person having the possession or custody of any instrument on which notices under that section may be endorsed shall cause the name of the trust corporation to whom notices may be given to be endorsed upon that instrument.

(3)   Notice given to any trust corporation whose name is so endorsed shall operate in the same way as a notice or endorsement under the foregoing section.

(4)   Where a trust corporation is acting for the purposes of this section a notice given to a trustee of the trust instrument of a dealing relating to the trust property shall forthwith be delivered or sent by post by the trustee to the trust corporation, and until received by the corporation shall not affect any priority.

(5)   A trust corporation shall not be nominated for the purposes of this section—
  (a)   unless that corporation consents to act; or
  (b)   where that corporation has any beneficial interest in or charge upon the trust property; or
  (c)   where a trust corporation is acting as the trustee or one of the trustees of the instrument creating the trust.

(6)   Where a trust corporation acting for the purposes of this section becomes entitled to any beneficial interest in or charge upon the trust property, another trust corporation shall be nominated in its place and all documents relating to notices affecting the trust shall be delivered to the corporation so nominated.

(7)   A trust corporation acting for the purposes of this section shall be bound to keep a separate register of notices of dealings in respect of each equitable interest and shall enter therein—
  (a)   the date of the notice;
  (b)   the name of the person giving the notice;
  (c)   short particulars of the equitable interest intended to be affected; and
  (d)   short particulars of the effect of the dealing if mentioned in the notice.

(8)   The trust corporation may, before making any entry in the register, require the applicant to pay a fee not exceeding the prescribed fee.

(9)   Subject to the payment of a fee not exceeding the prescribed fee, the trust corporation shall permit any person who would, if the corporation had been the trustee of the trust instrument, have been entitled to inspect notices served on the trustee, to inspect and take copies of the register and any notices held by the corporation.

(10) Subject to the payment by the applicant of a fee not exceeding the prescribed fee, the trust corporation shall reply to all inquiries respecting notices received by the corporation in like manner and in the same circumstances as if the corporation had been the trustee of the trust instrument.

(11) In this section 'prescribed fee' means the fee prescribed by the Lord Chancellor, in cases where the Public Trustee acts as a trust corporation for the purposes of this section.

PART V
LEASES AND TENANCIES

139.   Effect of extinguishment of reversion

(1)   Where a reversion expectant on a lease of land is surrendered or merged, the estate or interest which as against the lessee for the time being confers the next vested right to the land, shall be deemed the reversion for the purpose of preserving the same incidents and obligations as would have affected the original reversion had there been no surrender or merger thereof.

(2)   This section applies to surrenders or mergers effected after the first day of October, eighteen hundred and forty-five.

140.   Apportionment of conditions on severance

(1)   Notwithstanding the severance by conveyance, surrender, or otherwise of the reversionary estate in any land comprised in a lease, and notwithstanding the avoidance or cesser in any other manner of the term granted by a lease as to part only of the land comprised therein, every condition or right of re-entry, and every other condition contained in the lease, shall be apportioned, and shall remain annexed to the severed parts of the reversionary estate as severed, and shall be in force with respect to the term whereon each severed part is reversionary, or the term in the part of the land as to which the term has not been surrendered, or has not been avoided or has not otherwise ceased, in like manner as if the land comprised in each severed part, or the land as to which the term remains subsisting, as the case may be, had alone originally been comprised in the lease.

(2)   In this section 'right of re-entry' includes a right to determine the lease by notice to quit or otherwise; but where the notice is served by a person entitled to a severed part of the reversion so that it extends to part only of the land demised, the lessee may within one month determine the lease in regard to the rest of the land by giving to the owner of the reversionary estate therein a counter notice expiring at the same time as the original notice.

(3)   This section applies to leases made before or after the commencement of this Act and whether the severance of the reversionary estate or the partial avoidance or cesser of the term was effected before or after such commencement:

Provided that, where the lease was made before the first day of January eighteen hundred and eighty-two nothing in this section shall affect the operation of a severance of the reversionary estate or partial avoidance or cesser of the term which was effected before the commencement of this Act.

141.   Rent and benefit of lessee's covenants to run with the reversion

(1)   Rent reserved by a lease, and the benefit of every covenant or provision therein contained, having reference to the subject-matter thereof, and on the lessee's part to be observed or performed, and every condition of re-entry and other condition therein contained, shall be annexed and incident to and shall go with the reversionary estate in the land, or in any part thereof, immediately expectant on the term granted by the lease, notwithstanding severance of that reversionary estate, and without prejudice to any liability affecting a covenantor or his estate.

(2)   Any such rent, covenant or provision shall be capable of being recovered, received, enforced, and taken advantage of, by the person from time to time entitled, subject to the term, to the income of the whole or any part, as the case may require, of the land leased.

(3)   Where that person becomes entitled by conveyance or otherwise, such rent, covenant or provision may be recovered, received, enforced or taken advantage of by him notwithstanding that he becomes so entitled after the condition of re-entry of forfeiture has become enforceable, but this subsection does not render enforceable any condition of re- entry or other condition waived or released before such person becomes entitled as aforesaid.

(4)   This section applies to leases made before or after the commencement of this Act, but does not affect the operation of—
   (a)   any severance of the reversionary estate; or
   (b)   any acquisition by conveyance or otherwise of the right to receive or enforce any rent covenant or provision;
   effected before the commencement of this Act.

142.   Obligation of lessor's covenants to run with reversion

(1)   The obligation under a condition or of a covenant entered into by a lessor with reference to the subject-matter of the lease shall, if and as far as the lessor has power to bind the reversionary estate immediately expectant on the term granted by the lease, be annexed and incident to and shall go with that reversionary estate, or the several parts thereof, notwithstanding severance of that reversionary estate, and may be taken advantage of and enforced by the person in whom the term is from time to time vested by conveyance, devolution in law, or otherwise; and, if and as far as the lessor has power to bind the person from time to time entitled to that reversionary estate, the obligation aforesaid may be taken advantage of and enforced against any person so entitled.

(2)   This section applies to leases made before or after the commencement of this Act, whether the severance of the reversionary estate was effected before or after such commencement:

Provided that, where the lease was made before the first day of January eighteen hundred and eighty-two, nothing in this section shall affect the operation of any severance of the reversionary estate effected before such commencement.

This section takes effect without prejudice to any liability affecting a covenantor or his estate.

143.   Effect of licences granted to lessees

(1)   Where a licence is granted to a lessee to do any act, the licence, unless otherwise expressed, extends only—
   (a)   to the permission actually given; or

      (b)   to the specific breach of any provision or covenant referred to; or

      (c)   to any other matter thereby specifically authorised to be done; and the licence does not prevent any proceeding for any subsequent breach unless otherwise specified in the licence.

(2)   Notwithstanding any such licence—

      (a)   All rights under covenants and powers of re-entry contained in the lease remain in full force and are available as against any subsequent breach of covenant, condition or other matter not specifically authorised or waived, in the same manner as if no licence had been granted; and

      (b)   The condition or right of entry remains in force in all respects as if the licence had not been granted, save in respect of the particular matter authorised to be done.

(3)   Where in any lease there is a power or condition of re-entry on the lessee assigning, subletting or doing any other specified act without a licence, and a licence is granted—

      (a)   to any one or two or more lessees to do any act, or to deal with his equitable share or interest; or

      (b)   to any lessee, or to any one of two or more lessees to assign or underlet part only of the property, or to do any act in respect of part only of the property; the licence does not operate to extinguish the right of entry in case of any breach of covenant or condition by the co-lessees of the other shares or interests in the property, or by the lessee or lessees of the rest of the property (as the case may be) in respect of such shares or interests or remaining property, but the right of entry remains in force in respect of the shares, interests or property not the subject of the licence.

This subsection does not authorise the grant after the commencement of this Act of a licence to create an undivided share in a legal estate.

(4)   This section applies to licences granted after the thirteenth day of August, eighteen hundred and fifty-nine.

144. No fine to be exacted for licence to assign

In all leases containing a covenant, condition, or agreement against assigning, underletting, or parting with the possession, or disposing of the land or property leased without licence or consent, such covenant, condition, or agreement shall, unless the lease contains an express provision to the contrary, be deemed to be subject to a proviso to the effect that no fine or sum of money in the nature of a fine shall be payable for or in respect of such licence or consent; but this proviso does not preclude the right to require the payment of a reasonable sum in respect of any legal or other expense incurred in relation to such licence or consent.

145. Lessee to give notice of ejectment to lessor

Every lessee to whom there is delivered any writ for the recovery of premises demised to or held by him, or to whose knowledge any such writ comes, shall forthwith give notice thereof to his lessor or his bailiff or receiver, and, if he fails so to do, he shall be liable to forfeit to the person of whom he holds the premises an amount equal to the value of three years' improved or rack rent of the premises, to be recovered by action in any court having jurisdiction in respect of claims for such an amount.

146. Restrictions on and relief against forfeiture of leases and underleases

(1)   A right of re-entry or forfeiture under any proviso or stipulation in a lease for a breach of any covenant or condition in the lease shall not be enforceable, by action or otherwise, unless and until the lessor serves on the lessee a notice—

      (a)   specifying the particular breach complained of; and

      (b)   if the breach is capable of remedy, requiring the lessee to remedy the breach; and

      (c)   in any case, requiring the lessee to make compensation in money for the breach; and the lessee fails, within a reasonable time thereafter, to remedy the breach, if it is capable of remedy, and to make reasonable compensation in money, to the satisfaction of the lessor, for the breach.

(2)   Where a lessor is proceeding, by action or otherwise, to enforce such a right of re-entry or forfeiture, the lessee may, in the lessor's action, if any, or in any action brought by himself, apply to the court for relief; and the court may grant or refuse relief, as the court, having regard to the proceedings and conduct of the parties under the foregoing provisions of this section, and to all the other circumstances, thinks fit; and in case of relief may grant it on such terms, if any, as to costs, expenses, damages, compensation, penalty, or otherwise, including the granting of an injunction to restrain any like breach in the future, as the court, in the circumstances of each case, thinks fit.

(3)   A lessor shall be entitled to recover as a debt due to him from a lessee, and in addition to damages (if any), all reasonable costs and expenses properly incurred by the lessor in the employment of a solicitor and surveyor or valuer, or otherwise, in reference to any breach giving rise to a right of re-entry or forfeiture which, at the request of the lessee, is waived by the lessor, or from which the lessee is relieved, under the provisions of this Act.

(4)   Where a lessor is proceeding by action or otherwise to enforce a right of re-entry or forfeiture under any covenant, proviso, or stipulation in a lease, or for non-payment of rent, the court may, on application by any person claiming as under-lessee any estate or interest in the property comprised in the lease or any part thereof, either in the lessor's action (if any) or in any action brought by such person for that purpose, make an order vesting, for the whole term of the lease or any less term, the property comprised in the lease or any part thereof in any person entitled as under-lessee to any estate or interest in such property upon such conditions as to execution of any deed or other document, payment of rent, costs, expenses, damages, compensation, giving security, or otherwise, as the court in the circumstances of each case may think fit, but in no case shall any such under-lessee be entitled to require a lease to be granted to him for any longer than he had under his original sub-lease.

(5)   For the purposes of this section—
   (a)   'Lease' includes an original or derivative under-lease; also an agreement for a lease where the lessee has become entitled to have his lease granted; also a grant at a fee arm rent, or securing a rent by condition;
   (b)   'Lessee' includes an original or derivative under-lessee, and the persons deriving title under a lessee; also a grantee under any such grant as aforesaid and the persons deriving title under him;
   (c)   'Lessor' includes an original or derivative under-lessor, and the persons deriving title under a lessor; also a person making such grant as aforesaid and the persons deriving title under him;
   (d)   'Under-lease' includes an agreement for an under-lease where the under-lessee has become entitled to have his under-lease granted;
   (e)   'Under-lessee' includes any person deriving title under an under-lessee.

(6)   This section applies although the proviso or stipulation under which the right of re-entry or forfeiture accrues is inserted in the lease in pursuance of the directions of any Act of Parliament.

(7)   For the purposes of this section a lease limited to continue as long only as the lessee abstains from committing a breach of covenant shall be and take effect as a lease to continue for any longer term for which it could subsist, but determinable by a proviso for re-entry on such a breach.

(8)   This section does not extend—
   (i)   To a covenant or condition against assigning, underletting, parting with the possession, or disposing of the land leased where the breach occurred before the commencement of this Act; or
   (ii)   In the case of a mining lease, to a covenant or condition for allowing the lessor to have access to or inspect books, accounts, records, weighing machines or other things, or to enter or inspect the mine or the workings thereof.

(9)   This section does not apply to a condition for forfeiture on the bankruptcy of the lessee or on taking in execution of the lessee's interest if contained in a lease of—
   (a)   Agricultural or pastoral land;
   (b)   Mines or minerals;
   (c)   A house used or intended to be used as a public-house or beershop;
   (d)   A house let as a dwelling-house, with the use of any furniture, books, works of art, or other chattels not being in the nature of fixtures;
   (e)   Any property with respect to which the personal qualifications of the tenant are of importance for the preservation of the value or character of the property, or on the ground of neighbourhood to the lessor, or to any person holding under him.

(10) Where a condition of forfeiture on the bankruptcy of the lessee or on taking in execution of the lessee's interest is contained in any lease, other than a lease of any of the classes mentioned in the last sub-section, then—
   (a)   if the lessee's interest is sold within one year from the bankruptcy or taking in execution, this section applies to the forfeiture condition aforesaid;
   (b)   if the lessee's interest is not sold before the expiration of that year, this section only applies to the forfeiture condition aforesaid during the first year from the date of the bankruptcy or taking in execution.

(11) This section does not, save as otherwise mentioned, affect the law relating to re-entry or forfeiture or relief in case of non-payment of rent.

(12) This section has effect notwithstanding any stipulation to the contrary.

(13) The county court has jurisdiction under this section.

147. Relief against notice to effect decorative repairs

(1) After a notice is served on a lessee relating to the internal decorative repairs to a house or other building, he may apply to the court for relief, and if, having regard to all the circumstances of the case (including in particular the length of the lessee's term or interest remaining unexpired), the court is satisfied that the notice is unreasonable, it may, by order, wholly or partially relieve the lessee from liability for such repairs.

(2) This section does not apply:—

    (i)   where the liability arises under an express covenant or agreement to put the property in a decorative state of repair and the covenant or agreement has never been performed;

    (ii) to any matter necessary or proper—

        (a) for putting or keeping the property in a sanitary condition, or

        (b) for the maintenance or preservation of the structure;

    (iii) to any statutory liability to keep a house in all respects reasonably fit for human habitation;

    (iv) to any covenant or stipulation to yield up the house or other building in a specified state of repair at the end of the term.

(3) In this section 'lease' includes an underlease and an agreement for a lease, and 'lessee' has a corresponding meaning and includes any person liable to effect the repairs.

(4) This section applies whether the notice is served before or after the commencement of this Act, and has effect notwithstanding any stipulation to the contrary.

(5) The county court has jurisdiction under this section.

148. Waiver of a covenant in a lease

(1) Where any actual waiver by a lessor or the persons deriving title under him of the benefit of any covenant or condition in any lease is proved to have taken place in any particular instance, such waiver shall not be deemed to extend to any instance, or to any breach of covenant or condition save that to which such waiver specially relates, nor operate as a general waiver of the benefit of any such covenant or condition.

(2) This section applies unless a contrary intention appears and extends to waivers effected after the twenty-third day of July, eighteen hundred and sixty.

149. Abolition of interesse termini, and as to reversionary leases and leases for lives

(1) The doctrine of interesse termini is hereby abolished.

(2) As from the commencement of this Act all terms of years absolute shall, whether the interest is created before or after such commencement, be capable of taking effect at law or in equity, according to the estate interest or powers of the grantor, from the date fixed for commencement of the term, without actual entry.

(3) A term, at a rent or granted in consideration of a fine, limited after the commencement of this Act to take effect more than twenty-one years from the date of the instrument purporting to create it, shall be void, and any contract made after such commencement to create such a term shall likewise be void; but this subsection does not apply to any term taking effect in equity under a settlement, or created out of an equitable interest under a settlement, or under an equitable power for mortgage, indemnity or other like purposes.

(4) Nothing in subsections (1) and (2) of this section prejudicially affects the right of any person to recover any rent or to enforce or take advantage of any covenants or conditions, or, as respects terms or interests created before the commencement of this Act, operates to vary any statutory or other obligations imposed in respect of such terms or interests.

(5) Nothing in this Act affects the rule of law that a legal term, whether or not being a mortgage term, may be created to take effect in reversion expectant on a longer term, which rule is hereby confirmed.

(6)   Any lease or underlease, at a rent, or in consideration of a fine, for life or lives or for any term of years determinable with life or lives, or on the marriage of the lessee or on the formation of a civil partnership between the lessee and another person, or any contract therefor, made before or after the commencement of this Act, or created by virtue of Part V. of the Law of Property Act, 1922, shall take effect as a lease, underlease or contract therefor, for a term of ninety years determinable after the death or marriage of, or the formation of a civil partnership by, the original lessee or the survivor of the original lessees, by at least one month's notice in writing given to determine the same on one of the quarter days applicable to the tenancy, either by the lessor or the persons deriving title under him, to the person entitled to the leasehold interest, or if no such person is in existence by affixing the same to the premises, or by the lessee or other persons in whom the leasehold interest is vested to the lessor or the persons deriving title under him:
      Provided that—
   (a)   this subsection shall not apply to any term taking effect in equity under a settlement or created out of an equitable interest under a settlement for mortgage, indemnity, or other like purposes;
   (b)   the person in whom the leasehold interest is vested by virtue of Part V of the Law of Property Act, 1922, shall, for the purposes of this subsection, be deemed an original lessee;
   (c)   if the lease, underlease, or contract therefor is made determinable on the dropping of the lives of persons other than or besides the lessees, then the notice shall be capable of being served after the death of any person or of the survivor of any persons (whether or not including the lessees) on the cesser of whose life or lives the lease, underlease, or contract is made determinable, instead of after the death of the original lessee or of the survivor of the original lessees;
   (d)   if there are no quarter days specially applicable to the tenancy, notice may be given to determine the tenancy on one of the usual quarter days.
(7)   Subsection (8) applies where a lease, underlease or contract—
   (a)   relates to commonhold land, and
   (b)   would take effect by virtue of subsection (6) as a lease, underlease or contract of the kind mentioned in that subsection.
(8)   The lease, underlease or contract shall be treated as if it purported to be a lease, underlease or contract of the kind referred to in subsection 7(b) (and sections 17 and 18 of the Commonhold and Leasehold Reform Act 2002 (residential and non-residential leases) shall apply accordingly).

150. Surrender of a lease, without prejudice to underleases with a view to the grant of a new lease

(1)   A lease may be surrendered with a view to the acceptance of a new lease in place thereof, without a surrender of any under-lease derived thereout.
(2)   A new lease may be granted and accepted, in place of any lease so surrendered, without any such surrender of an under-lease as aforesaid, and the new lease operates as if all under-leases derived out of the surrendered lease had been surrendered before the surrender of that lease was effected.
(3)   The lessee under the new lease and any person deriving title under him is entitled to the same rights and remedies in respect of the rent reserved by and the covenants, agreements and conditions contained in any under-lease as if the original lease had not been surrendered but was or remained vested in him.
(4)   Each under-lessee and any person deriving title under him is entitled to hold and enjoy the land comprised in his under-lease (subject to the payment of any rent reserved by and to the observance of the covenants agreements and conditions contained in the under-lease) as if the lease out of which the under-lease was derived had not been surrendered.
(5)   The lessor granting the new lease and any person deriving title under him is entitled to the same remedies, under section 72(1) of the Tribunals, Courts and Enforcement Act 2007 (commercial rent arrears recovery) or by entry in and upon the land comprised in any such under-lease for rent reserved by or for breach of any covenant, agreement or condition contained in the new lease (so far only as the rents reserved by or the covenants, agreements or conditions contained in the new lease do not exceed or impose greater burdens than those reserved by or contained in the original lease out of which the under-lease is derived) as he would have had—

(a)   If the original lease had remained on foot; or

(b)   If a new under-lease derived out of the new lease had been granted to the under-lessee or a person deriving title under him; as the case may require.

(6)   This section does not affect the powers of the court to give relief against forfeiture.

151.   Provision as to attornments by tenants

(1)   Where land is subject to a lease—

(a)   the conveyance of a reversion in the land expectant on the determination of the lease; or

(b)   the creation or conveyance of a rentcharge to issue or issuing out of the land;

shall be valid without any attornment of the lessee:

Nothing in this subsection—

(i)   affects the validity of any payment of rent by the lessee to the person making the conveyance or grant before notice of the conveyance or grant is given to him by the person entitled thereunder; or

(ii)   renders the lessee liable for any breach of covenant to pay rent, on account of his failure to pay rent to the person entitled under the conveyance or grant before such notice is given to the lessee.

(2)   An attornment by the lessee in respect of any land to a person claiming to be entitled to the interest in the land of the lessor, if made without the consent of the lessor, shall be void.

This subsection does not apply to an attornment—

(a)   made pursuant to a judgment of a court of competent jurisdiction; or

(b)   to a mortgagee, by a lessee holding under a lease from the mortgagor where the right of redemption is barred; or

(c)   to any other person rightfully deriving title under the lessor.

152.   Leases invalidated by reason of non-compliance with terms of powers under which they are granted

(1)   Where in the intended exercise of any power of leasing, whether conferred by an Act of Parliament or any other instrument, a lease (in this section referred to as an invalid lease) is granted, which by reason of any failure to comply with the terms of the power is invalid, then—

(a)   as against the person entitled after the determination of the interest of the grantor to the reversion; or

(b)   as against any other person who, subject to any lease properly granted under the power, would have been entitled to the land comprised in the lease;

the lease, if it was made in good faith, and the lessee has entered, thereunder, shall take effect in equity as a contract for the grant, at the request of the lessee, of a valid lease under the power, of like effect as the invalid lease, subject to such variations as may be necessary in order to comply with the terms of the power:

Provided that a lessee under an invalid lease shall not, by virtue of any such implied contract, be entitled to obtain a variation of the lease if the other persons who would have been bound by the contract are willing and able to confirm the lease without variation.

(2)   Where a lease granted in the intended exercise of such a power is invalid by reason of the grantor not having power to grant the lease at the date thereof, but the grantor's interest in the land comprised therein continues after the time when he might, in the exercise of the power, have properly granted a lease in the like terms, the lease shall take effect as a valid lease in like manner as if it had been granted at that time.

(3)   Where during the continuance of the possession taken under an invalid lease the person for the time being entitled, subject to such possession, to the land comprised therein or to the rents and profits thereof, is able to confirm the lease without variation, the lessee, or other person who would have been bound by the lease had it been valid, shall, at the request of the person so able to confirm the lease, be bound to accept a confirmation thereof, and thereupon the lease shall have effect and be deemed to have had effect as a valid lease from the grant thereof.

Confirmation under this subsection may be by a memorandum in writing signed by or on behalf of the persons respectively confirming and accepting the confirmation of the lease.

(4)   Where a receipt or a memorandum in writing confirming an invalid lease is, upon or before the acceptance of the rent thereunder, signed by or on behalf of the person accepting the rent, that acceptance shall, as against that person, be deemed to be a confirmation of the lease.

(5)   The foregoing provisions of this section do not affect prejudicially—

     (a)   any right of action or other right or remedy to which, but for those provisions or any enactment replaced by those provisions, the lessee named in an invalid lease would or might have been entitled under any covenant on the part of the grantor for title or quiet enjoyment contained therein or implied thereby; or

     (b)   any right of re-entry or other right or remedy to which, but for those provisions or any enactment replaced thereby, the grantor or other person for the time being entitled to the reversion expectant on the termination of the lease, would or might have been entitled by reason of any breach of the covenants, conditions or provisions contained in the lease and binding on the lessee.

(6)   Where a valid power of leasing is vested in or may be exercised by a person who grants a lease which, by reason of the determination of the interest of the grantor or otherwise, cannot have effect and continuance according to the terms thereof independently of the power, the lease shall for the purposes of this section be deemed to have been granted in the intended exercise of the power although the power is not referred to in the lease.

(7)   This section does not apply to a lease of land held on charitable, ecclesiastical or public trusts.

(8)   This section takes effect without prejudice to the provision in this Act for the grant of leases in the name and on behalf of the estate owner of the land affected.

153. Enlargement of residue of long terms into fee simple estates

(1)   Where a residue unexpired of not less than two hundred years of a term, which, as originally created, was for not less than three hundred years, is subsisting in land, whether being the whole land originally comprised in the term, or part only thereof,—

     (a)   without any trust or right of redemption affecting the term in favour of the freeholder, or other person entitled in reversion expectant on the term; and

     (b)   without any rent, or with merely a peppercorn rent or other rent having no money value, incident to the reversion, or having had a rent, not being merely a peppercorn rent or other rent having no money value, originally so incident, which subsequently has been released or has become barred by lapse of time, or has in any other way ceased to be payable;

the term may be enlarged into a fee simple in the manner, and subject to the restrictions in this section provided.

(2)   This section applies to and includes every such term as aforesaid whenever created, whether or not having the freehold as the immediate reversion thereon; but does not apply to—

     (i)   Any term liable to be determined by re-entry for condition broken; or

     (ii)   Any term created by subdemise out of a superior term, itself incapable of being enlarged into fee simple.

(3)   This section extends to mortgage terms, where the right of redemption is barred.

(4)   A rent not exceeding the yearly sum of one pound which has not been collected or paid for a continuous period of twenty years or upwards shall, for the purposes of this section, be deemed to have ceased to be payable.

(5)   Where a rent incident to a reversion expectant on a term to which this section applies is deemed to have ceased to be payable for the purposes aforesaid, no claim for such rent or for any arrears thereof shall be capable of being enforced.

(6)   Each of the following persons, namely—

     (i)   Any person beneficially entitled in right of the term, whether subject to any incumbrance or not, to possession of any land comprised in the term, and, in the case of a married woman without the concurrence of her husband, whether or not she is entitled for her separate use or as her separate property;

     (ii)   Any person being in receipt of income as trustee, in right of the term, or having the term vested in him as a trustee of land, whether subject to any incumbrance or not;

     (iii)   Any person in whom, as personal representative of any deceased person, the term is vested, whether subject to any incumbrance or not;

shall, so far as regards the land to which he is entitled, or in which he is interested in right of the term, in any such character as aforesaid, have power by deed to declare to the effect that, from and after the execution of the deed, the term shall be enlarged into a fee simple.

(7) Thereupon, by virtue of the deed and of this Act, the term shall become and be enlarged accordingly, and the person in whom the term was previously vested shall acquire and have in the land a fee simple instead of the term.

(8) The estate in fee simple so acquired by enlargement shall be subject to all the same trusts, powers, executory limitations over, rights, and equities, and to all the same covenants and provisions relating to user and enjoyment, and to all the same obligations of every kind, as the term would have been subject to if it had not been so enlarged.

(9) But where—

(a) any land so held for the residue of a term has been settled in trust by reference to other land, being freehold land, so as to go along with that other land, or, in the case of settlements coming into operation before the commencement of this Act, so as to go along with that other land as far as the law permits; and

(b) at the time of enlargement, the ultimate beneficial interest in the term, whether subject to any subsisting particular estate or not, has not become absolutely and indefeasibly vested in any person, free from charges or powers of charging created by a settlement;

the estate in fee simple acquired as aforesaid shall, without prejudice to any conveyance for value previously made by a person having a contingent or defeasible interest in the term, be liable to be, and shall be, conveyed by means of a subsidiary vesting instrument and settled in like manner as the other land, being freehold land, aforesaid, and until so conveyed and settled shall devolve beneficially as if it had been so conveyed and settled.

(10) The estate in fee simple so acquired shall, whether the term was originally created without impeachment of waste or not, include the fee simple in all mines and minerals which at the time of enlargement have not been severed in right or in fact, or have not been severed or reserved by an inclosure Act or award.

154. Application of Part V to existing leases

This Part of this Act, except where otherwise expressly provided, applies to leases created before or after the commencement of this Act, and 'lease' includes an under-lease or other tenancy.

PART VI
POWERS

155. Release of powers simply collateral

A person to whom any power, whether coupled with an interest or not, is given may by deed release, or contract not to exercise, the power.

156. Disclaimer of power

(1) A person to whom any power, whether coupled with an interest or not, is given may by deed disclaim the power, and, after disclaimer, shall not be capable of exercising or joining in the exercise of the power.

(2) On such disclaimer, the power may be exercised by the other person or persons or the survivor or survivors of the other persons, to whom the power is given, unless the contrary is expressed in the instrument creating the power.

157. Protection of purchasers claiming under certain void appointments

(1) An instrument purporting to exercise a power of appointment over property, which, in default of and subject to any appointment, is held in trust for a class or number of persons of whom the appointee is one, shall not (save as hereinafter provided) be void on the ground of fraud on the power as against a purchaser in good faith:

Provided that, if the interest appointed exceeds, in amount or value, the interest in such property to which immediately before the execution of the instrument the appointee was presumptively entitled under the trust in default of appointment, having regard to any advances made in his favour and to any hotchpot provision, the protection afforded by this section to a purchaser shall not extend to such excess.

(2) In this section 'a purchaser in good faith' means a person dealing with an appointee of the age of not less than twenty-five years for valuable consideration in money or money's worth, and without notice of the fraud, or of any circumstances from which, if reasonable inquiries had been made, the fraud might have been discovered.

(3) Persons deriving title under any purchaser entitled to the benefit of this section shall be entitled to the like benefit.

(4) This section applies only to dealings effected after the commencement of this Act.

158. Validation of appointments where objects are excluded or take illusory shares

(1) No appointment made in exercise of any power to appoint any property among two or more objects shall be invalid on the ground that—

   (a) an unsubstantial, illusory, or nominal share only is appointed to or left unappointed to devolve upon any one or more of the objects of the power; or

   (b) any object of the power is thereby altogether excluded;

but every such appointment shall be valid notwithstanding that any one or more of the objects is not thereby, or in default of appointment, to take any share in the property.

(2) This section does not affect any provision in the instrument creating the power which declares the amount of any share from which any object of the power is not to be excluded.

(3) This section applies to appointments made before or after the commencement of this Act.

159. Execution of powers not testamentary

(1) A deed executed in the presence of and attested by two or more witnesses (in the manner in which deeds are ordinarily executed and attested) is so far as respects the execution and attestation thereof, a valid execution of a power of appointment by deed or by any instrument in writing, not testamentary, notwithstanding that it is expressly required that a deed or instrument in writing, made in exercise of the power, is to be executed or attested with some additional or other form of execution or attestation or solemnity.

(2) This section does not operate to defeat any direction in the instrument creating the power that—

   (a) the consent of any particular person is to be necessary to a valid execution;

   (b) in order to give validity to any appointment, any act is to be performed having no relation to the mode of executing and attesting the instrument.

(3) This section does not prevent the donee of a power from executing it in accordance with the power by writing, or otherwise than by an instrument executed and attested as a deed; and where a power is so executed this section does not apply.

(4) This section applies to appointments by deed made after the thirteenth day of August, eighteen hundred and fifty-nine.

160. Application of Part VI to existing powers

This Part of this Act applies to powers created or arising either before or after the commencement of this Act.

PART VII
PERPETUITIES AND ACCUMULATIONS

Perpetuities

161. Abolition of the double possibility rule

(1) The rule of law prohibiting the limitation, after a life interest to an unborn person, of an interest in land to the unborn child or other issue of an unborn person is hereby abolished, but without prejudice to any other rule relating to perpetuities.

(2) This section only applies to limitations or trusts created by an instrument coming into operation after the commencement of this Act.

PART IX
VOIDABLE DISPOSITIONS

173. Voluntary disposition of land how far voidable as against purchasers

(1)   Every voluntary disposition of land made with intent to defraud a subsequent purchaser is voidable at the instance of that purchaser.

(2)   For the purposes of this section, no voluntary disposition, whenever made, shall be deemed to have been made with intent to defraud by reason only that a subsequent conveyance for valuable consideration was made, if such subsequent conveyance was made after the twenty-eighth day of June, eighteen hundred and ninety-three.

174. Acquisitions of reversions at an under value

(1)   No acquisition made in good faith, without fraud or unfair dealing, of any reversionary interest in real or personal property, for money or money's worth, shall be liable to be opened or set aside merely on the ground of under value.

In this subsection 'reversionary interest' includes an expectancy or possibility.

(2)   This section does not affect the jurisdiction of the court to set aside or modify unconscionable bargains.

PART X
WILLS

175. Contingent and future testamentary gifts to carry the intermediate income

(1)   A contingent or future specific devise or bequest of property, whether real or personal, and a contingent residuary devise of freehold land, and a specific or residuary devise of freehold land to trustees upon trust for persons whose interests are contingent or executory shall, subject to the statutory provisions relating to accumulations, carry the intermediate income of that property from the death of the testator, except so far as such income, or any part thereof, may be otherwise expressly disposed of.

(2)   This section applies only to wills coming into operation after the commencement of this Act.

176. Power for tenant in tail in possession to dispose of property by specific devise or bequest

(1)   A tenant in tail of full age shall have power to dispose by will, by means of a devise or bequest referring specifically either to the property or to the instrument under which it was acquired or to entailed property generally—

   (a)   of all property of which he is tenant in tail in possession at his death; and

   (b)   of money (including the proceeds of property directed to be sold) subject to be invested in the purchase of property, of which if it had been so invested he would have been tenant in tail in possession at his death;

in like manner as if, after barring the entail, he had been tenant in fee-simple or absolute owner thereof for an equitable interest at his death, but, subject to and in default of any such disposition by will, such property shall devolve in the same manner as if this section had not been passed.

(2)   This section applies to entailed interests authorised to be created by this Act as well as to estates tail created before the commencement of this Act, but does not extend to a tenant in tail who is by statute restrained from barring or defeating his estate tail, whether the land or property in respect whereof he is so restrained was purchased with money provided by Parliament in consideration of public services or not, or to a tenant in tail after possibility of issue extinct, and does not render any interest which is not disposed of by the will of the tenant in tail liable for his debts or other liabilities.

(3)   In this section 'tenant in tail' includes an owner of a base fee in possession who has power to enlarge the base fee into a fee-simple without the concurrence of any other person.

(4)   This section only applies to wills executed after the commencement of this Act, or confirmed or republished by codicil executed after such commencement.

PART XI
MISCELLANEOUS

184. Presumption of survivorship in regard to claims to property

In all cases where, after the commencement of this Act, two or more persons have died in circumstances rendering it uncertain which of them survived the other or others, such deaths shall (subject to any order of the court), for all purposes affecting the title to property, be presumed to have occurred in order of seniority, and accordingly the younger shall be deemed to have survived the elder.

185. Merger

There is no merger by operation of law only of any estate the beneficial interest in which would not be deemed to be merged or extinguished in equity.

186. Rights of preemption capable of release

All statutory and other rights of preemption affecting a legal estate shall be and be deemed always to have been capable of release, and unless released shall remain in force as equitable interests only.

187. Legal easements

(1) Where an easement, right or privilege for a legal estate is created, it shall enure for the benefit of the land to which it is intended to be annexed.

(2) Nothing in this Act affects the right of a person to acquire, hold or exercise an easement, right or privilege over or in relation to land for a legal estate in common with any other person, or the power of creating or conveying such an easement right or privilege.

188. Power to direct division of chattels

(1) Where any chattels belong to persons in undivided shares, the persons interested in a moiety or upwards may apply to the court for an order for division of the chattels or any of them, according to a valuation or otherwise, and the court may make such order and give any consequential directions as it thinks fit.

(2) ...

189. Indemnities against rents

(1) ...

(2) The benefit of all covenants and powers given by way of indemnity against a rent or any part thereof payable in respect of land, or against the breach of any covenant or condition in relation to land, is and shall be deemed always to have been annexed to the land to which the indemnity is intended to relate, and may be enforced by the estate owner for the time being of the whole or any part of that land, notwithstanding that the benefit may not have been expressly apportioned or assigned to him or to any of his predecessors in title.

Redemption and Apportionment of Rents, etc.

190. Equitable apportionment of rents and remedies for non-payment or breach of covenant

(1) Where in a conveyance for valuable consideration, other than a mortgage, or part of land which is affected by a rentcharge, such rentcharge or a part thereof is, without the consent of the owner thereof, expressed to be—

(a) charged exclusively on the land conveyed or any part thereof in exoneration of the land retained or other land; or

(b) charged exclusively on the land retained or any part thereof in exoneration of the land conveyed or other land; or

(c) apportioned between the land conveyed or any part thereof, and the land retained by the grantor or any part thereof;

then, without prejudice to the rights of the owner of the rentcharge, such charge or apportionment shall be binding as between the grantor and the grantee under the conveyance and their respective successors in title.

(2) ...

(3) Where in a conveyance for valuable consideration, other than a mortgage, of part of land comprised in a lease, for the residue of the term or interest created by the lease, the rent reserved by such lease or a part thereof is, without the consent of the lessor, expressed to be—

  (a) charged exclusively on the land conveyed or any part thereof in exoneration of the land retained by the assignor or other land; or

  (b) charged exclusively on the land retained by the assignor or any part thereof in exoneration of the land conveyed or other land; or

  (c) apportioned between the land conveyed or any part thereof and the land retained by the assignor or any part thereof;

then, without prejudice to the rights of the lessor, such charge or apportionment shall be binding as between the assignor and the assignee under the conveyance and their respective successors in title.

(4) Subsection (5) applies where—

  (a) any default is made in payment of the whole or part of a rent by the person ('the defaulter') who, by reason of a charge or apportionment within subsection (3), is liable to pay it, and

  (b) the lessee for the time being of any other land comprised in the lease, in whom, as respects that land, the residue of the term or interest created by the lease is vested, ('the paying lessee') pays or is required to pay the whole or part of the rent which ought to have been paid by the defaulter.

(5) Section 72(1) of the Tribunals, Courts and Enforcement Act 2007 (commercial rent arrears recovery) applies, subject to the other provisions of Chapter 2 of Part 3 of that Act, to the recovery by the paying lessee from the defaulter of the rent paid by the paying lessee which ought to have been paid by the defaulter, as if the paying lessee were the landlord, and the defaulter his tenant, under the lease.

(6) This section applies only if and so far as a contrary intention is not expressed in the conveyance whereby the rent or any part thereof is expressed to be charged or apportioned as aforesaid, and takes effect subject to the terms of that conveyance and to the provisions therein contained.

(7) The remedies conferred by this section apply only where the conveyance whereby the rent or any part thereof is expressed to be charged or apportioned is made after the commencement of this Act, and do not apply where the rent is charged exclusively as aforesaid or legally apportioned with the consent of the lessor.

(8) The rule of law relating to perpetuities does not affect the powers or remedies conferred by this section or any like powers or remedies expressly conferred, before or after the commencement of this Act, by an instrument.

Commons and Waste Lands

193. Rights of the public over commons and waste lands

(1) Members of the public shall, subject as hereinafter provided, have rights of access for air and exercise to any land which is a metropolitan common within the meaning of the Metropolitan Commons Acts, 1866 to 1898, or manorial waste, or a common which is wholly or partly situated within an area which immediately before 1st April 1974 was a borough or urban district, and to any land which at the commencement of this Act is subject to rights of common and to which this section may from time to time be applied in manner hereinafter provided:

  Provided that—

  (a) such rights of access shall be subject to any Act, scheme, or provisional order for the regulation of the land, and to any byelaw, regulation or order made thereunder or under any other statutory authority; and

  (b) the Minister shall, on the application of any person entitled as lord of the manor or otherwise to the soil of the land, or entitled to any commonable rights affecting the land, impose such limitations on and conditions as to the exercise of the rights of access or as to the extent of the land to be affected as, in the opinion of the Minister, are necessary or desirable for preventing any estate, right or interest of a profitable or beneficial nature in, over, or affecting the land from being injuriously affected, for conserving flora, fauna or geological or physiographical features of the land, or for protecting any object of historical interest and, where any such limitations or conditions are so imposed, the rights of access shall be subject thereto; and

(c)   such rights of access shall not include any right to draw or drive upon the land a carriage, cart, caravan, truck, or other vehicle, or to camp or light any fire thereon; and

(d)   the rights of access shall cease to apply—
   (i)   to any land over which the commonable rights are extinguished under any statutory provision;
   (ii)   to any land over which the commonable rights are otherwise extinguished if the council of the county, county borough or metropolitan district in which the land is situated by resolution assent to its exclusion from the operation of this section, and the resolution is approved by the Minister.

...

Judgments, etc. affecting Land

195. Equitable charges in right of judgment debt, etc.

(1)–(3) ...

(4)   A recognisance, on behalf of the Crown or otherwise, whether entered into before or after the commencement of this Act, and an inquisition finding a debt due to the Crown, and any obligation or speciality made to or in favour of the Crown, whatever may have been its date, shall not operate as a charge on any interest in land, or on the unpaid purchase money for any land, unless or until a writ or order, for the purpose of enforcing it, is registered in the register of writs and orders at the Land Registry.

(5)   ...

196. Regulations respecting notices

(1)   Any notice required or authorised to be served or given by this Act shall be in writing.

(2)   Any notice required or authorised by this Act to be served on a lessee or mortgagor shall be sufficient, although only addressed to the lessee or mortgagor by that designation, without his name, or generally to the persons interested, without any name, and notwithstanding that any person to be affected by the notice is absent, under disability, unborn, or unascertained.

(3)   Any notice required or authorised by this Act to be served shall be sufficiently served if it is left at the last-known place of abode or business in the United Kingdom of the lessee, lessor, mortgagee, mortgagor, or other person to be served, or, in case of a notice required or authorised to be served on a lessee or mortgagor, is affixed or left for him on the land or any house or building comprised in the lease or mortgage, or, in case of a mining lease, is left for the lessee at the office or counting-house of the mine.

(4)   Any notice required or authorised by this Act to be served shall also be sufficiently served, if it is sent by post in a registered letter addressed to the lessee, lessor, mortgagee, mortgagor, or other person to be served, by name, at the aforesaid place of abode or business, office, or counting-house, and if that letter is not returned by the postal operator (within the meaning of Part 3 of the Postal Services Act 2011) concerned undelivered; and that service shall be deemed to be made at the time at which the registered letter would in the ordinary course by delivered.

(5)   The provisions of the section shall extend to notices required to be served by any instrument affecting property executed or coming into operation after the commencement of this Act unless a contrary intention appears.

(6)   This section does not apply to notices served in proceedings in the court.

198. Registration under the Land Charges Act, 1925, to be notice

(1)   The registration of any instrument or matter in any register kept under the Land Charges Act 1972 or the local land charges register, shall be deemed to constitute actual notice of such instrument or matter, and of the fact of such registration, to all persons and for all purposes connected with the land affected, as from the date of registration or other prescribed date and so long as the registration continues in force.

(2)   This section operates without prejudice to the provisions of this Act respecting the making of further advances by a mortgagee, and applies only to instruments and matters required or authorised to be registered in any such register.

199. Restrictions on constructive notice

(1) A purchaser shall not be prejudicially affected by notice of—

   (i)   any instrument or matter capable of registration under the provisions of the Land Charges Act, 1925, or any enactment which it replaces, which is void or not enforceable as against him under that Act or enactment, by reason of the non-registration thereof;

   (ii) any other instrument or matter or any fact or thing unless—

      (a) it is within his own knowledge, or would have come to his knowledge if such inquiries and inspections had been made as ought reasonably to have been made by him; or

      (b) in the same transaction with respect to which a question of notice to the purchaser arises, it has come to the knowledge of his counsel, as such, or of his solicitor or other agent, as such, or would have come to the knowledge of his solicitor or other agent, as such, if such inquiries and inspections had been made as ought reasonably to have been made by the solicitor or other agent.

(2) Paragraph (ii) of the last subsection shall not exempt a purchaser from any liability under, or any obligation to perform or observe, any covenant, condition, provision, or restriction contained in any instrument under which his title is derived, mediately or immediately; and such liability or obligation may be enforced in the same manner and to the same extent as if that paragraph had not been enacted.

(3) A purchaser shall not by reason of anything in this section be affected by notice in any case where he would not have been so affected if this section had not been enacted.

(4) This section applies to purchases made either before or after the commencement of this Act.

200. Notice of restrictive covenants and easements

(1) Where land having a common title with other land is disposed of to a purchaser (other than a lessee or a mortgagee) who does not hold or obtain possession of the documents forming the common title, such purchaser, notwithstanding any stipulation to the contrary, may require that a memorandum giving notice of any provision contained in the disposition to him restrictive of user of, or giving rights over, any other land comprised in the common title, shall, where practicable, be written or indorsed on, or, where impracticable, be permanently annexed to some one document selected by the purchaser but retained in the possession or power of the person who makes the disposition, and being or forming part of the common title.

(2) The title of any person omitting to require an indorsement to be made or a memorandum to be annexed shall not, by reason only of this enactment, be prejudiced or affected by the omission.

(3) This section does not apply to dispositions of registered land.

(4) Nothing in this section affects the obligation to register a land charge in respect of—

      (a) any restrictive covenant or agreement affecting freehold land; or

      (b) any estate contract; or

      (c) any equitable easement, liberty or privilege.

PART XII

CONSTRUCTION, JURISDICTION, AND GENERAL PROVISIONS

201. Provisions of Act to apply to incorporeal hereditaments

(1) The provisions of this Act relating to freehold land apply to manors, reputed manors, lordships, advowsons, perpetual rentcharges, and other incorporeal hereditaments, subject only to the qualifications necessarily arising by reason of the inherent nature of the hereditament affected.

(2) This Act does not affect the special restrictions imposed on dealing with advowsons by the Benefices Act, 1898, or any other statute or measure, nor affect the limitation of, or authorise any disposition to be made of, a title or dignity of honour which in its nature is inalienable.

(3) ...

202. Provisions as to enfranchisement of copyholds, etc.

For giving effect to this Act, the enfranchisement of copyhold land, and the conversion into long terms of perpetually renewable leaseholds, and of leases for lives and of leases for years terminable with life or lives or on marriage, effected by the Law of Property Act, 1922, as amended by any subsequent enactment, shall be deemed to have been effected immediately before the commencement of this Act.

205. General definitions

(1)   In this Act unless the context otherwise requires, the following expressions have the meanings hereby assigned to them respectively, that is to say:—

(i)   'Bankruptcy' includes liquidation by arrangement; also in relation to a corporation means the winding up thereof;

(ii)   'Conveyance' includes a mortgage, charge, lease, assent, vesting declaration, vesting instrument, disclaimer, release and every other assurance of property or of an interest therein by any instrument, except a will; 'convey' has a corresponding meaning; and 'disposition' includes a conveyance and also a devise, bequest, or an appointment of property contained in a will; and 'dispose of' has a corresponding meaning;

(iii)   'Building purposes' include the erecting and improving of, and the adding to, and the repairing of buildings; and a 'building lease' is a lease for building purposes or purposes connected therewith;

(iiiA) ...

(iv)   'Death duty' means estate duty and every other duty leviable or payable on a death;

(v)   'Estate owner' means the owner of a legal estate, but an infant is not capable of being an estate owner;

(vi)   'Gazette' means the London Gazette;

(vii)   'Incumbrance' includes a legal or equitable mortgage and a trust for securing money, and a lien, and a charge of a portion, annuity, or other capital or annual sum; and 'incumbrancer' has a meaning corresponding with that of incumbrance, and includes every person entitled to the benefit of an incumbrance, or to require payment or discharge thereof;

(viii) 'Instrument' does not include a statute, unless the statute creates a settlement;

(ix)   'Land' includes land of any tenure, and mines and minerals, whether or not held apart from the surface, buildings or parts of buildings (whether the division is horizontal, vertical or made in any other way) and other corporeal hereditaments, also a manor, an advowson, and a rent and other incorporeal hereditaments, and an easement, right, privilege, or benefit in, over, or derived from land; and 'mines and minerals' include any strata or seam of minerals or substances in or under any land, and powers of working and getting the same; and 'manor' includes a lordship, and reputed manor or lordship; and 'hereditament' means any real property which on an intestacy occurring before the commencement of this Act might have devolved upon an heir;

(x)   'Legal estates' mean the estates, interests and charges, in or over land (subsisting or created at law) which are by this Act authorised to subsist or to be created as legal estates; 'equitable interests' means all the other interests and charges in or over land; an equitable interest 'capable of subsisting as a legal estate' means such as could validly subsist or be created as a legal estate under this Act;

(xi)   'Legal powers' include the powers vested in a chargee by way of legal mortgage or in an estate owner under which a legal estate can be transferred or created; and 'equitable powers' mean all the powers in or over land under which equitable interests or powers only can be transferred or created;

(xii)   'Limitation Acts' mean the Real Property Limitation Acts, 1833, 1837 and 1874, and 'limitation' includes a trust;

(xiii) ...

(xiv)   A 'mining lease' means a lease for mining purposes, that is, the searching for, winning, working, getting, making merchantable, carrying away, or disposing of mines and minerals, or purposes connected therewith, and includes a grant or licence for mining purposes;

(xv) ...

(xvi) 'Mortgage' includes any charge or lien on any property for securing money or money's worth; 'legal mortgage' means a mortgage by demise or subdemise or a charge by way of legal mortgage and 'legal mortgagee' has a corresponding meaning; 'mortgage money' means money or money's worth secured by a mortgage; 'mortgagor' includes any person from time to time deriving title under the original mortgagor or entitled to redeem a mortgage according to his estate interest or right in the mortgaged property; 'mortgagee' includes a chargee by way of legal mortgage and any person from time to time deriving title under the original mortgagee; and 'mortgagee in possession' is, for the purposes of this Act, a mortgagee who, in right of the mortgage, has entered into and is in possession of the mortgaged property; and 'right of redemption' includes an option to repurchase only if the option in effect creates a right of redemption;

(xvii) 'Notice' includes constructive notice;

(xviii) 'Personal representative' means the executor, original or by representation, or administrator for the time being of a deceased person, and as regards any liability for the payment of death duties includes any person who takes possession of or intermeddles with the property of a deceased person without the authority of the personal representatives or the court;

(xix) 'Possession' includes receipt of rents and profits or the right to receive the same, if any; and 'income' includes rents and profits;

(xx) 'Property' includes any thing in action, and any interest in real or personal property;

(xxi) 'Purchaser' means a purchaser in good faith for valuable consideration and includes a lessee, mortgagee or other person who for valuable consideration acquires an interest in property except that in Part I of this Act and elsewhere where so expressly provided 'purchaser' only means a person who acquires an interest in or charge on property for money or money's worth; and in reference to a legal estate includes a chargee by way of legal mortgage; and where the context so requires 'purchaser' includes an intending purchaser; 'purchase' has a meaning corresponding with that of 'purchaser'; and 'valuable consideration' includes marriage, and formation of a civil partnership, but does not include a nominal consideration in money;

(xxii) 'Registered land' has the same meaning as in the Land Registration Act 2002;

(xxiii) 'Rent' includes a rent service or a rentcharge, or other rent, toll, duty, royalty, or annual or periodical payment in money or money's worth, reserved or issuing out of or charged upon land, but does not include mortgage interest; 'rentcharge' includes a fee farm rent; 'fine' includes a premium or foregift and any payment, consideration, or benefit in the nature of a fine, premium or foregift; 'lessor' includes an underlessor and a person deriving title under a lessor or underlessor; and 'lessee' includes an underlessee and a person deriving title under a lessee or underlessee, and 'lease' includes an underlease or other tenancy;

(xxiv) 'Sale' includes an extinguishment of manorial incidents, but in other respects means a sale properly so called;

(xxv) 'Securities' include stocks, funds and shares;

(xxvi) 'Tenant for life,' 'statutory owner,' 'settled land,' 'settlement,' 'vesting deed,' 'subsidiary vesting deed,' 'vesting order,' 'vesting instrument,' 'trust instrument,' 'capital money,' and 'trustees of the settlement' have the same meanings as in the Settled Land Act, 1925;

(xxvii) 'Term of years absolute' means a term of years (taking effect either in possession or in reversion whether or not at a rent) with or without impeachment for waste, subject or not to another legal estate, and either certain or liable to determination by notice, re-entry, operation of law, or by a provision for cesser on redemption, or in any other event (other than the dropping of a life, or the determination of a determinable life interest); but does not include any term of years determinable with life or lives or with the cesser of a determinable life interest, nor, if created after the commencement of this Act, a term of years which is not expressed to take effect in possession within twenty-one years after the creation thereof where required by this Act to take effect within that period; and in this definition the expression 'term of years' includes a term for less than a year, or for a year or years and a fraction of a year or from year to year;

(xxviii) 'Trust Corporation' means the Public Trustee or a corporation either appointed by the court in any particular case to be a trustee or entitled by rules made under subsection (3) of section four of the Public Trustee Act, 1906, to act as custodian trustee;

(xxix) 'Trust for sale,' in relation to land, means an immediate trust for sale, whether or not exercisable at the request or with the consent of any person; 'trustees for sale' mean the persons (including a personal representative) holding land on trust for sale;

(xxx) 'United Kingdom' means Great Britain and Northern Ireland;

(xxxi) 'Will' includes codicil.

(1A) Any reference in this Act to money being paid into court shall be construed as referring to the money being paid into the Senior Courts or any other court that has jurisdiction, and any reference in this Act to the court, in a context referring to the investment or application of money paid into court, shall be construed, in the case of money paid into the Senior Courts, as referring to the High Court, and in the case of money paid into another court, as referring to that other court.

(2) Where an equitable interest in or power over property arises by statute or operation of law, references to the creation of an interest or power include references to any interest or power so arising.

(3) References to registration under the Land Charges Act, 1925, apply to any registration made under any other statute which is by the Land Charges Act, 1925, to have effect as if the registration had been made under that Act.

207. Repeals as respects England and Wales

Without prejudice to the provisions of section thirty-eight of the Interpretation Act, 1889:—

(a) Nothing in this repeal shall affect the validity or legality of any dealing in property or other transaction completed before the commencement of this Act, or any title or right acquired or appointment made before such commencement, but, subject as aforesaid, this Act shall, except where otherwise expressly provided, apply to and in respect of instruments whether made or coming into operation before or after such commencement:

(b) Nothing in this repeal shall affect any rules, orders, or other instruments made under any enactment so repealed, but all such rules, orders and instruments shall continue in force as if made under the corresponding enactment in this Act:

(c) References in any document to any enactment repealed by this Act shall be construed as references to this Act or to the corresponding enactment in this Act.

208. Application to the Crown

(1) Nothing in this Act shall be construed as rendering any property of the Crown subject to distress, or liable to be taken or disposed of by means of any distress.

(2) This Act shall not in any manner (save as otherwise expressly provided and except so far as it relates to undivided shares, joint ownership, leases for lives or leases for years terminable with life or marriage) affect or alter the descent, devolution or tenure or the nature of the estates and interests of or in any land for the time being vested in His Majesty either in right of the Crown or of the Duchy of Lancaster or of or in any land for the time being belonging to the Duchy of Cornwall and held in right or in respect of the said Duchy, but so nevertheless that, after the commencement of this Act, no estates, interests or charges in or over any such lands as aforesaid shall be conveyed or created, except such estates, interests or charges as are capable under this Act of subsisting or of being conveyed or created.

(3) Subject as aforesaid the provisions of this Act bind the Crown.

SCHEDULES

Section 39

FIRST SCHEDULE
TRANSITIONAL PROVISIONS

PART I
CONVERSION OF CERTAIN EXISTING LEGAL ESTATES INTO EQUITABLE INTERESTS

All estates, interests and charges in or over land, including fees determinable whether by limitation or condition, which immediately before the commencement of this Act were estates, interests or charges, subsisting at law, or capable of taking effect as such, but which by virtue of Part I. of this Act are not capable of taking effect as legal estates, shall as from the commencement of this Act be converted into equitable interests, and shall not fail by reason of being so converted into equitable interests either in the land or in the proceeds of sale thereof, nor shall the priority of any such estate, charge or interest over other equitable interests be affected.

PART II
VESTING OF LEGAL ESTATES

1. Where the purposes of a term of years, created or limited out of leasehold land, are satisfied at the commencement of this Act, that term shall merge in the reversion expectant thereon and shall cease accordingly; but where the term was vested in the owner of the reversion, the merger and cesser shall take effect without prejudice to any protection which would have been afforded to the owner for the time being of that reversion had the term remained subsisting.

    Where the purposes are satisfied only as respects part of the land comprised in a term, this provision has effect as if a separate term had been created in regard to that part of the land.

2. Where immediately after the commencement of this Act any owner of a legal estate is entitled, subject or not to the payment of the costs of tracing the title and of conveyance, to require any other legal estate in the same land to be surrendered, released or conveyed to him so as to merge or be extinguished, the last-mentioned estate shall by virtue of this Part of this Schedule be extinguished, but without prejudice to any protection which would have been afforded to him had that estate remained subsisting.

3. Where immediately after the commencement of this Act any person is entitled, subject or not to the payment of the costs of tracing the title and of conveyance, to require any legal estate (not vested in trustees for sale) to be conveyed to or otherwise vested in him, such legal estate shall, by virtue of this Part of this Schedule, vest in manner hereinafter provided.

    The divesting of a legal estate by virtue of this paragraph shall not, where the person from whom the estate is so divested was a trustee, operate to prevent the legal estate being conveyed, or a legal estate being created, by him in favour of a purchaser for money or money's worth, if the purchaser has no notice of the trust and if the documents of title relating to the estate divested are produced by the trustee or by persons deriving title under him.

    This paragraph shall (without prejudice to any claim, in respect of fines, fees, and other customary payments) apply to a person who, under a surrender or any disposition having the effect of a surrender, or under a covenant to surrender or otherwise, was, immediately before the commencement of this Act, entitled to require a legal customary estate of inheritance to be vested in him, or who, immediately after such commencement becomes entitled to enfranchised land.

4. Any person who, immediately after the commencement of this Act, is entitled to an equitable interest capable of subsisting as a legal estate which has priority over any legal estate in the same land, shall be deemed to be entitled for the foregoing purposes to require a legal estate to be vested in him for an interest of a like nature not exceeding in extent or duration the equitable interest:

    Provided that this paragraph shall not—

    (a) apply where the equitable interest is capable of being overreached by virtue of a subsisting trust for sale or a settlement;

    (b) operate to prevent such person from acquiring any other legal estate under this Part of this Schedule to which he may be entitled.

5.   For the purposes of this Part of this Schedule, a tenant for life, statutory owner or personal representative, shall be deemed to be entitled to require to be vested in him any legal estate in settled land (whether or not vested in the Crown) which he is, by the Settled Land Act, 1925, given power to convey.

6.   Under the provisions of this Part of this Schedule, the legal estate affected (namely, any estate which a person is entitled to require to be vested in him as aforesaid) shall vest as follows:—

    (a)   Where at the commencement of this Act land is subject to a mortgage (not being an equitable charge unsecured by any estate), the legal estate affected shall vest in accordance with the provisions relating to mortgages contained in this Schedule;

    (b)   Where the land is at the commencement or by virtue of this Act or any Act coming into operation at the same time subject or is by virtue of any statute made subject to a trust for sale, the legal estate affected shall vest in the trustees for sale (including personal representatives holding land on trust for sale) but subject to any mortgage term subsisting or created by this Act;

    (c)   Where at the commencement of this Act or by virtue of any statute coming into operation at the same time the land is settled land, the legal estate affected shall vest in the tenant for life or statutory owner entitled under the Settled Land Act, 1925, to require a vesting deed to be executed in his favour, or in the personal representative, if any, in whom the land may be vested or the Public Trustee, as the case may require but subject to any mortgage term subsisting or created by this Act;

    (d)   In any case to which the foregoing sub-paragraphs do not apply the legal estate affected shall vest in the person of full age who, immediately after the commencement of this Act, is entitled (subject or not to the payment of costs and any customary payments) to require the legal estate to be vested in him, but subject to any mortgage term subsisting or created by this Act.

7.   Nothing in this Part of this Schedule shall operate—

    (a)   To vest in a mortgagee of a term of years absolute any nominal leasehold reversion which is held in trust for him subject to redemption; or

    (b)   To vest in a mortgagee any legal estate except a term of years absolute; or

    (c)   To vest in a person entitled to a leasehold interest, as respects such interest, any legal estate except a term of years absolute; or

    (d)   To vest in a person entitled to a rentcharge (either perpetual or held for a term of years absolute) as respects such rentcharge, any legal estate except a legal estate in the rentcharge; or

    (e)   To vest in a person entitled to an easement, right or privilege with reference thereto, any legal estate except a legal estate in the easement, right or privilege; or

    (f)   To vest any legal estate in a person for an undivided share, or

    (g)   To vest any legal estate in an infant; or

    (h)   To affect prejudicially the priority of any mortgage or other incumbrance or interest subsisting at the commencement of this Act; or

    (i)   To render invalid any limitation or trust which would have been capable of taking effect as an equitable limitation or trust; or

    (j)   To vest in a purchaser or his personal representatives any legal estate which he has contracted to acquire and in regard to which a contract, including an agreement to create a legal mortgage, is pending at the commencement of this Act, although the consideration may have been paid or satisfied and the title accepted, or to render unnecessary the conveyance of such estate; or

    (k)   To vest in the managing trustees or committee of management of a charity any legal estate vested in the Official Trustee of Charity Lands; or

    (l)   To vest in any person any legal estate which failed to pass to him by reason of his omission to be registered as proprietor under the Land Transfer Acts, 1875 and 1897, until brought into operation by virtue of the Land Registration Act, 1925.

    (m)   To vest in any person any legal estate affected by any rent covenants or conditions if, before any proceedings are commenced in respect of the rent covenants or conditions, and before any conveyance of the legal estate or dealing therewith inter vivos is effected, he or his personal representatives disclaim it in writing signed by him or them.

8.   Any legal estate acquired by virtue of this Part of this Schedule shall be held upon the trusts and subject to the powers, provisions, rents, covenants, conditions, rights of redemption (as respects terms of years absolute) and other rights, burdens and obligations, if any, upon or subject to which the estate acquired ought to be held.

9.   No stamp duty shall become payable by reason only of any vesting surrender or release effected by this Schedule.

PART III
PROVISIONS AS TO LEGAL ESTATE VESTED IN INFANT

1. Where immediately before the commencement of this Act a legal estate in land is vested in one or more infants beneficially, or where immediately after the commencement of this Act a legal estate in land would by virtue of this Act have become vested in one or more infants beneficially if he or they had been of full age, the legal estate shall vest in the manner provided by the Settled Land Act, 1925.

2. Where immediately before the commencement of this Act a legal estate in land is vested in an infant jointly with one or more other persons of full age beneficially, the legal estate shall by virtue of this Act vest in that other person or those other persons on the statutory trusts, but not so as to sever any joint tenancy in the net proceeds of sale or in the rents and profits until sale: Provided that, if by virtue of this paragraph the legal estate becomes vested in one person as trustee, then, if no other person is able and willing to do so, the parents or parent, testamentary or other guardian of the infant, if respectively able and willing to act, (in the order named) may, and at the request of any person interested shall (subject to the costs being provided for) by writing appoint an additional trustee and thereupon by virtue of this Act the legal estate shall vest in the additional trustee and existing trustee as joint tenants.

3. Where, immediately before the commencement of this Act, a legal estate in land is vested solely in an infant as a personal representative, or a trustee of a settlement, or on trust for sale or on any other trust, or by way of mortgage, or where immediately after the commencement of this Act a legal estate in land would by virtue of any provision of this Act or otherwise have been so vested if the infant were of full age, the legal estate and the mortgage debt (if any) and interest thereon shall, by virtue of this Act, vest in the Public Trustee, pending the appointment of trustees as hereinafter provided—

    (a) as to the land, upon the trusts, and subject to the equities affecting the same (but in the case of a mortgage estate for a term of years absolute in accordance with this Act); and

    (b) as to the mortgage debt and interest, upon such trusts as may be requisite for giving effect to the rights (if any) of the infant or other persons beneficially interested therein:

    Provided that—

    (i) The Public Trustee shall not be entitled to act in the trust, or charge any fee, or be liable in any manner, unless and until requested in writing to act by or on behalf of the persons interested in the land or the income thereof, or in the mortgage debt or interest thereon (as the case may be), which request may be made on behalf of the infant by his parents or parent, or testamentary or other guardian (in the order named), and those persons may, in the order aforesaid (if no other person is able and willing to do so) appoint new trustees in the place of the Public Trustee, and thereupon by virtue of this Act the land or term and mortgage money shall vest in the trustees so appointed upon the trusts and subject to the equities aforesaid: Provided that the Public Trustee may, before he accepts the trust, but subject to the payment of his costs, convey to a person of full age who becomes entitled;

    (ii) After the Public Trustee has been so requested to act, and has accepted the trust, no trustee shall (except by an order of the court) be appointed in his place without his consent;

    (iii) Any person interested in the land or the income thereof, or in the mortgage debt or in the interest thereon (as the case may be), may, at any time during the minority, apply to the court for the appointment of trustees of the trust, and the court may make such order as it thinks fit, and if thereby new trustees are appointed the legal estate (but in the case of a mortgage estate only for a term of years absolute as aforesaid) and the mortgage debt (if any) and interest shall, by virtue of this Act, vest in the trustees as joint tenants upon the trusts and subject to the equities aforesaid;

    (iv) Neither a purchaser of the land nor a transferee for money or money's worth of the mortgage shall be concerned in any way with the trusts affecting the legal estate or the mortgage debt and interest thereon;

    (v) The vesting in the Public Trustee of a legal estate or a mortgage debt by virtue of this Part of this Schedule shall not affect any directions previously given as to the payment of income or of interest on any mortgage money, but such instructions may, until he accepts the trust, continue to be acted on as if no such vesting had been effected.

3A. The county court has jurisdiction under proviso (iii) to paragraph 3 of this Part where the land which is to be dealt with in the court does not exceed £30,000 in capital value.

4.   Where, immediately before the commencement of this Act, a legal estate in land is vested in two or more persons jointly as personal representatives, trustees, or mortgagees, and anyone of them is an infant, or where immediately after the commencement of this Act a legal estate in land would, by virtue of this Act, or otherwise have been so vested if the infant were of full age, the legal estate in the land with the mortgage debt (if any) and the interest thereon shall, by virtue of this Act, vest in the other person or persons of full age—

(a)   as to the legal estate, upon the trusts and subject to the equities affecting the same (but in the case of a mortgage estate only for a term of years absolute as aforesaid); and

(b)   as to the mortgage debt and interest, upon such trusts as may be requisite for giving effect to the rights (if any) of the infant or other persons beneficially interested therein;

but neither a purchaser of the land nor a transferee for money or money's worth of the mortgage shall be concerned in any way with the trusts affecting the legal estate or the mortgage debt and interest thereon:

Provided that, if, by virtue of this paragraph, the legal estate and mortgage debt, if any, become vested in a sole trustee, then, if no other person is able and willing to do so, the parents or parent, testamentary or other guardian of the infant (in the order named) may, and at the request of any person interested shall, (subject to the costs being provided for) by writing appoint a new trustee in place of the infant, and thereupon by virtue of this Act the legal estate and mortgage money shall vest in the new and continuing trustees upon the trusts and subject to the equities aforesaid.

5.   This Part of this Schedule does not affect the estate or powers of an administrator durante minore aetate, nor, where there is a tenant for life or statutory owner of settled land, operate to vest the legal estate therein in the Public Trustee.

PART IV
PROVISIONS SUBJECTING LAND HELD IN UNDIVIDED SHARES TO A TRUST FOR SALE

1.   Where, immediately before the commencement of this Act, land is held at law or in equity in undivided shares vested in possession, the following provisions shall have effect:—

(1)   If the entirety of the land is vested in trustees or personal representatives (whether subject or not to incumbrances affecting the entirety or an undivided share) in trust for persons entitled in undivided shares, then—

(a)   if the land is subject to incumbrances affecting undivided shares or to incumbrances affecting the entirety which under this Act or otherwise are not secured by legal terms of years absolute, the entirety of the land shall vest free from such incumbrances in such trustees or personal representatives and be held by them upon the statutory trusts; and

(b)   in any other case, the land shall be held by such trustees or personal representatives upon the statutory trusts;

subject in the case of personal representatives, to their rights and powers for the purposes of administration.

(2)   If the entirety of the land (not being settled land) is vested absolutely and beneficially in not more than four persons of full age entitled thereto in undivided shares free from incumbrances affecting undivided shares, but subject or not to incumbrances affecting the entirety, it shall, by virtue of this Act, vest in them as joint tenants upon the statutory trusts.

(3)   If the entirety of the land is settled land (whether subject or not to incumbrances affecting the entirety or an undivided share) held under one and the same settlement, it shall, by virtue of this Act, vest, free from incumbrances affecting undivided shares, and from incumbrances affecting the entirety, which under this Act or otherwise are not secured by a legal mortgage, and free from any interests, powers, and charges subsisting under the settlement, which have priority to the interests of the persons entitled to the undivided shares, in the trustees (if any) of the settlement as joint tenants upon the statutory trusts.

Provided that if there are no such trustees, then—

(i)   pending their appointment, the land shall, by virtue of this Act, vest (free as aforesaid) in the Public Trustee upon the statutory trusts;

(ii)   the Public Trustee shall not be entitled to act in the trust, or charge any fee, or be liable in any manner, unless and until requested in writing to act by or on behalf of persons interested in more than an undivided half of the land or the income thereof;

(iii) after the Public Trustee has been so requested to act, and has accepted the trust, no trustee shall (except by an order of the Court) be appointed in the place of the Public Trustee without his consent;

(iv) if, before the Public Trustee has accepted the trust, trustees of the settlement are appointed, the land shall, by virtue of this Act, vest (free as aforesaid) in them as joint tenants upon the statutory trusts;

(v) if, before the Public Trustee has accepted the trust, the persons having power to appoint new trustees are unable or unwilling to make an appointment, or if the tenant for life having power to apply to the court for the appointment of trustees of the settlement neglects to make the application for at least three months after being requested by any person interested in writing so to do, or if the tenants for life of the undivided shares are unable to agree, any person interested under the settlement may apply to the court for the appointment of such trustees.

(3A) The county court has jurisdiction under proviso (v) to sub-paragraph (3) of this paragraph where the land to be dealt with in the court does not exceed £30,000 in capital value.

(4) In any case to which the foregoing provisions of this Part of this Schedule do not apply, the entirety of the land shall vest (free as aforesaid) in the Public Trustee upon the statutory trusts: Provided that—

(i) The Public Trustee shall not be entitled to act in the trust, or charge any fee, or be liable in any manner, unless and until requested in writing to act by or on behalf of the persons interested in more than an undivided half of the land or the income thereof;

(ii) After the Public Trustee had been so requested to act, and has accepted the trust, no trustee shall (except by an order of the court) be appointed in the place of the Public Trustee without his consent;

(iii) Subject as aforesaid, any persons interested in more than an undivided half of the land or the income thereof may appoint new trustees in the place of the Public Trustee with the consent of any incumbrances of undivided shares (but so that a purchaser shall not be concerned to see whether any such consent has been given) and thereupon the land shall by virtue of this Act vest in the persons so appointed (free as aforesaid) upon the statutory trusts; or such persons may (without such consent as aforesaid), at any time, whether or not the Public Trustee has accepted the trust, apply to the court for the appointment of trustees of the land, and the court may make such order as it thinks fit, and if thereby trustees of the land are appointed, the same shall by virtue of this Act, vest (free as aforesaid) in the trustees as joint tenants upon the statutory trusts;

(iv) If the persons interested in more than an undivided half of the land or the income thereof do not either request the Public Trustee to act, or (whether he refuses to act or has not been requested to act) apply to the court for the appointment of trustees in his place, within three months from the time when they have been requested in writing by any person interested so to do, then and in any such case, any person interested may apply to the court for the appointment of trustees in the place of the Public Trustee, and the court may make such order as it thinks fit, and if thereby trustees of the land are appointed the same shall by virtue of this Act, vest (free as aforesaid) in the trustees upon the statutory trusts.

(4A) The county court has jurisdiction under provisos (iii) and (iv) to sub-paragraph (4) of this paragraph where the land which is to be dealt with in the court does not exceed £30,000 in capital value.

(5) The vesting in the Public Trustee of land by virtue of this Part of this Schedule shall not affect any directions previously given as to the payment of income or of interest on any mortgage money, but such instructions may, until he accepts the trust, continue to be acted on as if no such vesting had been effected.

(6) The court or the Public Trustee may act on evidence given by affidavit or by statutory declaration as respects the undivided shares without investigating the title to the land.

(7) Where all the undivided shares in the land are vested in the same mortgagees for securing the same mortgage money and the rights of redemption affecting the land are the same as might have been subsisting if the entirety had been mortgaged by an owner before the undivided shares were created, the land shall, by virtue of this Act, vest in the mortgagees as joint tenants for a legal term of years absolute (in accordance with this Act) subject to cesser on redemption by the trustees for sale in whom the right of

redemption is vested by this Act, and for the purposes of this Part of this Schedule the mortgage shall be deemed an incumbrance affecting the entirety.

(8)   This Part of this Schedule does not (except where otherwise expressly provided) prejudice incumbrancers whose incumbrances affect the entirety of the land at the commencement of this Act, but (if the nature of the incumbrance admits) the land shall vest in them for legal terms of years absolute in accordance with this Act but not so as to affect subsisting priorities.

(9)   The trust for sale and powers of management vested in persons who hold the entirety of the land on trust for sale shall, save as hereinafter mentioned, not be exercisable without the consent of any incumbrancer, being of full age, affected whose incumbrance is divested by this Part of this Schedule, but a purchaser shall not be concerned to see or inquire whether any such consent has been given, nor, where the incumbrancer is not in possession, shall any such consent be required if, independently of this Part of this Schedule or any enactment replaced thereby the transaction would have been binding on him, had the same been effected by the mortgagor.

(10) This Part of this Schedule does not apply to land in respect of which a subsisting contract for sale (whether made under an order in a partition action or by or on behalf of all the tenants in common or coparceners) is in force at the commencement of this Act if the contract is completed in due course (in which case title may be made in like manner as if this Act, and any enactment thereby replaced, had not been passed), nor to the land in respect of which a partition action is pending at such commencement if an order for a partition or sale is subsequently made in such action within eighteen months from the commencement of this Act.

(11) The repeal of the enactments relating to partition shall operate without prejudice to any proceedings thereunder commenced before the commencement of this Act, and to the jurisdiction of the court to make any orders in reference thereto, and subject to the following provisions, namely:—

  (i)   In any such proceedings, and at any stage thereof, any person or persons interested individually or collectively in one half or upwards of the land to which the proceedings relate, may apply to the court for an order staying such proceedings;

  (ii)   The court may upon such application make an order staying the proceedings as regards the whole or any part, not being an undivided share, of the land;

  (iii) As from the date of such order the said enactments shall cease to apply to the land affected by the order and the provisions of this Part of this Schedule shall apply thereto;

  (iv)   The court may by such order appoint trustees of the land and the same shall by virtue of this Act vest (free as aforesaid) in the trustees as joint tenants upon the statutory trusts;

  (v)   The court may order that the costs of the proceedings and of the application shall be raised by the trustees, by legal mortgage of the land or any part thereof, and paid either wholly or partially into court or to the trustees;

  (vi)   The court may act on such evidence as appears to be sufficient, without investigating the title to the land.

(12) In this Part of this Schedule 'incumbrance' does not include a legal rentcharge affecting the entirety, land tax, tithe rentcharge, or any similar charge on the land not created by an instrument.

2.   Where undivided shares in land, created before the commencement of this Act, fall into possession after such commencement, and the land is not settled land when the shares fall into possession, the personal representatives (subject to their rights and powers for purposes of administration) or other estate owners in whom the entirety of the land is vested shall, by an assent or a conveyance, give effect to the foregoing provisions of this Part of this Schedule in like manner as if the shares had fallen into possession immediately before the commencement of this Act, and in the meantime the land shall be held on the statutory trusts.

3.   This Part of this Schedule shall not save as hereinafter mentioned apply to party structures and open spaces within the meaning of the next succeeding Part of this Schedule.

4.   Where, immediately before the commencement of this Act, there are two or more tenants for life of full age entitled under the same settlement in undivided shares, and, after the cesser of all their interests in the income of the settled land, the entirety of the land is limited so as to devolve together (not in undivided shares), their interests shall, but without prejudice to any beneficial interest, be converted into a joint tenancy, and the joint tenants and the survivor of them shall, until the said cesser occurs, constitute the tenant for life for the purposes of the Settled Land Act, 1925, and this Act.

PART V
PROVISIONS AS TO PARTY STRUCTURES AND OPEN SPACES

1.   Where, immediately before the commencement of this Act, a party wall or other party structure is held in undivided shares, the ownership thereof shall be deemed to be severed vertically as between the respective owners, and the owner of each part shall have such rights to support and of user over the rest of the structure as may be requisite for conferring rights corresponding to those subsisting at the commencement of this Act.

2.   Where, immediately before the commencement of this Act, an open space of land (with or without any building used in common for the purposes of any adjoining land) is held in undivided shares, in right whereof each owner has rights of access and user over the open space, the ownership thereof shall vest in the Public Trustee on the statutory trusts which shall be executed only with the leave of the court, and, subject to any order of the court to the contrary, each person who would have been a tenant in common shall, until the open space is conveyed to a purchaser, have rights of access and user over the open space corresponding to those which would have subsisted if the tenancy in common had remained subsisting.

3.   Any person interested may apply to the court for an order declaring the rights and interests under this Part of this Schedule, of the persons interested in any such party structure or open space, or generally may apply in relation to the provisions of this Part of this Schedule, and the court may make such order as it thinks fit.

PART VI

...

PART VII
CONVERSION OF EXISTING FREEHOLD MORTGAGES INTO MORTGAGES BY DEMISE

1.   All land, which immediately before the commencement of this Act, was vested in a first or only mortgagee for an estate in fee simple in possession, whether legal or equitable, shall, from and after the commencement of this Act, vest in the first or only mortgagee for a term of three thousand years from such commencement, without impeachment of waste, but subject to a provision for cesser corresponding to the right of redemption which, at such commencement, was subsisting with respect to the fee simple.

2.   All land, which immediately before the commencement of this Act, was vested in a second or subsequent mortgagee for an estate in fee simple in possession, whether legal or equitable, shall, from and after the commencement of this Act, vest in the second or subsequent mortgagee for a term one day longer than the term vested in the first or other mortgagee whose security ranks immediately before that of such second or subsequent mortgagee, without impeachment of waste, but subject to the term or terms vested in such first or other prior mortgagee and subject to a provision for cesser corresponding to the right of redemption which, at such commencement, was subsisting with respect to the fee simple.

3.   The estate in fee simple which, immediately before the commencement of this Act, was vested in any such mortgagee shall, from and after such commencement, vest in the mortgagor or tenant for life, statutory owner, trustee for sale, personal representative, or other person of full age who, if all money owing on the security of the mortgage and all other mortgages or charges (if any) had been discharged at the commencement of this Act, would have been entitled to have the fee simple conveyed to him, but subject to any mortgage term created by this Part of this Schedule or otherwise and to the money secured by any such mortgage or charge.

4.   If a sub-mortgage by conveyance of the fee simple is subsisting immediately before the commencement of this Act, the principal mortgagee shall take the principal term created by paragraphs 1 or 2 of this Part of this Schedule (as the case may require) and the sub-mortgagee shall take a derivative term less by one day than the term so created, without impeachment of waste, subject to a provision for cesser corresponding to the right of redemption subsisting under the sub-mortgage.

5.   This Part of this Schedule applies to land enfranchised by statute as well as to land which was freehold before the commencement of this Act, and (save where expressly excepted) whether or not the land is registered under the Land Registration Act, 1925, or the mortgage is made by way of trust for sale or otherwise.

6.   A mortgage affecting a legal estate made before the commencement of this Act which is not protected, either by a deposit of documents of title relating to the legal estate or by registration as a land charge, shall not, as against a purchaser in good faith without notice thereof, obtain any benefit by reason of being converted into a legal mortgage by this Schedule, but shall, in favour of such purchaser, be deemed to remain an equitable interest. This paragraph does not apply to mortgages or charges registered or protected under the Land Registration Act, 1925, or to mortgages or charges registered in a local deeds register.

7.   Nothing in this Part of this Schedule shall affect priorities or the right of any mortgagee to retain possession of documents, nor affect his title to or rights over any fixtures or chattels personal comprised in the mortgage.

8.   This Part of this Schedule does not apply unless a right of redemption is subsisting immediately before the commencement of this Act.

PART VIII
CONVERSION OF EXISTING LEASEHOLD MORTGAGES
INTO MORTGAGES BY SUBDEMISE

1.   All leasehold land, which immediately before the commencement of this Act, was vested in a first or only mortgagee by way of assignment of a term of years absolute shall, from and after the commencement of this Act, vest in the first or only mortgagee for a term equal to the term assigned by the mortgage, less the last ten days thereof, but subject to a provision for cesser corresponding to the right of redemption which at such commencement was subsisting with respect to the term assigned.

2.   All leasehold land, which immediately before the commencement of this Act, was vested in a second or subsequent mortgagee by way of assignment of a term of years absolute (whether legal or equitable) shall, from and after the commencement of this Act, vest in the second or subsequent mortgagee for a term one day longer than the term vested in the first or other mortgagee whose security ranks immediately before that of such second or subsequent mortgagee if the length of the last-mentioned term permits, and in any case for a term less by one day at least than the term assigned by the mortgage, but subject to the term or terms vested in such first or other prior mortgagee, and subject to a provision for cesser corresponding to the right of redemption which, at the commencement of this Act, was subsisting with respect to the term assigned by the mortgage.

3.   The term of years absolute which was assigned by any such mortgage shall from and after the commencement of this Act, vest in the mortgagor or tenant for life, statutory owner, trustee for sale, personal representative, or other person of full age who, if all the money owing on the security of the mortgage and all other mortgages or charges, if any, had been discharged at the commencement of this Act, would have been entitled to have the term assigned or surrendered to him, but subject to any derivative mortgage term created by this Part of this Schedule or otherwise and to the money secured by any such mortgage or charge.

4.   If a sub-mortgage by assignment of a term is subsisting immediately before the commencement of this Act, the principal mortgagee shall take the principal derivative term created by paragraphs 1 or 2 of this Part of this Schedule or the derivative term created by his mortgage (as the case may require), and the sub-mortgagee shall take a derivative term less by one day than the term so vested in the principal mortgagee, subject to a provision for cesser corresponding to the right of redemption subsisting under the sub-mortgage.

5.   A mortgage affecting a legal estate made before the commencement of this Act which is not protected, either by a deposit of documents of title relating to the legal estate or by registration as a land charge shall not, as against a purchaser in good faith without notice thereof, obtain any benefit by reason of being converted into a legal mortgage by this Schedule, but shall, in favour of such purchaser, be deemed to remain an equitable interest.
        This paragraph does not apply to mortgages or charges registered or protected under the Land Registration Act, 1925, or to mortgages or charges registered in a local deeds register.

6.   This Part of this Schedule applies to perpetually renewable leaseholds, and to leaseholds for lives, which are by statute converted into long terms, with the following variations, namely:—
    (a)   The term to be taken by a first or only mortgagee shall be ten days less than the term created by such statute:
    (b)   The term to be taken by a second or subsequent mortgagee shall be one day longer than the term vested in the first or other mortgagee whose security ranks immediately before that of the second or subsequent mortgagee, if the length of the last-mentioned term permits, and in any case for a term less by one day at least than the term created by such statute:

(c)　The term created by such statute shall, from and after the commencement of this Act, vest in the mortgagor or tenant for life, statutory owner, trustee for sale, personal representative, or other person of full age, who if all the money owing on the security of the mortgage and all other mortgages or charges, if any, had been discharged at the commencement of this Act, would have been entitled to have the term assigned or surrendered to him, but subject to any derivative mortgage term created by this Part of this Schedule or otherwise and to the money secured by any such mortgage or charge.

7.　This Part of this Schedule applies (save where expressly excepted) whether or not the leasehold land is registered under the Land Registration Act, 1925, or the mortgage is made by way of trust for sale or otherwise.

8.　Nothing in this Part of this Schedule shall affect priorities or the right of any mortgagee to retain possession of documents, nor affect his title to or rights over any fixtures or chattels personal comprised in the mortgage, but this Part of this Schedule does not apply unless a right of redemption is subsisting at the commencement of this Act.

LAND REGISTRATION ACT 1925
(1925, c. 21)

[Repealed]

PART VI
GENERAL PROVISIONS AS TO REGISTRATION AND THE EFFECT THEREOF

70.　Liability of registered land to overriding interests

(1)　All registered land shall, unless under the provisions of this Act the contrary is expressed on the register, be deemed to be subject to such of the following overriding interests as may be for the time being subsisting in reference thereto, and such interests shall not be treated as incumbrances within the meaning of this Act, (that is to say):—

(a)　Rights of common, drainage rights, customary rights (until extinguished), public rights, profits a prendre, rights of sheepwalk, rights of way, watercourses, rights of water, and other easements not being equitable easements required to be protected by notice on the register;

(b)　Liability to repair highways by reason of tenure, quit-rents, crown rents, heriots and other rents and charges (until extinguished) having their origin in tenure;

(c)　Liability to repair the chancel of any church;

(d)　Liability in respect of embankments, and sea and river walls;

(c)　... payments in lieu of tithe, and charges or annuities payable for the redemption of tithe rentcharges;

(f)　Subject to the provisions of this Act, rights acquired or in course of being acquired under the Limitation Acts;

(g)　The rights of every person in actual occupation of the land or in receipt of the rents and profits thereof, save where enquiry is made of such person and the rights are not disclosed;

(h)　In the case of a possessory, qualified, or good leasehold title, all estates, rights, interests, and powers excepted from the effect of registration;

(i)　Rights under local land charges unless and until registered or protected on the register in the prescribed manner;

(j)　Rights of fishing and sporting, seignorial and manorial rights of all descriptions (until extinguished), and franchises;

(k)　Leases granted for a term not exceeding twenty-one years;

(kk)　PPP leases;

(l)　In respect of land registered before the commencement of this Act, rights to mines and minerals, and rights of entry, search, and user, and other rights and reservations incidental to or required for the purpose of giving full effect to the enjoyment of rights to mines and minerals or of property in mines or minerals, being rights which, where the title was first registered before the first day of January, eighteen hundred and ninety-eight, were created before that date, and where the title was first registered after the thirty-first day of December, eighteen hundred and ninety-seven, were created before the date of first registration;

(m) any interest or right which is an overriding interest by virtue of paragraph 1(1) of Schedule 9 of the Coal Industry Act 1994.

Provided that, where it is proved to the satisfaction of the registrar that any land registered or about to be registered is exempt from land tax, or tithe rentcharge or payments in lieu of tithe, or from charges or annuities payable for the redemption of tithe rentcharge, the registrar may notify the fact on the register in the prescribed manner.

(2) Where at the time of first registration any easement, right, privilege, or benefit created by an instrument and appearing on the title adversely affects the land, the registrar shall enter a note thereof on the register.

(3) Where the existence of any overriding interest mentioned in this section is proved to the satisfaction of the registrar or admitted, he may (subject to any prescribed exceptions) enter notice of the same or of a claim thereto on the register, but no claim to an easement, right, or privilege not created by an instrument shall be noted against the title to the servient land if the proprietor of such land (after the prescribed notice is given to him) shows sufficient cause to the contrary.

(3A) Neither subsection (2) nor subsection (3) of this section shall apply in the case of a PPP lease.

(4) Neither subsection (2) nor subsection (3) of this section shall apply in the case of any such interest or right as is mentioned in subsection (1)(m) of this subsection.

ADMINISTRATION OF ESTATES ACT 1925
(1925, c. 23)

PART I
DEVOLUTION OF REAL ESTATE

1.   Devolution of real estate on personal representative

(1) Real estate to which a deceased person was entitled for an interest not ceasing on his death shall on his death, and notwithstanding any testamentary disposition thereof, devolve from time to time on the personal representative of the deceased, in like manner as before the commencement of this Act chattels real devolved on the personal representative from time to time of a deceased person.

(2) The personal representatives for the time being of a deceased person are deemed in law his heirs and assigns within the meaning of all trusts and powers.

(3) The personal representatives shall be the representative of the deceased in regard to his real estate to which he was entitled for an interest not ceasing on his death as well as in regard to his personal estate.

2.   Application to real estate of law affecting chattels real

(1) Subject to the provisions of this Act, all enactments and rules of law, and all jurisdiction of any court with respect to the appointment of administrators or to probate or letters of administration, or to dealings before probate in the case of chattels real, and with respect to costs and other matters in the administration of personal estate, in force before the commencement of this Act, and all powers, duties, rights, equities, obligations, and liabilities of a personal representative in force at the commencement of this Act with respect to chattels real, shall apply and attach to the personal representative and shall have effect with respect to real estate vested in him, and in particular all such powers of disposition and dealing as were before the commencement of this Act exercisable as respects chattels real by the survivor or survivors of two or more personal representatives, as well as by a single personal representative, or by all the personal representatives together, shall be exercisable by the personal representatives or representative of the deceased with respect to his real estate.

(2) Where as respects real estate there are two or more personal representatives, a conveyance of real estate devolving under this Part of this Act or a contract for such a conveyance shall not be made without the concurrence therein of all such representatives

or an order of the court, but where probate is granted to one or some of two or more persons named as executors, whether or not power is reserved to the other or others to prove, any conveyance of the real estate or contract for such a conveyance may be made by the proving executor or executors for the time being, without an order of the court, and shall be as effectual as if all the persons named as executors had concurred therein.

(3)   Without prejudice to the rights and powers of a personal representative, the appointment of a personal representative in regard to real estate shall not, save as hereinafter provided, affect—

    (a)   any rule as to marshalling or as to administration of assets;

    (b)   the beneficial interest in real estate under any testamentary disposition;

    (c)   any mode of dealing with any beneficial interest in real estate, or the proceeds of sale thereof;

    (d)   the right of any person claiming to be interested in the real estate to take proceedings for the protection or recovery thereof against any person other than the personal representative.

3.   Interpretation of Part I

(1)   In this Part of this Act 'real estate' includes—

    (i)   Chattels real, and land in possession, remainder, or reversion, and every interest in or over land to which a deceased person was entitled at the time of his death; and

    (ii)   Real estate held on trust (including settled land) or by way of mortgage or security, but not money secured or charged on land.

(2)   A testator shall be deemed to have been entitled at his death to any interest in real estate passing under any gift contained in his will which operates as an appointment under a general power to appoint by will, or operates under the testamentary power conferred by statute to dispose of an entailed interest.

(3)   An entailed interest of a deceased person shall (unless disposed of under the testamentary power conferred by statute) be deemed an interest ceasing on his death, but any further or other interest of the deceased in the same property in remainder or reversion which is capable of being disposed of by his will shall not be deemed to be an interest so ceasing.

(4)   The interest of a deceased person under a joint tenancy where another tenant survives the deceased is an interest ceasing on his death.

(5)   On the death of a corporator sole his interest in the corporation's real and personal estate shall be deemed to be an interest ceasing on his death and shall devolve to his successor. This subsection applies on the demise of the Crown as respects all property, real and personal, vested in the Crown as a corporation sole.

PART II

EXECUTORS AND ADMINISTRATORS

General Provisions

5.   Cesser of right of executor to prove

Where a person appointed executor by a will—

(i)   survives the testator but dies without having taken out probate of the will; or

(ii)   is cited to take out probate of the will and does not appear to the citation; or

(iii)   renounces probate of the will;

his rights in respect of the executorship shall wholly cease, and the representation to the testator and the administration of his real and personal estate shall devolve and be committed in like manner as if that person had not been appointed executor.

6.   Withdrawal of renunciation

(1)   Where an executor who has renounced probate has been permitted, whether before or after the commencement of this Act, to withdraw the renunciation and prove the will, the probate shall take effect and be deemed always to have taken effect without prejudice to the previous acts and dealings of and notices to any other personal representative who has previously proved the will or taken out letters of administration, and a memorandum of the subsequent probate shall be endorsed on the original probate or letters of administration.

(2)   This section applies whether the testator died before or after the commencement of this Act.

7.   Executor of executor represents original testator

(1)   An executor of a sole or last surviving executor of a testator is the executor of that testator. This provision shall not apply to an executor who does not prove the will of his testator, and, in the case of an executor who on his death leaves surviving him some other executor of his testator who afterwards proves the will of that testator, it shall cease to apply on such probate being granted.

(2)   So long as the chain of such representation is unbroken, the last executor in the chain is the executor of every preceding testator.

(3)   The chain of such representation is broken by—

(a)   an intestacy; or

(b)   the failure of a testator to appoint an executor; or

(c)   the failure to obtain probate of a will;

but is not broken by a temporary grant of administration if probate is subsequently granted.

(4)   Every person in the chain of representation to a testator—

(a)   has the same rights in respect of the real and personal estate of that testator as the original executor would have had if living; and

(b)   is, to the extent to which the estate whether real or personal of that testator has come to his hands, answerable as if he were an original executor.

8.   Right of proving executors to exercise powers

(1)   Where probate is granted to one or some of two or more persons named as executors, whether or not power is reserved to the others or other to prove, all the powers which are by law conferred on the personal representative may be exercised by the proving executor or executors for the time being and shall be as effectual as if all the persons named as executors had concurred therein.

(2)   This section applies whether the testator died before or after the commencement of this Act.

9.   Vesting of estate in Public Trustee where intestacy or lack of executors

(1)   Where a person dies intestate, his real and personal estate shall vest in the Public Trustee until the grant of administration.

(2)   Where a testator dies and—

(a)   at the time of his death there is no executor with power to obtain probate of the will, or

(b)   at any time before probate of the will is granted there ceases to be any executor with power to obtain probate,

the real and personal estate of which he disposes by the will shall vest in the Public Trustee until the grant of representation.

(3)   The vesting of real or personal estate in the Public Trustee by virtue of this section does not confer on him any beneficial interest in, or impose on him any duty, obligation or liability in respect of, the property.

15.   Executor not to act while administration is in force

Where administration has been granted in respect of any real or personal estate of a deceased person, no person shall have power to bring any action or otherwise act as executor of the deceased person in respect of the estate comprised in or affected by the grant until the grant has been recalled or revoked.

17.   Continuance of legal proceedings after revocation of temporary administration

(1)   If, while any legal proceeding is pending in any court by or against an administrator to whom a temporary administration has been granted, that administration is revoked, that court may order that the proceeding be continued by or against the new personal representative in like manner as if the same had been originally commenced by or against him, but subject to such conditions and variations, if any, as that court directs.

(2)   The county court has jurisdiction under this section where the proceedings are pending in that court.

21.   Rights and liabilities of administrator

Every person to whom administration of the real and personal estate of a deceased person is granted, shall, subject to the limitations contained in the grant, have the same rights and liabilities and be accountable in like manner as if he were the executor of the deceased.

21A. Debtor who becomes creditor's executor by representation or administrator to account for debt to estate

(1) Subject to subsection (2) of this section, where a debtor becomes his deceased creditor's executor by representation or administrator—

(a) his debt shall thereupon be extinguished; but

(b) he shall be accountable for the amount of the debt as part of the creditor's estate in any case where he would be so accountable if he had been appointed as an executor by the creditor's will.

(2) Subsection (1) of this section does not apply where the debtor's authority to act as executor or administrator is limited to part only of the creditor's estate which does not include the debt; and a debtor whose debt is extinguished by virtue of paragraph (a) shall not be accountable for its amount by virtue of paragraph (b) of that subsection in any case where the debt was barred by the Limitation Act 1939 before he became the creditor's executor or administrator.

(3) In this section 'debt' includes any liability, and 'debtor' and 'creditor' shall be construed accordingly.

Special Provisions as to Settled Land

22. Special executors as respects settled land

(1) A testator may appoint, and in default of such express appointment shall be deemed to have appointed, as his special executors in regard to settled land, the persons, if any, who are at his death the trustees of the settlement thereof, and probate may be granted to such trustees specially limited to the settled land. In this subsection 'settled land' means land vested in the testator which was settled previously to his death and not by his will.

(2) A testator may appoint other persons either with or without such trustees as aforesaid or any of them to be his general executors in regard to his other property and assets.

23. Provisions where, as respects settled land, representation is not granted to the trustees of the settlement

(1) Where settled land becomes vested in a personal representative, not being a trustee of the settlement, upon trust to convey the land to or assent to the vesting thereof in the tenant for life or statutory owner in order to give effect to a settlement created before the death of the deceased and not by his will, or would on the grant of representation to him, have become so vested, such representative may—

(a) before representation has been granted, renounce his office in regard only to such settled land without renouncing it in regard to other property;

(b) after representation has been granted, apply to the court for revocation of the grant in regard to the settled land without applying in regard to other property.

(2) Whether such renunciation or revocation is made or not, the trustees of the settlement, or any person beneficially interested thereunder, may apply to the High Court for an order appointing a special or additional personal representative in respect of the settled land, and a special or additional personal representative, if and when appointed under the order, shall be in the same position as if representation had originally been granted to him alone in place of the original personal representative, if any, or to him jointly with the original personal representative, as the case may be, limited to the settled land, but without prejudice to the previous acts and dealings, if any, of the personal representative originally constituted or the effect of notices given to such personal representative.

(3) The court may make such order as aforesaid subject to such security, if any, being given by or on behalf of the special or additional personal representative, as the court may direct, and shall, unless the court considers that special considerations apply, appoint such persons as may be necessary to secure that the persons to act as representatives in respect of the settled land shall, if willing to act, be the same persons as are the trustees of the settlement, and an office copy of the order when made shall be furnished to the principal registry of the Family Division of the High Court for entry, and a memorandum of the order shall be endorsed on the probate or administration.

(4) The person applying for the appointment of a special or additional personal representative shall give notice of the application to the principal registry of the Family Division of the High Court in the manner prescribed.

(5) Rules of court may be made for prescribing for all matters required for giving effect to the provisions of this section, and in particular—

    (a)   for notice of any application being given to the proper officer;

    (b)   for production of orders, probates, and administration to the registry;

    (c)   for the endorsement on a probate or administration of a memorandum of an order, subject or not to any exceptions;

    (d)   for the manner in which the costs are to be borne;

    (e)   for protecting purchasers and trustees and other persons in a fiduciary position, dealing in good faith with or giving notices to a personal representative before notice of any order has been endorsed on the probate or administration or a pending action has been registered in respect of the proceedings.

24.   Power for special personal representatives to dispose of settled land

(1)   The special personal representatives may dispose of the settled land without the concurrence of the general personal representatives, who may likewise dispose of the other property and assets of the deceased without the concurrence of the special personal representatives.

(2)   In this section the expression 'special personal representatives' means the representatives appointed to act for the purposes of settled land and includes any original personal representative who is to act with an additional personal representative for those purposes.

Duties, Rights and Obligations

25.   Duty of personal representatives

The personal representative of a deceased person shall be under a duty to—

    (a)   collect and get in the real and personal estate of the deceased and administer it according to law;

    (b)   when required to do so by the court, exhibit on oath in the court a full inventory of the estate and when so required render an account of the administration of the estate to the court;

    (c)   when required to do so by the High Court, deliver up the grant of probate or administration to that court.

26.   Rights of action by and against personal representative

(1)–(3) ...

(4) To recover rent due or accruing to the deceased, a personal representative may exercise any power under section 72(1) (commercial rent arrears recovery) or 81 (right to rent from sub-tenant) of the Tribunals, Courts and Enforcement Act 2007 that would have been exercisable by the deceased if he had still been living.

(5), (6) ...

27.   Protection of persons on probate or administration

(1)   Every person making or permitting to be made any payment or disposition in good faith under a representation shall be indemnified and protected in so doing, notwithstanding any defect or circumstance whatsoever affecting the validity of the representation.

(2)   Where a representation is revoked, all payments and dispositions made in good faith to a personal representative under the representation before the revocation thereof are a valid discharge to the person making the same; and the personal representative who acted under the revoked representation may retain and reimburse himself in respect of any payments or dispositions made by him which the person to whom representation is afterwards granted might have properly made.

28.   Liability of person fraudulently obtaining or retaining estate of deceased

If any person, to the defrauding of creditors or without full valuable consideration, obtains, receives or holds any real or personal estate of a deceased person or effects the release of any debt or liability due to the estate of the deceased, he shall be charged as executor in his own wrong to the extent of the real and personal estate received or coming to his hands, or the debt or liability released, after deducting—

    (a)   any debt for valuable consideration and without fraud due to him from the deceased person at the time of his death; and

    (b)   any payment made by him which might properly be made by a personal representative.

29.　Liability of estate of personal representative

Where a person as personal representative of a deceased person (including an executor in his own wrong) wastes or converts to his own use any part of the real or personal estate of the deceased, and dies, his personal representative shall to the extent of the available assets of the defaulter be liable and chargeable in respect of such waste or conversion in the same manner as the defaulter would have been if living.

31.　Power to make rules

Provision may be made by rules of court for giving effect to the provisions of this Part of this Act so far as relates to real estate and in particular for adapting the procedure and practice on the grant of letters of administration to the case of real estate.

PART III
ADMINISTRATION OF ASSETS

32.　Real and personal estate of deceased are assets for payment of debts

(1)　The real and personal estate, whether legal or equitable, of a deceased person, to the extent of his beneficial interest therein, and the real and personal estate of which a deceased person in pursuance of any general power (including the statutory power to dispose of entailed interests) disposes by his will, are assets for payment of his debts (whether by specialty or simple contract) and liabilities, and any disposition by will inconsistent with this enactment is void as against the creditors, and the court shall if necessary, administer the property for the purpose of the payment of the debts and liabilities.

　　This subsection takes effect without prejudice to the rights of incumbrancers.

(2)　If any person to whom any such beneficial interest devolves, or is given, or in whom any such interest vests, disposes thereof in good faith before an action is brought or process is sued out against him, he shall be personally liable for the value of the interest so disposed of by him, but that interest shall not be liable to be taken in execution in the action or under the process.

33.　Trust for sale

(1)　On the death of a person intestate as to any real or personal estate, that estate shall be held in trust by his personal representatives with the power to sell it.

(2)　The personal representatives shall pay out of—

　　(a)　the ready money of the deceased (so far as not disposed of by his will, if any); and

　　(b)　any net money arising from disposing of any other part of his estate (after payment of costs),

all such funeral, testamentary and administration expenses, debts and other liabilities as are properly payable thereout having regard to the rules of administration contained in this Part of this Act, and out of the residue of the said money the personal representative shall set aside a fund sufficient to provide for any pecuniary legacies bequeathed by the will (if any) of the deceased.

(3)　During the minority of any beneficiary or the subsistence of any life interest and pending the distribution of the whole or any part of the estate of the deceased, the personal representatives may invest the residue of the said money, or so much thereof as may not have been distributed, under the Trustee Act 2000.

(4)　The residue of the said money and any investments for the time being representing the same, and any part of the estate of the deceased which remains unsold and is not required for the administration purposes aforesaid, is in this Act referred to as 'the residuary estate of the intestate.'

(5)　The income (including net rents and profits of real estate and chattels real after payment of rates, taxes, rent, costs of insurance, repairs and other outgoings properly attributable to income) of so much of the real and personal estate of the deceased as may not be disposed of by his will, if any, or may not be required for the administration purposes aforesaid, may, however such estate is invested, as from the death of the deceased, be treated and applied as income, and for that purpose any necessary apportionment may be made between tenant for life and remainderman.

(6)　Nothing in this section affects the rights of any creditor of the deceased or the rights of the Crown in respect of death duties.

(7)　Where the deceased leaves a will, this section has effect subject to the provisions contained in the will.

34.   Administration of assets

(1)   ...

(2)   ...

(3)   Where the estate of a deceased person is solvent his real and personal estate shall, subject to rules of court and the provisions hereinafter contained as to charges on property of the deceased, and to the provisions, if any, contained in his will, be applicable towards the discharge of the funeral, testamentary and administration expenses, debts and liabilities payable thereout in the order mentioned in Part II of the First Schedule to this Act.

35.   Charges on property of deceased to be paid primarily out of the property charged

(1)   Where a person dies possessed of, or entitled to, or, under a general power of appointment (including the statutory power to dispose of entailed interests) by his will disposes of, an interest in property, which at the time of his death is charged with the payment of money, whether by way of legal mortgage, equitable charge or otherwise (including a lien for unpaid purchase money), and the deceased has not by will deed or other document signified a contrary or other intention, the interest so charged, shall as between the different persons claiming through the deceased, be primarily liable for the payment of the charge; and every part of the said interest, according to its value, shall bear a proportionate part of the charge on the whole thereof.

(2)   Such contrary or other intention shall not be deemed to be signified—

     (a)   by a general direction for the payment of debts or of all the debts of the testator out of his personal estate, or his residuary real and personal estate, or his residuary real estate; or

     (b)   by a charge of debts upon any such estate;

     unless such intention is further signified by words expressly or by necessary implication referring to all or some part of the charge.

(3)   Nothing in this section affects the right of a person entitled to the charge to obtain payment or satisfaction thereof either out of the other assets of the deceased or otherwise.

36.   Effect of assent or conveyance by personal representative

(1)   A personal representative may assent to the vesting, in any person who (whether by devise, bequest, devolution, appropriation or otherwise) may be entitled thereto, either beneficially or as a trustee or personal representative, of any estate or interest in real estate to which the testator or intestate was entitled or over which he exercised a general power of appointment by his will, including the statutory power to dispose of entailed interests, and which devolved upon the personal representative.

(2)   The assent shall operate to vest in that person the estate or interest to which the assent relates, and, unless a contrary intention appears, the assent shall relate back to the death of the deceased.

(3)   ...

(4)   An assent to the vesting of a legal estate shall be in writing, signed by the personal representative, and shall name the person in whose favour it is given and shall operate to vest in that person the legal estate to which it relates; and an assent not in writing or not in favour of a named person shall not be effectual to pass a legal estate.

(5)   Any person in whose favour an assent or conveyance of a legal estate is made by a personal representative may require that notice of the assent or conveyance be written or endorsed on or permanently annexed to the probate or letters of administration, at the cost of the estate of the deceased, and that the probate or letters of administration be produced, at the like cost, to prove that the notice has been placed thereon or annexed thereto.

(6)   A statement in writing by a personal representative that he has not given or made an assent or conveyance in respect of a legal estate, shall, in favour of a purchaser, but without prejudice to any previous disposition made in favour of another purchaser deriving title mediately or immediately under the personal representative, be sufficient evidence that an assent or conveyance has not been given or made in respect of the legal estate to which the statement relates, unless notice of a previous assent or conveyance affecting that estate has been placed on or annexed to the probate or administration.

     A conveyance by a personal representative of a legal estate to a purchaser accepted on the faith of such a statement shall (without prejudice as aforesaid and unless notice of a previous assent or conveyance affecting that estate has been placed on or annexed to the probate or administration) operate to transfer or create the legal estate expressed to be conveyed in like manner as if no previous assent or conveyance had been made by the personal representative.

A personal representative making a false statement, in regard to any such matter, shall be liable in like manner as if the statement had been contained in a statutory declaration.

(7) An assent or conveyance by a personal representative in respect of a legal estate shall, in favour of a purchaser, unless notice of a previous assent or conveyance affecting that legal estate has been placed on or annexed to the probate or administration, be taken as sufficient evidence that the person in whose favour the assent or conveyance is given or made is the person entitled to have the legal estate conveyed to him, and upon the proper trusts, if any, but shall not otherwise prejudicially affect the claim of any person rightfully entitled to the estate vested or conveyed or any charge thereon.

(8) A conveyance of a legal estate by a personal representative to a purchaser shall not be invalidated by reason only that the purchaser may have notice that all the debts, liabilities, funeral, and testamentary or administration expenses, duties, and legacies of the deceased have been discharged or provided for.

(9) An assent or conveyance given or made by a personal representative shall not, except in favour of a purchaser of a legal estate, prejudice the right of the personal representative or any other person to recover the estate or interest to which the assent or conveyance relates, or to be indemnified out of such estate or interest against any duties, debts, or liability to which such estate or interest would have been subject if there had not been any assent or conveyance.

(10) A personal representative may, as a condition of giving an assent or making a conveyance, require security for the discharge of any such duties, debt, or liability, but shall not be entitled to postpone the giving of an assent merely by reason of the subsistence of any such duties, debt or liability if reasonable arrangements have been made for discharging the same; and an assent may be given subject to any legal estate or charge by way of legal mortgage.

(11) This section shall not operate to impose any stamp duty in respect of an assent, and in this section 'purchaser' means a purchaser for money or money's worth.

(12) This section applies to assents and conveyances made after the commencement of this Act, whether the testator or intestate died before or after such commencement.

37. Validity of conveyance not affected by revocation of representation

(1) All conveyances of any interest in real or personal estate made to a purchaser either before or after the commencement of this Act by a person to whom probate or letters of administration have been granted are valid, notwithstanding any subsequent revocation or variation, either before or after the commencement of this Act, of the probate or administration.

(2) This section takes effect without prejudice to any order of the court made before the commencement of this Act, and applies whether the testator or intestate died before or after such commencement.

38. Right to follow property and powers of the court in relation thereto

(1) An assent or conveyance by a personal representative to a person other than a purchaser does not prejudice the rights of any person to follow the property to which the assent or conveyance relates, or any property representing the same, into the hands of the person in whom it is vested by the assent or conveyance, or of any other person (not being a purchaser) who may have received the same or in whom it may be vested.

(2) Notwithstanding any such assent or conveyance the court may, on the application of any creditor or other person interested,—

(a) order a sale, exchange, mortgage, charge, lease, payment, transfer or other transaction to be carried out which the court considers requisite for the purpose of giving effect to the rights of the persons interested;

(b) declare that the person, not being a purchaser, in whom the property is vested is a trustee for those purposes;

(c) give directions respecting the preparation and execution of any conveyance or other instrument or as to any other matter required for giving effect to the order;

(d) make any vesting order, or appoint a person to convey in accordance with the provisions of the Trustee Act 1925.

(3)   This section does not prejudice the rights of a purchaser or a person deriving title under him, but applies whether the testator or intestate died before or after the commencement of this Act.

(4)   The county court has jurisdiction under this section where the estate in respect of which the application is made does not exceed in amount or value the county court limit.

39.   Powers of management

(1)   In dealing with the real and personal estate of the deceased his personal representatives shall, for purposes of administration, or during a minority of any beneficiary or the subsistence of any life interest, or until the period of distribution arrives, have—

(i)   as respects the personal estate, the same powers and discretions, including power to raise money by mortgage or charge (whether or not by deposit of documents), as a personal representative had before the commencement of this Act, with respect to personal estate vested in him; and

(ii)   as respects the real estate, all the functions conferred on them by Part I of the Trusts of Land and Appointment of Trustees Act 1996;

(iii)   all the powers necessary so that every contract entered into by a personal representative shall be binding on and be enforceable against and by the personal representative for the time being of the deceased, and may be carried into effect, or be varied or rescinded by him, and, in the case of a contract entered into by a predecessor, as if it had been entered into by himself.

(1A)   Subsection (1) of this section is without prejudice to the powers conferred on personal representatives by the Trustee Act 2000.

(2)   Nothing in this section shall affect the right of any person to require an assent or conveyance to be made.

(3)   This section applies whether the testator or intestate died before or after the commencement of this Act.

40.   Powers of personal representative for raising money, etc.

(1)   For giving effect to beneficial interests the personal representative may limit or demise land for a term of years absolute, with or without impeachment for waste, to trustees on usual trusts for raising or securing any principal sum and the interest thereon for which the land, or any part thereof, is liable, and may limit or grant a rentcharge for giving effect to any annual or periodical sum for which the land or the income thereof or any part thereof is liable.

(2)   This section applies whether the testator or intestate died before or after the commencement of this Act.

41.   Powers of personal representative as to appropriation

(1)   The personal representative may appropriate any part of the real or personal estate, including things in action, of the deceased in the actual condition or state of investment thereof at the time of appropriation in or towards satisfaction of any legacy bequeathed by the deceased, or of any other interest or share in his property, whether settled or not, as to the personal representative may seem just and reasonable, according to the respective rights of the persons interested in the property of the deceased:
Provided that—

(i)   an appropriation shall not be made under this section so as to affect prejudicially any specific devise or bequest;

(ii)   an appropriation of property, whether or not being an investment authorised by law or by the will, if any, of the deceased for the investment of money subject to the trust, shall not (save as hereinafter mentioned) be made under this section except with the following consents:—

(a)   when made for the benefit of a person absolutely and beneficially entitled in possession, the consent of that person;

(b)   when made in respect of any settled legacy share or interest, the consent of either the trustee thereof, if any (not being also the personal representative), or the person who may for the time being be entitled to the income:

If the person whose consent is so required as aforesaid is an infant or lacks capacity (within the meaning of the Mental Capacity Act 2005) to give the consent, it shall be given on his behalf by his parents or parent, testamentary or other guardian, or a person appointed as deputy for him by the Court of Protection, or if, in the case of an infant, there is no such parent or guardian, by the court on the application of his next friend;

(iii)   no consent (save of such trustee as aforesaid) shall be required on behalf of a person who may come into existence after the time of appropriation, or who cannot be found or ascertained at that time;

(iv)   if no deputy is appointed for a person who lacks capacity to consent then, if the appropriation is of an investment authorised by law or by the will, if any, of the deceased for the investment of money subject to the trust, no consent shall be required on behalf of the said person;

(v)   if, independently of the personal representative, there is no trustee of a settled legacy share or interest, and no person of full age and capacity entitled to the income thereof, no consent shall be required to an appropriation in respect of such legacy share or interest, provided that the appropriation is of an investment authorised as aforesaid.

(1A) The county court has jurisdiction under proviso (ii) to subsection (1) of this section where the estate in respect of which the application is made does not exceed in amount or value the county court limit.

(2)   Any property duly appropriated under the powers conferred by this section shall thereafter be treated as an authorised investment, and may be retained or dealt with accordingly.

(3)   For the purposes of such appropriation, the personal representative may ascertain and fix the value of the respective parts of the real and personal estate and the liabilities of the deceased as he may think fit, and shall for that purpose employ a duly qualified valuer in any case where such employment may be necessary; and may make any conveyance (including an assent) which may be requisite for giving effect to the appropriation.

(4)   An appropriation made pursuant to this section shall bind all persons interested in the property of the deceased whose consent is not hereby made requisite.

(5)   The personal representative shall, in making the appropriation, have regard to the rights of any person who may thereafter come into existence, or who cannot be found or ascertained at the time of appropriation, and of any other person whose consent is not required by this section.

(6)   This section does not prejudice any other power of appropriation conferred by law or by the will (if any) of the deceased, and takes effect with any extended powers conferred by the will (if any) of the deceased, and where an appropriation is made under this section, in respect of a settled legacy, share or interest, the property appropriated shall remain subject to all trusts and powers of leasing, disposition, and management or varying investments which would have been applicable thereto or to the legacy, share or interest in respect of which the appropriation is made, if no such appropriation had been made.

(7)   If after any real estate has been appropriated in purported exercise of the powers conferred by this section, the person to whom it was conveyed disposes of it or any interest therein, then, in favour of a purchaser, the appropriation shall be deemed to have been made in accordance with the requirements of this section and after all requisite consents, if any, had been given.

(8)   In this section, a settled legacy, share or interest includes any legacy, share or interest to which a person is not absolutely entitled in possession at the date of the appropriation, also an annuity, and 'purchaser' means a purchaser for money or money's worth.

(9)   This section applies whether the deceased died intestate or not, and whether before or after the commencement of this Act, and extends to property over which a testator exercises a general power of appointment, including the statutory power to dispose of entailed interests, and authorises the setting apart of a fund to answer an annuity by means of the income of that fund or otherwise.

42.   Power to appoint trustees of infants' property

(1)   Where an infant is absolutely entitled under the will or on the intestacy of a person dying before or after the commencement of this Act (in this subsection called 'the deceased') to a devise or legacy, or to the residue of the estate of the deceased, or any share therein, and such devise, legacy, residue or share is not under the will, if any, of the deceased, devised or bequeathed to trustees for the infant, the personal representatives of the deceased may appoint a trust corporation or two or more individuals not exceeding four (whether or not including the personal representatives or one or more of the personal representatives), to be the trustee or trustees of such devise, legacy, residue or share for the infant, and to be trustees of any land devised or any land being or forming part of

such residue or share for the purposes of the Settled Land Act 1925, and of the statutory provisions relating to the management of land during a minority, and may execute or do any assurance or thing requisite for vesting such devise, legacy, residue or share in the trustee or trustees so appointed.

On such appointment the personal representatives, as such, shall be discharged from all further liability in respect of such devise, legacy, residue, or share, and the same may be retained in its existing condition or state of investment, or may be converted into money, and such money may be invested in any authorised investment.

(2) Where a personal representative has before the commencement of this Act retained or sold any such devise, legacy, residue or share, and invested the same or the proceeds thereof in any investments in which he was authorised to invest money subject to the trust, then, subject to any order of the court made before such commencement, he shall not be deemed to have incurred any liability on that account, or by reason of not having paid or transferred the money or property into court.

43. Obligations of personal representative as to giving possession of land and powers of the court

(1) A personal representative, before giving an assent or making a conveyance in favour of any person entitled, may permit that person to take possession of the land, and such possession shall not prejudicially affect the right of the personal representative to take or resume possession nor his power to convey the land as if he were in possession thereof, but subject to the interest of any lessee, tenant or occupier in possession or in actual occupation of the land.

(2) Any person who as against the personal representative claims possession of real estate, or the appointment of a receiver thereof, or a conveyance thereof, or an assent to the vesting thereof, or to be registered as proprietor thereof under the Land Registration Act 2002, may apply to the court for directions with reference thereto, and the court may make such vesting or other order as may be deemed proper, and the provisions of the Trustee Act 1925, relating to vesting orders and to the appointment of a person to convey, shall apply.

(3) This section applies whether the testator or intestate died before or after the commencement of this Act.

(4) The county court has jurisdiction under this section where the estate in respect of which the application is made does not exceed in amount or value the county court limit.

44. Power to postpone distribution

Subject to the foregoing provisions of this Act, a personal representative is not bound to distribute the estate of the deceased before the expiration of one year from the death.

PART IV
DISTRIBUTION OF RESIDUARY ESTATE

45. Abolition of descent to heir, curtesy, dower and escheat

(1) With regard to the real estate and personal inheritance of every person dying after the commencement of this Act, there shall be abolished—

(a) All existing modes rules and canons of descent, and of devolution by special occupancy or otherwise, of real estate, or of a personal inheritance, whether operating by the general law or by the custom of gavelkind or borough-English or by any other custom of any county, locality, or manor, or otherwise howsoever; and

(b) Tenancy by the curtesy and every other estate and interest of a husband in real estate as to which his wife dies intestate, whether arising under the general law or by custom or otherwise; and

(c) Dower and freebench and every other estate and interest of a wife in real estate as to which her husband dies intestate, whether arising under the general law or by custom or otherwise: Provided that where a right (if any) to freebench or other like right has attached before the commencement of this Act which cannot be barred by a testamentary or other disposition made by the husband, such right shall, unless released, remain in force as an equitable interest; and

(d) Escheat to the Crown or the Duchy of Lancaster or the Duke of Cornwall or to a mesne lord for want of heirs.

(2) Nothing in this section affects the descent or devolution of an entailed interest.

46.   Succession to real and personal estate on intestacy

(1)   The residuary estate of an intestate shall be distributed in the manner or be held on the trusts mentioned in this section, namely:—

    (i)   If the intestate leaves a spouse or civil partner, then in accordance with the following Table:

(1)	If the intestate leaves no issue:	the residuary estate shall be held in trust for the surviving spouse or civil partner absolutely.

(2)	If the intestate leaves issue:	(A)	the surviving spouse or civil partner shall take the personal chattels absolutely;
		(B)	the residuary estate of the intestate (other than the personal chattels) shall stand charged with the payment of a fixed net sum, free of death duties and costs, to the surviving spouse or civil partner, together with simple interest on it from the date of the death at the rate provided for by subsection (1A) until paid or appropriated; and
		(C)	subject to providing for the sum and interest referred to in paragraph (B), the residuary estate (other than the personal chattels) shall be held—
			(a) as to one half, in trust for the surviving spouse or civil partner absolutely, and
			(b) as to the other half, on the statutory trusts for the issue of the intestate.

The amount of the fixed net sum referred to in paragraph (B) of case (2) of this Table is to be determined in accordance with Schedule 1A.

    (ii)   If the intestate leaves issue but no spouse or civil partner, the residuary estate of the intestate shall be held on the statutory trusts for the issue of the intestate;

    (iii)   If the intestate leaves no spouse or civil partner and no issue but both parents, then the residuary estate of the intestate shall be held in trust for the father and mother in equal shares absolutely;

    (iv)   If the intestate leaves no spouse or civil partner and no issue but one parent, then the residuary estate of the intestate shall be held in trust for the surviving father or mother absolutely;

    (v)   If the intestate leaves no spouse or civil partner and no issue and no parent, then the residuary estate of the intestate shall be held in trust for the following persons living at the death of the intestate, and in the following order and manner, namely:— First, on the statutory trusts for the brothers and sisters of the whole blood of the intestate; but if no person takes an absolutely vested interest under such trusts; then
Secondly, on the statutory trusts for the brothers and sisters of the half blood of the intestate; but if no person takes an absolutely vested interest under such trusts; then
Thirdly, for the grandparents of the intestate and, if more than one survive the intestate, in equal shares; but if there is no member of this class; then
Fourthly, on the statutory trusts for the uncles and aunts of the intestate (being brothers or sisters of the whole blood of a parent of the intestate); but if no person takes an absolutely vested interest under such trusts; then
Fifthly, on the statutory trusts for the uncles and aunts of the intestate (being brothers or sisters of the half blood of a parent of the intestate)

    (vi)   In default of any person taking an absolute interest under the foregoing provisions, the residuary estate of the intestate shall belong to the Crown or to the Duchy of Lancaster or to the Duke of Cornwall for the time being, as the case may be, as bona vacantia, and in lieu of any right to escheat.
The Crown or the said Duchy or the said Duke may (without prejudice to the powers reserved by section nine of the Civil List Act 1910, or any other powers), out of the whole or any part of the property devolving on them respectively, provide, in accordance with the existing practice, for dependents, whether kindred or not, of the intestate, and other persons for whom the intestate might reasonably have been expected to make provision.

(1A) The interest rate referred to in paragraph (B) of case (2) of the Table in subsection (1)(i) is the Bank of England rate that had effect at the end of the day on which the intestate died.

(2)   A husband and wife shall for all purposes of distribution or division under the foregoing provisions of this section be treated as two persons.

(2A) Where the intestate's spouse or civil partner survived the intestate but died before the end of the period of 28 days beginning with the day on which the intestate died, this section shall have effect as respects the intestate as if the spouse or civil partner had not survived the intestate.

(3)   ...

(4)   The interest payable on the fixed net sum payable to a surviving spouse or civil partner shall be primarily payable out of income.

46A. Disclaimer or forfeiture on intestacy

(1)   This section applies where a person—
   (a)   is entitled in accordance with section 46 to an interest in the residuary estate of an intestate but disclaims it, or
   (b)   would have been so entitled had the person not been precluded by the forfeiture rule from acquiring it.

(2)   The person is to be treated for the purposes of this Part as having died immediately before the intestate.

(3)   But in a case within subsection (1)(b), subsection (2) does not affect the power conferred by section 2 of the Forfeiture Act 1982 (power of court to modify the forfeiture rule).

(4)   In this section 'forfeiture rule' has the same meaning as in the Forfeiture Act 1982.

47.   Statutory trusts in favour of issue and other classes of relatives of intestate

(1)   Where under this Part of this Act the residuary estate of an intestate, or any part thereof, is directed to be held on the statutory trusts for the issue of the intestate, the same shall be held upon the following trusts, namely:—
   (i)   In trust, in equal shares if more than one, for all or any the children or child of the intestate, living at the death of the intestate, who attain the age of eighteen years or marry under that age or form a civil partnership under that age, and for all or any of the issue living at the death of the intestate who attain the age of eighteen years or marry, or form a civil partnership, under that age of any child of the intestate who predeceases the intestate, such issue to take through all degrees, according to their stocks, in equal shares if more than one, the share which their parent would have taken if living at the death of the intestate, and so that (subject to section 46A) no issue shall take whose parent is living at the death of the intestate and so capable of taking;
   (ii)   The statutory power of advancement, and the statutory provisions which relate to maintenance and accumulation of surplus income, shall apply, but when an infant marries, or forms a civil partnership, such infant shall be entitled to give valid receipts for the income of the infant's share or interest;
   (iii)   ...
   (iv)   The personal representatives may permit any infant contingently interested to have the use and enjoyment of any personal chattels in such manner and subject to such conditions (if any) as the personal representatives may consider reasonable, and without being liable to account for any consequential loss.

(2)   If the trusts in favour of the issue of the intestate fail by reason of no child or other issue attaining an absolutely vested interest—
   (a)   the residuary estate of the intestate and the income thereof and all statutory accumulations, if any, of the income thereof, or so much thereof as may not have been paid or applied under any power affecting the same, shall go, devolve and be held under the provisions of this Part of this Act as if the intestate had died without leaving issue living at the death of the intestate;
   (b)   references in this Part of this Act to the intestate 'leaving no issue' shall be construed as 'leaving no issue who attain an absolutely vested interest';
   (c)   references in this Part of this Act to the intestate 'leaving issue' or 'leaving a child or other issue' shall be construed as 'leaving issue who attain an absolutely vested interest.'

(3) Where under this Part of this Act the residuary estate of an intestate or any part thereof is directed to be held on the statutory trusts for any class of relatives of the intestate, other than issue of the intestate, the same shall be held on trusts corresponding to the statutory trusts for the issue of the intestate (other than the provision for bringing any money or property into account) as if such trusts (other than as aforesaid) were repeated with the substitution of references to the members or member of that class for references to the children or child of the intestate.

(4) References in paragraph (i) of subsection (1) of the last foregoing section to the intestate leaving, or not leaving, a member of the class consisting of brothers or sisters of the whole blood of the intestate and issue of brothers or sisters of the whole blood of the intestate shall be construed as references to the intestate leaving, or not leaving, a member of that class who attains an absolutely vested interest.

(4A) Subsections (2) and (4) are subject to section 46A.

(4B) Subsections (4C) and (4D) apply if a beneficiary under the statutory trusts—
  (a) fails to attain an absolutely vested interest because the beneficiary dies without having reached 18 and without having married or formed a civil partnership, and
  (b) dies leaving issue.

(4C) The beneficiary is to be treated for the purposes of this Part as having died immediately before the intestate.

(4D) The residuary estate (together with the income from it and any statutory accumulations of income from it) or so much of it as has not been paid or applied under a power affecting it is to devolve accordingly.

(5) ...

48. Powers of personal representative in respect of interests of surviving spouse

(1) ...

(2) The personal representatives may raise—
  (a) the fixed net sum or any part thereof and the interest thereon payable to the surviving spouse or civil partner of the intestate on the security of the whole or any part of the residuary estate of the intestate (other than the personal chattels), so far as that estate may be sufficient for the purpose of the said sum and interest may not have been satisfied by an appropriation under the statutory power available in that behalf;
and the amount, if any, properly required for the payment of the costs of the transaction.

49. Application to cases of partial intestacy

(1) Where any person dies leaving a will effectively disposing of part of his property, this Part of this Act shall have effect as respects the part of his property not so disposed of subject to the provisions contained in the will and subject to the following modifications: —
  (aa), (a) ...
  (b) The personal representative shall, subject to his rights and powers for the purposes of administration, be a trustee for the persons entitled under this Part of this Act in respect of the part of the estate not expressly disposed of unless it appears by the will that the personal representative is intended to take such part beneficially.

(2), (3), (4) ...

50. Construction of documents

(1) References to any Statutes of Distribution in an instrument inter vivos made or in a will coming into operation after the commencement of this Act, shall be construed as references to this Part of this Act; and references in such an instrument or will to statutory next of kin shall be construed, unless the context otherwise requires, as referring to the persons who would take beneficially on an intestacy under the foregoing provisions of this Part of this Act.

(2) Trusts declared in an instrument inter vivos made, or in a will coming into operation, before the commencement of this Act by reference to the Statutes of Distribution, shall, unless the contrary thereby appears, be construed as referring to the enactments (other than the Intestates' Estates Act 1890) relating to the distribution of effects of intestates which were in force immediately before the commencement of this Act.

(3)   In subsection (1) of this section the reference to this Part of this Act, or the foregoing provisions of this Part of this Act, shall in relation to an instrument inter vivos made, or a will or codicil coming into operation, after the coming into force of section 18 of the Family Law Reform Act 1987 (but not in relation to instruments inter vivos made or wills or codicils coming into operation earlier) be construed as including references to that section.

51.   Savings

(1)   Nothing in this Part of this Act affects the right of any person to take beneficially, by purchase, as heir either general or special.

(2)   The foregoing provisions of this Part of this Act do not apply to any beneficial interest in real estate (not including chattels real) to which a person of unsound mind or defective living and of full age at the commencement of this Act, and unable, by reason of his incapacity, to make a will, who thereafter dies intestate in respect of such interest without having recovered his testamentary capacity, was entitled at his death, and any such beneficial interest (not being an interest ceasing on his death) shall, without prejudice to any will of the deceased, devolve in accordance with the general law in force before the commencement of this Act applicable to freehold land, and that law shall, notwithstanding any repeal, apply to the case. For the purposes of this subsection, a person of unsound mind or defective who dies intestate as respects any beneficial interest in real estate shall not be deemed to have recovered his testamentary capacity unless his receiver has been discharged.

(3)   Where an infant dies after the commencement of this Act without having been married or having formed a civil partnership, and without issue, and independently of this subsection he would, at his death, have been equitably entitled under a trust or settlement (including a will) to a vested estate in fee simple or absolute interest in freehold land, or in any property to devolve therewith or as freehold land, such infant shall be deemed to have had a life interest, and the trust or settlement shall be construed accordingly.

(4)   ...

52.   Interpretation of Part IV

In this Part of this Act 'real and personal estate' means every beneficial interest (including rights of entry and reverter) of the intestate in real and personal estate which (otherwise than in right of a power of appointment or of the testamentary power conferred by statute to dispose of entailed interests) he could, if of full age and capacity, have disposed of by his will and references (however expressed) to any relationship between two persons shall be construed in accordance with section 1 of the Family Law Reform Act 1987.

PART V
SUPPLEMENTAL

53.   General savings

(1)   Nothing in this Act shall derogate from the powers of the High Court which exist independently of this Act or alter the distribution of business between the several divisions of the High Court, or operate to transfer any jurisdiction from the High Court to any other court.

    ...

54.   Application of Act

Save as otherwise expressly provided, this Act does not apply in any case where the death occurred before the commencement of this Act.

55.   Definitions

In this Act, unless the context otherwise requires, the following expressions have the meanings hereby assigned to them respectively, that is to say:—

(1)   (i)   'Administration' means, with reference to the real and personal estate of a deceased person, letters of administration whether general or limited, or with the will annexed or otherwise:

      (ii)   'Administrator' means a person to whom administration is granted:

      (iii)   'Conveyance' includes a mortgage, charge by way of legal mortgage, lease, assent, vesting, declaration, vesting instrument, disclaimer, release and every other assurance of property or of an interest therein by any instrument, except a will, and 'convey' has a corresponding meaning, and 'disposition' includes a 'conveyance' also a devise bequest and an appointment of property contained in a will, and 'dispose of' has a corresponding meaning:

(iiiA) 'the County Court limit', in relation to any enactment contained in this Act, means the amount for the time being specified by an Order in Council under section 145 of the County Courts Act 1984 as the county court limit for the purposes of that enactment (or, where no such Order in Council has been made, the corresponding limit specified by Order in Council under section 192 of the County Courts Act 1959);

(iv) 'the Court' means the High Court and also the county court, where that court has jurisdiction

(v) 'Income' includes rents and profits:

(vi) 'Intestate' includes a person who leaves a will but dies intestate as to some beneficial interest in his real or personal estate:

(via) 'Land' has the same meaning as in the Law of Property Act 1925;

(vii) 'Legal estates' mean the estates charges and interests in or over land (subsisting or created at law) which are by statute authorised to subsist or to be created at law; and 'equitable interests' mean all other interests and charges in or over land:

(viii) ...

(ix) 'Pecuniary legacy' includes an annuity, a general legacy, a demonstrative legacy so far as it is not discharged out of the designated property, and any other general direction by a testator for the payment of money, including all death duties free from which any devise, bequest, or payment is made to take effect:

(x) 'Personal chattels' means tangible movable property, other than any such property which—

consists of money or securities for money, or

was used at the death of the intestate solely or mainly for business purposes, or

was held at the death of the intestate solely as an investment:

(xi) 'Personal representative' means the executor, original or by representation, or administrator for the time being of a deceased person, and as regards any liability for the payment of death duties includes any person who takes possession of or intermeddles with the property of a deceased person without the authority of the personal representatives or the court, and 'executor' includes a person deemed to be appointed executor as respects settled land:

(xii) 'Possession' includes the receipt of rents and profits or the right to receive the same, if any:

(xiii) 'Prescribed' means prescribed by rules of court:

(xiv) 'Probate' means the probate of a will:

(xv), (xvi) ...

(xvii) 'Property' includes a thing in action and any interest in real or personal property:

(xviii) 'Purchaser' means a lessee, mortgagee, or other person who in good faith acquires an interest in property for valuable consideration, also an intending purchaser and 'valuable consideration' includes marriage, and formation of a civil partnership, but does not include a nominal consideration in money:

(xix) 'Real estate' save as provided in Part IV of this Act means real estate, including chattels real, which by virtue of Part I of this Act devolves on the personal representative of a deceased person:

(xx) 'Representation' means the probate of a will and administration, and the expression 'taking out representation' refers to the obtaining of the probate of a will or of the grant of administration:

(xxi) 'Rent' includes a rent service or a rentcharge, or other rent, toll, duty, or annual or periodical payment in money or money's worth, issuing out of or charged upon land, but does not include mortgage interest; and 'rentcharge' includes a fee farm rent:

(xxii) ...

(xxiii) 'Securities' include stocks, funds, or shares:

(xxiv) 'Tenant for life,' 'statutory owner,' 'settled land,' 'settlement,' 'trustees of the settlement,' 'term of years absolute,' 'death duties,' and 'legal mortgage,' have the same meanings as in the Settled Land Act 1925, and 'entailed interest' and 'charge by way of legal mortgage' have the same meanings as in the Law of Property Act 1925:

(xxv) 'Treasury solicitor' means the solicitor for the affairs of His Majesty's Treasury, and includes the solicitor for the affairs of the Duchy of Lancaster:

(xxvi) 'Trust corporation' means the public trustee or a corporation either appointed by the court in any particular case to be a trustee or entitled by rules made under subsection (3) of section four of the Public Trustee Act 1906, to act as custodian trustee:

(xxvii)...

(xxviii) 'Will' includes codicil.

(2) References to a child or issue living at the death of any person include child or issue en ventre sa mere at the death.

(3) References to the estate of a deceased person include property over which the deceased exercises a general power of appointment (including the statutory power to dispose of entailed interests) by his will.

SCHEDULE 1

PART II
ORDER OF APPLICATION OF ASSETS WHERE THE ESTATE IS SOLVENT

1. Property of the deceased undisposed of by will, subject to the retention thereout of a fund sufficient to meet any pecuniary legacies.

2. Property of the deceased not specifically devised or bequeathed but included (either by a specific or general description) in a residuary gift, subject to the retention out of such property of a fund sufficient to meet any pecuniary legacies, so far as not provided for as aforesaid.

3. Property of the deceased specifically appropriated or devised or bequeathed (either by a specific or general description) for the payment of debts.

4. Property of the deceased charged with, or devised or bequeathed (either by a specific or general description) subject to a charge for the payment of debts.

5. The fund, if any, retained to meet pecuniary legacies.

6. Property specifically devised or bequeathed, rateably according to value,

7. Property appointed by will under a general power, including the statutory power to dispose of entailed interests, rateably according to value.

8. The following provisions shall also apply—
   (a) The order of application may be varied by the will of the deceased.
   (b) ...

LANDLORD AND TENANT ACT 1927
(1927, c. 36)

18. Provisions as to covenants to repair

(1) Damages for a breach of a covenant or agreement to keep or put premises in repair during the currency of a lease, or to leave or put premises in repair at the termination of a lease, whether such covenant or agreement is expressed or implied, and whether general or specific, shall in no case exceed the amount (if any) by which the value of the reversion (whether immediate or not) in the premises is diminished owing to the breach of such covenant or agreement as aforesaid; and in particular no damage shall be recovered for a breach of any such covenant or agreement to leave or put premises in repair at the termination of a lease, if it is shown that the premises, in whatever state of repair they might be, would at or shortly after the termination of the tenancy have been or be pulled down, or such structural alterations made therein as would render valueless the repairs covered by the covenant or agreement.

(2) A right of re-entry or forfeiture for a breach of any such covenant or agreement as aforesaid shall not be enforceable, by action or otherwise, unless the lessor proves that the fact that such a notice as is required by section one hundred and forty-six of the Law of Property Act,1925, had been served on the lessee was known either—
   (a) to the lessee; or
   (b) to an under-lessee holding under an under-lease which reserved a nominal reversion only to the lessee; or

(c) to the person who last paid the rent due under the lease either on his own behalf or as agent for the lessee or under-lessee;

and that a time reasonably sufficient to enable the repairs to be executed had elapsed since the time when the fact of the service of the notice came to the knowledge of any such person.

Where a notice has been sent by registered post addressed to a person at his last known place of abode in the United Kingdom, then, for the purposes of this subsection, that person shall be deemed, unless the contrary is proved, to have had knowledge of the fact that the notice had been served as from the time at which the letter would have been delivered in the ordinary course of post.

This subsection shall be construed as one with section one hundred and forty-six of the Law of Property Act, 1925.

(3) This section applies whether the lease was created before or after the commencement of this Act.

19.   Provisions as to covenants not to assign, etc. without licence or consent

(1) In all leases whether made before or after the commencement of this Act containing a covenant condition or agreement against assigning, under-letting, charging or parting with the possession of demised premises or any part thereof without licence or consent, such covenant condition or agreement shall, notwithstanding any express provision to the contrary, be deemed to be subject—

(a) to a proviso to the effect that such licence or consent is not to be unreasonably withheld, but this proviso does not preclude the right of the landlord to require payment of a reasonable sum in respect of any legal or other expenses incurred in connection with such licence or consent; and

(b) (if the lease is for more than forty years, and is made in consideration wholly or partially of the erection, or the substantial improvement, addition or alteration of buildings, and the lessor is not a Government department or local or public authority, or a statutory or public utility company) to a proviso to the effect that in the case of any assignment, under-letting, charging or parting with the possession (whether by the holders of the lease or any under-tenant whether immediate or not) effected more than seven years before the end of the term no consent or licence shall be required, if notice in writing of the transaction is given to the lessor within six months after the transaction is effected.

(1A) Where the landlord and the tenant under a qualifying lease have entered into an agreement specifying for the purposes of this subsection—

(a) any circumstances in which the landlord may withhold his licence or consent to an assignment of the demised premises or any part of them, or

(b) any conditions subject to which any such licence or consent may be granted,

then the landlord—

(i) shall not be regarded as unreasonably withholding his licence or consent to any such assignment if he withholds it on the ground (and it is the case) that any such circumstances exist, and

(ii) if he gives any such licence or consent subject to any such conditions, shall not be regarded as giving it subject to unreasonable conditions;

and section 1 of the Landlord and Tenant Act 1988 (qualified duty to consent to assignment etc.) shall have effect subject to the provisions of this subsection.

(1B) Subsection (1A) of this section applies to such an agreement as is mentioned in that subsection—

(a) whether it is contained in the lease or not, and

(b) whether it is made at the time when the lease is granted or at any other time falling before the application for the landlord's licence or consent is made.

(1C) Subsection (1A) shall not, however, apply to any such agreement to the extent that any circumstances or conditions specified in it are framed by reference to any matter falling to be determined by the landlord or by any other person for the purposes of the agreement, unless under the terms of the agreement—

(a) that person's power to determine that matter is required to be exercised reasonably, or

(b) the tenant is given an unrestricted right to have any such determination reviewed by a person independent of both landlord and tenant whose identity is ascertainable by reference to the agreement, and in the latter case the agreement provides for the determination made by any such independent person on the review to be conclusive as to the matter in question.

(1D) In its application to a qualifying lease, subsection (1)(b) of this section shall not have effect in relation to any assignment of the lease.

(1E) In subsections (1A) and (1D) of this section—

    (a)   'qualifying lease' means any lease which is a new tenancy for the purposes of section 1 of the Landlord and Tenant (Covenants) Act 1995 other than a residential lease, namely a lease by which a building or part of a building is let wholly or mainly as a single private residence; and

    (b)   references to assignment include parting with possession on assignment.

(2)   In all leases whether made before or after the commencement of this Act containing a covenant condition or agreement against the making of improvements without licence or consent, such covenant condition or agreement shall be deemed, notwithstanding any express provision to the contrary, to be subject to a proviso that such licence or consent is not to be unreasonably withheld; but this proviso does not preclude the right to require as a condition of such licence or consent the payment of a reasonable sum in respect of any damage to or diminution in the value of the premises or any neighbouring premises belonging to the landlord, and of any legal or other expenses properly incurred in connection with such licence or consent nor, in the case of an improvement which does not add to the letting value of the holding, does it preclude the right to require as a condition of such licence or consent, where such a requirement would be reasonable, an undertaking on the part of the tenant to reinstate the premises in the condition in which they were before the improvement was executed.

(3)   In all leases whether made before or after the commencement of this Act containing a covenant condition or agreement against the alteration of the user of the demised premises, without licence or consent, such covenant condition or agreement shall, if the alteration does not involve any structural alteration of the premises, be deemed, notwithstanding any express provision to the contrary, to be subject to a proviso that no fine or sum of money in the nature of a fine, whether by way of increase of rent or otherwise, shall be payable for or in respect of such licence or consent; but this proviso does not preclude the right of the landlord to require payment of a reasonable sum in respect of any damage to or diminution in the value of the premises or any neighbouring premises belonging to him and of any legal or other expenses incurred in connection with such licence or consent.

Where a dispute as to the reasonableness of any such sum has been determined by a court of competent jurisdiction, the landlord shall be bound to grant the licence or consent on payment of the sum so determined to be reasonable.

(4)   This section shall not apply to leases of agricultural holdings within the meaning of the Agricultural Holdings Act 1986 which are leases in relation to which that Act applies, or to farm business tenancies within the meaning of the Agricultural Tenancies Act 1995, and paragraph (b) of subsection (1), subsection (2) and subsection (3) of this section shall not apply to mining leases.

LEASEHOLD PROPERTY (REPAIRS) ACT 1938
(1938, c. 34)

1.   Restriction on enforcement of repairing covenants in long leases of small houses

(1)   Where a lessor serves on a lessee under sub-section (1) of section one hundred and forty-six of the Law of Property Act, 1925, a notice that relates to a breach of a covenant or agreement to keep or put in repair during the currency of the lease all or any of the property comprised in the lease, and at the date of the service of the notice three years or more of the term of the lease remain unexpired, the lessee may within twenty-eight days from that date serve on the lessor a counter-notice to the effect that he claims the benefit of this Act.

(2)   A right to damages for a breach of such a covenant as aforesaid shall not be enforceable by action commenced at any time at which three years or more of the term of the lease

remain unexpired unless the lessor has served on the lessee not less than one month before the commencement of the action such a notice as is specified in subsection (1) of section one hundred and forty-six of the Law of Property Act, 1925, and where a notice is served under this subsection, the lessee may, within twenty-eight days from the date of the service thereof, serve on the lessor a counter-notice to the effect that he claims the benefit of this Act.

(3)   Where a counter-notice is served by a lessee under this section, then, notwithstanding anything in any enactment or rule of law, no proceedings, by action or otherwise, shall be taken by the lessor for the enforcement of any right of re-entry or forfeiture under any proviso or stipulation in the lease for breach of the covenant or agreement in question, or for damages for breach thereof, otherwise than with the leave of the court.

(4)   A notice served under subsection (1) of section one hundred and forty-six of the Law of Property Act, 1925, in the circumstances specified in subsection (1) of this section, and a notice served under subsection (2) of this section shall not be valid unless it contains a statement, in characters not less conspicuous than those used in any other part of the notice, to the effect that the lessee is entitled under this Act to serve on the lessor a counter-notice claiming the benefit of this Act, and a statement in the like characters specifying the time within which, and the manner in which, under this Act a counter-notice may be served and specifying the name and address for service of the lessor.

(5)   Leave for the purposes of this section shall not be given unless the lessor proves—
   (a)   that the immediate remedying of the breach in question is requisite for preventing substantial diminution in the value of his reversion, or that the value thereof has been substantially diminished by the breach;
   (b)   that the immediate remedying of the breach is required for giving effect in relation to the premises to the purposes of any enactment, or of any byelaw or other provision having effect under an enactment, or for giving effect to any order of a court or requirement of any authority under any enactment or any such byelaw or other provision as aforesaid;
   (c)   in a case in which the lessee is not in occupation of the whole of the premises as respects which the covenant or agreement is proposed to be enforced, that the immediate remedying of the breach is required in the interests of the occupier of those premises or of part thereof;
   (d)   that the breach can be immediately remedied at an expense that is relatively small in comparison with the much greater expense that would probably be occasioned by postponement of the necessary work; or
   (e)   special circumstances which in the opinion of the court, render it just and equitable that leave should be given.

(6)   The court may, in granting or in refusing leave for the purposes of this section, impose such terms and conditions on the lessor or on the lessee as it may think fit.

3.   Saving for obligation to repair on taking possession

This Act shall not apply to a breach of a covenant or agreement in so far as it imposes on the lessee an obligation to put premises in repair that is to be performed upon the lessee taking possession of the premises or within a reasonable time thereafter.

7.   Application of certain provisions of 15 and 16 Geo 5 c 20

(1)   In this Act the expressions 'lessor', 'lessee' and 'lease' have the meanings assigned to them respectively by sections one hundred and forty-six and one hundred and fifty-four of the Law of Property Act, 1925, except that they do not include any reference to such a grant as is mentioned in the said section one hundred and forty-six, or to the person making, or to the grantee under such a grant, or to persons deriving title under such a person; and 'lease' means a lease for a term of seven years or more, not being a lease of an agricultural holding within the meaning of the Agricultural Holdings Act 1986 which is a lease in relation to which that Act applies and not being a farm business tenancy within the meaning of the Agricultural Tenancies Act 1995.

(2)   The provisions of section one hundred and ninety-six of the said Act (which relate to the service of notices) shall extend to notices and counter-notices required or authorised by this Act.

INTESTATES' ESTATES ACT 1952
(1952, c. 64)

PART I
AMENDMENTS OF LAW OF INTESTATE SUCCESSION

5.   **Rights of surviving spouse or civil partner as respects the matrimonial or civil partnership home**

The Second Schedule to this Act shall have effect for enabling the surviving spouse or civil partner of a person dying intestate after the commencement of this Act to acquire the matrimonial or civil partnership home.

SCHEDULE 2

RIGHTS OF SURVIVING SPOUSE OR CIVIL PARTNER AS RESPECTS THE MATRIMONIAL OR CIVIL PARTNERSHIP HOME

1.   (1)   Subject to the provisions of this Schedule, where the residuary estate of the intestate comprises of interest in a dwelling-house in which the surviving spouse or civil partner was resident at the time of the intestate's death, the surviving spouse or civil partner may require the personal representative in exercise of the power conferred by section forty-one of the principal Act (and with due regard to the requirements of that section as to valuation) to appropriate the said interest in the dwelling-house in or towards satisfaction of any absolute interest of the surviving spouse or civil partner in the real and personal estate of the intestate.

        (2)   The right conferred by this paragraph shall not be exercisable where the interest is—
        (a)   a tenancy which at the date of the death of the intestate was a tenancy which would determine within the period of two years from that date; or
        (b)   a tenancy which the landlord by notice given for that date could determine within the remainder of that period.

        (3)   Nothing in subsection (5) of section forty-one of the principal Act (which requires the personal representative, in making an appropriation to any person under that section, to have regard to the rights of others) shall prevent the personal representative from giving effect to the right conferred by this paragraph.

        (4)   ...

        (5)   Where part of a building was, at the date of the death of the intestate, occupied as a separate dwelling, that dwelling shall for the purposes of this Schedule be treated as a dwelling-house.

2.   Where—
        (a)   the dwelling-house forms part of a building and an interest in the whole of the building is comprised in the residuary estate; or
        (b)   the dwelling-house is held with agricultural land and an interest in the agricultural land is comprised in the residuary estate; or
        (c)   the whole or part of the dwelling-house was at the time of the intestate's death used as a hotel or lodging house; or
        (d)   a part of the dwelling-house was at the time of the intestate's death used for purposes other than domestic purposes,
        the right conferred by paragraph 1 of this Schedule shall not be exercisable unless the court, on being satisfied that the exercise of that right is not likely to diminish the value of assets in the residuary estate (other than the said interest in the dwelling-house) or make them more difficult to dispose of, so orders.

3.   (1)   The right conferred by paragraph 1 of this Schedule
        (a)   shall not be exercisable after the expiration of twelve months from the first taking out of representation with respect to the intestate's estate;
        (b)   shall not be exercisable after the death of the surviving spouse or civil partner;
        (c)   shall be exercisable, except where the surviving spouse or civil partner is the sole personal representative, by notifying the personal representative (or, where there are two or more personal representatives of whom one is the surviving spouse or civil partner, all of them except the surviving spouse or civil partner) in writing.

(2)   A notification in writing under paragraph (c) of the foregoing sub-paragraph shall not be revocable except with the consent of the personal representative; but the surviving spouse or civil partner may require the personal representative to have the said interest in the dwelling-house valued in accordance with section forty-one of the principal Act and to inform him or her of the result of that valuation before he or she decides whether to exercise the right.

(3)   The court may extend the period of 12 months referred to in sub-paragraph (1)(a) if the surviving spouse or civil partner applies for it to be extended and satisfies the court that a period limited to 12 months would operate unfairly—

    (a)   in consequence of the representation first taken out being probate of a will subsequently revoked on the ground that the will was invalid, or

    (b)   in consequence of a question whether a person had an interest in the estate, or as to the nature of an interest in the estate, not having been determined at the time when representation was first taken out, or

    (c)   in consequence of some other circumstances affecting the administration or distribution of the estate.

(4)   For the purposes of the construction of the references in this paragraph to the first taking out of representation, there shall be left out of account—

    (a)   a grant limited to settled land or to trust property,

    (b)   any other grant that does not permit any of the estate to be distributed,

    (c)   a grant limited to real estate or to personal estate, unless a grant limited to the remainder of the estate has previously been made or is made at the same time,

    (d)   a grant, or its equivalent, made outside the United Kingdom (but see sub-paragraph (5)).

(5)   A grant sealed under section 2 of the Colonial Probates Act 1892 counts as a grant made in the United Kingdom for the purposes of sub-paragraph (4), but is to be taken as dated on the date of sealing.

4.   (1)   During the period of twelve months mentioned in paragraph 3 of this Schedule the personal representative shall not without the written consent of the surviving spouse or civil partner sell or otherwise dispose of the said interest in the dwelling-house except in the course of administration owing to want of other assets.

    (2)   An application to the court under paragraph 2 of this Schedule may be made by the personal representative as well as by the surviving spouse or civil partner, and if, on an application under that paragraph, the court does not order that the right conferred by paragraph 1 of this Schedule shall be exercisable by the surviving spouse or civil partner, the court may authorise the personal representative to dispose of the said interest in the dwelling-house within the said period of twelve months.

    (3)   Where the court under sub-paragraph (3) of paragraph 3 of this Schedule extends the said period of twelve months, the court may direct that this paragraph shall apply in relation to the extended period as it applied in relation to the original period of twelve months.

    (4)   This paragraph shall not apply where the surviving spouse or civil partner is the sole personal representative or one of two or more personal representatives.

    (5)   Nothing in this paragraph shall confer any right on the surviving spouse or civil partner as against a purchaser from the personal representative.

5.   (1)   Where the surviving spouse or civil partner is one of two or more personal representatives, the rule that a trustee may not be a purchaser of trust property shall not prevent the surviving spouse or civil partner from purchasing out of the estate of the intestate an interest in a dwelling-house in which the surviving spouse or civil partner was resident at the time of the intestate's death.

    (2)   The power of appropriation under section forty-one of the principal Act shall include power to appropriate an interest in a dwelling-house in which the surviving spouse or civil partner was resident at the time of the intestate's death partly in satisfaction of an interest of the surviving spouse or civil partner in the real and personal estate of the intestate and partly in return for a payment of money by the surviving spouse or civil partner to the personal representative.

6.   (1)   Where the surviving spouse or civil partner lacks capacity (within the meaning of the Mental Capacity Act 2005) to make a requirement or give a consent under this Schedule, the requirement or consent may be made or given by a deputy appointed by the Court of Protection with power in that respect or, if no deputy has that power, by that court.

(2) A requirement or consent made or given under this Schedule by a surviving spouse or civil partner who is an infant shall be as valid and binding as it would be if he or she were of age, and, as respects an appropriation in pursuance of paragraph 1 of this Schedule, the provisions of section forty-one of the principal Act as to obtaining the consent of the infant's parent or guardian, or of the court on behalf of the infant, shall not apply.

7. (1) Except where the context otherwise requires, references in this Schedule to a dwelling-house include references to any garden or portion of ground attached to and usually occupied with the dwelling-house or otherwise required for the amenity or convenience of the dwelling-house.

(2) This Schedule shall be construed as one with Part IV of the principal Act.

LANDLORD AND TENANT ACT 1954
(1954, c. 56)

PART II
SECURITY OF TENURE FOR BUSINESS, PROFESSIONAL AND OTHER TENANTS

Tenancies to which Part II applies

23. Tenancies to which Part II applies

(1) Subject to the provisions of this Act, this Part of this Act applies to any tenancy where the property comprised in the tenancy is or includes premises which are occupied by the tenant and are so occupied for the purposes of a business carried on by him or for those and other purposes.

(1A) Occupation or the carrying on of a business—

(a) by a company in which the tenant has a controlling interest; or

(b) where the tenant is a company, by a person with a controlling interest in the company,

shall be treated for the purposes of this section as equivalent to occupation or, as the case may be, the carrying on of a business by the tenant.

(1B) Accordingly references (however expressed) in this Part of this Act to the business of, or to use, occupation or enjoyment by, the tenant shall be construed as including references to the business of, or to use, occupation or enjoyment by, a company falling within subsection (1A)(a) above or a person falling within subsection (1A)(b) above.

(2) In this Part of this Act the expression 'business' includes a trade, profession or employment and includes any activity carried on by a body of persons, whether corporate or unincorporate.

(3) In the following provisions of this Part of this Act the expression 'the holding', in relation to a tenancy to which this Part of this Act applies, means the property comprised in the tenancy, there being excluded any part thereof which is occupied neither by the tenant nor by a person employed by the tenant and so employed for the purposes of a business by reason of which the tenancy is one to which this Part of this Act applies.

(4) Subject to subsection (5), where the tenant is carrying on a business, in all or any part of the property comprised in a tenancy, in breach of a prohibition (however expressed) of use for business purposes which subsists under the terms of the tenancy and extends to the whole of that property, this Part of this Act shall not apply to the tenancy unless the immediate landlord or his predecessor in title has consented to the breach or the immediate landlord has acquiesced therein.

In this subsection the reference to a prohibition of use for business purposes does not include a prohibition of use for the purposes of a specified business, or of use for purposes of any but a specified business, but save as aforesaid includes a prohibition of use for the purposes of some one or more only of the classes of business specified in the definition of that expression in subsection (2) of this section.

(5) Where the tenant's breach of a prohibition (however expressed) of use for business purposes which subsists under the terms of the tenancy and extends to the whole of the property consists solely of carrying on a home business, this Part of this Act does not apply to the tenancy, even if the immediate landlord or the immediate landlord's predecessor in title has consented to the breach or the immediate landlord has acquiesced in the breach.

(6) In subsection (5) 'home business' has the same meaning as in section 43ZA.

Continuation and renewal of tenancies

24. Continuation of tenancies to which Part II applies and grant of new tenancies

(1)   A tenancy to which this Part of this Act applies shall not come to an end unless terminated in accordance with the provisions of this Part of this Act; and, subject to the following provisions of this Act either the tenant or the landlord under such a tenancy may apply to the court for an order for the grant of a new tenancy—

(a)   if the landlord has given notice under section 25 of this Act to terminate the tenancy, or

(b)   if the tenant has made a request for a new tenancy in accordance with section 26 of this Act.

(2)   The last foregoing subsection shall not prevent the coming to an end of a tenancy by notice to quit given by the tenant, by surrender or forfeiture, or by the forfeiture of a superior tenancy unless—

(a)   in the case of a notice to quit, the notice was given before the tenant had been in occupation in right of the tenancy for one month; ...

(b)   ...

(2A) Neither the tenant nor the landlord may make an application under subsection (1) above if the other has made such an application and the application has been served.

(2B) Neither the tenant nor the landlord may make such an application if the landlord has made an application under section 29(2) of this Act and the application has been served.

(2C) The landlord may not withdraw an application under subsection (1) above unless the tenant consents to its withdrawal.

(3)   Notwithstanding anything in subsection (1) of this section,—

(a)   where a tenancy to which this Part of this Act applies ceases to be such a tenancy, it shall not come to an end by reason only of the cesser, but if it was granted for a term of years certain and has been continued by subsection (1) of this section then (without prejudice to the termination thereof in accordance with any terms of the tenancy) it may be terminated by not less than three nor more than six months' notice in writing given by the landlord to the tenant;

(b)   where, at a time when a tenancy is not one to which this Part of this Act applies, the landlord gives notice to quit, the operation of the notice shall not be affected by reason that the tenancy becomes one to which this Part of this Act applies after the giving of the notice.

24A. Applications for determination of interim rent while tenancy continues

(1)   Subject to subsection (2) below, if—

(a)   the landlord of a tenancy to which this Part of this Act applies has given notice under section 25 of this Act to terminate the tenancy; or

(b)   the tenant of such a tenancy has made a request for a new tenancy in accordance with section 26 of this Act,

either of them may make an application to the court to determine a rent (an 'interim rent') which the tenant is to pay while the tenancy ('the relevant tenancy') continues by virtue of section 24 of this Act and the court may order payment of an interim rent in accordance with section 24C or 24D of this Act.

(2)   Neither the tenant nor the landlord may make an application under subsection (1) above if the other has made such an application and has not withdrawn it.

(3)   No application shall be entertained under subsection (1) above if it is made more than six months after the termination of the relevant tenancy.

24B. Date from which interim rent is payable

(1)   The interim rent determined on an application under section 24A(1) of this Act shall be payable from the appropriate date.

(2)   If an application under section 24A(1) of this Act is made in a case where the landlord has given a notice under section 25 of this Act, the appropriate date is the earliest date of termination that could have been specified in the landlord's notice.

(3)   If an application under section 24A(1) of this Act is made in a case where the tenant has made a request for a new tenancy under section 26 of this Act, the appropriate date is the earliest date that could have been specified in the tenant's request as the date from which the new tenancy is to begin.

24C. **Amount of interim rent where new tenancy of whole premises granted and landlord not opposed**

(1)   This section applies where—

(a)   the landlord gave a notice under section 25 of this Act at a time when the tenant was in occupation of the whole of the property comprised in the relevant tenancy for purposes such as are mentioned in section 23(1) of this Act and stated in the notice that he was not opposed to the grant of a new tenancy; or

(b)   the tenant made a request for a new tenancy under section 26 of this Act at a time when he was in occupation of the whole of that property for such purposes and the landlord did not give notice under subsection (6) of that section,

and the landlord grants a new tenancy of the whole of the property comprised in the relevant tenancy to the tenant (whether as a result of an order for the grant of a new tenancy or otherwise).

(2)   Subject to the following provisions of this section, the rent payable under and at the commencement of the new tenancy shall also be the interim rent.

(3)   Subsection (2) above does not apply where—

(a)   the landlord or the tenant shows to the satisfaction of the court that the interim rent under that subsection differs substantially from the relevant rent; or

(b)   the landlord or the tenant shows to the satisfaction of the court that the terms of the new tenancy differ from the terms of the relevant tenancy to such an extent that the interim rent under that subsection is substantially different from the rent which (in default of such agreement) the court would have determined under section 34 of this Act to be payable under a tenancy which commenced on the same day as the new tenancy and whose other terms were the same as the relevant tenancy.

(4)   In this section 'the relevant rent' means the rent which (in default of agreement between the landlord and the tenant) the court would have determined under section 34 of this Act to be payable under the new tenancy if the new tenancy had commenced on the appropriate date (within the meaning of section 24B of this Act).

(5)   The interim rent in a case where subsection (2) above does not apply by virtue only of subsection (3)(a) above is the relevant rent.

(6)   The interim rent in a case where subsection (2) above does not apply by virtue only of subsection (3)(b) above, or by virtue of subsection (3)(a) and (b) above, is the rent which it is reasonable for the tenant to pay while the relevant tenancy continues by virtue of section 24 of this Act.

(7)   In determining the interim rent under subsection (6) above the court shall have regard—

(a)   to the rent payable under the terms of the relevant tenancy; and

(b)   to the rent payable under any sub-tenancy of part of the property comprised in the relevant tenancy,

but otherwise subsections (1) and (2) of section 34 of this Act shall apply to the determination as they would apply to the determination of a rent under that section if a new tenancy of the whole of the property comprised in the relevant tenancy were granted to the tenant by order of the court and the duration of that new tenancy were the same as the duration of the new tenancy which is actually granted to the tenant.

(8)   In this section and section 24D of this Act 'the relevant tenancy' has the same meaning as in section 24A of this Act.

24D. **Amount of interim rent in any other case**

(1)   The interim rent in a case where section 24C of this Act does not apply is the rent which it is reasonable for the tenant to pay while the relevant tenancy continues by virtue of section 24 of this Act.

(2)   In determining the interim rent under subsection (1) above the court shall have regard—

(a)   to the rent payable under the terms of the relevant tenancy; and

(b)   to the rent payable under any sub-tenancy of part of the property comprised in the relevant tenancy,

but otherwise subsections (1) and (2) of section 34 of this Act shall apply to the determination as they would apply to the determination of a rent under that section if a new tenancy from year to year of the whole of the property comprised in the relevant tenancy were granted to the tenant by order of the court.

(3)   If the court—

(a)   has made an order for the grant of a new tenancy and has ordered payment of interim rent in accordance with section 24C of this Act, but

    (b)   either—
        (i)   it subsequently revokes under section 36(2) of this Act the order for the grant of a new tenancy; or
        (ii)   the landlord and tenant agree not to act on the order,

the court on the application of the landlord or the tenant shall determine a new interim rent in accordance with subsections (1) and (2) above without a further application under section 24A(1) of this Act.

25.   Termination of tenancy by the landlord

(1)   The landlord may terminate a tenancy to which this Part of this Act applies by a notice given to the tenant in the prescribed form specifying the date at which the tenancy is to come to an end (hereinafter referred to as 'the date of termination'):

Provided that this subsection has effect subject to the provisions of section 29B(4) of this Act and the provisions of Part IV of this Act as to the interim continuation of tenancies pending the disposal of applications to the court.

(2)   Subject to the provisions of the next following subsection, a notice under this section shall not have effect unless it is given not more than twelve nor less than six months before the date of termination specified therein.

(3)   In the case of a tenancy which apart from this Act could have been brought to an end by notice to quit given by the landlord—

    (a)   the date of termination specified in a notice under this section shall not be earlier than the earliest date on which apart from this Part of this Act the tenancy could have been brought to an end by notice to quit given by the landlord on the date of the giving of the notice under this section; and

    (b)   where apart from this Part of this Act more than six months' notice to quit would have been required to bring the tenancy to an end, the last foregoing subsection shall have effect with the substitution for twelve months of a period six months longer than the length of notice to quit which would have been required as aforesaid.

(4)   In the case of any other tenancy, a notice under this section shall not specify a date of termination earlier than the date on which apart from this Part of this Act the tenancy would have come to an end by effluxion of time.

(5)   ...

(6)   A notice under this section shall not have effect unless it states whether the landlord is opposed to the grant of a new tenancy to the tenant.

(7)   A notice under this section which states that the landlord is opposed to the grant of a new tenancy to the tenant shall not have effect unless it also specifies one or more of the grounds specified in section 30(1) of this Act as the ground or grounds for his opposition.

(8)   A notice under this section which states that the landlord is not opposed to the grant of a new tenancy to the tenant shall not have effect unless it sets out the landlord's proposals as to—

    (a)   the property to be comprised in the new tenancy (being either the whole or part of the property comprised in the current tenancy);

    (b)   the rent to be payable under the new tenancy; and

    (c)   the other terms of the new tenancy.

26.   Tenant's request for a new tenancy

(1)   A tenant's request for a new tenancy may be made where the current tenancy is a tenancy granted for a term of years certain exceeding one year, whether or not continued by section twenty-four of this Act, or granted for a term of years certain and thereafter from year to year.

(2)   A tenant's request for a new tenancy shall be for a tenancy beginning with such date, not more than twelve nor less than six months after the making of the request, as may be specified therein:

Provided that the said date shall not be earlier than the date on which apart from this Act the current tenancy would come to an end by effluxion of time or could be brought to an end by notice to quit given by the tenant.

(3)   A tenant's request for a new tenancy shall not have effect unless it is made by notice in the prescribed form given to the landlord and sets out the tenant's proposals as to the property to be comprised in the new tenancy (being either the whole or part of the property comprised in the current tenancy), as to the rent to be payable under the new tenancy and as to the other terms of the new tenancy.

(4)   A tenant's request for a new tenancy shall not be made if the landlord has already given notice under the last foregoing section to terminate the current tenancy, or if the tenant has already given notice to quit or notice under the next following section; and no such notice shall be given by the landlord or the tenant after the making by the tenant of a request for a new tenancy.

(5)   Where the tenant makes a request for a new tenancy in accordance with the foregoing provisions of this section, the current tenancy shall, subject to the provisions of sections 29B(4) and 36(2) of this Act and the provisions of Part IV of this Act as to the interim continuation of tenancies, terminate immediately before the date specified in the request for the beginning of the new tenancy.

(6)   Within two months of the making of a tenant's request for a new tenancy the landlord may give notice to the tenant that he will oppose an application to the court for the grant of a new tenancy, and any such notice shall state on which of the grounds mentioned in section thirty of this Act the landlord will oppose the application.

27.   Termination by tenant of tenancy for fixed term

(1)   Where the tenant under a tenancy to which this Part of this Act applies, being a tenancy granted for a term of years certain, gives to the immediate landlord, not later than three months before the date on which apart from this Act the tenancy would come to an end by effluxion of time, a notice in writing that the tenant does not desire the tenancy to be continued, section twenty-four of this Act shall not have effect in relation to the tenancy unless the notice is given before the tenant has been in occupation in right of the tenancy for one month.

(1A) Section 24 of this Act shall not have effect in relation to a tenancy for a term of years certain where the tenant is not in occupation of the property comprised in the tenancy at the time when, apart from this Act, the tenancy would come to an end by effluxion of time.

(2)   A tenancy granted for a term of years certain which is continuing by virtue of section twenty-four of this Act shall not come to an end by reason only of the tenant ceasing to occupy the property comprised in the tenancy but may be brought to an end on any day by not less than three months' notice in writing given by the tenant to the immediate landlord, whether the notice is given after the date on which apart from this Act the tenancy would have come to an end or before that date, but not before the tenant has been in occupation in right of the tenancy for one month.

(3)   Where a tenancy is terminated under subsection (2) above, any rent payable in respect of a period which begins before, and ends after, the tenancy is terminated shall be apportioned, and any rent paid by the tenant in excess of the amount apportioned to the period before termination shall be recoverable by him.

28.   Renewal of tenancies by agreement

Where the landlord and tenant agree for the grant to the tenant of a future tenancy of the holding, or of the holding with other land, on terms and from a date specified in the agreement, the current tenancy shall continue until that date but no longer, and shall not be a tenancy to which this Part of this Act applies.

Applications to court

29.   Order by court for grant of new tenancy or termination of current tenancy

(1)   Subject to the provisions of this Act, on an application under section 24(1) of this Act, the court shall make an order for the grant of a new tenancy and accordingly for the termination of the current tenancy immediately before the commencement of the new tenancy.

(2)   Subject to the following provisions of this Act, a landlord may apply to the court for an order for the termination of a tenancy to which this Part of this Act applies without the grant of a new tenancy—

    (a)   if he has given notice under section 25 of this Act that he is opposed to the grant of a new tenancy to the tenant; or

    (b)   if the tenant has made a request for a new tenancy in accordance with section 26 of this Act and the landlord has given notice under subsection (6) of that section.

(3)   The landlord may not make an application under subsection (2) above if either the tenant or the landlord has made an application under section 24(1) of this Act.

(4)   Subject to the provisions of this Act, where the landlord makes an application under subsection (2) above—

     (a)   if he establishes, to the satisfaction of the court, any of the grounds on which he is entitled to make the application in accordance with section 30 of this Act, the court shall make an order for the termination of the current tenancy in accordance with section 64 of this Act without the grant of a new tenancy; and

     (b)   if not, it shall make an order for the grant of a new tenancy and accordingly for the termination of the current tenancy immediately before the commencement of the new tenancy.

(5)   The court shall dismiss an application by the landlord under section 24(1) of this Act if the tenant informs the court that he does not want a new tenancy.

(6)   The landlord may not withdraw an application under subsection (2) above unless the tenant consents to its withdrawal.

29A.   Time limits for applications to court

(1)   Subject to section 29B of this Act, the court shall not entertain an application—

     (a)   by the tenant or the landlord under section 24(1) of this Act; or

     (b)   by the landlord under section 29(2) of this Act, if it is made after the end of the statutory period.

(2)   In this section and section 29B of this Act 'the statutory period' means a period ending—

     (a)   where the landlord gave a notice under section 25 of this Act, on the date specified in his notice; and

     (b)   where the tenant made a request for a new tenancy under section 26 of this Act, immediately before the date specified in his request.

(3)   Where the tenant has made a request for a new tenancy under section 26 of this Act, the court shall not entertain an application under section 24(1) of this Act which is made before the end of the period of two months beginning with the date of the making of the request, unless the application is made after the landlord has given a notice under section 26(6) of this Act.

29B.   Agreements extending time limits

(1)   After the landlord has given a notice under section 25 of this Act, or the tenant has made a request under section 26 of this Act, but before the end of the statutory period, the landlord and tenant may agree that an application such as is mentioned in section 29A(1) of this Act, may be made before the end of a period specified in the agreement which will expire after the end of the statutory period.

(2)   The landlord and tenant may from time to time by agreement further extend the period for making such an application, but any such agreement must be made before the end of the period specified in the current agreement.

(3)   Where an agreement is made under this section, the court may entertain an application such as is mentioned in section 29A(1) of this Act if it is made before the end of the period specified in the agreement.

(4)   Where an agreement is made under this section, or two or more agreements are made under this section, the landlord's notice under section 25 of this Act or tenant's request under section 26 of this Act shall be treated as terminating the tenancy at the end of the period specified in the agreement or, as the case may be, at the end of the period specified in the last of those agreements.

30.   Opposition by landlord to application for a new tenancy

(1)   The grounds on which a landlord may oppose an application under section 24(1) of this Act, or make an application under section 29(2) of this Act, are such of the following grounds as may be stated in the landlord's notice under section twenty-five of this Act or, as the case may be, under subsection (6) of section twenty-six thereof, that is to say: —

     (a)   where under the current tenancy the tenant has any obligations as respects the repair and maintenance of the holding, that the tenant ought not to be granted a new tenancy in view of the state of repair of the holding, being a state resulting from the tenant's failure to comply with the said obligations;

(b)   that the tenant ought not to be granted a new tenancy in view of his persistent delay in paying rent which has become due;

(c)   that the tenant ought not to be granted a new tenancy in view of other substantial breaches by him of his obligations under the current tenancy, or for any other reason connected with the tenant's use or management of the holding;

(d)   that the landlord has offered and is willing to provide or secure the provision of alternative accommodation for the tenant, that the terms on which the alternative accommodation is available are reasonable having regard to the terms of the current tenancy and to all other relevant circumstances, and that the accommodation and the time at which it will be available are suitable for the tenant's requirements (including the requirement to preserve goodwill) having regard to the nature and class of his business and to the situation and extent of, and facilities afforded by, the holding;

(e)   where the current tenancy was created by the sub-letting of part only of the property comprised in a superior tenancy and the landlord is the owner of an interest in reversion expectant on the termination of that superior tenancy, that the aggregate of the rents reasonably obtainable on separate lettings of the holding and the remainder of that property would be substantially less than the rent reasonably obtainable on a letting of that property as a whole, that on the termination of the current tenancy the landlord requires possession of the holding for the purpose of letting or otherwise disposing of the said property as a whole, and that in view thereof the tenant ought not to be granted a new tenancy;

(f)   that on the termination of the current tenancy the landlord intends to demolish or reconstruct the premises comprised in the holding or a substantial part of those premises or to carry out substantial work of construction on the holding or part thereof and that he could not reasonably do so without obtaining possession of the holding;

(g)   subject as hereinafter provided, that on the termination of the current tenancy the landlord intends to occupy the holding for the purposes, or partly for the purposes, of a business to be carried on by him therein, or as his residence.

(1A) Where the landlord has a controlling interest in a company, the reference in subsection (1)(g) above to the landlord shall be construed as a reference to the landlord or that company.

(1B) Subject to subsection (2A) below, where the landlord is a company and a person has a controlling interest in the company, the reference in subsection (1)(g) above to the landlord shall be construed as a reference to the landlord or that person.

(2)   The landlord shall not be entitled to oppose an application under section 24(1) of this Act, or make an application under section 29(2) of this Act, on the ground specified in paragraph (g) of the last foregoing subsection if the interest of the landlord, or an interest which has merged in that interest and but for the merger would be the interest of the landlord, was purchased or created after the beginning of the period of five years which ends with the termination of the current tenancy, and at all times since the purchase or creation thereof the holding has been comprised in a tenancy or successive tenancies of the description specified in subsection (1) of section twenty-three of this Act.

(2A) Subsection (1B) above shall not apply if the controlling interest was acquired after the beginning of the period of five years which ends with the termination of the current tenancy, and at all times since the acquisition of the controlling interest the holding has been comprised in a tenancy or successive tenancies of the description specified in section 23(1) of this Act.

31.   Dismissal of application for new tenancy where landlord successfully opposes

(1)   If the landlord opposes an application under subsection (1) of section twenty-four of this Act on grounds on which he is entitled to oppose it in accordance with the last foregoing section and establishes any of those grounds to the satisfaction of the court, the court shall not make an order for the grant of a new tenancy.

(2)   Where the landlord opposes an application under section 24(1) of this Act, or makes an application under section 29(2) of this Act, on one or more of the grounds specified in section 30(1)(d) to (f) of this Act but establishes none of those grounds, and none of the other grounds specified in section 30(1) of this Act, to the satisfaction of the court, then

if the court would have been satisfied on any of the grounds specified in section 30(1)(d) to (f) of this Act if the date of termination specified in the landlord's notice or, as the case may be, the date specified in the tenant's request for a new tenancy as the date from which the new tenancy is to begin, had been such later date as the court may determine, being a date not more than one year later than the date so specified, —

(a)   the court shall make a declaration to that effect, stating of which of the said grounds the court would have been satisfied as aforesaid and specifying the date determined by the court as aforesaid, but shall not make an order for the grant of a new tenancy;

(b)   if, within fourteen days after the making of the declaration, the tenant so requires the court shall make an order substituting the said date for the date specified in the said landlord's notice or tenant's request, and thereupon that notice or request shall have effect accordingly.

31A.   Grant of new tenancy in some cases where section 30(1)(f) applies

(1)   Where the landlord opposes an application under section 24(1) of this Act on the ground specified in paragraph (f) of section 30(1) of this Act, or makes an application under section 29(2) of this Act on that ground, the court shall not hold that the landlord could not reasonably carry out the demolition, reconstruction or work of construction intended without obtaining possession of the holding if—

(a)   the tenant agrees to the inclusion in the terms of the new tenancy of terms giving the landlord access and other facilities for carrying out the work intended and, given that access and those facilities, the landlord could reasonably carry out the work without obtaining possession of the holding and without interfering to a substantial extent or for a substantial time with the use of the holding for the purposes of the business carried on by the tenant; or

(b)   the tenant is willing to accept a tenancy of an economically separable part of the holding and either paragraph (a) of this section is satisfied with respect to that part or possession of the remainder of the holding would be reasonably sufficient to enable the landlord to carry out the intended work.

(2)   For the purposes of subsection (1)(b) of this section a part of a holding shall be deemed to be an economically separable part if, and only if, the aggregate of the rents which, after the completion of the intended work, would be reasonably obtainable on separate lettings of that part and the remainder of the premises affected by or resulting from the work would not be substantially less than the rent which would then be reasonably obtainable on a letting of those premises as a whole.

32.   Property to be comprised in new tenancy

(1)   Subject to the following provisions of this section, an order under section twenty-nine of this Act for the grant of a new tenancy shall be an order for the grant of a new tenancy of the holding; and in the absence of agreement between the landlord and the tenant as to the property which constitutes the holding the court shall in the order designate that property by reference to the circumstances existing at the date of the order.

(1A) Where the court, by virtue of paragraph (b) of section 31A(1) of this Act, makes an order under section 29 of this Act for the grant of a new tenancy in a case where the tenant is willing to accept a tenancy of part of the holding, the order shall be an order for the grant of a new tenancy of that part only.

(2)   The foregoing provisions of this section shall not apply in a case where the property comprised in the current tenancy includes other property besides the holding and the landlord requires any new tenancy ordered to be granted under section twenty-nine of this Act to be a tenancy of the whole of the property comprised in the current tenancy; but in any such case—

(a)   any order under the said section twenty-nine for the grant of a new tenancy shall be an order for the grant of a new tenancy of the whole of the property comprised in the current tenancy, and

(b)   references in the following provisions of this Part of this Act to the holding shall be construed as references to the whole of that property.

(3)   Where the current tenancy includes rights enjoyed by the tenant in connection with the holding, those rights shall be included in a tenancy ordered to be granted under section twenty-nine of this Act except as otherwise agreed between the landlord and the tenant or, in default of such agreement, determined by the court.

33.   Duration of new tenancy

Where on an application under this Part of this Act the court makes an order for the grant of a new tenancy, the new tenancy shall be such tenancy as may be agreed between the landlord and the tenant, or, in default of such an agreement, shall be such a tenancy as may be determined by the court to be reasonable in all the circumstances, being, if it is a tenancy for a term of years certain, a tenancy for a term not exceeding fifteen years, and shall begin on the coming to an end of the current tenancy.

34.   Rent under new tenancy

(1) The rent payable under a tenancy granted by order of the court under this Part of this Act shall be such as may be agreed between the landlord and the tenant or as, in default of such agreement, may be determined by the court to be that at which, having regard to the terms of the tenancy (other than those relating to rent), the holding might reasonably be expected to be let in the open market by a willing lessor, there being disregarded—

    (a) any effect on rent of the fact that the tenant has or his predecessors in title have been in occupation of the holding,

    (b) any goodwill attached to the holding by reason of the carrying on thereat of the business of the tenant (whether by him or by a predecessor of his in that business),

    (c) any effect on rent of an improvement to which this paragraph applies,

    (d) in the case of a holding comprising licensed premises, any addition to its value attributable to the licence, if it appears to the court that having regard to the terms of the current tenancy and any other relevant circumstances the benefit of the licence belongs to the tenant.

(2) Paragraph (c) of the foregoing subsection applies to any improvement carried out by a person who at the time it was carried out was the tenant, but only if it was carried out otherwise than in pursuance of an obligation to his immediate landlord, and either it was carried out during the current tenancy or the following conditions are satisfied, that is to say,—

    (a) that it was completed not more than twenty-one years before the application to the court was made; and

    (b) that the holding or any part of it affected by the improvement has at all times since the completion of the improvement been comprised in tenancies of the description specified in section 23(1) of this Act; and

    (c) that at the termination of each of those tenancies the tenant did not quit.

(2A) If this Part of this Act applies by virtue of section 23(1A) of this Act, the reference in subsection (1)(d) above to the tenant shall be construed as including—

    (a) a company in which the tenant has a controlling interest, or

    (b) where the tenant is a company, a person with a controlling interest in the company.

(3) Where the rent is determined by the court the court may, if it thinks fit, further determine that the terms of the tenancy shall include such provision for varying the rent as may be specified in the determination.

(4) It is hereby declared that the matters which are to be taken into account by the court in determining the rent include any effect on rent of the operation of the provisions of the Landlord and Tenant (Covenants) Act 1995.

35.   Other terms of new tenancy

(1) The terms of a tenancy granted by order of the court under this Part of this Act (other than terms as to the duration thereof and as to the rent payable thereunder), including, where different persons own interests which fulfil the conditions specified in section 44(1) of this Act in different parts of it, terms as to the apportionment of the rent, shall be such as may be agreed between the landlord and the tenant or as, in default of such agreement, may be determined by the court; and in determining those terms the court shall have regard to the terms of the current tenancy and to all relevant circumstances.

(2) In subsection (1) of this section the reference to all relevant circumstances includes (without prejudice to the generality of that reference) a reference to the operation of the provisions of the Landlord and Tenant (Covenants) Act 1995.

36.   Carrying out of order for new tenancy

(1) Where under this Part of this Act the court makes an order for the grant of a new tenancy, then, unless the order is revoked under the next following subsection or the landlord and the tenant agree not to act upon the order, the landlord shall be bound to execute or make

in favour of the tenant, and the tenant shall be bound to accept, a lease or agreement for a tenancy of the holding embodying the terms agreed between the landlord and the tenant or determined by the court in accordance with the foregoing provisions of this Part of this Act; and where the landlord executes or makes such a lease or agreement the tenant shall be bound, if so required by the landlord, to execute a counterpart or duplicate thereof.

(2)   If the tenant, within fourteen days after the making of an order under this Part of this Act for the grant of a new tenancy, applies to the court for the revocation of the order the court shall revoke the order; and where the order is so revoked, then, if it is so agreed between the landlord and the tenant or determined by the court, the current tenancy shall continue, beyond the date at which it would have come to an end apart from this subsection, for such period as may be so agreed or determined to be necessary to afford to the landlord a reasonable opportunity for reletting or otherwise disposing of the premises which would have been comprised in the new tenancy; and while the current tenancy continues by virtue of this subsection it shall not be a tenancy to which this Part of this Act applies.

(3)   Where an order is revoked under the last foregoing subsection any provision thereof as to payment of costs shall not cease to have effect by reason only of the revocation; but the court may, if it thinks fit, revoke or vary any such provision or, where no costs have been awarded in the proceedings for the revoked order, award such costs.

(4)   A lease executed or agreement made under this section, in a case where the interest of the lessor is subject to a mortgage, shall be deemed to be one authorised by section ninety-nine of the Law of Property Act 1925 (which confers certain powers of leasing on mortgagors in possession), and subsection (13) of that section (which allows those powers to be restricted or excluded by agreement) shall not have effect in relation to such a lease or agreement.

37.   Compensation where order for new tenancy precluded on certain grounds

(1)   Subject to the provisions of this Act, in a case specified in subsection (1A), (1B) or (1C) below (a 'compensation case') the tenant shall be entitled on quitting the holding to recover from the landlord by way of compensation an amount determined in accordance with this section.

(1A) The first compensation case is where on the making of an application by the tenant under section 24(1) of this Act the court is precluded (whether by subsection (1) or subsection

(2)   of section 31 of this Act) from making an order for the grant of a new tenancy by reason of any of the grounds specified in paragraphs (e), (f) and (g) of section 30(1) of this Act (the 'compensation grounds') and not of any grounds specified in any other paragraph of section 30(1).

(1B) The second compensation case is where on the making of an application under section 29(2) of this Act the court is precluded (whether by section 29(4)(a) or section 31(2) of this Act) from making an order for the grant of a new tenancy by reason of any of the compensation grounds and not of any other grounds specified in section 30(1) of this Act.

(1C) The third compensation case is where—

    (a)   the landlord's notice under section 25 of this Act or, as the case may be, under section 26(6) of this Act, states his opposition to the grant of a new tenancy on any of the compensation grounds and not on any other grounds specified in section 30(1) of this Act; and

    (b)   either—

        (i)   no application is made by the tenant under section 24(1) of this Act or by the landlord under section 29(2) of this Act; or

        (ii)   such an application is made but is subsequently withdrawn.

(2)   Subject to the following provisions of this section, compensation under this section shall be as follows, that is to say,—

    (a)   where the conditions specified in the next following subsection are satisfied in relation to the whole of the holding it shall be the product of the appropriate multiplier and twice the rateable value of the holding,

    (b)   in any other case it shall be the product of the appropriate multiplier and the rateable value of the holding.

(3)   The said conditions are—
    (a)   that, during the whole of the fourteen years immediately preceding the termination of the current tenancy, premises being or comprised in the holding have been occupied for the purposes of a business carried on by the occupier or for those and other purposes;
    (b)   that, if during those fourteen years there was a change in the occupier of the premises, the person who was the occupier immediately after the change was the successor to the business carried on by the person who was the occupier immediately before the change.
(3A) If the conditions specified in subsection (3) above are satisfied in relation to part of the holding but not in relation to the other part, the amount of compensation shall be the aggregate of sums calculated separately as compensation in respect of each part, and accordingly, for the purpose of calculating compensation in respect of a part any reference in this section to the holding shall be construed as a reference to that part.
(3B) Where section 44(1A) of this Act applies, the compensation shall be determined separately for each part and compensation determined for any part shall be recoverable only from the person who is the owner of an interest in that part which fulfils the conditions specified in section 44(1) of this Act.
(4)   Where the court is precluded from making an order for the grant of a new tenancy under this Part of this Act in a compensation case, the court shall on the application of the tenant certify that fact.
(5)   For the purposes of subsection (2) of this section the rateable value of the holding shall be determined as follows:—
    (a)   where in the valuation list in force at the date on which the landlord's notice under section twenty-five or, as the case may be, subsection (6) of section twenty-six of this Act is given a value is then shown as the annual value (as hereinafter defined) of the holding, the rateable value of the holding shall be taken to be that value;
    (b)   where no such value is so shown with respect to the holding but such a value or such values is or are so shown with respect to premises comprised in or comprising the holding or part of it, the rateable value of the holding shall be taken to be such value as is found by a proper apportionment or aggregation of the value or values so shown;
    (c)   where the rateable value of the holding cannot be ascertained in accordance with the foregoing paragraphs of this subsection, it shall be taken to be the value which, apart from any exemption from assessment to rates, would on a proper assessment be the value to be entered in the said valuation list as the annual value of the holding;
and any dispute arising, whether in proceedings before the court or otherwise, as to the determination for those purposes of the rateable value of the holding shall be referred to the Commissioners of Inland Revenue for decision by a valuation officer.
An appeal shall lie to the Upper Tribunal from any decision of a valuation officer under this subsection, but subject thereto any such decision shall be final.
(5A) If part of the holding is domestic property, as defined in section 66 of the Local Government Finance Act 1988,—
    (a)   the domestic property shall be disregarded in determining the rateable value of the holding under subsection (5) of this section; and
    (b)   if, on the date specified in subsection (5)(a) of this section, the tenant occupied the whole or any part of the domestic property, the amount of compensation to which he is entitled under subsection (1) of this section shall be increased by the addition of a sum equal to his reasonable expenses in removing from the domestic property.
(5B) Any question as to the amount of the sum referred to in paragraph (b) of subsection (5A) of this section shall be determined by agreement between the landlord and the tenant or, in default of agreement, by the court.
(5C) If the whole of the holding is domestic property, as defined in section 66 of the Local Government Finance Act 1988, for the purposes of subsection (2) of this section the rateable value of the holding shall be taken to be an amount equal to the rent at which it is estimated the holding might reasonably be expected to let from year to year if the tenant undertook to pay all usual tenant's rates and taxes and to bear the cost of the repairs and insurance and the other expenses (if any) necessary to maintain the holding in a state to command that rent.

(5D) The following provisions shall have effect as regards a determination of an amount mentioned in subsection (5C) of this section—

(a)   the date by reference to which such a determination is to be made is the date on which the landlord's notice under section 25 or, as the case may be, subsection (6) of section 26 of this Act is given;

(b)   any dispute arising, whether in proceedings before the court or otherwise, as to such a determination shall be referred to the Commissioners of Inland Revenue for decision by a valuation officer;

(c)   an appeal shall lie to the Upper Tribunal from such a decision but subject to that, such a decision shall be final.

(5E) Any deduction made under paragraph 2A of Schedule 6 to the Local Government Finance Act 1988 (deduction from valuation of hereditaments used for breeding horses etc.) shall be disregarded, to the extent that it relates to the holding, in determining the rateable value of the holding under subsection (5) of this section.

(6)   The Commissioners of Inland Revenue may by statutory instrument make rules prescribing the procedure in connection with references under this section.

(7)   In this section—

the reference to the termination of the current tenancy is a reference to the date of termination specified in the landlord's notice under section twenty-five of this Act or, as the case may be, the date specified in the tenant's request for a new tenancy as the date from which the new tenancy is to begin;

the expression 'annual value' means rateable value except that where the rateable value differs from the net annual value the said expression means net annual value;

the expression 'valuation officer' means any officer of the Commissioners of Inland Revenue for the time being authorised by a certificate of the Commissioners to act in relation to a valuation list.

(8)   In subsection (2) of this section 'the appropriate multiplier' means such multiplier as the Secretary of State may by order made by statutory instrument prescribe and different multipliers may be so prescribed in relation to different cases.

(9)   A statutory instrument containing an order under subsection (8) of this section shall be subject to annulment in pursuance of a resolution of either House of Parliament.

37A.   Compensation for possession obtained by misrepresentation

(1)   Where the court—

(a)   makes an order for the termination of the current tenancy but does not make an order for the grant of a new tenancy, or

(b)   refuses an order for the grant of a new tenancy,

and it subsequently made to appear to the court that the order was obtained, or the court was induced to refuse the grant, by misrepresentation or the concealment of material facts, the court may order the landlord to pay to the tenant such sum as appears sufficient as compensation for damage or loss sustained by the tenant as the result of the order or refusal.

(2)   Where—

(a)   the tenant has quit the holding—

(i)   after making but withdrawing an application under section 24(1) of this Act; or

(ii)   without making such an application; and

(b)   it is made to appear to the court that he did so by reason of misrepresentation or the concealment of material facts,

the court may order the landlord to pay to the tenant such sum as appears sufficient as compensation for damage or loss sustained by the tenant as the result of quitting the holding.

38.   Restriction on agreements excluding provisions of Part II

(1)   Any agreement relating to a tenancy to which this Part of this Act applies (whether contained in the instrument creating the tenancy or not) shall be void (except as provided by section 38A of this Act) in so far as it purports to preclude the tenant from making an application or request under this Part of this Act or provides for the termination or the surrender of the tenancy in the event of his making such an application or request or for the imposition of any penalty or disability on the tenant in that event.

(2) Where—

    (a)   during the whole of the five years immediately preceding the date on which the tenant under a tenancy to which this Part of this Act applies is to quit the holding, premises being or comprised in the holding have been occupied for the purposes of a business carried on by the occupier or for those and other purposes, and

    (b)   if during those five years there was a change in the occupier of the premises, the person who was the occupier immediately after the change was the successor to the business carried on by the person who was the occupier immediately before the change,

any agreement (whether contained in the instrument creating the tenancy or not and whether made before or after the termination of that tenancy) which purports to exclude or reduce compensation under section 37 of this Act shall to that extent be void, so however that this subsection shall not affect any agreement as to the amount of any such compensation which is made after the right to compensation has accrued.

(3)   In a case not falling within section 37 of this Act the right to compensation conferred by the last foregoing section may be excluded or modified by agreement.

(4)   ...

38A.   Agreements to exclude provisions of Part 2

(1)   The persons who will be the landlord and the tenant in relation to a tenancy to be granted for a term of years certain which will be a tenancy to which this Part of this Act applies may agree that the provisions of sections 24 to 28 of this Act shall be excluded in relation to that tenancy.

(2)   The persons who are the landlord and the tenant in relation to a tenancy to which this Part of this Act applies may agree that the tenancy shall be surrendered on such date or in such circumstances as may be specified in the agreement and on such terms (if any) as may be so specified.

(3)   An agreement under subsection (1) above shall be void unless—

    (a)   the landlord has served on the tenant a notice in the form, or substantially in the form, set out in Schedule 1 to the Regulatory Reform (Business Tenancies) (England and Wales) Order 2003 ('the 2003 Order'); and

    (b)   the requirements specified in Schedule 2 to that Order are met.

(4)   An agreement under subsection (2) above shall be void unless—

    (a)   the landlord has served on the tenant a notice in the form, or substantially in the form, set out in Schedule 3 to the 2003 Order; and

    (b)   the requirements specified in Schedule 4 to that Order are met.

General and supplementary provisions

41A.   Partnerships

(1)   The following provisions of this section shall apply where—

    (a)   a tenancy is held jointly by two or more persons (in this section referred to as the joint tenants); and

    (b)   the property comprised in the tenancy is or includes premises occupied for the purposes of a business; and

    (c)   the business (or some other business) was at some time during the existence of the tenancy carried on in partnership by all the persons who were then the joint tenants or by those and other persons and the joint tenants' interest in the premises was then partnership property; and

    (d)   the business is carried on (whether alone or in partnership with other persons) by one or some only of the joint tenants and no part of the property comprised in the tenancy is occupied, in right of the tenancy, for the purposes of a business carried on (whether alone or in partnership with other persons) by the other or others.

(2)   In the following provisions of this section those of the joint tenants who for the time being carry on the business are referred to as the business tenants and the others as the other joint tenants.

(3)   Any notice given by the business tenants which, had it been given by all the joint tenants, would have been—

    (a)   a tenant's request for a new tenancy made in accordance with section 26 of this Act; or

    (b)   a notice under subsection (1) or subsection (2) of section 27 of this Act;

shall be treated as such if it states that it is given by virtue of this section and sets out the facts by virtue of which the persons giving it are the business tenants; and references in those sections and in section 24A of this Act to the tenant shall be construed accordingly.

(4) A notice given by the landlord to the business tenants which, had it been given to all the joint tenants, would have been a notice under section 25 of this Act shall be treated as such a notice, and references in that section to the tenant shall be construed accordingly.

(5) An application under section 24(1) of this Act for a new tenancy may, instead of being made by all the joint tenants, be made by the business tenants alone; and where it is so made—

    (a) this Part of this Act shall have effect, in relation to it, as if the references therein to the tenant included references to the business tenants alone; and

    (b) the business tenants shall be liable, to the exclusion of the other joint tenants, for the payment of rent and the discharge of any other obligation under the current tenancy for any rental period beginning after the date specified in the landlord's notice under section 25 of this Act or, as the case may be, beginning on or after the date specified in their request for a new tenancy.

(6) Where the court makes an order under section 29 of this Act for the grant of a new tenancy it may order the grant to be made to the business tenants or to them jointly with the persons carrying on the business in partnership with them, and may order the grant to be made subject to the satisfaction, within a time specified by the order, of such conditions as to guarantors, sureties or otherwise as appear to the court equitable, having regard to the omission of the other joint tenants from the persons who will be the tenant under the new tenancy.

(7) The business tenants shall be entitled to recover any amount payable by way of compensation under section 37 or section 59 of this Act.

43. Tenancies excluded from Part II

(1) This Part of this Act does not apply—

    (a) to a tenancy of an agricultural holding which is a tenancy in relation to which the Agricultural Holdings Act 1986 applies or a tenancy which would be a tenancy of an agricultural holding in relation to which that Act applied if subsection (3) of section 2 of that Act did not have effect or, in a case where approval was given under subsection (1) of that section, if that approval had not been given;

    (aa) to a farm business tenancy;

    (b) to a tenancy created by a mining lease; (c), (d)...

(2) This Part of this Act does not apply to a tenancy granted by reason that the tenant was the holder of an office, appointment or employment from the grantor thereof and continuing only so long as the tenant holds the office, appointment or employment, or terminable by the grantor on the tenant's ceasing to hold it, or coming to an end at a time fixed by reference to the time at which the tenant ceases to hold it:

Provided that this subsection shall not have effect in relation to a tenancy granted after the commencement of this Act unless the tenancy was granted by an instrument in writing which expressed the purpose for which the tenancy was granted.

(3) This Part of this Act does not apply to a tenancy granted for a term certain not exceeding six months unless—

    (a) the tenancy contains provision for renewing the term or for extending it beyond six months from its beginning; or

    (b) the tenant has been in occupation for a period which, together with any period during which any predecessor in the carrying on of the business carried on by the tenant was in occupation, exceeds twelve months.

43ZA. Further exclusion of home business tenancies from Part 2

(1) This Part of this Act does not apply to a home business tenancy.

(2) A home business tenancy is a tenancy under which—

    (a) a dwelling-house is let as a separate dwelling,

    (b) the tenant or, where there are joint tenants, each of them, is an individual, and

    (c) the terms of the tenancy—

        (i) require the tenant or, where there are joint tenants, at least one of them, to occupy the dwelling-house as a home (whether or not as that individual's only or principal home),

       (ii)   permit a home business to be carried on in the dwelling-house, or permit the immediate landlord to give consent for a home business to be carried on in the dwelling-house, and

       (iii)   do not permit a business other than a home business to be carried on in the dwelling-house.

(3)   The terms of a tenancy permit the carrying on of a home business if they permit the carrying on of a particular home business, a particular description of home business or any home business.

(4)   A 'home business' is a business of a kind which might reasonably be carried on at home.

(5)   A business is not to be treated as a home business if it involves the supply of alcohol for consumption on licensed premises which form all or part of the dwelling-house.

(6)   The appropriate national authority may by regulations prescribe cases in which businesses are, or are not, to be treated as home businesses.

(7)   Regulations under this section—

    (a)   may include transitional or saving provision,

    (b)   may make different provision for different purposes,

    (c)   are to be made by statutory instrument,

    (d)   may not be made unless—

       (i)   in the case of regulations made by the Secretary of State, a draft of the statutory instrument containing the regulations has been laid before Parliament and approved by a resolution of each House of Parliament,

       (ii)   in the case of regulations made by the Welsh Ministers, a draft of the statutory instrument containing the regulations has been laid before, and approved by a resolution of, the National Assembly for Wales.

(8)   For the purposes of this section, a dwelling-house which is let for mixed residential and business use is capable of being let as a dwelling.

(9)   If, under a tenancy, a dwelling-house is let together with other land, then, for the purposes of this section—

    (a)   if the main purpose of the letting is the provision of a home for the tenant, the other land is to be treated as part of the dwelling-house, and

    (b)   if the main purpose of the letting is not as mentioned in paragraph (a), the tenancy is to be treated as not being one under which a dwelling-house is let as a separate dwelling.

(10) In this section—

'the appropriate national authority' means—

    (a)   in relation to England, the Secretary of State, and

    (b)   in relation to Wales, the Welsh Ministers;

'dwelling-house' may be a house or part of a house;

'let' includes sub-let;

'licensed premises' has the same meaning as in the Licensing Act 2003 (see section 193 of that Act);

'supply of alcohol' has the same meaning as in the Licensing Act 2003 (see section 14 of that Act).

PART IV
MISCELLANEOUS AND SUPPLEMENTARY

64.   Interim continuation of tenancies pending determination by court

(1)   In any case where—

    (a)   a notice to terminate a tenancy has been given under Part I or Part II of this Act or a request for a new tenancy has been made under Part II thereof, and

    (b)   an application to the court has been made under the said Part I or under section 24(1) or 29(2) of this Act, as the case may be, and

    (c)   apart from this section the effect of the notice or request would be to terminate the tenancy before the expiration of the period of three months beginning with the date on which the application is finally disposed of,

the effect of the notice or request shall be to terminate the tenancy at the expiration of the said period of three months and not at any other time.

(2)   The reference in paragraph (c) of subsection (1) of this section to the date on which an application is finally disposed of shall be construed as a reference to the earliest

date by which the proceedings on the application (including any proceedings on or in consequence of an appeal) have been determined and any time for appealing or further appealing has expired, except that if the application is withdrawn or any appeal is abandoned the reference shall be construed as a reference to the date of the withdrawal or abandonment.

69. Interpretation

(1) In this Act the following expressions have the meanings hereby assigned to them respectively, that is to say: —

'agricultural holding' has the same meaning as in the Agricultural Holdings Act 1986;

'development corporation' has the same meaning as in the Town and Country Planning Act 1971;

'farm business tenancy' has the same meaning as in the Agricultural Tenancies Act 1995;

'local authority' means any local authority within the meaning of the Town and Country Planning Act 1990, any National Park authority, the Broads Authority, the London Fire and Emergency Planning Authority, a joint authority established by Part IV of the Local Government Act 1985, an economic prosperity board established under section 88 of the Local Democracy, Economic Development and Construction Act 2009 or a combined authority established under section 103 of that Act;

'mortgage' includes a charge or lien and 'mortgagor' and 'mortgagee' shall be construed accordingly;

'notice to quit' means a notice to terminate a tenancy (whether a periodical tenancy or a tenancy for a term of years certain) given in accordance with the provisions (whether express or implied) of that tenancy;

'repairs' includes any work of maintenance, decoration or restoration, and references to repairing, to keeping or yielding up in repair and to state of repair shall be construed accordingly;

'statutory undertakers' has the same meaning as in the Town and Country Planning Act 1971;

'tenancy' means a tenancy created either immediately or derivatively out of the freehold, whether by a lease or underlease, by an agreement for a lease or underlease or by a tenancy agreement or in pursuance of any enactment (including this Act), but does not include a mortgage term or any interest arising in favour of a mortgagor by his attorning tenant to his mortgagee, and references to the granting of a tenancy and to demised property shall be construed accordingly;

'terms', in relation to a tenancy, includes conditions.

(2) References in this Act to an agreement between the landlord and the tenant (except in section seventeen and subsections (1) and (2) of section thirty-eight thereof) shall be construed as references to an agreement in writing between them.

VARIATION OF TRUSTS ACT 1958
(1958, c. 53)

1. Jurisdiction of courts to vary trusts

(1) Where property, whether real or personal, is held on trusts arising, whether before or after the passing of this Act, under any will, settlement or other disposition, the court may if it thinks fit by order approve on behalf of—

    (a) any person having, directly or indirectly, an interest, whether vested or contingent, under the trusts who by reason of infancy or other incapacity is incapable of assenting, or

    (b) any person (whether ascertained or not) who may become entitled, directly or indirectly, to an interest under the trusts as being at a future date or on the happening of a future event a person of any specified description or a member of any specified class of persons, so however that this paragraph shall not include any person who would be of that description, or a member of that class, as the case may be, if the said date had fallen or the said event had happened at the date of the application to the court, or

    (c) any person unborn, or

(d)   any person in respect of any discretionary interest of his under protective trusts where the interest of the principal beneficiary has not failed or determined.

any arrangement (by whomsoever proposed, and whether or not there is any other person beneficially interested who is capable of assenting thereto) varying or revoking all or any of the trusts, or enlarging the powers of the trustees of managing or administering any of the property subject to the trusts:

Provided that except by virtue of paragraph (d) of this subsection the court shall not approve an arrangement on behalf of any person unless the carrying out thereof would be for the benefit of that person.

(2)   In the foregoing subsection 'protective trusts' means the trusts specified in paragraphs (i) and (ii) of subsection (1) of section thirty-three of the Trustee Act, 1925, or any like trusts, 'the principal beneficiary' has the same meaning as in the said subsection (1) and 'discretionary interest' means an interest arising under the trust specified in paragraph (ii) of the said subsection (1) or any like trust.

(3)   The jurisdiction conferred by subsection (1) of this section shall be exercisable by the High Court, except that the question whether the carrying out of any arrangement would be for the benefit of a person falling within paragraph (a) of the said subsection (1) who lacks capacity (within the meaning of the Mental Capacity Act 2005) to give his assent is to be determined by the Court of Protection.

(4)   ...

(5)   Nothing in the foregoing provisions of this section shall apply to trusts affecting property settled by Act of Parliament.

(6)   Nothing in this section shall be taken to limit the powers of the Court of Protection.

PERPETUITIES AND ACCUMULATIONS ACT 1964
(1964, c. 55)

Perpetuities

1. Power to specify perpetuity period

(1)   Subject to section 9(2) of this Act and subsection (2) below, where the instrument by which any disposition is made so provides, the perpetuity period applicable to the disposition under the rule against perpetuities, instead of being of any other duration, shall be of a duration equal to such number of years not exceeding eighty as is specified in that behalf in the instrument.

(2)   Subsection (1) above shall not have effect where the disposition is made in exercise of a special power of appointment, but where a period is specified under that subsection in the instrument creating such a power the period shall apply in relation to any disposition under the power as it applies in relation to the power itself.

2. Presumptions and evidence as to future parenthood

(1)   Where in any proceedings there arises on the rule against perpetuities a question which turns on the ability of a person to have a child at some future time, then—

(a)   subject to paragraph (b) below, it shall be presumed that a male can have a child at the age of fourteen years or over, but not under that age, and that a female can have a child at the age of twelve years or over, but not under that age or over the age of fifty-five years; but

(b)   in the case of a living person evidence may be given to show that he or she will or will not be able to have a child at the time in question.

(2)   Where any such question is decided by treating a person as unable to have a child at a particular time, and he or she does so, the High Court may make such order as it thinks fit for placing the persons interested in the property comprised in the disposition, so far as may be just, in the position they would have held if the question had not been so decided.

(3)   Subject to subsection (2) above, where any such question is decided in relation to a disposition by treating a person as able or unable to have a child at a particular time, then he or she shall be so treated for the purpose of any question which may arise on the rule against perpetuities in relation to the same disposition in any subsequent proceedings.

(4)   In the foregoing provisions of this section references to having a child are references to begetting or giving birth to a child, but those provisions (except subsection (1)(b) shall apply in relation to the possibility that a person will at any time have a child by adoption, legitimation or other means as they apply to his or her ability at that time to beget or give birth to a child.

3. **Uncertainty as to remoteness**

(1) Where, apart from the provisions of this section and section 4 and 5 of this Act, a disposition would be void on the ground that the interest disposed of might not become vested until too remote a time, the disposition shall be treated, until such time (if any) as it becomes established that the vesting must occur, if at all, after the end of the perpetuity period, as if the disposition were not subject to the rule against perpetuities; and its becoming so established shall not affect the validity of anything previously done in relation to the interest disposed of by way of advancement, application of intermediate income or otherwise.

(2) Where, apart from the said provisions, a disposition consisting of the conferring of a general power of appointment would be void on the ground that the power might not become exercisable until too remote a time, the disposition shall be treated, until such time (if any) as it becomes established that the power will not be exercisable within the perpetuity period, as if the disposition were not subject to the rule against perpetuities.

(3) Where, apart from the said provisions, a disposition consisting of the conferring of any power, option or other right would be void on the ground that the right might be exercised at too remote a time, the disposition shall be treated as regards any exercise of the right within the perpetuity period as if it were not subject to the rule against perpetuities and, subject to the said provisions, shall be treated as void for remoteness only if, and so far as, the right is not fully exercised within that period.

(4) Where this section applies to a disposition and the duration of the perpetuity period is not determined by virtue of section 1 or 9(2) of this Act, it shall be determined as follows:—

   (a) where any persons failing within subsection (5) below are individuals in being and ascertainable at the commencement of the perpetuity period the duration of the period shall be determined by reference to their lives and no others, but so that the lives of any description of persons falling within paragraph (b) or (c) of that subsection shall be disregarded if the number of persons of that description is such as to render it impracticable to ascertain the date of death of the survivor;

   (b) where there are no lives under paragraph (a) above the period shall be twenty-one years.

(5) The said persons are as follows:—

   (a) the person by whom the disposition was made;

   (b) a person to whom or in whose favour the disposition was made, that is to say—

      (i) in the case of a disposition to a class of persons, any member or potential member of the class;

      (ii) in the case of an individual disposition to a person taking only on certain conditions being satisfied, any person as to whom some of the conditions are satisfied and the remainder may in time be satisfied;

      (iii) in the case of a special power of appointment exercisable in favour of members of a class, any member or potential member of the class;

      (iv) in the case of a special power of appointment exercisable in favour of one person only, that person or, where the object of the power is ascertainable only on certain conditions being satisfied, any person as to whom some of the conditions are satisfied and the remainder may in time be satisfied;

      (v) in the case of any power, option or other right, the person on whom the right is conferred;

   (c) a person having a child or grandchild within sub-paragraphs (i) to (iv) of paragraph

   (b) above, or any of those children or grandchildren, if subsequently born, would by virtue of his or her descent fall within those sub-paragraphs;

   (d) any person on the failure or determination of whose prior interest the disposition is limited to take effect.

4. **Reduction of age and exclusion of class members to avoid remoteness**

(1) Where a disposition is limited by reference to the attainment by any person or persons of a specified age exceeding twenty-one years, and it is apparent at the time the disposition is made or becomes apparent at a subsequent time—

   (a) that the disposition would, apart from this section, be void for remoteness, but

   (b) that it would not be so void if the specified age had been twenty-one years, the disposition shall be treated for all purposes as if, instead of being limited by reference to the age in fact specified, it had been limited by reference to the age nearest to that age which would, if specified instead, have prevented the disposition from being so void.

(2) Where in the case of any disposition different ages exceeding twenty-one years are specified in relation to different persons—

    (a) the reference in paragraph (b) of subsection (1) above to the specified age shall be construed as a reference to all the specified ages, and

    (b) that subsection shall operate to reduce each such age so far as is necessary to save the disposition from being void for remoteness.

(3) Where the inclusion of any persons, being potential members of a class of unborn persons who at birth would become members or potential members of the class, prevents the foregoing provisions of this section from operating to save a disposition from being void for remoteness, those persons shall thenceforth be deemed for all the purposes of the disposition to be excluded from the class, and the said provisions shall thereupon have effect accordingly.

(4) Where, in the case of a disposition to which subsection (3) above does not apply, it is apparent at the time the disposition is made or becomes apparent at a subsequent time that, apart from this subsection, the inclusion of any persons, being potential members of a class or unborn persons who at birth would become members or potential members of the class, would cause the disposition to be treated as void for remoteness, those persons shall, unless their exclusion would exhaust the class, thenceforth be deemed for all the purposes of the disposition to be excluded from the class.

(5) Where this section has effect in relation to a disposition to which section 3 above applies, the operation of this section shall not affect the validity of anything previously done in relation to the interest disposed of by way of advancement, application or intermediate income or otherwise.

(6) ...

(7) For the avoidance of doubt it is hereby declared that a question arising under section 3 of this Act or subsection (1)(a) above of whether a disposition would be void apart from this section is to be determined as if subsection (6) above had been a separate section of this Act.

5.   Condition relating to death of surviving spouse

Where a disposition is limited by reference to the time of death of the survivor of a person in being at the commencement of the perpetuity period and any spouse of that person, and that time has not arrived at the end of the perpetuity period, the disposition shall be treated for all purposes, where to do so would save it from being void for remoteness, as if it had been limited by reference to the time immediately before the end of that period.

6.   Saving and acceleration of expectant interests

A disposition shall not be treated as void for remoteness by reason only that the interest disposed of is ulterior to and dependent upon an interest under a disposition which is so void, and the vesting of an interest shall not be prevented from being accelerated on the failure of a prior interest by reason only that the failure arises because of remoteness.

7.   Powers of appointment

For the purposes of the rule against perpetuities, a power of appointment shall be treated as a special power unless—

(a) in the instrument creating the power it is expressed to be exercisable by one person only, and

(b) it could, at all times during its currency when that person is of full age and capacity, be exercised by him so as immediately to transfer to himself the whole of the interest governed by the power without the consent of any other person or compliance with any other condition, not being a formal condition relating only to the mode of exercise of the power:

Provided that for the purpose of determining whether a disposition made under a power of appointment exercisable by will only is void for remoteness, the power shall be treated as a general power where it would have fallen to be so treated if exercisable by deed.

8.   Administrative powers of trustees

(1)   The rule against perpetuities shall not operate to invalidate a power conferred on trustees or other persons to sell, lease, exchange or otherwise dispose of any property for full consideration, or to do any other act in the administration (as opposed to the distribution) of any property, and shall not prevent the payment to trustees or other persons or reasonable remuneration for their services.

(2)   Subsection (1) above shall apply for the purpose of enabling a power to be exercised at any time after the commencement of this Act notwithstanding that the power is conferred by an instrument which took effect before that commencement.

9.   Options relating to land

(1)   The rule against perpetuities shall not apply to a disposition consisting of the conferring of an option to acquire for valuable consideration an interest reversionary (whether directly or indirectly) on the term of a lease if—

     (a)   the option is exercisable only by the lessee or his successors in title, and

     (b)   it ceases to be exercisable at or before the expiration of one year following the determination of the lease.

This subsection shall apply in relation to an agreement for a lease as it applies in relation to a lease, and 'lessee' shall be construed accordingly.

(2)   In the case of a disposition consisting of the conferring of an option to acquire for valuable consideration any interest in land, the perpetuity period under the rule against perpetuities shall be twenty-one years, and section 1 of this Act shall not apply:

Provided that this subsection shall not apply to a right of preemption conferred on a public or local authority in respect of land used or to be used for religious purposes where the right becomes exercisable only if the land ceases to be used for such purposes.

10.   Avoidance of contractual and other rights in cases of remoteness

Where a disposition inter vivos would fall to be treated as void for remoteness if the rights and duties thereunder were capable of transmission to persons other than the original parties and had been so transmitted, it shall be treated as void as between the person by whom it was made and the person to whom or in whose favour it was made or any successor of his, and no remedy shall lie in contract or otherwise for giving effect to it or making restitution for its lack of effect.

11.   Rights for enforcement of rentcharges

(1)   The rule against perpetuities shall not apply to any powers or remedies for recovering or compelling the payment of an annual sum to which section 121 or 122 of the Law of Property Act 1925 applies, or otherwise becoming exercisable or enforceable on the breach of any condition or other requirement relating to that sum.

...

12.   Possibilities of reverter, conditions subsequent, exceptions and reservations

(1)   In the case of—

     (a)   a possibility of reverter on the determination of a determinable fee simple, or

     (b)   a possibility of a resulting trust on the determination of any other determinable interest in property,

the rule against perpetuities shall apply in relation to the provision causing the interest to be determinable as it would apply if that provision were expressed in the form of a condition subsequent giving rise, on breach thereof, to a right of re-entry or an equivalent right in the case of property other than land, and where the provision falls to be treated as void for remoteness the determinable interest shall become an absolute interest.

(2)   Where a disposition is subject to any such provision, or to any such condition subsequent, or to any exception or reservation, the disposition shall be treated for the purposes of this Act as including a separate disposition of any rights arising by virtue of the provision, condition subsequent, exception or reservation.

Accumulations

14. Right to stop accumulations

Section 2 above shall apply to any question as to the right of beneficiaries to put an end to accumulations of income under any disposition as it applies to questions arising on the rule against perpetuities.

Supplemental

15. Short title, interpretation and extent

(1) This Act may be cited as the Perpetuities and Accumulations Act 1964.

(2) In this Act—

'disposition' includes the conferring of a power of appointment and any other disposition of an interest in or right over property, and references to the interest disposed of shall be construed accordingly;

'in being' means living or en ventre sa mere;

'power of appointment' includes any discretionary power to transfer a beneficial interest in property without the furnishing of valuable consideration;

'will' includes a codicil;

and for the purposes of this Act a disposition contained in a will shall be deemed to be made at the death of the testator.

(3) For the purposes of this Act a person shall be treated as a member of a class if in his case all the conditions identifying a member of the class are satisfied, and shall be treated as a potential member if in his case some only of those conditions are satisfied but there is a possibility that the remainder will in time be satisfied.

(4) Nothing in this Act shall affect the operation of the rule of law rendering void for remoteness certain dispositions under which property is limited to be applied for purposes other than the benefit of any person or class of persons in cases where the property may be so applied after the end of the perpetuity period.

(5) The foregoing sections of this Act shall apply (except as provided in section 8(2) above) only in relation to instruments taking effect after the commencement of this Act, and in the case of an instrument made in the exercise of a special power of appointment shall apply only where the instrument creating the power takes effect after that commencement:

Provided that section 7 above shall apply in all cases for construing the foregoing reference to a special power of appointment.

(5A) The foregoing sections of this Act shall not apply in relation to an instrument taking effect on or after the day appointed under section 22(2) of the Perpetuities and Accumulations Act 2009 (commencement), but this shall not prevent those sections applying in relation to an instrument so taking effect if—

(a) it is a will executed before that day, or

(b) it is an instrument made in the exercise of a special power of appointment, and the instrument creating the power took effect before that day.

(5B) Subsection (5A) above shall not affect the operation of sections 4(6) and 11(2) above.

(6) This Act shall apply in relation to a disposition made otherwise than by an instrument as if the disposition had been contained in an instrument taking effect when the disposition was made.

(7) This Act binds the Crown.

...

LAW OF PROPERTY (JOINT TENANTS) ACT 1964
(1964, c. 63)

1. Assumptions on sale of land by survivor of joint tenants

(1) For the purposes of section 36(2) of the Law of Property Act 1925, as amended by section 7 of and the Schedule to the Law of Property (Amendment) Act 1926, the survivor of two or more joint tenants shall, in favour of a purchaser of the legal estate, be deemed to be solely and beneficially interested if the conveyance includes a statement that he is so interested.

Provided that the foregoing provisions of this subsection shall not apply if, at any time before the date of the conveyance by the survivor—

(a)   a memorandum of severance (that is to say a note or memorandum signed by the joint tenants or one of them and recording that the joint tenancy was severed in equity on a date therein specified) had been endorsed on or annexed to the conveyance by virtue of which the legal estate was vested in the joint tenants; or

(b)   a bankruptcy order made against any of the joint tenants, or a petition for such an order, had been registered under the Land Charges Act 1925, being an order or petition of which the purchaser has notice, by virtue of the registration, on the date of the conveyance by the survivor.

(2)   The foregoing provisions of this section shall apply with the necessary modifications in relation to a conveyance by the personal representatives of the survivor of joint tenants as they apply in relation to a conveyance by such a survivor.

2.   Retrospective and transitional provisions

Section 1 of this Act shall be deemed to have come into force on 1st January 1926, and for the purposes of that section in its application to a conveyance executed before the passing of this Act a statement signed by the vendor or by his personal representatives that he was solely and beneficially interested shall be treated as if it had been included in the conveyance.

3.   Exclusion of registered land

This Act shall not apply to registered land.

WILLS ACT 1968
(1968, c. 28)

1.   Restriction of operation of Wills Act 1837, s. 15

(1)   For the purposes of section 15 of the Wills Act 1837 (avoidance of gifts to attesting witnesses and their spouses) the attestation of a will by a person to whom or to whose spouse there is given or made any such disposition as is described in that section shall be disregarded if the will is duly executed without his attestation and without that of any other such person.

(2)   This section applies to the will of any person dying after the passing of this Act, whether executed before or after the passing of this Act.

LAW OF PROPERTY ACT 1969
(1969, c. 59)

Note. References to the Land Charges Act 1925 should be read as references to the Land Charges Act 1972.

PART III
AMENDMENT OF LAW RELATING TO DISPOSITIONS OF ESTATES AND INTERESTS IN LAND AND TO LAND CHARGES

23.   Reduction of statutory period of title

Section 44(1) of the Law of Property Act 1925 (under which the period of commencement of title which may be required under a contract expressing no contrary intention is thirty years except in certain cases) shall have effect, in its application to contracts made after the commencement of this Act, as if it specified fifteen years instead of thirty years as the period of commencement of title which may be so required.

24.   Contracts for purchase of land affected by land charge, etc.

(1)   Where under a contract for the sale or other disposition of any estate or interest in land the title to which is not registered under the Land Registration Act 2002 or any enactment replaced by it any question arises whether the purchaser had knowledge, at

the time of entering into the contract, of a registered land charge, that question shall be determined by reference to his actual knowledge and without regard to the provisions of section 198 of the Law of Property Act 1925 (under which registration under the Land Charges Act 1925 or any enactment replaced by it is deemed to constitute actual notice).

(2) Where any estate or interest with which such a contract is concerned is affected by a registered land charge and the purchaser, at the time of entering into the contract, had not received notice and did not otherwise actually know that the estate or interest was affected by the charge, any provision of the contract shall be void so far as it purports to exclude the operation of subsection (1) above or to exclude or restrict any right or remedy that might otherwise be exercisable by the purchaser on the ground that the estate or interest is affected by the charge.

(3) In this section—

'purchaser' includes a lessee, mortgagee or other person acquiring or intending to acquire an estate or interest in land; and

'registered land charge' means any instrument or matter registered, otherwise than in a register of local land charges, under the Land Charges Act 1925 or any Act replaced by it.

(4) For the purposes of this section any knowledge acquired in the course of a transaction by a person who is acting therein as counsel, or as solicitor or other agent, for another shall be treated as the knowledge of that other.

(5) This section does not apply to contracts made before the commencement of this Act.

25. Compensation in certain cases for loss due to undisclosed land charges

(1) Where a purchaser of any estate or interest in land under a disposition to which this section applies has suffered loss by reason that the estate or interest is affected by a registered land charge, then if—

(a) the date of completion was after the commencement of this Act; and

(b) on that date the purchaser had no actual knowledge of the charge, and

(c) the charge was registered against the name of an owner of an estate in the land who was not as owner of any such estate a party to any transaction, or concerned in any event, comprised in the relevant title;

the purchaser shall be entitled to compensation for the loss.

(2) For the purposes of subsection (1)(b) above, the question whether any person had actual knowledge of a charge shall be determined without regard to the provisions of section 198 of the Law of Property Act 1925 (under which registration under the Land Charges Act 1925 or any enactment replaced by it is deemed to constitute actual notice).

(3) Where a transaction comprised in the relevant title was effected or evidenced by a document which expressly provided that it should take effect subject to an interest or obligation capable of registration in any of the relevant registers, the transaction which created that interest or obligation shall be treated for the purposes of subsection (1)(c) above as comprised in the relevant title.

(4) Any compensation for loss under this section shall be paid by the Chief Land Registrar, and where the purchaser of the estate or interest in question has incurred expenditure for the purpose—

(a) of securing that the estate or interest is no longer affected by the registered land charge or is so affected to a less extent; or

(b) of obtaining compensation under this section;

the amount of the compensation shall include the amount of the expenditure (so far as it would not otherwise fall to be treated as compensation for loss) reasonably incurred by the purchaser for that purpose.

(5) In the case of an action to recover compensation under this section, the cause of action shall be deemed for the purposes of the Limitation Act 1980 to accrue at the time when the registered land charge affecting the estate or interest in question comes to the notice of the purchaser.

...

(9) This section applies to the following dispositions, that is to say—

(a) any sale or exchange and, subject to the following provisions of this subsection, any mortgage of an estate or interest in land;

(b) any grant of a lease for a term of years derived out of a leasehold interest;

(c) any compulsory purchase, by whatever procedure, of land; and

(d) any conveyance of a fee simple in land under Part I of the Leasehold Reform Act 1967;

but does not apply to the grant of a term of years derived out of the freehold or the mortgage of such a term by the lessee; and references in this section to a purchaser shall be construed accordingly.

(10) In this section—
'date of completion', in relation to land which vests in the Land Commission or another acquiring authority by virtue of a general vesting declaration under the Land Commission Act 1967 or the Town and County Planning Act 1968, means the date on which it so vests;
'mortgage' includes any charge;
'registered land charge' means any instrument or matter registered, otherwise than in a register of local land charges, under the Land Charges Act 1925 or any Act replaced by it, except that—

    (a)   in relation to an assignment of a lease or underlease or a mortgage by an assignee under such an assignment, it does not include any instrument or matter affecting the title to the freehold or to any relevant leasehold reversion; and

    (b)   in relation to the grant of an underlease or the mortgage by the underlessee of the term of years created by an underlease, it does not include any instrument or matter affecting the title to the freehold or to any leasehold reversion superior to the leasehold interest out of which the term of years is derived—

'relevant registers' means the registers kept under section 1 of the Land Charges Act 1925;
'relevant title' means—

    (a)   in relation to a disposition made under a contract, the title which the purchaser was, apart from any acceptance by him (by agreement or otherwise) of a shorter or an imperfect title, entitled to require; or

    (b)   in relation to any other disposition, the title which he would have been entitled to require if the disposition had been made under a contract to which section 44(1) of the Law of Property Act 1925 applied and that contract had been made on the date of completion.

(11) For the purposes of this section any knowledge acquired in the course of a transaction by a person who is acting therein as counsel, or as solicitor or other agent, for another shall be treated as the knowledge of that other.

ADMINISTRATION OF JUSTICE ACT 1970
(1970, c. 31)

PART IV

36. Additional powers of court in action by mortgagee for possession of dwelling-house

(1)   Where the mortgagee under a mortgage of land which consists of or includes a dwelling-house brings an action in which he claims possession of the mortgaged property, not being an action for foreclosure in which a claim for possession of the mortgaged property is also made, the court may exercise any of the powers conferred on it by subsection (2) below if it appears to the court that in the event of its exercising the power the mortgagor is likely to be able within a reasonable period to pay any sums due under the mortgage or to remedy a default consisting of a breach of any other obligation arising under or by virtue of the mortgage.

(2)   The court—
    (a)   may adjourn the proceedings, or
    (b)   on giving judgment, or making an order, for delivery of possession of the mortgaged property, or at any time before the execution of such judgment or order, may—
        (i)   stay or suspend execution of the judgment or order, or
        (ii)   postpone the date for delivery of possession, for such period or periods as the court thinks reasonable.

(3)   Any such adjournment, stay, suspension or postponement as is referred to in subsection (2) above may be made subject to such conditions with regard to payment by the mortgagor of any sum secured by the mortgage or the remedying of any default as the court thinks fit.

(4)   The court may from time to time vary or revoke any condition imposed by virtue of this section.

...

38A.   This Part of this Act shall not apply to a mortgage securing an agreement which is a regulated agreement within the meaning of the Consumer Credit Act 1974.

39.   Interpretation of Part IV

(1)   In this Part of this Act—
'dwelling house' includes any building or part thereof which is used as a dwelling; 'mortgage' includes a charge and 'mortgagor' and 'mortgagee' shall be construed accordingly;
'mortgagor' and 'mortgagee' includes any person deriving title under the original mortgagor or mortgagee.

(2)   The fact that part of the premises comprised in a dwelling-house is used as a shop or office or for business, trade or professional purposes shall not prevent the dwelling-house from being a dwelling-house for the purposes of this Part of this Act.

MATRIMONIAL PROCEEDINGS AND PROPERTY ACT 1970
(1970, c. 45)

Provisions relating to property of married persons

37.   Contributions by spouse in money or money's worth to the improvement of property

It is hereby declared that where a husband or wife contributes in money or money's worth to the improvement of real or personal property in which or in the proceeds of sale of which either or both of them has or have a beneficial interest, the husband or wife so contributing shall, if the contribution is of a substantial nature and subject to any agreement between them to the contrary express or implied, be treated as having then acquired by virtue of his or her contribution a share or an enlarged share, as the case may be, in that beneficial interest of such an extent as may have been then agreed or, in default of such agreement, as may seem in all the circumstances just to any court before which the question of the existence or extent of the beneficial interest of the husband or wife arises (whether in proceedings between them or in any other proceedings).

POWERS OF ATTORNEY ACT 1971
(1971 c. 27)

5.   Protection of donee and third persons where power of attorney is revoked

(1)   A donee of a power of attorney who acts in pursuance of the power at a time when it has been revoked shall not, by reason of the revocation, incur any liability (either to the donor or to any other person) if at that time he did not know that the power had been revoked.

(2)   Where a power of attorney has been revoked and a person, without knowledge of the revocation, deals with the donee of the power, the transaction between them shall, in favour of that person, be as valid as if the power had then been in existence.

(3)   Where the power is expressed in the instrument creating it to be irrevocable and to be given by way of security then, unless the person dealing with the donee knows that it was not in fact given by way of security, he shall be entitled to assume that the power is incapable of revocation except by the donor acting with the consent of the donee and shall accordingly be treated for the purposes of subsection (2) of this section as having knowledge of the revocation only if he knows that it has been revoked in that manner.

(4)   Where the interest of a purchaser depends on whether a transaction between the donee of a power of attorney and another person was valid by virtue of subsection (2) of this section, it shall be conclusively presumed in favour of the purchaser that that person did not at the material time know of the revocation of the power if—

(a)   the transaction between that person and the donee was completed within twelve months of the date on which the power came into operation; or

(b)   that person makes a statutory declaration, before or within three months after the completion of the purchase, that he did not at the material time know of the revocation of the power.

(5)   Without prejudice to subsection (3) of this section, for the purposes of this section knowledge of the revocation of a power of attorney includes knowledge of the occurrence of any event (such as the death of the donor) which has the effect of revoking the power.

(6)   In this section 'purchaser' and 'purchase' have the meanings specified in section 205(1) of the Law of Property Act 1925.

(7)   This section applies whenever the power of attorney was created but only to acts and transactions after the commencement of this Act.

6.   Additional protection for transferees under stock exchange transactions

(1)   Without prejudice to section 5 of this Act, where—
   (a)   the donee of a power of attorney executes, as transferor, an instrument transferring registered securities; and
   (b)   the instrument is executed for the purposes of a stock exchange transaction,
   it shall be conclusively presumed in favour of the transferee that the power had not been revoked at the date of the instrument if a statutory declaration to that effect is made by the donee of the power on or within three months after that date.

(2)   In this section 'registered securities' and 'stock exchange transaction' have the same meanings as in the Stock Transfer Act 1963.

7.   Execution of instruments etc. by donee of power of attorney

(1)   If the donee of a power of attorney is an individual, he may, if he thinks fit—
   (a)   execute any instrument with his own signature, and
   (b)   do any other thing in his own name,
   by the authority of the donor of the power; and any instrument executed or thing done in that manner shall, subject to subsection (1A) of this section, be as effective as if executed by the donee in any manner which would constitute due execution of that instrument by the donor or, as the case may be, as if done by the donee in the name of the donor.

(1A)   Where an instrument is executed by the donee as a deed, it shall be effective as if executed by the donee in a manner which would constitute due execution of it as a deed by the donor only if it is executed in accordance with section 1(3)(a) of the Law of Property (Miscellaneous Provisions) Act 1989.

(2)   For the avoidance of doubt it is hereby declared that an instrument to which subsection (3) of section 74 of the Law of Property Act 1925 applies may be executed either as provided in that subsection or as provided in this section.

(3)   ...

(4)   This section applies whenever the power of attorney was created.

LAND CHARGES ACT 1972
(1972, c. 61)

Preliminary

1.   The registers and the index

(1)   The registrar shall continue to keep at the registry in the prescribed manner the following registers, namely—
   (a)   a register of land charges;
   (b)   a register of pending actions;
   (c)   a register of writs and orders affecting land;
   (d)   ...
   (e)   a register of annuities,
   and shall also continue to keep there an index whereby all entries made in any of those registers can readily be traced.

(2)   Every application to register shall be in the prescribed form and shall contain the prescribed particulars.

(3)   Where any charge or other matter is registrable in more than one of the registers kept under this Act it shall be sufficient if it is registered in one register, and if it is so registered the person entitled to the benefit of it shall not be prejudicially affected by the provision of this Act as to the effect of non-registration in any other such register.

(3A) Where any charge or other matter is registrable in a register kept under this Act and was also, before the commencement of the Local Land Charges Act 1975, registrable in a local land charges register, then, if before the commencement of the said Act it was registered in the appropriate local land charges register it shall be treated for the purposes of the provisions of this Act as to the effect of non-registration as if it had been registered in the appropriate register under this Act, and any certificate setting out the result of an official search of the appropriate local land charges register shall, in relation to it, have effect as if it were a certificate setting out the result of an official search under this Act.

(4)   Schedule 1 to this Act shall have effect in relation to the register of annuities.

(5)   An office copy of an entry in any register kept under this section shall be admissible in evidence in all proceedings and between all parties to the same extent as the original would be admissible.

(6)   Subject to the provisions of this Act, registration may be vacated pursuant to an order of the court.

(6A) The county court has jurisdiction under subsection (6) above—

    (a)   in the case of a land charge of Class C(i), C(ii) or D(i) if the amount does not exceed £30,000;

    (b)   in the case of a land charge of Class C(iii), if it is for a specified capital sum of money, not exceeding £30,000 or, where it is not for a specified capital sum, if the land affected does not exceed the county court limit in capital value or in net annual value for rating;

    (c)   in the case of a land charge of Class A, Class B, Class C(iv), Class D(ii), Class D(iii) or Class E, if the land affected does not exceed £30,000;

    (d)   in the case of a land charge of Class F, if the land affected by it is the subject of an order made by the court under section 1 of the Matrimonial Homes Act 1983 or section 33 of the Family Law Act 1996 or an application for an order under either of those sections relating to that land has been made to the court.

    (e)   in a case where an application under section 23 of the Deeds of Arrangement Act 1914 could be entertained by the court.

(6B) ...

(7)   In this section 'index' includes any device or combination of devices serving the purpose of an index.

Registration in register of land charges

2.   The register of land charges

(1)   If a charge on or obligation affecting land falls into one of the classes described in this section, it may be registered in the register of land charges as a land charge of that class.

(2)   A Class A land charge is—

    (a)   a rent or annuity or principal money payable by instalments or otherwise, with or without interest, which is not a charge created by deed but is a charge upon land (other than a rate) created pursuant to the application of some person under the provisions of any Act of Parliament, for securing to any person either the money spent by him or the costs, charges and expenses incurred by him under such Act, or the money advanced by him for repaying the money spent or the costs, charges and expenses incurred by another person under the authority of an Act of Parliament; or

    (b)   a rent or annuity or principal money payable as mentioned in paragraph (a) above which is not a charge created by deed but is a charge upon land (other than a rate) created pursuant to the application of some person under any of the enactments mentioned in Schedule 2 to this Act.

(3)   A Class B land charge is a charge on land (not being a local land charge) of any of the kinds described in paragraph (a) of subsection (2) above, created otherwise than pursuant to the application of any person.

(4)   A Class C land charge is any of the following (not being a local land charge), namely—

    (i)   a puisne mortgage;

    (ii)   a limited owner's charge;

    (iii)   a general equitable charge;

    (iv)   an estate contract;

and for this purpose—

(i)   a puisne mortgage is a legal mortgage which is not protected by a deposit of documents relating to the legal estate affected;

(ii)   a limited owner's charge is an equitable charge acquired by a tenant for life or statutory owner under the Inheritance Tax Act 1984 or under any other statute by reason of the discharge by him of any inheritance tax or other liabilities and to which special priority is given by the statute;

(iii)   a general equitable charge is any equitable charge which—

    (a)   is not secured by a deposit of documents relating to the legal estate affected; and

    (b)   does not arise or affect an interest arising under a trust of land or a settlement; and

    (c)   is not a charge given by way of indemnity against rents equitably apportioned or charged exclusively on land in exoneration of other land and against the breach or non-observance of covenants or conditions; and

    (d)   is not included in any other class of land charge;

(iv)   an estate contract is a contract by an estate owner or by a person entitled at the date of the contract to have a legal estate conveyed to him to convey or create a legal estate, including a contract conferring either expressly or by statutory implication a valid option to purchase, a right of preemption or any other like right.

(5)   A Class D land charge is any of the following, (not being a local land charge), namely—

(i)   an Inland Revenue charge;

(ii)   a restrictive covenant;

(iii)   an equitable easement;

and for this purpose—

(i)   an Inland Revenue charge is a charge on land, being a charge acquired by the Board under the Inheritance Tax Act 1984;

(ii)   a restrictive covenant is a covenant or agreement (other than a covenant or agreement between a lessor and a lessee) restrictive of the user of land and entered into on or after 1st January 1926,

(iii)   an equitable easement is an easement, right or privilege over or affecting land created or arising on or after 1st January 1926, and being merely an equitable interest.

(6)   A Class E land charge is an annuity created before 1st January 1926 and not registered in the register of annuities.

(7)   A Class F land charge is a charge affecting any land by virtue of the Part IV of the Family Law Act 1996.

(8)   A charge or obligation created before 1st January 1926 can only be registered as a Class B land charge or a Class C land charge if it is acquired under a conveyance made on or after that date.

3.   Registration of land charges

(1)   A land charge shall be registered in the name of the estate owner whose estate is intended to be affected.

(1A)   Where a person has died and a land charge created before his death would apart from his death have been registered in his name, it shall be so registered notwithstanding his death.

(2)   A land charge registered before lst January 1926 under any enactment replaced by the Land Charges Act 1925 in the name of a person other than the estate owner may remain so registered until it is registered in the name of the estate owner in the prescribed manner.

(3)   A puisne mortgage created before 1st January 1926 may be registered as a land charge before any transfer of the mortgage is made.

(4)   The expenses incurred by the person entitled to the charge in registering a land charge of Class A, Class B or Class C (other than an estate contract) or by the Board in registering an Inland Revenue charge shall be deemed to form part of the land charge, and shall be recoverable accordingly on the day for payment of any part of the land charge next after such expenses are incurred.

(5)   Where a land charge is not created by an instrument, short particulars of the effect of the charge shall be furnished with the application to register the charge.

(6)   An application to register an Inland Revenue charge shall state the tax in respect of which the charge is claimed and, so far as possible, shall define the land affected, and such particulars shall be entered or referred to in the register.

(7)   In the case of a land charge for securing money created by a company before 1st January 1970 or so created at any time as a floating charge, registration under any of the enactments mentioned in subsection (8) below shall be sufficient in place of registration under this Act, and shall have effect as if the land charge had been registered under this Act.

(8)   The enactments referred to in subsection (7) above are section 93 of the Companies (Consolidation) Act 1908, section 79 of the Companies Act 1929, section 95 of the Companies Act 1948, sections 395 to 398 of the Companies Act 1985 and Part 25 of the Companies Act 2006 and regulations made under section 1052 of that Act.

4.   Effect of land charges and protection of purchasers

(1)   A land charge of Class A (other than a land improvement charge registered after 31st December 1969) or of Class B shall, when registered, take effect as if it had been created by a deed of charge by way of legal mortgage, but without prejudice to the priority of the charge.

(2)   A land charge of Class A created after 31st December 1888 shall be void as against a purchaser of the land charged with it or of any interest in such land, unless the land charge is registered in the register of land charges before the completion of the purchase.

(3)   After the expiration of one year from the first conveyance occurring on or after 1st January 1889 of a land charge of Class A created before that date the person entitled to the land charge shall not be able to recover the land charge or any part of it as against a purchaser of the land charged with it or of any interest in the land, unless the land charge is registered in the register of land charges before the completion of the purchase.

(4)   If a land improvement charge was registered as a land charge of Class A before 1st January 1970, any body corporate which, but for the charge, would have power to advance money on the security of the estate or interest affected by it shall have that power notwithstanding the charge.

(5)   A land charge of Class B and a land charge of Class C (other than an estate contract) created or arising on or after 1st January 1926 shall be void as against a purchaser of the land charged with it, or of any interest in such land, unless the land charge is registered in the appropriate register before the completion of the purchase.

(6)   An estate contract and a land charge of Class D created or entered into on or after 1st January 1926 shall be void as against a purchaser for money or money's worth (or in the case of an Inland Revenue charge, a purchaser within the meaning of the Inheritance Tax Act 1984) of a legal estate in the land charged with it, unless the land charge is registered in the appropriate register before the completion of the purchase.

(7)   After the expiration of one year from the first conveyance occurring on or after 1st January 1926 of a land charge of Class B or Class C created before that date the person entitled to the land charge shall not be able to enforce or recover the land charge or any part of it as against a purchaser of the land charged with it, or of any interest in the land, unless the land charge is registered in the appropriate register before the completion of the purchase.

(8)   A land charge of Class F shall be void as against a purchaser of the land charged with it, or of any interest in such land, unless the land charge is registered in the appropriate register before the completion of the purchase.

Registration in registers of pending actions, writs and orders and deeds of arrangement

5.   The register of pending actions

(1)   There may be registered in the register of pending actions—
    (a)   a pending land action;
    (b)   a petition in bankruptcy filed on or after 1st January 1926.

(2)   Subject to general rules under section 16 of this Act, every application for registration under this section shall contain particulars of the title of the proceedings and the name, address and description of the estate owner or other person whose estate or interest is intended to be affected.

(3) An application for registration shall also state—
   (a) if it relates to a pending land action, the court in which and the day on which the action was commenced; and
   (b) if it relates to a petition in bankruptcy, the court in which and the day on which the petition was filed.
(4) The registrar shall forthwith enter the particulars in the register, in the name of the estate owner or other person whose estate or interest is intended to be affected.
(4A) Where a person has died and a pending land action would apart from his death have been registered in his name, it shall be so registered notwithstanding his death.
(5) An application to register a petition in bankruptcy against a firm shall state the names and addresses of the partners, and the registration shall be effected against each partner as well as against the firm.
(6) No fee shall be charged for the registration of a petition in bankruptcy if the application for registration is made by the registrar of the court in which the petition is filed.
(7) A pending land action shall not bind a purchaser without express notice of it unless it is for the time being registered under this section.
(8) A petition in bankruptcy shall not bind a purchaser of a legal estate in good faith, for money or money's worth, unless it is for the time being registered under this section.
(9) ...
(10) The court, if it thinks fit, may, upon the determination of the proceedings, or during the pendency of the proceedings if satisfied that they are not prosecuted in good faith, make an order vacating a registration under this section, and direct the party on whose behalf it was made to pay all or any of the costs and expenses occasioned by the registration and by its vacation.
(11) The county court has jurisdiction under subsection (10) of this section where the action was brought or the petition in bankruptcy was filed by the court.

6.   The register of writs and orders affecting land

(1) There may be registered in the register of writs and orders affecting land—
   (a) any writ or order affecting land issued or made by any court for the purpose of enforcing a judgment or recognisance—
   (b) any order appointing a receiver or sequestrator of land;
   (c) any bankruptcy order whether or not the bankrupt's estate is known to include land
   (c) any receiving order in bankruptcy made on or after 1st January 1926, whether or not it is known to affect land.
   (d) any access order under the Access to Neighbouring Land Act 1992.
(1A) No writ or order affecting an interest under a trust of land may be registered under subsection (1) above.
(2) Every entry made pursuant to this section shall be made in the name of the estate owner or other person whose land, if any, is affected by the writ or order registered.
(2A) Where a person has died and any such writ or order as is mentioned in subsection (1)(a) or (b) above would apart from his death have been registered in his name, it shall be so registered notwithstanding his death.
(3) No fee shall be charged for the registration of a bankruptcy order if the application for registration is made by an official receiver.
(4) Except as provided by subsection (5) below and by section 37(5) of the Senior Courts Act 1981 and section 107(3) of the County Courts Act 1984 (which make special provision as to receiving orders in respect of land of judgment debtors) every such writ and order as is mentioned in subsection (1) above, and every delivery in execution or other proceeding taken pursuant to any such writ or order, or in obedience to any such writ or order, shall be void as against a purchaser of the land unless the writ or order is for the time being registered under this section.
(5) Subject to subsection (6) below, the title of a trustee in bankruptcy shall be void as against a purchaser of a legal estate in good faith for money or money's worth unless the bankruptcy order is for the time being registered under this section.
(6) Where a petition in bankruptcy has been registered under section 5 above, the title of the trustee in bankruptcy shall be void as against a purchaser of a legal estate in good faith for money or money's worth claiming under a conveyance made after the date of registration, unless at the date of the conveyance either the registration of the petition is in force or a receiving order on the petition is registered under this section.

7   ...

8.   Expiry and renewal of registrations

A registration under section 5, section 6 or section 7 of this Act shall cease to have effect at the end of the period of five years from the date on which it is made, but may be renewed from time to time and, if so renewed, shall have effect for five years from the date of renewal.

Searches and official searches

9.   Searches

(1)   Any person may search in any register kept under this Act on paying the prescribed fee.

(2)   Without prejudice to subsection (1) above, the registrar may provide facilities for enabling persons entitled to search in any such register to see photographic or other images or copies of any portion of the register which they may wish to examine.

10.   Official searches

(1)   Where any person requires search to be made at the registry for entries of any matters or documents, entries of which are required or allowed to be made in the registry by this Act, he may make a requisition in that behalf to the registrar, which may be either—

    (a)   a written requisition delivered at or sent by post to the registry, or

    (b)   a requisition communicated by teleprinter, telephone or other means in such manner as may be prescribed in relation to the means in question, in which case it shall be treated as made to the registrar if, but only if, he accepts it;

and the registrar shall not accept a requisition made in accordance with paragraph (b) above unless it is made by a person maintaining a credit account at the registry, and may at his discretion refuse to accept it notwithstanding that it is made by such a person.

(2)   The prescribed fee shall be payable in respect of every requisition made under this section; and that fee—

    (a)   in the case of a requisition made in accordance with subsection (1)(a) above, shall be paid in such manner as may be prescribed for the purposes of this paragraph unless the requisition is made by a person maintaining a credit account at the registry and the fee is debited to that account;

    (b)   in the case of a requisition made in accordance with subsection (1)(b) above, shall be debited to the credit account of the person by whom the requisition is made.

(3)   Where a requisition is made under subsection (1) above and the fee payable in respect of it is paid or debited in accordance with subsection (2) above, the registrar shall thereupon make the search required and—

    (a)   shall issue a certificate setting out the result of the search; and

    (b)   without prejudice to paragraph (a) above, may take such other steps as he considers appropriate to communicate that result to the person by whom the requisition was made.

(4)   In favour of a purchaser or an intending purchaser, as against persons interested under or in respect of matters or documents entries of which are required or allowed as aforesaid, the certificate, according to its tenor, shall be conclusive, affirmatively or negatively, as the case may be.

(5)   If any officer, clerk or person employed in the registry commits, or is party or privy to, any act of fraud or collusion, or is wilfully negligent, in the making of or otherwise in relation to any certificate under this section, he shall be guilty of an offence and shall be liable on conviction on indictment to imprisonment for a term not exceeding two years, or on summary conviction to imprisonment for a term not exceeding three months or to a fine not exceeding the prescribed sum, or to both such imprisonment and fine.

(6)   Without prejudice to subsection (5) above, no officer, clerk or person employed in the registry shall, in the absence of fraud on his part, be liable for any loss which may be suffered—

    (a)   by reason of any discrepancy between—

        (i)   the particulars which are shown in a certificate under this section as being the particulars in respect of which the search for entries was made, and

        (ii)   the particulars in respect of which a search for entries was required by the person who made the requisition; or

    (b)   by reason of any communication of the result of a search under this section made otherwise than by issuing a certificate under this section.

Miscellaneous and supplementary

11. Date of effective registration and priority notices

(1) Any person intending to make an application for the registration of any contemplated charge, instrument or other matter in pursuance of this Act or any rule made under this Act may give a priority notice in the prescribed form at least the relevant number of days before the registration is to take effect.

(2) Where a notice is given under subsection (1) above, it shall be entered in the register to which the intended application when made will relate.

(3) If the application is presented within the relevant number of days thereafter and refers in the prescribed manner to the notice, the registration shall take effect as if the registration had been made at the time when the charge, instrument or matter was created, entered into, made or arose, and the date at which the registration so takes effect shall be deemed to be the date of registration.

(4) Where—
   (a) any two charges, instruments or matters are contemporaneous; and
   (b) one of them (whether or not protected by a priority notice) is subject to or dependent on the other; and
   (c) the latter is protected by a priority notice,
   the subsequent or dependent charge, instrument or matter shall be deemed to have been created, entered into or made, or to have arisen, after the registration of the other.

(5) Where a purchaser has obtained a certificate under section 10 above, any entry which is made in the register after the date of the certificate and before the completion of the purchase, and is not made pursuant to a priority notice entered on the register on or before the date of the certificate, shall not affect the purchaser if the purchase is completed before the expiration of the relevant number of days after the date of the certificate.

(6) The relevant number of days is—
   (a) for the purposes of subsection (1) and (5) above, fifteen;
   (b) for the purposes of subsection (3) above, thirty,
   or such other number as may be prescribed; but in reckoning the relevant number of days for any of the purposes of this section any days when the registry is not open to the public shall be excluded.

12. Protection of solicitors, trustees, etc.

A solicitor, or a trustee, personal representative, agent or other person in a fiduciary position, shall not be answerable—

(a) in respect of any loss occasioned by reliance on an office copy of an entry in any register kept under this Act;

(b) for any loss that may arise from error in a certificate under section 10 above obtained by him.

13. Saving for overreaching powers

(1) The registration of any charge, annuity or other interest under this Act shall not prevent the charge, annuity or interest being overreached under any other Act, except where otherwise provided by that other Act.

(2) The registration as a land charge of a puisne mortgage or charge shall not operate to prevent that mortgage or charge being overreached in favour of a prior mortgagee or a person deriving title under him where, by reason of a sale or foreclosure, or otherwise, the right of the puisne mortgagee or subsequent chargee to redeem is barred.

14. Exclusion of matters affecting registered land or created by instruments necessitating registration of land

(1) This Act shall not apply to instruments or matters required to be registered or re- registered on or after 1st January 1926, if and so far as they affect registered land, and can be protected under the Land Registration Act 2002.

(2) Nothing in this Act imposes on the registrar any obligation to ascertain whether or not an instrument or matter affects registered land.

(3) Where an instrument executed on or after 27th July 1971 conveys, grants or assigns an estate in land and creates a land charge affecting that estate, this Act shall not apply to

the land charge, so far as it affects that estate, if under section 7 of the Land Registration Act 2002 (effect of failure to comply with requirement of registration) the instrument will, unless the necessary application for registration under that Act is made within the time allowed by or under section 6 of that Act, become void so far as respects the conveyance, grant or assignment of that estate.

17. Interpretation

(1)   In this Act, unless the context otherwise requires:—

'annuity' means a rentcharge or an annuity for a life or lives or for any term of years or greater estate determinable on a life or on lives and created after 25th April 1855 and before 1st January 1926, but does not include an annuity created by a marriage settlement or will;

'the Board' means the Commissioners of Inland Revenue;

'conveyance' includes a mortgage, charge, lease, assent, vesting declaration, vesting instrument, release and every other assurance of property, or of an interest in property, by any instrument except a will, and 'convey' has a corresponding meaning;

'court' means the High Court, or the county court in a case where that court has jurisdiction;

'estate owner', 'legal estate', 'equitable interest', 'charge by way of legal mortgage', and 'will' have the same meanings as in the Law of Property Act 1925;

'judgment' includes any order or decree having the effect of a judgment;

'land' includes land of any tenure and mines and minerals, whether or not severed from the surface, buildings or parts of buildings (whether the division is horizontal, vertical or made in any other way) and other corporeal hereditaments, also a manor, an advowson and a rent and other incorporeal hereditaments, and an easement, right, privilege or benefit in, over or derived from land, but not an undivided share in land, and 'hereditament' means real property which, on an intestacy occurring before 1st January 1926, might have devolved on an heir;

'land improvement charge' means any charge under the Improvement of Land Act 1864 or under any special improvement Act within the meaning of the Improvement of Land Act 1899;

'pending land action' means any action or proceeding pending in court relating to land or any interest in or charge on land;

'prescribed' means prescribed by rules made pursuant to this Act;

'purchaser' means any person (including a mortgagee or lessee) who, for valuable consideration, takes any interest in land or in a charge on land, and 'purchase' has a corresponding meaning;

'registrar' means the Chief Land Registrar, 'registry' means Her Majesty's Land Registry, and 'registered land' has the same meaning as in the Land Registration Act 2002;

'tenant for life', 'statutory owner', 'vesting instrument' and 'settlement' have the same meanings as in the Settled Land Act 1925.

...

(3)   Any reference in this Act to any enactment is a reference to it as amended by or under any other enactment, including this Act.

ADMINISTRATION OF JUSTICE ACT 1973
(1973, c. 15)

8. Extension of powers by court in action by mortgagee of dwelling-house

(1)   Where by a mortgage of land which consists of or includes a dwelling-house, or by any agreement between the mortgagee under such a mortgage and the mortgagor, the mortgagor is entitled or is to be permitted to pay the principal sum secured by instalments or otherwise to defer payment of it in whole or in part, but provision is also made for earlier payment in the event of any default by the mortgagor or of a demand by the mortgagee or otherwise, then for purposes of section 36 of the Administration of Justice Act 1970 (under which a court has power to delay giving a mortgagee possession of the mortgaged property so as to allow the mortgagor a reasonable time to pay any sums due under the mortgage) a court may treat as due under the mortgage on account

of the principal sum secured and of interest on it only such amounts as the mortgagor would have expected to be required to pay if there had been no such provision for earlier payment.

(2) A court shall not exercise by virtue of subsection (1) above the powers conferred by section 36 of the Administration of Justice Act 1970 unless it appears to the court not only that the mortgagor is likely to be able within a reasonable period to pay any amounts regarded (in accordance with subsection (1) above) as due on account of the principal sum secured, together with the interest on those amounts, but also that he is likely to be able by the end of that period to pay any further amounts that he would have expected to be required to pay by then on account of that sum and of interest on it if there had been no such provision as is referred to in subsection (1) above for earlier payment.

(3) Where subsection (1) above would apply to an action in which a mortgagee only claimed possession of the mortgaged property, and the mortgagee brings an action for foreclosure (with or without also claiming possession of the property), then section 36 of the Administration of Justice Act 1970 together with subsections (1) and (2) above shall apply as they would apply if it were an action in which the mortgagee only claimed possession of the mortgaged property, except that—

(a) section 36(2)(b) shall apply only in relation to any claim for possession; and

(b) section 36(5) shall not apply.

(4) For purposes of this section the expressions 'dwelling-house', 'mortgage', mortgagee' and 'mortgagor' shall be construed in the same way as for the purposes of Part IV of the Administration of Justice Act 1970.

...

MATRIMONIAL CAUSES ACT 1973
(1973, c. 18)

24. Property adjustment orders in connection with divorce proceedings, etc.

(1) On granting a decree of divorce, a decree of nullity of marriage or a decree of judicial separation or at any time thereafter (whether, in the case of a decree of divorce or of nullity of marriage, before or after the decree is made absolute), the court may make any one or more of the following orders, that is to say—

(a) an order that a party to the marriage shall transfer to the other party, to any child of the family or to such person as may be specified in the order for the benefit of such a child such property as may be so specified, being property to which the first-mentioned party is entitled, either in possession or reversion;

(b) an order that a settlement of such property as may be so specified, being property to which a party to the marriage is so entitled, be made to the satisfaction of the court for the benefit of the other party to the marriage and of the children of the family or either or any of them;

(c) an order varying for the benefit of the parties to the marriage and of the children of the family or either or any of them any ante-nuptial or post-nuptial settlement (including such a settlement made by will or codicil) made on the parties to the marriage ...;

(d) an order extinguishing or reducing the interest of either of the parties to the marriage under any such settlement ...;

subject, however, in the case of an order under paragraph (a) above, to the restrictions imposed by section 29(1) and (3) below on the making of orders for a transfer of property in favour of children who have attained the age of eighteen.

(2) The court may make an order under subsection (1)(c) above notwithstanding that there are no children of the family.

(3) ...

24A. Orders for sale of property

Note. References to orders made under s 22ZA (orders for payment in respect of legal services) have been omitted from the text of this section.

(1) Where the court makes ... under section 23 or 24 of this Act a secured periodical payments order, an order for the payment of a lump sum or a property adjustment order,

then, on making that order or at any time thereafter, the court may make a further order for the sale of such property as may be specified in the order, being property in which or in the proceeds of sale of which either or both of the parties to the marriage has or have a beneficial interest, either in possession or reversion.

(2)   Any order made under subsection (1) above may contain such consequential or supplementary provisions as the court thinks fit and, without prejudice to the generality of the foregoing provision, may include—

(a)   provision requiring the making of a payment out of the proceeds of sale of the property to which the order relates, and

(b)   provision requiring any such property to be offered for sale to a person, or class of persons, specified in the order.

(3)   Where an order is made under subsection (1) above on or after the grant of a decree of divorce or nullity of marriage, the order shall not take effect unless the decree has been made absolute.

(4)   Where an order is made under subsection (1) above, the court may direct that the order, or such provision thereof as the court may specify, shall not take effect until the occurrence of an event specified by the court or the expiration of a period so specified.

(5)   Where an order under subsection (1) above contains a provision requiring the proceeds of sale of the property to which the order relates to be used to secure periodical payments to a party to the marriage, the order shall cease to have effect on the death or re-marriage of, or formation of a civil partnership by, that person.

(6)   Where a party to a marriage has a beneficial interest in any property, or in the proceeds of sale thereof, and some other person who is not a party to the marriage also has a beneficial interest in that property or in the proceeds of sale thereof, then, before deciding whether to make an order under this section in relation to that property, it shall be the duty of the court to give that other person an opportunity to make representations with respect to the order; and any representations made by that other person shall be included among the circumstances to which the court is required to have regard under section 25(1) below.

25.   Matters to which court is to have regard in deciding how to exercise its powers under ss … 24 [and] 24A …

Note: References to orders made under s 23 (financial provision orders), s 24B (pension sharing orders) and s 24E (pension compensation sharing orders) have been omitted from the text of this section.

(1)   It shall be the duty of the court in deciding whether to exercise its powers under section … 24 [or] 24A … above and, if so, in what manner, to have regard to all the circumstances of the case, first consideration being given to the welfare while a minor of any child of the family who has not attained the age of eighteen.

(2)   As regards the exercise of the powers of the court under section … 24 [or] 24A … above in relation to a party to the marriage, the court shall in particular have regard to the following matters—

(a)   the income, earning capacity, property and other financial resources which each of the parties to the marriage has or is likely to have in the foreseeable future, including in the case of earning capacity any increase in that capacity which it would in the opinion of the court be reasonable to expect a party to the marriage to take steps to acquire;

(b)   the financial needs, obligations and responsibilities which each of the parties to the marriage has or is likely to have in the foreseeable future;

(c)   the standard of living enjoyed by the family before the breakdown of the marriage;

(d)   the age of each party to the marriage and the duration of the marriage;

(e)   any physical or mental disability of either of the parties to the marriage;

(f)   the contributions which each of the parties has made or is likely in the foreseeable future to make to the welfare of the family, including any contribution by looking after the home or caring for the family;

(g)   the conduct of each of the parties, if that conduct is such that it would in the opinion of the court be inequitable to disregard it;

(h)   in the case of proceedings for divorce or nullity of marriage, the value to each of the parties to the marriage of any benefit which, by reason of the dissolution or annulment of the marriage, that party will lose the chance of acquiring.

(3) As regards the exercise of the powers of the court under section ... 24 or 24A above in relation to a child of the family, the court shall in particular have regard to the following matters—

(a) the financial needs of the child;

(b) the income, earning capacity (if any), property and other financial resources of the child;

(c) any physical or mental disability of the child;

(d) the manner in which he was being and in which the parties to the marriage expected him to be educated or trained;

(e) the considerations mentioned in relation to the parties to the marriage in paragraphs (a), (b), (c) and (e) of subsection (2) above.

(4) As regards the exercise of the powers of the court under section ... 24 or 24A above against a party to a marriage in favour of a child of the family who is not the child of that party, the court shall also have regard—

(a) to whether that party assumed any responsibility for the child's maintenance, and, if so, to the extent to which, and the basis upon which, that party assumed such responsibility and to the length of time for which that party discharged such responsibility;

(b) to whether in assuming and discharging such responsibility that party did so knowing that the child was not his or her own;

(c) to the liability of any other person to maintain the child.

(5) ...

37. Avoidance of transactions intended to prevent or reduce financial relief

(1) For the purposes of this section 'financial relief' means relief under any of the provisions of sections 22, 23, 24, 24B, 27, 31 (except subsection (6)) and 35 above, and any reference in this section to defeating a person's claim for financial relief is a reference to preventing financial relief from being granted to that person, or to that person for the benefit of a child of the family, or reducing the amount of any financial relief which might be so granted, or frustrating or impeding the enforcement of any order which might be or has been made at his instance under any of those provisions.

(2) Where proceedings for financial relief are brought by one person against another, the court may, on the application of the first-mentioned person—

(a) if it is satisfied that the other party to the proceedings is, with the intention of defeating the claim for financial relief, about to make any disposition or to transfer out of the jurisdiction or otherwise deal with any property, make such order as it thinks fit for restraining the other party from so doing or otherwise for protecting the claim;

(b) if it is satisfied that the other party has, with that intention, made a reviewable disposition and that if the disposition were set aside financial relief or different financial relief would be granted to the applicant, make an order setting aside the disposition;

(c) if it is satisfied, in a case where an order has been obtained under any of the provisions mentioned in subsection (1) above by the applicant against the other party, that the other party has, with that intention, made a reviewable disposition, make an order setting aside the disposition;

and an application for the purposes of paragraph (b) above shall be made in the proceedings for the financial relief in question.

(3) Where the court makes an order under subsection (2)(b) or (c) above setting aside a disposition it shall give such consequential directions as it thinks fit for giving effect to the order (including directions requiring the making of any payments or the disposal of any property).

(4) Any disposition made by the other party to the proceedings for financial relief in question (whether before or after the commencement of those proceedings) is a reviewable disposition for the purposes of subsection (2)(b) and (c) above unless it was made for valuable consideration (other than marriage) to a person who, at the time of the disposition, acted in relation to it in good faith and without notice of any intention on the part of the other party to defeat the applicant's claim for financial relief.

(5) Where an application is made under this section with respect to a disposition which took place less than three years before the date of the application or with respect to a

disposition or other dealing with property which is about to take place and the court is satisfied—

(a)   in a case falling within subsection (2)(a) or (b) above, that the disposition or other dealing would (apart from this section) have the consequence, or

(b)   in a case falling within subsection (2)(c) above, that the disposition has had the consequence,

of defeating the applicant's claim for financial relief, it shall be presumed, unless the contrary is shown, that the person who disposed of or is about to dispose of or deal with the property did so or, as the case may be, is about to do so, with the intention of defeating the applicant's claim for financial relief.

(6)   In this section 'disposition' does not include any provision contained in a will or codicil but, with that exception, includes any conveyance, assurance or gift of property of any description, whether made by an instrument or otherwise.

(7)   This section does not apply to a disposition made before 1st January 1968.

INHERITANCE (PROVISION FOR FAMILY AND DEPENDANTS) ACT 1975
(1975, c. 63)

1.   Application for financial provision from deceased's estate

(1)   Where after the commencement of this Act a person dies domiciled in England and Wales and is survived by any of the following persons:—

(a)   the spouse or civil partner of the deceased;

(b)   a former spouse or former civil partner of the deceased, but not one who has formed a subsequent marriage or civil partnership;

(ba)   any person (not being a person included in paragraph (a) or (b) above) to whom subsection (1A) or (1B) below applies

(c)   a child of the deceased;

(d)   any person (not being a child of the deceased) who in relation to any marriage or civil partnership to which the deceased was at any time a party, or otherwise in relation to any family in which the deceased at any time stood in the role of a parent, was treated by the deceased as a child of the family;

(e)   any person (not being a person included in the foregoing paragraphs of this subsection) who immediately before the death of the deceased was being maintained, either wholly or partly, by the deceased;

that person may apply to the court for an order under section 2 of this Act on the ground that the disposition of the deceased's estate effected by his will or the law relating to intestacy, or the combination of his will and that law, is not such as to make reasonable financial provision for the applicant.

(1A)   This section applies to a person if the deceased died on or after 1st January 1996 and, during the whole of the period of two years ending immediately before the date when the deceased died, the person was living—

(a)   in the same household as the deceased, and

(b)   as the husband or wife of the deceased.

(1B)   This subsection applies to a person if for the whole of the period of two years ending immediately before the date when the deceased died the person was living—

(a)   in the same household as the deceased, and

(b)   as the civil partner of the deceased.

(2)   In this Act 'reasonable financial provision'—

(a)   in the case of an application made by virtue of subsection (1)(a) above by the husband or wife of the deceased (except where the marriage with the deceased was the subject of a decree of judicial separation and at the date of death the decree was in force and the separation was continuing), means such financial provision as it would be reasonable in all the circumstances of the case for a husband or wife to receive, whether or not that provision is required for his or her maintenance;

(aa)   in the case of an application made by virtue of subsection (1)(a) above by the civil partner of the deceased (except where, at the date of death, a separation order under Chapter 2 of Part 2 of the Civil Partnership Act 2004 was in force in relation to the civil partnership and the separation was continuing), means such financial provision as it would be reasonable in all the circumstances of the case for a civil partner to receive, whether or not that provision is required for his or her maintenance;

(b)   in the case of any other application made by virtue of subsection (1) above, means such financial provision as it would be reasonable in all the circumstances of the case for the applicant to receive for his maintenance.

(2A) The reference in subsection (1)(d) above to a family in which the deceased stood in the role of a parent includes a family of which the deceased was the only member (apart from the applicant).

(3)   For the purposes of subsection (1)(e) above, a person shall be treated as being maintained by the deceased, either wholly or partly, as the case may be, if the deceased, otherwise than for full valuable consideration, was making a substantial contribution in money or money's worth towards the reasonable needs of that person.

2.   Powers of court to make orders

(1)   Subject to the provisions of this Act, where an application is made for an order under this section, the court may, if it is satisfied that the disposition of the deceased's estate effected by his will or the law relating to intestacy, or the combination of his will and that law, is not such as to make reasonable financial provision for the applicant, make any one or more of the following orders: —

(a)   an order for the making to the applicant out of the net estate of the deceased of such periodical payments and for such term as may be specified in the order;

(b)   an order for the payment to the applicant out of that estate of a lump sum of such amount as may be so specified;

(c)   an order for the transfer to the applicant of such property comprised in that estate as may be so specified;

(d)   an order for the settlement for the benefit of the applicant of such property comprised in that estate as may be so specified;

(e)   an order for the acquisition out of property comprised in that estate of such property as may be so specified and for the transfer of the property so acquired to the applicant or for the settlement thereof for his benefit;

(f)   an order varying any ante-nuptial or post-nuptial settlement (including such a settlement made by will) made on the parties to a marriage to which the deceased was one of the parties, the variation being for the benefit of the surviving party to that marriage, or any child of that marriage, or any person who was treated by the deceased as a child of the family in relation to that marriage;

(g)   an order varying any settlement made—

    (i)   during the subsistence of a civil partnership formed by the deceased, or

    (ii)   in anticipation of the formation of a civil partnership by the deceased,

on the civil partners (including such a settlement made by will), the variation being for the benefit of the surviving civil partner, or any child of both the civil partners, or any person who was treated by the deceased as a child of the family in relation to that civil partnership;

(h)   an order varying for the applicant's benefit the trusts on which the deceased's estate is held (whether arising under the will, or the law relating to intestacy, or both).

(2)   An order under subsection (1)(a) above providing for the making out of the net estate of the deceased of periodical payments may provide for—

(a)   payments of such amount as may be specified in the order,

(b)   payments equal to the whole of the income of the net estate or of such portion thereof as may be so specified,

(c)   payments equal to the whole of the income of such part of the net estate as the court may direct to be set aside or appropriated for the making out of the income thereof of payments under this section,

or may provide for the amount of the payments or any of them to be determined in any other way the court thinks fit.

(3)   Where an order under subsection (1)(a) above provides for the making of payments of an amount specified in the order, the order may direct that such part of the net estate as may be so specified shall be set aside or appropriated for the making out of the income

thereof of those payments; but no larger part of the net estate shall be so set aside or appropriated than is sufficient, at the date of the order, to produce by the income thereof the amount required for the making of those payments.

(3A) In assessing for the purposes of an order under this section the extent (if any) to which the net estate is reduced by any debts or liabilities (including any inheritance tax paid or payable out of the estate), the court may assume that the order has already been made.

(4) An order under this section may contain such consequential and supplemental provisions as the court thinks necessary or expedient for the purpose of giving effect to the order or for the purpose of securing that the order operates fairly as between one beneficiary of the estate of the deceased and another and may, in particular, but without prejudice to the generality of this subsection —

   (a) order any person who holds any property which forms part of the net estate of the deceased to make such payment or transfer such property as may be specified in the order;

   (b) vary the disposition of the deceased's estate effected by the will or the law relating to intestacy, or by both the will and the law relating to intestacy, in such manner as the court thinks fair and reasonable having regard to the provisions of the order and all the circumstances of the case;

   (c) confer on the trustees of any property which is the subject of an order under this section such powers as appear to the court to be necessary or expedient.

3. Matters to which court is to have regard in exercising powers under s. 2

(1) Where an application is made for an order under section 2 of this Act, the court shall, in determining whether the disposition of the deceased's estate effected by his will or the law relating to intestacy, or the combination of his will and that law, is such as to make reasonable financial provision for the applicant and, if the court considers that reasonable financial provision has not been made, in determining whether and in what manner it shall exercise its powers under that section, have regard to the following matters, that is to say—

   (a) the financial resources and financial needs which the applicant has or is likely to have in the foreseeable future;

   (b) the financial resources and financial needs which any other applicant for an order under section 2 of this Act has or is likely to have in the foreseeable future;

   (c) the financial resources and financial needs which any beneficiary of the estate of the deceased has or is likely to have in the foreseeable future;

   (d) any obligations and responsibilities which the deceased had towards any applicant for an order under the said section 2 or towards any beneficiary of the estate of the deceased;

   (e) the size and nature of the net estate of the deceased;

   (f) any physical or mental disability of any applicant for an order under the said section 2 or any beneficiary of the estate of the deceased;

   (g) any other matter, including the conduct of the applicant or any other person, which in the circumstances of the case the court may consider relevant.

(2) This subsection applies, without prejudice to the generality of paragraph (g) of subsection (1) above, where an application for an order under section 2 of this Act is made by virtue of section 1(1)(a) or (b) of this Act. The court shall, in addition to the matters specifically mentioned in paragraphs (a) to (f) of that subsection, have regard to—

   (a) the age of the applicant and the duration of the marriage or civil partnership;

   (b) the contribution made by the applicant to the welfare of the family of the deceased, including any contribution made by looking after the home or caring for the family.

In the case of an application by the wife or husband of the deceased, the court shall also, unless at the date of death a decree of judicial separation was in force and the separation was continuing, have regard to the provision which the applicant might reasonably have expected to receive if on the day on which the deceased died the marriage, instead of being terminated by death, had been terminated by a degree of divorce; but nothing requires the court to treat such provision as setting an upper or lower limit on the provision which may be made by an order under section 2. In the case of an application by the civil partner of the deceased, the court shall also, unless at the date of the death a separation order under Chapter 2 of Part 2 of the Civil Partnership Act 2004 was in force and the separation was continuing, have regard to the provision which the applicant might reasonably have expected to receive if on the day on which the deceased died the civil partnership, instead of being terminated by death, had been terminated by a dissolution order ; but nothing requires the court to treat such provision as setting an upper or lower limit on the provision which may be made by an order under section 2.

(2A) Without prejudice to the generality of paragraph (g) of subsection (1) above, where an application for an order under section 2 of this Act is made by virtue of section 1(1)(ba) of this Act, the court shall, in addition to the matters specifically mentioned in paragraphs (a) to (f) of that subsection, have regard to—

    (a)   the age of the applicant and the length of the period during which the applicant lived as the husband or wife or civil partner of the deceased and in the same household as the deceased;

    (b)   the contribution made by the applicant to the welfare of the family of the deceased, including any contribution made by looking after the home or caring for the family.

(3) Without prejudice to the generality of paragraph (g) of subsection (1) above, where an application for an order under section 2 of this Act is made by virtue of section 1(1)(c) or 1(1)(d) of this Act, the court shall, in addition to the matters specifically mentioned in paragraphs (a) to (f) of that subsection, have regard to the manner in which the applicant was being or in which he might expect to be educated or trained, and where the application is made by virtue of section 1(1)(d) the court shall also have regard—

    (a)   to whether the deceased maintained the applicant and, if so, to the length of time for which and basis on which the deceased did so, and to the extent of the contribution made by way of maintenance;

    (aa)   to whether and, if so, to what extent the deceased assumed responsibility for the maintenance of the applicant;

    (b)   to whether in maintaining or assuming responsibility for maintaining the applicant the deceased did so knowing that the applicant was not his own child;

    (c)   to the liability of any other person to maintain the applicant.

(4) Without prejudice to the generality of paragraph (g) of subsection (1) above, where an application for an order under section 2 of this Act is made by virtue of section 1(1)(e) of this Act, the court shall, in addition to the matters specifically mentioned in paragraphs (a) to (f) of that subsection, have regard—

    (a)   to the length of time for which and basis on which the deceased maintained the applicant, and to the extent of the contribution made by way of maintenance;

    (b)   to whether and, if so, to what extent the deceased assumed responsibility for the maintenance of the applicant.

(5) In considering the matters to which the court is required to have regard under this section, the court shall take into account the facts as known to the court at the date of the hearing.

(6) In considering the financial resources of any person for the purposes of this section the court shall take into account his earning capacity and in considering the financial needs of any person for the purposes of this section the court shall take into account his financial obligations and responsibilities.

4.   Time-limit for applications

An application for an order under section 2 of this Act shall not, except with the permission of the court, be made after the end of the period of six months from the date on which representation with respect to the estate of the deceased is first taken out (but nothing prevents the making of an application before such representation is first taken out).

5.   Interim orders

(1) Where on an application for an order under section 3 of this Act it appears to the court—

    (a)   that the applicant is in immediate need of financial assistance, but it is not yet possible to determine what order (if any) should be made under that section; and

    (b)   that property forming part of the net estate of the deceased is or can be made available to meet the need of the applicant;

the court may order that, subject to such conditions or restrictions, if any, as the court may impose and to any further order of the court, there shall be paid to the applicant out of the net estate of the deceased such sum or sums and (if more than one) at such intervals as the court thinks reasonable; and the court may order that, subject to the provisions of this Act, such payments are to be made until such date as the court may specify, not being later than the date on which the court either makes an order under the said section 2 or decides not to exercise its powers under that section.

(2)   Subsections (2), (3) and (4) of section 2 of this Act shall apply in relation to an order under this section as they apply in relation to an order under that section.

(3)   In determining what order, if any, should be made under this section the court shall, so far as the urgency of the case admits, have regard to the same matters as those to which the court is required to have regard under section 3 of this Act.

(4)   An order made under section 2 of this Act may provide that any sum paid to the applicant by virtue of this section shall be treated to such an extent and in such manner as may be provided by that order as having been paid on account of any payment provided for by that order.

6.   Variation, discharge, etc. of orders for periodical payments

(1)   Subject to the provisions of this Act, where the court has made an order under section 2(1)(a) of this Act (in this section referred to as 'the original order') for the making of periodical payments to any person (in this section referred to as 'the original recipient'), the court, on an application under this section, shall have power by order to vary or discharge the original order or to suspend any provision of it temporarily and to revive the operation of any provision so suspended.

(2)   Without prejudice to the generality of subsection (1) above, an order made on an application for the variation of the original order may—

(a)   provide for the making out of any relevant property of such periodical payments and for such term as may be specified in the order to any person who has applied, or would but for section 4 of this Act be entitled to apply, for an order under section 2 of this Act (whether or not, in the case of any application, an order was made in favour of the applicant);

(b)   provide for the payment out of any relevant property of a lump sum of such amount as may be so specified to the original recipient or to any such person as is mentioned in paragraph (a) above;

(c)   provide for the transfer of the relevant property, or such part thereof as may be so specified, to the original recipient or to any such person as is so mentioned.

(3)   Where the original order provides that any periodical payments payable thereunder to the original recipient are to cease on the occurrence of an event specified in the order (other than the formation of a subsequent marriage or civil partnership by a former spouse or former civil partner) or on the expiration of a period so specified, then, if, before the end of the period of six months from the date of the occurrence of that event or of the expiration of that period, an application is made for an order under this section, the court shall have power to make any order which it would have had power to make if the application had been made before the date (whether in favour of the original recipient or any such person as is mentioned in subsection (2)(a) above and whether having effect from that date or from such later date as the court may specify).

(4)   Any reference in this section to the original order shall include a reference to an order made under this section and any reference in this section to the original recipient shall include a reference to any person to whom periodical payments are required to be made by virtue of an order under this section.

(5)   An application under this section may be made by any of the following persons, that is to say—

(a)   any person who by virtue of section 1(1) of this Act has applied, or would but for section 4 of this Act be entitled to apply, for an order under section 2 of this Act,

(b)   the personal representatives of the deceased,

(c)   the trustees of any relevant property, and

(d)   any beneficiary of the estate of the deceased.

(6)   An order under this section may only affect—

(a)   property the income of which is at the date of the order applicable wholly or in part for the making of periodical payments to any person who has applied for an order under this Act, or

(b)   in the case of an application under subsection (3) above in respect of payments which have ceased to be payable on the occurrence of an event or the expiration of a period, property the income of which was so applicable immediately before the occurrence of that event or the expiration of that period, as the case may be, and any such property as is mentioned in paragraph (a) or (b) above is in subsections (2) and (5) above referred to as 'relevant property'.

(7)   In exercising the powers conferred by this section the court shall have regard to all circumstances of the case, including any change in any of the matters to which the court was required to have regard when making the order to which the application relates.

(8)   Where the court makes an order under this section, it may give such consequential directions as it thinks necessary or expedient having regard to the provisions of the order.

(9)   No such order as is mentioned in section 2(1)(d), (e) or (f), 9, 10 or 11 of this Act shall be made on an application under this section.

(10) For the avoidance of doubt it is hereby declared that, in relation to an order which provides for the making of periodical payments which are to cease on the occurrence of an event specified in the order (other than the formation of a subsequent marriage or civil partnership by a former spouse or former civil partner) or on the expiration of a period so specified, the power to vary an order includes power to provide for the making of periodical payments after the expiration of that period or the occurrence of that event.

7.   Payment of lump sums by instalments

(1)   An order under section 2(1)(b) or 6(2)(b) of this Act for the payment of a lump sum may provide for the payment of that sum by instalments of such amount as may be specified in the order.

(2)   Where an order is made by virtue of subsection (1) above, the court shall have power, on an application made by the person to whom the lump sum is payable, by the personal representatives of the deceased or by the trustees of the property out of which the lump sum is payable, to vary that order by varying the number of instalments payable, the amount of any instalment and the date on which any instalment becomes payable.

8.   Property treated as part of 'net estate'

(1)   Where a deceased person has in accordance with the provisions of any enactment nominated any person to receive any sum of money or other property on his death and that nomination is in force at the time of his death, that sum of money, after deducting therefrom any inheritance tax payable in respect thereof, or that other property, to the extent of the value thereof at the date of the death of the deceased after deducting therefrom any inheritance tax so payable, shall be treated for the purposes of this Act as part of the net estate of the deceased; but this subsection shall not render any person liable for having paid that sum or transferred that other property to the person named in the nomination in accordance with the directions given in the nomination.

(2)   Where any sum of money or other property is received by any person as a donatio mortis causa made by a deceased person, that sum of money, after deducting therefrom any inheritance tax payable thereon, or that other property, to the extent of the value thereof at the date of the death of the deceased after deducting therefrom any inheritance tax so payable, shall be treated for the purposes of this Act as part of the net estate of the deceased; but this subsection shall not render any person liable for having paid that sum or transferred that other property in order to give effect to that donatio mortis causa.

(3)   The amount of inheritance tax to be deducted for the purposes of this section shall not exceed the amount of that tax which has been borne by the person nominated by the deceased or, as the case may be, the person who has received a sum of money or other property as a donatio mortis causa.

9.   Property held on a joint tenancy

(1)   Where a deceased person was immediately before his death beneficially entitled to a joint tenancy of any property, then, if an application is made for an order under section 2 of this Act, the court for the purpose of facilitating the making of financial provision for the applicant under this Act may order that the deceased's severable share of that property shall, to such extent as appears to the court to be just in all the circumstances of the case, be treated for the purposes of this Act as part of the net estate of the deceased.

(1A) Where an order is made under subsection (1) the value of the deceased's severable share of the property concerned is taken for the purposes of this Act to be the value that the share would have had at the date of the hearing of the application for an order under section 2 had the share been severed immediately before the deceased's death, unless the court orders that the share is to be valued at a different date.

(2)   In determining the extent to which any severable share is to be treated as part of the net estate of the deceased by virtue of an order under subsection (1) above, the court shall have regard to any inheritance tax payable in respect of that severable share.

(3)   Where an order is made under subsection (1) above, the provisions of this section shall not render any person liable for anything done by him before the order was made.

(4)   For the avoidance of doubt it is hereby declared that for the purposes of this section there may be a joint tenancy of a chose in action.

Powers of court in relation to transactions intended to defeat applications
for financial provision

10.   Dispositions intended to defeat applications for financial provisions

(1)   Where an application is made to the court for an order under section 2 of this Act, the applicant may, in the proceedings on that application, apply to the court for an order under subsection (2) below.

(2)   Where on an application under subsection (1) above the court is satisfied—

     (a)   that, less than six years before the date of the death of the deceased, the deceased with the intention of defeating an application for financial provision under this Act made a disposition, and

     (b)   that full valuable consideration for that disposition was not given by the person to whom or for the benefit of whom the disposition was made (in this section referred to as the donee') or by any other person, and

     (c)   that the exercise of the powers conferred by this section would facilitate the making of financial provision for the applicant under this Act,

then, subject to the provisions of this section and of sections 12 and 13 of this Act, the court may order the donee (whether or not at the date of the order he holds any interest in the property disposed of to him or for his benefit by the deceased) to provide, for the purpose of the making of that financial provision, such sum of money or other property as may be specified in the order.

(3)   Where an order is made under subsection (2) above as respects any disposition made by the deceased which consisted of the payment of money to or for the benefit of the donee, the amount of any sum of money or the value of any property ordered to be provided under that subsection shall not exceed the amount of the payment made by the deceased after deducting therefrom any inheritance tax borne by the donee in respect of that payment.

(4)   Where an order is made under subsection (2) above as respects any disposition made by the deceased which consisted of the transfer of property (other than a sum of money) to or for the benefit of the donee, the amount of any sum of money or the value of any property ordered to be provided under that subsection shall not exceed the value at the date of the death of the deceased of the property disposed of by him to or for the benefit of the donee (or if that property has been disposed of by the person to whom it was transferred by the deceased, the value at the date of that disposal thereof) after deducting therefrom any inheritance tax borne by the donee in respect of the transfer of that property by the deceased.

(5)   Where an application (in this subsection referred to as 'the original application') is made for an order under subsection (2) above in relation to any disposition, then, if on an application under this subsection by the donee or by any applicant for an order under section 2 of this Act the court is satisfied—

     (a)   that, less than six years before the date of the death of the deceased, the deceased with the intention of defeating an application for financial provision under this Act made a disposition other than the disposition which is the subject of the original application, and

     (b)   that full valuable consideration for that other disposition was not given by the person to whom or for the benefit of whom that other disposition was made or by any other person,

the court may exercise in relation to the person to whom or for the benefit of whom that other disposition was made the powers which the court would have had under subsection (2) above if the original application had been made in respect of that other disposition and the court had been satisfied as to the matters set out in paragraphs (a), (b) and (c) of that subsection; and where any application is made under this subsection, any reference in this section (except in subsection (2)(b)) to the donee shall include a reference to the person to whom or for the benefit of whom that other disposition was made.

(6)   In determining whether and in what manner to exercise its powers under this section, the court shall have regard to the circumstances in which any disposition was made and any valuable consideration which was given therefor, the relationship, if any, of the donee to the deceased, the conduct and financial resources of the donee and all the other circumstances of the case.

(7)   In this section 'disposition' does not include—

(a)   any provision in a will, any such nomination as is mentioned in section 8(1) of this Act or any donatio mortis causa, or

(b)   any appointment of property made, otherwise than by will, in the exercise of a special power of appointment,

but, subject to these exceptions, includes any payment of money (including the payment of a premium under a policy of assurance) and any conveyance, assurance, appointment or gift of property of any description, whether made by an instrument or otherwise.

(8)   The provisions of this section do not apply to any disposition made before the commencement of this Act.

11.   Contracts to leave property by will

(1)   Where an application is made to a court for an order under section 2 of this Act, the applicant may, in the proceedings on that application, apply to the court for an order under this section.

(2)   Where on an application under subsection (1) above the court is satisfied—

(a)   that the deceased made a contract by which he agreed to leave by his will a sum of money or other property to any person or by which he agreed that a sum of money or other property would be paid or transferred to any person out of his estate, and

(b)   that the deceased made that contract with the intention of defeating an application for financial provision under this Act, and

(c)   that when the contract was made full valuable consideration for that contract was not given or promised by the person with whom or for the benefit of whom the contract was made (in this section referred to as 'the donee') or by any other person, and

(d)   that the exercise of the powers conferred by this section would facilitate the making of financial provision for the applicant under this Act,

then, subject to the provisions of this section and of sections 12 and 13 of this Act, the court may make any one or more of the following orders, that is to say—

(i)   if any money has been paid or any other property has been transferred to or for the benefit of the donee in accordance with the contract, an order directing the donee to provide, for the purpose of the making of that financial provision, such sum of money or other property as may be specified in the order;

(ii)   if the money or all the money has not been paid or the property or all the property has not been transferred in accordance with the contract, an order directing the personal representatives not to make any payment or transfer any property, or not to make any further payment or transfer any further property, as the case may be, in accordance therewith or directing the personal representatives only to make such payment or transfer such property as may be specified in the order.

(3)   Notwithstanding anything in subsection (2) above, the court may exercise its powers thereunder in relation to any contract made by the deceased only to the extent that the court considers that the amount of any sum of money paid or to be paid or the value of any property transferred or to be transferred in accordance with the contract exceeds the value of any valuable consideration given or to be given for that contract, and for this purpose the court shall have regard to the value of property at the date of the hearing.

(4)   In determining whether and in what manner to exercise its powers under this section, the court shall have regard to the circumstances in which the contract was made, the relationship, if any, of the donee to the deceased, the conduct and financial resources of the donee and all the other circumstances of the case.

(5)   Where an order has been made under subsection (2) above in relation to any contract, the rights of any person to enforce that contract or to recover damages or to obtain other relief for the breach thereof shall be subject to any adjustment made by the court under section 12(3) of this Act and shall survive to such extent only as is consistent with giving effect to the terms of that order.

(6)   The provisions of this section do not apply to a contract made before the commencement of this Act.

12.   Provisions supplementary to ss. 10 and 11

(1)   Where the exercise of any of the powers conferred by section 10 or 11 of this Act is conditional on the court being satisfied that a disposition or contract was made by a deceased person with the intention of defeating an application for financial provision under this Act, that condition shall be fulfilled if the court is of the opinion that, on a balance of probabilities, the intention of the deceased (though not necessarily his sole intention) in making the disposition or contract was to prevent an order for financial provision being made under this Act or to reduce the amount of the provision which might otherwise be granted by an order thereunder.

(2)   Where an application is made under section 11 of this Act with respect to any contract made by the deceased and no valuable consideration was given or promised by any person for that contract then, notwithstanding anything in subsection (1) above, it shall be presumed, unless the contrary is shown, that the deceased made that contract with the intention of defeating an application for financial provision under this Act.

(3)   Where the court makes an order under section 10 or 11 of this Act it may give such consequential directions as it thinks fit (including directions requiring the making of any payment or the transfer of any property) for giving effect to the order or for securing a fair adjustment of the rights of the persons affected thereby.

(4)   Any power conferred on the court by the said section 10 or 11 to order the donee, in relation to any disposition or contract, to provide any sum of money or other property shall be exercisable in like manner in relation to the personal representative of the donee, and

(a)   any reference in section 10(4) to the disposal of property by the donee shall include a reference to disposal by the personal representative of the donee, and

(b)   any reference in section 10(5) to an application by the donee under that subsection shall include a reference to an application by the personal representative of a donee;

but the court shall not have power under the said section 10 or 11 to make an order in respect of any property forming part of the estate of the donee which has been distributed by the personal representative; and the personal representative shall not be liable for having distributed any such property before he has notice of the making of an application under the said section 10 or 11 on the ground that he ought to have taken into account the possibility that such an application would be made.

13.   Provisions as to trustees in relation to ss. 10 and 11

(1)   Where an application is made for—

(a)   an order under section 10 of this Act in respect of a disposition made by the deceased to any person as a trustee, or

(b)   an order under section 11 of this Act in respect of any payment made or property transferred, in accordance with a contract made by the deceased, to any person as a trustee,

the powers of the court under the said section 10 or 11 to order that trustee to provide a sum of money or other property shall be subject to the following limitation (in addition, in a case of an application under section 10, to any provision regarding the deduction of inheritance tax) namely, that the amount of any sum of money or the value of any property ordered to be provided—

(i)   in the case of an application in respect of a disposition which consisted of the payment of money or an application in respect of the payment of money in accordance with a contract, shall not exceed the aggregate of so much of that money as is at the date of the order in the hands of the trustee and the value at that date of any property which represents that money or is derived therefrom and is at that date in the hands of the trustee;

(ii) in the case of an application in respect of a disposition which consisted of the transfer of property (other than a sum of money) or an application in respect of the transfer of property (other than a sum of money) in accordance with a contract, shall not exceed the aggregate of the value at the date of the order of so much of that property as is at that date in the hands of the trustee and the value at that date of any property which represents the first-mentioned property or is derived therefrom and is at that date in the hands of the trustee.

(2) Where any such application is made in respect of a disposition made to any person as a trustee or in respect of any payment made or property transferred in pursuance of a contract to any person as a trustee, the trustee shall not be liable for having distributed any money or other property on the ground that he ought to have taken into account the possibility that such an application would be made.

(3) Where any such application is made in respect of a disposition made to any person as a trustee or in respect of any payment made or property transferred in accordance with a contract to any person as a trustee, any reference in the said section 10 or 11 to the donee shall be construed as including a reference to the trustee or trustees for the time being of the trust in question and any reference in subsection (1) or (2) above to a trustee shall be construed in the same way.

Special provisions relating to cases of divorce, separation etc.

14.   Provision as to cases where no financial relief was granted in divorce proceedings etc.

(1) Where, within twelve months from the date on which a decree of divorce or nullity of marriage has been made absolute or a decree of judicial separation has been granted, a party to the marriage dies and—

(a) an application for a financial provision order under section 23 of the Matrimonial Causes Act 1973 or a property adjustment order under section 24 of that Act has not been made by the other party to that marriage, or

(b) such an application has been made but the proceedings thereon have not been determined at the time of the death of the deceased,

then, if an application for an order under section 2 of this Act is made by that other party, the court shall, notwithstanding anything in section 1 or section 3 of this Act, have power, if it thinks it just to do so, to treat that party for the purposes of that application as if the decree of divorce or nullity of marriage had not been made absolute or the decree of judicial separation has not been granted, as the case may be.

(2) This section shall not apply in relation to a decree of judicial separation unless at the date of the death of the deceased the order was in force and the separation was continuing.

14A. Provision as to cases where no financial relief was granted in proceedings for the dissolution etc. of a civil partnership

(1) Subsection (2) below applies where—

(a) a dissolution order, nullity order, separation order or presumption of death order has been made under Chapter 2 of Part 2 of the Civil Partnership Act 2004 in relation to a civil partnership,

(b) one of the civil partners dies within twelve months from the date on which the order is made, and

(c) either—

(i) an application for a financial provision order under Part 1 of Schedule 5 to that Act or a property adjustment order under Part 2 of that Schedule has not been made by the other civil partner, or

(ii) such an application has been made but the proceedings on the application have not been determined at the time of the death of the deceased.

(2) If an application for an order under section 2 of this Act is made by the surviving civil partner, the court shall, notwithstanding anything in section 1 or section 3 of this Act, have power, if it thinks it just to do so, to treat the surviving civil partner as if the order mentioned in subsection (1)(a) above had not been made.

(3) This section shall not apply in relation to a separation order unless at the date of the death of the deceased the separation order was in force and the separation was continuing.

15.   Restriction imposed in divorce proceedings etc. on application under this Act

(1)   On the grant of a decree of divorce, a decree of nullity of marriage or a decree of judicial separation or at any time thereafter the court, if it considers it just to do so, may, on the application of either party to the marriage, order that the other party to the marriage shall not on the death of the applicant be entitled to apply for an order under section 2 of this Act.

In this subsection 'the court' means the High Court or the family court.

(2)   In the case of a decree of divorce or nullity of marriage an order may be made under subsection (1) above before or after the decree is made absolute, but if it is made before the decree is made absolute it shall not take effect unless the decree is made absolute.

(3)   Where an order made under subsection (1) above on the grant of a decree of divorce or nullity of marriage has come into force with respect to a party to a marriage, then, on the death of the other party to that marriage, the court shall not entertain any application for an order under section 2 of this Act made by the first-mentioned party.

(4)   Where an order made under subsection (1) above on the grant of a decree of judicial separation has come into force with respect to any party to a marriage, then, if the other party to that marriage dies while the decree is in force and the separation is continuing, the court shall not entertain any application for an order under section 2 of this Act made by the first-mentioned party.

15ZA. Restriction imposed in proceedings for the dissolution etc. of a civil partnership on application under this Act

(1)   On making a dissolution order, nullity order, separation order or presumption of death order under Chapter 2 of Part 2 of the Civil Partnership Act 2004, or at any time after making such an order, the court, if it considers it just to do so, may, on the application of either of the civil partners, order that the other civil partner shall not on the death of the applicant be entitled to apply for an order under section 2 of this Act.

(2)   In subsection (1) above 'the court' means the High Court or the family court.

(3)   In the case of a dissolution order, nullity order or presumption of death order ('the main order') an order may be made under subsection (1) above before (as well as after) the main order is made final, but if made before the main order is made final it shall not take effect unless the main order is made final.

(4)   Where an order under subsection (1) above made in connection with a dissolution order, nullity order or presumption of death order has come into force with respect to a civil partner, then, on the death of the other civil partner, the court shall not entertain any application for an order under section 2 of this Act made by the surviving civil partner.

(5)   Where an order under subsection (1) above made in connection with a separation order has come into force with respect to a civil partner, then, if the other civil partner dies while the separation order is in force and the separation is continuing, the court shall not entertain any application for an order under section 2 of this Act made by the surviving civil partner.

15A.   Restriction imposed in proceedings under the Matrimonial and Family Proceedings Act 1984 on application under this Act

(1)   On making an order under section 17 of the Matrimonial and Family Proceedings Act 1984 (orders for financial provision and property adjustment following overseas divorces etc.) the court, if it considers it just to do so, may, on the application of either party to the marriage order that the other party to the marriage shall not on the death of the applicant be entitled to apply for an order under section 2 of this Act.

In this subsection 'the court' means the High Court or the family court.

(2)   Where an order under subsection (1) above has been made with respect to a party to a marriage which has been dissolved or annulled then, on the death of the other party to that marriage, the court shall not entertain an application under section 2 of this Act by the first-mentioned party.

(3)   Where an order under subsection (1) above has been made with respect to a party to a marriage the parties to which have been legally separated, then, if the other party to the marriage dies while the legal separation is in force, the court shall not entertain an application under section 2 of this Act made by the first-mentioned party.

15B. **Restriction imposed in proceedings under Schedule 7 to the Civil Partnership Act 2004 on application under this Act**

(1) On making an order under paragraph 9 of Schedule 7 to the Civil Partnership Act 2004 (orders for financial provision, property adjustment and pension-sharing following overseas dissolution etc. of civil partnership) the court, if it considers it just to do so, may, on the application of either of the civil partners, order that the other civil partner shall not on the death of the applicant be entitled to apply for an order under section 2 of this Act.

(2) In subsection (1) above 'the court' means the High Court or the family court.

(3) Where an order under subsection (1) above has been made with respect to one of the civil partners in a case where a civil partnership has been dissolved or annulled, then, on the death of the other civil partner, the court shall not entertain an application under section 2 of this Act made by the surviving civil partner.

(4) Where an order under subsection (1) above has been made with respect to one of the civil partners in a case where civil partners have been legally separated, then, if the other civil partner dies while the legal separation is in force, the court shall not entertain an application under section 2 of this Act made by the surviving civil partner.

16. **Variation and discharge of secured periodical payments orders made under Matrimonial Causes Act 1973**

(1) Where an application for an order under section 2 of this Act is made to the court by any person who was at the time of the death of the deceased entitled to payments from the deceased under a secured periodical payments order made under the Matrimonial Causes Act 1973 or Schedule 5 to the Civil Partnership Act 2004, then, in the proceedings on that application, the court shall have power, if an application is made under this section by that person or by the personal representative of the deceased, to vary or discharge that periodical payments order or to revive the operation of any provision thereof which has been suspended under section 31 of that Act of 1973 or Part 11 of that Schedule.

(2) In exercising the powers conferred by this section the court shall have regard to all the circumstances of the case, including any order which the court proposes to make under section 2 or section 5 of this Act and any change (whether resulting from the death of the deceased or otherwise) in any of the matters to which the court was required to have regard when making the secured periodical payments order.

(3) The power exercisable by the court under this section in relation to an order shall be exercisable also in relation to any instrument executed in pursuance of the order.

17. **Variation and revocation of maintenance agreements**

(1) Where an application for an order under section 2 of this Act is made to the court by any person who was at the time of the death of the deceased entitled to payments from the deceased under a maintenance agreement which provided for the continuation of payments under the agreement after the death of the deceased, then, in the proceedings on that application, the court shall have power, if an application is made under this section by that person or by the personal representative of the deceased, to vary or revoke that agreement.

(2) In exercising the powers conferred by this section the court shall have regard to all the circumstances of the case, including any order which the court proposes to make under section 2 or section 5 of this Act and any change (whether resulting from the death of the deceased or otherwise) in any of the circumstances in the light of which the agreement was made.

(3) If a maintenance agreement is varied by the court under this section the like consequences shall ensue as if the variation had been made immediately before the death of the deceased by agreement between the parties and for valuable consideration.

(4) In this section 'maintenance agreement', in relation to a deceased person, means any agreement made, whether in writing or not and whether before or after the commencement of this Act, by the deceased with any person with whom he formed a marriage or civil partnership, being an agreement which contained provisions governing the rights and liabilities towards one another when living separately of the parties to that marriage or of the civil partners (whether or not the marriage or civil partnership has been dissolved or annulled) in respect of the making or securing of payments or

the disposition or use of any property, including such rights and liabilities with respect to the maintenance or education of any child, whether or not a child of the deceased or a person who was treated by the deceased as a child of the family in relation to that marriage or civil partnership.

18.   Availability of court's powers under this Act in applications under ss. 31 and 36 of the Matrimonial Causes Act 1973

(1)   Where—

    (a)   a person against whom a secured periodical payments order was made under the Matrimonial Causes Act 1973 has died and an application is made under section 31(6) of that Act for the variation or discharge of that order or for the revival of the operation of any provision thereof which has been suspended, or

    (b)   a party to a maintenance agreement within the meaning of section 34 of that Act has died, the agreement being one which provides for the continuation of payments thereunder after the death of one of the parties, and an application is made under section 36(1) of that Act for the alteration of the agreement under section 35 thereof,

the court shall have power to direct that the application made under the said section 31(6) or 36(1) shall be deemed to have been accompanied by an application for an order under section 2 of this Act.

(2)   Where the court gives a direction under subsection (1) above it shall have power, in the proceedings on the application under the said section 31(6) or 36(1), to make any order which the court would have had power to make under the provisions of this Act if the application under the said section 31(6) or 36(1), as the case may be, had been made jointly with an application for an order under the said section 2; and the court shall have power to give such consequential directions as may be necessary for enabling the court to exercise any of the powers available to the court under this Act in the case of an application for an order under section 2.

(3)   Where an order made under section 15(1) of this Act is in force with respect to a party to a marriage, the court shall not give a direction under subsection (1) above with respect to any application made under the said section 31(6) or 36(1) by that party on the death of the other party.

18A.   Availability of court's powers under this Act in applications under paragraphs 60 and 73 of Schedule 5 to the Civil Partnership Act 2004

(1)   Where—

    (a)   a person against whom a secured periodical payments order was made under Schedule 5 to the Civil Partnership Act 2004 has died and an application is made under paragraph 60 of that Schedule for the variation or discharge of that order or for the revival of the operation of any suspended provision of the order, or

    (b)   a party to a maintenance agreement within the meaning of Part 13 of that Schedule has died, the agreement being one which provides for the continuation of payments under the agreement after the death of one of the parties, and an application is made under paragraph 73 of that Schedule for the alteration of the agreement under paragraph 69 of that Schedule,

the court shall have power to direct that the application made under paragraph 60 or 73 of that Schedule shall be deemed to have been accompanied by an application for an order under section 2 of this Act.

(2)   Where the court gives a direction under subsection (1) above it shall have power, in the proceedings on the application under paragraph 60 or 73 of that Schedule, to make any order which the court would have had power to make under the provisions of this Act if the application under that paragraph had been made jointly with an application for an order under section 2 of this Act; and the court shall have power to give such consequential directions as may be necessary for enabling the court to exercise any of the powers available to the court under this Act in the case of an application for an order under section 2.

(3)   Where an order made under section 15ZA(1) of this Act is in force with respect to a civil partner, the court shall not give a direction under subsection (1) above with respect to any application made under paragraph 60 or 73 of that Schedule by that civil partner on the death of the other civil partner.

Miscellaneous and supplementary provisions

19.   Effect, duration and form of orders

(1)   Where an order is made under section 2 of this Act then for all purposes, including the purposes of the enactments relating to inheritance tax, the will or the law relating to intestacy, or both the will and the law relating to intestacy, as the case may be, shall have effect and be deemed to have had effect as from the deceased's death subject to the provisions of the order.

(2)   Any order made under section 2 or 5 of this Act in favour of—

(a)   an applicant who was the former spouse or former civil partner of the deceased, or

(b)   an applicant who was the husband or wife of the deceased in a case where the marriage with the deceased was the subject of a decree of judicial separation and at the date of death the decree was in force, at the date of death, a separation order under the Family Law Act 1996 was in force in relation to the marriage with the deceased and the separation was continuing, or

(c)   an applicant who was the civil partner of the deceased in a case where, at the date of death, a separation order under Chapter 2 of Part 2 of the Civil Partnership Act 2004 was in force in relation to their civil partnership and the separation was continuing,

shall, in so far as it provides for the making of periodical payments, cease to have effect on the formation by the applicant of a subsequent marriage or civil partnership, except in relation to any arrears due under the order on the date of the formation of the subsequent marriage or civil partnership.

(3)   A copy of every order made under this Act other than an order made under section 15(1) or 15ZA(1) of this Act shall be sent to the principal registry of the Family Division for entry and filing, and a memorandum of the order shall be endorsed on, or permanently annexed to, the probate or letters of administration under which the estate is being administered.

20.   Provisions as to personal representatives

(1)   The provisions of this Act shall not render the personal representative of a deceased person liable for having distributed any part of the estate of the deceased, after the end of the period of six months from the date on which representation with respect to the estate of the deceased is first taken out, on the ground that he ought to have taken into account the possibility—

(a)   that the court might permit the making of an application for an order under section 2 of this Act after the end of that period, or

(b)   that, where an order has been made under the said section 2, the court might exercise in relation thereto the powers conferred on it by section 6 of this Act,

but this subsection shall not prejudice any power to recover, by reason of the making of an order under this Act, any part of the estate so distributed.

(2)   Where the personal representative of a deceased person pays any sum directed by an order under section 5 of this Act to be paid out of the deceased's net estate, he shall not be under any liability by reason of that estate not being sufficient to make the payment, unless at the time of making the payment he has reasonable cause to believe that the estate is not sufficient.

(3)   Where a deceased person entered into a contract by which he agreed to leave by his will any sum of money or other property to any person or by which he agreed that a sum of money or other property would be paid or transferred to any person out of his estate, then, if the personal representative of the deceased has reason to believe that the deceased entered into the contract with the intention of defeating an application for financial provision under this Act, he may, notwithstanding anything in that contract, postpone the payment of that sum of money or the transfer of that property until the expiration of the period of six months from the date on which representation with respect to the estate of the deceased is first taken out or, if during that period an application is made for an order under section 2 of this Act, until the determination of the proceedings on that application.

23.   Determination of date on which representation was first taken out

(1)   The following are to be left out of account when considering for the purposes of this Act when representation with respect to the estate of a deceased person was first taken out—

(a)   a grant limited to settled land or to trust property,

  (b)   any other grant that does not permit any of the estate to be distributed,
  (c)   a grant limited to real estate or to personal estate, unless a grant limited to the remainder of the estate has previously been made or is made at the same time,
  (d)   a grant, or its equivalent, made outside the United Kingdom (but see subsection (2) below).
(2) A grant sealed under section 2 of the Colonial Probates Act 1892 counts as a grant made in the United Kingdom for the purposes of this section, but is to be taken as dated on the date of sealing.

24.   Effect of this Act on s 46(1)(vi) of Administration of Estates Act 1925

Section 46(1)(vi) of the Administration of Estates Act 1925, in so far as it provides for the devolution of property on the Crown, the Duchy of Lancaster or the Duke of Cornwall as bona vacantia, shall have effect subject to the provisions of this Act.

25.   Interpretation

(1) In this Act—

'beneficiary', in relation to the estate of a deceased person, means—
  (a)   a person who under the will of the deceased or under the law relating to intestacy is beneficially interested in the estate or would be so interested if an order had not been made under this Act, and
  (b)   a person who has received any sum of money or other property which by virtue of section 8(1) or 8(2) of this Act is treated as part of the net estate of the deceased or would have received that sum or other property if an order had not been made under this Act;

'child' includes an illegitimate child and a child en ventre sa mere at the death of the deceased;

'the court' means unless the context otherwise requires the High Court, or where the county court has jurisdiction by virtue of section 25 of the County Courts Act 1984, the county court;

'former civil partner' means a person whose civil partnership with the deceased was during the lifetime of the deceased either—
  (a)   dissolved or annulled by an order made under the law of any part of the British Islands, or
  (b)   dissolved or annulled in any country or territory outside the British Islands by a dissolution or annulment which is entitled to be recognised as valid by the law of England and Wales;

'former spouse' means a person whose marriage with the deceased was during the lifetime of the deceased either—
  (a)   dissolved or annulled by a decree of divorce or a decree of nullity of marriage granted under the law of any part of the British Islands; or
  (b)   dissolved or annulled in any country or territory outside the British Islands by a divorce or annulment which is entitled to be recognised as valid by the law of England and Wales;

'net estate', in relation to a deceased person, means—
  (a)   all property of which the deceased had power to dispose by his will (otherwise than by virtue of a special power of appointment) less the amount of his funeral, testamentary and administration expenses, debts and liabilities, including any inheritance tax payable out of his estate on his death;
  (b)   any property in respect of which the deceased held a general power of appointment (not being a power exercisable by will) which has not been exercised,
  (c)   any sum of money or other property which is treated for the purposes of this Act as part of the net estate of the deceased by virtue of section 8(1) or (2) of this Act;
  (d)   any property which is treated for the purposes of this Act as part of the net estate of the deceased by virtue of an order made under section 9 of the Act;
  (e)   any sum of money or other property which is, by reason of a disposition or contract made by the deceased, ordered under section 10 or 11 of this Act to be provided for the purpose of the making of financial provision under this Act;

'property' includes any chose in action;

'reasonable financial provision' has the meaning assigned to it by section 1 of this Act;

'valuable consideration' does not include a marriage or a promise of marriage;

'will' includes codicil.

(2) For the purposes of paragraph (a) of the definition of 'net estate' in subsection (1) above a person who is not of full age and capacity shall be treated as having power to dispose by will of all property of which he would have had power to dispose by will if he had been of full age and capacity.

(3) Any reference in this Act to provision out of the net estate of a deceased person includes a reference to provision extending to the whole of that estate.

(4) For the purposes of this Act any reference to a spouse, wife or husband shall be treated as including a reference to a person who in good faith entered into a void marriage with the deceased unless either—

   (a) the marriage of the deceased and that person was dissolved or annulled during the lifetime of the deceased and the dissolution or annulment is recognised by the law of England and Wales, or

   (b) that person has during the lifetime of the deceased formed a subsequent marriage or civil partnership.

(4A) For the purposes of this Act any reference to a civil partner shall be treated as including a reference to a person who in good faith formed a void civil partnership with the deceased unless either—

   (a) the civil partnership between the deceased and that person was dissolved or annulled during the lifetime of the deceased and the dissolution or annulment is recognised by the law of England and Wales, or

   (b) that person has during the lifetime of the deceased formed a subsequent civil partnership or marriage.

(5) Any reference in this Act to the formation of, or to a person who has formed, a subsequent marriage or civil partnership includes (as the case may be) a reference to the formation of, or to a person who has formed, a marriage or civil partnership which is by law void or voidable.

(5A) The formation of a marriage or civil partnership shall be treated for the purposes of this Act as the formation of a subsequent marriage or civil partnership, in relation to either of the spouses or civil partners, notwithstanding that the previous marriage or civil partnership of that spouse or civil partner was void or voidable.

(6) Any reference in this Act to an order or decree made under the Matrimonial Causes Act 1973 or under any section of that Act shall be construed as including a reference to an order or decree which is deemed to have been made under that Act or under that section thereof, as the case may be.

(6A) Any reference in this Act to an order made under, or under any provision of, the Civil Partnership Act 2004 shall be construed as including a reference to anything which is deemed to be an order made (as the case may be) under that Act or provision.

(7) Any reference in this Act to any enactment is a reference to that enactment as amended by or under any subsequent enactment.

PROTECTION FROM EVICTION ACT 1977
(1977, c. 43)

PART I
UNLAWFUL EVICTION AND HARASSMENT

1.   Unlawful eviction and harassment of occupier

(1) In this section 'residential occupier', in relation to any premises, means a person occupying the premises as a residence, whether under a contract or by virtue of any enactment or rule of law giving him the right to remain in occupation or restricting the right of any other person to recover possession of the premises.

(2) If any person unlawfully deprives the residential occupier of any premises of his occupation of the premises or any part thereof, or attempts to do so, he shall be guilty of an offence unless he proves that he believed, and had reasonable cause to believe, that the residential occupier had ceased to reside in the premises.

(3) If any person with intent to cause the residential occupier of any premises—

   (a) to give up the occupation of the premises or any part thereof; or

    (b)   to refrain from exercising any right or pursuing any remedy in respect of the premises or part thereof;

does acts likely to interfere with the peace or comfort of the residential occupier or members of his household, or persistently withdraws or withholds services reasonably required for the occupation of the premises as a residence, he shall be guilty of an offence.

(3A) Subject to subsection (3B) below, the landlord of a residential occupier or an agent of the landlord shall be guilty of an offence if—

    (a)   he does acts likely to interfere with the peace or comfort of the residential occupier or members of his household, or

    (b)   he persistently withdraws or withholds services reasonably required for the occupation of the premises in question as a residence,

and (in either case) he knows, or has reasonable cause to believe, that that conduct is likely to cause the residential occupier to give up the occupation of the whole or part of the premises or to refrain from exercising any right or pursuing any remedy in respect of the whole or part of the premises.

(3B) A person shall not be guilty of an offence under subsection (3A) above if he proves that he had reasonable grounds for doing the acts or withdrawing or withholding the services in question.

(3C) In subsection (3A) above 'landlord', in relation to a residential occupier of any premises, means the person who, but for—

    (a)   the residential occupier's right to remain in occupation of the premises, or

    (b)   a restriction on the person's right to recover possession of the premises,

would be entitled to occupation of the premises and any superior landlord under whom that person derives title.

(4)   A person guilty of an offence under this section shall be liable—

    (a)   on summary conviction, to a fine not exceeding the prescribed sum or to imprisonment for a term not exceeding 6 months or to both;

    (b)   on conviction on indictment, to a fine or to imprisonment for a term not exceeding 2 years or to both.

(5)   Nothing in this section shall be taken to prejudice any liability or remedy to which a person guilty of an offence thereunder may be subject in civil proceedings.

(6)   Where an offence under this section committed by a body corporate is proved to have been committed with the consent or connivance of, or to be attributable to any neglect on the part of, any director, manager or secretary or other similar officer of the body corporate or any person who was purporting to act in any such capacity, he as well as the body corporate shall be guilty of that offence and shall be liable to be proceeded against and punished accordingly.

2.   Restriction on re-entry without due process of law

Where any premises are let as a dwelling on a lease which is subject to a right of re-entry or forfeiture it shall not be lawful to enforce that right otherwise than by proceedings in the court while any person is lawfully residing in the premises or part of them.

3.   Prohibition of eviction without due process of law

(1)   Where any premises have been let as a dwelling under a tenancy which is neither a statutorily protected tenancy nor an excluded tenancy and—

    (a)   the tenancy (in this section referred to as the former tenancy) has come to an end, but

    (b)   the occupier continues to reside in the premises or part of them,

it shall not be lawful for the owner to enforce against the occupier, otherwise than by proceedings in the court, his right to recover possession of the premises.

(2)   In this section 'the occupier', in relation to any premises, means any person lawfully residing in the premises or part of them at the termination of the former tenancy.

(2A) Subsections (1) and (2) above apply in relation to any restricted contract (within the meaning of the Rent Act 1977) which—

    (a)   creates a licence; and

    (b)   is entered into after the commencement of section 69 of the Housing Act 1980; as they apply in relation to a restricted contract which creates a tenancy.

(2B) Subsections (1) and (2) above apply in relation to any premises occupied as a dwelling under a licence, other than an excluded licence, as they apply in relation to premises let as a dwelling under a tenancy, and in those subsections the expressions 'let' and 'tenancy' shall be construed accordingly.

(2C) References in the preceding provisions of this section and section 4(2) below to an excluded tenancy do not apply to—

(a)   a tenancy entered into before the date on which the Housing Act 1988 came into force, or

(b)   a tenancy entered into on or after that date but pursuant to a contract made before that date,

but, subject to that, 'excluded tenancy' and 'excluded licence' shall be construed in accordance with section 3A below.

PART II
NOTICE TO QUIT

5.   Validity of notices to quit

(1)   Subject to subsection (1B) below no notice by a landlord or a tenant to quit any premises let (whether before or after the commencement of this Act) as a dwelling shall be valid unless—

(a)   it is in writing and contains such information as may be prescribed, and

(b)   it is given not less than 4 weeks before the date on which it is to take effect.

(1A) Subject to subsection (1B) below, no notice by a licensor or a licensee to determine a periodic licence to occupy premises as a dwelling (whether the licence was granted before or after the passing of this Act) shall be valid unless—

(a)   it is in writing and contains such information as may be prescribed, and

(b)   it is given not less than 4 weeks before the date on which it is to take effect. (1B) Nothing in subsection (1) or subsection (1A) above applies to—

(a)   premises let on an excluded tenancy which is entered into on or after the date on which the Housing Act 1988 came into force unless it is entered into pursuant to a contract made before that date; or

(b)   premises occupied under an excluded licence.

(2)   In this section 'prescribed' means prescribed by regulations made by the Secretary of State by statutory instrument, and a statutory instrument containing any such regulations shall be subject to annulment in pursuance of a resolution of either House of Parliament.

(3)   Regulations under this section may make different provision in relation to different descriptions of lettings and different circumstances.

CRIMINAL LAW ACT 1977
(1977, c. 45)

PART II
OFFENCES RELATING TO ENTERING AND REMAINING ON PROPERTY

6.   Violence for securing entry

(1)   Subject to the following provisions of this section, any person who, without lawful authority, uses or threatens violence for the purpose of securing entry into any premises for himself or for any other person is guilty of an offence, provided that—

(a)   there is someone present on those premises at the time who is opposed to the entry which the violence is intended to secure; and

(b)   the person using or threatening the violence knows that that is the case.

(1A) Subsection (1) above does not apply to a person who is a displaced residential occupier or a protected intending occupier of the premises in question or who is acting on behalf of such an occupier; and if the accused adduces sufficient evidence that he was, or was acting on behalf of, such an occupier he shall be presumed to be, or to be acting on behalf of, such an occupier unless the contrary is proved by the prosecution.

(2)   Subject to subsection (1A) above, the fact that a person has any interest in or right to possession or occupation of any premises shall not for the purposes of subsection (1)

above constitute lawful authority for the use or threat of violence by him or anyone else for the purpose of securing his entry into those premises.

(3)   ...

(4)   It is immaterial for the purposes of this section—

  (a)   whether the violence in question is directed against the person or against property; and

  (b)   whether the entry which the violence is intended to secure is for the purpose of acquiring possession of the premises in question or for any other purpose.

(5)   A person guilty of an offence under this section shall be liable on summary conviction to imprisonment for a term not exceeding six months or to a fine not exceeding level 5 on the standard scale or to both.

LIMITATION ACT 1980
(1980, c. 58)

Actions to recover land and rent

15.   Time limit for actions to recover land

(1)   No action shall be brought by any person to recover any land after the expiration of twelve years from the date on which the right of action accrued to him or, if it first accrued to some person through whom he claims, to that person.

(2)   Subject to the following provisions of this section, where—

  (a)   the estate or interest claimed was an estate or interest in reversion or remainder or any other future estate or interest and the right of action to recover the land accrued on the date on which the estate or interest fell into possession by the determination of the preceding estate or interest; and

  (b)   the person entitled to the preceding estate or interest (not being a term of years absolute) was not in possession of the land on that date;

  no action shall be brought by the person entitled to the succeeding estate or interest after the expiration of twelve years from the date on which the right of action accrued to the person entitled to the preceding estate or interest or six years from the date on which the right of action accrued to the person entitled to the succeeding estate or interest, whichever period last expires.

(3)   Subsection (2) above shall not apply to any estate or interest which falls into possession on the determination of an entailed interest and which might have been barred by the person entitled to the entailed interest.

(4)   No person shall bring an action to recover any estate or interest in land under an assurance taking effect after the right of action to recover the land had accrued to the person by whom the assurance was made or some person through whom he claimed or some person entitled to a preceding estate or interest, unless the action is brought within the period during which the person by whom the assurance was made could have brought such an action.

(5)   Where any person is entitled to any estate or interest in land in possession and, while so entitled, is also entitled to any future estate or interest in that land, and his right to recover the estate or interest in possession is barred under this Act, no action shall be brought by that person, or by any person claiming through him, in respect of the future estate or interest, unless in the meantime possession of the land has been recovered by a person entitled to an intermediate estate or interest.

(6)   Part I of Schedule 1 to this Act contains provisions for determining the date of accrual of rights of action to recover land in the cases there mentioned.

(7)   Part II of that Schedule contains provisions modifying the provisions of this section in their application to actions brought by, or by a person claiming through, the Crown or any spiritual or eleemosynary corporation sole.

16.   Time limit for redemption actions

When a mortgagee of land has been in possession of any of the mortgaged land for a period of twelve years, no action to redeem the land of which the mortgagee has been so in possession shall be brought after the end of that period by the mortgagor or any person claiming through him.

17. Extinction of title to land after expiration of time limit

Subject to—

(a)   section 18 of this Act,

(b)   …

at the expiration of the period prescribed by this Act for any person to bring an action to recover land (including a redemption action) the title of that person to the land shall be extinguished.

18. Settled land and land held on trust

(1)   Subject to section 21(1) and (2) of this Act, the provisions of this Act shall apply to equitable interests in land as they apply to legal estates.

Accordingly a right of action to recover the land shall, for the purposes of this Act but not otherwise, be treated as accruing to a person entitled in possession to such an equitable interest in the like manner and circumstances, and on the same date, as it would accrue if his interest were a legal estate in the land (and any relevant provision of Part I of Schedule 1 to this Act shall apply in any such case accordingly).

(2)   Where the period prescribed by this Act has expired for the bringing of an action to recover land by a tenant for life or a statutory owner of settled land—

(a)   his legal estate shall not be extinguished if and so long as the right of action to recover the land of any person entitled to a beneficial interest in the land either has not accrued or has not been barred by this Act; and

(b)   the legal estate shall accordingly remain vested in the tenant for life or statutory owner and shall devolve in accordance with the Settled Land Act 1925;

but if and when every such right of action has been barred by this Act, his legal estate shall be extinguished.

(3)   Where any land is held upon trust and the period prescribed by this Act has expired for the bringing of an action to recover the land by the trustees, the estate of the trustees shall not be extinguished if and so long as the right of action to recover the land of any person entitled to a beneficial interest in the land either has not accrued or has not been barred by this Act; but if and when every such right of action has been so barred the estate of the trustees shall be extinguished.

(4)   Where—

(a)   any settled land is vested in a statutory owner; or

(b)   any land is held upon trust;

an action to recover the land may be brought by the statutory owner or trustees on behalf of any person entitled to a beneficial interest in possession in the land whose right of action has not been barred by this Act, notwithstanding that the right of action of the statutory owner or trustees would apart from this provision have been barred by this Act.

19. Time limit for actions to recover rent

No action shall be brought, and the power conferred by section 72(1) of the Tribunals, Courts and Enforcement Act 2007 shall not be exercisable, to recover arrears of rent, or damages in respect of arrears of rent, after the expiration of six years from the date on which the arrears became due.

Commonhold

19A Actions for breach of commonhold duty

An action in respect of a right or duty of a kind referred to in section 37(1) of the Commonhold and Leasehold Reform Act 2002 (enforcement) shall not be brought after the expiration of six years from the date on which the cause of action accrued.

*Actions to recover money secured by a mortgage or charge or to recover
proceeds of the sale of land*

20. Time limit for actions to recover money secured by a mortgage or charge or to recover proceeds of the sale of land

(1)   No action shall be brought to recover—

(a)   any principal sum of money secured by a mortgage or other charge on property (whether real or personal); or

(b)   proceeds of the sale of land;

after the expiration of twelve years from the date on which the right to receive the money accrued.

(2)   No foreclosure action in respect of mortgaged personal property shall be brought after the expiration of twelve years from the date on which the right to foreclose accrued.

But if the mortgagee was in possession of the mortgaged property after that date, the right to foreclose on the property which was in his possession shall not be treated as having accrued for the purposes of this subsection until the date on which his possession discontinued.

(3)   The right to receive any principal sum of money secured by a mortgage or other charge and the right to foreclose on the property subject to the mortgage or charge shall not be treated as accruing so long as that property comprises any future interest or any life insurance policy which has not matured or been determined.

(4)   Nothing in this section shall apply to a foreclosure action in respect of mortgaged land, but the provisions of this Act relating to actions to recover land shall apply to such an action.

(5)   Subject to subsections (6) and (7) below, no action to recover arrears of interest payable in respect of any sum of money secured by a mortgage or other charge or payable in respect of proceeds of the sale of land, or to recover damages in respect of such arrears shall be brought after the expiration of six years from the date on which the interest became due.

(6)   Where—
   (a)   a prior mortgagee or other incumbrancer has been in possession of the property charged; and
   (b)   an action is brought within one year of the discontinuance of that possession by the subsequent incumbrancer;

the subsequent incumbrancer may recover by that action all the arrears of interest which fell due during the period of possession by the prior incumbrancer or damages in respect of those arrears, notwithstanding that the period exceeded six years.

(7)   Where—
   (a)   the property subject to the mortgage or charge comprises any future interest or fife insurance policy; and
   (b)   it is a term of the mortgage or charge that arrears of interest shall be treated as part of the principal sum of money secured by the mortgage or charge; interest shall not be treated as becoming due before the right to recover the principal sum of money has accrued or is treated as having accrued.

Actions in respect of trust property or the personal estate of deceased persons

21.   Time limit for actions in respect of trust property

(1)   No period of limitation prescribed by this Act shall apply to an action by a beneficiary under a trust, being an action—
   (a)   in respect of any fraud or fraudulent breach of trust to which the trustee was a party or privy; or
   (b)   to recover from the trustee trust property or the proceeds of trust property in the possession of the trustee, or previously received by the trustee and converted to his use.

(2)   Where a trustee who is also a beneficiary under the trust receives or retains trust property or its proceeds as his share on a distribution of trust property under the trust, his liability in any action brought by virtue of subsection (1)(b) above to recover that property or its proceeds after the expiration of the period of limitation prescribed by this Act for bringing an action to recover trust property shall be limited to the excess over his proper share.

This subsection only applies if the trustee acted honestly and reasonably in making the distribution.

(3)   Subject to the preceding provisions of this section, an action by a beneficiary to recover trust property or in respect of any breach of trust, not being an action for which a period of limitation is prescribed by any other provision of this Act, shall not be brought after the expiration of six years from the date on which the right of action accrued.

For the purposes of this subsection, the right of action shall not be treated as having accrued to any beneficiary entitled to a future interest in the trust property until the interest fell into possession.

(4)   No beneficiary as against whom there would be a good defence under this Act shall derive any greater or other benefit from a judgment or order obtained by any other beneficiary that he could have obtained if he had brought the action and this Act had been pleaded in defence.

22.   Time limit for actions claiming personal estate of a deceased person

Subject to section 21(1) and (2) of this Act—

(a)   no action in respect of any claim to the personal estate of a deceased person or to any share or interest in any such estate (whether under a will or on intestacy) shall be brought after the expiration of twelve years from the date on which the right to receive the share or interest accrued; and

(b)   no action to recover arrears of interest in respect of any legacy, or damages in respect of such arrears, shall be brought after the expiration of six years from the date on which the interest became due.

Actions for an account

23.   Time limit in respect of actions for an account

An action for an account shall not be brought after the expiration of any time limit under this Act which is applicable to the claim which is the basis of the duty to account.

26.   Administration to date back to death

For the purposes of the provisions of this Act relating to actions for the recovery of land ... an administrator of the estate of a deceased person shall be treated as claiming as if there had been no interval of time between the death of the deceased person and the grant of the letters of administration.

27.   Cure of defective disentailing assurance

(1)   This section applies where—

(a)   a person entitled in remainder to an entailed interest in any land makes an assurance of his interest which fails to bar the issue in tail or the estates and interests taking effect on the determination of the entailed interest, or fails to bar those estates and interests only; and

(b)   any person takes possession of the land by virtue of the assurance.

(2)   If the person taking possession of the land by virtue of the assurance, or any other person whatsoever (other than a person entitled to possession by virtue of the settlement) is in possession of the land for a period of twelve years from the commencement of the time when the assurance could have operated as an effective bar, the assurance shall thereupon operate, and be treated as having always operated, to bar the issue in tail and the estates and interests taking effect on the determination of the entailed interest.

(3)   The reference in subsection (2) above to the time when the assurance could have operated as an effective bar is a reference to the time at which the assurance, as it had then been executed by the person entitled to the entailed interest, would have operated, without the consent of any other person, to bar the issue in tail and the estates and interests taking effect on the determination of the entailed interest.

27A.   Actions for recovery of property obtained through unlawful conduct

(1)   None of the time limits given in the preceding provisions of this Act applies to any proceedings under Chapter 2 of Part 5 of the Proceeds of Crime Act 2002 (civil recovery of proceeds of unlawful conduct).

(2)   Proceedings under that Chapter for a recovery order in respect of any recoverable property shall not be brought after the expiration of the period of 20 years from the date on which the relevant person's cause of action accrued.

(3)   Proceedings under that Chapter are brought when—

(a)   a claim form is issued,

(aa)   an application is made for a property freezing order, or

(b)   an application is made for an interim receiving order, whichever is the earliest.

(4)   The relevant person's cause of action accrues in respect of any recoverable property—

(a)   in the case of proceedings for a recovery order in respect of property obtained through unlawful conduct, when the property is so obtained,

(b)   in the case of proceedings for a recovery order in respect of any other recoverable property, when the property obtained through unlawful conduct which it represents is so obtained.

(5)   If—

(a)   a person would (but for the preceding provisions of this Act) have a cause of action in respect of the conversion of a chattel, and

(b)   proceedings are started under that Chapter for a recovery order in respect of the chattel, section 3(2) of this Act does not prevent his asserting on an application under section 281 of that Act that the property belongs to him, or the court making a declaration in his favour under that section.

(6)   If the court makes such a declaration, his title to the chattel is to be treated as not having been extinguished by section 3(2) of this Act.

(7)   Expressions used in this section and Part 5 of that Act have the same meaning in this section as in that Part.

(8)   In this section 'relevant person' means—
    (a)   the National Crime Agency,
    (b)   the Director of Public Prosecutions, or
    (c)   ...
    (d)   the Director of the Serious Fraud Office.

27AB. Actions to prohibit dealing with property subject to an external request

(1)   None of the time limits given in the preceding provisions of this Act applies to any proceedings under Part 4A of the Proceeds of Crime Act 2002 (External Requests and Orders) Order 2005 (giving effect to external request by means of civil proceedings).

(2)   Proceedings under that Part for a prohibition order in respect of relevant property shall not be brought after the expiration of the period of 20 years from the date on which the relevant person's cause of action accrued.

(3)   Proceedings under that Part are brought when an application is made for a prohibition order.

(4)   The relevant person's cause of action accrues in respect of relevant property when the property is obtained (or when it is believed to have been obtained) as a result of or in connection with criminal conduct.

(5)   In this section—
    (a)   'criminal conduct' is to be construed in accordance with section 447(8) of the Act,
    (b)   expressions used in this section and Part 4A of the Proceeds of Crime Act 2002 (External Requests and Orders) Order 2005 have the same meaning in this section as in that Part.

(6)   In this section 'relevant person' means—
    (a)   the National Crime Agency,
    (b)   the Director of Public Prosecutions, or
    (c)   ...
    (d)   the Director of the Serious Fraud Office.

27B. Actions for recovery of property for purposes of an external order

(1)   None of the time limits given in the preceding provisions of this Act applies to any proceedings under Chapter 2 of Part 5 of the Proceeds of Crime Act 2002 (External Requests and Orders) Order 2005 (civil proceedings for the realisation of property to give effect to an external order).

(2)   Proceedings under that Chapter for a recovery order in respect of any recoverable property shall not be brought after the expiration of the period of 20 years from the date on which the relevant person's cause of action accrued.

(3)   Proceedings under that Chapter are brought when—
    (a)   a claim form is issued, or
    (b)   an application is made for a property freezing order, or
    (c)   an application is made for an interim receiving order, whichever is earliest.

(4)   The relevant person's cause of action accrues in respect of any recoverable property—
    (a)   in the case of proceedings for a recovery order in respect of property obtained, or believed to have been obtained, as a result of or in connection with criminal conduct, when the property is so obtained,
    (b)   in the case of proceedings for a recovery order in respect of any other recoverable property, when the property obtained, or believed to have been obtained, as a result of or in connection with criminal conduct which it represents is so obtained.

(5)   If—
    (a)   a person would (but for the preceding provisions of this Act) have a cause of action in respect of the conversion of a chattel, and
    (b)   proceedings are started under that Chapter for a recovery order in respect of the chattel,

section 3(2) of this Act does not prevent his asserting on an application under article 192 of that Order that the property belongs to him, or the court making a declaration in his favour under that article.

(6)   If the court makes such a declaration, his title to the chattel is to be treated as not having been extinguished by section 3(2) of this Act.

(7)   In this section—
    (a)   'criminal conduct' is to be construed in accordance with section 447(8) of the Proceeds of Crime Act 2002, and
    (b)   expressions used in this section which are also used in Part 5 of the Proceeds of Crime Act 2002 (External Requests and Orders) Order 2005 have the same meaning in this section as in that Part.

(8)   In this section 'relevant person' means—
    (a)   the National Crime Agency,
    (b)   the Director of Public Prosecutions, or
    (c)   ...
    (d)   the Director of the Serious Fraud Office.

PART II
EXTENSION OR EXCLUSION OF ORDINARY TIME LIMITS

Disability

28.   Extension of limitation period in case of disability

(1)   Subject to the following provisions of this section, if on the date when any right of action accrued for which a period of limitation is prescribed by this Act, the person to whom it accrued was under a disability, the action may be brought at any time before the expiration of six years from the date when he ceased to be under a disability or died (whichever first occurred) notwithstanding that the period of limitation has expired.

(2)   This section shall not affect any case where the right of action first accrued to some person (not under a disability) through whom the person under a disability claims.

(3)   When a right of action which has accrued to a person under a disability accrues, on the death of that person while still under a disability, to another person under a disability, no further extension of time shall be allowed by reason of the disability of the second person.

(4)   No action to recover land or money charged on land shall be brought by virtue of this section by any person after the expiration of thirty years from the date on which the right of action accrued to that person or some person through whom he claims.

Acknowledgment and part payment

29.   Fresh accrual of action on acknowledgment or part payment

(1)   Subsections (2) and (3) below apply where any right of action (including a foreclosure action) to recover land ... or any right of a mortgagee of personal property to bring a foreclosure action in respect of the property has accrued.

(2)   If the person in possession of the land, benefice or personal property in question acknowledges the title of the person to whom the right of action has accrued—
    (a)   the right shall be treated as having accrued on and not before the date of the acknowledgment; and
    (b)   in the case of a right of action to recover land which has accrued to a person entitled to an estate or interest taking effect on the determination of an entailed interest against whom time is running under section 27 of this Act, section 27 shall thereupon cease to apply to the land.

(3)   In the case of a foreclosure or other action by a mortgagee, if the person in possession of the land, benefice or personal property in question or the person liable for the mortgage debt makes any payment in respect of the debt (whether of principal or interest) the right shall be treated as having accrued on and not before the date of the payment.

(4)   Where a mortgagee is by virtue of the mortgage in possession of any mortgaged land and either—
    (a)   receives any sum in respect of the principal or interest of the mortgage debt; or
    (b)   acknowledges the title of the mortgagor, or his equity of redemption;
an action to redeem the land in his possession may be brought at any time before the expiration of twelve years from the date of the payment or acknowledgment.

(5)   Subject to subsection (6) below, where any right of action has accrued to recover—
      (a)   any debt or other liquidated pecuniary claim; or
      (b)   any claim to the personal estate of a deceased person or to any share or interest
            in any such estate;
      and the person liable or accountable for the claim acknowledges the claim or makes any
      payment in respect of it the right shall be treated as having accrued on and not before
      the date of the acknowledgment or payment.
(6)   A payment of a part of the rent or interest due at any time shall not extend the period
      for claiming the remainder then due, but any payment of interest shall be treated as a
      payment in respect of the principal debt.
(7)   Subject to subsection (6) above, a current period of limitation may be repeatedly
      extended under this section by further acknowledgments or payments, but a right of
      action, once barred by this Act, shall not be revived by any subsequent acknowledgment
      or payment.

30.   Formal provisions as to acknowledgments and part payments

(1)   To be effective for the purposes of section 29 of this Act, an acknowledgment must be in
      writing and signed by the person making it.
(2)   For the purposes of section 29, any acknowledgment or payment—
      (a)   may be sent by the agent of the person by whom it is required to be made under
            that section; and
      (b)   shall be made to the person, or to an agent of the person, whose title or claim
            is being acknowledged or, as the case may be, in respect of whose claim the
            payment is being made.

31.   Effect of acknowledgment or part payment on persons other than the maker or recipient

(1)   An acknowledgment of the title to any land, benefice, or mortgaged personalty by any
      person in possession of it shall bind all other persons in possession during the ensuing
      period of limitation.
(2)   A payment in respect of a mortgage debt by the mortgagor or any other person liable for
      the debt, or by any person in possession of the mortgaged property, shall, so far as any
      right of the mortgagee to foreclose or otherwise to recover the property is concerned,
      bind all other persons in possession of the mortgaged property during the ensuing
      period of limitation.
(3)   Where two or more mortgagees are by virtue of the mortgage in possession of the
      mortgaged land, an acknowledgment of the mortgagor's title or of his equity of
      redemption by one of the mortgagees shall only bind him and his successors and shall
      not bind any other mortgagee or his successors.
(4)   Where in a case within subsection (3) above the mortgagee by whom the acknowledgment
      is given is entitled to a part of the mortgaged land and not to any ascertained part of
      the mortgage debt the mortgagor shall be entitled to redeem that part of the land on
      payment, with interest, of the part of the mortgage debt which bears the same proportion
      to the whole of the debt as the value of the part of the land bears to the whole of the
      mortgaged land.
(5)   Where there are two or more mortgagors, and the title or equity of redemption of one of the
      mortgagors is acknowledged as mentioned above in this section, the acknowledgment
      shall be treated as having been made to all the mortgagors.
(6)   An acknowledgment of any debt or other liquidated pecuniary claim shall bind the
      acknowledgor and his successors but not any other person.
(7)   A payment made in respect of any debt or other liquidated pecuniary claim shall bind all
      persons liable in respect of the debt or claim.
(8)   An acknowledgment by one of several personal representatives of any claim to the
      personal estate of the deceased person or to any share or interest in any such estate, or
      a payment by one of several personal representatives in respect of any such claim, shall
      bind the estate of the deceased person.
(9)   In this section 'successor', in relation to any mortgagee or person liable in respect of
      any debt or claim, means his personal representatives and any other person on whom
      the rights under the mortgage or, as the case may be, the liability in respect of the debt
      or claim devolve (whether on death or bankruptcy or the disposition of property or the
      determination of a limited estate or interest in settled property or otherwise).

Fraud, concealment and mistake

32.   Postponement of limitation period in case of fraud, concealment or mistake

(1)   Subject to subsection (3) ... below, where in the case of any action for which a period of limitation is prescribed by this Act, either—

(a)   the action is based upon the fraud of the defendant; or

(b)   any fact relevant to the plaintiff s right of action has been deliberately concealed from him by the defendant; or

(c)   the action is for relief from the consequences of a mistake;

the period of limitation shall not begin to run until the plaintiff has discovered the fraud, concealment or mistake (as the case may be) or could with reasonable diligence have discovered it.

References in this subsection to the defendant include references to the defendant's agent and to any person through whom the defendant claims and his agent.

(2)   For the purposes of subsection (1) above, deliberate commission of a breach of duty in circumstances in which it is unlikely to be discovered for some time amounts to deliberate concealment of the facts involved in that breach of duty.

(3)   Nothing in this section shall enable any action—

(a)   to recover, or recover the value of, any property; or

(b)   to enforce any charge against, or set aside any transaction affecting, any property;

to be brought against the purchaser of the property or any person claiming through him in any case where the property has been purchased for valuable consideration by an innocent third party since the fraud or concealment or (as the case may be) the transaction in which the mistake was made took place.

(4)   A purchaser is an innocent third party for the purposes of this section—

(a)   in the case of fraud or concealment of any fact relevant to the plaintiff's right of action, if he was not a party to the fraud or (as the case may be) to the concealment of that fact and did not at the time of the purchase know or have reason to believe that the fraud or concealment had taken place; and

(b)   in the case of mistake, if he did not at that time of the purchase know or have reason to believe that the mistake had been made.

38.   Interpretation

(1)   In this Act, unless the context otherwise requires—

'action' includes any proceeding in a court of law, including an ecclesiastical court;

'land' includes corporeal hereditaments, tithes and any legal or equitable estate or interest therein, but except as provided above in this definition does not include any incorporeal hereditament;

'personal estate' and 'personal property' do not include chattels real;

'rent' includes a rentcharge and a rentservice;

'rentcharge' means any annuity or periodical sum of money charged upon or payable out of land, except a rent service or interest on a mortgage on land;

'settled land', 'statutory owner' and 'tenant for life' have the same meanings respectively as in the Settled Land Act 1925;

'trust' and 'trustee' have the same meanings respectively as in the Trustee Act 1925; and

...

(2)   For the purposes of this Act a person shall be treated as under a disability while he is an infant, or lacks capacity (within the meaning of the Mental Capacity Act 2005) to conduct legal proceedings.

(3), (4)   ...

(5)   Subject to subsection (6) below, a person shall be treated as claiming through another person if he became entitled by, through, under, or by the act of that other person to the right claimed, and any person whose estate or interest might have been barred by a person entitled to an entailed interest in possession shall be treated as claiming through the person so entitled.

(6)   A person becoming entitled to any estate or interest by virtue of a special power of appointment shall not be treated as claiming through the appointor.

(7)   References in this Act to a right of action to recover land shall include references to a right to enter into possession of the land or, in the case of tithes, to distrain for arrears of tithe, and references to the bringing of such an action shall include references to the making of such an entry or distress.

(8) References in this Act to the possession of land shall, in the case of tithes and rentcharges, be construed as references to the receipt of the tithe or rent, and references to the date of dispossession or discontinuance of possession of land shall, in the case of rentcharges, be construed as references to the date of the last receipt of rent.

(9) References in Part II of this Act to a right of action shall include references to—

    (a)   a cause of action;

    (b)   a right to receive money secured by a mortgage or charge on any property,

    (c)   a right to recover proceeds of the sale of land; and

    (d)   a right to receive a share of interest in the personal estate of a deceased person.

SCHEDULES

SCHEDULE I
PROVISIONS WITH RESPECT TO ACTIONS TO RECOVER LAND

PART I
ACCRUAL OF RIGHTS OF ACTION TO RECOVER LAND

Accrual of right of action in case of present interests in land

1.   Where the person bringing an action to recover land, or some person through whom he claims, has been in possession of the land, and has while entitled to the land been dispossessed or discontinued his possession, the right of action shall be treated as having accrued on the date of the dispossession or discontinuance.

2.   Where any person brings an action to recover any land of a deceased person (whether under a will or on intestacy) and the deceased person—

    (a)   was on the date of his death in possession of the land or, in the case of a rent charge created by will or taking effect upon his death, in possession of the land charged; and

    (b)   was the last person entitled to the land to be in possession of it;

the right of action shall be treated as having accrued on the date of his death.

3.   Where any person brings an action to recover land, being an estate or interest in possession assured otherwise than by will to him, or to some person through whom he claims, and—

    (a)   the person making the assurance was on the date when the assurance took effect in possession of the land or, in the case of a rentcharge created by the assurance, in possession of the land charged; and

    (b)   no person has been in possession of the land by virtue of the assurance; the right of action shall be treated as having accrued on the date when the assurance took effect.

Accrual of right of action in case of future interests

4.   The right of action to recover any land shall, in a case where—

    (a)   the estate or interest claimed was an estate or interest in reversion or remainder or any other future estate or interest, and

    (b)   no person has taken possession of the land by virtue of the estate or interest claimed;

be treated as having accrued on the date on which the estate or interest fell into possession by the determination of the preceding estate or interest.

5.   (1)   Subject to sub-paragraph (2) below, a tenancy from year to year or other period, without a lease in writing, shall for the purposes of this Act be treated as being determined at the expiration of the first year or other period; and accordingly the right of action of the person entitled to the land subject to the tenancy shall be treated as having accrued at the date on which in accordance with this sub-paragraph the tenancy is determined.

    (2)   Where any rent has subsequently been received in respect of the tenancy, the right of action shall be treated as having accrued on the date of the last receipt of rent.

6.   (1)   Where—

    (a)   any person is in possession of land by virtue of a lease in writing by which a rent of not less than ten pounds a year is reserved; and

    (b)   the rent is received by some person wrongfully claiming to be entitled to the land in reversion immediately expectant on the determination of the lease; and

    (c)   no rent is subsequently received by the person rightfully so entitled; the right of action to recover the land of the person rightfully so entitled shall be treated as having accrued on the date when the rent was first received by the person wrongfully claiming to be so entitled and not on the date of the determination of the lease.

    (2)   Sub-paragraph (1) above shall not apply to any lease granted by the Crown.

Accrual of right of action in case of forfeiture or breach of condition

7.   (1)   Subject to sub-paragraph (2) below, a right of action to recover land by virtue of a forfeiture or breach of condition shall be treated as having accrued on the date on which the forfeiture was incurred or the condition broken.

(2)   If any such right has accrued to a person entitled to an estate or interest in reversion or remainder and the land was not recovered by virtue of that right, the right of action to recover the land shall not be treated as having accrued to that person until his estate or interest fell into possession, as if no such forfeiture or breach of condition had occurred.

Right of action not to accrue or continue unless there is adverse possession

8.   (1)   No right of action to recover land shall be treated as accruing unless the land is in the possession of some person in whose favour the period of limitation can run (referred to below in this paragraph as 'adverse possession'); and where under the preceding provisions of this Schedule any such right of action is treated as accruing on a certain date and no person is in adverse possession on that date, the right of action shall not be treated as accruing unless and until adverse possession is taken of the land.

(2)   Where a right of action to recover land has accrued and after its accrual, before the right is barred, the land ceases to be in adverse possession, the right of action shall no longer be treated as having accrued and no fresh right of action shall be treated as accruing unless and until the land is again taken into adverse possession.

(3)   For the purposes of this paragraph—
   (a)   possession of any land subject to a rentcharge by a person (other than the person entitled to the rentcharge) who does not pay the rent shall be treated as adverse possession of the rentcharge; and
   (b)   receipt of rent under a lease by a person wrongfully claiming to be entitled to the land in reversion immediately expectant on the determination of the lease shall be treated as adverse possession of the land.

(4)   For the purpose of determining whether a person occupying any land is in adverse possession of the land it shall not be assumed by implication of law that his occupation is by permission of the person entitled to the land merely by virtue of the fact that his occupation is not inconsistent with the latter's present or future enjoyment of the land.
      This provision shall not be taken as prejudicing a finding to the effect that a person's occupation of any land is by implied permission of the person entitled to the land in any case where such a finding is justified on the actual facts of the case.

Possession of beneficiary not adverse to others interested in settled land or land subject to a trust of land

9.   Where any settled land or any land subject to a trust of land is in the possession of a person entitled to a beneficial interest in the land (not being a person solely or absolutely entitled to the land or the proceeds), no right of action to recover the land shall be treated for the purposes of this Act as accruing during that possession to any person in whom the land is vested as tenant for life, statutory owner or trustee, or to any other person entitled to a beneficial interest in the land.

SENIOR COURTS ACT 1981
(1981, c. 54)

GENERAL PROVISIONS

Law and equity

49.   Concurrent administration of law and equity

(1)   Subject to the provisions of this or any other Act, every court exercising jurisdiction in England or Wales in any civil cause or matter shall continue to administer law and equity on the basis that, wherever there is any conflict or variance between the rules of equity and the rules of the common law with reference to the same matter, the rules of equity shall prevail.

(2) Every such court shall give the same effect as hitherto—
  (a) to all equitable estates, titles, rights, reliefs, defences and counterclaims, and to all equitable duties and liabilities; and
  (b) subject thereto, to all legal claims and demands and all estates, titles, rights, duties, obligations and liabilities existing by the common law or by any custom or created by any statute,

and, subject to the provisions of this or any other Act, shall so exercise its jurisdiction in every cause or matter before it as to secure that, as far as possible, all matters in dispute between the parties are completely and finally determined, and all multiplicity of legal proceedings with respect to any of those matters is avoided.

(3) Nothing in this Act shall affect the power of the Court of Appeal or the High Court to stay any proceedings before it, where it thinks fit to do so, either of its own motion or on the application of any person, whether or not a party to the proceedings.

50. Power to award damages as well as, or in substitution for, injunction or specific performance

Where the Court of Appeal or the High Court has jurisdiction to entertain an application for an injunction or specific performance, it may award damages in addition to, or in substitution for, an injunction or specific performance.

Powers of Court in relation to personal representatives

112. Summons to executor to prove or renounce

The High Court may summon any person named as executor in a will to prove, or renounce probate of, the will, and to do such other things concerning the will as the court had power to order such a person to do immediately before the commencement of this Act.

113. Power of court to sever grant

(1) Subject to subsection (2), the High Court may grant probate or administration in respect of any part of the estate of a deceased person, limited in any way the court thinks fit.
(2) Where the estate of a deceased person is known to be insolvent, the grant of representation to it shall not be severed under subsection (1) except as regards a trust estate in which he had no beneficial interest.

114. Number of personal representatives

(1) Probate or administration shall not be granted by the High Court to more than four persons in respect of the same part of the estate of a deceased person.
(2) Where under a will or intestacy any beneficiary is a minor or a life interest arises, any grant of administration by the High Court shall be made either to a trust corporation (with or without an individual) or to not less than two individuals, unless it appears to the court to be expedient in all the circumstances to appoint an individual as sole administrator.
(3) For the purpose of determining whether a minority or life interest arises in any particular case, the court may act on such evidence as may be prescribed.
(4) If at any time during the minority of a beneficiary or the subsistence of a life interest under a will or intestacy there is only one personal representative (not being a trust corporation), the High Court may, on the application of any person interested or the guardian or receiver of any such person, and in accordance with probate rules, appoint one or more additional personal representatives to act while the minority or life interest subsists and until the estate is fully administered.
(5) An appointment of an additional personal representative under subsection (4) to act with an executor shall not have the effect of including him in any chain of representation.

116. Power of court to pass over prior claims to grant

(1) If by reason of any special circumstances it appears to the High Court to be necessary or expedient to appoint as administrator some person other than the person who, but for this section, would in accordance with probate rules have been entitled to the grant, the court may in its discretion appoint as administrator such person as it thinks expedient.
(2) Any grant of administration under this section may be limited in any way the court thinks fit.

117. Administration pending suit

(1) Where any legal proceedings concerning the validity of the will of a deceased person, or for obtaining, recalling or revoking any grant, are pending, the High Court may grant administration of the estate of the deceased person in question to an administrator pending suit, who shall, subject to subsection (2), have all the rights, duties and powers of a general administrator.

(2) An administrator pending suit shall be subject to the immediate control of the court and act under its direction; and, except in such circumstances as may be prescribed, no distribution of the estate, or any part of the estate, of the deceased person in question shall be made by such an administrator without the leave of the court.

(3) The court may, out of the estate of the deceased, assign an administrator pending suit such reasonable remuneration as it thinks fit.

118. Effect of appointment of minor as executor

Where a testator by his will appoints a minor to be an executor, the appointment shall not operate to vest in the minor the estate, or any part of the estate, of the testator, or to constitute him a personal representative for any purpose, unless and until probate is granted to him in accordance with probate rules.

119. Administration with will annexed

(1) Administration with the will annexed shall be granted, subject to and in accordance with probate rules, in every class of case in which the High Court had power to make such a grant immediately before the commencement of this Act.

(2) Where administration with the will annexed is granted, the will of the deceased shall be performed and observed in the same manner as if probate of it had been granted to an executor.

120. Power to require administrators to produce sureties

(1) As a condition of granting administration to any person the High Court may, subject to the following provisions of this section and subject to and in accordance with probate rules, require one or more sureties to guarantee that they will make good, within any limit imposed by the court on the total liability of the surety or sureties, any loss which any person interested in the administration of the estate of the deceased may suffer in consequence of a breach by the administrator of his duties as such.

(2) A guarantee given in pursuance of any such requirement shall enure for the benefit of every person interested in the administration of the estate of the deceased as if contained in a contract under seal made by the surety or sureties with every such person and, where there are two or more sureties, as if they had bound themselves jointly and severally.

(3) No action shall be brought on any such guarantee without the leave of the High Court.

(4) Stamp duty shall not be chargeable on any such guarantee.

(5) This section does not apply where administration is granted to the Treasury Solicitor, the Official Solicitor, the Public Trustee, the Solicitor for the affairs of the Duchy of Lancaster or the Duchy of Cornwall or the Crown Solicitor for Northern Ireland, or to the consular officer of a foreign state to which section 1 of the Consular Conventions Act 1949 applies, or in such other cases as may be prescribed.

Revocation of grants and cancellation of resealing at instance of court

121. Revocation of grants and cancellation of resealing at instance of court

(1) Where it appears to the High Court that a grant either ought not to have been made or contains an error, the court may call in the grant and, if satisfied that it would be revoked at the instance of a party interested, may revoke it.

(2) A grant may be revoked under subsection (1) without being called in, if it cannot be called in.

(3) Where it appears to the High Court that a grant resealed under the Colonial Probates Acts 1892 and 1927 ought not to have been resealed, the court may call in the relevant document and, if satisfied that the resealing would be cancelled at the instance of a party interested, may cancel the resealing.

In this and the following subsection 'the relevant document' means the original grant or, where some other document was sealed by the court under those Acts, that document.

(4) A resealing may be cancelled under subsection (3) without the relevant document being called in, if it cannot be called in.

122. Examination of person with knowledge of testamentary document

(1)   Where it appears that there are reasonable grounds for believing that any person has knowledge of any document which is or purports to be a testamentary document, the High Court may, whether or not any legal proceedings are pending, order him to attend for the purpose of being examined in open court.

(2)   The court may—

    (a)   require any person who is before it in compliance with an order under subsection (1) to answer any question relating to the document concerned; and

    (b)   if appropriate, order him to bring in the document in such manner as the court may direct.

(3)   Any person who, having been required by the court to do so under this section, fails to attend for examination, answer any question or bring in any document shall be guilty of contempt of court.

123. Subpoena to bring in testamentary document

Where it appears that any person has in his possession, custody or power any document which is or purports to be a testamentary document, the High Court may, whether or not any legal proceedings are pending, issue a subpoena requiring him to bring in the document in such manner as the court may in the subpoena direct.

Provisions as to documents

124. Place for deposit of original wills and other documents

All original wills and other documents which are under the control of the High Court in the Principal Registry or in any district probate registry shall be deposited and preserved in such places as may be provided for in directions given in accordance with Part 1 of Schedule 2 to the Constitutional Reform Act 2005; and any wills or other documents so deposited shall, subject to the control of the High Court and to probate rules, be open to inspection.

125. Copies of wills and grants

An office copy, or a sealed and certified copy, of any will or part of a will open to inspection under section 124 or of any grant may, on payment of the fee prescribed by an order under section 92 of the Courts Act 2003 (fees), be obtained—

(a)   from the registry in which in accordance with section 124 the will or documents relating to the grant are preserved; or

(b)   where in accordance with that section the will or such documents are preserved in some place other than a registry, from the Principal Registry; or

(c)   subject to the approval of the Senior Registrar of the Family Division, from the Principal Registry in any case where the will was proved in or the grant was issued from a district probate registry.

126. Depositories for wills of living persons

(1)   There shall be provided, under the control and direction of the High Court, safe and convenient depositories for the custody of the wills of living persons; and any person may deposit his will in such a depository on payment of the fee prescribed by an order under section 92 of the Courts Act 2003 (fees) and subject to such conditions as may be prescribed by regulations made by the President of the Family Division with the concurrence of the Lord Chancellor.

(2)   Any regulations made under this section shall be made by statutory instrument which shall be laid before Parliament after being made; and the Statutory Instruments Act 1946 shall apply to a statutory instrument containing regulations under this section in like manner as if they had been made by a Minister of the Crown.

Probate rules

127. Probate rules

(1)   Rules of court (in this Part referred to as 'probate rules') may be made in accordance with Part 1 of Schedule 1 to the Constitutional Reform Act 2005 for regulating and prescribing the practice and procedure of the High Court with respect to non-contentious or common form probate business.

(2)   Without prejudice to the generality of subsection (1), probate rules may make provision for regulating the classes of persons entitled to grants of probate or administration in particular circumstances and the relative priorities of their claims thereto.

(3)   ...

FORFEITURE ACT 1982
(1982, c. 34)

1.   The 'forfeiture rule'

(1)   In this Act, the 'forfeiture rule' means the rule of public policy which in certain circumstances precludes a person who has unlawfully killed another from acquiring a benefit in consequence of the killing.

(2)   References in this Act to a person who has unlawfully killed another include a reference to a person who has unlawfully aided, abetted, counselled or procured the death of that other and references in this Act to unlawful killing shall be interpreted accordingly.

2.   Power to modify the rule

(1)   Where a court determines that the forfeiture rule has precluded a person (in this section referred to as 'the offender') who has unlawfully killed another from acquiring any interest in property mentioned in subsection (4) below, the court may make an order under this section modifying the effect of that rule.

(2)   The court shall not make an order under this section modifying the effect of the forfeiture rule in any case unless it is satisfied that, having regard to the conduct of the offender and of the deceased and to such other circumstances as appear to the court to be material, the justice of the case requires the effect of the rule to be so modified in that case.

(3)   In any case where a person stands convicted of an offence of which unlawful killing is an element, the court shall not make an order under this section modifying the effect of the forfeiture rule in that case unless proceedings for the purpose are brought before the expiry of the period of three months beginning with his conviction.

(4)   The interests in property referred to in subsection (1) above are—

    (a)   any beneficial interest in property which (apart from the forfeiture rule) the offender would have acquired—

        (i)   under the deceased's will ... or the law relating to intestacy or by way of ius relicti, ius relictae or legitim;

        (ii)   on the nomination of the deceased in accordance with the provisions of any enactment,

        (iii)   as a donatio mortis causa made by the deceased;

        (iv)   under a special destination (whether relating to heritable or moveable property); or

    (b)   any beneficial interest in property which (apart from the forfeiture rule) the offender would have acquired in consequence of the death of the deceased, being property which, before the death, was held on trust for any person.

(5)   An order under this section may modify the effect of the forfeiture rule in respect of any interest in property to which the determination referred to in subsection (1) above relates and may do so in either or both of the following ways, that is—

    (a)   where there is more than one such interest, by excluding the application of the rule in respect of any (but not all) of those interests; and

    (b)   in the case of any such interest in property, by excluding the application of the rule in respect of part of the property.

(6)   On the making of an order under this section, the forfeiture rule shall have effect for all purposes (including purposes relating to anything done before the order is made) subject to the modifications made by the order.

(7)   The court shall not make an order under this section modifying the effect of the forfeiture rule in respect of any interest in property which, in consequence of the rule, has been acquired before the coming into force of this section by a person other than the offender or a person claiming through him.

(8)   In this section—

'property' includes any chose in action or incorporeal moveable property; and 'will' includes codicil.

3. **Application for financial provision not affected by the rule**
   (1) The forfeiture rule shall not be taken to preclude any person from making any application under a provision mentioned in subsection (2) below or the making of any order on the application.
   (2) The provisions referred to in subsection (1) above are—
      (a) any provision of the Inheritance (Provision for Family and Dependants) Act 1975;
      (b) sections 31(6) and 36(1) of the Matrimonial Causes Act 1973 (variation by court in England and Wales of periodical payments orders and maintenance agreements in respect of marriages);
      (c) paragraphs 60(2) and 73(2) of Schedule 5 to the Civil Partnership Act 2004 (variation by court in England and Wales of periodical payments orders and maintenance agreements in respect of civil partnerships); and
      (d) section 13(4) of the Family Law (Scotland) Act 1985 (variation etc. of periodical allowances in respect of marriages and civil partnerships).

5. **Exclusion of murderers**
Nothing in this Act or in any order made under section 2 or referred to in section 3(1) of this Act

... shall affect the application of the forfeiture rule in the case of a person who stands convicted of murder.

ADMINISTRATION OF JUSTICE ACT 1982
(1982, c. 53)

Rectification and interpretation of wills

20. **Rectification**
   (1) If a court is satisfied that a will is so expressed that it fails to carry out the testator's intentions, in consequence—
      (a) of a clerical error; or
      (b) of a failure to understand his instructions,
      it may order that the will shall be rectified so as to carry out his intentions.

   (2) An application for an order under this section shall not, except with the permission of the court, be made after the end of the period of six months from the date on which representation with respect to the estate of the deceased is first taken out.
   (3) The provisions of this section shall not render the personal representatives of a deceased person liable for having distributed any part of the estate of the deceased, after the end of the period of six months from the date on which representation with respect to the estate of the deceased is first taken out, on the ground that they ought to have taken into account the possibility that the court might permit the making of an application for an order under this section after the end of that period; but this subsection shall not prejudice any power to recover, by reason of the making of an order under this section, any part of the estate so distributed.
   (4) The following are to be left out of account when considering for the purposes of this section when representation with respect to the estate of a deceased person was first taken out—
      (a) a grant limited to settled land or to trust property,
      (b) any other grant that does not permit any of the estate to be distributed,
      (c) a grant limited to real estate or to personal estate, unless a grant limited to the remainder of the estate has previously been made or is made at the same time,
      (d) a grant, or its equivalent, made outside the United Kingdom (but see subsection (5)).
   (5) A grant sealed under section 2 of the Colonial Probates Act 1892 counts as a grant made in the United Kingdom for the purposes of subsection (4), but is to be taken as dated on the date of sealing.

21. **Interpretation of wills—general rules as to evidence**
   (1) This section applies to a will—
      (a) in so far as any part of it is meaningless;
      (b) in so far as the language used in any part of it is ambiguous on the face of it;

(c) in so far as evidence, other than evidence of the testator's intention, shows that the language used in any part of it is ambiguous in the light of surrounding circumstances.

(2) In so far as this section applies to a will extrinsic evidence, including evidence of the testator's intention, may be admitted to assist in its interpretation.

22. Presumption as to effect of gifts to spouses

Except where a contrary intention is shown it shall be presumed that if a testator devises or bequeaths property to his spouse in terms which in themselves would give an absolute interest to the spouse, but by the same instrument purports to give his issue an interest in the same property, the gift to the spouse is absolute notwithstanding the purported gift to the issue.

LANDLORD AND TENANT ACT 1985
(1985, c. 70)

Information to be given to tenant

1. Disclosure of landlord's identity

(1) If the tenant of premises occupied as a dwelling makes a written request for the landlord's name and address to—

(a) any person who demands, or the last person who received, rent payable under the tenancy, or

(b) any other person for the time being acting as agent for the landlord, in relation to the tenancy,

that person shall supply the tenant with a written statement of the landlord's name and address within the period of 21 days beginning with the day on which he receives the request.

(2) A person who, without reasonable excuse, fails to comply with subsection (1) commits a summary offence and is liable on conviction to a fine not exceeding level 4 on the standard scale.

(3) In this section and section 2—

(a) 'tenant' includes a statutory tenant; and

(b) 'landlord' means the immediate landlord.

Provision of rent books

4. Provision of rent books

(1) Where a tenant has a right to occupy premises as a residence in consideration of a rent payable weekly, the landlord shall provide a rent book or other similar document for use in respect of the premises.

(2) Subsection (1) does not apply to premises if the rent includes a payment in respect of board and the value of that board to the tenant forms a substantial proportion of the whole rent.

(3) In this section and sections 5 to 7—

(a) 'tenant' includes a statutory tenant and a person having a contractual right to occupy the premises; and

(b) 'landlord', in relation to a person having such a contractual right, means the person who granted the right or any successor in title of his, as the case may require.

Repairing obligations

11. Repairing obligations in short leases

(1) In a lease to which this section applies (as to which, see sections 13 and 14) there is implied a covenant by the lessor—

(a) to keep in repair the structure and exterior of the dwelling-house (including drains, gutters and external pipes),

(b) to keep in repair and proper working order the installations in the dwelling-house for the supply of water, gas and electricity and for sanitation (including basins, sinks, baths and sanitary conveniences, but not other fixtures, fittings and appliances for making use of the supply of water, gas or electricity), and

(c) to keep in repair and proper working order the installations in the dwelling-house for space heating and heating water.

(1A) If a lease to which this section applies is a lease of a dwelling-house which forms part only of a building, then, subject to subsection (1B), the covenant implied by subsection (1) shall have effect as if—

    (a)   the reference in paragraph (a) of that subsection to the dwelling-house included a reference to any part of the building in which the lessor has an estate or interest; and

    (b)   any reference in paragraphs (b) and (c) of that subsection to an installation in the dwelling-house included a reference to an installation which, directly or indirectly, serves the dwelling-house and which either—

        (i)   forms part of any part of a building in which the lessor has an estate or interest; or

        (ii)   is owned by the lessor or under his control.

(1B) Nothing in subsection (1A) shall be construed as requiring the lessor to carry out any works or repairs unless the disrepair (or failure to maintain in working order) is such as to affect the lessee's enjoyment of the dwelling-house or of any common parts, as defined in section 60(1) of the Landlord and Tenant Act 1987, which the lessee, as such, is entitled to use.

(2) The covenant implied by subsection (1) ('the lessor's repairing covenant') shall not be construed as requiring the lessor—

    (a)   to carry out works or repairs for which the lessee is liable by virtue of his duty to use the premises in a tenant-like manner, or would be so liable but for an express covenant on his part,

    (b)   to rebuild or reinstate the premises in the case of destruction or damage by fire, or by tempest, flood or other inevitable accident, or

    (c)   to keep in repair or maintain anything which the lessee is entitled to remove from the dwelling-house.

(3) In determining the standard of repair required by the lessor's repairing covenant, regard shall be had to the age, character and the dwelling-house and the locality in which it is situated.

(3A) In any case where—

    (a)   the lessor's repairing covenant has effect as mentioned in subsection (1A), and

    (b)   in order to comply with the covenant the lessor needs to carry out works or repairs otherwise than in, or to an installation in, the dwelling-house, and

    (c)   the lessor does not have a sufficient right in the part of the building or the installation concerned to enable him to carry out the required works or repairs,

then, in any proceedings relating to a failure to comply with the lessor's repairing covenant, so far as it requires the lessor to carry out the works or repairs in question, it shall be a defence for the lessor to prove that he used all reasonable endeavours to obtain, but was unable to obtain, such rights as would be adequate to enable him to carry out the works or repairs.

(4) A covenant by the lessee for the repair of the premises is of no effect so far as it relates to the matters mentioned in subsection (1)(a) to (c), except so far as it imposes on the lessee any of the requirements mentioned in subsection (2)(a) or (c).

(5) The reference in subsection (4) to a covenant by the lessee for the repair of the premises includes a covenant—

    (a)   to put in repair or deliver up in repair,

    (b)   to paint, point or render,

    (c)   to pay money in lieu of repairs by the lessee, or

    (d)   to pay money on account of repairs by the lessor.

(6) In a case in which the lessor's repairing covenant is implied there is also implied a covenant by the lessee that the lessor, or any person authorised by him in writing, may at reasonable times of the day and on giving 24 hours' notice in writing to the occupier, enter the premises comprised in the lease for the purpose of viewing their condition and state of repair.

13.   Leases to which s 11 applies: general rule

(1) Section 11 (repairing obligations) applies to a lease of a dwelling-house granted on or after 24th October 1961 for a term of less than seven years.

(1A) Section 11 also applies to a lease of a dwelling-house in England granted on or after the day on which section 166 of the Localism Act 2011 came into force which is—

(a)   a secure tenancy for a fixed term of seven years or more granted by a person within section 80(1) of the Housing Act 1985 (secure tenancies: the landlord condition), or

(b)   an assured tenancy for a fixed term of seven years or more that—
    (i)   is not a shared ownership lease, and
    (ii)   is granted by a private registered provider of social housing. (1B) In subsection (1A)—

'assured tenancy' has the same meaning as in Part 1 of the Housing Act 1988;

'secure tenancy' has the meaning given by section 79 of the Housing Act 1985; and

'shared ownership lease' means a lease—

(a)   granted on payment of a premium calculated by reference to a percentage of the value of the dwelling-house or of the cost of providing it, or

(b)   under which the lessee (or the lessee's personal representatives) will or may be entitled to a sum calculated by reference, directly or indirectly, to the value of the dwelling-house.

(2)   In determining whether a lease is one to which section 11 applies—

(a)   any part of the term which falls before the grant shall be left out of account and the lease shall be treated as a lease for a term commencing with the grant,

(b)   a lease which is determinable at the option of the lessor before the expiration of seven years from the commencement of the term shall be treated as a lease for a term of less than seven years, and

(c)   a lease (other than a lease to which paragraph (b) applies) shall not be treated as a lease for a term of less than seven years if it confers on the lessee an option for renewal for a term which, together with the original term, amounts to seven years or more.

(3)   This section has effect subject to—
section 14 (leases to which section 11 applies: exceptions), and
section 32(2) (provisions not applying to tenancies within Part II of the Landlord and Tenant Act 1954).

14.   Leases to which s 11 applies: exceptions

(1)   Section 11 (repairing obligations) does not apply to a new lease granted to an existing tenant, or to a former tenant still in possession, if the previous lease was not a lease to which section 11 applied (and, in the case of a lease granted before 24th October 1961, would not have been if it had been granted on or after that date).

(2)   In subsection (1) —
'existing tenant' means a person who is when, or immediately before, the new lease is granted, the lessee under another lease of the dwelling-house;
'former tenant still in possession' means a person who—

(a)   was the lessee under another lease of the dwelling-house which terminated at some time before the new lease was granted, and

(b)   between the termination of that other lease and the grant of the new lease was continuously in possession of the dwelling-house or of the rents and profits of the dwelling-house; and

'the previous lease' means the other lease referred to in the above definitions.

(3)   Section 11 does not apply to a lease of a dwelling-house which is a tenancy of an agricultural holding within the meaning of the Agricultural Holdings Act 1986 and in relation to which that Act applies or to a farm business tenancy within the meaning of the Agricultural Tenancies Act 1995.

(4)   Section 11 does not apply to a lease granted on or after 3rd October 1980 to—
a local authority,
a National Park authority,
a new town corporation,
a Mayoral development corporation, an urban development corporation,
the Development Board for Rural Wales,
a non-profit registered provider of social housing, a registered social landlord,
a co-operative housing association,
an educational institution or other body specified, or of a class specified, by regulations under section 8 of the Rent Act 1977 or paragraph 8 of Schedule 1 to the Housing Act 1988 (bodies making student lettings), or
a housing action trust established under Part III of the Housing Act 1988.

(5)   Section 11 does not apply to a lease granted on or after 3rd October 1980 to—
    (a)   Her Majesty in right of the Crown (unless the lease is under the management of the Crown Estate Commissioners), or
    (b)   a government department or a person holding in trust for Her Majesty for the purposes of a government department.

17.   Specific performance of landlord's repairing obligations

(1)   In proceedings in which a tenant of a dwelling alleges a breach on the part of his landlord of a repairing covenant relating to any part of the premises in which the dwelling is comprised, the court may order specific performance of the covenant whether or not the breach relates to a part of the premises let to the tenant and notwithstanding any equitable rule restricting the scope of the remedy, whether on the basis of a lack of mutuality or otherwise.

(2)   In this section—
    (a)   'tenant' includes a statutory tenant,
    (b)   in relation to a statutory tenant the reference to the premises let to him is to the premises of which he is a statutory tenant,
    (c)   'landlord', in relation to a tenant, includes any person against whom the tenant has a right to enforce a repairing covenant, and
    (d)   'repairing covenant' means a covenant to repair, maintain, renew, construct or replace any property.

INSOLVENCY ACT 1986
(1986, c. 45)

CHAPTER V
EFFECT OF BANKRUPTCY ON CERTAIN RIGHTS, TRANSACTIONS, ETC.

Rights under trusts of land

335A.   Rights under trusts of land

(1)   Any application by a trustee of a bankrupt's estate under section 14 of the Trusts of Land and Appointment of Trustees Act 1996 (powers of court in relation to trusts of land) for an order under that section for the sale of land shall be made to the court having jurisdiction in relation to the bankruptcy.

(2)   On such an application the court shall make such order as it thinks just and reasonable having regard to—
    (a)   the interests of the bankrupt's creditors;
    (b)   where the application is made in respect of land which includes a dwelling house which is or has been the home of the bankrupt or the bankrupt's spouse or civil partner or former spouse or former civil partner—
        (i)   the conduct of the spouse, civil partner, former spouse or former civil partner, so far as contributing to the bankruptcy,
        (ii)   the needs and financial resources of the spouse, civil partner, former spouse or formal civil partner, and
        (iii) the needs of any children; and
    (c)   all the circumstances of the case other than the needs of the bankrupt.

(3)   Where such an application is made after the end of the period of one year beginning with the first vesting under Chapter IV of this Part of the bankrupt's estate in a trustee, the court shall assume, unless the circumstances of the case are exceptional, that the interests of the bankrupt's creditors outweigh all other considerations.

(4)   The powers conferred on the court by this section are exercisable on an application whether it is made before or after the commencement of this section.

Rights of occupation

336.   Rights of occupation etc. of bankrupt's spouse or civil partner

(1)   Nothing occurring in the initial period of the bankruptcy (that is to say, the period beginning with the day of the making of the bankruptcy application or (as the case

may be) the presentation of the bankruptcy petition and ending with the vesting of the bankrupt's estate in a trustee) is to be taken as having given rise to any home rights under Part IV of the Family Law Act 1996 in relation to a dwelling house comprised in the bankrupt's estate.

(2) Where a spouse's or civil partner's home rights under the Act of 1996 are a charge on the estate or interest of the other spouse or civil partner, or of trustees for the other spouse or civil partner, and the other spouse or civil partner is made bankrupt—

(a) the charge continues to subsist notwithstanding the bankruptcy and, subject to the provisions of that Act, binds the trustee of the bankrupt's estate and persons deriving title under that trustee, and

(b) any application for an order under section 33 of that Act shall be made to the court having jurisdiction in relation to the bankruptcy.

(3) ...

(4) On such an application as is mentioned in subsection (2) the court shall make such order under section 33 of the Act of 1996 as it thinks just and reasonable having regard to—

(a) the interests of the bankrupt's creditors,

(b) the conduct of the spouse or former spouse or civil partner or former civil partner, so far as contributing to the bankruptcy,

(c) the needs and financial resources of the spouse or former spouse or civil partner or former civil partner,

(d) the needs of any children, and

(e) all the circumstances of the case other than the needs of the bankrupt.

(5) Where such an application is made after the end of the period of one year beginning with the first vesting under Chapter IV of this Part of the bankrupt's estate in a trustee, the court shall assume, unless the circumstances of the case are exceptional, that the interests of the bankrupt's creditors outweigh all other considerations.

337. Rights of occupation of bankrupt

(1) This section applies where—

(a) a person who is entitled to occupy a dwelling house by virtue of a beneficial estate or interest is made bankrupt, and

(b) any persons under the age of 18 with whom that person had at some time occupied that dwelling house had their home with that person at the time when the bankruptcy application was made or (as the case may be) the bankruptcy petition was presented and at the commencement of the bankruptcy.

(2) Whether or not the bankrupt's spouse or civil partner (if any) has home rights under Part IV of the Family Law Act 1996—

(a) the bankrupt has the following rights as against the trustee of his estate—

(i) if in occupation, a right not to be evicted or excluded from the dwelling house or any part of it, except with the leave of the court,

(ii) if not in occupation, a right with the leave of the court to enter into and occupy the dwelling house, and

(b) the bankrupt's rights are a charge, having the like priority as an equitable interest created immediately before the commencement of the bankruptcy, on so much of his estate or interest in the dwelling house as vests in the trustee.

(3) The Act of 1996 has effect, with the necessary modifications, as if—

(a) the rights conferred by paragraph (a) of subsection (2) were home rights under that Act,

(b) any application for such leave as is mentioned in that paragraph were an application for an order under section 33 of that Act, and

(c) any charge under paragraph (b) of that subsection on the estate or interest of the trustee were a charge under that Act on the estate or interest of a spouse or civil partner.

(4) Any application for leave such as is mentioned in subsection (2)(a) or otherwise by virtue of this section for an order under section 33 of the Act of 1996 shall be made to the court having jurisdiction in relation to the bankruptcy.

(5) On such an application the court shall make such order under section 33 of the Act of 1996 as it thinks just and reasonable having regard to the interests of the creditors, to the bankrupt's financial resources, to the needs of the children and to all the circumstances of the case other than the needs of the bankrupt.

(6)   Where such an application is made after the end of the period of one year beginning with the first vesting ... of the bankrupt's estate in a trustee, the court shall assume, unless the circumstances of the case are exceptional, that the interests of the bankrupt's creditors outweigh all other considerations.

338.   Payments in respect of premises occupied by bankrupt

Where any premises comprised in a bankrupt's estate are occupied by him (whether by virtue of the preceding section or otherwise) on condition that he makes payments towards satisfying any liability arising under a mortgage of the premises or otherwise towards the outgoings of the premises, the bankrupt does not, by virtue of those payments, acquire any interest in the premises.

Adjustment of prior transactions, etc.

339.   Transactions at an undervalue

(1)   Subject as follows in this section and sections 341 and 342, where an individual is made bankrupt and he has at a relevant time (defined in section 341) entered into a transaction with any person at an undervalue, the trustee of the bankrupt's estate may apply to the court for an order under this section.

(2)   The court shall, on such an application, make such order as it thinks fit for restoring the position to what it would have been if that individual had not entered into that transaction.

(3)   For the purposes of this section and sections 341 and 342, an individual enters into a transaction with a person at an undervalue if—

(a)   he makes a gift to that person or he otherwise enters into a transaction with that person on terms that provide for him to receive no consideration,

(b)   he enters into a transaction with that person in consideration of marriage or the formation of a civil partnership, or

(c)   he enters into a transaction with that person for a consideration the value of which, in money or money's worth, is significantly less than the value, in money or money's worth, of the consideration provided by the individual.

340.   Preferences

(1)   Subject as follows in this and the next two sections, where an individual is made bankrupt and he has at a relevant time (defined in section 341) given a preference to any person, the trustee of the bankrupt's estate may apply to the court for an order under this section.

(2)   The court shall, on such an application, make such order as it thinks fit for restoring the position to what it would have been if that individual had not given that preference.

(3)   For the purposes of this and the next two sections, an individual gives a preference to a person if—

(a)   that person is one of the individual's creditors or a surety or guarantor for any of his debts or other liabilities, and

(b)   the individual does anything or suffers anything to be done which (in either case) has the effect of putting that person into a position which, in the event of the individual's bankruptcy, will be better than the position he would have been in if that thing had not been done.

(4)   The court shall not make an order under this section in respect of a preference given to any person unless the individual who gave the preference was influenced in deciding to give it by a desire to produce in relation to that person the effect mentioned in subsection (3)(b) above.

(5)   An individual who has given a preference to a person who, at the time the preference was given, was an associate of his (otherwise than by reason only of being his employee) is presumed, unless the contrary is shown, to have been influenced in deciding to give it by such a desire as is mentioned in subsection (4).

(6)   The fact that something has been done in pursuance of the order of a court does not, without more, prevent the doing or suffering of that thing from constituting the giving of a preference.

341.   'Relevant time' under ss. 339, 340

(1)   Subject as follows, the time at which an individual enters into a transaction at an undervalue or gives a preference is a relevant time if the transaction is entered into or the preference given—

    (a)   in the case of a transaction at an undervalue, at a time in the period of 5 years ending with the day of the making of the bankruptcy application as a result of which, or (as the case may be) the presentation of the bankruptcy petition on which, the individual is made bankrupt,

    (b)   in the case of a preference which is not a transaction at an undervalue and is given to a person who is an associate of the individual (otherwise than by reason only of being his employee), at a time in the period of 2 years ending with that day, and

    (c)   in any other case of a preference which is not a transaction at an undervalue, at a time in the period of 6 months ending with that day.

(2)   Where an individual enters into a transaction at an undervalue or gives a preference at a time mentioned in paragraph (a), (b) or (c) of subsection (1) (not being, in the case of a transaction at an undervalue, a time less than 2 years before the end of the period mentioned in paragraph (a)), that time is not a relevant time for the purposes of sections 339 and 340 unless the individual—

    (a)   is insolvent at that time, or

    (b)   becomes insolvent in consequence of the transaction or preference;

but the requirements of this subsection are presumed to be satisfied, unless the contrary is shown, in relation to any transaction at an undervalue which is entered into by an individual with a person who is an associate of his (otherwise than by reason only of being his employee).

(3)   For the purposes of subsection (2), an individual is insolvent if—

    (a)   he is unable to pay his debts as they fall due, or

    (b)   the value of his assets is less than the amount of his liabilities, taking into account his contingent and prospective liabilities.

(4)–(5)…

342. Orders under ss. 339, 340

(1)   Without prejudice to the generality of section 339(2) or 340(2), an order under either of those sections with respect to a transaction or preference entered into or given by an individual who is subsequently made bankrupt may (subject as follows)—

    (a)   require any property transferred as part of the transaction, or in connection with the giving of the preference, to be vested in the trustee of the bankrupt's estate as part of that estate;

    (b)   require any property to be so vested if it represents in any person's hands the application either of the proceeds of sale of property so transferred or of money so transferred;

    (c)   release or discharge (in whole or in part) any security given by the individual;

    (d)   require any person to pay, in respect of benefits received by him from the individual, such sums to the trustee of his estate as the court may direct,

    (e)   provide for any surety or guarantor whose obligations to any person were released or discharged (in whole or in part) under the transaction or by the giving of the preference to be under such new or revived obligations to that person as the court thinks appropriate;

    (f)   provide for security to be provided for the discharge of any obligation imposed by or arising under the order, for such an obligation to be charged on any property and for the security or charge to have the same priority as a security or charge released or discharged (in whole or in part) under the transaction or by the giving of the preference; and

    (g)   provide for the extent to which any person whose property is vested by the order in the trustee of the bankrupt's estate, or on whom obligations are imposed by the order, is to be able to prove in the bankruptcy for debts or other liabilities which arose from, or were released or discharged (in whole or in part) under or by, the transaction or the giving of the preference.

(2)   An order under section 339 or 340 may affect the property of, or impose any obligation on, any person whether or not he is the person with whom the individual in question entered into the transaction or, as the case may be, the person to whom the preference was given; but such an order—

    (a)   shall not prejudice any interest in property which was acquired from a person other than that individual and was acquired in good faith and for value, or prejudice any interest deriving from such an interest, and

(b)   shall not require a person who received a benefit from the transaction or preference in good faith and for value to pay a sum to the trustee of the bankrupt's estate, except where he was a party to the transaction or the payment is to be in respect of a preference given to that person at a time when he was a creditor of that individual.

(2A)   Where a person has acquired an interest in property from a person other than the individual in question, or has received a benefit from the transaction or preference, and at the time of that acquisition a receipt—

(a)   he had notice of the relevant surrounding circumstances and of the relevant proceedings, or

(b)   he was an associate of, or was connected with, either the individual in question or the person with whom that individual gave the preference,

then, unless the contrary is shown, it shall be presumed for the purposes of paragraph (a) or (as the case may be) paragraph (b) of subsection (2) that the interest was acquired or the benefit was received otherwise than in good faith.

(3)   Any sums required to be paid to the trustee in accordance with an order under section 339 or 340 shall be comprised in the bankrupt's estate.

(4)   For the purposes of subsection (2A)(a), the relevant surrounding circumstances are (as the case may require)—

(a)   the fact that the individual in question entered into the transaction at an undervalue; or

(b)   the circumstances which amounted to the giving of the preference by the individual in question.

(5)   For the purposes of subsection (2A)(a), a person has notice of the relevant proceedings if he has notice—

(a)   of the fact that the bankruptcy application as a result of which, or (as the case may be) the bankruptcy petition on which, the individual in question is made bankrupt has been made or presented; or

(b)   of the fact that the individual in question has been made bankrupt.

...

PART XVI
PROVISIONS AGAINST DEBT AVOIDANCE (ENGLAND AND WALES ONLY)

423.   Transactions defrauding creditors

(1)   This section relates to transactions entered into at an undervalue, and a person enters into such a transaction with another person if—

(a)   he makes a gift to the other person or he otherwise enters into a transaction with the other on terms that provide for him to receive no consideration;

(b)   he enters into a transaction with the other in consideration of marriage or the formation of a civil partnership; or

(c)   he enters into a transaction with the other for a consideration the value of which, in money or money's worth, is significantly less than the value, in money or money's worth, of the consideration provided by himself.

(2)   Where a person has entered into such a transaction, the court may, if satisfied under the next subsection, make such order as it thinks fit for—

(a)   restoring the position to what it would have been if the transaction had not been entered into, and

(b)   protecting the interests of persons who are victims of the transaction.

(3)   In the case of a person entering into such a transaction, an order shall only be made if the court is satisfied that it was entered into by him for the purpose—

(a)   of putting assets beyond the reach of a person who is making, or may at some time make, a claim against him, or

(b)   of otherwise prejudicing the interests of such a person in relation to the claim which he is making or may make.

(4)   In this section 'the court' means the High Court or—

(a)   if the person entering into the transaction is an individual, any other court which would have jurisdiction in relation to a bankruptcy petition relating to him;

(b)   if that person is a body capable of being wound up, any other court having jurisdiction to wind it up.

(5)   In relation to a transaction at an undervalue, references here and below to a victim of the transaction are to a person who is, or is capable of being, prejudiced by it; and in the following two sections the person entering into the transaction is referred to as 'the debtor'.

424.   Those who may apply for an order under s. 423

(1)   An application for an order under section 423 shall not be made in relation to a transaction except—

(a)   in a case where the debtor has been made bankrupt or is a body corporate which is being wound up or is in administration, by the official receiver, by the trustee of the bankrupt's estate or the liquidator or administrator of the body corporate or (with the leave of the court) by a victim of the transaction;

(b)   in a case where a victim of the transaction is bound by a voluntary arrangement approved under Part I or Part VIII of this Act, by the supervisor of the voluntary arrangement or by any person who (whether or not so bound) is such a victim; or

(c)   in any other case, by a victim of the transaction.

(2)   An application made under any of the paragraphs of subsection (1) is to be treated as made on behalf of every victim of the transaction.

425.   Provision which may be made by order under s. 423

(1)   Without prejudice to the generality of section 423, an order made under that section with respect to a transaction may (subject as follows)—

(a)   require any property transferred as part of the transaction to be vested in any person, either absolutely or for the benefit of all the persons on whose behalf the application for the order is treated as made;

(b)   require any property to be so vested if it represents, in any person's hands, the application either of the proceeds of sale of property so transferred or of money so transferred;

(c)   release or discharge (in whole or in part) any security given by the debtor;

(d)   require any person to pay to any other person in respect of benefits received from the debtor such sums as the court may direct;

(e)   provide for any surety or guarantor whose obligations to any person were released or discharged (in whole or in part) under the transaction to be under such new or revived obligations as the court thinks appropriate;

(f)   provide for security to be provided for the discharge of any obligation imposed by or arising under the order, for such an obligation to be charged on any property and for such security or charge to have the same priority as a security or charge released or discharged (in whole are in part) under the transaction.

(2)   An order under section 423 may affect the property of, or impose any obligation on, any person whether or not he is the person with whom the debtor entered into the transaction; but such an order—

(a)   shall not prejudice any interest in property which was acquired from a person other than the debtor and was acquired in good faith, for value and without notice of the relevant circumstances, or prejudice any interest deriving from such an interest, and

(b)   shall not require a person who received a benefit from the transaction in good faith, for value and without notice of the relevant circumstances to pay any sum unless he was a party to the transaction.

(3)   For the purposes of this section the relevant circumstances in relation to a transaction are the circumstances by virtue of which an order under section 423 may be made in respect of the transaction.

(4)   In this section 'security' means any mortgage, charge, lien or other security.

LANDLORD AND TENANT ACT 1988
(1988, c. 26)

1.   Qualified duty to consent to assigning, underletting etc. of premises

(1)   This section applies in any case where—

(a)   a tenancy includes a covenant on the part of the tenant not to enter into one or more of the following transactions, that is—

        (i)   assigning,
        (ii)   underletting,
        (iii)   charging, or
        (iv)   parting with the possession of,

the premises comprised in the tenancy or any part of the premises without the consent of the landlord or some other person, but

(b) the covenant is subject to the qualification that the consent is not to be unreasonably withheld (whether or not it is also subject to any other qualification).

(2) In this section and section 2 of this Act—

(a) references to a proposed transaction are to any assignment, underletting, charging or parting with possession to which the covenant relates, and

(b) references to the person who may consent to such a transaction are to the person who under the covenant may consent to the tenancy entering into the proposed transaction.

(3) Where there is served on the person who may consent to a proposed transaction a written application by the tenant for consent to the transaction, he owes a duty to the tenant within a reasonable time—

(a) to give consent, except in a case where it is reasonable not to give consent,

(b) to serve on the tenant written notice of his decision whether or not to give consent specifying in addition—

        (i)   if the consent is given subject to conditions, the conditions,
        (ii)   if the consent is withheld, the reasons for withholding it.

(4) Giving consent subject to any condition that is not a reasonable condition does not satisfy the duty under subsection (3)(a) above.

(5) For the purposes of this Act it is reasonable for a person not to give consent to a proposed transaction only in a case where, if he withheld consent and the tenant completed the transaction, the tenant would be in breach of a covenant.

(6) It is for the person who owed any duty under subsection (3) above—

(a) if he gave consent and the question arises whether he gave it within a reasonable time, to show that he did,

(b) if he gave consent subject to any condition and the question arises whether the condition was a reasonable condition, to show that it was,

(c) if he did not give consent and the question arises whether it was reasonable for him not to do so, to show that it was reasonable,

and, if the question arises whether he served notice under that subsection within a reasonable time, to show that he did.

2.   Duty to pass on applications

(1) If, in a case where section 1 of this Act applies, any person receives a written application by the tenant for consent to a proposed transaction and that person—

(a) is a person who may consent to the transaction or (though not such a person) is the landlord, and

(b) believes that another person, other than a person who he believes has received the application or a copy of it, is a person who may consent to the transaction,

he owes a duty to the tenant (whether or not he owes him any duty under section 1 of this Act) to take such steps as are reasonable to secure the receipt within a reasonable time by the other person of a copy of the application.

(2) The reference in section 1(3) of this Act to the service of an application on a person who may consent to a proposed transaction includes a reference to the receipt by him of an application or a copy of an application (whether it is for his consent or that of another).

3.   Qualified duty to approve consent by another

(1) This section applies in any case where—

(a) a tenancy includes a covenant on the part of the tenant not without the approval of the landlord to consent to the sub-tenant—

        (i)   assigning,
        (ii)   underletting,
        (iii)   charging, or
        (iv)   parting with the possession of,

the premises comprised in the sub-tenancy or any part of the premises, but

(b) the covenant is subject to the qualification that the approval is not to be unreasonably withheld (whether or not it is also subject to any other qualification).

(2) Where there is served on the landlord a written application by the tenant for approval or a copy of a written application to the tenant by the sub-tenant for consent to a transaction to which the covenant relates the landlord owes a duty to the sub-tenant within a reasonable time—
    (a) to give approval, except in a case where it is reasonable not to give approval,
    (b) to serve on the tenant and the sub-tenant written notice of his decision whether or not to give approval specifying in addition—
        (i) if approval is given subject to conditions, the conditions,
        (ii) if approval is withheld, the reasons for withholding it.

(3) Giving approval subject to any condition that is not a reasonable condition does not satisfy the duty under subsection (2)(a) above.

(4) For the purposes of this section it is reasonable for the landlord not to give approval only in a case where, if he withheld approval and the tenant gave his consent, the tenant would be in breach of covenant.

(5) It is for a landlord who owed any duty under subsection (2) above—
    (a) if he gave approval and the question arises whether he gave it within a reasonable time, to show that he did,
    (b) if he gave approval subject to any condition and the question arises whether the condition was a reasonable condition, to show that it was,
    (c) if he did not give approval and the question arises whether it was reasonable for him not to do so, to show that it was reasonable,
and, if the question arises whether he served notice under that subsection within a reasonable time, to show that he did.

4. Breach of duty

A claim that a person has broken any duty under this Act may be made the subject of civil proceedings in like manner as any other claim in tort for breach of statutory duty.

5. Interpretation

(1) In this Act—
'covenant' includes condition and agreement, 'consent' includes licence,
'landlord' includes any superior landlord from whom the tenant's immediate landlord directly or indirectly holds,
'tenancy', subject to subsection (3) below, means any lease or other tenancy (whether made before or after the coming into force of this Act) and includes—
    (a) a sub-tenancy, and
    (b) an agreement for a tenancy
and references in this Act to the landlord and to the tenant are to be interpreted accordingly, and
'tenant' , where the tenancy is affected by a mortgage (within the meaning of the Law of Property Act 1925) and the mortgage proposes to exercise his statutory or express power of sale, includes the mortgagee.

(2) An application or notice is to be treated as served for the purposes of this Act if—
    (a) served in any manner provided in the tenancy, and
    (b) in respect of any matter for which the tenancy makes no provision, served in any manner provided by section 23 of the Landlord and Tenant Act 1927.

(3) This Act does not apply to a secure tenancy (defined in section 79 of the Housing Act 1985) or to an introductory tenancy (within the meaning of Chapter I of Part V of the Housing Act 1996).

(4) This Act applies only to applications for consent or approval served after its coming into force.

LAW OF PROPERTY (MISCELLANEOUS PROVISIONS) ACT 1989
(1989, c. 34)

1. Deeds and their execution

(1) Any rule of law which—
    (a) restricts the substances on which a deed may be written;
    (b) requires a seal for the valid execution of an instrument as a deed by an individual; or
    (c) requires authority by one person to another to deliver an instrument as a deed on his behalf to be given by deed, is abolished.

(2) An instrument shall not be a deed unless—
- (a) it makes it clear on its face that it is intended to be a deed by the person making it or, as the case may be, by the parties to it (whether describing itself as a deed or expressing itself to be executed or signed as a deed or otherwise); and
- (b) it is validly executed as a deed—
  - (i) by that person or a person authorised to execute it in the name or on behalf of that person, or
  - (ii) by one or more of those parties or a person authorised to execute it in the name or on behalf of one or more of those parties.

(2A) For the purposes of subsection (2)(a) above, an instrument shall not be taken to make it clear on its face that it is intended to be a deed merely because it is executed under seal.

(3) An instrument is validly executed as a deed by an individual if, and only if—
- (a) it is signed—
  - (i) by him in the presence of a witness who attests the signature; or
  - (ii) at his direction and in his presence and the presence of two witnesses who each attest the signature; and
- (b) it is delivered as a deed.

(4) In subsection (2) and (3) above 'sign', in relation to an instrument, includes—
- (a) an individual signing the name of the person or party on whose behalf he executes the instrument; and
- (b) making one's mark on the instrument, and 'signature' is to be construed accordingly.

(4A) Subsection (3) above applies in the case of an instrument executed by an individual in the name or on behalf of another person whether or not that person is also an individual.

(5) Where a relevant lawyer, or an agent or employee of a relevant lawyer, in the course of or in connection with a transaction, purports to deliver an instrument as a deed on behalf of a party to the instrument, it shall be conclusively presumed in favour of a purchaser that he is authorised so to deliver the instrument.

(6) In subsection (5) above—
'purchaser' has the same meaning as in the Law of Property Act 1925; and
'relevant lawyer' means a person who, for the purposes of the Legal Services Act 2007, is an authorised person in relation to an activity which constitutes a reserved instrument activity (within the meaning of that Act).

(7) Where an instrument under seal that constitutes a deed is required for the purposes of an Act passed before this section comes into force, this section shall have effect as to signing, sealing or delivery of an instrument by an individual in place of any provision of that Act as to signing, sealing or delivery.

…

(10) The references in this section to the execution of a deed by an individual do not include execution by a corporation sole and the reference in subsection (7) above to signing, sealing or delivery by an individual does not include signing, sealing or delivery by such a corporation.

(11) Nothing in this section applies in relation to instruments delivered as deeds before this section comes into force.

2. Contracts for sale etc. of land to be made by signed writing

(1) A contract for the sale or other disposition of an interest in land can only be made in writing and only by incorporating all the terms which the parties have expressly agreed in one document or, where contracts are exchanged, in each.

(2) The terms may be incorporated in a document either by being set out in it or by reference to some other document.

(3) The document incorporating the terms or, where contracts are exchanged, one of the documents incorporating them (but not necessarily the same one) must be signed by or on behalf of each party to the contract.

(4) Where a contract for the sale or other disposition of an interest in land satisfies the conditions of this section by reason only of the rectification of one or more documents in pursuance of an order of a court, the contract shall come into being, or be deemed to have come into being, at such time as may be specified in the order.

(5) This section does not apply in relation to—
- (a) a contract to grant such a lease as is mentioned in section 54(2) of the Law of Property Act 1925 (short leases);

(b)   a contract made in the course of a public auction; or

(c)   a contract regulated under the Financial Services and Markets Act 2000, other than a regulated mortgage contract, a regulated home reversion plan, a regulated home purchase plan or a regulated sale and rent back agreement;

and nothing in this section affects the creation or operation of resulting, implied or constructive trusts.

(6)   In this section—

'disposition' has the same meaning as in the Law of Property Act 1925;

'interest in land' means any estate, interest or charge in or over land;

'regulated mortgage contract', 'regulated home reversion plan', 'regulated home purchase plan' and 'regulated sale and rent back agreement' must be read with—

(a)   section 22 of the Financial Services and Markets Act 2000,

(b)   any relevant order under that section, and

(c)   Schedule 2 of that Act.

(7)   Nothing in this section shall apply in relation to contracts made before this section comes into force.

(8)   Section 40 of the Law of Property Act 1925 (which is superseded by this section) shall cease to have effect.

3.   **Abolition of rule in *Bain v Fothergill***

The rule of law known as the rule in *Bain v Fothergill* is abolished in relation to contracts made after this section comes into force.

ACCESS TO NEIGHBOURING LAND ACT 1992
(1992, c. 23)

1.   **Access orders**

(1)   A person—

(a)   who, for the purpose of carrying out works to any land (the 'dominant land'), desires to enter upon any adjoining or adjacent land (the 'servient land'), and

(b)   who needs, but does not have, the consent of some other person to that entry,

may make an application to the court for an order under this section ('an access order') against that other person.

(2)   On application under this section, the court shall make an access order if, and only if, it is satisfied—

(a)   that the works are reasonably necessary for the preservation of the whole or any part of the dominant land; and

(b)   that they cannot be carried out, or would be substantially more difficult to carry out, without entry upon the servient land;

but this subsection is subject to subsection (3) below.

(3)   The court shall not make an access order in any case where it is satisfied that, were it to make such an order—

(a)   the respondent or any other person would suffer interference with, or disturbance of, his use or enjoyment of the servient land, or

(b)   the respondent, or any other person (whether of full age or capacity or not) in occupation of the whole or any part of the servient land, would suffer hardship,

to such a degree by reason of the entry (notwithstanding any requirement of this Act or any term or condition that may be imposed under it) that it would be unreasonable to make the order.

(4)   Where the court is satisfied on an application under this section that it is reasonably necessary to carry out any basic preservation works to the dominant land, those works shall be taken for the purposes of this Act to be reasonably necessary for the preservation of the land; and in this subsection 'basic preservation works' means any of the following, that is to say—

(a)   the maintenance, repair or renewal of any part of a building or other structure comprised in, or situate on, the dominant land;

(b)   the clearance, repair or renewal of any drain, sewer, pipe or cable so comprised or situate;

(c)   the treatment, cutting back, felling, removal or replacement of any hedge, tree, shrub or other growing thing which is so comprised and which is, or is in danger of becoming, damaged, diseased, dangerous, insecurely rooted or dead;

(d)   the filling in, or clearance, of any ditch so comprised;

but this subsection is without prejudice to the generality of the works which may, apart from it, be regarded by the court as reasonably necessary for the preservation of any land.

(5)   If the court considers it fair and reasonable in all the circumstances of the case, works may be regarded for the purposes of this Act as being reasonably necessary for the preservation of any land (or, for the purposes of subsection (4) above, as being basic preservation works which it is reasonably necessary to carry out to any land) notwithstanding that the works incidentally involve—

(a)   the making of some alteration, adjustment or improvement to the land, or

(b)   the demolition of the whole or any part of a building or structure comprised in or situate upon the land.

(6)   Where any works are reasonably necessary for the preservation of the whole or any part of the dominant land, the doing to the dominant land of anything which is requisite for, incidental to, or consequential on, the carrying out of those works shall be treated for the purposes of this Act as the carrying out of works which are reasonably necessary for the preservation of that land; and references in this Act to works, or to the carrying out of works, shall be construed accordingly.

(7)   Without prejudice to the generality of subsection (6) above, if it is reasonably necessary for a person to inspect the dominant land—

(a)   for the purpose of ascertaining whether any works may be reasonably necessary for the preservation of the whole or any part of that land,

(b)   for the purpose of making any map or plan, or ascertaining the course of any drain, sewer, pipe or cable, in preparation for, or otherwise in connection with, the carrying out of works which are so reasonably necessary, or

(c)   otherwise in connection with the carrying out of any such works,

the making of such an inspection shall be taken for the purposes of this Act to be the carrying out to the dominant land of works which are reasonably necessary for the preservation of that land; and references in this Act to works, or to the carrying out of works, shall be construed accordingly.

2.   Terms and conditions of access orders

(1)   An access order shall specify—

(a)   the works to the dominant land that may be carried out by entering upon the servient land in pursuance of the order;

(b)   the particular area of servient land that may be entered upon by virtue of the order for the purpose of carrying out those works to the dominant land; and

(c)   the date on which, or the period during which, the land may be so entered upon;

and in the following provisions of this Act any reference to the servient land is a reference to the area specified in the order in pursuance of paragraph (b) above.

(2)   An access order may impose upon the applicant or the respondent such terms and conditions as appear to the court to be reasonably necessary for the purpose of avoiding or restricting—

(a)   any loss, damage, or injury which might otherwise be caused to the respondent or any other person by reason of the entry authorised by the order; or

(b)   any inconvenience or loss of privacy that might otherwise be so caused to the respondent or any other person.

(3)   Without prejudice to the generality of subsection (2) above, the terms and conditions which may be imposed under that subsection include provisions with respect to—

(a)   the manner in which the specified works are to be carried out;

(b)   the days on which, and the hours between which, the work involved may be executed;

(c)   the persons who may undertake the carrying out of the specified works or enter upon the servient land under or by virtue of the order;

(d)   the taking of any such precautions by the applicant as may be specified in the order.

(4) An access order may also impose terms and conditions —
    (a) requiring the applicant to pay, or to secure that such person connected with him as may be specified in the order pays, compensation for —
        (i) any loss, damage or injury, or
        (ii) any substantial loss of privacy or other substantial inconvenience,
        which will, or might, be caused to the respondent or any other person by reason of the entry authorised by the order;
    (b) requiring the applicant to secure that he, or such person connected with him as may be specified in the order, is insured against any such risks as may be so specified; or
    (c) requiring such a record to be made of the condition of the servient land, or of such part of it as may be so specified, as the court may consider expedient with a view to facilitating the determination of any question that may arise concerning damage to that land.

(5) An access order may include provision requiring the applicant to pay the respondent such sum by way of consideration for the privilege of entering the servient land in pursuance of the order as appears to the court to be fair and reasonable having regard to all the circumstances of the case, including, in particular —
    (a) the likely financial advantage of the order to the applicant and any persons connected with him; and
    (b) the degree of inconvenience likely to be caused to the respondent or any other person by the entry;
but no payment shall be ordered under this subsection if and to the extent that the works which the applicant desires to carry out by means of the entry are works to residential land.

(6) For the purposes of subsection (5)(a) above, the likely financial advantage of an access order to the applicant and any persons connected with him shall in all cases be taken to be a sum of money equal to the greater of the following amounts, that is to say —
    (a) the amount (if any) by which so much of any likely increase in the value of any land —
        (i) which consists of or includes the dominant land, and
        (ii) which is owned or occupied by the same person as the dominant land,
    as may reasonably be regarded as attributable to the carrying out of the specified works exceeds the likely cost of carrying out those works with the benefit of the access order; and
    (b) the difference (if it would have been possible to carry out the specified works without entering upon the servient land) between —
        (i) the likely cost of carrying out those works without entering upon the servient land; and
        (ii) the likely cost of carrying them out with the benefit of the access order.

(7) For the purposes of subsection (5) above, 'residential land' means so much of any land as consists of —
    (a) a dwelling or part of a dwelling;
    (b) a garden, yard, private garage or outbuilding which is used and enjoyed wholly or mainly with a dwelling; or
    (c) in the case of a building which includes one or more dwellings, any part of the building which is used and enjoyed wholly or mainly with those dwellings or any of them.

(8) The persons who are to be regarded for the purposes of this section as 'connected with' the applicants are —
    (a) the owner of any estate or interest in, or right over, the whole or any part of the dominant land;
    (b) the occupier of the whole or any part of the dominant land; and
    (c) any person whom the applicant may authorise under section 3(7) below to exercise the power of entry conferred by the access order.

(9) The court may make provision —
    (a) for the reimbursement by the applicant of any expenses reasonably incurred by the respondent in connection with the application which are not otherwise recoverable as costs;
    (b) for the giving of security by the applicant for any sum that might become payable to the respondent or any other person by virtue of this section or section 3 below.

3. **Effect of access order**

(1) An access order requires the respondent, so far as he has power to do so, to permit the applicant or any of his associates to do anything which the applicant or associate is authorised or required to do under or by virtue of the order or this section.

(2) Except as otherwise provided by or under this Act, an access order authorises the applicant or any of his associates, without the consent of the respondent, —

    (a) to enter upon the servient land for the purpose of carrying out the specified works;

    (b) to bring on to that land, leave there during the period permitted by the order and, before the end of that period, remove, such materials, plant and equipment as are reasonably necessary for the carrying out of those works; and

    (c) to bring on to that land any waste arising from the carrying out of those works, if it is reasonably necessary to do so in the course of removing it from the dominant land;

but nothing in this Act or in any access order shall authorise the applicant or any of his associates to leave anything in, on or over the servient land (otherwise than in discharge of their duty to make good that land) after their entry for the purpose of carrying out works to the dominant land ceases to be authorised under or by virtue of the order.

(3) An access order requires the applicant—

    (a) to secure that any waste arising from the carrying out of the specified works is removed from the servient land forthwith;

    (b) to secure that, before the entry ceases to be authorised under or by virtue of the order, the servient land is, so far as reasonably practicable, made good; and

    (c) to indemnify the respondent against any damage which may be caused to the servient land or any goods by the applicant or any of his associates which would not have been so caused had the order not been made;

but this subsection is subject to subsections (4) and (5) below.

(4) In making an access order, the court may vary or exclude, in whole or in part, —

    (a) any authorisation that would otherwise by conferred by subsection (2)(b) or (c) above; or

    (b) any requirement that would otherwise by imposed by subsection (3) above.

(5) Without prejudice to the generality of subsection (4) above, if the court is satisfied that it is reasonably necessary for any such waste as may arise from the carrying out of the specified works to be left on the servient land for some period before removal, the access order may, in place of subsection (3)(a) above, include provision—

    (a) authorising the waste to be left on that land for such period as may be permitted by the order; and

    (b) requiring the applicant to secure that the waste is removed before the end of that period.

(6) Where the applicant or any of his associates is authorised or required under or by virtue of an access order or this section to enter, or do any other thing, upon the servient land, he shall not (as respects that access order) be taken to be a trespasser from the beginning on account of his, or any other person's, subsequent conduct.

(7) For the purposes of this section, the applicant's 'associates' are such number of persons (whether or not servants or agents of his) whom he may reasonably authorise under this subsection to exercise the power of entry conferred by the access order as may be reasonably necessary for carrying out the specified works.

4. **Persons bound by access order, unidentified persons and bar on contracting out**

(1) In addition to the respondent, an access order shall, subject to the provisions of the Land Charges Act 1972 and the Land Registration Act 2002, be binding on—

    (a) any of his successors in title to the servient land; and

    (b) any person who has an estate or interest in, or right over, the whole or any part of the servient land which was created after the making of the order and who derives his title to that estate, interest or right under the respondent;

and references to the respondent shall be construed accordingly.

(2) If and to the extent that the court considers it just and equitable to allow him to do so, a person on whom an access order becomes binding by virtue of subsection (1)(a) or (b) above shall be entitled, as respects anything falling to be done after the order becomes binding on him, to enforce the order or any of its terms or conditions as if he were the respondent, and references to the respondent shall be construed accordingly.

(3) Rules of court may—
  (a) provide a procedure which may be followed where the applicant does not know, and cannot reasonably ascertain, the name of any person whom he desires to make respondent to the application; and
  (b) make provision enabling such an applicant to make such a person respondent by description instead of by name;
  and in this subsection 'applicant' includes a person who proposes to make an application for an access order.
(4) Any agreement, whenever made, shall be void if and to the extent that it would, apart from this subsection, prevent a person from applying for an access order or restrict his right to do so.

5. Registration of access orders and of applications for such orders

...

(4) In any case where—
  (a) an access order is discharged under section 6(1)(a) below, and
  (b) the order has been protected by an entry registered under the Land Charges Act 1972 or by a notice under the Land Registration Act 2002,
  the court may by order direct that the entry or notice shall be cancelled.
(5) The rights conferred on a person by or under an access order shall not be capable of falling within paragraph 2 of Schedule 1 or 3 to the Land Registration Act 2002 (overriding status of interest of person in actual occupation).
(6) An application for an access order shall be regarded as a pending land action for the purposes of the Land Charges Act 1972 and the Land Registration Act 2002.

6. Variation of orders and damages for breach

(1) Where an access order or an order under this subsection has been made, the court may, on the application of any party to the proceedings in which the order was made or of any other person on whom the order is binding—
  (a) discharge or vary the order or any of its terms or conditions;
  (b) suspend any of its terms or conditions; or
  (c) revive any term or condition suspended under paragraph (b) above;
  and in the application of subsections (1) and (2) of section 4 above in relation to an access order, any order under this subsection which relates to the access order shall be treated for the purposes of those subsections as included in the access order.
(2) If any person contravenes or fails to comply with any requirement, term or condition imposed upon him by or under this Act, the court may, without prejudice to any other remedy available, make an order for the payment of damages by him to any other person affected by the contravention or failure who makes an application for relief under this subsection.

8. Interpretation and application

(1) Any reference in this Act to an 'entry' upon any servient land includes a reference to the doing on that land of anything necessary for carrying out the works to the dominant land which are reasonably necessary for its preservation; and 'enter' shall be construed accordingly.
(2) This Act applies in relation to any obstruction of, or other interference with, a right over, or interest in, any land as it applies in relation to an entry upon that land; and 'enter' and 'entry' shall be construed accordingly.
(3) In this Act—
  'access order' has the meaning given by section 1(1) above;
  'applicant' means a person making an application for an access order and, subject to section 4 above, 'the respondent' means the respondent, or any of the respondents, to such an application;
  'the court' means the High Court or the county court;
  'the dominant land' and 'the servient land' respectively have the meanings given by section 1(1) above, but subject, in the case of servient land, to section 2(1) above;
  'land' does not include a highway;
  'the specified works' means the works specified in the access order in pursuance of section 2(1)(a) above.

LANDLORD AND TENANT (COVENANTS) ACT 1995
(1995, c. 30)

Preliminary

1. Tenancies to which the Act applies

(1) Sections 3 to 16 and 21 apply only to new tenancies.

(2) Sections 17 to 20 apply to both new and other tenancies.

(3) For the purposes of this section a tenancy is a new tenancy if it is granted on or after the date on which this Act comes into force otherwise than in pursuance of—
    (a) an agreement entered into before that date, or
    (b) an order of a court made before that date.

(4) Subsection (3) has effect subject to section 20(1) in the case of overriding leases granted under section 19.

(5) Without prejudice to the generality of subsection (3), that subsection applies to the grant of a tenancy where by virtue of any variation of a tenancy there is a deemed surrender and regrant as it applies to any other grant of a tenancy.

(6) Where a tenancy granted on or after the date on which this Act comes into force is so granted in pursuance of an option granted before that date, the tenancy shall be regarded for the purposes of subsection (3) as granted in pursuance of an agreement entered into before that date (and accordingly is not a new tenancy), whether or not the option was exercised before that date.

(7) In subsection (6) 'option' includes right of first refusal.

2. Covenants to which the Act applies

(1) This Act applies to a landlord covenant or a tenant covenant of a tenancy—
    (a) whether or not the covenant has reference to the subject matter of the tenancy, and
    (b) whether the covenant is express, implied or imposed by law, but does not apply to a covenant falling within subsection (2).

(2) Nothing in this Act affects any covenant imposed in pursuance of—
    (a) section 35 or 155 of the Housing Act 1985 (covenants for repayment of discount on early disposals);
    (b) paragraph 1 of Schedule 6A to that Act (covenants requiring redemption of landlord's share); or
    (c) section 11 or 13 of the Housing Act 1996 or paragraph 1 or 3 of Schedule 2 to the Housing Associations Act 1985 (covenants for repayment of discount on early disposals or for restricting disposals).

Transmission of covenants

3. Transmission of benefit and burden of covenants

(1) The benefit and burden of all landlord and tenant covenants of a tenancy—
    (a) shall be annexed and incident to the whole, and to each and every part, of the premises demised by the tenancy and of the reversion in them, and
    (b) shall in accordance with this section pass on an assignment of the whole or any part of those premises or of the reversion in them.

(2) Where the assignment is by the tenant under the tenancy, then as from the assignment the assignee—
    (a) becomes bound by the tenant covenants of the tenancy except to the extent that—
        (i) immediately before the assignment they did not bind the assignor, or
        (ii) they fall to be complied with in relation to any demised premises not comprised in the assignment; and
    (b) becomes entitled to the benefit of the landlord covenants of the tenancy except to the extent that they fall to be complied with in relation to any such premises.

(3) Where the assignment is by the landlord under the tenancy, then as from the assignment the assignee—
    (a) becomes bound by the landlord covenants of the tenancy except to the extent that—
        (i) immediately before the assignment they did not bind the assignor, or
        (ii) they fall to be complied with in relation to any demised premises not comprised in the assignment; and
    (b) becomes entitled to the benefit of the tenant covenants of the tenancy except to the extent that they fall to be complied with in relation to any such premises.

(4) In determining for the purposes of subsection (2) or (3) whether any covenant bound the assignor immediately before the assignment, any waiver or release of the covenant which (in whatever terms) is expressed to be personal to the assignor shall be disregarded.

(5) Any landlord or tenant covenant of a tenancy which is restrictive of the user of land shall, as well as being capable of enforcement against an assignee, be capable of being enforced against any other person who is the owner or occupier of any demised premises to which the covenant relates, even though there is no express provision in the tenancy to that effect.

(6) Nothing in this section shall operate—

    (a) in the case of a covenant which (in whatever terms) is expressed to be personal to any person, to make the covenant enforceable by or (as the case may be) against any other person; or

    (b) to make a covenant enforceable against any person if, apart from this section, it would not be enforceable against him by reason of its not having been registered under the Land Registration Act 2002 or the Land Charges Act 1972.

(7) To the extent that there remains in force any rule of law by virtue of which the burden of a covenant whose subject matter is not in existence at the time when it is made does not run with the land affected unless the covenantor covenants on behalf of himself and his assigns, that rule of law is hereby abolished in relation to tenancies.

4. Transmission of rights of re-entry

The benefit of a landlord's right of re-entry under a tenancy—

    (a) shall be annexed and incident to the whole, and to each and every part, of the reversion in the premises demised by the tenancy, and

    (b) shall pass on an assignment of the whole or any part of the reversion in those premises.

Release of covenants on assignment

5. Tenant released from covenants on assignment of tenancy

(1) This section applies where a tenant assigns premises demised to him under a tenancy.

(2) If the tenant assigns the whole of the premises demised to him, he—

    (a) is released from the tenant covenants of the tenancy, and

    (b) ceases to be entitled to the benefit of the landlord covenants of the tenancy, as from the assignment.

(3) If the tenant assigns part only of the premises demised to him, then as from the assignment he—

    (a) is released from the tenant covenants of the tenancy, and

    (b) ceases to be entitled to the benefit of the landlord covenants of the tenancy,

only to the extent that those covenants fall to be complied with in relation to that part of the demised premises.

(4) This section applies as mentioned in subsection (1) whether or not the tenant is tenant of the whole of the premises comprised in the tenancy.

6. Landlord may be released from covenants on assignment of reversion

(1) This section applies where a landlord assigns the reversion in premises of which he is the landlord under a tenancy.

(2) If the landlord assigns the reversion in the whole of the premises of which he is the landlord—

    (a) he may apply to be released from the landlord covenants of the tenancy in accordance with section 8; and

    (b) if he is so released from all of those covenants, he ceases to be entitled to the benefit of the tenant covenants of the tenancy as from the assignment.

(3) If the landlord assigns the reversion in part only of the premises of which he is the landlord—

    (a) he may apply to be so released from the landlord covenants of the tenancy to the extent that they fall to be complied with in relation to that part of those premises; and

    (b) if he is, to that extent, so released from all of those covenants, then as from the assignment he ceases to be entitled to the benefit of the tenant covenants only to the extent that they fall to be complied with in relation to that part of those premises.

(4) This section applies as mentioned in subsection (1) whether or not the landlord is landlord of the whole of the premises comprised in the tenancy.

7.   Former landlord may be released from covenants on assignment of reversion

(1)   This section applies where—

    (a)   a landlord assigns the reversion in premises of which he is the landlord under a tenancy, and

    (b)   immediately before the assignment a former landlord of the premises remains bound by a landlord covenant of the tenancy ('the relevant covenant').

(2)   If immediately before the assignment the former landlord does not remain the landlord of any other premises demised by the tenancy, he may apply to be released from the relevant covenant in accordance with section 8.

(3)   In any other case the former landlord may apply to be so released from the relevant covenant to the extent that it falls to be complied with in relation to any premises comprised in the assignment.

(4)   If the former landlord is so released from every landlord covenant by which he remained bound immediately before the assignment, he ceases to be entitled to the benefit of the tenant covenants of the tenancy.

(5)   If the former landlord is so released from every such landlord covenant to the extent that it falls to be complied with in relation to any premises comprised in the assignment, he ceases to be entitled to the benefit of the tenant covenants of the tenancy to the extent that they fall to be so complied with.

(6)   This section applies as mentioned in subsection (1)—

    (a)   whether or not the landlord making the assignment is landlord of the whole of the premises comprised in the tenancy; and

    (b)   whether or not the former landlord has previously applied (whether under section 6 or this section) to be released from the relevant covenant.

8.   Procedure for seeking release from a covenant under section 6 or 7

(1)   For the purposes of section 6 or 7 an application for the release of a covenant to any extent is made by serving on the tenant, either before or within the period of four weeks beginning with the date of the assignment in question, a notice informing him of—

    (a)   the proposed assignment or (as the case may be) the fact that the assignment has taken place, and

    (b)   the request for the covenant to be released to that extent.

(2)   Where an application for the release of a covenant is made in accordance with subsection (1), the covenant is released to the extent mentioned in the notice if—

    (a)   the tenant does not, within the period of four weeks beginning with the day on which the notice is served, serve on the landlord or former landlord a notice in writing objecting to the release, or

    (b)   the tenant does so serve such a notice but the court, on the application of the landlord or former landlord, makes a declaration that it is reasonable for the covenant to be so released, or

    (c)   the tenant serves on the landlord or former landlord a notice in writing consenting to the release and, if he has previously served a notice objecting to it, stating that that notice is withdrawn.

(3)   Any release from a covenant in accordance with this section shall be regarded as occurring at the time when the assignment in question takes place.

(4)   In this section—

    (a)   'the tenant' means the tenant of the premises comprised in the assignment in question (or, if different parts of those premises are held under the tenancy by different tenants, each of those tenants);

    (b)   any reference to the landlord or the former landlord is a reference to the landlord referred to in section 6 or the former landlord referred to in section 7, as the case may be; and

    (c)   'the court' means the county court.

Apportionment of liability between assignor and assignee

9.   Apportionment of liability under covenants binding both assignor and assignee of tenancy or reversion

(1)   This section applies where—

    (a)   a tenant assigns part only of the premises demised to him by a tenancy;

(b)   after the assignment both the tenant and his assignee are to be bound by a non-attributable tenant covenant of the tenancy; and

(c)   the tenant and his assignee agree that as from the assignment liability under the covenant is to be apportioned between them in such manner as is specified in the agreement.

(2)   This section also applies where—

(a)   a landlord assigns the reversion in part only of the premises of which he is the landlord under a tenancy;

(b)   after the assignment both the landlord and his assignee are to be bound by a non-attributable landlord covenant of the tenancy; and

(c)   the landlord and his assignee agree that as from the assignment liability under the covenant is to be apportioned between them in such manner as is specified in the agreement.

(3)   Any such agreement as is mentioned in subsection (1) or (2) may apportion liability in such a way that a party to the agreement is exonerated from all liability under a covenant.

(4)   In any case falling within subsection (1) or (2) the parties to the agreement may apply for the apportionment to become binding on the appropriate person in accordance with section 10.

(5)   In any such case the parties to the agreement may also apply for the apportionment to become binding on any person (other than the appropriate person) who is for the time being entitled to enforce the covenant in question; and section 10 shall apply in relation to such an application as it applies in relation to an application made with respect to the appropriate person.

(6)   For the purposes of this section a covenant is, in relation to an assignment, a 'non-attributable' covenant if it does not fall to be complied with in relation to any premises comprised in the assignment.

(7)   In this section 'the appropriate person' means either—

(a)   the landlord of the entire premises referred to in subsection (1)(a) (or, if different parts of those premises are held under the tenancy by different landlords, each of those landlords), or

(b)   the tenant of the entire premises referred to in subsection (2)(a) (or, if different parts of those premises are held under the tenancy by different tenants, each of those tenants),

depending on whether the agreement in question falls within subsection (1) or subsection (2).

10.   Procedure for making apportionment bind other party to lease

(1)   For the purposes of section 9 the parties to an agreement falling within subsection (1) or
(2)   of that section apply for an apportionment to become binding on the appropriate person if, either before or within the period of four weeks beginning with the date of the assignment in question, they serve on that person a notice informing him of—

(a)   the proposed assignment or (as the case may be) the fact that the assignment has taken place;

(b)   the prescribed particulars of the agreement; and

(c)   their request that the apportionment should become binding on him.

(2)   Where an application for an apportionment to become binding has been made in accordance with subsection (1), the apportionment becomes binding on the appropriate person if—

(a)   he does not, within the period of four weeks beginning with the day on which the notice is served under subsection (1), serve on the parties to the agreement a notice in writing objecting to the apportionment becoming binding on him, or

(b)   he does so serve such a notice but the court, on the application of the parties to the agreement, makes a declaration that it is reasonable for the apportionment to become binding on him, or

(c)   he serves on the parties to the agreement a notice in writing consenting to the apportionment becoming binding on him and, if he has previously served a notice objecting thereto, stating that the notice is withdrawn.

(3)   Where any apportionment becomes binding in accordance with this section, this shall be regarded as occurring at the time when the assignment in question takes place.

(4)   In this section—
      'the appropriate person' has the same meaning as in section 9;
      'the court' means the county court;
      'prescribed' means prescribed by virtue of section 27.

Excluded assignments

11.   Assignments in breach of covenant or by operation of law

(1)   This section provides for the operation of sections 5 to 10 in relation to assignments in breach of a covenant of a tenancy or assignments by operation of law ('excluded assignments').

(2)   In the case of an excluded assignment subsection (2) or (3) of section 5—
      (a)   shall not have the effect mentioned in that subsection in relation to the tenant as from that assignment, but
      (b)   shall have that effect as from the next assignment (if any) of the premises assigned by him which is not an excluded assignment.

(3)   In the case of an excluded assignment subsection (2) or (3) of section 6 or 7—
      (a)   shall not enable the landlord or former landlord to apply for such a release as is mentioned in that subsection as from that assignment, but
      (b)   shall apply on the next assignment (if any) of the reversion assigned by the landlord which is not an excluded assignment so as to enable the landlord or former landlord to apply for any such release as from that subsequent assignment.

(4)   Where subsection (2) or (3) of section 6 or 7 does so apply—
      (a)   any reference in that section to the assignment (except where it relates to the time as from which the release takes effect) is a reference to the excluded assignment; but
      (b)   in that excepted case and in section 8 as it applies in relation to any application under that section made by virtue of subsection (3) above, any reference to the assignment or proposed assignment is a reference to any such subsequent assignment as is mentioned in that subsection.

(5)   In the case of an excluded assignment section 9—
      (a)   shall not enable the tenant or landlord and his assignee to apply for an agreed apportionment to become binding in accordance with section 10 as from that assignment, but
      (b)   shall apply on the next assignment (if any) of the premises or reversion assigned by the tenant or landlord which is not an excluded assignment so as to enable him and his assignee to apply for such an apportionment to become binding in accordance with section 10 as from that subsequent assignment.

(6)   Where section 9 does so apply—
      (a)   any reference in that section to the assignment or the assignee under it is a reference to the excluded assignment and the assignee under that assignment; but
      (b)   in section 10 as it applies in relation to any application under section 9 made by virtue of subsection (5) above, any reference to the assignment or proposed assignment is a reference to any such subsequent assignment as is mentioned in that subsection.

(7)   If any such subsequent assignment as is mentioned in subsection (2), (3) or (5) above comprises only part of the premises assigned by the tenant or (as the case may be) only part of the premises the reversion in which was assigned by the landlord on the excluded assignment—
      (a)   the relevant provision or provisions of section 5, 6, 7 or 9 shall only have the effect mentioned in that subsection to the extent that the covenants or covenant in question fall or falls to be complied with in relation to that part of those premises; and
      (b)   that subsection may accordingly apply on different occasions in relation to different parts of those premises.

Third party covenants

12.   Covenants with management companies etc.

(1)   This section applies where—
      (a)   a person other than the landlord or tenant ('the third party') is under a covenant of a tenancy liable (as principal) to discharge any function with respect to all or any of the demised premises ('the relevant function'); and

    (b)   that liability is not the liability of a guarantor or any other financial liability referable to the performance or otherwise of a covenant of the tenancy by another party to it.

(2)   To the extent that any covenant of the tenancy confers any rights against the third party with respect to the relevant function, then for the purposes of the transmission of the benefit of the covenant in accordance with this Act it shall be treated as if it were—

    (a)   a tenant covenant of the tenancy to the extent that those rights are exercisable by the landlord; and

    (b)   a landlord covenant of the tenancy to the extent that those rights are exercisable by the tenant.

(3)   To the extent that any covenant of the tenancy confers any rights exercisable by the third party with respect to the relevant function, then for the purposes mentioned in subsection (4), it shall be treated as if it were—

    (a)   a tenant covenant of the tenancy to the extent that those rights are exercisable against the tenant; and

    (b)   a landlord covenant of the tenancy to the extent that those rights are exercisable against the landlord.

(4)   The purposes mentioned in subsection (3) are—

    (a)   the transmission of the burden of the covenant in accordance with this Act; and

    (b)   any release from, or apportionment of liability in respect of, the covenant in accordance with this Act.

(5)   In relation to the release of the landlord from any covenant which is to be treated as a landlord covenant by virtue of subsection (3), section 8 shall apply as if any reference to the tenant were a reference to the third party.

Joint liability under covenants

13. Covenants binding two or more persons

(1)   Where in consequence of this Act two or more persons are bound by the same covenant, they are so bound both jointly and severally.

(2)   Subject to section 24(2), where by virtue of this Act—

    (a)   two or more persons are bound jointly and severally by the same covenant, and

    (b)   any of the persons so bound is released from the covenant, the release does not extend to any other of those persons.

(3)   For the purpose of providing for contribution between persons who, by virtue of this Act, are bound jointly and severally by a covenant, the Civil Liability (Contribution) Act 1978 shall have effect as if—

    (a)   liability to a person under a covenant were liability in respect of damage suffered by that person;

    (b)   references to damage accordingly included a breach of a covenant of a tenancy; and

    (c)   section 7(2) of that Act were omitted.

Enforcement of covenants

15. Enforcement of covenants

(1)   Where any tenant covenant of a tenancy, or any right of re-entry contained in a tenancy, is enforceable by the reversioner in respect of any premises demised by the tenancy, it shall also be so enforceable by—

    (a)   any person (other than the reversioner) who, as the holder of the immediate reversion in those premises, is for the time being entitled to the rents and profits under the tenancy in respect of those premises, or

    (b)   any mortgagee in possession of the reversion in those premises who is so entitled.

(2)   Where any landlord covenant of a tenancy is enforceable against the reversioner in respect of any premises demised by the tenancy, it shall also be so enforceable against any person falling within subsection (1)(a) or (b).

(3)   Where any landlord covenant of a tenancy is enforceable by the tenant in respect of any premises demised by the tenancy, it shall also be so enforceable by any mortgagee in possession of those premises under a mortgage granted by the tenant.

(4)   Where any tenant covenant of a tenancy, or any right of re-entry contained in a tenancy, is enforceable against the tenant in respect of any premises demised by the tenancy, it shall also be so enforceable against any such mortgagee.

(5) Nothing in this section shall operate—

    (a) in the case of a covenant which (in whatever terms) is expressed to be personal to any person, to make the covenant enforceable by or (as the case may be) against any other person; or

    (b) to make a covenant enforceable against any person if, apart from this section, it would not be enforceable against him by reason of its not having been registered under the Land Registration Act 2002 or the Land Charges Act 1972.

(6) In this section—

    'mortgagee' and 'mortgage' include 'chargee' and 'charge' respectively;

    'the reversioner', in relation to a tenancy, means the holder for the time being of the interest of the landlord under the tenancy.

Liability of former tenant etc. in respect of covenants

16. Tenant guaranteeing performance of covenant by assignee

(1) Where on an assignment a tenant is to any extent released from a tenant covenant of a tenancy by virtue of this Act ('the relevant covenant'), nothing in this Act (and in particular section 25) shall preclude him from entering into an authorised guarantee agreement with respect to the performance of that covenant by the assignee.

(2) For the purposes of this section an agreement is an authorised guarantee agreement if—

    (a) under it the tenant guarantees the performance of the relevant covenant to any extent by the assignee; and

    (b) it is entered into in the circumstances set out in subsection (3); and

    (c) its provisions conform with subsections (4) and (5).

(3) Those circumstances are as follows—

    (a) by virtue of a covenant against assignment (whether absolute or qualified) the assignment cannot be effected without the consent of the landlord under the tenancy or some other person;

    (b) any such consent is given subject to a condition (lawfully imposed) that the tenant is to enter into an agreement guaranteeing the performance of the covenant by the assignee; and

    (c) the agreement is entered into by the tenant in pursuance of that condition.

(4) An agreement is not an authorised guarantee agreement to the extent that it purports—

    (a) to impose on the tenant any requirement to guarantee in any way the performance of the relevant covenant by any person other than the assignee; or

    (b) to impose on the tenant any liability, restriction or other requirement (of whatever nature) in relation to any time after the assignee is released from that covenant by virtue of this Act.

(5) Subject to subsection (4), an authorised guarantee agreement may—

    (a) impose on the tenant any liability as sole or principal debtor in respect of any obligation owed by the assignee under the relevant covenant;

    (b) impose on the tenant liabilities as guarantor in respect of the assignee's performance of that covenant which are no more onerous than those to which he would be subject in the event of his being liable as sole or principal debtor in respect of any obligation owed by the assignee under that covenant;

    (c) require the tenant, in the event of the tenancy assigned by him being disclaimed, to enter into a new tenancy of the premises comprised in the assignment—

        (i)   whose term expires not later than the term of the tenancy assigned by the tenant, and

        (ii) whose tenant covenants are no more onerous than those of that tenancy;

    (d) make provision incidental or supplementary to any provision made by virtue of any of paragraphs (a) to (c).

(6) Where a person ('the former tenant') is to any extent released from a covenant of a tenancy by virtue of section 11(2) as from an assignment and the assignor under the assignment enters into an authorised guarantee agreement with the landlord with respect to the performance of that covenant by the assignee under the assignment—

    (a) the landlord may require the former tenant to enter into an agreement under which he guarantees, on terms corresponding to those of that authorised guarantee agreement, the performance of that covenant by the assignee under the assignment; and

      (b)   if its provisions conform with subsections (4) and (5), any such agreement shall be an authorised guarantee agreement for the purposes of this section; and

      (c)   in the application of this section in relation to any such agreement—

          (i)   subsections (2)(b) and (c) and (3) shall be omitted, and

          (ii)   any reference to the tenant or to the assignee shall be read as a reference to the former tenant or to the assignee under the assignment.

(7)   For the purposes of subsection (1) it is immaterial that—

      (a)   the tenant has already made an authorised guarantee agreement in respect of a previous assignment by him of the tenancy referred to in that subsection, it having been subsequently revested in him following a disclaimer on behalf of the previous assignee, or

      (b)   the tenancy referred to in that subsection is a new tenancy entered into by the tenant in pursuance of an authorised guarantee agreement;

    and in any such case subsections (2) to (5) shall apply accordingly.

(8)   It is hereby declared that the rules of law relating to guarantees (and in particular those relating to the release of sureties) are, subject to its terms, applicable in relation to any authorised guarantee agreement as in relation to any other guarantee agreement.

17. Restriction on liability of former tenant or his guarantor for rent or service charge etc.

(1)   This section applies where a person ('the former tenant') is as a result of an assignment no longer a tenant under a tenancy but—

      (a)   (in the case of a tenancy which is a new tenancy) he has under an authorised guarantee agreement guaranteed the performance by his assignee of a tenant covenant of the tenancy under which any fixed charge is payable; or

      (b)   (in the case of any tenancy) he remains bound by such a covenant.

(2)   The former tenant shall not be liable under that agreement or (as the case may be) the covenant to pay any amount in respect of any fixed charge payable under the covenant unless, within the period of six months beginning with the date when the charge becomes due, the landlord serves on the former tenant a notice informing him—

      (a)   that the charge is now due; and

      (b)   that in respect of the charge the landlord intends to recover from the former tenant such amount as is specified in the notice and (where payable) interest calculated on such basis as is so specified.

(3)   Where a person ('the guarantor') has agreed to guarantee the performance by the former tenant of such a covenant as is mentioned in subsection (1), the guarantor shall not be liable under the agreement to pay any amount in respect of any fixed charge payable under the covenant unless, within the period of six months beginning with the date when the charge becomes due, the landlord serves on the guarantor a notice informing him—

      (a)   that the charge is now due; and

      (b)   that in respect of the charge the landlord intends to recover from the guarantor such amount as is specified in the notice and (where payable) interest calculated on such basis as is so specified.

(4)   Where the landlord has duly served a notice under subsection (2) or (3), the amount (exclusive of interest) which the former tenant or (as the case may be) the guarantor is liable to pay in respect of the fixed charge in question shall not exceed the amount specified in the notice unless—

      (a)   his liability in respect of the charge is subsequently determined to be for a greater amount,

      (b)   the notice informed him of the possibility that that liability would be so determined, and

      (c)   within the period of three months beginning with the date of the determination, the landlord serves on him a further notice informing him that the landlord intends to recover that greater amount from him (plus interest, where payable).

(5)   For the purposes of subsection (2) or (3) any fixed charge which has become due before the date on which this Act comes into force shall be treated as becoming due on that date; but neither of those subsections applies to any such charge if before that date proceedings have been instituted by the landlord for the recovery from the former tenant of any amount in respect of it.

(6)   In this section—

    'fixed charge', in relation to tenancy, means—

(a)   rent,

(b)   any service charge as defined by section 18 of the Landlord and Tenant Act 1985 (the words 'of a dwelling' being disregarded for this purpose), and

(c)   any amount payable under a tenant covenant of the tenancy providing for the payment of a liquidated sum in the event of a failure to comply with any such covenant;

'landlord', in relation to a fixed charge, includes any person who has a right to enforce payment of the charge.

18. Restriction of liability of former tenant or his guarantor where tenancy subsequently varied

(1)   This section applies where a person ('the former tenant') is as a result of an assignment no longer a tenant under a tenancy but—

(a)   (in the case of a new tenancy) he has under an authorised guarantee agreement guaranteed the performance by his assignee of any tenant covenant of the tenancy; or

(b)   (in the case of any tenancy) he remains bound by such a covenant.

(2)   The former tenant shall not be liable under the agreement or (as the case may be) the covenant to pay any amount in respect of the covenant to the extent that the amount is referable to any relevant variation of the tenant covenants of the tenancy effected after the assignment.

(3)   Where a person ('the guarantor') has agreed to guarantee the performance by the former tenant of a tenant covenant of the tenancy, the guarantor (where his liability to do so is not wholly discharged by any such variation of the tenant covenants of the tenancy) shall not be liable under the agreement to pay any amount in respect of the covenant to the extent that the amount is referable to any such variation.

(4)   For the purposes of this section a variation of the tenant covenants of a tenancy is a 'relevant variation' if either—

(a)   the landlord has, at the time of the variation, an absolute right to refuse to allow it; or

(b)   the landlord would have had such a right if the variation had been sought by the former tenant immediately before the assignment by him but, between the time of that assignment and the time of the variation, the tenant covenants of the tenancy have been so varied as to deprive the landlord of such a right.

(5)   In determining whether the landlord has or would have had such a right at any particular time regard shall be had to all the circumstances (including the effect of any provision made by or under any enactment).

(6)   Nothing in this section applies to any variation of the tenant covenants of a tenancy effected before the date on which this Act comes into force.

(7)   In this section 'variation' means a variation whether effected by deed or otherwise.

Overriding leases

19. Right of former tenant or his guarantor to overriding lease

(1)   Where in respect of any tenancy ('the relevant tenancy') any person ('the claimant') makes full payment of an amount which he has been duly required to pay in accordance with section 17, together with any interest payable, he shall be entitled (subject to and in accordance with this section) to have the landlord under that tenancy grant him an overriding lease of the premises demised by the tenancy.

(2)   For the purposes of this section 'overriding lease' means a tenancy of the reversion expectant on the relevant tenancy which—

(a)   is granted for a term equal to the remainder of the term of the relevant tenancy plus three days or the longest period (less than three days) that will not wholly displace the landlord's reversionary interest expectant on the relevant tenancy, as the case may require; and

(b)   (subject to subsections (3) and (4) and to any modifications agreed to by the claimant and the landlord) otherwise contains the same covenants as the relevant tenancy, as they have effect immediately before the grant of the lease.

(3)   An overriding lease shall not be required to reproduce any covenant of the relevant tenancy to the extent that the covenant is (in whatever terms) expressed to be a personal covenant between the landlord and the tenant under that tenancy.

(4)   If any right, liability or other matter arising under a covenant of the relevant tenancy falls to be determined or otherwise operates (whether expressly or otherwise) by reference to the commencement of that tenancy—

    (a)   the corresponding covenant of the overriding lease shall be so framed that that right, liability or matter falls to be determined or otherwise operates by reference to the commencement of that tenancy; but

    (b)   the overriding lease shall not be required to reproduce any covenant of that tenancy to the extent that it has become spent by the time that that lease is granted.

(5)   A claim to exercise the right to an overriding lease under this section is made by the claimant making a request for such a lease to the landlord; and any such request—

    (a)   must be made to the landlord in writing and specify the payment by virtue of which the claimant claims to be entitled to the lease ('the qualifying payment'); and

    (b)   must be so made at the time of making the qualifying payment or within the period of 12 months beginning with the date of that payment.

(6)   Where the claimant duly makes such a request—

    (a)   the landlord shall (subject to subsection (7)) grant and deliver to the claimant an overriding lease of the demised premises within a reasonable time of the request being received by the landlord; and

    (b)   the claimant—

        (i)   shall thereupon deliver to the landlord a counterpart of the lease duly executed by the claimant, and

        (ii) shall be liable for the landlord's reasonable costs of and incidental to the grant of the lease.

(7)   The landlord shall not be under any obligation to grant an overriding lease of the demised premises under this section at a time when the relevant tenancy has been determined; and a claimant shall not be entitled to the grant of such a lease if at the time when he makes his request—

    (a)   the landlord has already granted such a lease and that lease remains in force; or

    (b)   another person has already duly made a request for such a lease to the landlord and that request has been neither withdrawn nor abandoned by that person.

(8)   Where two or more requests are duly made on the same day, then for the purposes of subsection (7)—

    (a)   a request made by a person who was liable for the qualifying payment as a former tenant shall be treated as made before a request made by a person who was so liable as a guarantor; and

    (b)   a request made by a person whose liability in respect of the covenant in question commenced earlier than any such liability of another person shall be treated as made before a request made by that other person.

(9)   Where a claimant who has duly made a request for an overriding lease under this section subsequently withdraws or abandons the request before he is granted such a lease by the landlord, the claimant shall be liable for the landlord's reasonable costs incurred in pursuance of the request down to the time of its withdrawal or abandonment; and for the purposes of this section—

    (a)   a claimant's request is withdrawn by the claimant notifying the landlord in writing that he is withdrawing his request; and

    (b)   a claimant is to be regarded as having abandoned his request if—

        (i)   the landlord has requested the claimant in writing to take, within such reasonable period as is specified in the landlord's request, all or any of the remaining steps required to be taken by the claimant before the lease can be granted, and

        (ii) the claimant fails to comply with the landlord's request,

    and is accordingly to be regarded as having abandoned it at the time when that period expires.

(10) Any request or notification under this section may be sent by post.

(11) The preceding provisions of this section shall apply where the landlord is the tenant under an overriding lease granted under this section as they apply where no such lease has been granted; and accordingly there may be two or more such leases interposed between the first such lease and the relevant tenancy.

20.   Overriding leases: supplementary provisions

(1)   For the purposes of section 1 an overriding lease shall be a new tenancy only if the relevant tenancy is a new tenancy.

(2)   Every overriding lease shall state—

    (a)   that it is a lease granted under section 19, and

    (b)   whether it is or is not a new tenancy for the purposes of section 1;

and any such statement shall comply with such requirements as may be prescribed by land registration rules under the Land Registration Act 2002.

(3)   A claim that the landlord has failed to comply with subsection (6)(a) of section 19 may be made the subject of civil proceedings in like manner as any other claim in tort for breach of statutory duty; and if the claimant under that section fails to comply with subsection (6)(b)(i) of that section he shall not be entitled to exercise any of the rights otherwise exercisable by him under the overriding lease.

(4)   An overriding lease—

    (a)   shall be deemed to be authorised as against the persons interested in any mortgage of the landlord's interest (however created or arising); and

    (b)   shall be binding on any such persons;

and if any such person is by virtue of such a mortgage entitled to possession of the documents of title relating to the landlord's interest—

    (i)   the landlord shall within one month of the execution of the lease deliver to that person the counterpart executed in pursuance of section 19(6)(b)(i); and

    (ii)   if he fails to do so, the instrument creating or evidencing the mortgage shall apply as if the obligation to deliver a counterpart were included in the terms of the mortgage as set out in that instrument.

(5)   It is hereby declared—

    (a)   that the fact that an overriding lease takes effect subject to the relevant tenancy shall not constitute a breach of any covenant of the lease against subletting or parting with possession of the premises demised by the lease or any part of them; and

    (b)   that each of sections 16, 17 and 18 applies where the tenancy referred to in subsection (1) of that section is an overriding lease as it applies in other cases falling within that subsection.

(6)   No tenancy shall be registrable under the Land Charges Act 1972 or be taken to be an estate contract within the meaning of that Act by reason of any right or obligation that may arise under section 19, and any right arising from a request made under that section shall not be capable of falling within paragraph 2 of Schedule 1 or 3 to the Land Registration Act 2002; but any such request shall be registrable under the Land Charges Act 1972, or may be the subject of a notice under the Land Registration Act 2002, as if it were an estate contract.

(7)   In this section—

    (a)   'mortgage' includes 'charge'; and

    (b)   any expression which is also used in section 19 has the same meaning as in that section.

Forfeiture and disclaimer

21.   Forfeiture or disclaimer limited to part only of demised premises

(1)   Where—

    (a)   as a result of one or more assignments a person is the tenant of part only of the premises demised by a tenancy, and

    (b)   under a proviso or stipulation in the tenancy there is a right of re-entry or forfeiture for a breach of a tenant covenant of the tenancy, and

    (c)   the right is (apart from this subsection) exercisable in relation to that part and other land demised by the tenancy,

the right shall nevertheless, in connection with a breach of any such covenant by that person, be taken to be a right exercisable only in relation to that part.

(2)   Where—

    (a)   a company which is being wound up, or a trustee in bankruptcy, is as a result of one or more assignments the tenant of part only of the premises demised by a tenancy, and

(b)   the liquidator of the company exercises his power under section 178 of the Insolvency Act 1986, or the trustee in bankruptcy exercises his power under section 315 of that Act, to disclaim property demised by the tenancy,

the power is exercisable only in relation to the part of the premises referred to in paragraph (a).

Supplemental

23.   Effects of becoming subject to liability under, or entitled to benefit of, covenant etc.

(1)   Where as a result of an assignment a person becomes, by virtue of this Act, bound by or entitled to the benefit of a covenant, he shall not by virtue of this Act have any liability or rights under the covenant in relation to any time falling before the assignment.

(2)   Subsection (1) does not preclude any such rights being expressly assigned to the person in question.

(3)   Where as a result of an assignment a person becomes, by virtue of this Act, entitled to a right of re-entry contained in a tenancy, that right shall be exercisable in relation to any breach of a covenant of the tenancy occurring before the assignment as in relation to one occurring thereafter, unless by reason of any waiver or release it was not so exercisable immediately before the assignment.

24.   Effects of release from liability under, or loss of benefit of, covenant

(1)   Any release of a person from a covenant by virtue of this Act does not affect any liability of his arising from a breach of the covenant occurring before the release.

(2)   Where—
(a)   by virtue of this Act a tenant is released from a tenant covenant of a tenancy, and
(b)   immediately before the release another person is bound by a covenant of the tenancy imposing any liability or penalty in the event of a failure to comply with that tenant covenant,

then, as from the release of the tenant, that other person is released from the covenant mentioned in paragraph (b) to the same extent as the tenant is released from that tenant covenant.

(3)   Where a person bound by a landlord or tenant covenant of a tenancy—
(a)   assigns the whole or part of his interest in the premises demised by the tenancy, but
(b)   is not released by virtue of this Act from the covenant (with the result that subsection (1) does not apply),

the assignment does not affect any liability of his arising from a breach of the covenant occurring before the assignment.

(4)   Where by virtue of this Act a person ceases to be entitled to the benefit of a covenant, this does not affect any rights of his arising from a breach of the covenant occurring before he ceases to be so entitled.

25.   Agreement void if it restricts operation of the Act

(1)   Any agreement relating to a tenancy is void to the extent that—
(a)   it would apart from this section have effect to exclude, modify or otherwise frustrate the operation of any provision of this Act, or
(b)   it provides for—
(i)   the termination or surrender of the tenancy, or
(ii)   the imposition on the tenant of any penalty, disability or liability,
in the event of the operation of any provision of this Act, or
(c)   it provides for any of the matters referred to in paragraph (b)(i) or (ii) and does so (whether expressly or otherwise) in connection with, or in consequence of, the operation of any provision of this Act.

(2)   To the extent that an agreement relating to a tenancy constitutes a covenant (whether absolute or qualified) against the assignment, or parting with the possession, of the premises demised by the tenancy or any part of them—
(a)   the agreement is not void by virtue of subsection (1) by reason only of the fact that as such the covenant prohibits or restricts any such assignment or parting with possession; but
(b)   paragraph (a) above does not otherwise affect the operation of that subsection in relation to the agreement (and in particular does not preclude its application to the agreement to the extent that it purports to regulate the giving of, or the making of any application for, consent to any such assignment or parting with possession).

(3)   In accordance with section 16(1) nothing in this section applies to any agreement to the extent that it is an authorised guarantee agreement; but (without prejudice to the generality of subsection (1) above) an agreement is void to the extent that it is one falling within section 16(4)(a) or (b).

(4)   This section applies to an agreement relating to a tenancy whether or not the agreement is—

(a)   contained in the instrument creating the tenancy; or

(b)   made before the creation of the tenancy.

26.   Miscellaneous savings etc.

(1)   Nothing in this Act is to be read as preventing—

(a)   a party to a tenancy from releasing a person from a landlord covenant or a tenant covenant of the tenancy; or

(b)   the parties to a tenancy from agreeing to an apportionment of liability under such a covenant.

(2)   Nothing in this Act affects the operation of section 3(3A) of the Landlord and Tenant Act 1985 (preservation of former landlord's liability until tenant notified of new landlord).

(3)   No apportionment which has become binding in accordance with section 10 shall be affected by any order or decision made under or by virtue of any enactment not contained in this Act which relates to apportionment.

28.   Interpretation

(1)   In this Act (unless the context otherwise requires)—

'assignment' includes equitable assignment and in addition (subject to section 11) assignment in breach of a covenant of a tenancy or by operation of law;

'authorised guarantee agreement' means an agreement which is an authorised guarantee agreement for the purposes of section 16;

'collateral agreement', in relation to a tenancy, means any agreement collateral to the tenancy, whether made before or after its creation; 'consent' includes licence;

'covenant' includes term, condition and obligation, and references to a covenant (or any description of covenant) of a tenancy include a covenant (or a covenant of that description) contained in a collateral agreement;

'landlord' and 'tenant', in relation to a tenancy, mean the person for the time being entitled to the reversion expectant on the term of the tenancy and the person so entitled to that term respectively;

'landlord covenant', in relation to a tenancy, means a covenant falling to be complied with by the landlord of premises demised by the tenancy;

'new tenancy' means a tenancy which is a new tenancy for the purposes of section 1;

'reversion' means the interest expectant on the termination of a tenancy;

'tenancy' means any lease or other tenancy and includes—

(a)   a sub-tenancy, and

(b)   an agreement for a tenancy,

but does not include a mortgage term;

'tenant covenant', in relation to a tenancy, means a covenant falling to be complied with by the tenant of premises demised by the tenancy.

(2)   For the purposes of any reference in this Act to a covenant falling to be complied with in relation to a particular part of the premises demised by a tenancy, a covenant falls to be so complied with if—

(a)   it in terms applies to that part of the premises, or

(b)   in its practical application it can be attributed to that part of the premises (whether or not it can also be so attributed to other individual parts of those premises).

(3)   Subsection (2) does not apply in relation to covenants to pay money; and, for the purposes of any reference in this Act to a covenant falling to be complied with in relation to a particular part of the premises demised by a tenancy, a covenant of a tenancy which is a covenant to pay money falls to be so complied with if—

(a)   the covenant in terms applies to that part; or

(b)   the amount of the payment is determinable specifically by reference—

(i)   to that part, or

        (ii)   to anything falling to be done by or for a person as tenant or occupier of that part (if it is a tenant covenant), or

        (iii)   to anything falling to be done by or for a person as landlord of that part (if it is a landlord covenant).

(4) Where two or more persons jointly constitute either the landlord or the tenant in relation to a tenancy, any reference in this Act to the landlord or the tenant is a reference to both or all of the persons who jointly constitute the landlord or the tenant, as the case may be (and accordingly nothing in section 13 applies in relation to the rights and liabilities of such persons between themselves).

(5) References in this Act to the assignment by a landlord of the reversion in the whole or part of the premises demised by a tenancy are to the assignment by him of the whole of his interest (as owner of the reversion) in the whole or part of those premises.

(6) For the purposes of this Act—

    (a)   any assignment (however effected) consisting in the transfer of the whole of the landlord's interest (as owner of the reversion) in any premises demised by a tenancy shall be treated as an assignment by the landlord of the reversion in those premises even if it is not effected by him; and

    (b)   any assignment (however effected) consisting in the transfer of the whole of the tenant's interest in any premises demised by a tenancy shall be treated as an assignment by the tenant of those premises even if it is not effected by him.

TREASURE ACT 1996
(1996, c. 24)

Meaning of 'treasure'

1.   Meaning of 'treasure'

(1) Treasure is—

    (a)   any object at least 300 years old when found which—

        (i)   is not a coin but has metallic content of which at least 10 per cent by weight is precious metal;

        (ii)   when found, is one of at least two coins in the same find which are at least 300 years old at that time and have that percentage of precious metal; or

        (iii) when found, is one of at least ten coins in the same find which are at least 300 years old at that time;

    (b)   any object at least 200 years old when found which belongs to a class designated under section 2(1);

    (c)   any object which would have been treasure trove if found before the commencement of section 4;

    (d)   any object which, when found, is part of the same find as—

        (i)   an object within paragraph (a), (b) or (c) found at the same time or earlier; or

        (ii)   an object found earlier which would be within paragraph (a) or (b) if it had been found at the same time.

(2) Treasure does not include objects which are—

    (a)   unworked natural objects, or

    (b)   minerals as extracted from a natural deposit,

or which belong to a class designated under section 2(2).

2.   Power to alter meaning

(1) The Secretary of State may by order, for the purposes of section 1(1)(b), designate any class of object which he considers to be of outstanding historical, archaeological or cultural importance.

(2) The Secretary of State may by order, for the purposes of section 1(2), designate any class of object which (apart from the order) would be treasure.

   ...

3.   Supplementary

(1) This section supplements section 1.

(2)   'Coin' includes any metal token which was, or can reasonably be assumed to have been, used or intended for use as or instead of money.

(3)   'Precious metal' means gold or silver.

(4)   When an object is found, it is part of the same find as another object if—

    (a)   they are found together,

    (b)   the other object was found earlier in the same place where they had been left together.

    (c)   the other object was found earlier in a different place, but they had been left together and had become separated before being found.

(5)   If the circumstances in which objects are found can reasonably be taken to indicate that they were together at some time before being found, the objects are to be presumed to have been left together, unless shown not to have been.

(6)   An object which can reasonably be taken to be at least a particular age is to be presumed to be at least that age, unless shown not to be.

(7)   An object is not treasure if it is wreck within the meaning of Part IX of the Merchant Shipping Act 1995.

Ownership of treasure

4.   Ownership of treasure which is found

(1)   When treasure is found, it vests, subject to prior interests and rights—

    (a)   in the franchisee, if there is one;

    (b)   otherwise, in the Crown.

(2)   Prior interests and rights are any which, or which derive from any which—

    (a)   were held when the treasure was left where it was found, or

    (b)   if the treasure had been moved before being found, were held when it was left where it was before being moved.

(3)   If the treasure would have been treasure trove if found before the commencement of this section, neither the Crown nor any franchisee has any interest in it or right over it except in accordance with this Act.

(4)   This section applies—

    (a)   whatever the nature of the place where the treasure was found, and

    (b)   whatever the circumstances in which it was left (including being lost or being left with no intention of recovery).

5.   Meaning of 'franchisee'

(1)   The franchisee for any treasure is the person who—

    (a)   was, immediately before the commencement of section 4, or

    (b)   apart from this Act, as successor in title, would have been, the franchisee of the Crown in right of treasure trove for the place where the treasure was found.

(2)   It is as franchisees in right of treasure trove that Her Majesty and the Duke of Cornwall are to be treated as having enjoyed the rights to treasure trove which belonged respectively to the Duchy of Lancaster and the Duchy of Cornwall immediately before the commencement of section 4.

6.   Treasure vesting in the Crown

(1)   Treasure vesting in the Crown under this Act is to be treated as part of the hereditary revenues of the Crown to which section 1 of the Civil List Act 1952 applies (surrender of hereditary revenues to the Exchequer).

(2)   Any such treasure may be transferred, or otherwise disposed of, in accordance with directions given by the Secretary of State.

(3)   The Crown's title to any such treasure may be disclaimed at any time by the Secretary of State.

…

Coroners' jurisdiction

7.   Jurisdiction of coroners

(1)   The jurisdiction of coroners which is referred to in section 30 of the Coroners Act 1988 (treasure) is exercisable in relation to anything which is treasure for the purposes of this Act.

(2) That jurisdiction is not exercisable for the purposes of the law relating to treasure trove in relation to anything found after the commencement of section 4.

(3) The Act of 1988 and anything saved by virtue of section 36(5) of that Act (saving for existing law and practice etc.) has effect subject to this section.

(4) An inquest held by virtue of this section is to be held without a jury, unless the coroner orders otherwise.

8. Duty of finder to notify coroner

(1) A person who finds an object which he believes or has reasonable grounds for believing is treasure must notify the coroner for the district in which the object was found before the end of the notice period.

(2) The notice period is fourteen days beginning with—
   (a) the day after the find; or
   (b) if later, the day on which the finder first believes or has reason to believe the object is treasure.

(3) Any person who fails to comply with subsection (1) is guilty of an offence and liable on summary conviction to—
   (a) imprisonment for a term not exceeding three months;
   (b) a fine of an amount not exceeding level 5 on the standard scale; or
   (c) both.

(4) In proceedings for an offence under this section, it is a defence for the defendant to show that he had, and has continued to have, a reasonable excuse for failing to notify the coroner.

(5) If the office of coroner for a district is vacant, the person acting as coroner for that district is the coroner for the purposes of subsection (1).

9. Procedure for inquests

(1) In this section, 'inquest' means an inquest held under section 7.

(2) A coroner proposing to conduct an inquest must notify—
   (a) the British Museum, if his district is in England; or
   (b) the National Museum of Wales, if it is in Wales.

(3) Before conducting the inquest, the coroner must take reasonable steps to notify—
   (a) any person who it appears to him may have found the treasure; and
   (b) any person who, at the time the treasure was found, occupied land which it appears to him may be where it was found.

(4) During the inquest the coroner must take reasonable steps to notify any such person not already notified.

(5) Before or during the inquest, the coroner must take reasonable steps—
   (a) to obtain from any person notified under subsection (3) or (4) the names and addresses of interested persons; and
   (b) to notify any interested person whose name and address he obtains.

(6) The coroner must take reasonable steps to give any interested person notified under subsection (3), (4) or (5) an opportunity to examine witnesses at the inquest.

(7) In subsections (5) and (6), 'interested person' means a person who appears to the coroner to be likely to be concerned with the inquest—
   (a) as the finder of the treasure or otherwise involved in the find;
   (b) as the occupier, at the time the treasure was found, of the land where it was found, or
   (c) as having had an interest in that land at that time or since.

Rewards, codes of practice and report

10. Rewards

(1) This section applies if treasure—
   (a) has vested in the Crown under section 4; and
   (b) is to be transferred to a museum.

(2) The Secretary of State must determine whether a reward is to be paid by the museum before the transfer.

(3) If the Secretary of State determines that a reward is to be paid, he must also determine, in whatever way he thinks fit—
   (a) the treasure's market value:
   (b) the amount of the reward;

    (c)   to whom the reward is to be payable; and

    (d)   if it is to be payable to more than one person, how much each is to receive.

(4)   The total reward must not exceed the treasure's market value.

(5)   The reward may be payable to—

    (a)   the finder or any other person involved in the find:

    (b)   the occupier of the land at the time of the find;

    (c)   any person who had an interest in the land at that time, or has had such an interest at any time since then.

(6)   Payment of the reward is not enforceable against a museum or the Secretary of State.

(7)   In a determination under this section, the Secretary of State must take into account anything relevant in the code of practice issued under section 11.

(8)   This section also applies in relation to treasure which has vested in a franchisee under section 4, if the franchisee makes a request to the Secretary of State that it should.

FAMILY LAW ACT 1996
(1996, c. 27)

PART IV
FAMILY HOMES AND DOMESTIC VIOLENCE

Rights to occupy matrimonial or civil partnership home

30.   Rights concerning home where one spouse or civil partner has no estate, etc.

(1)   This section applies if—

    (a)   one spouse or civil partner ('A') is entitled to occupy a dwelling-house by virtue of—

        (i)   a beneficial estate or interest or contract; or

        (ii)   any enactment giving A the right to remain in occupation; and

    (b)   the other spouse or civil partner ('B') is not so entitled.

(2)   Subject to the provisions of this Part, B has the following rights ('home rights')—

    (a)   if in occupation, a right not to be evicted or excluded from the dwelling-house or any part of it by A except with the leave of the court given by an order under section 33;

    (b)   if not in occupation, a right with the leave of the court so given to enter into and occupy the dwelling-house.

(3)   If B is entitled under this section to occupy a dwelling-house or any part of a dwelling-house, any payment or tender made or other thing done by B in or towards satisfaction of any liability of A in respect of rent, mortgage payments or other outgoings affecting the dwelling-house is, whether or not it is made or done in pursuance of an order under section 40, as good as if made or done by A.

(4)   B's occupation by virtue of this section—

    (a)   is to be treated, for the purposes of the Rent (Agriculture) Act 1976 and the Rent Act 1977 (other than Part V and sections 103 to 106 of that Act), as occupation by A as A's residence, and

    (b)   if B occupies the dwelling-house as B's only or principal home, is to be treated, for the purposes of the Housing Act 1985, Part I of the Housing Act 1988 and Chapter I of Part V of the Housing Act 1996 and the Prevention of Social Housing Fraud Act 2013, as occupation by A as A's only or principal home.

(5)   If B—

    (a)   is entitled under this section to occupy a dwelling-house or any part of a dwelling-house, and

    (b)   makes any payment in or towards satisfaction of any liability of A in respect of mortgage payments affecting the dwelling-house,

the person to whom the payment is made may treat it as having been made by A, but the fact that that person has treated any such payment as having been so made does not affect any claim of B against A to an interest in the dwelling-house by virtue of the payment.

(6) If B is entitled under this section to occupy a dwelling-house or part of a dwelling-house by reason of an interest of A under a trust, all the provisions of subsections (3) to (5) apply in relation to the trustees as they apply in relation to A.

(7) This section does not apply to a dwelling-house which—

    (a) in the case of spouses, has at no time been, and was at no time intended by them to be, a matrimonial home of theirs; and

    (b) in the case of civil partners, has at no time been, and was at no time intended by them to be, a civil partnership home of theirs.

(8) B's home rights continue—

    (a) only so long as the marriage or civil partnership subsists, except to the extent that an order under section 33(5) otherwise provides; and

    (b) only so long as A is entitled as mentioned in subsection (1) to occupy the dwelling-house, except where provision is made by section 31 for those rights to be a charge on an estate or interest in the dwelling-house.

(9) It is hereby declared that a person—

    (a) who has an equitable interest in a dwelling-house or in its proceeds of sale, but

    (b) is not a person in whom there is vested (whether solely or as joint tenant) a legal estate in fee simple or a legal term of years absolute in the dwelling-house,

is to be treated, only for the purpose of determining whether he has home rights, as not being entitled to occupy the dwelling-house by virtue of that interest.

31. Effect of home rights as charge on dwelling-house

(1) Subsections (2) and (3) apply if, at any time during a marriage or civil partnership, A is entitled to occupy a dwelling-house by virtue of a beneficial estate or interest.

(2) B's home rights are a charge on the estate or interest.

(3) The charge created by subsection (2) has the same priority as if it were an equitable interest created at whichever is the latest of the following dates—

    (a) the date on which A acquires the estate or interest;

    (b) the date of the marriage or of the formation of the civil partnership; and

    (c) 1st January 1968 (the commencement date of the Matrimonial Homes Act 1967).

(4) Subsections (5) and (6) apply if, at any time when B's home rights are a charge on an interest of A under a trust, there are, apart from A or B, no persons, living or unborn, who are or could become beneficiaries under the trust.

(5) The rights are a charge also on the estate or interest of the trustees for A.

(6) The charge created by subsection (5) has the same priority as if it were an equitable interest created (under powers overriding the trusts) on the date when it arises.

(7) In determining for the purposes of subsection (4) whether there are any persons who are not, but could become, beneficiaries under the trust, there is to be disregarded any potential exercise of a general power of appointment exercisable by either or both of A and B alone (whether or not the exercise of it requires the consent of another person).

(8) Even though B's home rights are a charge on an estate or interest in the dwelling-house, those rights are brought to an end by—

    (a) the death of A, or

    (b) the termination (otherwise than by death) of the marriage or civil partnership, unless the court directs otherwise by an order made under section 33(5).

(9) If—

    (a) B's home rights are a charge on an estate or interest in the dwelling-house, and

    (b) that estate or interest is surrendered to merge in some other estate or interest expectant on it in such circumstances that, but for the merger, the person taking the estate or interest would be bound by the charge,

the surrender has effect subject to the charge and the persons thereafter entitled to the other estate or interest are, for so long as the estate or interest surrendered would have endured if not so surrendered, to be treated for all purposes of this Part as deriving title to the other estate or interest under A or, as the case may be, under the trustees for A, by virtue of the surrender.

(10) If the title to the legal estate by virtue of which A is entitled to occupy a dwelling-house (including any legal estate held by trustees for A) is registered under the Land Registration Act 2002 or any enactment replaced by that Act—

    (a) registration of a land charge affecting the dwelling-house by virtue of this Part is to be effected by registering a notice under that Act; and

    (b) B's home rights are not to be capable of falling within paragraph 2 of Schedule 1 or 3 to that Act.

(11) ...

(12) If—
    (a)   B's home rights are a charge on the estate of A or of trustees of A, and
    (b)   that estate is the subject of a mortgage,
then if, after the date of the creation of the mortgage ('the first mortgage'), the charge is registered under section 2 of the Land Charges Act 1972, the charge is, for the purposes of section 94 of the Law of Property Act 1925 (which regulates the rights of mortgagees to make further advances ranking in priority to subsequent mortgages), to be deemed to be a mortgage subsequent in date to the first mortgage.

(13) It is hereby declared that a charge under subsection (2) or (5) is not registrable under subsection (10) or under section 2 of the Land Charges Act 1972 unless it is a charge on a legal estate.

32. Further provisions relating to home rights

Schedule 4 (provisions supplementary to sections 30 and 31) has effect.

Occupation orders

33. Occupation orders where applicant has estate or interest etc. or has home rights

(1) If—
    (a)   a person ('the person entitled')—
        (i)   is entitled to occupy a dwelling-house by virtue of a beneficial estate or interest or contract or by virtue of any enactment giving him the right to remain in occupation, or
        (ii)   has home rights in relation to a dwelling-house, and
    (b)   the dwelling-house—
        (i)   is or at any time has been the home of the person entitled and of another person with whom he is associated, or
        (ii)   was at any time intended by the person entitled and any such other person to be their home,
    the person entitled may apply to the court for an order containing any of the provisions specified in subsections (3), (4) and (5).

(2) If an agreement to marry is terminated, no application under this section may be made by virtue of section 62(3)(e) by reference to that agreement after the end of the period of three years beginning with the day on which it is terminated.

(2A) If a civil partnership agreement (as defined by section 73 of the Civil Partnership Act 2004) is terminated, no application under this section may be made by virtue of section 62(3)(eza) by reference to that agreement after the end of the period of three years beginning with the day on which it is terminated.

(3) An order under this section may—
    (a)   enforce the applicant's entitlement to remain in occupation as against the other person ('the respondent');
    (b)   require the respondent to permit the applicant to enter and remain in the dwelling-house or part of the dwelling-house;
    (c)   regulate the occupation of the dwelling-house by either or both parties;
    (d)   if the respondent is entitled as mentioned in subsection (1)(a)(i), prohibit, suspend or restrict the exercise by him of his right to occupy the dwelling-house;
    (e)   if the respondent has home rights in relation to the dwelling-house and the applicant is the other spouse or civil partner, restrict or terminate those rights;
    (f)   require the respondent to leave the dwelling-house or part of the dwelling-house; or
    (g)   exclude the respondent from a defined area in which the dwelling-house is included.

(4) An order under this section may declare that the applicant is entitled as mentioned in subsection (1)(a)(i) or has home rights.

(5) If the applicant has home rights and the respondent is the other spouse or civil partner, an order under this section made during the marriage or civil partnership may provide that those rights are not brought to an end by—
    (a)   the death of the other spouse or civil partner; or
    (b)   the termination (otherwise than by death) of the marriage or civil partnership.

(6)   In deciding whether to exercise its powers under subsection (3) and (if so) in what manner, the court shall have regard to all the circumstances including—

    (a)   the housing needs and housing resources of each of the parties and of any relevant child;

    (b)   the financial resources of each of the parties;

    (c)   the likely effect of any order, or of any decision by the court not to exercise its powers under subsection (3), on the health, safety or well-being of the parties and of any relevant child; and

    (d)   the conduct of the parties in relation to each other and otherwise.

(7)   If it appears to the court that the applicant or any relevant child is likely to suffer significant harm attributable to conduct of the respondent if an order under this section containing one or more of the provisions mentioned in subsection (3) is not made, the court shall make the order unless it appears to it that—

    (a)   the respondent or any relevant child is likely to suffer significant harm if the order is made; and

    (b)   the harm likely to be suffered by the respondent or child in that event is as great as, or greater than, the harm attributable to conduct of the respondent which is likely to be suffered by the applicant or child if the order is not made.

(8)   The court may exercise its powers under subsection (5) in any case where it considers that in all the circumstances it is just and reasonable to do so.

(9)   An order under this section—

    (a)   may not be made after the death of either of the parties mentioned in subsection (1); and

    (b)   except in the case of an order made by virtue of subsection (5)(a), ceases to have effect on the death of either party.

(10) An order under this section may, in so far as it has continuing effect, be made for a specified period, until the occurrence of a specified event or until further order.

34.   Effect of order under s 33 where rights are charge on dwelling-house

(1)   If B's home rights are a charge on the estate or interest of A or of trustees for A—

    (a)   an order under section 33 against A has, except so far as a contrary intention appears, the same effect against persons deriving title under A or under the trustees and affected by the charge, and

    (b)   sections 33(1), (3), (4) and (10) and 30(3) to (6) apply in relation to any person deriving title under A or under the trustees and affected by the charge as they apply in relation to A.

(2)   The court may make an order under section 33 by virtue of subsection (1)(b) if it considers that in all the circumstances it is just and reasonable to do so.

35.   One former spouse or former civil partner with no existing right to occupy

(1)   This section applies if—

    (a)   one former spouse or former civil partner is entitled to occupy a dwelling-house by virtue of a beneficial estate or interest or contract, or by virtue of any enactment giving him the right to remain in occupation;

    (b)   the other former spouse or former civil partner is not so entitled; and

    (c)   the dwelling-house—

        (i)   in the case of former spouses, was at any time their matrimonial home or was at any time intended by them to be their matrimonial home, or

        (ii)   in the case of former civil partners, was at any time their civil partnership home or was at any time intended by them to be their civil partnership home.

(2)   The former spouse or former civil partner not so entitled may apply to the court for an order under this section against the other former spouse or former civil partner ('the respondent').

(3)   If the applicant is in occupation, an order under this section must contain provision—

    (a)   giving the applicant the right not to be evicted or excluded from the dwelling-house or any part of it by the respondent for the period specified in the order; and

    (b)   prohibiting the respondent from evicting or excluding the applicant during that period.

(4) If the applicant is not in occupation, an order under this section must contain provision—
    (a) giving the applicant the right to enter into and occupy the dwelling-house for the period specified in the order; and
    (b) requiring the respondent to permit the exercise of that right.

(5) An order under this section may also—
    (a) regulate the occupation of the dwelling-house by either or both of the parties;
    (b) prohibit, suspend or restrict the exercise by the respondent of his right to occupy the dwelling-house;
    (c) require the respondent to leave the dwelling-house or part of the dwelling-house; or
    (d) exclude the respondent from a defined area in which the dwelling-house is included.

(6) In deciding whether to make an order under this section containing provision of the kind mentioned in subsection (3) or (4) and (if so) in what manner, the court shall have regard to all the circumstances including—
    (a) the housing needs and housing resources of each of the parties and of any relevant child;
    (b) the financial resources of each of the parties;
    (c) the likely effect of any order, or of any decision by the court not to exercise its powers under subsection (3) or (4), on the health, safety or well-being of the parties and of any relevant child;
    (d) the conduct of the parties in relation to each other and otherwise;
    (e) the length of time that has elapsed since the parties ceased to live together;
    (f) the length of time that has elapsed since the marriage or civil partnership was dissolved or annulled; and
    (g) the existence of any pending proceedings between the parties—
        (i) for an order under section 23A or 24 of the Matrimonial Causes Act 1973 (property adjustment orders in connection with divorce proceedings etc.);
        (ia) for a property adjustment order under Part 2 of Schedule 5 to the Civil Partnership Act 2004;
        (ii) for an order under paragraph 1(2)(d) or (e) of Schedule 1 to the Children Act 1989 (orders for financial relief against parents); or
        (iii) relating to the legal or beneficial ownership of the dwelling-house.

(7) In deciding whether to exercise its power to include one or more of the provisions referred to in subsection (5) ('a subsection (5) provision') and (if so) in what manner, the court shall have regard to all the circumstances including the matters mentioned in subsection (6)(a) to (e).

(8) If the court decides to make an order under this section and it appears to it that, if the order does not include a subsection (5) provision, the applicant or any relevant child is likely to suffer significant harm attributable to conduct of the respondent, the court shall include the subsection (5) provision in the order unless it appears to the court that—
    (a) the respondent or any relevant child is likely to suffer significant harm if the provision is included in the order; and
    (b) the harm likely to be suffered by the respondent or child in that event is as great as or greater than the harm attributable to conduct of the respondent which is likely to be suffered by the applicant or child if the provision is not included.

(9) An order under this section—
    (a) may not be made after the death of either of the former spouses or former civil partners; and
    (b) ceases to have effect on the death of either of them.

(10) An order under this section must be limited so as to have effect for a specified period not exceeding six months, but may be extended on one or more occasions for a further specified period not exceeding six months.

(11) A former spouse or former civil partner who has an equitable interest in the dwelling-house or in the proceeds of sale of the dwelling-house but in whom there is not vested (whether solely or as joint tenant) a legal estate in fee simple or a legal term of years absolute in the dwelling-house is to be treated (but only for the purpose of determining whether he is eligible to apply under this section) as not being entitled to occupy the dwelling-house by virtue of that interest.

(12) Subsection (11) does not prejudice any right of such a former spouse or former civil partner to apply for an order under section 33.

(13) So long as an order under this section remains in force, subsections (3) to (6) of section 30 apply in relation to the applicant—

    (a)   as if he were B (the person entitled to occupy the dwelling-house by virtue of that section); and

    (b)   as if the respondent were A (the person entitled as mentioned in subsection (1)(a) of that section).

36. One cohabitant or former cohabitant with no existing right to occupy

(1) This section applies if—

    (a)   one cohabitant or former cohabitant is entitled to occupy a dwelling-house by virtue of a beneficial estate or interest or contract or by virtue of any enactment giving him the right to remain in occupation;

    (b)   the other cohabitant or former cohabitant is not so entitled; and

    (c)   that dwelling-house is the home in which they cohabit or a home in which they at any time cohabited or intended to cohabit.

(2) The cohabitant or former cohabitant not so entitled may apply to the court for an order under this section against the other cohabitant or former cohabitant ('the respondent').

(3) If the applicant is in occupation, an order under this section must contain provision—

    (a)   giving the applicant the right not to be evicted or excluded from the dwelling-house or any part of it by the respondent for the period specified in the order; and

    (b)   prohibiting the respondent from evicting or excluding the applicant during that period.

(4) If the applicant is not in occupation, an order under this section must contain provision—

    (a)   giving the applicant the right to enter into and occupy the dwelling-house for the period specified in the order; and

    (b)   requiring the respondent to permit the exercise of that right.

(5) An order under this section may also—

    (a)   regulate the occupation of the dwelling-house by either or both of the parties;

    (b)   prohibit, suspend or restrict the exercise by the respondent of his right to occupy the dwelling-house;

    (c)   require the respondent to leave the dwelling-house or part of the dwelling-house; or

    (d)   exclude the respondent from a defined area in which the dwelling-house is included.

(6) In deciding whether to make an order under this section containing provision of the kind mentioned in subsection (3) or (4) and (if so) in what manner, the court shall have regard to all the circumstances including—

    (a)   the housing needs and housing resources of each of the parties and of any relevant child;

    (b)   the financial resources of each of the parties;

    (c)   the likely effect of any order, or of any decision by the court not to exercise its powers under subsection (3) or (4), on the health, safety or well-being of the parties and of any relevant child;

    (d)   the conduct of the parties in relation to each other and otherwise;

    (e)   the nature of the parties' relationship and in particular the level of commitment involved in it;

    (f)   the length of time during which they have cohabited;

    (g)   whether there are or have been any children who are children of both parties or for whom both parties have or have had parental responsibility;

    (h)   the length of time that has elapsed since the parties ceased to live together; and

    (i)   the existence of any pending proceedings between the parties—

        (i)   for an order under paragraph 1 (2)(d) or (e) of Schedule to the Children Act 1989 (orders for financial relief against parents); or

        (ii)   relating to the legal or beneficial ownership of the dwelling-house.

(7) In deciding whether to exercise its powers to include one or more of the provisions referred to in subsection (5) ('a subsection (5) provision') and (if so) in what manner, the court shall have regard to all the circumstances including—

    (a)   the matters mentioned in subsection (6)(a) to (d); and

    (b)   the questions mentioned in subsection (8).

(8)   The questions are—
  (a)   whether the applicant or any relevant child is likely to suffer significant harm attributable to conduct of the respondent if the subsection (5) provision is not included in the order; and
  (b)   whether the harm likely to be suffered by the respondent or child if the provision is included is as great as or greater than the harm attributable to conduct of the respondent which is likely to be suffered by the applicant or child if the provision is not included.

(9)   An order under this section—
  (a)   may not be made after the death of either of the parties; and
  (b)   ceases to have effect on the death of either of them.

(10) An order under this section must be limited so as to have effect for a specified period not exceeding six months, but may be extended on one occasion for a further specified period not exceeding six months.

(11) A person who has an equitable interest in the dwelling-house or in the proceeds of sale of the dwelling-house but in whom there is not vested (whether solely or as joint tenant) a legal estate in fee simple or a legal term of years absolute in the dwelling-house is to be treated (but only for the purpose of determining whether he is eligible to apply under this section) as not being entitled to occupy the dwelling-house by virtue of that interest.

(12) Subsection (11) does not prejudice any right of such a person to apply for an order under section 33.

(13) So long as the order remains in force, subsections (3) to (6) of section 30 apply in relation to the applicant—
  (a)   as if he were B (the person entitled to occupy the dwelling-house by virtue of that section); and
  (b)   as if the respondent were A (the person entitled as mentioned in subsection (1)(a) of that section).

37.   Neither spouse or civil partner entitled to occupy

(1)   This section applies if—
  (a)   one spouse or former spouse and the other spouse or former spouse occupy a dwelling-house which is or was the matrimonial home; but
  (b)   neither of them is entitled to remain in occupation—
    (i)   by virtue of a beneficial estate or interest or contract; or
    (ii)   by virtue of any enactment giving him the right to remain in occupation.

(1A) This section also applies if—
  (a)   one civil partner or former civil partner and the other civil partner or former civil partner occupy a dwelling-house which is or was the civil partnership home; but
  (b)   neither of them is entitled to remain in occupation—
    (i)   by virtue of a beneficial estate or interest or contract; or
    (ii)   by virtue of any enactment giving him the right to remain in occupation.

(2)   Either of the parties may apply to the court for an order against the other under this section.

(3)   An order under this section may—
  (a)   require the respondent to permit the applicant to enter and remain in the dwelling-house or part of the dwelling-house;
  (b)   regulate the occupation of the dwelling-house by either or both of the parties;
  (c)   require the respondent to leave the dwelling-house or part of the dwelling-house; or
  (d)   exclude the respondent from a defined area in which the dwelling-house is included.

(4)   Subsections (6) and (7) of section 33 apply to the exercise by the court of its powers under this section as they apply to the exercise by the court of its powers under subsection (3) of that section.

(5)   An order under this section must be limited so as to have effect for a specified period not exceeding six months, but may be extended on one or more occasions for a further specified period not exceeding six months.

38.   Neither cohabitant or former cohabitant entitled to occupy

(1)   This section applies if—
   (a)   one cohabitant or former cohabitant and the other cohabitant or former cohabitant occupy a dwelling-house which is the home in which they cohabit or cohabited; but
   (b)   neither of them is entitled to remain in occupation—
      (i)   by virtue of a beneficial estate or interest or contract; or
      (ii)   by virtue of any enactment giving him the right to remain in occupation.
(2)   Either of the parties may apply to the court for an order against the other under this section.
(3)   An order under this section may—
   (a)   require the respondent to permit the applicant to enter and remain in the dwelling-house or part of the dwelling-house;
   (b)   regulate the occupation of the dwelling-house by either or both of the parties;
   (c)   require the respondent to leave the dwelling-house or part of the dwelling-house; or
   (d)   exclude the respondent from a defined area in which the dwelling-house is included.
(4)   In deciding whether to exercise its powers to include one or more of the provisions referred to in subsection (3) ('a subsection (3) provision') and (if so) in what manner, the court shall have regard to all the circumstances including—
   (a)   the housing needs and housing resources of each of the parties and of any relevant child;
   (b)   the financial resources of each of the parties;
   (c)   the likely effect of any order, or of any decision by the court not to exercise its powers under subsection (3), on the health, safety or well-being of the parties and of any relevant child;
   (d)   the conduct of the parties in relation to each other and otherwise; and
   (e)   the questions mentioned in subsection (5).
(5)   The questions are—
   (a)   whether the applicant or any relevant child is likely to suffer significant harm attributable to conduct of the respondent if the subsection (3) provision is not included in the order; and
   (b)   whether the harm likely to be suffered by the respondent or child if the provision is included is as great as or greater than the harm attributable to conduct of the respondent which is likely to be suffered by the applicant or child if the provision is not included.
(6)   An order under this section shall be limited so as to have effect for a specified period not exceeding six months, but may be extended on one occasion for a further specified period not exceeding six months.

39.   Supplementary provisions

(1)   In this Part an 'occupation order' means an order under section 33, 35, 36, 37 or 38.
(2)   An application for an occupation order may be made in other family proceedings or without any other family proceedings being instituted.
(3)   If—
   (a)   an application for an occupation order is made under section 33, 35, 36, 37 or 38, and
   (b)   the court considers that it has no power to make the order under the section concerned, but that it has power to make an order under one of the other sections, the court may make an order under that other section.
(4)   The fact that a person has applied for an occupation order under sections 35 to 38, or that an occupation order has been made, does not affect the right of any person to claim a legal or equitable interest in any property in any subsequent proceedings (including subsequent proceedings under this Part).

40.   Additional provisions that may be included in certain occupation orders

(1)   The court may on, or at any time after, making an occupation order under section 33, 35 or 36—
   (a)   impose on either party obligations as to—
      (i)   the repair and maintenance of the dwelling-house; or
      (ii)   the discharge of rent, mortgage payments or other outgoings affecting the dwelling-house;

  (b) order a party occupying the dwelling-house or any part of it (including a party who is entitled to do so by virtue of a beneficial estate or interest or contract or by virtue of any enactment giving him the right to remain in occupation) to make periodical payments to the other party in respect of the accommodation, if the other party would (but for the order) be entitled to occupy the dwelling-house by virtue of a beneficial estate or interest or contract or by virtue of any such enactment;

  (c) grant either party possession or use of furniture or other contents of the dwelling-house;

  (d) order either party to take reasonable care of any furniture or other contents of the dwelling-house;

  (e) order either party to take reasonable steps to keep the dwelling-house and any furniture or other contents secure.

(2) In deciding whether and, if so, how to exercise its powers under this section, the court shall have regard to all the circumstances of the case including—

  (a) the financial needs and financial resources of the parties; and

  (b) the financial obligations which they have, or are likely to have in the foreseeable future, including financial obligations to each other and to any relevant child.

(3) An order under this section ceases to have effect when the occupation order to which it relates ceases to have effect.

Dwelling-house subject to mortgage

54. Dwelling-house subject to mortgage

(1) In determining for the purposes of this Part whether a person is entitled to occupy a dwelling-house by virtue of an estate or interest, any right to possession of the dwelling-house conferred on a mortgagee of the dwelling-house under or by virtue of his mortgage is to be disregarded.

(2) Subsection (1) applies whether or not the mortgagee is in possession.

(3) Where a person ('A') is entitled to occupy a dwelling-house by virtue of an estate or interest, a connected person does not by virtue of—

  (a) any home rights conferred by section 30, or

  (b) any rights conferred by an order under section 35 or 36,

  have any larger right against the mortgagee to occupy the dwelling-house than A has by virtue of his estate or interest and of any contract with the mortgagee.

(4) Subsection (3) does not apply, in the case of home rights, if under section 31 those rights are a charge, affecting the mortgagee, on the estate or interest mortgaged.

(5) In this section 'connected person', in relation to any person, means that person's spouse, former spouse, civil partner, former civil partner, cohabitant or former cohabitant.

55. Actions by mortgagees: joining connected persons as parties

(1) This section applies if a mortgagee of land which consists of or includes a dwelling-house brings an action in any court for the enforcement of his security.

(2) A connected person who is not already a party to the action is entitled to be made a party in the circumstances mentioned in subsection (3).

(3) The circumstances are that—

  (a) the connected person is enabled by section 30(3) or (6) (or by section 30(3) or (6) as applied by section 35(13) or 36(13)), to meet the mortgagor's liabilities under the mortgage;

  (b) he has applied to the court before the action is finally disposed of in that court; and

  (c) the court sees no special reason against his being made a party to the action and is satisfied—

   (i) that he may be expected to make such payments or do such other things in or towards satisfaction of the mortgagor's liabilities or obligations as might affect the outcome of the proceedings; or

   (ii) that the expectation of it should be considered under section 36 of the Administration of Justice Act 1970.

(4) In this section 'connected person' has the same meaning as in section 54.

56. Actions by mortgagees: service of notice on certain persons

(1) This section applies if a mortgagee of land which consists, or substantially consists, of a dwelling-house brings an action for the enforcement of his security, and at the relevant time there is—

     (a)   in the case of unregistered land, a land charge of Class F registered against the person who is the estate owner at the relevant time or any person who, where the estate owner is a trustee, preceded him as trustee during the subsistence of the mortgage; or

     (b)   in the case of registered land, a subsisting registration of—

        (i)   a notice under section 31(10);

        (ii)   a notice under section 2(8) of the Matrimonial Homes Act 1983; or

        (iii)   a notice or caution under section 2(7) of the Matrimonial Homes Act 1967.

  (2)   If the person on whose behalf—

     (a)   the land charge is registered, or

     (b)   the notice or caution is entered,

     is not a party to the action, the mortgagee must serve notice of the action on him.

  (3)   If—

     (a)   an official search has been made on behalf of the mortgagee which would disclose any land charge of Class F, notice or caution within subsection (1)(a) or (b),

     (b)   a certificate of the result of the search has been issued, and

     (c)   the action is commenced within the priority period, the relevant time is the date of the certificate.

  (4)   In any other case the relevant time is the time when the action is commenced.

  (5)   The priority period is, for both registered and unregistered land, the period for which, in accordance with section 11(5) and (6) of the Land Charges Act 1972, a certificate on an official search operates in favour of a purchaser.

SCHEDULE 4

PROVISIONS SUPPLEMENTARY TO SECTIONS 30 AND 31

Restriction on registration where spouse or civil partner entitled to more than one charge

2.   Where one spouse or civil partner is entitled by virtue of section 31 to a registrable charge in respect of each of two or more dwelling-houses, only one of the charges to which that spouse or civil partner is so entitled shall be registered under section 31(10) or under section 2 of the Land Charges Act 1972 at any one time, and if any of those charges is registered under either of those provisions the Chief Land Registrar, on being satisfied that any other of them is so registered, shall cancel the registration of the charge first registered.

Contract for sale of house affected by registered charge to include term
requiring cancellation of registration before completion

3.   (1)   Where one spouse or civil partner is entitled by virtue of section 31 to a charge on an estate in a dwelling-house and the charge is registered under section 31(10) or section 2 of the Land Charges Act 1972, it shall be a term of any contract for the sale of that estate whereby the vendor agrees to give vacant possession of the dwelling-house on completion of the contract that the vendor will before such completion procure the cancellation of the registration of the charge at his expense.

    (2)   Sub-paragraph (1) shall not apply to any such contract made by a vendor who is entitled to sell the estate in the dwelling-house freed from any such charge.

    (3)   If, on the completion of such a contract as is referred to in sub-paragraph (1), there is delivered to the purchaser or his legal representative an application by the spouse or civil partner entitled to the charge for the cancellation of the registration of that charge, the term of the contract for which sub-paragraph (1) provides shall be deemed to have been performed.

    (4)   This paragraph applies only if and so far as a contrary intention is not expressed in the contract.

    (5)   This paragraph shall apply to a contract for exchange as it applies to a contract for sale.

    (6)   This paragraph shall, with the necessary modifications, apply to a contract for the grant of a lease or underlease of a dwelling-house as it applies to a contract for the sale of an estate in a dwelling-house.

Cancellation of registration after termination of marriage or civil partnership, etc.

4.   (1)   Where a spouse's or civil partner's home rights are a charge on an estate in the dwelling-house and the charge is registered under section 31(10) or under section 2 of the Land Charges Act 1972, the Chief Land Registrar shall, subject to sub-paragraph (2), cancel the registration of the charge if he is satisfied—

    (a)   in the case of a marriage—

        (i)   by the production of a certificate or other sufficient evidence, that either spouse is dead,

        (ii)   by the production of an official copy of a decree or order of a court, that the marriage has been terminated otherwise than by death, or

        (iii)   by the production of an order of the court, that the spouse's home rights constituting the charge have been terminated by the order, and

    (b)   in the case of a civil partnership—

        (i)   by the production of a certificate or other sufficient evidence, that either civil partner is dead,

        (ii)   by the production of an official copy of an order or decree of a court, that the civil partnership has been terminated otherwise than by death, or

        (iii)   by the production of an order of the court, that the civil partner's home rights constituting the charge have been terminated by the order.

(2)   Where—

    (a)   the marriage or civil partnership in question has been terminated by the death of the spouse or civil partner entitled to an estate in the dwelling-house or otherwise than by death, and

    (b)   an order affecting the charge of the spouse or civil partner not so entitled had been made under section 33(5),

then if, after the making of the order, registration of the charge was renewed or the charge registered in pursuance of sub-paragraph (3), the Chief Land Registrar shall not cancel the registration of the charge in accordance with sub-paragraph (1) unless he is also satisfied that the order has ceased to have effect.

(3)   Where such an order has been made, then, for the purposes of sub-paragraph (2), the spouse or civil partner entitled to the charge affected by the order may—

    (a)   if before the date of the order the charge was registered under section 31(10) or under section 2 of the Land Charges Act 1972, renew the registration of the charge, and

    (b)   if before the said date the charge was not so registered, register the charge under section 31(10) or under section 2 of the Land Charges Act 1972.

(4)   Renewal of the registration of a charge in pursuance of sub-paragraph (3) shall be effected in such manner as may be prescribed, and an application for such renewal or for registration of a charge in pursuance of that sub-paragraph shall contain such particulars of any order affecting the charge made under section 33(5) as may be prescribed.

(5)   The renewal in pursuance of sub-paragraph (3) of the registration of a charge shall not affect the priority of the charge.

(6)   In this paragraph 'prescribed' means prescribed by rules made under section 16 of the Land Charges Act 1972 or by land registration rules under the Land Registration Act 2002, as the circumstances of the case require.

Release of home rights

5.   (1)   A spouse or civil partner entitled to home rights may by a release in writing release those rights or release them as respects part only of the dwelling-house affected by them.

    (2)   Where a contract is made for the sale of an estate or interest in a dwelling-house, or for the grant of a lease or underlease of a dwelling-house, being (in either case) a dwelling-house affected by a charge registered under section 31(10) or under section 2 of the Land Charges Act 1972, then, without prejudice to sub-paragraph (1), the home rights constituting the charge shall be deemed to have been released on the happening of whichever of the following events first occurs—

        (a)   the delivery to the purchaser or lessee, as the case may be, or his legal representative on completion of the contract of an application by the spouse or civil partner entitled to the charge for the cancellation of the registration of the charge; or

        (b)   the lodging of such an application at Her Majesty's Land Registry.

Postponement of priority of charge

6.   A spouse or civil partner entitled by virtue of section 31 to a charge on an estate or interest may agree in writing that any other charge on, or interest in, that estate or interest shall rank in priority to the charge to which that spouse or civil partner is so entitled.

TRUSTS OF LAND AND APPOINTMENT OF TRUSTEES ACT 1996
(1996, c. 47)

PART I
TRUSTS OF LAND

Introductory

1.　Meaning of 'trust of land'
(1)　In this Act—
    (a)　'trust of land' means (subject to subsection (3)) any trust of property which consists of or includes land, and
    (b)　'trustees of land' means trustees of a trust of land.
(2)　The reference in subsection (1)(a) to a trust—
    (a)　is to any description of trust (whether express, implied, resulting or constructive), including a trust for sale and a bare trust, and
    (b)　includes a trust created, or arising, before the commencement of this Act.
(3)　The reference to land in subsection (1)(a) does not include land which (despite section 2) is settled land or which is land to which the Universities and College Estates Act 1925 applies.

Settlements and trusts for sale as trusts of land

2.　Trusts in place of settlements
(1)　No settlement created after the commencement of this Act is a settlement for the purposes of the Settled Land Act 1925; and no settlement shall be deemed to be made under that Act after that commencement.
(2)　Subsection (1) does not apply to a settlement created on the occasion of an alteration in any interest in, or of a person becoming entitled under, a settlement which—
    (a)　is in existence at the commencement of this Act, or
    (b)　derives from a settlement within paragraph (a) or this paragraph.
(3)　But a settlement created as mentioned in subsection (2) is not a settlement for the purposes of the Settled Land Act 1925 if provision to the effect that it is not is made in the instrument, or any of the instruments, by which it is created.
(4)　Where at any time after the commencement of this Act there is in the case of any settlement which is a settlement for the purposes of the Settled Land Act 1925 no relevant property which is, or is deemed to be, subject to the settlement, the settlement permanently ceases at that time to be a settlement for the purposes of that Act.
    In this subsection 'relevant property' means land and personal chattels to which section 67(1) of the Settled Land Act 1925 (heirlooms) applies.
(5)　No land held on charitable, ecclesiastical or public trusts shall be or be deemed to be settled land after the commencement of this Act, even if it was or was deemed to be settled land before that commencement.
(6)　Schedule 1 has effect to make provision consequential on this section (including provision to impose a trust in circumstances in which, apart from this section, there would be a settlement for the purposes of the Settled Land Act 1925 (and there would not otherwise be a trust)).

3.　Abolition of doctrine of conversion
(1)　Where land is held by trustees subject to a trust for sale, the land is not to be regarded as personal property; and where personal property is subject to a trust for sale in order that the trustees may acquire land, the personal property is not to be regarded as land.
(2)　Subsection (1) does not apply to a trust created by a will if the testator died before the commencement of this Act.
(3)　Subject to that, subsection (1) applies to a trust whether it is created, or arises, before or after that commencement.

4.　Express trusts for sale as trusts of land
(1)　In the case of every trust for sale of land created by a disposition there is to be implied, despite any provision to the contrary made by the disposition, a power for the trustees to postpone sale of the land; and the trustees are not liable in any way for postponing sale of the land, in the exercise of their discretion, for an indefinite period.

(2)　Subsection (1) applies to a trust whether it is created, or arises, before or after the commencement of this Act.

(3)　Subsection (1) does not affect any liability incurred by trustees before that commencement.

5.　Implied trusts for sale as trusts of land

(1)　Schedule 2 has effect in relation to statutory provisions which impose a trust for sale of land in certain circumstances so that in those circumstances there is instead a trust of the land (without a duty to sell).

(2)　Section 1 of the Settled Land Act 1925 does not apply to land held on any trust arising by virtue of that Schedule (so that any such land is subject to a trust of land).

Functions of trustees of land

6.　General powers of trustees

(1)　For the purpose of exercising their functions as trustees, the trustees of land have in relation to the land subject to the trust all the powers of an absolute owner.

(2)　Where in the case of any land subject to a trust of land each of the beneficiaries interested in the land is a person of full age and capacity who is absolutely entitled to the land, the powers conferred on the trustees by subsection (1) include the power to convey the land to the beneficiaries even though they have not required the trustees to do so; and where land is conveyed by virtue of this subsection—

(a)　the beneficiaries shall do whatever is necessary to secure that it vests in them, and

(b)　if they fail to do so, the court may make an order requiring them to do so.

(3)　The trustees of land have power to acquire land under the power conferred by section 8 of the Trustee Act 2000.

(4)　...

(5)　In exercising the powers conferred by this section trustees shall have regard to the rights of the beneficiaries.

(6)　The powers conferred by this section shall not be exercised in contravention of, or of any order made in pursuance of, any other enactment or any rule of law or equity.

(7)　The reference in subsection (6) to an order includes an order of any court or of the Charity Commission.

(8)　Where any enactment other than this section confers on trustees authority to act subject to any restriction, limitation or condition, trustees of land may not exercise the powers conferred by this section to do any act which they are prevented from doing under the other enactment by reason of the restriction, limitation or condition.

(9)　The duty of care under section 1 of the Trustee Act 2000 applies to trustees of land when exercising the powers conferred by this section.

7.　Partition by trustees

(1)　The trustees of land may, where beneficiaries of full age are absolutely entitled in undivided shares to land subject to the trust, partition the land, or any part of it, and provide (by way of mortgage or otherwise) for the payment of any equality money.

(2)　The trustees shall give effect to any such partition by conveying the partitioned land in severalty (whether or not subject to any legal mortgage created for raising equality money), either absolutely or in trust, in accordance with the rights of those beneficiaries.

(3)　Before exercising their powers under subsection (2) the trustees shall obtain the consent of each of those beneficiaries.

(4)　Where a share in the land is affected by an incumbrance, the trustees may either give effect to it or provide for its discharge from the property allotted to that share as they think fit.

(5)　If a share in the land is absolutely vested in a minor, subsections (1) to (4) apply as if he were of full age, except that the trustees may act on his behalf and retain land or other property representing his share in trust for him.

(6)　Subsection (1) is subject to sections 21 (part-unit: interests) and 22 (part-unit: charging) of the Commonhold and Leasehold Reform Act 2002.

8.　Exclusion and restriction of powers

(1)　Sections 6 and 7 do not apply in the case of a trust of land created by a disposition in so far as provision to the effect that they do not apply is made by the disposition.

(2)　If the disposition creating such a trust makes provision requiring any consent to be obtained to the exercise of any power conferred by section 6 or 7, the power may not be exercised without that consent.

(3)   Subsection (1) does not apply in the case of charitable, ecclesiastical or public trusts.

(4)   Subsections (1) and (2) have effect subject to any enactment which prohibits or restricts the effect of provision of the description mentioned in them.

9.   Delegation by trustees

(1)   The trustees of land may, by power of attorney, delegate to any beneficiary or beneficiaries of full age and beneficially entitled to an interest in possession in land subject to the trust any of their functions as trustees which relate to the land.

(2)   Where trustees purport to delegate to a person by a power of attorney under subsection (1) functions relating to any land and another person in good faith deals with him in relation to the land, he shall be presumed in favour of that other person to have been a person to whom the functions could be delegated unless that other person has knowledge at the time of the transaction that he was not such a person.

And it shall be conclusively presumed in favour of any purchaser whose interest depends on the validity of that transaction that that other person dealt in good faith and did not have such knowledge if that other person makes a statutory declaration to that effect before or within three months after the completion of the purchase.

(3)   A power of attorney under subsection (1) shall be given by all the trustees jointly and (unless expressed to be irrevocable and to be given by way of security) may be revoked by any one or more of them; and such a power is revoked by the appointment as a trustee of a person other than those by whom it is given (though not by any of those persons dying or otherwise ceasing to be a trustee).

(4)   Where a beneficiary to whom functions are delegated by a power of attorney under subsection (1) ceases to be a person beneficially entitled to an interest in possession in land subject to the trust—

(a)   if the functions are delegated to him alone, the power is revoked,

(b)   if the functions are delegated to him and to other beneficiaries to be exercised by them jointly (but not separately), the power is revoked if each of the other beneficiaries ceases to be so entitled (but otherwise functions exercisable in accordance with the power are so exercisable by the remaining beneficiary or beneficiaries), and

(c)   if the functions are delegated to him and to other beneficiaries to be exercised by them separately (or either separately or jointly), the power is revoked in so far as it relates to him.

(5)   A delegation under subsection (1) may be for any period or indefinite.

(6)   A power of attorney under subsection (1) cannot be an enduring power of attorney or lasting power of attorney within the meaning of the Mental Capacity Act 2005.

(7)   Beneficiaries to whom functions have been delegated under subsection (1) are, in relation to the exercise of the functions, in the same position as trustees (with the same duties and liabilities); but such beneficiaries shall not be regarded as trustees for any other purposes (including, in particular, the purposes of any enactment permitting the delegation of functions by trustees or imposing requirements relating to the payment of capital money).

(8)   ...

(9)   Neither this section nor the repeal by this Act of section 29 of the Law of Property Act 1925 (which is superseded by this section) affects the operation after the commencement of this Act of any delegation effected before that commencement.

9A.   Duties of trustees in connection with delegation etc.

(1)   The duty of care under section 1 of the Trustee Act 2000 applies to trustees of land in deciding whether to delegate any of their functions under section 9.

(2)   Subsection (3) applies if the trustees of land—

(a)   delegate any of their functions under section 9, and

(b)   the delegation is not irrevocable.

(3)   While the delegation continues, the trustees—

(a)   must keep the delegation under review,

(b)   if circumstances make it appropriate to do so, must consider whether there is a need to exercise any power of intervention that they have, and

(c)   if they consider that there is a need to exercise such a power, must do so.

(4)   'Power of intervention' includes—

(a)   a power to give directions to the beneficiary;

(b)   a power to revoke the delegation.

(5) The duty of care under section 1 of the 2000 Act applies to trustees in carrying out any duty under subsection (3).

(6) A trustee of land is not liable for any act or default of the beneficiary, or beneficiaries, unless the trustee fails to comply with the duty of care in deciding to delegate any of the trustees' functions under section 9 or in carrying out any duty under subsection (3).

(7) Neither this section nor the repeal of section 9(8) by the Trustee Act 2000 affects the operation after the commencement of this section of any delegation effected before that commencement.

Consents and consultation

10. Consents

(1) If a disposition creating a trust of land requires the consent of more than two persons to the exercise by the trustees of any function relating to the land, the consent of any two of them to the exercise of the function is sufficient in favour of a purchaser.

(2) Subsection (1) does not apply to the exercise of a function by trustees of land held on charitable, ecclesiastical or public trusts.

(3) Where at any time a person whose consent is expressed by a disposition creating a trust of land to be required to the exercise by the trustees of any function relating to the land is not of full age—
   (a) his consent is not, in favour of a purchaser, required to the exercise of the function, but
   (b) the trustees shall obtain the consent of a parent who has parental responsibility for him (within the meaning of the Children Act 1989) or of a guardian of his.

11. Consultation with beneficiaries

(1) The trustees of land shall in the exercise of any function relating to land subject to the trust—
   (a) so far as practicable, consult the beneficiaries of full age and beneficially entitled to an interest in possession in the land, and
   (b) so far as consistent with the general interest of the trust, give effect to the wishes of those beneficiaries, or (in case of dispute) of the majority (according to the value of their combined interests).

(2) Subsection (1) does not apply—
   (a) in relation to a trust created by a disposition in so far as provision that it does not apply is made by the disposition,
   (b) in relation to a trust created or arising under a will made before the commencement of this Act, or
   (c) in relation to the exercise of the power mentioned in section 6(2).

(3) Subsection (1) does not apply to a trust created before the commencement of this Act by a disposition, or a trust created after that commencement by reference to such a trust, unless provision to the effect that it is to apply is made by a deed executed—
   (a) in a case in which the trust was created by one person and he is of full capacity, by that person, or
   (b) in a case in which the trust was created by more than one person, by such of the persons who created the trust as are alive and of full capacity.

(4) A deed executed for the purposes of subsection (3) is irrevocable.

Right of beneficiaries to occupy trust land

12. The right to occupy

(1) A beneficiary who is beneficially entitled to an interest in possession in land subject to a trust of land is entitled by reason of his interest to occupy the land at any time if at that time—
   (a) the purposes of the trust include making the land available for his occupation (or for the occupation of beneficiaries of a class of which he is a member or of beneficiaries in general), or
   (b) the land is held by the trustees so as to be so available.

(2) Subsection (1) does not confer on a beneficiary a right to occupy land if it is either unavailable or unsuitable for occupation by him.

(3) This section is subject to section 13.

13.   Exclusion and restriction of right to occupy

(1)   Where two or more beneficiaries are (or apart from this subsection would be) entitled under section 12 to occupy land, the trustees of land may exclude or restrict the entitlement of any one or more (but not all) of them.

(2)   Trustees may not under subsection (1)—

(a)   unreasonably exclude any beneficiary's entitlement to occupy land, or

(b)   restrict any such entitlement to an unreasonable extent.

(3)   The trustees of land may from time to time impose reasonable conditions on any beneficiary in relation to his occupation of land by reason of his entitlement under section 12.

(4)   The matters to which trustees are to have regard in exercising the powers conferred by this section include—

(a)   the intentions of the person or persons (if any) who created the trust,

(b)   the purposes for which the land is held, and

(c)   the circumstances and wishes of each of the beneficiaries who is (or apart from any previous exercise by the trustees of those powers would be) entitled to occupy the land under section 12.

(5)   The conditions which may be imposed on a beneficiary under subsection (3) include, in particular, conditions requiring him—

(a)   to pay any outgoings or expenses in respect of the land, or

(b)   to assume any other obligation in relation to the land or to any activity which is or is proposed to be conducted there.

(6)   Where the entitlement of any beneficiary to occupy land under section 12 has been excluded or restricted, the conditions which may be imposed on any other beneficiary under subsection (3) include, in particular, conditions requiring him to—

(a)   make payments by way of compensation to the beneficiary whose entitlement has been excluded or restricted, or

(b)   forgo any payment or other benefit to which he would otherwise be entitled under the trust so as to benefit that beneficiary.

(7)   The powers conferred on trustees by this section may not be exercised—

(a)   so as prevent any person who is in occupation of land (whether or not by reason of an entitlement under section 12) from continuing to occupy the land, or

(b)   in a manner likely to result in any such person ceasing to occupy the land, unless he consents or the court has given approval.

(8)   The matters to which the court is to have regard in determining whether to give approval under subsection (7) include the matters mentioned in subsection (4)(a) to (c).

Powers of court

14.   Applications for order

(1)   Any person who is a trustee of land or has an interest in property subject to a trust of land may make an application to the court for an order under this section.

(2)   On an application for an order under this section the court may make any such order—

(a)   relating to the exercise by the trustees of any of their functions (including an order relieving them of any obligation to obtain the consent of, or to consult, any person in connection with the exercise of any of their functions), or

(b)   declaring the nature or extent of a person's interest in property subject to the trust, as the court thinks fit.

(3)   The court may not under this section make any order as to the appointment or removal of trustees.

(4)   The powers conferred on the court by this section are exercisable on an application whether it is made before or after the commencement of this Act.

15.   Matters relevant in determining applications

(1)   The matters to which the court is to have regard in determining an application for an order under section 14 include—

(a)   the intentions of the person or persons (if any) who created the trust,

(b)   the purposes for which the property subject to the trust is held,

(c)   the welfare of any minor who occupies or might reasonably be expected to occupy any land subject to the trust as his home, and

(d)   the interests of any secured creditor of any beneficiary.

(2)   In the case of an application relating to the exercise in relation to any land of the powers conferred on the trustees by section 13, the matters to which the court is to have regard also include the circumstances and wishes of each of the beneficiaries who is (or apart from any previous exercise by the trustees of those powers would be) entitled to occupy the land under section 12.

(3)   In the case of any other application, other than one relating to the exercise of the power mentioned in section 6(2), the matters to which the court is to have regard also include the circumstances and wishes of any beneficiaries of full age and entitled to an interest in possession in property subject to the trust or (in case of dispute) of the majority (according to the value of their combined interests).

(4)   This section does not apply to an application if section 335A of the Insolvency Act 1986 ... applies to it.

Purchaser protection

16.   Protection of purchasers

(1)   A purchaser of land which is or has been subject to a trust need not be concerned to see that any requirement imposed on the trustees by section 6(5), 7(3) or 11(1) has been complied with.

(2)   Where—
    (a)   trustees of land who convey land which (immediately before it is conveyed) is subject to the trust contravene section 6(6) or (8), but
    (b)   the purchaser of the land from the trustees has no actual notice of the contravention,
the contravention does not invalidate the conveyance.

(3)   Where the powers of trustees of land are limited by virtue of section 8—
    (a)   the trustees shall take all reasonable steps to bring the limitation to the notice of any purchaser of the land from them, but
    (b)   the limitation does not invalidate any conveyance by the trustees to a purchaser who has no actual notice of the limitation.

(4)   Where trustees of land convey land which (immediately before it is conveyed) is subject to the trust to persons believed by them to be beneficiaries absolutely entitled to the land under the trust and of full age and capacity—
    (a)   the trustees shall execute a deed declaring that they are discharged from the trust in relation to that land, and
    (b)   if they fail to do so, the court may make an order requiring them to do so.

(5)   A purchaser of land to which a deed under subsection (4) relates is entitled to assume that, as from the date of the deed, the land is not subject to the trust unless he has actual notice that the trustees were mistaken in their belief that the land was conveyed to beneficiaries absolutely entitled to the land under the trust and of full age and capacity.

(6)   Subsections (2) and (3) do not apply to land held on charitable, ecclesiastical or public trusts.

(7)   This section does not apply to registered land.

Supplementary

17.   Applications of provisions to trusts of proceeds of sale

(1)   ...

(2)   Section 14 applies in relation to a trust of proceeds of sale of land and trustees of such a trust as in relation to a trust of land and trustees of land.

(3)   In this section 'trust of proceeds of sale of land' means (subject to subsection (5)) any trust of property (other than a trust of land) which consists of or includes—
    (a)   any proceeds of a disposition of land held in trust (including settled land), or
    (b)   any property representing any such proceeds.

(4)   The references in subsection (3) to a trust—
    (a)   are to any description of trust (whether express, implied, resulting or constructive), including a trust for sale and a bare trust, and
    (b)   include a trust created, or arising, before the commencement of this Act.

(5)   A trust which (despite section 2) is a settlement for the purposes of the Settled Land Act 1925 cannot be a trust of proceeds of sale of land.

(6)   In subsection (3)—

(a)   'disposition' includes any disposition made, or coming into operation, before the commencement of this Act, and

(b)   the reference to settled land includes personal chattels to which section 67(1) of the Settled Land Act 1925 (heirlooms) applies.

18. Application of Part to personal representatives

(1)   The provisions of this Part relating to trustees, other than sections 10, 11 and 14, apply to personal representatives, but with appropriate modifications and without prejudice to the functions of personal representatives for the purposes of administration.

(2)   The appropriate modifications include—

(a)   the substitution of references to persons interested in the due administration of the estate for references to beneficiaries, and

(b)   the substitution of references to the will for references to the disposition creating the trust.

(3)   Section 3(1) does not apply to personal representatives if the death occurs before the commencement of this Act.

PART II
APPOINTMENT AND RETIREMENT OF TRUSTEES

19. Appointment and retirement of trustee at instance of beneficiaries

(1)   This section applies in the case of a trust where—

(a)   there is no person nominated for the purpose of appointing new trustees by the instrument, if any, creating the trust, and

(b)   the beneficiaries under the trust are of full age and capacity and (taken together) are absolutely entitled to the property subject to the trust.

(2)   The beneficiaries may give a direction or directions of either or both of the following descriptions—

(a)   a written direction to a trustee or trustees to retire from the trust, and

(b)   a written direction to the trustees or trustee for the time being (or, if there are none, to the personal representative of the last person who was a trustee) to appoint by writing to be a trustee or trustees the person or persons specified in the direction.

(3)   Where—

(a)   a trustee has been given a direction under subsection (2)(a),

(b)   reasonable arrangements have been made for the protection of any rights of his in connection with the trust,

(c)   after he has retired there will be either a trust corporation or at least two persons to act as trustees to perform the trust, and

(d)   either another person is to be appointed to be a new trustee on his retirement (whether in compliance with a direction under subsection (2)(b) or otherwise) or the continuing trustees by deed consent to his retirement,

he shall make a deed declaring his retirement and shall be deemed to have retired and be discharged from the trust.

(4)   Where a trustee retires under subsection (3) he and the continuing trustees (together with any new trustee) shall (subject to any arrangements for the protection of his rights) do anything necessary to vest the trust property in the continuing trustees (or the continuing and new trustees).

(5)   This section has effect subject to the restrictions imposed by the Trustee Act 1925 on the number of trustees.

20. Appointment of substitute for trustee who lacks capacity

(1)   This section applies where—

(a)   a trustee lacks capacity (within the meaning of the Mental Capacity Act 2005) to exercise his functions as trustee,

(b)   there is no person who is both entitled and willing and able to appoint a trustee in place of him under section 36(1) of the Trustee Act 1925, and

(c)   the beneficiaries under the trust are of full age and capacity and (taken together) are absolutely entitled to the property subject to the trust.

(2)   The beneficiaries may give to—
    (a)   a deputy appointed for the trustee by the Court of Protection,
    (b)   an attorney acting for him under the authority of an enduring power of attorney or lasting power of attorney registered under the Mental Capacity Act 2005,
    (c)   a person authorised for the purpose by the Court of Protection,
a written direction to appoint by writing the person or persons specified in the direction to be a trustee or trustees in place of the incapable trustee.

21.   Supplementary

(1)   For the purposes of section 19 or 20 a direction is given by beneficiaries if—
    (a)   a single direction is jointly given by all of them, or
    (b)   (subject to subsection (2)) a direction is given by each of them (whether solely or jointly with one or more, but not all, of the others),
and none of them by writing withdraws the direction given by him before it has been complied with.

(2)   Where more than one direction is given each must specify for appointment or retirement the same person or persons.

(3)   Subsection (7) of section 36 of the Trustee Act 1925 (powers of trustees appointed under that section) applies to a trustee appointed under section 19 or 20 as if he were appointed under that section.

(4)   A direction under section 19 or 20 must not specify a person or persons for appointment if the appointment of that person or those persons would be in contravention of section 35(1) of the Trustee Act 1925 or section 24(1) of the Law of Property Act 1925 (requirements as to identity of trustees).

(5)   Sections 19 and 20 do not apply in relation to a trust created by a disposition in so far as provision that they do not apply is made by the disposition.

(6)   Sections 19 and 20 do not apply in relation to a trust created before the commencement of this Act by a disposition in so far as provision to the effect that they do not apply is made by a deed executed—
    (a)   in a case in which the trust was created by one person and he is of full capacity, by that person, or
    (b)   in a case in which the trust was created by more than one person, by such of the persons who created the trust as are alive and of full capacity.

(7)   A deed executed for the purposes of subsection (6) is irrevocable.

(8)   Where a deed is executed for the purposes of subsection (6)—
    (a)   it does not affect anything done before its execution to comply with a direction under section 19 or 20, but
    (b)   a direction under section 19 or 20 which has been given but not complied with before its execution shall cease to have effect.

PART III
SUPPLEMENTARY

22.   Meaning of 'beneficiary'

(1)   In this Act 'beneficiary', in relation to a trust, means any person who under the trust has an interest in property subject to the trust (including a person who has such an interest as a trustee or a personal representative).

(2)   In this Act references to a beneficiary who is beneficially entitled do not include a beneficiary who has an interest in property subject to the trust only by reason of being a trustee or personal representative.

(3)   For the purposes of this Act a person who is a beneficiary only by reason of being an annuitant is not to be regarded as entitled to an interest in possession in land subject to the trust.

23.   Other interpretation provisions

(1)   In this Act 'purchaser' has the same meaning as in Part I of the Law of Property Act 1925.

(2)   Subject to that, where an expression used in this Act is given a meaning by the Law of Property Act 1925 it has the same meaning as in that Act unless the context otherwise requires.

(3)   In this Act 'the court' means—
    (a)   the High Court, or
    (b)   the county court.

SCHEDULES

Section 2

SCHEDULE 1
PROVISIONS CONSEQUENTIAL ON SECTION 2

Minors

1. (1) Where after the commencement of this Act a person purports to convey a legal estate in land to a minor, or two or more minors, alone, the conveyance—
    (a) is not effective to pass the legal estate, but
    (b) operates as a declaration that the land is held in trust for the minor or minors (or if he purports to convey it to the minor or minors in trust for any persons, for those persons).
    (2) Where after the commencement of this Act a person purports to convey a legal estate in land to—
    (a) a minor or two or more minors, and
    (b) another person who is, or other persons who are, of full age,
    the conveyance operates to vest the land in the other person or persons in trust for the minor or minors and the other person or persons (or if he purports to convey it to them in trust for any persons, for those persons).
    (3) Where immediately before the commencement of this Act a conveyance is operating (by virtue of section 27 of the Settled Land Act 1925) as an agreement to execute a settlement in favour of a minor or minors—
    (a) the agreement ceases to have effect on the commencement of this Act, and
    (b) the conveyance subsequently operates instead as a declaration that the land is held in trust for the minor or minors.

2. Where after the commencement of this Act a legal estate in land would, by reason of intestacy or in any other circumstances not dealt with in paragraph 1, vest in a person who is a minor if he were a person of full age, the land is held in trust for the minor.

Family charges

3. Where, by virtue of an instrument coming into operation after the commencement of this Act, land becomes charged voluntarily (or in consideration of marriage or the formation of a civil partnership) or by way of family arrangement, whether immediately or after an interval, with the payment of—
    (a) a rentcharge for the life of a person or a shorter period, or
    (b) capital, annual or periodical sums for the benefit of a person,
    the instrument operates as a declaration that the land is held in trust for giving effect to the charge.

Charitable, ecclesiastical and public trusts

4. (1) This paragraph applies in the case of land held on charitable, ecclesiastical or public trusts (other than land to which the Universities and College Estates Act 1925 applies).
    (2) Where there is a conveyance of such land—
    (a) if neither section 122(2) nor section 125(1) of the Charities Act 2011 applies to the conveyance, it shall state that the land is held on such trusts, and
    (b) if neither section 122(3) nor section 125(2) of that Act has been complied with in relation to the conveyance and a purchaser has notice that the land is held on such trusts, he must see that any consents or orders necessary to authorise the transaction have been obtained.
    (3) Where any trustees or the majority of any set of trustees have power to transfer or create any legal estate in the land, the estate shall be transferred or created by them in the names and on behalf of the persons in whom it is vested.

Entailed interests

5. (1) Where a person purports by an instrument coming into operation after the commencement of this Act to grant to another person an entailed interest in real or personal property, the instrument—
    (a) is not effective to grant an entailed interest, but
    (b) operates instead as a declaration that the property is held in trust absolutely for the person to whom an entailed interest in the property was purportedly granted.

(2)   Where a person purports by an instrument coming into operation after the commencement of this Act to declare himself a tenant in tail of real or personal property, the instrument is not effective to create an entailed interest.

Property held on settlement ceasing to exist

6.   Where a settlement ceases to be a settlement for the purposes of the Settled Land Act 1925 because no relevant property (within the meaning of section 2(4)) is, or is deemed to be, subject to the settlement, any property which is or later becomes subject to the settlement is held in trust for the persons interested under the settlement.

HUMAN RIGHTS ACT 1998
(1998, c. 42)

Legislation

3.   Interpretation of legislation

(1)   So far as it is possible to do so, primary legislation and subordinate legislation must be read and given effect in a way which is compatible with Convention rights.

(2)   This section—

(a)   applies to primary legislation and subordinate legislation whenever enacted;

(b)   does not affect the validity, continuing operation or enforcement of any incompatible primary legislation; and

(c)   does not affect the validity, continuing operation or enforcement of any incompatible subordinate legislation if (disregarding any possibility of revocation) primary legislation prevents removal of the incompatibility.

SCHEDULES

SCHEDULE 1
THE ARTICLES

PART I
THE CONVENTION RIGHTS AND FREEDOMS

Right to respect for private and family life

Article 8

1.   Everyone has the right to respect for his private and family life, his home and his correspondence.

2.   There shall be no interference by a public authority with the exercise of this right except such as is in accordance with the law and is necessary in a democratic society in the interests of national security, public safety or the economic well-being of the country, for the prevention of disorder or crime, for the protection of health or morals, or for the protection of the rights and freedoms of others.

PART II
THE FIRST PROTOCOL

Protection of property

Article 1

Every natural or legal person is entitled to the peaceful enjoyment of his possessions. No one shall be deprived of his possessions except in the public interest and subject to the conditions provided for by law and by the general principles of international law.

The preceding provisions shall not, however, in any way impair the right of a State to enforce such laws as it deems necessary to control the use of property in accordance with the general interest or to secure the payment of taxes or other contributions or penalties.

TRUSTEE DELEGATION ACT 1999
(1999, c. 15)

Attorney of trustee with beneficial interest in land

1.   **Exercise of trustee functions by attorney**

(1)   The donee of a power of attorney is not prevented from doing an act in relation to—
    (a)   land,
    (b)   capital proceeds of a conveyance of land, or
    (c)   income from land,
    by reason only that the act involves the exercise of a trustee function of the donor if, at the time when the act is done, the donor has a beneficial interest in the land, proceeds or income.

(2)   In this section—
    (a)   'conveyance' has the same meaning as in the Law of Property Act 1925, and
    (b)   references to a trustee function of the donor are to a function which the donor has as trustee (either alone or jointly with any other person or persons).

(3)   Subsection (1) above—
    (a)   applies only if and so far as a contrary intention is not expressed in the instrument creating the power of attorney, and
    (b)   has effect subject to the terms of that instrument.

(4)   The donor of the power of attorney—
    (a)   is liable for the acts or defaults of the donee in exercising any function by virtue of subsection (1) above in the same manner as if they were acts or defaults of the donor, but
    (b)   is not liable by reason only that a function is exercised by the donee by virtue of that subsection.

(5)   Subsections (1) and (4) above—
    (a)   apply only if and so far as a contrary intention is not expressed in the instrument (if any) creating the trust, and
    (b)   have effect subject to the terms of such an instrument.

(6)   The fact that it appears that, in dealing with any shares or stock, the donee of the power of attorney is exercising a function by virtue of subsection (1) above does not affect with any notice of any trust a person in whose books the shares are, or stock is, registered or inscribed.

(7)   In any case where (by way of exception to section 3(1) of the Trusts of Land and Appointment of Trustees Act 1996) the doctrine of conversion continues to operate, any person who, by reason of the continuing operation of that doctrine, has a beneficial interest in the proceeds of sale of land shall be treated for the purposes of this section and section 2 below as having a beneficial interest in the land.

(8)   The donee of a power of attorney is not to be regarded as exercising a trustee function by virtue of subsection (1) above if he is acting under a trustee delegation power; and for this purpose a trustee delegation power is a power of attorney given under—
    (a)   a statutory provision, or
    (b)   a provision of the instrument (if any) creating a trust,
    under which the donor of the power is expressly authorised to delegate the exercise of all or any of his trustee functions by power of attorney.

(9)   Subject to section 4(6) below, this section applies only to powers of attorney created after the commencement of this Act.

2.   **Evidence of beneficial interest**

(1)   This section applies where the interest of a purchaser depends on the donee of a power of attorney having power to do an act in relation to any property by virtue of section 1(1) above. In this subsection 'purchaser' has the same meaning as in Part I of the Law of Property Act 1925.

(2)   Where this section applies an appropriate statement is, in favour of the purchaser, conclusive evidence of the donor of the power having a beneficial interest in the property at the time of the doing of the act.

(3)   In this section 'an appropriate statement' means a signed statement made by the donee—
      (a)   when doing the act in question, or
      (b)   at any other time within the period of three months beginning with the day on which the act is done,
     that the donor has a beneficial interest in the property at the time of the donee doing the act.

(4)   If an appropriate statement is false, the donee is liable in the same way as he would be if the statement were contained in a statutory declaration.

Miscellaneous provisions about attorney acting for trustee

7.   Two-trustee rules

(1)   A requirement imposed by an enactment—
      (a)   that capital money be paid to, or dealt with as directed by, at least two trustees or that a valid receipt for capital money be given otherwise than by a sole trustee, or
      (b)   that, in order for an interest or power to be overreached, a conveyance or deed be executed by at least two trustees,
     is not satisfied by money being paid to or dealt with as directed by, or a receipt for money being given by, a relevant attorney or by a conveyance or deed being executed by such an attorney.

(2)   In this section 'relevant attorney' means a person (other than a trust corporation within the meaning of the Trustee Act 1925) who is acting either—
      (a)   both as a trustee and as attorney for one or more other trustees, or
      (b)   as attorney for two or more trustees,
     and who is not acting together with any other person or persons.

(3)   This section applies whether a relevant attorney is acting under a power created before or after the commencement of this Act (but in the case of such an attorney acting under an enduring power created before that commencement is without prejudice to any continuing application of section 3(3) of the Enduring Powers of Attorney Act 1985 to the enduring power after the commencement).

Authority of attorney to act in relation to land

10.   Extent of attorney's authority to act in relation to land

(1)   Where the donee of a power of attorney is authorised by the power to do an act of any description in relation to any land, his authority to do an act of that description at any time includes authority to do it with respect to any estate or interest in the land which is held at that time by the donor (whether alone or jointly with any other person or persons).

(2)   Subsection (1) above—
      (a)   applies only if and so far as a contrary intention is not expressed in the instrument creating the power of attorney, and
      (b)   has effect subject to the terms of that instrument.

(3)   This section applies only to powers of attorney created after the commencement of this Act.

Supplementary

11.   Interpretation

(1)   In this Act—
     'land' has the same meaning as in the Trustee Act 1925, and 'enduring power' has the same meaning as in the Enduring Powers of Attorney Act 1985.

(2)   References in this Act to the creation of a power of attorney are to the execution by the donor of the instrument creating it.

CONTRACTS (RIGHTS OF THIRD PARTIES) ACT 1999
(1999, c. 31)

1.   Right of third party to enforce contractual term

(1)   Subject to the provisions of this Act, a person who is not a party to a contract (a 'third party') may in his own right enforce a term of the contract if—

(a)   the contract expressly provides that he may, or

(b)   subject to subsection (2), the term purports to confer a benefit on him.

(2)   Subsection (1)(b) does not apply if on a proper construction of the contract it appears that the parties did not intend the term to be enforceable by the third party.

(3)   The third party must be expressly identified in the contract by name, as a member of a class or as answering a particular description but need not be in existence when the contract is entered into.

(4)   This section does not confer a right on a third party to enforce a term of a contract otherwise than subject to and in accordance with any other relevant terms of the contract.

(5)   For the purpose of exercising his right to enforce a term of the contract, there shall be available to the third party any remedy that would have been available to him in an action for breach of contract if he had been a party to the contract (and the rules relating to damages, injunctions, specific performance and other relief shall apply accordingly).

(6)   Where a term of a contract excludes or limits liability in relation to any matter references in this Act to the third party enforcing the term shall be construed as references to his availing himself of the exclusion or limitation.

(7)   In this Act, in relation to a term of a contract which is enforceable by a third party—

'the promisor' means the party to the contract against whom the term is enforceable by the third party, and

'the promisee' means the party to the contract by whom the term is enforceable against the promisor.

TRUSTEE ACT 2000
(2000, c. 29)

PART I
THE DUTY OF CARE

1.   The duty of care

(1)   Whenever the duty under this subsection applies to a trustee, he must exercise such care and skill as is reasonable in the circumstances, having regard in particular—

(a)   to any special knowledge or experience that he has or holds himself out as having, and

(b)   if he acts as trustee in the course of a business or profession, to any special knowledge or experience that it is reasonable to expect of a person acting in the course of that kind of business or profession.

(2)   In this Act the duty under subsection (1) is called 'the duty of care'.

2.   Application of duty of care

Schedule 1 makes provision about when the duty of care applies to a trustee.

PART II
INVESTMENT

3.   General power of investment

(1)   Subject to the provisions of this Part, a trustee may make any kind of investment that he could make if he were absolutely entitled to the assets of the trust.

(2)   In this Act the power under subsection (1) is called 'the general power of investment'.

(3)   The general power of investment does not permit a trustee to make investments in land other than in loans secured on land (but see also section 8).

(4)   A person invests in a loan secured on land if he has rights under any contract under which—

(a)   one person provides another with credit, and

(b)   the obligation of the borrower to repay is secured on land.

(5)   'Credit' includes any cash loan or other financial accommodation.

(6)   'Cash' includes money in any form.

4.   Standard investment criteria

(1)   In exercising any power of investment, whether arising under this Part or otherwise, a trustee must have regard to the standard investment criteria.

(2)   A trustee must from time to time review the investments of the trust and consider whether, having regard to the standard investment criteria, they should be varied.

(3)   The standard investment criteria, in relation to a trust, are—

    (a)   the suitability to the trust of investments of the same kind as any particular investment proposed to be made or retained and of that particular investment as an investment of that kind, and

    (b)   the need for diversification of investments of the trust, in so far as is appropriate to the circumstances of the trust.

5.   Advice

(1)   Before exercising any power of investment, whether arising under this Part or otherwise, a trustee must (unless the exception applies) obtain and consider proper advice about the way in which, having regard to the standard investment criteria, the power should be exercised.

(2)   When reviewing the investments of the trust, a trustee must (unless the exception applies) obtain and consider proper advice about whether, having regard to the standard investment criteria, the investments should be varied.

(3)   The exception is that a trustee need not obtain such advice if he reasonably concludes that in all the circumstances it is unnecessary or inappropriate to do so.

(4)   Proper advice is the advice of a person who is reasonably believed by the trustee to be qualified to give it by his ability in and practical experience of financial and other matters relating to the proposed investment.

6.   Restriction or exclusion of this Part etc.

(1)   The general power of investment is—

    (a)   in addition to powers conferred on trustees otherwise than by this Act, but

    (b)   subject to any restriction or exclusion imposed by the trust instrument or by any enactment or any provision of subordinate legislation.

(2)   For the purposes of this Act, an enactment or a provision of subordinate legislation is not to be regarded as being, or as being part of, a trust instrument.

(3)   In this Act 'subordinate legislation' has the same meaning as in the Interpretation Act 1978.

7.   Existing trusts

(1)   This Part applies in relation to trusts whether created before or after its commencement.

(2)   No provision relating to the powers of a trustee contained in a trust instrument made before 3rd August 1961 is to be treated (for the purposes of section 6(1)(b)) as restricting or excluding the general power of investment.

(3)   A provision contained in a trust instrument made before the commencement of this Part which—

    (a)   has effect under section 3(2) of the Trustee Investments Act 1961 as a power to invest under that Act, or

    (b)   confers power to invest under that Act,

is to be treated as conferring the general power of investment on a trustee.

PART III
ACQUISTION OF LAND

8.   Power to acquire freehold and leasehold land

(1)   A trustee may acquire freehold or leasehold land in the United Kingdom—

    (a)   as an investment,

    (b)   for occupation by a beneficiary, or

    (c)   for any other reason.

(2)   'Freehold or leasehold land' means—

    (a)   in relation to England and Wales, a legal estate in land.

    (b)   in relation to Scotland—

        (i)   the estate or interest of the proprietor of the dominium utile or, in the case of land not held on feudal tenure, the estate or interest of the owner, or

        (ii)   a tenancy, and

(c)   in relation to Northern Ireland, a legal estate in land, including land held under a fee farm grant.

(3)   For the purpose of exercising his functions as a trustee, a trustee who acquires land under this section has all the powers of an absolute owner in relation to the land.

9.   Restriction or exclusion of this Part etc.

The powers conferred by this Part are—

(a)   in addition to powers conferred on trustees otherwise than by this Part, but

(b)   subject to any restriction or exclusion imposed by the trust instrument or by any enactment or any provision of subordinate legislation.

10.   Existing trusts

(1)   This Part does not apply in relation to—

(a)   a trust of property which consists of or includes land which (despite section 2 of the Trusts of Land and Appointment of Trustees Act 1996) is settled land, or

(b)   a trust to which the Universities and College Estates Act 1925 applies.

(2)   Subject to subsection (1), this Part applies in relation to trusts whether created before or after its commencement.

PART IV
AGENTS, NOMINEES AND CUSTODIANS

Agents

11.   Power to employ agents

(1)   Subject to the provisions of this Part, the trustees of a trust may authorise any person to exercise any or all of their delegable functions as their agent.

(2)   In the case of a trust other than a charitable trust, the trustees' delegable functions consist of any function other than—

(a)   any function relating to whether or in what way any assets of the trust should be distributed,

(b)   any power to decide whether any fees or other payment due to be made out of the trust funds should be made out of income or capital.

(c)   any power to appoint a person to be a trustee of the trust, or

(d)   any power conferred by any other enactment or the trust instrument which permits the trustees to delegate any of their functions or to appoint a person to act as a nominee or custodian.

(3)   In the case of a charitable trust, the trustees' delegable functions are—

(a)   any function consisting of carrying out a decision that the trustees have taken;

(b)   any function relating to the investment of assets subject to the trust (including, in the case of land held as an investment, managing the land and creating or disposing of an interest in the land);

(c)   any function relating to the raising of funds for the trust otherwise than by means of profits of a trade which is an integral part of carrying out the trust's charitable purpose;

(d)   any other function prescribed by an order made by the Secretary of State.

(4)   For the purposes of subsection (3)(c) a trade is an integral part of carrying out a trust's charitable purpose if, whether carried on in the United Kingdom or elsewhere, the profits are applied solely to the purposes of the trust and either—

(a)   the trade is exercised in the course of the actual carrying out of a primary purpose of the trust, or

(b)   the work in connection with the trade is mainly carried out by beneficiaries of the trust.

(5)   The power to make an order under subsection (3)(d) is exercisable by statutory instrument which shall be subject to annulment in pursuance of a resolution of either House of Parliament.

12.   Persons who may act as agents

(1)   Subject to subsection (2), the persons whom the trustees may under section 11 authorise to exercise functions as their agent include one or more of their number.

(2)   The trustees may not authorise two (or more) persons to exercise the same function unless they are to exercise the function jointly.

(3)   The trustees may not under section 11 authorise a beneficiary to exercise any function as their agent (even if the beneficiary is also a trustee).

(4)   The trustees may under section 11 authorise a person to exercise functions as their agent even though he is also appointed to act as their nominee or custodian (whether under section 16, 17 or 18 or any other power).

13. Linked functions etc.

(1)   Subject to subsections (2) and (5), a person who is authorised under section 11 to exercise a function is (whatever the terms of the agency) subject to any specific duties or restrictions attached to the function.

For example, a person who is authorised under section 11 to exercise the general power of investment is subject to the duties under section 4 in relation to that power.

(2)   A person who is authorised under section 11 to exercise a power which is subject to a requirement to obtain advice is not subject to the requirement if he is the kind of person from whom it would have been proper for the trustees, in compliance with the requirement, to obtain advice.

(3)   Subsections (4) and (5) apply to a trust to which section 11(1) of the Trusts of Land and Appointment of Trustees Act 1996 (duties to consult beneficiaries and give effect to their wishes) applies.

(4)   The trustees may not under section 11 authorise a person to exercise any of their functions on terms that prevent them from complying with section 11(1) of the 1996 Act.

(5)   A person who is authorised under section 11 to exercise any function relating to land subject to the trust is not subject to section 11(1) of the 1996 Act.

14. Terms of agency

(1)   Subject to subsection (2) and sections 15(2) and 29 to 32, the trustees may authorise a person to exercise functions as their agent on such terms as to remuneration and other matters as they may determine.

(2)   The trustees may not authorise a person to exercise functions as their agent on any of the terms mentioned in subsection (3) unless it is reasonably necessary for them to do so.

(3)   The terms are—
       (a)   a term permitting the agent to appoint a substitute;
       (b)   a term restricting the liability of the agent or his substitute to the trustees or any beneficiary;
       (c)   a term permitting the agent to act in circumstances capable of giving rise to a conflict of interest.

15. Asset management: special restrictions

(1)   The trustees may not authorise a person to exercise any of their asset management functions as their agent except by an agreement which is in or evidenced in writing.

(2)   The trustees may not authorise a person to exercise any of their asset management functions as their agent unless—
       (a)   they have prepared a statement that gives guidance as to how the functions should be exercised ('a policy statement'), and
       (b)   the agreement under which the agent is to act includes a term to the effect that he will secure compliance with—
              (i)   the policy statement, or
              (ii)   if the policy statement is revised or replaced under section 22, the revised or replacement policy statement.

(3)   The trustees must formulate any guidance given in the policy statement with a view to ensuring that the functions will be exercised in the best interests of the trust.

(4)   The policy statement must be in or evidenced in writing.

(5)   The asset management functions of trustees are their functions relating to—
       (a)   the investment of assets subject to the trust.
       (b)   the acquisition of property which is to be subject to the trust, and
       (c)   managing property which is subject to the trust and disposing of, or creating or disposing of an interest in, such property.

Nominees and custodians

16.   Power to appoint nominees

(1)   Subject to the provisions of this Part, the trustees of a trust may—

    (a)   appoint a person to act as their nominee in relation to such of the assets of the trust as they determine (other than settled land), and

    (b)   take such steps as are necessary to secure that those assets are vested in a person so appointed.

(2)   An appointment under this section must be in or evidenced in writing.

(3)   This section does not apply to any trust having a custodian trustee or in relation to any assets vested in the official custodian for charities.

17.   Power to appoint custodians

(1)   Subject to the provisions of this Part, the trustees of a trust may appoint a person to act as a custodian in relation to such of the assets of the trust as they may determine.

(2)   For the purposes of this Act a person is a custodian in relation to assets if he undertakes the safe custody of the assets or of any documents or records concerning the assets.

(3)   An appointment under this section must be in or evidenced in writing.

(4)   This section does not apply to any trust having a custodian trustee or in relation to any assets vested in the official custodian for charities.

18.   Investment in bearer securities

(1)   If trustees retain or invest in securities payable to bearer, they must appoint a person to act as a custodian of the securities.

(2)   Subsection (1) does not apply if the trust instrument or any enactment or provision of subordinate legislation contains provision which (however expressed) permits the trustees to retain or invest in securities payable to bearer without appointing a person to act as a custodian.

(3)   An appointment under this section must be in or evidenced in writing.

(4)   This section does not apply to any trust having a custodian trustee or in relation to any securities vested in the official custodian for charities.

19.   Persons who may be appointed as nominees or custodians

(1)   A person may not be appointed under section 16, 17 or 18 as a nominee or custodian unless one of the relevant conditions is satisfied.

(2)   The relevant conditions are that—

    (a)   the person carries on a business which consists of or includes acting as a nominee or custodian;

    (b)   the person is a body corporate which is controlled by the trustees;

    (c)   the person is a body corporate recognised under section 9 of the Administration of Justice Act 1985.

(3)   The question whether a body corporate is controlled by trustees is to be determined in accordance with section 1124 of the Corporation Tax Act 2010.

(4)   The trustees of a charitable trust which is not an exempt charity must act in accordance with any guidance given by the Charity Commission concerning the selection of a person for appointment as a nominee or custodian under section 16, 17 or 18.

(5)   Subject to subsections (1) and (4), the persons whom the trustees may under section 16, 17 or 18 appoint as a nominee or custodian include—

    (a)   one of their number, if that one is a trust corporation, or

    (b)   two (or more) of their number, if they are to act as joint nominees or joint custodians.

(6)   The trustees may under section 16 appoint a person to act as their nominee even though he is also—

    (a)   appointed to act as their custodian (whether under section 17 or 18 or any other power), or

    (b)   authorised to exercise functions as their agent (whether under section 11 or any other power).

(7)   Likewise, the trustees may under section 17 or 18 appoint a person to act as their custodian even though he is also—

    (a)   appointed to act as their nominee (whether under section 16 or any other power), or

    (b)   authorised to exercise functions as their agent (whether under section 11 or any other power).

20.   Terms of appointment of nominees and custodians

(1)   Subject to subsection (2) and sections 29 to 32, the trustees may under section 16, 17 or 18 appoint a person to act as a nominee or custodian on such terms as to remuneration and other matters as they may determine.

(2)   The trustees may not under section 16, 17 or 18 appoint a person to act as a nominee or custodian on any of the terms mentioned in subsection (3) unless it is reasonably necessary for them to do so.

(3)   The terms are—
   (a)   a term permitting the nominee or custodian to appoint a substitute;
   (b)   a term restricting the liability of the nominee or custodian or his substitute to the trustees or to any beneficiary;
   (c)   a term permitting the nominee or custodian to act in circumstances capable of giving rise to a conflict of interest.

Review of and liability for agents, nominees and custodians etc.

21.   Application of sections 22 and 23

(1)   Sections 22 and 23 apply in a case where trustees have, under section 11, 16, 17 or 18—
   (a)   authorised a person to exercise functions as their agent, or
   (b)   appointed a person to act as a nominee or custodian.

(2)   Subject to subsection (3), sections 22 and 23 also apply in a case where trustees have, under any power conferred on them by the trust instrument or by any enactment or any provision of subordinate legislation
   (a)   authorised a person to exercise functions as their agent, or
   (b)   appointed a person to act as a nominee or custodian.

(3)   If the application of section 22 or 23 is inconsistent with the terms of the trust instrument or the enactment or provision of subordinate legislation, the section in question does not apply.

22.   Review of agents, nominees and custodians etc.

(1)   While the agent, nominee or custodian continues to act for the trust, the trustees—
   (a)   must keep under review the arrangements under which the agent, nominee or custodian acts and how those arrangements are being put into effect,
   (b)   if circumstances make it appropriate to do so, must consider whether there is a need to exercise any power of intervention that they have, and
   (c)   if they consider that there is a need to exercise such a power, must do so.

(2)   If the agent has been authorised to exercise asset management functions, the duty under subsection (1) includes, in particular—
   (a)   a duty to consider whether there is any need to revise or replace the policy statement made for the purposes of section 15,
   (b)   if they consider that there is a need to revise or replace the policy statement, a duty to do so, and
   (c)   a duty to assess whether the policy statement (as it has effect for the time being) is being complied with.

(3)   Subsections (3) and (4) of section 15 apply to the revision or replacement of a policy statement under this section as they apply to the making of a policy statement under that section.

(4)   'Power of intervention' includes—
   (a)   a power to give directions to the agent, nominee or custodian;
   (b)   a power to revoke the authorisation or appointment.

23.   Liability for agents, nominees and custodians etc.

(1)   A trustee is not liable for any act or default of the agent, nominee or custodian unless he has failed to comply with the duty of care applicable to him, under paragraph 3 of Schedule 1—
   (a)   when entering into the arrangements under which the person acts as agent, nominee or custodian, or
   (b)   when carrying out his duties under section 22.

(2)   If a trustee has agreed a term under which the agent, nominee or custodian is permitted to appoint a substitute, the trustee is not liable for any act or default of the substitute unless he has failed to comply with the duty of care applicable to him, under paragraph 3 of Schedule 1—
   (a)   when agreeing that term, or
   (b)   when carrying out his duties under section 22 in so far as they relate to the use of the substitute.

Supplementary

24.   Effect of trustees exceeding their powers

A failure by the trustees to act within the limits of the powers conferred by this Part—

   (a)   in authorising a person to exercise a function of theirs as an agent, or

   (b)   in appointing a person to act as a nominee or custodian, does not invalidate the authorisation or appointment.

25.   Sole trustees

(1)   Subject to subsection (2), this Part applies in relation to a trust having a sole trustee as it applies in relation to other trusts (and references in this Part to trustees — except in sections 12(1) and (3) and 19(5) — are to be read accordingly).

(2)   Section 18 does not impose a duty on a sole trustee if that trustee is a trust corporation.

26.   Restriction or exclusion of this Part etc.

The powers conferred by this Part are—

   (a)   in addition to powers conferred on trustees otherwise than by this Act, but

   (b)   subject to any restriction or exclusion imposed by the trust instrument or by any enactment or any provision of subordinate legislation.

27.   Existing trusts

This Part applies in relation to trusts whether created before or after its commencement.

PART V
REMUNERATION

28.   Trustee's entitlement to payment under trust instrument

(1)   Except to the extent (if any) to which the trust instrument makes inconsistent provision, subsections (2) to (4) apply to a trustee if—

   (a)   there is a provision in the trust instrument entitling him to receive payment out of trust funds in respect of services provided by him to or on behalf of the trust, and

   (b)   the trustee is a trust corporation or is acting in a professional capacity.

(2)   The trustee is to be treated as entitled under the trust instrument to receive payment in respect of services even if they are services which are capable of being provided by a lay trustee.

(3)   Subsection (2) applies to a trustee of a charitable trust who is not a trust corporation only—

   (a)   if he is not a sole trustee, and

   (b)   to the extent that a majority of the other trustees have agreed that It should apply to him.

(4)   Any payments to which the trustee is entitled in respect of services are to be treated as remuneration for services (and not as a gift) for the purposes of—

   (a)   section 15 of the Wills Act 1837 (gifts to an attesting witness to be void), and

   (b)   section 34(3) of the Administration of Estates Act 1925 (order in which estate to be paid out).

(5)   For the purposes of this Part, a trustee acts in a professional capacity if he acts in the course of a profession or business which consists of or includes the provision of services in connection with—

   (a)   the management or administration of trusts generally or a particular kind of trust, or

   (b)   any particular aspect of the management or administration of trusts generally or a particular kind of trust, and the services he provides to or on behalf of the trust fall within that description.

(6)   For the purposes of this Part, a person acts as a lay trustee if he—

   (a)   is not a trust corporation, and

   (b)   does not act in a professional capacity.

29.   Remuneration of certain trustees

(1)   Subject to subsection (5), a trustee who—

   (a)   is a trust corporation, but

        (b)   is not a trustee of a charitable trust, is entitled to receive reasonable remuneration out of the trust funds for any services that the trust corporation provides to or on behalf of the trust.

  (2)   Subject to subsection (5), a trustee who—
        (a)   acts in a professional capacity, but
        (b)   is not a trust corporation, a trustee of a charitable trust or a sole trustee, is entitled to receive reasonable remuneration out of the trust funds for any services that he provides to or on behalf of the trust if each other trustee has agreed in writing that he may be remunerated for the services.

  (3)   'Reasonable remuneration' means, in relation to the provision of services by a trustee, such remuneration as is reasonable in the circumstances for the provision of those services to or on behalf of that trust by that trustee and for the purposes of subsection (1) includes, in relation to the provision of services by a trustee who is a deposit taker and provides the services in that capacity, the deposit taker's reasonable charges for the provision of such services.

  (3A) In subsection (3), 'deposit taker' means—
        (a)   a person who has permission under Part 4A of the Financial Services and Markets Act 2000 to accept deposits, or
        (b)   an EEA firm of the kind mentioned in paragraph 5(b) of Schedule 3 to that Act which has permission under paragraph 15 of that Schedule (as a result of qualifying for authorisation under paragraph 12(1) of that Schedule) to accept deposits.

  (3B) A reference in subsection (3A) to a person or firm with permission to accept deposits does not include a person or firm with permission to do so only for the purposes of, or in the course of, carrying on another regulated activity in accordance with that permission.

  (3C) Subsections (3A) and (3B) must be read with—
        (a)   section 22 of the Financial Services and Markets Act 2000,
        (b)   any relevant order under that section, and
        (c)   Schedule 2 to that Act.

  (4)   A trustee is entitled to remuneration under this section even if the services in question are capable of being provided by a lay trustee.

  (5)   A trustee is not entitled to remuneration under this section if any provision about his entitlement to remuneration has been made—
        (a)   by the trust instrument, or
        (b)   by any enactment or any provision of subordinate legislation.

  (6)   This section applies to a trustee who has been authorised under a power conferred by Part IV or the trust instrument—
        (a)   to exercise functions as an agent of the trustees, or
        (b)   to act as a nominee or custodian, as it applies to any other trustee.

30.   Remuneration of trustees of charitable trusts

  (1)   The Secretary of State may by regulations make provision for the remuneration of trustees of charitable trusts who are trust corporations or act in a professional capacity.

  (2)   The power under subsection (1) includes power to make provision for the remuneration of a trustee who has been authorised under a power conferred by Part IV or any other enactment or any provision of subordinate legislation, or by the trust instrument—
        (a)   to exercise functions as an agent of the trustees, or
        (b)   to act as a nominee or custodian.

  (3)   Regulations under this section may—
        (a)   make different provision for different cases:
        (b)   contain such supplemental, incidental, consequential and transitional provision as the Secretary of State considers appropriate.

  (4)   The power to make regulations under this section is exercisable by statutory instrument, but no such instrument shall be made unless a draft of it has been laid before Parliament and approved by a resolution of each House of Parliament.

31.   Trustees' expenses

  (1)   A trustee—
        (a)   is entitled to be reimbursed from the trust funds, or
        (b)   may pay out of the trust funds,
    expenses properly incurred by him when acting on behalf of the trust.

(2)   This section applies to a trustee who has been authorised under a power conferred by Part IV or any other enactment or any provision of subordinate legislation, or by the trust instrument—

    (a)   to exercise functions as an agent of the trustees, or

    (b)   to act as a nominee or custodian, as it applies to any other trustee.

32.   Remuneration and expenses of agents, nominees and custodians

(1)   This section applies if, under a power conferred by Part IV or any other enactment or any provision of subordinate legislation, or by the trust instrument, a person other than a trustee has been—

    (a)   authorised to exercise functions as an agent of the trustees, or

    (b)   appointed to act as a nominee or custodian.

(2)   The trustees may remunerate the agent, nominee or custodian out of the trust funds for services if—

    (a)   he is engaged on terms entitling him to be remunerated for those services, and

    (b)   the amount does not exceed such remuneration as is reasonable in the circumstances for the provision of those services by him to or on behalf of that trust.

(3)   The trustees may reimburse the agent, nominee or custodian out of the trust funds for any expenses properly incurred by him in exercising functions as an agent, nominee or custodian.

33.   Application

(1)   Subject to subsection (2), sections 28, 29, 31 and 32 apply in relation to services provided to or on behalf of, or (as the case may be) expenses incurred on or after their commencement on behalf of, trusts whenever created.

(2)   Nothing in section 28 or 29 is to be treated as affecting the operation of—

    (a)   section 15 of the Wills Act 1837, or

    (b)   section 34(3) of the Administration of Estates Act 1925, in relation to any death occurring before the commencement of section 28 or (as the case may be) section 29.

PART VI
MISCELLANEOUS AND SUPPLEMENTARY

35.   Personal representatives

(1)   Subject to the following provisions of this section, this Act applies in relation to a personal representative administering an estate according to the law as it applies to a trustee carrying out a trust for beneficiaries.

(2)   For this purpose this Act is to be read with the appropriate modifications and in particular—

    (a)   references to the trust instrument are to be read as references to the will,

    (b)   references to a beneficiary or to beneficiaries, apart from the reference to a beneficiary in section 8(1)(b), are to be read as references to a person or the persons interested in the due administration of the estate, and

    (c)   the reference to a beneficiary in section 8(1)(b) is to be read as a reference to a person who under the will of the deceased or under the law relating to intestacy is beneficially interested in the estate.

(3)   Remuneration to which a personal representative is entitled under section 28 or 29 is to be treated as an administration expense for the purposes of—

    (a)   section 34(3) of the Administration of Estates Act 1925 (order in which estate to be paid out), and

    (b)   any provision giving reasonable administration expenses priority over the preferential debts listed in Schedule 6 to the Insolvency Act 1986.

(4)   Nothing in subsection (3) is to be treated as affecting the operation of the provisions mentioned in paragraphs (a) and (b) of that subsection in relation to any death occurring before the commencement of this section.

36.   Pension schemes

(1)   In this section 'pension scheme' means an occupational pension scheme (within the meaning of the Pension Schemes Act 1993) established under a trust and subject to the law of England and Wales.

(2) Part I does not apply in so far as it imposes a duty of care in relation to —
  (a) the functions described in paragraphs 1 and 2 of Schedule 1, or
  (b) the functions described in paragraph 3 of that Schedule to the extent that they relate to trustees —
    (i) authorising a person to exercise their functions with respect to investment, or
    (ii) appointing a person to act as their nominee or custodian.
(3) Nothing in Part II or III applies to the trustees of any pension scheme.
(4) Part IV applies to the trustees of a pension scheme subject to the restrictions in subsections (5) to (8).
(5) The trustees of a pension scheme may not under Part IV authorise any person to exercise any functions relating to investment as their agent.
(6) The trustees of a pension scheme may not under Part IV authorise a person who is —
  (a) an employer in relation to the scheme, or
  (b) connected with or an associate of such an employer, to exercise any of their functions as their agent.
(7) For the purposes of subsection (6) —
  (a) 'employer', in relation to a scheme, has the same meaning as in the Pensions Act 1995;
  (b) sections 249 and 435 of the Insolvency Act 1986 apply for the purpose of determining whether a person is connected with or an associate of an employer.

39. Interpretation
(1) In this Act —
  'asset' includes any right or interest;
  'charitable trust' means a trust under which property is held for charitable purposes and 'charitable purposes' has the meaning given by section 11 of the Charities Act 2011;
  'custodian trustee' has the same meaning as in the Public Trustee Act 1906;
  'enactment' includes any provision of a Measure of the Church Assembly or of the General Synod of the Church of England;
  'exempt charity' has the same meaning as in the Charities Act 2011;
  'functions' includes powers and duties;
  'legal mortgage' has the same meaning as in the Law of Property Act 1925;
  'personal representative' has the same meaning as in the Trustee Act 1925;
  'settled land' has the same meaning as in the Settled Land Act 1925;
  'trust corporation' has the same meaning as in the Trustee Act 1925;
  'trust funds' means income or capital funds of the trust.
  ...

LAND REGISTRATION ACT 2002
(2002, c. 9)

PART 1 PRELIMINARY

1. Register of title
(1) There is to continue to be a register of title kept by the registrar.
(2) Rules may make provision about how the register is to be kept and may, in particular, make provision about —
  (a) the information to be included in the register,
  (b) the form in which information included in the register is to be kept, and
  (c) the arrangement of that information.

2. Scope of title registration
This Act makes provision about the registration of title to —
(a) unregistered legal estates which are interests of any of the following kinds —
  (i) an estate in land,
  (ii) a rentcharge,
  (iii) a franchise,
  (iv) a profit a prendre in gross, and
  (v) any other interest or charge which subsists for the benefit of, or is a charge on, an interest the title to which is registered; and
(b) interests capable of subsisting at law which are created by a disposition of an interest the title to which is registered.

PART 2
FIRST REGISTRATION OF TITLE

CHAPTER 1
FIRST REGISTRATION

Voluntary registration

3. When title may be registered

(1) This section applies to any unregistered legal estate which is an interest of any of the following kinds—
  (a) an estate in land,
  (b) a rentcharge,
  (c) a franchise, and
  (d) a profit a prendre in gross.

(2) Subject to the following provisions, a person may apply to the registrar to be registered as the proprietor of an unregistered legal estate to which this section applies if—
  (a) the estate is vested in him, or
  (b) he is entitled to require the estate to be vested in him.

(3) Subject to subsection (4), an application under subsection (2) in respect of a leasehold estate may only be made if the estate was granted for a term of which more than seven years are unexpired.

(4) In the case of an estate in land, subsection (3) does not apply if the right to possession under the lease is discontinuous.

(4A) A person may not make an application under subsection (2) in respect of a leasehold estate in land under a relevant social housing tenancy.

(5) A person may not make an application under subsection (2)(a) in respect of a leasehold estate vested in him as a mortgagee where there is a subsisting right of redemption.

(6) A person may not make an application under subsection (2)(b) if his entitlement is as a person who has contracted to buy under a contract.

(7) If a person holds in the same right both—
  (a) a lease in possession, and
  (b) a lease to take effect in possession on, or within a month of, the end of the lease in possession, then, to the extent that they relate to the same land, they are to be treated for the purposes of this section as creating one continuous term.

Compulsory registration

4. When title must be registered

(1) The requirement of registration applies on the occurrence of any of the following events—
  (a) the transfer of a qualifying estate—
    (i) for valuable or other consideration, by way of gift or in pursuance of an order of any court,
    (ii) by means of an assent (including a vesting assent); or
    (iii) giving effect to a partition of land subject to a trust of land;
  (aa) the transfer of a qualifying estate—
    (i) by a deed that appoints, or by virtue of section 334 of the Charities Act 2011 has effect as if it appointed, a new trustee or is made in consequence of the appointment of a new trustee, or
    (ii) by a vesting order under section 44 of the Trustee Act 1925 that is consequential on the appointment of a new trustee;
  (b) the transfer of an unregistered legal estate in land in circumstances where section 171A of the Housing Act 1985 applies (disposal by landlord which leads to a person no longer being a secure tenant);
  (c) the grant out of a qualifying estate of an estate in land—
    (i) for a term of years absolute of more than seven years from the date of the grant, and
    (ii) for valuable or other consideration, by way of gift or in pursuance of an order of any court;

     (d)   the grant out of a qualifying estate of an estate in land for a term of years absolute to take effect in possession after the end of the period of three months beginning with the date of the grant;

     (e)   the grant of a lease in pursuance of Part 5 of the Housing Act 1985 (the right to buy) out of an unregistered legal estate in land;

     (f)   the grant of a lease out of an unregistered legal estate in land in such circumstances as are mentioned in paragraph (b);

     (g)   the creation of a protected first legal mortgage of a qualifying estate.

(2)   For the purposes of subsection (1), a qualifying estate is an unregistered legal estate which is—

     (a)   a freehold estate in land, or

     (b)   a leasehold estate in land for a term which, at the time of the transfer, grant or creation, has more than seven years to run.

(3)   In subsection (1)(a), the reference to transfer does not include transfer by operation of law.

(4)   Subsection (1)(a) does not apply to—

     (a)   the assignment of a mortgage term, or

     (b)   the assignment or surrender of a lease to the owner of the immediate reversion where the term is to merge in that reversion.

(5)   Subsection (1)(c) does not apply to the grant of an estate to a person as a mortgagee.

(5A) Subsection (1) does not apply to the transfer or grant of a leasehold estate in land under a relevant social housing tenancy.

(6)   For the purposes of subsection (1)(a) and (c), if the estate transferred or granted has a negative value, it is to be regarded as transferred or granted for valuable or other consideration.

(7)   In subsection (1)(a) and (c), references to transfer or grant by way of gift include transfer or grant for the purpose of—

     (a)   constituting a trust under which the settlor does not retain the whole of the beneficial interest, or

     (b)   uniting the bare legal title and the beneficial interest in property held under a trust under which the settlor did not, on constitution, retain the whole of the beneficial interest.

(8)   For the purposes of subsection (1)(g)—

     (a)   a legal mortgage is protected if it takes effect on its creation as a mortgage to be protected by the deposit of documents relating to the mortgaged estate, and

     (b)   a first legal mortgage is one which, on its creation, ranks in priority ahead of any other mortgages then affecting the mortgaged estate.

(9)   In this section—

'land' does not include mines and minerals held apart from the surface; 'vesting assent' has the same meaning as in the Settled Land Act 1925.

5.   Power to extend section 4

(1)   The Secretary of State may by order—

     (a)   amend section 4 so as to add to the events on the occurrence of which the requirement of registration applies such relevant event as he may specify in the order, and

     (b)   make such consequential amendments of any provision of, or having effect under, any Act as he thinks appropriate.

(2)   For the purposes of subsection (1)(a), a relevant event is an event relating to an unregistered legal estate which is an interest of any of the following kinds—

     (a)   an estate in land,

     (b)   a rentcharge,

     (c)   a franchise, and

     (d)   a profit a prendre in gross.

(3)   The power conferred by subsection (1) may not be exercised so as to require the title to an estate granted to a person as a mortgagee to be registered.

(4)   Before making an order under this section the Secretary of State must consult such persons as he considers appropriate.

6.   Duty to apply for registration of title

(1)   If the requirement of registration applies, the responsible estate owner, or his successor in title, must, before the end of the period for registration, apply to the registrar to be registered as the proprietor of the registrable estate.

(2) If the requirement of registration applies because of section 4(1)(g)—
    (a) the registrable estate is the estate charged by the mortgage, and
    (b) the responsible estate owner is the owner of that estate.

(3) If the requirement of registration applies otherwise than because of section 4(1)(g)—
    (a) the registrable estate is the estate which is transferred or granted, and
    (b) the responsible estate owner is the transferee or grantee of that estate.

(4) The period for registration is 2 months beginning with the date on which the relevant event occurs, or such longer period as the registrar may provide under subsection (5).

(5) If on the application of any interested person the registrar is satisfied that there is good reason for doing so, he may by order provide that the period for registration ends on such later date as he may specify in the order.

(6) Rules may make provision enabling the mortgagee under any mortgage falling within section 4(1)(g) to require the estate charged by the mortgage to be registered whether or not the mortgagor consents.

7. Effect of non-compliance with section 6

(1) If the requirement of registration is not complied with, the transfer, grant or creation becomes void as regards the transfer, grant or creation of a legal estate.

(2) On the application of subsection (1)—
    (a) in a case falling within section 4(1)(a) or (b), the title to the legal estate reverts to the transferor who holds it on a bare trust for the transferee,
    (aa) in a case falling within section 4(1)(aa), the title to the legal estate reverts to the person in whom it was vested immediately before the transfer, and
    (b) in a case falling within section 4(1)(c) to (g), the grant or creation has effect as a contract made for valuable consideration to grant or create the legal estate concerned.

(3) If an order under section 6(5) is made in a case where subsection (1) has already applied, that application of the subsection is to be treated as not having occurred.

(4) The possibility of reverter under subsection (1) is to be disregarded for the purposes of determining whether a fee simple is a fee simple absolute.

8. Liability for making good void transfers etc.

If a legal estate is retransferred, regranted or recreated because of a failure to comply with the requirement of registration, the transferee, grantee or, as the case may be, the mortgagor—
    (a) is liable to the other party for all the proper costs of and incidental to the retransfer, regrant or recreation of the legal estate, and
    (b) is liable to indemnify the other party in respect of any other liability reasonably incurred by him because of the failure to comply with the requirement of registration.

Classes of title

9. Titles to freehold estates

(1) In the case of an application for registration under this Chapter of a freehold estate, the classes of title with which the applicant may be registered as proprietor are—
    (a) absolute title,
    (b) qualified title, and
    (c) possessory title; and the following provisions deal with when each of the classes of title is available.

(2) A person may be registered with absolute title if the registrar is of the opinion that the person's title to the estate is such as a willing buyer could properly be advised by a competent professional adviser to accept.

(3) In applying subsection (2), the registrar may disregard the fact that a person's title appears to him to be open to objection if he is of the opinion that the defect will not cause the holding under the title to be disturbed.

(4) A person may be registered with qualified title if the registrar is of the opinion that the person's title to the estate has been established only for a limited period or subject to certain reservations which cannot be disregarded under subsection (3).

(5) A person may be registered with possessory title if the registrar is of the opinion—
    (a) that the person is in actual possession of the land, or in receipt of the rents and profits of the land, by virtue of the estate, and
    (b) that there is no other class of title with which he may be registered.

10.   Titles to leasehold estates

(1)   In the case of an application for registration under this Chapter of a leasehold estate, the classes of title with which the applicant may be registered as proprietor are—

    (a)   absolute title,

    (b)   good leasehold title,

    (c)   qualified title, and

    (d)   possessory title; and the following provisions deal with when each of the classes of title is available.

(2)   A person may be registered with absolute title if—

    (a)   the registrar is of the opinion that the person's title to the estate is such as a willing buyer could properly be advised by a competent professional adviser to accept, and

    (b)   the registrar approves the lessor's title to grant the lease.

(3)   A person may be registered with good leasehold title if the registrar is of the opinion that the person's title to the estate is such as a willing buyer could properly be advised by a competent professional adviser to accept.

(4)   In applying subsection (2) or (3), the registrar may disregard the fact that a person's title appears to him to be open to objection if he is of the opinion that the defect will not cause the holding under the title to be disturbed.

(5)   A person may be registered with qualified title if the registrar is of the opinion that the person's title to the estate, or the lessor's title to the reversion, has been established only for a limited period or subject to certain reservations which cannot be disregarded under subsection (4).

(6)   A person may be registered with possessory title if the registrar is of the opinion—

    (a)   that the person is in actual possession of the land, or in receipt of the rents and profits of the land, by virtue of the estate, and

    (b)   that there is no other class of title with which he may be registered.

Effect of first registration

11.   Freehold estates

(1)   This section is concerned with the registration of a person under this Chapter as the proprietor of a freehold estate.

(2)   Registration with absolute title has the effect described in subsections (3) to (5).

(3)   The estate is vested in the proprietor together with all interests subsisting for the benefit of the estate.

(4)   The estate is vested in the proprietor subject only to the following interests affecting the estate at the time of registration—

    (a)   interests which are the subject of an entry in the register in relation to the estate,

    (b)   unregistered interests which fall within any of the paragraphs of Schedule 1, and

    (c)   interests acquired under the Limitation Act 1980 of which the proprietor has notice.

(5)   If the proprietor is not entitled to the estate for his own benefit, or not entitled solely for his own benefit, then, as between himself and the persons beneficially entitled to the estate, the estate is vested in him subject to such of their interests as he has notice of.

(6)   Registration with qualified title has the same effect as registration with absolute title, except that it does not affect the enforcement of any estate, right or interest which appears from the register to be excepted from the effect of registration.

(7)   Registration with possessory title has the same effect as registration with absolute title, except that it does not affect the enforcement of any estate, right or interest adverse to, or in derogation of, the proprietor's title subsisting at the time of registration or then capable of arising.

12.   Leasehold estates

(1)   This section is concerned with the registration of a person under this Chapter as the proprietor of a leasehold estate.

(2)   Registration with absolute title has the effect described in subsections (3) to (5).

(3)   The estate is vested in the proprietor together with all interests subsisting for the benefit of the estate.

(4)   The estate is vested subject only to the following interests affecting the estate at the time of registration—
    (a)   implied and express covenants, obligations and liabilities incident to the estate,
    (b)   interests which are the subject of an entry in the register in relation to the estate,
    (c)   unregistered interests which fall within any of the paragraphs of Schedule 1, and
    (d)   interests acquired under the Limitation Act 1980 of which the proprietor has notice.

(5)   If the proprietor is not entitled to the estate for his own benefit, or not entitled solely for his own benefit, then, as between himself and the persons beneficially entitled to the estate, the estate is vested in him subject to such of their interests as he has notice of.

(6)   Registration with good leasehold title has the same effect as registration with absolute title, except that it does not affect the enforcement of any estate, right or interest affecting, or in derogation of, the title of the lessor to grant the lease.

(7)   Registration with qualified title has the same effect as registration with absolute title except that it does not affect the enforcement of any estate, right or interest which appears from the register to be excepted from the effect of registration.

(8)   Registration with possessory title has the same effect as registration with absolute title, except that it does not affect the enforcement of any estate, right or interest adverse to, or in derogation of, the proprietor's title subsisting at the time of registration or then capable of arising.

Dependent estates

13.   Appurtenant rights and charges

Rules may—
(a)   make provision for the registration of the proprietor of a registered estate as the proprietor of an unregistered legal estate which subsists for the benefit of the registered estate;
(b)   make provision for the registration of a person as the proprietor of an unregistered legal estate which is a charge on a registered estate.

Supplementary

14.   Rules about first registration

Rules may—
(a)   make provision about the making of applications for registration under this Chapter;
(b)   make provision about the functions of the registrar following the making of such an application, including provision about—
    (i)   the examination of title, and
    (ii)   the entries to be made in the register where such an application is approved;
(c)   make provision about the effect of any entry made in the register in pursuance of such an application.

CHAPTER 2
CAUTIONS AGAINST FIRST REGISTRATION

15.   Right to lodge

(1)   A person may lodge a caution against the registration of title to an unregistered legal estate if he claims to be—
    (a)   the owner of a qualifying estate, or
    (b)   entitled to an interest affecting a qualifying estate.

(2)   For the purposes of subsection (1), a qualifying estate is a legal estate which—
    (a)   relates to land to which the caution relates, and
    (b)   is an interest of any of the following kinds—
        (i)   an estate in land,
        (II)   a rentcharge,
        (iii)   a franchise, and
        (iv)   a profit a prendre in gross.

(3)   ...

(4)   The right under subsection (1) is exercisable by application to the registrar.

16.   Effect

(1)   Where an application for registration under this Part relates to a legal estate which is the subject of a caution against first registration, the registrar must give the cautioner notice of the application and of his right to object to it.

(2)   The registrar may not determine an application to which subsection (1) applies before the end of such period as rules may provide, unless the cautioner has exercised his right to object to the application or given the registrar notice that he does not intend to do so.

(3)   Except as provided by this section, a caution against first registration has no effect and, in particular, has no effect on the validity or priority of any interest of the cautioner in the legal estate to which the caution relates.

(4)   For the purposes of subsection (1), notice given by a person acting on behalf of an applicant for registration under this Part is to be treated as given by the registrar if—

(a)   the person is of a description provided by rules, and

(b)   notice is given in such circumstances as rules may provide.

17.   Withdrawal

The cautioner may withdraw a caution against first registration by application to the registrar.

18.   Cancellation

(1)   A person may apply to the registrar for cancellation of a caution against first registration if he is—

(a)   the owner of the legal estate to which the caution relates, or

(b)   a person of such other description as rules may provide.

(2)   Subject to rules, no application under subsection (1)(a) may be made by a person who—

(a)   consented in such manner as rules may provide to the lodging of the caution, or

(b)   derives title to the legal estate by operation of law from a person who did so.

(3)   Where an application is made under subsection (1), the registrar must give the cautioner notice of the application and of the effect of subsection (4).

(4)   If the cautioner does not exercise his right to object to the application before the end of such period as rules may provide, the registrar must cancel the caution.

19.   Cautions register

(1)   The registrar must keep a register of cautions against first registration.

(2)   Rules may make provision about how the cautions register is to be kept and may, in particular, make provision about—

(a)   the information to be included in the register,

(b)   the form in which information included in the register is to be kept, and

(c)   the arrangement of that information.

20.   Alteration of register by court

(1)   The court may make an order for alteration of the cautions register for the purpose of—

(a)   correcting a mistake, or

(b)   bringing the register up to date.

(2)   An order under subsection (1) has effect when served on the registrar to impose a duty on him to give effect to it.

(3)   Rules may make provision about—

(a)   the circumstances in which there is a duty to exercise the power under subsection (1),

(b)   the form of an order under that subsection, and

(c)   service of such an order.

21.   Alteration of register by registrar

(1)   The registrar may alter the cautions register for the purpose of—

(a)   correcting a mistake, or

(b)   bringing the register up to date.

(2)   Rules may make provision about—

(a)   the circumstances in which there is a duty to exercise the power under subsection (1),

(b)   how the cautions register is to be altered in exercise of that power,

(c)   applications for the exercise of that power, and

(d)   procedure in relation to the exercise of that power, whether on application or otherwise.

(3)   Where an alteration is made under this section, the registrar may pay such amount as he thinks fit in respect of any costs reasonably incurred by a person in connection with the alteration.

22.   Supplementary
In this Chapter, 'the cautioner', in relation to a caution against first registration, means the person who lodged the caution, or such other person as rules may provide.

PART 3
DISPOSITIONS OF REGISTERED LAND

Powers of disposition

23.   Owner's powers
(1)   Owner's powers in relation to a registered estate consist of—
    (a)   power to make a disposition of any kind permitted by the general law in relation to an interest of that description, other than a mortgage by demise or sub-demise, and
    (b)   power to charge the estate at law with the payment of money.
(2)   Owner's powers in relation to a registered charge consist of—
    (a)   power to make a disposition of any kind permitted by the general law in relation to an interest of that description, other than a legal sub-mortgage, and
    (b)   power to charge at law with the payment of money indebtedness secured by the registered charge.
(3)   In subsection (2)(a), 'legal sub-mortgage' means—
    (a)   a transfer by way of mortgage,
    (b)   a sub-mortgage by sub-demise, and
    (c)   a charge by way of legal mortgage.

24.   Right to exercise owner's powers
A person is entitled to exercise owner's powers in relation to a registered estate or charge if he is—
    (a)   the registered proprietor, or
    (b)   entitled to be registered as the proprietor.

25.   Mode of exercise
(1)   A registrable disposition of a registered estate or charge only has effect if it complies with such requirements as to form and content as rules may provide.
(2)   Rules may apply subsection (1) to any other kind of disposition which depends for its effect on registration.

26.   Protection of disponees
(1)   Subject to subsection (2), a person's right to exercise owner's powers in relation to a registered estate or charge is to be taken to be free from any limitation affecting the validity of a disposition.
(2)   Subsection (1) does not apply to a limitation—
    (a)   reflected by an entry in the register, or
    (b)   imposed by, or under, this Act.
(3)   This section has effect only for the purpose of preventing the title of a disponee being questioned (and so does not affect the lawfulness of a disposition).

Registrable dispositions

27.   Dispositions required to be registered
(1)   If a disposition of a registered estate or registered charge is required to be completed by registration, it does not operate at law until the relevant registration requirements are met.
(2)   In the case of a registered estate, the following are the dispositions which are required to be completed by registration—
    (a)   a transfer,

    (b)   where the registered estate is an estate in land, the grant of a term of years absolute—

        (i)   for a term of more than seven years from the date of the grant,

        (ii)   to take effect in possession after the end of the period of three months beginning with the date of the grant,

        (iii)   under which the right to possession is discontinuous,

        (iv)   in pursuance of Part 5 of the Housing Act 1985 (the right to buy), or

        (v)   in circumstances where section 171A of that Act applies (disposal by landlord which leads to a person no longer being a secure tenant),

    (c)   where the registered estate is a franchise or manor, the grant of a lease,

    (d)   the express grant or reservation of an interest of a kind falling within section 1(2) (a) of the Law of Property Act 1925, other than one which is capable of being registered under Part 1 of the Commons Act 2006,

    (e)   the express grant or reservation of an interest of a kind falling within section 1(2)(b) or (e) of the Law of Property Act 1925, and

    (f)   the grant of a legal charge.

(3)   In the case of a registered charge, the following are the dispositions which are required to be completed by registration—

    (a)   a transfer, and

    (b)   the grant of a sub-charge.

(4)   Schedule 2 to this Act (which deals with the relevant registration requirements) has effect.

(5)   This section applies to dispositions by operation of law as it applies to other dispositions, but with the exception of the following—

    (a)   a transfer on the death or bankruptcy of an individual proprietor,

    (b)   a transfer on the dissolution of a corporate proprietor, and

    (c)   the creation of a legal charge which is a local land charge.

(5A) This section does not apply to—

    (a)   the grant of a term of years absolute under a relevant social housing tenancy, or

    (b)   the express grant of an interest falling within section 1(2) of the Law of Property Act 1925, where the interest is created for the benefit of a leasehold estate in land under a relevant social housing tenancy.

(6)   Rules may make provision about applications to the registrar for the purpose of meeting registration requirements under this section.

(7)   In subsection (2)(d), the reference to express grant does not include grant as a result of the operation of section 62 of the Law of Property Act 1925.

Effect of dispositions on priority

28.   Basic rule

(1)   Except as provided by sections 29 and 30, the priority of an interest affecting a registered estate or charge is not affected by a disposition of the estate or charge.

(2)   It makes no difference for the purposes of this section whether the interest or disposition is registered.

29.   Effect of registered dispositions: estates

(1)   If a registrable disposition of a registered estate is made for valuable consideration, completion of the disposition by registration has the effect of postponing to the interest under the disposition any interest affecting the estate immediately before the disposition whose priority is not protected at the time of registration.

(2)   For the purposes of subsection (1), the priority of an interest is protected—

    (a)   in any case, if the interest—

        (i)   is a registered charge or the subject of a notice in the register,

        (ii)   falls within any of the paragraphs of Schedule 3, or

        (iii)   appears from the register to be excepted from the effect of registration, and

    (b)   in the case of a disposition of a leasehold estate, if the burden of the interest is incident to the estate.

(3)   Subsection (2)(a)(ii) does not apply to an interest which has been the subject of a notice in the register at any time since the coming into force of this section.

(4) Where the grant of a leasehold estate in land out of a registered estate does not involve a registrable disposition, this section has effect as if—
- (a) the grant involved such a disposition, and
- (b) the disposition were registered at the time of the grant.

30. Effect of registered dispositions: charges

(1) If a registrable disposition of a registered charge is made for valuable consideration, completion of the disposition by registration has the effect of postponing to the interest under the disposition any interest affecting the charge immediately before the disposition whose priority is not protected at the time of registration.

(2) For the purposes of subsection (1), the priority of an interest is protected—
- (a) in any case, if the interest—
  - (i) is a registered charge or the subject of a notice in the register,
  - (ii) falls within any of the paragraphs of Schedule 3, or
  - (iii) appears from the register to be excepted from the effect of registration, and
- (b) in the case of a disposition of a charge which relates to a leasehold estate, if the burden of the interest is incident to the estate.

(3) Subsection (2)(a)(ii) does not apply to an interest which has been the subject of a notice in the register at any time since the coming into force of this section.

31. Inland Revenue charges

The effect of a disposition of a registered estate or charge on a charge under section 237 of the Inheritance Tax Act 1984 (charge for unpaid tax) is to be determined, not in accordance with sections 28 to 30 above, but in accordance with sections 237(6) and 238 of that Act (under which a purchaser in good faith for money or money's worth takes free from the charge in the absence of registration).

PART 4
NOTICES AND RESTRICTIONS

Notices

32. Nature and effect

(1) A notice is an entry in the register in respect of the burden of an interest affecting a registered estate or charge.

(2) The entry of a notice is to be made in relation to the registered estate or charge affected by the interest concerned.

(3) The fact that an interest is the subject of a notice does not necessarily mean that the interest is valid, but does mean that the priority of the interest, if valid, is protected for the purposes of sections 29 and 30.

33. Excluded Interests

No notice may be entered in the register in respect of any of the following—
- (a) an interest under—
  - (i) a trust of land, or
  - (ii) a settlement under the Settled Land Act 1925,
- (b) a leasehold estate in land which—
  - (i) is granted for a term of years of three years or less from the date of the grant, and
  - (ii) is not required to be registered,
- (ba) an interest under a relevant social housing tenancy,
- (c) a restrictive covenant made between a lessor and lessee, so far as relating to the demised premises,
- (d) an interest which is capable of being registered under Part 1 of the Commons Act 2006, and
- (e) an interest in any coal or coal mine, the rights attached to any such interest and the rights of any person under section 38, 49 or 51 of the Coal Industry Act 1994.

34. Entry on application

(1) A person who claims to be entitled to the benefit of an interest affecting a registered estate or charge may, if the interest is not excluded by section 33, apply to the registrar for the entry in the register of a notice in respect of the interest.

(2) Subject to rules, an application under this section may be for—
   (a) an agreed notice, or
   (b) a unilateral notice.

(3) The registrar may only approve an application for an agreed notice if—
   (a) the applicant is the relevant registered proprietor, or a person entitled to be registered as such proprietor,
   (b) the relevant registered proprietor, or a person entitled to be registered as such proprietor, consents to the entry of the notice, or
   (c) the registrar is satisfied as to the validity of the applicant's claim.

(4) In subsection (3), references to the relevant registered proprietor are to the proprietor of the registered estate or charge affected by the interest to which the application relates.

35. Unilateral notices

(1) If the registrar enters a notice in the register in pursuance of an application under section 34(2)(b) ('a unilateral notice'), he must give notice of the entry to—
   (a) the proprietor of the registered estate or charge to which it relates, and
   (b) such other persons as rules may provide.

(2) A unilateral notice must—
   (a) indicate that it is such a notice, and
   (b) identify who is the beneficiary of the notice.

(3) The person shown in the register as the beneficiary of a unilateral notice, or such other person as rules may provide, may apply to the registrar for the removal of the notice from the register.

36. Cancellation of unilateral notices

(1) A person may apply to the registrar for the cancellation of a unilateral notice if he is—
   (a) the registered proprietor of the estate or charge to which the notice relates, or
   (b) a person entitled to be registered as the proprietor of that estate or charge.

(2) Where an application is made under subsection (1), the registrar must give the beneficiary of the notice notice of the application and of the effect of subsection (3).

(3) If the beneficiary of the notice does not exercise his right to object to the application before the end of such period as rules may provide, the registrar must cancel the notice.

(4) In this section—
'beneficiary', in relation to a unilateral notice, means the person shown in the register as the beneficiary of the notice, or such other person as rules may provide;
'unilateral notice' means a notice entered in the register in pursuance of an application under section 34(2)(b).

37. Unregistered interests

(1) If it appears to the registrar that a registered estate is subject to an unregistered interest which—
   (a) falls within any of the paragraphs of Schedule 1, and
   (b) is not excluded by section 33, he may enter a notice in the register in respect of the interest.

(2) The registrar must give notice of an entry under this section to such persons as rules may provide.

38. Registrable dispositions

Where a person is entered in the register as the proprietor of an interest under a disposition falling within section 27(2)(b) to (e), the registrar must also enter a notice in the register in respect of that interest.

39. Supplementary

Rules may make provision about the form and content of notices in the register.

Restrictions

40. Nature

(1) A restriction is an entry in the register regulating the circumstances in which a disposition of a registered estate or charge may be the subject of an entry in the register.

(2)   A restriction may, in particular—
    (a)   prohibit the making of an entry in respect of any disposition, or a disposition of a kind specified in the restriction;
    (b)   prohibit the making of an entry—
        (i)   indefinitely,
        (ii)   for a period specified in the restriction, or
        (iii) until the occurrence of an event so specified.
(3)   Without prejudice to the generality of subsection (2)(b)(iii), the events which may be specified include—
    (a)   the giving of notice,
    (b)   the obtaining of consent, and
    (c)   the making of an order by the court or registrar.
(4)   The entry of a restriction is to be made in relation to the registered estate or charge to which it relates.

41.   Effect

(1)   Where a restriction is entered in the register, no entry in respect of a disposition to which the restriction applies may be made in the register otherwise than in accordance with the terms of the restriction, subject to any order under subsection (2).
(2)   The registrar may by order—
    (a)   disapply a restriction in relation to a disposition specified in the order or dispositions of a kind so specified, or
    (b)   provide that a restriction has effect, in relation to a disposition specified in the order or dispositions of a kind so specified, with modifications so specified.
(3)   The power under subsection (2) is exercisable only on the application of a person who appears to the registrar to have a sufficient interest in the restriction.

42.   Power of registrar to enter

(1)   The registrar may enter a restriction in the register if it appears to him that it is necessary or desirable to do so for the purpose of—
    (a)   preventing invalidity or unlawfulness in relation to dispositions of a registered estate or charge,
    (b)   securing that interests which are capable of being overreached on a disposition of a registered estate or charge are overreached, or
    (c)   protecting a right or claim in relation to a registered estate or charge.
(2)   No restriction may be entered under subsection (1)(c) for the purpose of protecting the priority of an interest which is, or could be, the subject of a notice.
(3)   The registrar must give notice of any entry made under this section to the proprietor of the registered estate or charge concerned, except where the entry is made in pursuance of an application under section 43.
(4)   For the purposes of subsection (1)(c), a person entitled to the benefit of a charging order relating to an interest under a trust shall be treated as having a right or claim in relation to the trust property.

43.   Applications

(1)   A person may apply to the registrar for the entry of a restriction under section 42(1) if—
    (a)   he is the relevant registered proprietor, or a person entitled to be registered as such proprietor,
    (b)   the relevant registered proprietor, or a person entitled to be registered as such proprietor, consents to the application, or
    (c)   he otherwise has a sufficient interest in the making of the entry.
(2)   Rules may—
    (a)   require the making of an application under subsection (1) in such circumstances, and by such person, as the rules may provide;
    (b)   make provision about the form of consent for the purposes of subsection (1)(b);
    (c)   provide for classes of person to be regarded as included in subsection (1)(c);
    (d)   specify standard forms of restriction.
(3)   If an application under subsection (1) is made for the entry of a restriction which is not in a form specified under subsection (2)(d), the registrar may only approve the application if it appears to him—

(a)   that the terms of the proposed restriction are reasonable, and
(b)   that applying the proposed restriction would—
      (i)   be straightforward, and
      (ii)   not place an unreasonable burden on him.

(4) In subsection (1), references to the relevant registered proprietor are to the proprietor of the registered estate or charge to which the application relates.

44. Obligatory restrictions

(1) If the registrar enters two or more persons in the register as the proprietor of a registered estate in land, he must also enter in the register such restrictions as rules may provide for the purpose of securing that interests which are capable of being overreached on a disposition of the estate are overreached.

(2) Where under any enactment the registrar is required to enter a restriction without application, the form of the restriction shall be such as rules may provide.

45. Notifiable applications

(1) Where an application under section 43(1) is notifiable, the registrar must give notice of the application, and of the right to object to it, to—
(a)   the proprietor of the registered estate or charge to which it relates, and
(b)   such other persons as rules may provide.

(2) The registrar may not determine an application to which subsection (1) applies before the end of such period as rules may provide, unless the person, or each of the persons, notified under that subsection has exercised his right to object to the application or given the registrar notice that he does not intend to do so.

(3) For the purposes of this section, an application under section 43(1) is notifiable unless it is—
(a)   made by or with the consent of the proprietor of the registered estate or charge to which the application relates, or a person entitled to be registered as such proprietor,
(b)   made in pursuance of rules under section 43(2)(a), or
(c)   an application for the entry of a restriction reflecting a limitation under an order of the court or registrar, or an undertaking given in place of such an order.

46. Power of court to order entry

(1) If it appears to the court that it is necessary or desirable to do so for the purpose of protecting a right or claim in relation to a registered estate or charge, it may make an order requiring the registrar to enter a restriction in the register.

(2) No order under this section may be made for the purpose of protecting the priority of an interest which is, or could be, the subject of a notice.

(3) The court may include in an order under this section a direction that an entry made in pursuance of the order is to have overriding priority.

(4) If an order under this section includes a direction under subsection (3), the registrar must make such entry in the register as rules may provide.

(5) The court may make the exercise of its power under subsection (3) subject to such terms and conditions as it thinks fit.

47. Withdrawal

A person may apply to the registrar for the withdrawal of a restriction if—
(a)   the restriction was entered in such circumstances as rules may provide, and
(b)   he is of such a description as rules may provide.

PART 5
CHARGES

Relative priority

48. Registered charges

(1) Registered charges on the same registered estate, or on the same registered charge, are to be taken to rank as between themselves in the order shown in the register.

(2)   Rules may make provision about—
 (a)   how the priority of registered charges as between themselves is to be shown in the register, and
 (b)   applications for registration of the priority of registered charges as between themselves.

49.   Tacking and further advances

(1)   The proprietor of a registered charge may make a further advance on the security of the charge ranking in priority to a subsequent charge if he has not received from the subsequent chargee notice of the creation of the subsequent charge.

(2)   Notice given for the purposes of subsection (1) shall be treated as received at the time when, in accordance with rules, it ought to have been received.

(3)   The proprietor of a registered charge may also make a further advance on the security of the charge ranking in priority to a subsequent charge if—
 (a)   the advance is made in pursuance of an obligation, and
 (b)   at the time of the creation of the subsequent charge the obligation was entered in the register in accordance with rules.

(4)   The proprietor of a registered charge may also make a further advance on the security of the charge ranking in priority to a subsequent charge if—
 (a)   the parties to the prior charge have agreed a maximum amount for which the charge is security, and
 (b)   at the time of the creation of the subsequent charge the agreement was entered in the register in accordance with rules.

(5)   Rules may—
 (a)   disapply subsection (4) in relation to charges of a description specified in the rules, or
 (b)   provide for the application of that subsection to be subject, in the case of charges of a description so specified, to compliance with such conditions as may be so specified.

(6)   Except as provided by this section, tacking in relation to a charge over registered land is only possible with the agreement of the subsequent chargee.

50.   Overriding statutory charges: duty of notification

If the registrar enters a person in the register as the proprietor of a charge which—
(a)   is created by or under an enactment, and
(b)   has effect to postpone a charge which at the time of registration of the statutory charge is—
 (i)   entered in the register, or
 (ii)   the basis for an entry in the register,
he must in accordance with rules give notice of the creation of the statutory charge to such person as rules may provide.

Powers as chargee

51.   Effect of completion by registration

On completion of the relevant registration requirements, a charge created by means of a registrable disposition of a registered estate has effect, if it would not otherwise do so, as a charge by deed by way of legal mortgage.

52.   Protection of disponees

(1)   Subject to any entry in the register to the contrary, the proprietor of a registered charge is to be taken to have, in relation to the property subject to the charge, the powers of disposition conferred by law on the owner of a legal mortgage.

(2)   Subsection (1) has effect only for the purpose of preventing the title of a disponee being questioned (and so does not affect the lawfulness of a disposition).

53.   Powers as sub-chargee

The registered proprietor of a sub-charge has, in relation to the property subject to the principal charge or any intermediate charge, the same powers as the sub-chargor.

Realisation of security

54. Proceeds of sale: chargee's duty

For the purposes of section 105 of the Law of Property Act 1925 (mortgagee's duties in relation to application of proceeds of sale), in its application to the proceeds of sale of registered land, a person shall be taken to have notice of anything in the register immediately before the disposition on sale.

55. Local land charges

A charge over registered land which is a local land charge may only be realised if the title to the charge is registered.

Miscellaneous

56. Receipt in case of joint proprietors

Where a charge is registered in the name of two or more proprietors, a valid receipt for the money secured by the charge may be given by—
(a) the registered proprietors,
(b) the survivors or survivor of the registered proprietors, or
(c) the personal representative of the last survivor of the registered proprietors.

57. Entry of right of consolidation

Rules may make provision about entry in the register of a right of consolidation in relation to a registered charge.

PART 6
REGISTRATION: GENERAL

Registration as proprietor

58. Conclusiveness

(1) If, on the entry of a person in the register as the proprietor of a legal estate, the legal estate would not otherwise be vested in him, it shall be deemed to be vested in him as a result of the registration.
(2) Subsection (1) does not apply where the entry is made in pursuance of a registrable disposition in relation to which some other registration requirement remains to be met.

59. Dependent estates

(1) The entry of a person in the register as the proprietor of a legal estate which subsists for the benefit of a registered estate must be made in relation to the registered estate.
(2) The entry of a person in the register as the proprietor of a charge on a registered estate must be made in relation to that estate.
(3) The entry of a person in the register as the proprietor of a sub-charge on a registered charge must be made in relation to that charge.

Boundaries

60. Boundaries

(1) The boundary of a registered estate as shown for the purposes of the register is a general boundary, unless shown as determined under this section.
(2) A general boundary does not determine the exact line of the boundary.
(3) Rules may make provision enabling or requiring the exact line of the boundary of a registered estate to be determined and may, in particular, make provision about—
(a)   the circumstances in which the exact line of a boundary may or must be determined,
(b)   how the exact line of a boundary may be determined,
(c)   procedure in relation to applications for determination, and
(d)   the recording of the fact of determination in the register or the index maintained under section 68.
(4) Rules under this section must provide for applications for determination to be made to the registrar.

61.   Accretion and diluvion

(1)   The fact that a registered estate in land is shown in the register as having a particular boundary does not affect the operation of accretion or diluvion.

(2)   An agreement about the operation of accretion or diluvion in relation to a registered estate in land has effect only if registered in accordance with rules.

Quality of title

62.   Power to upgrade title

(1)   Where the title to a freehold estate is entered in the register as possessory or qualified, the registrar may enter it as absolute if he is satisfied as to the title to the estate.

(2)   Where the title to a leasehold estate is entered in the register as good leasehold, the registrar may enter it as absolute if he is satisfied as to the superior title.

(3)   Where the title to a leasehold estate is entered in the register as possessory or qualified the registrar may—

    (a)   enter it as good leasehold if he is satisfied as to the title to the estate, and

    (b)   enter it as absolute if he is satisfied both as to the title to the estate and as to the superior title.

(4)   Where the title to a freehold estate in land has been entered in the register as possessory for at least twelve years, the registrar may enter it as absolute if he is satisfied that the proprietor is in possession of the land.

(5)   Where the title to a leasehold estate in land has been entered in the register as possessory for at least twelve years, the registrar may enter it as good leasehold if he is satisfied that the proprietor is in possession of the land.

(6)   None of the powers under subsections (1) to (5) is exercisable if there is outstanding any claim adverse to the title of the registered proprietor which is made by virtue of an estate, right or interest whose enforceability is preserved by virtue of the existing entry about the class of title.

(7)   The only persons who may apply to the registrar for the exercise of any of the powers under subsections (1) to (5) are—

    (a)   the proprietor of the estate to which the application relates,

    (b)   a person entitled to be registered as the proprietor of that estate,

    (c)   the proprietor of a registered charge affecting that estate, and

    (d)   a person interested in a registered estate which derives from that estate.

(8)   In determining for the purposes of this section whether he is satisfied as to any title, the registrar is to apply the same standards as those which apply under section 9 or 10 to first registration of title.

(9)   The Secretary of State may by order amend subsection (4) or (5) by substituting for the number of years for the time being specified in that subsection such number of years as the order may provide.

63.   Effect of upgrading title

(1)   On the title to a registered freehold or leasehold estate being entered under section 62 as absolute, the proprietor ceases to hold the estate subject to any estate, right or interest whose enforceability was preserved by virtue of the previous entry about the class of title.

(2)   Subsection (1) also applies on the title to a registered leasehold estate being entered under section 62 as good leasehold, except that the entry does not affect or prejudice the enforcement of any estate, right or interest affecting, or in derogation of, the title of the lessor to grant the lease.

64.   Use of register to record defects in title

(1)   If it appears to the registrar that a right to determine a registered estate in land is exercisable, he may enter the fact in the register.

(2)   Rules may make provision about entries under subsection (1) and may, in particular, make provision about—

    (a)   the circumstances in which there is a duty to exercise the power conferred by that subsection,

    (b)   how entries under that subsection are to be made, and

    (c)   the removal of such entries.

Alteration of register

65.   Alteration of register
Schedule 4 (which makes provision about alteration of the register) has effect.

Information etc.

66.   Inspection of the registers etc.
(1)   Any person may inspect and make copies of, or of any part of—
    (a)   the register of title,
    (b)   any document kept by the registrar which is referred to in the register of title,
    (c)   any other document kept by the registrar which relates to an application to him, or
    (d)   the register of cautions against first registration.
(2)   The right under subsection (1) is subject to rules which may, in particular—
    (a)   provide for exceptions to the right, and
    (b)   impose conditions on its exercise, including conditions requiring the payment of fees.

67.   Official copies of the registers etc.
(1)   An official copy of, or of a part of—
    (a)   the register of title,
    (b)   any document which is referred to in the register of title and kept by the registrar,
    (c)   any other document kept by the registrar which relates to an application to him, or
    (d)   the register of cautions against first registration, is admissible in evidence to the same extent as the original.
(2)   A person who relies on an official copy in which there is a mistake is not liable for loss suffered by another by reason of the mistake.
(3)   Rules may make provision for the issue of official copies and may, in particular, make provision about—
    (a)   the form of official copies,
    (b)   who may issue official copies,
    (c)   applications for official copies, and
    (d)   the conditions to be met by applicants for official copies, including conditions requiring the payment of fees.

68.   Index
(1)   The registrar must keep an index for the purpose of enabling the following matters to be ascertained in relation to any parcel of land—
    (a)   whether any registered estate relates to the land,
    (b)   how any registered estate which relates to the land is identified for the purposes of the register,
    (c)   whether the land is affected by any, and, if so what, caution against first registration, and
    (d)   such other matters as rules may provide.
(2)   Rules may—
    (a)   make provision about how the index is to be kept and may, in particular, make provision about—
        (i)   the information to be included in the index,
        (ii)   the form in which information included in the index is to be kept, and
        (iii)   the arrangement of that information;
    (b)   make provision about official searches of the index.

69.   Historical information
(1)   The registrar may on application provide information about the history of a registered title.
(2)   Rules may make provision about applications for the exercise of the power conferred by subsection (1).
(3)   The registrar may—
    (a)   arrange for the provision of information about the history of registered titles, and
    (b)   authorise anyone who has the function of providing information under paragraph (a) to have access on such terms as the registrar thinks fit to any relevant information kept by him.

70.   **Official searches**

Rules may make provision for official searches of the register, including searches of pending applications for first registration, and may, in particular, make provision about—

(a)   the form of applications for searches,

(b)   the manner in which such applications may be made,

(c)   the form of official search certificates, and

(d)   the manner in which such certificates may be issued.

Applications

71.   **Duty to disclose unregistered interests**

Where rules so provide—

(a)   a person applying for registration under Chapter 1 of Part 2 must provide to the registrar such information as the rules may provide about any interest affecting the estate to which the application relates which—

(i)   falls within any of the paragraphs of Schedule 1, and

(ii)   is of a description specified by the rules;

(b)   a person applying to register a registrable disposition of a registered estate must provide to the registrar such information as the rules may provide about any unregistered interest affecting the estate which—

(i)   falls within any of the paragraphs of Schedule 3, and

(ii)   is of description specified by the rules.

72.   **Priority protection**

(1)   For the purposes of this section, an application for an entry in the register is protected if—

(a)   it is one to which a priority period relates, and

(b)   it is made before the end of that period.

(2)   Where an application for an entry in the register is protected, any entry made in the register during the priority period relating to the application is postponed to any entry made in pursuance of it.

(3)   Subsection (2) does not apply if—

(a)   the earlier entry was made in pursuance of a protected application, and

(b)   the priority period relating to that application ranks ahead of the one relating to the application for the other entry.

(4)   Subsection (2) does not apply if the earlier entry is one to which a direction under section 46(3) applies.

(5)   The registrar may defer dealing with an application for an entry in the register if it appears to him that subsection (2) might apply to the entry were he to make it.

(6)   Rules may—

(a)   make provision for priority periods in connection with—

(i)   official searches of the register, including searches of pending applications for first registration, or

(ii)   the noting in the register of a contract for the making of a registrable disposition of a registered estate or charge;

(b)   make provision for the keeping of records in relation to priority periods and the inspection of such records.

(7)   Rules under subsection (6)(a) may, in particular, make provision about—

(a)   the commencement and length of a priority period,

(b)   the applications for registration to which such a period relates,

(c)   the order in which competing priority periods rank, and

(d)   the application of subsections (2) and (3) in cases where more than one priority period relates to the same application.

73.   **Objections**

(1)   Subject to subsections (2) and (3), anyone may object to an application to the registrar.

(2)   In the case of an application under section 18, only the person who lodged the caution to which the application relates, or such other person as rules may provide, may object.

(3)   In the case of an application under section 36, only the person shown in the register as the beneficiary of the notice to which the application relates, or such other person as rules may provide, may object.

(4)   The right to object under this section is subject to rules.

(5) Where an objection is made under this section, the registrar—
    (a) must give notice of the objection to the applicant, and
    (b) may not determine the application until the objection has been disposed of.

(6) Subsection (5) does not apply if the objection is one which the registrar is satisfied is groundless.

(7) If it is not possible to dispose by agreement of an objection to which subsection (5) applies, the registrar must refer the matter to the First-tier Tribunal.

(8) Rules may make provision about references under subsection (7).

74. Effective date of registration

An entry made in the register in pursuance of—
    (a) an application for registration of an unregistered legal estate, or
    (b) an application for registration in relation to a disposition required to be completed by registration,

has effect from the time of the making of the application.

Proceedings before the registrar

75. Production of documents

(1) The registrar may require a person to produce a document for the purposes of proceedings before him.

(2) The power under subsection (1) is subject to rules.

(3) A requirement under subsection (1) shall be enforceable as an order of the court.

(4) A person aggrieved by a requirement under subsection (1) may appeal to the county court, which may make any order which appears appropriate.

76. Costs

(1) The registrar may make orders about costs in relation to proceedings before him.

(2) The power under subsection (1) is subject to rules which may, in particular, make provision about—
    (a) who may be required to pay costs,
    (b) whose costs a person may be required to pay,
    (c) the kind of costs which a person may be required to pay, and
    (d) the assessment of costs.

(3) Without prejudice to the generality of subsection (2), rules under that subsection may include provision about—
    (a) costs of the registrar, and
    (b) liability for costs thrown away as the result of neglect or delay by a legal representative of a party to proceedings.

(4) An order under subsection (1) shall be enforceable as an order of the court.

(5) A person aggrieved by an order under subsection (1) may appeal to the county court, which may make any order which appears appropriate.

Miscellaneous

77. Duty to act reasonably

(1) A person must not exercise any of the following rights without reasonable cause—
    (a) the right to lodge a caution under section 15,
    (b) the right to apply for the entry of a notice or restriction, and
    (c) the right to object to an application to the registrar.

(2) The duty under this section is owed to any person who suffers damage in consequence of its breach.

78. Notice of trust not to affect registrar

The registrar shall not be affected with notice of a trust.

PART 7
SPECIAL CASES

The Crown

79. Voluntary registration of demesne land

(1) Her Majesty may grant an estate in fee simple absolute in possession out of demesne land to Herself.

(2) The grant of an estate under subsection (1) is to be regarded as not having been made unless an application under section 3 is made in respect of the estate before the end of the period for registration.

(3) The period for registration is two months beginning with the date of the grant, or such longer period as the registrar may provide under subsection (4).

(4) If on the application of Her Majesty the registrar is satisfied that there is a good reason for doing so, he may by order provide that the period for registration ends on such later date as he may specify in the order.

(5) If an order under subsection (4) is made in a case where subsection (2) has already applied, that application of the subsection is to be treated as not having occurred.

80. Compulsory registration of grants out of demesne land

(1) Section 4(1) shall apply as if the following were included among the events listed—
    (a) the grant by Her Majesty out of demesne land of an estate in fee simple absolute in possession, otherwise than under section 79;
    (b) the grant by Her Majesty out of demesne land of an estate in land—
        (i) for a term of years absolute of more than seven years from the date of the grant, and
        (ii) for valuable or other consideration, by way of gift or in pursuance of an order of any court.

(2) In subsection (1)(b)(ii), the reference to grant by way of gift includes grant for the purpose of constituting a trust under which Her Majesty does not retain the whole of the beneficial interest.

(3) Subsection (1) does not apply to the grant of an estate in mines and minerals held apart from the surface.

(4) The Secretary of State may by order—
    (a) amend this section so as to add to the events in subsection (1) such events relating to demesne land as he may specify in the order, and
    (b) make such consequential amendments of any provision of, or having effect under, any Act as he thinks appropriate.

(5) In its application by virtue of subsection (1), section 7 has effect with the substitution for subsection (2) of—
'(2) On the application of subsection (1), the grant has effect as a contract made for valuable consideration to grant the legal estate concerned'.

81. Demesne land: cautions against first registration

(1) Section 15 shall apply as if demesne land were held by Her Majesty for an unregistered estate in fee simple absolute in possession.

(2) The provisions of this Act relating to cautions against first registration shall, in relation to cautions lodged by virtue of subsection (1), have effect subject to such modifications as rules may provide.

82. Escheat etc.

(1) Rules may make provision about—
    (a) the determination of a registered freehold estate in land, and
    (b) the registration of an unregistered freehold legal estate in land in respect of land to which a former registered freehold estate in land related.

(2) Rules under this section may, in particular—
    (a) make provision for determination to be dependent on the meeting of such registration requirements as the rules may specify;
    (b) make provision for entries relating to a freehold estate in land to continue in the register, notwithstanding determination, for such time as the rules may provide;
    (c) make provision for the making in the register in relation to a former freehold estate in land of such entries as the rules may provide;
    (d) make provision imposing requirements to be met in connection with an application for the registration of such an unregistered estate as is mentioned in subsection (1) (b).

83. Crown and Duchy land: representation

(1) With respect to a Crown or Duchy interest, the appropriate authority—
    (a) may represent the owner of the interest for all purposes of this Act,
    (b) is entitled to receive such notice as that person is entitled to receive under this Act, and

    (c)   may make such applications and do such other acts as that person is entitled to make or do under this Act.

(2)   In this section—

    'the appropriate authority' means—

    (a)   in relation to an interest belonging to Her Majesty in right of the Crown and forming part of the Crown Estate, the Crown Estate Commissioners;

    (b)   in relation to any other interest belonging to Her Majesty in right of the Crown, the government department having the management of the interest or, if there is no such department, such person as Her Majesty may appoint in writing under the Royal Sign Manual;

    (c)   in relation to an interest belonging to Her Majesty in right of the Duchy of Lancaster, the Chancellor of the Duchy;

    (d)   in relation to an interest belonging to the Duchy of Cornwall, such person as the Duke of Cornwall, or the possessor for the time being of the Duchy of Cornwall, appoints;

    (e)   in relation to an interest belonging to a government department, or held in trust for Her Majesty for the purposes of a government department, that department;

    'Crown interest' means an interest belonging to Her Majesty in right of the Crown, or belonging to a government department, or held in trust for Her Majesty for the purposes of a government department;

    'Duchy interest' means an interest belonging to Her Majesty in right of the Duchy of Lancaster, or belonging to the Duchy of Cornwall;

    'interest' means any estate, interest or charge in or over land and any right or claim in relation to land.

84.   Disapplication of requirements relating to Duchy land

Nothing in any enactment relating to the Duchy of Lancaster or the Duchy of Cornwall shall have effect to impose any requirement with respect to formalities or enrolment in relation to a disposition by a registered proprietor.

85.   Bona vacantia

Rules may make provision about how the passing of a registered estate or charge as bona vacantia is to be dealt with for the purposes of this Act.

Pending actions etc.

86.   Bankruptcy

(1)   In this Act, references to an interest affecting an estate or charge do not include a petition in bankruptcy or bankruptcy order.

(2)   As soon as practicable after registration of a petition in bankruptcy as a pending action under the Land Charges Act 1972, the registrar must enter in the register in relation to any registered estate or charge which appears to him to be affected a notice in respect of the pending action.

(3)   Unless cancelled by the registrar in such manner as rules may provide, a notice entered under subsection (2) continues in force until—

    (a)   a restriction is entered in the register under subsection (4), or

    (b)   the trustee in bankruptcy is registered as proprietor.

(4)   As soon as practicable after registration of a bankruptcy order under the Land Charges Act 1972, the registrar must, in relation to any registered estate or charge which appears to him to be affected by the order, enter in the register a restriction reflecting the effect of the Insolvency Act 1986.

(5)   Where the proprietor of a registered estate or charge is made bankrupt, the title of his trustee in bankruptcy is void as against a person to whom a registrable disposition of the estate or charge is made if—

    (a)   the disposition is made for valuable consideration,

    (b)   the person to whom the disposition is made acts in good faith, and

    (c)   at the time of the disposition—

        (i)   no notice or restriction is entered under this section in relation to the registered estate or charge, and

        (ii)   the person to whom the disposition is made has no notice of the bankruptcy petition or the adjudication.

(6)   Subsection (5) only applies if the relevant registration requirements are met in relation to the disposition, but, when they are met, has effect as from the date of the disposition.

(7) Nothing in this section requires a person to whom a registrable disposition is made to make any search under the Land Charges Act 1972.

87. Pending land actions, writs, orders and deeds of arrangement

(1) Subject to the following provisions, references in this Act to an interest affecting an estate or charge include—
   (a) a pending land action within the meaning of the Land Charges Act 1972,
   (b) a writ or order of the kind mentioned in section 6(1)(a) of that Act (writ or order affecting land issued or made by any court for the purposes of enforcing a judgment or recognisance), and
   (c) an order appointing a receiver or sequestrator.
(2) No notice may be entered in the register in respect of—
   (a) an order appointing a receiver or sequestrator.
(3) None of the matters mentioned in subsection (1) shall be capable of falling within paragraph 2 of Schedule 1 or 3.
(4) In its application to any of the matters mentioned in subsection (1), this Act shall have effect subject to such modifications as rules may provide.

Miscellaneous

88. Incorporeal hereditaments

In its application to—
(a) rentcharges,
(b) franchises,
(c) profits a prendre in gross, or
(d) manors,
this Act shall have effect subject to such modification as rules may provide.

89. Settlements

(1) Rules may make provision for the purposes of this Act in relation to the application to registered land of the enactments relating to settlements under the Settled Land Act 1925 (c. 18).
(2) Rules under this section may include provision modifying any of those enactments in its application to registered land.
(3) In this section, 'registered land' means an interest the title to which is, or is required to be, registered.

90. PPP leases relating to transport in London

(1) No application for registration under section 3 may be made in respect of a leasehold estate in land under a PPP lease.
(2) The requirement of registration does not apply on the grant or transfer of a leasehold estate in land under a PPP lease.
(3) For the purposes of section 27, the following are not dispositions requiring to be completed by registration—
   (a) the grant of a term of years absolute under a PPP lease;
   (b) the express grant of an interest falling within section 1(2) of the Law of Property Act 1925, where the interest is created for the benefit of a leasehold estate in land under a PPP lease.
(4) No notice may be entered in the register in respect of an interest under a PPP lease.
(5) Schedules 1 and 3 have effect as if they included a paragraph referring to a PPP lease.
(6) In this section, 'PPP lease' has the meaning given by section 218 of the Greater London Authority Act 1999 (which makes provision about leases created for public-private partnerships relating to transport in London).

PART 8
ELECTRONIC CONVEYANCING

91. Electronic dispositions: formalities

(1) This section applies to a document in electronic form where—
   (a) the document purports to effect a disposition which falls within subsection (2), and
   (b) the conditions in subsection (3) are met.

    (2)   A disposition falls within this subsection if it is—
        (a)   a disposition of a registered estate or charge,
        (b)   a disposition of an interest which is the subject of a notice in the register, or
        (c)   a disposition which triggers the requirement of registration, which is of a kind specified by rules.

    (3)   The conditions referred to above are that—
        (a)   the document makes provision for the time and date when it takes effect,
        (b)   the document has the electronic signature of each person by whom it purports to be authenticated,
        (c)   each electronic signature is certified, and
        (d)   such other conditions as rules may provide are met.

    (4)   A document to which this section applies is to be regarded as—
        (a)   in writing, and
        (b)   signed by each individual, and sealed by each corporation, whose electronic signature it has.

    (5)   A document to which this section applies is to be regarded for the purposes of any enactment as a deed.

    (6)   If a document to which this section applies is authenticated by a person as agent, it is to be regarded for the purposes of any enactment as authenticated by him under the written authority of his principal.

    (7)   If notice of an assignment made by means of a document to which this section applies is given in electronic form in accordance with rules, it is to be regarded for the purposes of any enactment as given in writing.

    (8)   The right conferred by section 75 of the Law of Property Act 1925 (purchaser's right to have the execution of a conveyance attested) does not apply to a document to which this section applies.

    (9)   In relation to the execution of a document by a company in accordance with section 44(2) of the Companies Act 2006 (signature on behalf of the company)—
        (a)   subsection (4) above has effect in relation to paragraph (a) of that provision (signature by two authorised signatories) but not paragraph (b) (signature by director in presence of witness);
        (b)   the other provisions of section 44 apply accordingly (the references to a document purporting to be signed in accordance with subsection (2) of that section being read as references to its purporting to be authenticated in accordance with this section);
        (c)   where subsection (4) above has effect in relation to a person signing on behalf of more than one company, the requirement of subsection (6) of that section is treated as met if the document specifies the different capacities in which the person signs.

  (9A)   If subsection (3) of section 53 of the Co-operative and Community Benefit Societies Act 2014 (execution of documents) applies to a document because of subsection (4) above, subsection (5) of that section (presumption of due execution) shall have effect in relation to the document with the substitution of 'authenticated' for 'signed'.

  (10)   In this section, references to an electronic signature and to the certification of such a signature are to be read in accordance with section 7(2) and (3) of the Electronic Communications Act 2000.

92.   Land registry network

    (1)   The registrar may provide, or arrange for the provision of, an electronic communications network for use for such purposes as he thinks fit relating to registration or the carrying on of transactions which—
        (a)   involve registration, and
        (b)   are capable of being effected electronically.

    (2)   Schedule 5 (which makes provision in connection with a network provided under subsection (1) and transactions carried on by means of such a network) has effect.

93.   Power to require simultaneous registration

    (1)   This section applies to a disposition of—
        (a)   a registered estate or charge, or
        (b)   an interest which is the subject of a notice in the register, where the disposition is of a description specified by rules.

(2)   A disposition to which this section applies, or a contract to make such a disposition, only has effect if it is made by means of a document in electronic form and if, when the document purports to take effect—

     (a)   it is electronically communicated to the registrar, and

     (b)   the relevant registration requirements are met.

(3)   For the purposes of subsection (2)(b), the relevant registration requirements are—

     (a)   in the case of a registrable disposition, the requirements under Schedule 2, and

     (b)   in the case of any other disposition, or a contract, such requirements as rules may provide.

(4)   Section 27(1) does not apply to a disposition to which this section applies.

(5)   Before making rules under this section the Secretary of State must consult such persons as he considers appropriate.

(6)   In this section, 'disposition', in relation to a registered charge, includes postponement.

94.   Electronic settlement

The registrar may take such steps as he thinks fit for the purpose of securing the provision of a system of electronic settlement in relation to transactions involving registration.

95.   Supplementary

Rules may—

     (a)   make provision about the communication of documents in electronic form to the registrar;

     (b)   make provision about the electronic storage of documents communicated to the registrar in electronic form.

PART 9
ADVERSE POSSESSION

96.   Disapplication of periods of limitation

(1)   No period of limitation under section 15 of the Limitation Act 1980 (time limits in relation to recovery of land) shall run against any person, other than a chargee, in relation to an estate in land or rentcharge the title to which is registered.

(2)   No period of limitation under section 16 of that Act (time limits in relation to redemption of land) shall run against any person in relation to such an estate in land or rentcharge.

(3)   Accordingly, section 17 of that Act (extinction of title on expiry of time limit) does not operate to extinguish the title of any person where, by virtue of this section, a period of limitation does not run against him.

97.   Registration of adverse possessor

Schedule 6 (which makes provision about the registration of an adverse possessor of an estate in land or rentcharge) has effect.

98.   Defences

(1)   A person has a defence to an action for possession of land if—

     (a)   on the day immediately preceding that on which the action was brought he was entitled to make an application under paragraph 1 of Schedule 6 to be registered as the proprietor of an estate in the land, and

     (b)   had he made such an application on that day, the condition in paragraph 5(4) of that Schedule would have been satisfied.

(2)   A judgment for possession of land ceases to be enforceable at the end of the period of two years beginning with the date of the judgment if the proceedings in which the judgment is given were commenced against a person who was at that time entitled to make an application under paragraph 1 of Schedule 6.

(3)   A person has a defence to an action for possession of land if on the day immediately preceding that on which the action was brought he was entitled to make an application under paragraph 6 of Schedule 6 to be registered as the proprietor of an estate in the land.

(4)   A judgment for possession of land ceases to be enforceable at the end of the period of two years beginning with the date of the judgment if, at the end of that period, the person against whom the judgment was given is entitled to make an application under paragraph 6 of Schedule 6 to be registered as the proprietor of an estate in the land.

(5) Where in any proceedings a court determines that—
  (a) a person is entitled to a defence under this section, or
  (b) a judgment for possession has ceased to be enforceable against a person by virtue of subsection (4), the court must order the registrar to register him as the proprietor of the estate in relation to which he is entitled to make an application under Schedule 6.

(6) The defences under this section are additional to any other defences a person may have.

(7) Rules may make provision to prohibit the recovery of rent due under a rentcharge from a person who has been in adverse possession of the rentcharge.

PART 10

LAND REGISTRY

Administration

99. The land registry

(1) There is to continue to be an office called Her Majesty's Land Registry which is to deal with the business of registration under this Act.

(2) The land registry is to consist of—
  (a) the Chief Land Registrar, who is its head, and
  (b) the staff appointed by him; and references in this Act to a member of the land registry are to be read accordingly.

(3) The Secretary of State shall appoint a person to be the Chief Land Registrar.

(4) Schedule 7 (which makes further provision about the land registry) has effect.

100. Conduct of business

(1) Any function of the registrar may be carried out by any member of the land registry who is authorised for the purpose by the registrar.

(2) The Secretary of State may by regulations make provision about the carrying out of functions during any vacancy in the office of registrar.

(2A) Subsections (1) and (2) apply to all functions of the registrar, whether or not conferred by this Act.

(3) The Secretary of State may by order designate a particular office of the land registry as the proper office for the receipt of applications or a specified description of application.

(4) The registrar may prepare and publish such forms and directions as he considers necessary or desirable for facilitating the conduct of the business of registration under this Act.

101. Annual report

(1) The registrar must make an annual report on the business of the land registry to the Secretary of State.

(2) The registrar must publish every report under this section and may do so in such manner as he thinks fit.

(3) The Secretary of State must lay copies of every report under this section before Parliament.

Fees and indemnities

102. Fee orders

The Secretary of State may with the advice and assistance of the body referred to in section 127(2) (the Rule Committee), and the consent of the Treasury, by order—
  (a) prescribe fees to be paid in respect of dealings with the land registry, except under section 69(3)(b) or 105;
  (b) make provision about the payment of prescribed fees.

103. Indemnities

Schedule 8 (which makes provision for the payment of indemnities by the registrar) has effect.

Miscellaneous

104. General information about land

The registrar may publish information about land in England and Wales if it appears to him to be information in which there is legitimate public interest.

105. Services relating to land or other property

(1) The registrar may provide, or arrange for the provision of—

    (a) consultancy or advisory services about land or other property in England and Wales or elsewhere,

    (b) information services about land or other property in England and Wales, or

    (c) services relating to documents or registers which relate to land or other property in England and Wales.

(2) The terms on which services are provided under this section by the registrar, in particular terms as to payment, shall be such as he thinks fit.

106. Incidental powers: companies

(1) If the registrar considers it expedient to do so in connection with his functions under section 69(3)(a), 92(1), 94 or 105(1) or paragraph 10 of Schedule 5, or under the Local Land Charges Act 1975, he may—

    (a) form, or participate in the formation of, a company, or

    (b) purchase, or invest in, a company.

(2) In this section—

'company' means a company as defined in section 1(1) of the Companies Act 2006; 'invest' means invest in any way (whether by acquiring assets, securities or rights or otherwise).

(3) This section is without prejudice to any powers of the registrar exercisable otherwise than by virtue of this section.

PART 11
ADJUDICATION

108. Jurisdiction

(1) The First-tier Tribunal has the following functions—

    (a) determining matters referred to it under section 73(7), and

    (b) determining appeals under paragraph 4 of Schedule 5.

(2) Also, the First-tier Tribunal may, on application, make any order which the High Court could make for the rectification or setting aside of a document which—

    (a) effects a qualifying disposition of a registered estate or charge,

    (b) is a contract to make such a disposition, or

    (c) effects a transfer of an interest which is the subject of a notice in the register.

(3) For the purposes of subsection (2)(a), a qualifying disposition is—

    (a) a registrable disposition, or

    (b) a disposition which creates an interest which may be the subject of a notice in the register.

(4) The general law about the effect of an order of the High Court for the rectification or setting aside of a document shall apply to an order under this section.

(5) The Lord Chancellor may require the registrar to make payments towards expenses of the Lord Chancellor in support of the functions conferred on the First-tier Tribunal by this section.

110. Functions in relation to disputes

(1) In proceedings on a reference under section 73(7), the First-tier Tribunal may, instead of deciding a matter, direct a party to the proceedings to commence proceedings within a specified time in the court for the purpose of obtaining the court's decision on the matter.

(2) Tribunal Procedure Rules may make provision about the reference under subsection (1) of matters to the court and may, in particular, make provision about—

    (a) adjournment of the proceedings before the First-tier Tribunal pending the outcome of the proceedings before the court, and

    (b) the powers of the First-tier Tribunal in the event of failure to comply with a direction under subsection (1).

(3) Tribunal Procedure Rules may make provision about the functions of the First-tier Tribunal in consequence of a decision on a reference under section 73(7) and may, in particular, make provision enabling the First-tier Tribunal to determine, or give directions about the determination of—

    (a) the application to which the reference relates, or

    (b) such other present or future application to the registrar as Tribunal Procedure Rules may provide.

(4)   If, in the case of a reference under section 73(7) relating to an application under paragraph 1 of Schedule 6, the First-tier Tribunal determines that it would be unconscionable because of an equity by estoppel for the registered proprietor to seek to dispossess the applicant, but that the circumstances are not such that the applicant ought to be registered as proprietor, the First-tier Tribunal—

(a)   must determine how the equity due to the applicant is to be satisfied, and

(b)   may for that purpose make any order that the High Court could make in the exercise of its equitable jurisdiction.

111.   Appeals

(1)   Subject to this section, a person aggrieved by a decision of the First-tier Tribunal under this Act may appeal to the Upper Tribunal.

(2)   An appeal may not be brought under subsection (1) on a point of law (as to which see instead section 11 of the Tribunals, Courts and Enforcement Act 2007 (right of appeal to Upper Tribunal)).

(2A)   An appeal may not be brought under subsection (1) in the case of a decision under paragraph 4 of Schedule 5 (but this does not prevent an appeal on a point of law under section 11 of the Tribunals, Courts and Enforcement Act 2007).

(2B)   An appeal may not be brought under subsection (1) if the decision is set aside under section 9 of the Tribunals, Courts and Enforcement Act 2007 (review of decision of First-tier Tribunal).

(2C)   An appeal may be brought under subsection (1) only if, on an application made by the person concerned, the First-tier Tribunal or Upper Tribunal has given its permission for the appeal to be brought.

(3)   If on an appeal under this section or under section 11 of the Tribunals, Courts and Enforcement Act 2007 relating to an application under paragraph 1 of Schedule 6 the Upper Tribunal determines that it would be unconscionable because of an equity by estoppel for the registered proprietor to seek to dispossess the applicant, but that the circumstances are not such that the applicant ought to be registered as proprietor, the Upper Tribunal must determine how the equity due to the applicant is to be satisfied.

(4)   In any case where the Upper Tribunal is determining an appeal under subsection (1), section 12(2) to (4) of the Tribunals, Courts and Enforcement Act 2007 (proceedings on appeal to the Upper Tribunal) apply.

112.   Enforcement of orders etc.

A requirement of the First-tier Tribunal shall be enforceable as an order of the court.

PART 12
MISCELLANEOUS AND GENERAL

Miscellaneous

115.   Rights of pre-emption

(1)   A right of pre-emption in relation to registered land has effect from the time of creation as an interest capable of binding successors in title (subject to the rules about the effect of dispositions on priority).

(2)   This section has effect in relation to rights of pre-emption created on or after the day on which this section comes into force.

116.   Proprietary estoppel and mere equities

It is hereby declared for the avoidance of doubt that, in relation to registered land, each of the following—

(a)   an equity by estoppel, and

(b)   a mere equity,

has effect from the time the equity arises as an interest capable of binding successors in title (subject to the rules about the effect of dispositions on priority).

117.   Reduction in unregistered interests with automatic protection

(1)   Paragraphs 10 to 14 of Schedules 1 and 3 shall cease to have effect at the end of the period of ten years beginning with the day on which those Schedules come into force.

(2)   If made before the end of the period mentioned in subsection (1), no fee may be charged for—

   (a)   an application to lodge a caution against first registration by virtue of an interest falling within any of paragraphs 10 to 14 of Schedule 1, or

   (b)   an application for the entry in the register of a notice in respect of an interest falling within any of paragraphs 10 to 14 of Schedule 3.

118.   Power to reduce qualifying term

(1)   The Secretary of State may by order substitute for the term specified in any of the following provisions—

   (a)   section 3(3),
   (b)   section 4(1)(c)(i) and (2)(b),
   (c)   section 15(3)(a)(ii),
   (d)   section 27(2)(b)(i),
   (e)   section 80(1)(b)(i),
   (f)   paragraph 1 of Schedule 1,
   (g)   paragraphs 4(1), 5(1) and 6(1) of Schedule 2, and
   (h)   paragraph 1 of Schedule 3, such shorter term as he thinks fit.

(2)   An order under this section may contain such transitional provision as the Secretary of State thinks fit.

(3)   Before making an order under this section, the Secretary of State must consult such persons as he considers appropriate.

119.   Power to deregister manors

On the application of the proprietor of a registered manor, the registrar may remove the title to the manor from the register.

120.   Conclusiveness of filed copies etc.

(1)   This section applies where—

   (a)   a disposition relates to land to which a registered estate relates, and
   (b)   an entry in the register relating to the registered estate refers to a document kept by the registrar which is not an original.

(2)   As between the parties to the disposition, the document kept by the registrar is to be taken—

   (a)   to be correct, and
   (b)   to contain all the material parts of the original document.

(3)   No party to the disposition may require production of the original document.

(4)   No party to the disposition is to be affected by any provision of the original document which is not contained in the document kept by the registrar.

121.   Forwarding of applications to registrar of companies

(1)   The Secretary of State may by rules make provision about the transmission by the registrar to the registrar of companies of applications under—

   (a)   Part 25 of the Companies Act 2006 (registration of charges over property of companies registered in the United Kingdom), or

   (b)   regulations under section 1052 of that Act (registration of charges over property in the United Kingdom of overseas companies).

(2)   In subsection (1) 'the registrar of companies' has the same meaning as in the Companies Acts (see section 1060 of the Companies Act 2006).

Offences etc.

123.   Suppression of information

(1)   A person commits an offence if in the course of proceedings relating to registration under this Act he suppresses information with the intention of—

   (a)   concealing a person's right or claim, or
   (b)   substantiating a false claim.

(2)   A person guilty of an offence under this section is liable—

   (a)   on conviction on indictment, to imprisonment for a term not exceeding two years or to a fine;

   (b)   on summary conviction, to imprisonment for a term not exceeding six months or to a fine not exceeding the statutory maximum, or to both.

124. Improper alteration of the registers

(1) A person commits an offence if he dishonestly induces another—
   (a) to change the register of title or cautions register, or
   (b) to authorise the making of such a change.
(2) A person commits an offence if he intentionally or recklessly makes an unauthorised change in the register of title or cautions register.
(3) A person guilty of an offence under this section is liable—
   (a) on conviction on indictment, to imprisonment for a term not exceeding 2 years or to a fine;
   (b) on summary conviction, to imprisonment for a term not exceeding six months or to a fine not exceeding the statutory maximum, or to both.
(4) In this section, references to changing the register of title include changing a document referred to in it.

125. Privilege against self-incrimination

(1) The privilege against self-incrimination, so far as relating to offences under this Act, shall not entitle a person to refuse to answer any question or produce any document or thing in any legal proceedings other than criminal proceedings.
(2) No evidence obtained under subsection (1) shall be admissible in any criminal proceedings under this Act against the person from whom it was obtained or that person's spouse or civil partner.

Land registration rules

126. Miscellaneous and general powers

Schedule 10 (which contains miscellaneous and general land registration rule-making powers) has effect.

127. Exercise of powers

(1) Power to make land registration rules is exercisable by the Secretary of State with the advice and assistance of the Rule Committee.
...

Supplementary

129. Crown application

This Act binds the Crown.

130. Application to internal waters

This Act applies to land covered by internal waters of the United Kingdom which are—
(a) within England or Wales, or
(b) adjacent to England or Wales and specified for the purposes of this section by order made by the Secretary of State.

131. 'Proprietor in possession'

(1) For the purposes of this Act, land is in the possession of the proprietor of a registered estate in land if it is physically in his possession, or in that of a person who is entitled to be registered as the proprietor of the registered estate.
(2) In the case of the following relationships, land which is (or is treated as being) in the possession of the second-mentioned person is to be treated for the purposes of subsection (1) as in the possession of the first-mentioned person—
   (a) landlord and tenant;
   (b) mortgagor and mortgagee;
   (c) licensor and licensee;
   (d) trustee and beneficiary.
(3) In subsection (1), the reference to entitlement does not include entitlement under Schedule 6.

132. General interpretation

(1) In this Act—
'assured tenancy' has the same meaning as in Part 1 of the Housing Act 1988;
'caution against first registration' means a caution lodged under section 15;
'cautions register' means the register kept under section 19(1);

'charge' means any mortgage, charge or lien for securing money or money's worth;

'demesne land' means land belonging to Her Majesty in right of the Crown which is not held for an estate in fee simple absolute in possession;

'dwelling-house' has the same meaning as in Part 1 of the Housing Act 1988;

'flexible tenancy' has the meaning given by section 107A of the Housing Act 1985;

'land' includes—

(a)   buildings and other structures,

(b)   land covered with water, and

(c)   mines and minerals, whether or not held with the surface;

'land registration rules' means any rules under this Act, other than rules under section 93, Part 11, section 121 or paragraph 1, 2 or 3 of Schedule 5;

'legal estate' has the same meaning as in the Law of Property Act 1925; 'legal mortgage' has the same meaning as in the Law of Property Act 1925;

'long tenancy' means a tenancy granted for a term certain of more than 21 years, whether or not it is (or may become) terminable before the end of that term by notice given by the tenant or by re-entry or forfeiture;

'mines and minerals' includes any strata or seam of minerals or substances in or under any land, and powers of working and getting any such minerals or substances;

'registrar' means the Chief Land Registrar;

'register' means the register of title, except in the context of cautions against first registration;

'registered' means entered in the register;

'registered charge' means a charge the title to which is entered in the register; 'registered estate' means a legal estate the title to which is entered in the register, other than a registered charge;

'registered land' means a registered estate or registered charge;

'registrable disposition' means a disposition which is required to be completed by registration under section 27;

'relevant social housing tenancy' means—

(a)   a flexible tenancy, or

(b)   an assured tenancy of a dwelling-house in England granted by a private registered provider of social housing, other than a long tenancy or a shared ownership lease;

'requirement of registration' means the requirement of registration under section 4;

'shared ownership lease' means a lease of a dwelling-house—

(a)   granted on payment of a premium calculated by reference to a percentage of the value of the dwelling-house or of the cost of providing it, or

(b)   under which the lessee (or the lessee's personal representatives) will or may be entitled to a sum calculated by reference, directly or indirectly, to the value of the dwelling-house;

'sub-charge' means a charge under section 23(2)(b);

'term of years absolute' has the same meaning as in the Law of Property Act 1925;

'valuable   consideration' does not include marriage consideration or a nominal consideration in money.

(2)   In subsection (1), in the definition of 'demesne land', the reference to land belonging to Her Majesty does not include land in relation to which a freehold estate in land has determined, but in relation to which there has been no act of entry or management by the Crown.

(3)   In this Act—

(a)   references to the court are to the High Court or the county court,

(b)   references to an interest affecting an estate or charge are to an adverse right affecting the title to the estate or charge, and

(c)   references to the right to object to an application to the registrar are to the right under section 73.

Final provisions

134.   Transition

(1)   The Secretary of State may by order make such transitional provisions and savings as he thinks fit in connection with the coming into force of any of the provisions of this Act.

(2)   Schedule 12 (which makes transitional provisions and savings) has effect.

(3)   Nothing in Schedule 12 affects the power to make transitional provisions and savings under subsection (1); and an order under that subsection may modify any provision made by that Schedule.

135. Repeals

The enactments specified in Schedule 13 (which include certain provisions which are already spent) are hereby repealed to the extent specified there.

SCHEDULES

SCHEDULE 1
UNREGISTERED INTERESTS WHICH OVERRIDE FIRST REGISTRATION

Leasehold estates in land

1.   A leasehold estate in land granted for a term not exceeding seven years from the date of the grant, except for a lease the grant of which falls within section 4(1) (d), (e) or (f).

Relevant social housing tenancies

1A.   A leasehold estate in land under a relevant social housing tenancy.

Interests of persons in actual occupation

2.   An interest belonging to a person in actual occupation, so far as relating to land of which he is in actual occupation, except for an interest under a settlement under the Settled Land Act 1925.

Easements and profits a prendre

3.   A legal easement or profit a prendre.

Customary and public rights

4.   A customary right.
5.   A public right.

Local land charges

6.   A local land charge.

Mines and minerals

7.   An interest in any coal or coal mine, the rights attached to any such interest and the rights of any person under section 38, 49 or 51 of the Coal Industry Act 1994.
8.   In the case of land to which title was registered before 1898, rights to mines and minerals (and incidental rights) created before 1898.
9.   In the case of land to which title was registered between 1898 and 1925 inclusive, rights to mines and minerals (and incidental rights) created before the date of registration of the title.

SCHEDULE 2
REGISTRABLE DISPOSITIONS: REGISTRATION REQUIREMENTS

PART 1
REGISTERED ESTATES

Introductory

1.   This Part deals with the registration requirements relating to those dispositions of registered estates which are required to be completed by registration.

Transfer

2.   (1)   In the case of a transfer of whole or part, the transferee, or his successor in title, must be entered in the register as the proprietor.
       (2)   In the case of a transfer of part, such details of the transfer as rules may provide must be entered in the register in relation to the registered estate out of which the transfer is made.

Lease of estate in land

3. (1) This paragraph applies to a disposition consisting of the grant out of an estate in land of a term of years absolute.
    (2) In the case of a disposition to which this paragraph applies—
        (a) the grantee, or his successor in title, must be entered in the register as the proprietor of the lease, and
        (b) a notice in respect of the lease must be entered in the register.

Lease of franchise or manor

4. (1) This paragraph applies to a disposition consisting of the grant out of a franchise or manor of a lease for a term of more than seven years from the date of the grant.
    (2) In the case of a disposition to which this paragraph applies—
        (a) the grantee, or his successor in title, must be entered in the register as the proprietor of the lease, and
        (b) a notice in respect of the lease must be entered in the register.

5. (1) This paragraph applies to a disposition consisting of the grant out of a franchise or manor of a lease for a term not exceeding seven years from the date of the grant.
    (2) In the case of a disposition to which this paragraph applies, a notice in respect of the lease must be entered in the register.

Creation of independently registrable legal interest

6. (1) This paragraph applies to a disposition consisting of the creation of a legal rentcharge or profit a prendre in gross, other than one created for, or for an interest equivalent to, a term of years absolute not exceeding seven years from the date of creation.
    (2) In the case of a disposition to which this paragraph applies—
        (a) the grantee, or his successor in title, must be entered in the register as the proprietor of the interest created, and
        (b) a notice in respect of the interest created must be entered in the register.
    (3) In sub-paragraph (1), the reference to a legal rentcharge or profit a prendre in gross is to one falling within section 1(2) of the Law of Property Act 1925.

Creation of other legal interest

7. (1) This paragraph applies to a disposition which—
        (a) consists of the creation of an interest of a kind falling within section 1(2)(a), (b) or (e) of the Law of Property Act 1925, and
        (b) is not a disposition to which paragraph 4, 5 or 6 applies.
    (2) In the case of a disposition to which this paragraph applies—
        (a) a notice in respect of the interest created must be entered in the register, and
        (b) if the interest is created for the benefit of a registered estate, the proprietor of the registered estate must be entered in the register as its proprietor.
    (3) Rules may provide for sub-paragraph (2) to have effect with modifications in relation to a right of entry over or in respect of a term of years absolute.

Creation of legal charge

8. In the case of the creation of a charge, the chargee, or his successor in title, must be entered in the register as the proprietor of the charge.

PART 2
REGISTERED CHARGES

Introductory

9. This Part deals with the registration requirements relating to those dispositions of registered charges which are required to be completed by registration.

Transfer

10. In the case of a transfer, the transferee, or his successor in title, must be entered in the register as the proprietor.

Creation of sub-charge

11.   In the case of the creation of a sub-charge, the sub-chargee, or his successor in title, must be entered in the register as the proprietor of the sub-charge.

SCHEDULE 3
UNREGISTERED INTERESTS WHICH OVERRIDE REGISTERED DISPOSITIONS

Leasehold estates in land

1.   A leasehold estate in land granted for a term not exceeding seven years from the date of the grant, except for—
       (a)   a lease the grant of which falls within section 4(1)(d), (e) or (f);
       (b)   a lease the grant of which constitutes a registrable disposition.

Relevant social housing tenancies

1A.   A leasehold estate in land under a relevant social housing tenancy.

Interests of persons in actual occupation

2.   An interest belonging at the time of the disposition to a person in actual occupation, so far as relating to land of which he is in actual occupation, except for—
       (a)   an interest under a settlement under the Settled Land Act 1925;
       (b)   an interest of a person of whom inquiry was made before the disposition and who failed to disclose the right when he could reasonably have been expected to do so;
       (c)   an interest—
              (i)   which belongs to a person whose occupation would not have been obvious on a reasonably careful inspection of the land at the time of the disposition, and
              (ii)   of which the person to whom the disposition is made does not have actual knowledge at that time;
       (d)   a leasehold estate in land granted to take effect in possession after the end of the period of three months beginning with the date of the grant and which has not taken effect in possession at the time of the disposition.

Easements and profits a prendre

3.   (1)   A legal easement or profit a prendre, except for an easement, or a profit a prendre which is not registered under Part 1 of the Commons Act 2006, which at the time of the disposition—
              (a)   is not within the actual knowledge of the person to whom the disposition is made, and
              (b)   would not have been obvious on a reasonably careful inspection of the land over which the easement or profit is exercisable.
       (2)   The exception in sub-paragraph (1) does not apply if the person entitled to the easement or profit proves that it has been exercised in the period of one year ending with the day of the disposition.

Customary and public rights

4.   A customary right.
5.   A public right.

Local land charges

6.   A local land charge.

Mines and minerals

7.   An interest in any coal or coal mine, the rights attached to any such interest and the rights of any person under section 38, 49 or 51 of the Coal Industry Act 1994.
8.   In the case of land to which title was registered before 1898, rights to mines and minerals (and incidental rights) created before 1898.
9.   In the case of land to which title was registered between 1898 and 1925 inclusive, rights to mines and minerals (and incidental rights) created before the date of registration of the title.

SCHEDULE 4
ALTERATION OF THE REGISTER

Introductory

1.   In this Schedule, references to rectification, in relation to alteration of the register, are to alteration which—
    (a)   involves the correction of a mistake, and
    (b)   prejudicially affects the title of a registered proprietor.

Alteration pursuant to a court order

2.   (1)   The court may make an order for alteration of the register for the purpose of—
    (a)   correcting a mistake,
    (b)   bringing the register up to date, or
    (c)   giving effect to any estate, right or interest excepted from the effect of registration.
    (2)   An order under this paragraph has effect when served on the registrar to impose a duty on him to give effect to it.

3.   (1)   This paragraph applies to the power under paragraph 2, so far as relating to rectification.
    (2)   If alteration affects the title of the proprietor of a registered estate in land, no order may be made under paragraph 2 without the proprietor's consent in relation to land in his possession unless—
    (a)   he has by fraud or lack of proper care caused or substantially contributed to the mistake, or
    (b)   it would for any other reason be unjust for the alteration not to be made.
    (3)   If in any proceedings the court has power to make an order under paragraph 2, it must do so, unless there are exceptional circumstances which justify its not doing so.
    (4)   In sub-paragraph (2), the reference to the title of the proprietor of a registered estate in land includes his title to any registered estate which subsists for the benefit of the estate in land.

4.   Rules may—
    (a)   make provision about the circumstances in which there is a duty to exercise the power under paragraph 2, so far as not relating to rectification;
    (b)   make provision about the form of an order under paragraph 2;
    (c)   make provision about service of such an order.

Alteration otherwise than pursuant to a court order

5.   The registrar may alter the register for the purpose of—
    (a)   correcting a mistake,
    (b)   bringing the register up to date,
    (c)   giving effect to any estate, right or interest excepted from the effect of registration, or
    (d)   removing a superfluous entry.

6.   (1)   This paragraph applies to the power under paragraph 5, so far as relating to rectification.
    (2)   No alteration affecting the title of the proprietor of a registered estate in land may be made under paragraph 5 without the proprietor's consent in relation to land in his possession unless—
    (a)   he has by fraud or lack of proper care caused or substantially contributed to the mistake, or
    (b)   it would for any other reason be unjust for the alteration not to be made.
    (3)   If on an application for alteration under paragraph 5 the registrar has power to make the alteration, the application must be approved, unless there are exceptional circumstances which justify not making the alteration.
    (4)   In sub-paragraph (2), the reference to the title of the proprietor of a registered estate in land includes his title to any registered estate which subsists for the benefit of the estate in land.

7.   Rules may—
    (a)   make provision about the circumstances in which there is a duty to exercise the power under paragraph 5, so far as not relating to rectification;
    (b)   make provision about how the register is to be altered in exercise of that power;
    (c)   make provision about applications for alteration under that paragraph, including provision requiring the making of such applications;
    (d)   make provision about procedure in relation to the exercise of that power, whether on application or otherwise.

Rectification and derivative interests

8.   The powers under this Schedule to alter the register, so far as relating to rectification, extend to changing for the future the priority of any interest affecting the registered estate or charge concerned.

Costs in non-rectification cases

9.   (1)   If the register is altered under this Schedule in a case not involving rectification, the registrar may pay such amount as he thinks fit in respect of any costs or expenses reasonably incurred by a person in connection with the alteration which have been incurred with the consent of the registrar.

           (2)   The registrar may make a payment under sub-paragraph (1) notwithstanding the absence of consent if—

                (a)   it appears to him—

                      (i)   that the costs or expenses had to be incurred urgently, and

                      (ii)   that it was not reasonably practicable to apply for his consent, or

                (b)   he has subsequently approved the incurring of the costs or expenses.

SCHEDULE 5
LAND REGISTRY NETWORK

Access to network

1.   (1)   A person who is not a member of the land registry may only have access to a land registry network under authority conferred by means of an agreement with the registrar.

           (2)   An agreement for the purposes of sub-paragraph (1) ('network access agreement') may authorise access for—

                (a)   the communication, posting or retrieval of information,

                (b)   the making of changes to the register of title or cautions register,

                (c)   the issue of official search certificates,

                (d)   the issue of official copies, or

                (e)   such other conveyancing purposes as the registrar thinks fit.

           (3)   Rules may regulate the use of network access agreements to confer authority to carry out functions of the registrar.

           (4)   The registrar must, on application, enter into a network access agreement with the applicant if the applicant meets such criteria as rules may provide.

Terms of access

2.   (1)   The terms on which access to a land registry network is authorised shall be such as the registrar thinks fit, subject to sub-paragraphs (3) and (4), and may, in particular, include charges for access.

           (2)   The power under sub-paragraph (1) may be used, not only for the purpose of regulating the use of the network, but also for—

                (a)   securing that the person granted access uses the network to carry on such qualifying transactions as may be specified in, or under, the agreement,

                (b)   such other purpose relating to the carrying on of qualifying transactions as rules may provide, or

                (c)   enabling network transactions to be monitored.

           (3)   It shall be a condition of a network access agreement which enables the person granted access to use the network to carry on qualifying transactions that he must comply with any rules for the time being in force under paragraph 5.

           (4)   Rules may regulate the terms on which access to a land registry network is authorised.

Termination of access

3.   (1)   The person granted access by a network access agreement may terminate the agreement at any time by notice to the registrar.

           (2)   Rules may make provision about the termination of a network access agreement by the registrar and may, in particular, make provision about—

                (a)   the grounds of termination,

                (b)   the procedure to be followed in relation to termination, and

                (c)   the suspension of termination pending appeal.

(3) Without prejudice to the generality of sub-paragraph (2)(a), rules under that provision may authorise the registrar to terminate a network access agreement if the person granted access—

(a) fails to comply with the terms of the agreement,

(b) ceases to be a person with whom the registrar would be required to enter into a network access agreement conferring the authority which the agreement confers, or

(c) does not meet such conditions as the rules may provide.

Appeals

4. (1) A person who is aggrieved by a decision of the registrar with respect to entry into, or termination of, a network access agreement may appeal against the decision to the First-tier Tribunal.

(2) On determining an appeal under this paragraph, the First-tier Tribunal may give such directions as the Tribunal considers appropriate to give effect to its determination.

(3) Rules may make provision about appeals under this paragraph.

Network transaction rules

5. (1) Rules may make provision about how to go about network transactions.

(2) Rules under sub-paragraph (1) may, in particular, make provision about dealings with the land registry, including provision about—

(a) the procedure to be followed, and

(b) the supply of information (including information about unregistered interests).

Overriding nature of network access obligations

6. To the extent that an obligation not owed under a network access agreement conflicts with an obligation owed under such an agreement by the person granted access, the obligation not owed under the agreement is discharged.

Do-it-yourself conveyancing

7. (1) If there is a land registry network, the registrar has a duty to provide such assistance as he thinks appropriate for the purpose of enabling persons engaged in qualifying transactions who wish to do their own conveyancing to do so by means of the network.

(2) The duty under sub-paragraph (1) does not extend to the provision of legal advice.

Presumption of authority

8. Where—

(a) a person who is authorised under a network access agreement to do so uses the network for the making of a disposition or contract, and

(b) the document which purports to effect the disposition or to be the contract—

(i) purports to be authenticated by him as agent, and

(ii) contains a statement to the effect that he is acting under the authority of his principal, he shall be deemed, in favour of any other party, to be so acting.

Management of network transactions

9. (1) The registrar may use monitoring information for the purpose of managing network transactions and may, in particular, disclose such information to persons authorised to use the network, and authorise the further disclosure of information so disclosed, if he considers it is necessary or desirable to do so.

(2) The registrar may delegate his functions under sub-paragraph (1), subject to such conditions as he thinks fit.

(3) In sub-paragraph (1), 'monitoring information' means information provided in pursuance of provision in a network access agreement included under paragraph 2(2)(c).

Supplementary

10. The registrar may provide, or arrange for the provision of, education and training in relation to the use of a land registry network.

11. (1) Power to make rules under paragraph 1, 2 or 3 is exercisable by the Secretary of State.

(2)   Before making such rules, the Secretary of State must consult such persons as he considers appropriate.

(3)   In making rules under paragraph 1 or 3(2)(a), the Secretary of State must have regard, in particular, to the need to secure—

(a)   the confidentiality of private information kept on the network,

(b)   competence in relation to the use of the network (in particular for the purpose of making changes), and

(c)   the adequate insurance of potential liabilities in connection with use of the network.

12.   In this Schedule—

'land registry network' means a network provided under section 92(1);

'network access agreement' has the meaning given by paragraph 1(2);

'network transaction' means a transaction carried on by means of a land registry network;

'qualifying transaction' means a transaction which—

(a)   involves registration, and

(b)   is capable of being effected electronically.

SCHEDULE 6
REGISTRATION OF ADVERSE POSSESSOR

Note. In relation to registered rentcharges see the Land Registration Rules 2003, Sch 8.

Right to apply for registration

1.   (1)   Subject to paragraph 16, a person may apply to the registrar to be registered as the proprietor of a registered estate in land if he has been in adverse possession of the estate for the period of ten years ending on the date of the application.

(2)   Subject to paragraph 16, a person may also apply to the registrar to be registered as the proprietor of a registered estate in land if—

(a)   he has in the period of six months ending on the date of the application ceased to be in adverse possession of the estate because of eviction by the registered proprietor, or a person claiming under the registered proprietor,

(b)   on the day before his eviction he was entitled to make an application under sub-paragraph (1), and

(c)   the eviction was not pursuant to a judgment for possession.

(3)   However, a person may not make an application under this paragraph if—

(a)   he is a defendant in proceedings which involve asserting a right to possession of the land, or

(b)   judgment for possession of the land has been given against him in the last two years.

(4)   For the purposes of sub-paragraph (1), the estate need not have been registered throughout the period of adverse possession.

Notification of application

2.   (1)   The registrar must give notice of an application under paragraph 1 to—

(a)   the proprietor of the estate to which the application relates,

(b)   the proprietor of any registered charge on the estate,

(c)   where the estate is leasehold, the proprietor of any superior registered estate,

(d)   any person who is registered in accordance with rules as a person to be notified under this paragraph, and

(e)   such other persons as rules may provide.

(2)   Notice under this paragraph shall include notice of the effect of paragraph 4.

Treatment of application

3.   (1)   A person given notice under paragraph 2 may require that the application to which the notice relates be dealt with under paragraph 5.

(2)   The right under this paragraph is exercisable by notice to the registrar given before the end of such period as rules may provide.

4.   If an application under paragraph 1 is not required to be dealt with under paragraph 5, the applicant is entitled to be entered in the register as the new proprietor of the estate.

5.   (1)   If an application under paragraph 1 is required to be dealt with under this paragraph, the applicant is only entitled to be registered as the new proprietor of the estate if any of the following conditions is met.

    (2)   The first condition is that—

        (a)   it would be unconscionable because of an equity by estoppel for the registered proprietor to seek to dispossess the applicant, and

        (b)   the circumstances are such that the applicant ought to be registered as the proprietor.

    (3)   The second condition is that the applicant is for some other reason entitled to be registered as the proprietor of the estate.

    (4)   The third condition is that—

        (a)   the land to which the application relates is adjacent to land belonging to the applicant,

        (b)   the exact line of the boundary between the two has not been determined under rules under section 60,

        (c)   for at least ten years of the period of adverse possession ending on the date of the application, the applicant (or any predecessor in title) reasonably believed that the land to which the application relates belonged to him, and

        (d)   the estate to which the application relates was registered more than one year prior to the date of the application.

    (5)   In relation to an application under paragraph 1(2), this paragraph has effect as if the reference in sub-paragraph (4)(c) to the date of the application were to the day before the date of the applicant's eviction.

Right to make further application for registration

6.   (1)   Where a person's application under paragraph 1 is rejected, he may make a further application to be registered as the proprietor of the estate if he is in adverse possession of the estate from the date of the application until the last day of the period of two years beginning with the date of its rejection.

    (1A)   Sub-paragraph (1) is subject to paragraph 16.

    (2)   However, a person may not make an application under this paragraph if—

        (a)   he is a defendant in proceedings which involve asserting a right to possession of the land,

        (b)   judgment for possession of the land has been given against him in the last two years, or

        (c)   he has been evicted from the land pursuant to a judgment for possession.

7.   If a person makes an application under paragraph 6, he is entitled to be entered in the register as the new proprietor of the estate.

Restriction on applications

8.   (1)   No one may apply under this Schedule to be registered as the proprietor of an estate in land during, or before the end of twelve months after the end of, any period in which the existing registered proprietor is for the purposes of the Limitation (Enemies and War Prisoners) Act 1945—

        (a)   an enemy, or

        (b)   detained in enemy territory.

    (2)   No-one may apply under this Schedule to be registered as the proprietor of an estate in land during any period in which the existing registered proprietor is—

        (a)   unable because of mental disability to make decisions about issues of the kind to which such an application would give rise, or

        (b)   unable to communicate such decisions because of mental disability or physical impairment.

    (3)   For the purposes of sub-paragraph (2), 'mental disability' means a disability or disorder of the mind or brain, whether permanent or temporary, which results in an impairment or disturbance of mental functioning.

    (4)   Where it appears to the registrar that sub-paragraph (1) or (2) applies in relation to an estate in land, he may include a note to that effect in the register.

Effect of registration

9. (1) Where a person is registered as the proprietor of an estate in land in pursuance of an application under this Schedule, the title by virtue of adverse possession which he had at the time of the application is extinguished.

    (2) Subject to sub-paragraph (3), the registration of a person under this Schedule as the proprietor of an estate in land does not affect the priority of any interest affecting the estate.

    (3) Subject to sub-paragraph (4), where a person is registered under this Schedule as the proprietor of an estate, the estate is vested in him free of any registered charge affecting the estate immediately before his registration.

    (4) Sub-paragraph (3) does not apply where registration as proprietor is in pursuance of an application determined by reference to whether any of the conditions in paragraph 5 applies.

Apportionment and discharge of charges

10. (1) Where—
     (a) a registered estate continues to be subject to a charge notwithstanding the registration of a person under this Schedule as the proprietor, and
     (b) the charge affects property other than the estate, the proprietor of the estate may require the chargee to apportion the amount secured by the charge at that time between the estate and the other property on the basis of their respective values.

     (2) The person requiring the apportionment is entitled to a discharge of his estate from the charge on payment of—
     (a) the amount apportioned to the estate, and
     (b) the costs incurred by the chargee as a result of the apportionment.

     (3) On a discharge under this paragraph, the liability of the chargor to the chargee is reduced by the amount apportioned to the estate.

     (4) Rules may make provision about apportionment under this paragraph, in particular, provision about—
     (a) procedure,
     (b) valuation,
     (c) calculation of costs payable under sub-paragraph (2)(b), and
     (d) payment of the costs of the chargor.

Meaning of "adverse possession"

11. (1) A person is in adverse possession of an estate in land for the purposes of this Schedule if, but for section 96, a period of limitation under section 15 of the Limitation Act 1980 would run in his favour in relation to the estate.

     (2) A person is also to be regarded for those purposes as having been in adverse possession of an estate in land—
     (a) where he is the successor in title to an estate in the land, during any period of adverse possession by a predecessor in title to that estate, or
     (b) during any period of adverse possession by another person which comes between, and is continuous with, periods of adverse possession of his own.

     (3) In determining whether for the purposes of this paragraph a period of limitation would run under section 15 of the Limitation Act 1980, there are to be disregarded—
     (a) the commencement of any legal proceedings, and
     (b) paragraph 6 of Schedule 1 to that Act.

Trusts

12. A person is not to be regarded as being in adverse possession of an estate for the purposes of this Schedule at any time when the estate is subject to a trust, unless the interest of each of the beneficiaries in the estate is an interest in possession.

Crown foreshore

13. (1) Where—
     (a) a person is in adverse possession of an estate in land,
     (b) the estate belongs to Her Majesty in right of the Crown or the Duchy of Lancaster or to the Duchy of Cornwall, and

      (c)   the land consists of foreshore, paragraph 1(1) is to have effect as if the reference to ten years were to sixty years.

(2)   For the purposes of sub-paragraph (1), land is to be treated as foreshore if it has been foreshore at any time in the previous ten years.

(3)   In this paragraph, 'foreshore' means the shore and bed of the sea and of any tidal water, below the line of the medium high tide between the spring and neap tides.

Rentcharges

14.   Rules must make provision to apply the preceding provisions of this Schedule to registered rentcharges, subject to such modifications and exceptions as the rules may provide.

Procedure

15.   Rules may make provision about the procedure to be followed pursuant to an application under this Schedule.

Extension of time limits because of mediation in certain cross-border disputes

16.   (1)   In this paragraph—

      (a)   'Mediation Directive' means Directive 2008/52/EC of the European Parliament and of the Council of 21 May 2008 on certain aspects of mediation in civil and commercial matters,

      (b)   'mediation' has the meaning given by article 3(a) of the Mediation Directive,

      (c)   'mediator' has the meaning given by article 3(b) of the Mediation Directive, and

      (d)   'relevant dispute' means a dispute to which article 8(1) of the Mediation Directive applies (certain cross-border disputes).

(2)   Sub-paragraph (3) applies where—

      (a)   a period of time is prescribed by paragraph 1(1), 1(2)(a) or 6(1) in relation to the whole or part of a relevant dispute,

      (b)   a mediation in relation to the relevant dispute starts before the period expires, and

      (c)   if not extended by this paragraph, the period would expire before the mediation ends or less than eight weeks after it ends.

(3)   The period expires instead at the end of eight weeks after the mediation ends (subject to sub-paragraph (4)).

(4)   If a period has been extended by this paragraph, sub-paragraphs (2) and (3) apply to the extended period as they apply to a period mentioned in sub-paragraph (2)(a).

(5)   Where more than one period applies in relation to a relevant dispute, the extension by sub-paragraph (3) of one of those periods does not affect the others.

(6)   For the purposes of this paragraph, a mediation starts on the date of the agreement to mediate that is entered into by the parties and the mediator.

(7)   For the purposes of this paragraph, a mediation ends on date of the first of these to occur—

      (a)   the parties reach an agreement in resolution of the relevant dispute,

      (b)   a party completes the notification of the other parties that it has withdrawn from the mediation,

      (c)   a party to whom a qualifying request is made fails to give a response reaching the other parties within 14 days of the request,

      (d)   the parties, after being notified that the mediator's appointment has ended (by death, resignation or otherwise), fail to agree within 14 days to seek to appoint a replacement mediator,

      (e)   the mediation otherwise comes to an end pursuant to the terms of the agreement to mediate.

(8)   For the purpose of sub-paragraph (7), a qualifying request is a request by a party that another (A) confirm to all parties that A is continuing with the mediation.

(9)   In the case of any relevant dispute, references in this paragraph to a mediation are references to the mediation so far as it relates to that dispute, and references to a party are to be read accordingly.

SCHEDULE 8
INDEMNITIES

Entitlement

1.   (1)   A person is entitled to be indemnified by the registrar if he suffers loss by reason of—
             (a)   rectification of the register,
             (b)   a mistake whose correction would involve rectification of the register,
             (c)   a mistake in an official search,
             (d)   a mistake in an official copy,
             (e)   a mistake in a document kept by the registrar which is not an original and is referred to in the register,
             (f)   the loss or destruction of a document lodged at the registry for inspection or safe custody,
             (g)   a mistake in the cautions register, or
             (h)   failure by the registrar to perform his duty under section 50.
       (2)   For the purposes of sub-paragraph (1)(a)—
             (a)   any person who suffers loss by reason of the change of title under section 62 is to be regarded as having suffered loss by reason of rectification of the register, and
             (b)   the proprietor of a registered estate or charge claiming in good faith under a forged disposition is, where the register is rectified, to be regarded as having suffered loss by reason of such rectification as if the disposition had not been forged.
       (3)   No indemnity under sub-paragraph (1)(b) is payable until a decision has been made about whether to alter the register for the purpose of correcting the mistake; and the loss suffered by reason of the mistake is to be determined in the light of that decision.

Mines and minerals

2.   No indemnity is payable under this Schedule on account of—
             (a)   any mines or minerals, or
             (b)   the existence of any right to work or get mines or minerals, unless it is noted in the register that the title to the registered estate concerned includes the mines or minerals.

Costs

3.   (1)   In respect of loss consisting of costs or expenses incurred by the claimant in relation to the matter, an indemnity under this Schedule is payable only on account of costs or expenses reasonably incurred by the claimant with the consent of the registrar.
       (2)   The requirement of consent does not apply where—
             (a)   the costs or expenses must be incurred by the claimant urgently, and
             (b)   it is not reasonably practicable to apply for the registrar's consent.
       (3)   If the registrar approves the incurring of costs or expenses after they have been incurred, they shall be treated for the purposes of this paragraph as having been incurred with his consent.

4.   (1)   If no indemnity is payable to a claimant under this Schedule, the registrar may pay such amount as he thinks fit in respect of any costs or expenses reasonably incurred by the claimant in connection with the claim which have been incurred with the consent of the registrar.
       (2)   The registrar may make a payment under sub-paragraph (1) notwithstanding the absence of consent if—
             (a)   it appears to him—
                   (i)   that the costs or expenses had to be incurred urgently, and
                   (ii)   that it was not reasonably practicable to apply for his consent, or
             (b)   he has subsequently approved the incurring of the costs or expenses.

Claimant's fraud or lack of care

5.   (1)   No indemnity is payable under this Schedule on account of any loss suffered by a claimant—
             (a)   wholly or partly as a result of his own fraud, or
             (b)   wholly as a result of his own lack of proper care.

(2) Where any loss is suffered by a claimant partly as a result of his own lack of proper care, any indemnity payable to him is to be reduced to such extent as is fair having regard to his share in the responsibility for the loss.

(3) For the purposes of this paragraph any fraud or lack of care on the part of a person from whom the claimant derives title (otherwise than under a disposition for valuable consideration which is registered or protected by an entry in the register) is to be treated as if it were fraud or lack of care on the part of the claimant.

Valuation of estates etc.

6. Where an indemnity is payable in respect of the loss of an estate, interest or charge, the value of the estate, interest or charge for the purposes of the indemnity is to be regarded as not exceeding—

    (a) in the case of an indemnity under paragraph 1(1)(a), its value immediately before rectification of the register (but as if there were to be no rectification), and

    (b) in the case of an indemnity under paragraph 1(1)(b), its value at the time when the mistake which caused the loss was made.

Determination of indemnity by court

7. (1) A person may apply to the court for the determination of any question as to—

    (a) whether he is entitled to an indemnity under this Schedule, or

    (b) the amount of such an indemnity.

  (2) Paragraph 3(1) does not apply to the costs of an application to the court under this paragraph or of any legal proceedings arising out of such an application.

Time limits

8. For the purposes of the Limitation Act 1980—

    (a) a liability to pay an indemnity under this Schedule is a simple contract debt, and

    (b) the cause of action arises at the time when the claimant knows, or but for his own default might have known, of the existence of his claim.

Interest

9. Rules may make provision about the payment of interest on an indemnity under this Schedule, including—

    (a) the circumstances in which interest is payable, and

    (b) the periods for and rates at which it is payable.

Recovery of indemnity by registrar

10. (1) Where an indemnity under this Schedule is paid to a claimant in respect of any loss, the registrar is entitled (without prejudice to any other rights he may have)—

    (a) to recover the amount paid from any person who caused or substantially contributed to the loss by his fraud, or

    (b) for the purpose of recovering the amount paid, to enforce the rights of action referred to in sub-paragraph (2).

  (2) Those rights of action are—

    (a) any right of action (of whatever nature and however arising) which the claimant would have been entitled to enforce had the indemnity not been paid, and

    (b) where the register has been rectified, any right of action (of whatever nature and however arising) which the person in whose favour the register has been rectified would have been entitled to enforce had it not been rectified.

  (3) References in this paragraph to an indemnity include interest paid on an indemnity under rules under paragraph 9.

Interpretation

11. (1) For the purposes of this Schedule, references to a mistake in something include anything mistakenly omitted from it as well as anything mistakenly included in it.

  (2) In this Schedule, references to rectification of the register are to alteration of the register which—

    (a) involves the correction of a mistake, and

    (b) prejudicially affects the title of a registered proprietor.

SCHEDULE 10
MISCELLANEOUS AND GENERAL POWERS

PART 1
MISCELLANEOUS

Dealings with estates subject to compulsory first registration

1.   (1)   Rules may make provision—
       (a)   applying this Act to a pre-registration dealing with a registrable legal estate as if the dealing had taken place after the date of first registration of the estate, and
       (b)   about the date on which registration of the dealing is effective.
      (2)   For the purposes of sub-paragraph (1)—
       (a)   a legal estate is registrable if a person is subject to a duty under section 6 to make an application to be registered as the proprietor of it, and
       (b)   a pre-registration dealing is one which takes place before the making of such an application.

Regulation of title matters between sellers and buyers

2.   (1)   Rules may make provision about the obligations with respect to—
       (a)   proof of title, or
       (b)   perfection of title, of the seller under a contract for the transfer, or other disposition, for valuable consideration of a registered estate or charge.
      (2)   Rules under this paragraph may be expressed to have effect notwithstanding any stipulation to the contrary.

Implied covenants

3.   Rules may—
     (a)   make provision about the form of provisions extending or limiting any covenant implied by virtue of Part 1 of the Law of Property (Miscellaneous Provisions) Act 1994 (c. 36) (implied covenants for title) on a registrable disposition;
     (b)   make provision about the application of section 77 of the Law of Property Act 1925 (c. 20) (implied covenants in conveyance subject to rents) to transfers of registered estates;
     (c)   make provision about reference in the register to implied covenants, including provision for the state of the register to be conclusive in relation to whether covenants have been implied.

Land certificates

4.   Rules may make provision about—
     (a)   when a certificate of registration of title to a legal estate may be issued,
     (b)   the form and content of such a certificate, and
     (c)   when such a certificate must be produced or surrendered to the registrar.

PART 2
GENERAL

Notice

5.   (1)   Rules may make provision about the form, content and service of notice under this Act.
      (2)   Rules under this paragraph about the service of notice may, in particular—
       (a)   make provision requiring the supply of an address for service and about the entry of addresses for service in the register;
       (b)   make provision about—
         (i)   the time for service,
         (ii)   the mode of service, and
         (iii)   when service is to be regarded as having taken place.

Applications

6. Rules may—
   (a) make provision about the form and content of applications under this Act;
   (b) make provision requiring applications under this Act to be supported by such evidence as the rules may provide;
   (c) make provision about when an application under this Act is to be taken as made;
   (d) make provision about the order in which competing applications are to be taken to rank;
   (e) make provision for an alteration made by the registrar for the purpose of correcting a mistake in an application or accompanying document to have effect in such circumstances as the rules may provide as if made by the applicant or other interested party or parties.

Statutory statements

7. Rules may make provision about the form of any statement required under an enactment to be included in an instrument effecting a registrable disposition or a disposition which triggers the requirement of registration.

Residual power

8. Rules may make any other provision which it is expedient to make for the purposes of carrying this Act into effect, whether similar or not to any provision which may be made under the other powers to make land registration rules.

SCHEDULE 12
TRANSITION

Existing entries in the register

1. Nothing in the repeals made by this Act affects the validity of any entry in the register.
2. (1) This Act applies to notices entered under the Land Registration Act 1925 as it applies to notices entered in pursuance of an application under section 34(2)(a).
   (2) This Act applies to restrictions and inhibitions entered under the Land Registration Act 1925 as it applies to restrictions entered under this Act.
   (3) Notwithstanding their repeal by this Act, sections 55 and 56 of the Land Registration Act 1925 shall continue to have effect so far as relating to cautions against dealings lodged under that Act.
   (4) Rules may make provision about cautions against dealings entered under the Land Registration Act 1925.
   (5) In this paragraph, references to the Land Registration Act 1925 include a reference to any enactment replaced (directly or indirectly) by that Act.
3. An entry in the register which, immediately before the repeal of section 144(1)(xi) of the Land Registration Act 1925, operated by virtue of rule 239 of the Land Registration Rules as a caution under section 54 of that Act shall continue to operate as such a caution.

Existing cautions against first registration

4. Notwithstanding the repeal of section 56(3) of the Land Registration Act 1925, that provision shall continue to have effect in relation to cautions against first registration lodged under that Act, or any enactment replaced (directly or indirectly) by that Act.

Pending applications

5. Notwithstanding the repeal of the Land Registration Act 1925, that Act shall continue to have effect in relation to an application for the entry in the register of a notice, restriction, inhibition or caution against dealings which is pending immediately before the repeal of the provision under which the application is made.
6. Notwithstanding the repeal of section 53 of the Land Registration Act 1925, subsections (1) and (2) of that section shall continue to have effect in relation to an application to lodge a caution against first registration which is pending immediately before the repeal of those provisions.

Former overriding interests

7.   For the period of three years beginning with the day on which Schedule 1 comes into force, it has effect with the insertion after paragraph 14 of—

'15.   A right acquired under the Limitation Act 1980 before the coming into force of this Schedule.'

8.   Schedule 3 has effect with the insertion after paragraph 2 of—

'2A (1) An interest which, immediately before the coming into force of this Schedule, was an overriding interest under section 70(1)(g) of the Land Registration Act 1925 by virtue of a person's receipt of rents and profits, except for an interest of a person of whom inquiry was made before the disposition and who failed to disclose the right when he could reasonably have been expected to do so.

(2) Sub-paragraph (1) does not apply to an interest if at any time since the coming into force of this Schedule it has been an interest which, had the Land Registration Act 1925 continued in force, would not have been an overriding interest under section 70(1)(g) of that Act by virtue of a person's receipt of rents and profits.'

9.   (1)   This paragraph applies to an easement or profit a prendre which was an overriding interest in relation to a registered estate immediately before the coming into force of Schedule 3, but which would not fall within paragraph 3 of that Schedule if created after the coming into force of that Schedule.

(2)   In relation to an interest to which this paragraph applies, Schedule 3 has effect as if the interest were not excluded from paragraph 3.

10.   For the period of three years beginning with the day on which Schedule 3 comes into force, paragraph 3 of the Schedule has effect with the omission of the exception.

11.   For the period of three years beginning with the day on which Schedule 3 comes into force, it has effect with the insertion after paragraph 14 of—

'15.   A right under paragraph 18(1) of Schedule 12.'

12.   Paragraph 1 of each of Schedules 1 and 3 shall be taken to include an interest which immediately before the coming into force of the Schedule was an overriding interest under section 70(1)(k) of the Land Registration Act 1925.

13.   Paragraph 6 of each of Schedules 1 and 3 shall be taken to include an interest which immediately before the coming into force of the Schedule was an overriding interest under section 70(1)(i) of the Land Registration Act 1925 and whose status as such was preserved by section 19(3) of the Local Land Charges Act 1975 (transitional provision in relation to change in definition of 'local land charge').

Cautions against first registration

14.   (1)   For the period of two years beginning with the day on which section 15 comes into force, it has effect with the following omissions—

(a)   in subsection (1), the words 'Subject to subsection (3),', and

(b)   subsection (3).

(2)   Any caution lodged by virtue of sub-paragraph (1) which is in force immediately before the end of the period mentioned in that sub-paragraph shall cease to have effect at the end of that period, except in relation to applications for registration made before the end of that period.

(3)   This paragraph does not apply to section 15 as applied by section 81.

15.   (1)   As applied by section 81, section 15 has effect for the period of ten years beginning with the day on which it comes into force, or such longer period as rules may provide, with the omission of subsection (3)(a)(i).

(2)   Any caution lodged by virtue of sub-paragraph (1) which is in force immediately before the end of the period mentioned in that sub-paragraph shall cease to have effect at the end of that period, except in relation to applications for registration made before the end of that period.

16.   This Act shall apply as if the definition of 'caution against first registration' in section 132 included cautions lodged under section 53 of the Land Registration Act 1925.

Applications under section 34 or 43 by cautioners

17.   Where a caution under section 54 of the Land Registration Act 1925 is lodged in respect of a person's estate, right, interest or claim, he may only make an application under section 34 or 43 above in respect of that estate, right, interest or claim if he also applies to the registrar for the withdrawal of the caution.

Adverse possession

18. (1) Where a registered estate in land is held in trust for a person by virtue of section 75(1) of the Land Registration Act 1925 immediately before the coming into force of section 97, he is entitled to be registered as the proprietor of the estate.

(2) A person has a defence to any action for the possession of land (in addition to any other defence he may have) if he is entitled under this paragraph to be registered as the proprietor of an estate in the land.

(3) Where in an action for possession of land a court determines that a person is entitled to a defence under this paragraph, the court must order the registrar to register him as the proprietor of the estate in relation to which he is entitled under this paragraph to be registered.

(4) Entitlement under this paragraph shall be disregarded for the purposes of section 131(1).

(5) Rules may make transitional provision for cases where a rentcharge is held in trust under section 75(1) of the Land Registration Act 1925 immediately before the coming into force of section 97.

Indemnities

19. (1) Schedule 8 applies in relation to claims made before the commencement of that Schedule which have not been settled by agreement or finally determined by that time (as well as to claims for indemnity made after the commencement of that Schedule).

(2) But paragraph 3(1) of that Schedule does not apply in relation to costs and expenses incurred in respect of proceedings, negotiations or other matters begun before 27 April 1997.

Implied indemnity covenants on transfers of pre-1996 leases

20. (1) On a disposition of a registered leasehold estate by way of transfer, the following covenants are implied in the instrument effecting the disposition, unless the contrary intention is expressed—

(a) in the case of a transfer of the whole of the land comprised in the registered lease, the covenant in sub-paragraph (2), and

(b) in the case of a transfer of part of the land comprised in the lease—

(i) the covenant in sub-paragraph (3), and

(ii) where the transferor continues to hold land under the lease, the covenant in sub-paragraph (4).

(2) The transferee covenants with the transferor that during the residue of the term granted by the registered lease the transferee and the persons deriving title under him will—

(a) pay the rent reserved by the lease,

(b) comply with the covenants and conditions contained in the lease, and

(c) keep the transferor and the persons deriving title under him indemnified against all actions, expenses and claims on account of any failure to comply with paragraphs (a) and (b).

(3) The transferee covenants with the transferor that during the residue of the term granted by the registered lease the transferee and the persons deriving title under him will—

(a) where the rent reserved by the lease is apportioned, pay the rent apportioned to the part transferred,

(b) comply with the covenants and conditions contained in the lease so far as affecting the part transferred, and

(c) keep the transferor and the persons deriving title under him indemnified against all actions, expenses and claims on account of any failure to comply with paragraphs (a) and (b).

(4) The transferor covenants with the transferee that during the residue of the term granted by the registered lease the transferor and the persons deriving title under him will—

(a) where the rent reserved by the lease is apportioned, pay the rent apportioned to the part retained,

(b) comply with the covenants and conditions contained in the lease so far as affecting the part retained, and

(c) keep the transferee and the persons deriving title under him indemnified against all actions, expenses and claims on account of any failure to comply with paragraphs (a) and (b).

(5) This paragraph does not apply to a lease which is a new tenancy for the purposes of section 1 of the Landlord and Tenant (Covenants) Act 1995.

COMMONHOLD AND LEASEHOLD REFORM ACT 2002
(2002, c. 15)

PART 1
COMMONHOLD

Nature of commonhold

1.   Commonhold land

(1)   Land is commonhold land if—

    (a)   the freehold estate in the land is registered as a freehold estate in commonhold land,

    (b)   the land is specified in the articles of association of a commonhold association as the land in relation to which the association is to exercise functions, and

    (c)   a commonhold community statement makes provision for rights and duties of the commonhold association and unit-holders (whether or not the statement has come into force).

(2)   In this Part a reference to a commonhold is a reference to land in relation to which a commonhold association exercises functions.

(3)   In this Part—

'commonhold association' has the meaning given by section 34,

'commonhold community statement' has the meaning given by section 31,

'commonhold unit' has the meaning given by section 11,

'common parts' has the meaning given by section 25, and

'unit-holder' has the meaning given by sections 12 and 13.

(4)   Sections 7 and 9 make provision for the vesting in the commonhold association of the fee simple in possession in the common parts of a commonhold.

Registration

2.   Application

(1)   The Registrar shall register a freehold estate in land as a freehold estate in commonhold land if—

    (a)   the registered freeholder of the land makes an application under this section, and

    (b)   no part of the land is already commonhold land.

(2)   An application under this section must be accompanied by the documents listed in Schedule 1.

(3)   A person is the registered freeholder of land for the purposes of this Part if—

    (a)   he is registered as the proprietor of a freehold estate in the land with absolute title, or

    (b)   he has applied, and the Registrar is satisfied that he is entitled, to be registered as mentioned in paragraph (a).

3.   Consent

(1)   An application under section 2 may not be made in respect of a freehold estate in land without the consent of anyone who—

    (a)   is the registered proprietor of the freehold estate in the whole or part of the land,

    (b)   is the registered proprietor of a leasehold estate in the whole or part of the land granted for a term of more than 21 years,

    (c)   is the registered proprietor of a charge over the whole or part of the land, or

    (d)   falls within any other class of person which may be prescribed.

(2)   Regulations shall make provision about consent for the purposes of this section; in particular, the regulations may make provision—

    (a)   prescribing the form of consent;

    (b)   about the effect and duration of consent (including provision for consent to bind successors);

    (c)   about withdrawal of consent (including provision preventing withdrawal in specified circumstances);

    (d)   for consent given for the purpose of one application under section 2 to have effect for the purpose of another application;

    (e)   for consent to be deemed to have been given in specified circumstances;

    (f)   enabling a court to dispense with a requirement for consent in specified circumstances.

(3)   An order under subsection (2)(f) dispensing with a requirement for consent—

    (a)   may be absolute or conditional, and

    (b)   may make such other provision as the court thinks appropriate.

4. Land which may not be commonhold

Schedule 2 (which provides that an application under section 2 may not relate wholly or partly to land of certain kinds) shall have effect.

5. Registered details

(1)   The Registrar shall ensure that in respect of any commonhold land the following are kept in his custody and referred to in the register—

    (a)   the prescribed details of the commonhold association;

    (b)   the prescribed details of the registered freeholder of each commonhold unit;

    (c)   a copy of the commonhold community statement;

    (d)   a copy of the articles of association of the commonhold association.

(2)   The Registrar may arrange for a document or information to be kept in his custody and referred to in the register in respect of commonhold land if the document or information—

    (a)   is not mentioned in subsection (1), but

    (b)   is submitted to the Registrar in accordance with a provision made by or by virtue of this Part.

(3)   Subsection (1)(b) shall not apply during a transitional period within the meaning of section 8.

6. Registration in error

(1)   This section applies where a freehold estate in land is registered as a freehold estate in commonhold land and—

    (a)   the application for registration was not made in accordance with section 2,

    (b)   the certificate under paragraph 7 of Schedule 1 was inaccurate, or

    (c)   the registration contravened a provision made by or by virtue of this Part.

(2)   The register may not be altered by the Registrar under Schedule 4 to the Land Registration Act 2002 (alteration of register).

(3)   The court may grant a declaration that the freehold estate should not have been registered as a freehold estate in commonhold land.

(4)   A declaration under subsection (3) may be granted only on the application of a person who claims to be adversely affected by the registration.

(5)   On granting a declaration under subsection (3) the court may make any order which appears to it to be appropriate.

(6)   An order under subsection (5) may, in particular—

    (a)   provide for the registration to be treated as valid for all purposes;

    (b)   provide for alteration of the register;

    (c)   provide for land to cease to be commonhold land;

    (d)   require a director or other specified officer of a commonhold association to take steps to alter or amend a document;

    (e)   require a director or other specified officer of a commonhold association to take specified steps;

    (f)   make an award of compensation (whether or not contingent upon the occurrence or non-occurrence of a specified event) to be paid by one specified person to another;

    (g)   apply, disapply or modify a provision of Schedule 8 to the Land Registration Act 2002 (indemnity).

Effect of registration

7. Registration without unit-holders

(1)   This section applies where—

    (a)   a freehold estate in land is registered as a freehold estate in commonhold land in pursuance of an application under section 2, and

    (b)   the application is not accompanied by a statement under section 9(1)(b).

(2)   On registration—
    (a)   the applicant shall continue to be registered as the proprietor of the freehold estate in the commonhold land, and
    (b)   the rights and duties conferred and imposed by the commonhold community statement shall not come into force (subject to section 8(2)(b)).

(3)   Where after registration a person other than the applicant becomes entitled to be registered as the proprietor of the freehold estate in one or more, but not all, of the commonhold units—
    (a)   the commonhold association shall be entitled to be registered as the proprietor of the freehold estate in the common parts,
    (b)   the Registrar shall register the commonhold association in accordance with paragraph (a) (without an application being made),
    (c)   the rights and duties conferred and imposed by the commonhold community statement shall come into force, and
    (d)   any lease of the whole or part of the commonhold land shall be extinguished by virtue of this section.

(4)   For the purpose of subsection (3)(d) 'lease' means a lease which—
    (a)   is granted for any term, and
    (b)   is granted before the commonhold association becomes entitled to be registered as the proprietor of the freehold estate in the common parts.

8.   Transitional period

(1)   In this Part 'transitional period' means the period between registration of the freehold estate in land as a freehold estate in commonhold land and the event mentioned in section 7(3).

(2)   Regulations may provide that during a transitional period a relevant provision—
    (a)   shall not have effect, or
    (b)   shall have effect with specified modifications.

(3)   In subsection (2) 'relevant provision' means a provision made—
    (a)   by or by virtue of this Part,
    (b)   by a commonhold community statement, or
    (c)   by the articles of the commonhold association.

(4)   The Registrar shall arrange for the freehold estate in land to cease to be registered as a freehold estate in commonhold land if the registered proprietor makes an application to the Registrar under this subsection during the transitional period.

(5)   The provisions about consent made by or under sections 2 and 3 and Schedule 1 shall apply in relation to an application under subsection (4) as they apply in relation to an application under section 2.

(6)   A reference in this Part to a commonhold association exercising functions in relation to commonhold land includes a reference to a case where a commonhold association would exercise functions in relation to commonhold land but for the fact that the time in question falls in a transitional period.

9.   Registration with unit-holders

(1)   This section applies in relation to a freehold estate in commonhold land if—
    (a)   it is registered as a freehold estate in commonhold land in pursuance of an application under section 2, and
    (b)   the application is accompanied by a statement by the applicant requesting that this section should apply.

(2)   A statement under subsection (1)(b) must include a list of the commonhold units giving in relation to each one the prescribed details of the proposed initial unit-holder or joint unit-holders.

(3)   On registration—
    (a)   the commonhold association shall be entitled to be registered as the proprietor of the freehold estate in the common parts,
    (b)   a person specified by virtue of subsection (2) as the initial unit-holder of a commonhold unit shall be entitled to be registered as the proprietor of the freehold estate in the unit,
    (c)   a person specified by virtue of subsection (2) as an initial joint unit-holder of a commonhold unit shall be entitled to be registered as one of the proprietors of the freehold estate in the unit,

(d) the Registrar shall make entries in the register to reflect paragraphs (a) to (c) (without applications being made),

(e) the rights and duties conferred and imposed by the commonhold community statement shall come into force, and

(f) any lease of the whole or part of the commonhold land shall be extinguished by virtue of this section.

(4) For the purpose of subsection (3)(f) 'lease' means a lease which—

(a) is granted for any term, and

(b) is granted before the commonhold association becomes entitled to be registered as the proprietor of the freehold estate in the common parts.

10. Extinguished lease: liability

(1) This section applies where—

(a) a lease is extinguished by virtue of section 7(3)(d) or 9(3)(f), and

(b) the consent of the holder of that lease was not among the consents required by section 3 in respect of the application under section 2 for the land to become commonhold land.

(2) If the holder of a lease superior to the extinguished lease gave consent under section 3, he shall be liable for loss suffered by the holder of the extinguished lease.

(3) If the holders of a number of leases would be liable under subsection (2), liability shall attach only to the person whose lease was most proximate to the extinguished lease.

(4) If no person is liable under subsection (2), the person who gave consent under section 3 as the holder of the freehold estate out of which the extinguished lease was granted shall be liable for loss suffered by the holder of the extinguished lease.

Commonhold unit

11. Definition

(1) In this Part 'commonhold unit' means a commonhold unit specified in a commonhold community statement in accordance with this section.

(2) A commonhold community statement must—

(a) specify at least two parcels of land as commonhold units, and

(b) define the extent of each commonhold unit.

(3) In defining the extent of a commonhold unit a commonhold community statement—

(a) must refer to a plan which is included in the statement and which complies with prescribed requirements,

(b) may refer to an area subject to the exclusion of specified structures, fittings, apparatus or appurtenances within the area,

(c) may exclude the structures which delineate an area referred to, and

(d) may refer to two or more areas (whether or not contiguous).

(4) A commonhold unit need not contain all or any part of a building.

12. Unit-holder

A person is the unit-holder of a commonhold unit if he is entitled to be registered as the proprietor of the freehold estate in the unit (whether or not he is registered).

13. Joint unit-holders

(1) Two or more persons are joint unit-holders of a commonhold unit if they are entitled to be registered as proprietors of the freehold estate in the unit (whether or not they are registered).

(2) In the application of the following provisions to a unit with joint unit-holders a reference to a unit-holder is a reference to the joint unit-holders together—

(a) ...

(b) section 15(1),

(c) ...

(d) section 20(1),

(e) section 23(1),

(f) section 35(1)(b), and

(g) ...

(h) ...

(i) section 47(2).

(3) In the application of the following provisions to a unit with joint unit-holders a reference to a unit-holder includes a reference to each joint unit-holder and to the joint unit-holders together—

    (a)   section 1(1)(c),
    (aa)   section 14(3),
    (ab)   section 15(3),
    (b)   section 16,
    (ba)   section 19(2) and (3),
    (c)   section 31(1)(b), (3)(b), (5)(j) and (7),
    (d)   section 32(4)(a) and (c),
    (e)   section 35(1)(a), (2) and (3),
    (f)   section 37(2),
    (fa)   section 38(1),
    (fb)   section 39(2)
    (g)   section 40(1), and
    (h)   section 58(3)(a).

(4) Regulations under this Part which refer to a unit-holder shall make provision for the construction of the reference in the case of joint unit-holders.

(5) Regulations may amend subsection (2) or (3).

(6) Regulations may make provision for the construction in the case of joint unit-holders of a reference to a unit-holder in—

    (a)   an enactment,
    (b)   a commonhold community statement,
    (c)   the articles of association of a commonhold association, or
    (d)   another document.

14.   Use and maintenance

(1) A commonhold community statement must make provision regulating the use of commonhold units.

(2) A commonhold community statement must make provision imposing duties in respect of the insurance, repair and maintenance of each commonhold unit.

(3) A duty under subsection (2) may be imposed on the commonhold association or the unit-holder.

15.   Transfer

(1) In this Part a reference to the transfer of a commonhold unit is a reference to the transfer of a unit-holder's freehold estate in a unit to another person—

    (a)   whether or not for consideration,
    (b)   whether or not subject to any reservation or other terms, and
    (c)   whether or not by operation of law.

(2) A commonhold community statement may not prevent or restrict the transfer of a commonhold unit.

(3) On the transfer of a commonhold unit the new unit-holder shall notify the commonhold association of the transfer.

(4) Regulations may—

    (a)   prescribe the form and manner of notice under subsection (3);
    (b)   prescribe the time within which notice is to be given;
    (c)   make provision (including provision requiring the payment of money) about the effect of failure to give notice.

16.   Transfer: effect

(1) A right or duty conferred or imposed—

    (a)   by a commonhold community statement, or
    (b)   in accordance with section 20, shall affect a new unit-holder in the same way as it affected the former unit-holder.

(2) A former unit-holder shall not incur a liability or acquire a right—

    (a)   under or by virtue of the commonhold community statement, or
    (b)   by virtue of anything done in accordance with section 20.

(3) Subsection (2)—

    (a)   shall not be capable of being disapplied or varied by agreement, and
    (b)   is without prejudice to any liability or right incurred or acquired before a transfer takes effect.

(4) In this section—
'former unit-holder' means a person from whom a commonhold unit has been transferred (whether or not he has ceased to be the registered proprietor), and
'new unit-holder' means a person to whom a commonhold unit is transferred (whether or not he has yet become the registered proprietor).

17. Leasing: residential

(1) It shall not be possible to create a term of years absolute in a residential commonhold unit unless the term satisfies prescribed conditions.
(2) The conditions may relate to—
    (a) length;
    (b) the circumstances in which the term is granted;
    (c) any other matter.
(3) Subject to subsection (4), an instrument or agreement shall be of no effect to the extent that it purports to create a term of years in contravention of subsection (1).
(4) Where an instrument or agreement purports to create a term of years in contravention of subsection (1) a party to the instrument or agreement may apply to the court for an order—
    (a) providing for the instrument or agreement to have effect as if it provided for the creation of a term of years of a specified kind;
    (b) providing for the return or payment of money;
    (c) making such other provision as the court thinks appropriate.
(5) A commonhold unit is residential if provision made in the commonhold community statement by virtue of section 14(1) requires it to be used only—
    (a) for residential purposes, or
    (b) for residential and other incidental purposes.

18. Leasing: non-residential

An instrument or agreement which creates a term of years absolute in a commonhold unit which is not residential (within the meaning of section 17) shall have effect subject to any provision of the commonhold community statement.

19. Leasing: supplementary

(1) Regulations may—
    (a) impose obligations on a tenant of a commonhold unit;
    (b) enable a commonhold community statement to impose obligations on a tenant of a commonhold unit.
(2) Regulations under subsection (1) may, in particular, require a tenant of a commonhold unit to make payments to the commonhold association or a unit-holder in discharge of payments which—
    (a) are due in accordance with the commonhold community statement to be made by the unit-holder, or
    (b) are due in accordance with the commonhold community statement to be made by another tenant of the unit.
(3) Regulations under subsection (1) may, in particular, provide—
    (a) for the amount of payments under subsection (2) to be set against sums owed by the tenant (whether to the person by whom the payments were due to be made or to some other person);
    (b) for the amount of payments under subsection (2) to be recovered from the unit-holder or another tenant of the unit.
(4) Regulations may modify a rule of law about leasehold estates (whether deriving from the common law or from an enactment) in its application to a term of years in a commonhold unit.
(5) Regulations under this section—
    (a) may make provision generally or in relation to specified circumstances, and
    (b) may make different provision for different descriptions of commonhold land or commonhold unit.

20. Other transactions

(1) A commonhold community statement may not prevent or restrict the creation, grant or transfer by a unit-holder of—
    (a) an interest in the whole or part of his unit, or
    (b) a charge over his unit.

(2)   Subsection (1) is subject to sections 17 to 19 (which impose restrictions about leases).

(3)   It shall not be possible to create an interest of a prescribed kind in a commonhold unit unless the commonhold association—
    (a)   is a party to the creation of the interest, or
    (b)   consents in writing to the creation of the interest.

(4)   A commonhold association may act as described in subsection (3)(a) or (b) only if—
    (a)   the association passes a resolution to take the action, and
    (b)   at least 75 per cent. of those who vote on the resolution vote in favour.

(5)   An instrument or agreement shall be of no effect to the extent that it purports to create an interest in contravention of subsection (3).

(6)   In this section 'interest' does not include—
    (a)   a charge, or
    (b)   an interest which arises by virtue of a charge.

21.   Part-unit: interests

(1)   It shall not be possible to create an interest in part only of a commonhold unit.

(2)   But subsection (1) shall not prevent—
    (a)   the creation of a term of years absolute in part only of a residential commonhold unit where the term satisfies prescribed conditions,
    (b)   the creation of a term of years absolute in part only of a non-residential commonhold unit, or
    (c)   the transfer of the freehold estate in part only of a commonhold unit where the commonhold association consents in writing to the transfer.

(3)   An instrument or agreement shall be of no effect to the extent that it purports to create an interest in contravention of subsection (1).

(4)   Subsection (5) applies where—
    (a)   land becomes commonhold land or is added to a commonhold unit, and
    (b)   immediately before that event there is an interest in the land which could not be created after that event by reason of subsection (1).

(5)   The interest shall be extinguished by virtue of this subsection to the extent that it could not be created by reason of subsection (1).

(6)   Section 17(2) and (4) shall apply (with any necessary modifications) in relation to subsection (2)(a) and (b) above.

(7)   Where part only of a unit is held under a lease, regulations may modify the application of a provision which—
    (a)   is made by or by virtue of this Part, and
    (b)   applies to a unit-holder or a tenant or both.

(8)   Section 20(4) shall apply in relation to subsection (2)(c) above.

(9)   Where the freehold interest in part only of a commonhold unit is transferred, the part transferred—
    (a)   becomes a new commonhold unit by virtue of this subsection, or
    (b)   in a case where the request for consent under subsection (2)(c) states that this paragraph is to apply, becomes part of a commonhold unit specified in the request.

(10)   Regulations may make provision, or may require a commonhold community statement to make provision, about—
    (a)   registration of units created by virtue of subsection (9);
    (b)   the adaptation of provision made by or by virtue of this Part or by or by virtue of a commonhold community statement to a case where units are created or modified by virtue of subsection (9).

22.   Part-unit: charging

(1)   It shall not be possible to create a charge over part only of an interest in a commonhold unit.

(2)   An instrument or agreement shall be of no effect to the extent that it purports to create a charge in contravention of subsection (1).

(3)   Subsection (4) applies where—
    (a)   land becomes commonhold land or is added to a commonhold unit, and
    (b)   immediately before that event there is a charge over the land which could not be created after that event by reason of subsection (1).

(4)   The charge shall be extinguished by virtue of this subsection to the extent that it could not be created by reason of subsection (1).

23.   Changing size
(1)   An amendment of a commonhold community statement which redefines the extent of a commonhold unit may not be made unless the unit-holder consents—
   (a)   in writing, and
   (b)   before the amendment is made.
(2)   But regulations may enable a court to dispense with the requirement for consent on the application of a commonhold association in prescribed circumstances.

24.   Changing size: charged unit
(1)   This section applies to an amendment of a commonhold community statement which redefines the extent of a commonhold unit over which there is a registered charge.
(2)   The amendment may not be made unless the registered proprietor of the charge consents—
   (a)   in writing, and
   (b)   before the amendment is made.
(3)   But regulations may enable a court to dispense with the requirement for consent on the application of a commonhold association in prescribed circumstances.
(4)   If the amendment removes land from the commonhold unit, the charge shall by virtue of this subsection be extinguished to the extent that it relates to the land which is removed.
(5)   If the amendment adds land to the unit, the charge shall by virtue of this subsection be extended so as to relate to the land which is added.
(6)   Regulations may make provision—
   (a)   requiring notice to be given to the Registrar in circumstances to which this section applies;
   (b)   requiring the Registrar to alter the register to reflect the application of subsection (4) or (5).

Common parts

25.   Definition
(1)   In this Part 'common parts' in relation to a commonhold means every part of the commonhold which is not for the time being a commonhold unit in accordance with the commonhold community statement.
(2)   A commonhold community statement may make provision in respect of a specified part of the common parts (a 'limited use area') restricting—
   (a)   the classes of person who may use it;
   (b)   the kind of use to which it may be put.
(3)   A commonhold community statement—
   (a)   may make provision which has effect only in relation to a limited use area, and
   (b)   may make different provision for different limited use areas.

26.   Use and maintenance
A commonhold community statement must make provision—
   (a)   regulating the use of the common parts;
   (b)   requiring the commonhold association to insure the common parts;
   (c)   requiring the commonhold association to repair and maintain the common parts.

27.   Transactions
(1)   Nothing in a commonhold community statement shall prevent or restrict—
   (a)   the transfer by the commonhold association of its freehold estate in any part of the common parts, or
   (b)   the creation by the commonhold association of an interest in any part of the common parts.
(2)   In this section 'interest' does not include—
   (a)   a charge, or
   (b)   an interest which arises by virtue of a charge.

28.   Charges: general prohibition
(1)   It shall not be possible to create a charge over common parts.
(2)   An instrument or agreement shall be of no effect to the extent that it purports to create a charge over common parts.
(3)   Where by virtue of section 7 or 9 a commonhold association is registered as the proprietor of common parts, a charge which relates wholly or partly to the common parts shall be extinguished by virtue of this subsection to the extent that it relates to the common parts.

(4)   Where by virtue of section 30 land vests in a commonhold association following an amendment to a commonhold community statement which has the effect of adding land to the common parts, a charge which relates wholly or partly to the land added shall be extinguished by virtue of this subsection to the extent that it relates to that land.

(5)   This section is subject to section 29 (which permits certain mortgages).

29.   New legal mortgages

(1)   Section 28 shall not apply in relation to a legal mortgage if the creation of the mortgage is approved by a resolution of the commonhold association.

(2)   A resolution for the purposes of subsection (1) must be passed—
    (a)   before the mortgage is created, and
    (b)   unanimously.

(3)   In this section 'legal mortgage' has the meaning given by section 205(1)(xvi) of the Law of Property Act 1925 (interpretation).

30.   Additions to common parts

(1)   This section applies where an amendment of a commonhold community statement—
    (a)   specifies land which forms part of a commonhold unit, and
    (b)   provides for that land (the 'added land') to be added to the common parts.

(2)   The amendment may not be made unless the registered proprietor of any charge over the added land consents—
    (a)   in writing, and
    (b)   before the amendment is made.

(3)   But regulations may enable a court to dispense with the requirement for consent on the application of a commonhold association in specified circumstances.

(4)   On the filing of the amended statement under section 33—
    (a)   the commonhold association shall be entitled to be registered as the proprietor of the freehold estate in the added land, and
    (b)   the Registrar shall register the commonhold association in accordance with paragraph (a) (without an application being made).

Commonhold community statement

31.   Form and content: general

(1)   A commonhold community statement is a document which makes provision in relation to specified land for—
    (a)   the rights and duties of the commonhold association, and
    (b)   the rights and duties of the unit-holders.

(2)   A commonhold community statement must be in the prescribed form.

(3)   A commonhold community statement may—
    (a)   impose a duty on the commonhold association;
    (b)   impose a duty on a unit-holder;
    (c)   make provision about the taking of decisions in connection with the management of the commonhold or any other matter concerning it.

(4)   Subsection (3) is subject to—
    (a)   any provision made by or by virtue of this Part, and
    (b)   any provision of the articles of the commonhold association.

(5)   In subsection (3)(a) and (b) 'duty' includes, in particular, a duty—
    (a)   to pay money;
    (b)   to undertake works;
    (c)   to grant access;
    (d)   to give notice;
    (e)   to refrain from entering into transactions of a specified kind in relation to a commonhold unit;
    (f)   to refrain from using the whole or part of a commonhold unit for a specified purpose or for anything other than a specified purpose;
    (g)   to refrain from undertaking works (including alterations) of a specified kind;
    (h)   to refrain from causing nuisance or annoyance;
    (i)   to refrain from specified behaviour;
    (j)   to indemnify the commonhold association or a unit-holder in respect of costs arising from the breach of a statutory requirement.

(6)   Provision in a commonhold community statement imposing a duty to pay money (whether in pursuance of subsection (5)(a) or any other provision made by or by virtue of this Part) may include provision for the payment of interest in the case of late payment.

(7)   A duty conferred by a commonhold community statement on a commonhold association or a unit-holder shall not require any other formality.

(8)   A commonhold community statement may not provide for the transfer or loss of an interest in land on the occurrence or non-occurrence of a specified event.

(9)   Provision made by a commonhold community statement shall be of no effect to the extent that—
   (a)   it is prohibited by virtue of section 32,
   (b)   it is inconsistent with any provision made by or by virtue of this Part,
   (c)   it is inconsistent with anything which is treated as included in the statement by virtue of section 32, or
   (d)   it is inconsistent with the articles of association of the commonhold association.

32.   Regulations

(1)   Regulations shall make provision about the content of a commonhold community statement.

(2)   The regulations may permit, require or prohibit the inclusion in a statement of—
   (a)   specified provision, or
   (b)   provision of a specified kind, for a specified purpose or about a specified matter.

(3)   The regulations may—
   (a)   provide for a statement to be treated as including provision prescribed by or determined in accordance with the regulations;
   (b)   permit a statement to make provision in place of provision which would otherwise be treated as included by virtue of paragraph (a).

(4)   The regulations may—
   (a)   make different provision for different descriptions of commonhold association or unit-holder;
   (b)   make different provision for different circumstances;
   (c)   make provision about the extent to which a commonhold community statement may make different provision for different descriptions of unit-holder or common parts.

(5)   The matters to which regulations under this section may relate include, but are not limited to—
   (a)   the matters mentioned in sections 11, 14, 15, 20, 21, 25, 26, 27, 38, 39 and 58, and
   (b)   any matter for which regulations under section 37 may make provision.

33.   Amendment

(1)   Regulations under section 32 shall require a commonhold community statement to make provision about how it can be amended.

(2)   The regulations shall, in particular, make provision under section 32(3)(a) (whether or not subject to provision under section 32(3)(b)).

(3)   An amendment of a commonhold community statement shall have no effect unless and until the amended statement is registered in accordance with this section.

(4)   If the commonhold association makes an application under this subsection the Registrar shall arrange for an amended commonhold community statement to be kept in his custody, and referred to in the register, in place of the unamended statement.

(5)   An application under subsection (4) must be accompanied by a certificate given by the directors of the commonhold association that the amended commonhold community statement satisfies the requirements of this Part.

(6)   Where an amendment of a commonhold community statement redefines the extent of a commonhold unit, an application under subsection (4) must be accompanied by any consent required by section 23(1) or 24(2) (or an order of a court dispensing with consent).

(7)   Where an amendment of a commonhold community statement has the effect of changing the extent of the common parts, an application under subsection (4) must be accompanied by any consent required by section 30(2) (or an order of a court dispensing with consent).

(8)   Where the Registrar amends the register on an application under subsection (4) he shall make any consequential amendments to the register which he thinks appropriate.

Commonhold association

34. Constitution

(1) A commonhold association is a private company limited by guarantee—

  (a) the articles of which state that an object of the company is to exercise the functions of a commonhold association in relation to specified commonhold land, and

  (b) the statement of guarantee of which specifies £1 as the amount of the contribution required from each member in the event of the company being wound up.

(2) Schedule 3 (which makes provision about the constitution of a commonhold association) shall have effect.

35. Duty to manage

(1) The directors of a commonhold association shall exercise their powers so as to permit or facilitate so far as possible—

  (a) the exercise by each unit-holder of his rights, and

  (b) the enjoyment by each unit-holder of the freehold estate in his unit.

(2) The directors of a commonhold association shall, in particular, use any right, power or procedure conferred or created by virtue of section 37 for the purpose of preventing, remedying or curtailing a failure on the part of a unit-holder to comply with a requirement or duty imposed on him by virtue of the commonhold community statement or a provision of this Part.

(3) But in respect of a particular failure on the part of a unit-holder (the 'defaulter') the directors of a commonhold association—

  (a) need not take action if they reasonably think that inaction is in the best interests of establishing or maintaining harmonious relationships between all the unit-holders, and that it will not cause any unit-holder (other than the defaulter) significant loss or significant disadvantage, and

  (b) shall have regard to the desirability of using arbitration, mediation or conciliation procedures (including referral under a scheme approved under section 42) instead of legal proceedings wherever possible.

(4) A reference in this section to a unit-holder includes a reference to a tenant of a unit.

36. Voting

(1) This section applies in relation to any provision of this Part (a 'voting provision') which refers to the passing of a resolution by a commonhold association.

(2) A voting provision is satisfied only if every member is given an opportunity to vote in accordance with any relevant provision of the articles of association or the commonhold community statement.

(3) A vote is cast for the purposes of a voting provision whether it is cast in person or in accordance with a provision which—

  (a) provides for voting by post, by proxy or in some other manner, and

  (b) is contained in the articles of association or the commonhold community statement.

(4) A resolution is passed unanimously if every member who casts a vote votes in favour.

Termination: voluntary winding-up

43. Winding-up resolution

(1) A winding-up resolution in respect of a commonhold association shall be of no effect unless—

  (a) the resolution is preceded by a declaration of solvency,

  (b) the commonhold association passes a termination-statement resolution before it passes the winding-up resolution, and

  (c) each resolution is passed with at least 80 per cent. of the members of the association voting in favour.

(2) In this Part—

  'declaration of solvency' means a directors' statutory declaration made in accordance with section 89 of the Insolvency Act 1986,

  'termination-statement resolution' means a resolution approving the terms of a termination statement (within the meaning of section 47), and 'winding-up resolution' means a resolution for voluntary winding-up within the meaning of section 84 of that Act.

44.   100 per cent. agreement

(1)   This section applies where a commonhold association—

    (a)   has passed a winding-up resolution and a termination-statement resolution with 100 per cent. of the members of the association voting in favour, and

    (b)   has appointed a liquidator under section 91 of the Insolvency Act 1986.

(2)   The liquidator shall make a termination application within the period of six months beginning with the day on which the winding-up resolution is passed.

(3)   If the liquidator fails to make a termination application within the period specified in subsection (2) a termination application may be made by—

    (a)   a unit-holder, or

    (b)   a person falling within a class prescribed for the purposes of this subsection.

45.   80 per cent. agreement

(1)   This section applies where a commonhold association—

    (a)   has passed a winding-up resolution and a termination-statement resolution with at least 80 per cent. of the members of the association voting in favour, and

    (b)   has appointed a liquidator under section 91 of the Insolvency Act 1986.

(2)   The liquidator shall within the prescribed period apply to the court for an order determining—

    (a)   the terms and conditions on which a termination application may be made, and

    (b)   the terms of the termination statement to accompany a termination application.

(3)   The liquidator shall make a termination application within the period of three months starting with the date on which an order under subsection (2) is made.

(4)   If the liquidator fails to make an application under subsection (2) or (3) within the period specified in that subsection an application of the same kind may be made by—

    (a)   a unit-holder, or

    (b)   a person falling within a class prescribed for the purposes of this subsection.

46.   Termination application

(1)   A 'termination application' is an application to the Registrar that all the land in relation to which a particular commonhold association exercises functions should cease to be commonhold land.

(2)   A termination application must be accompanied by a termination statement.

(3)   On receipt of a termination application the Registrar shall note it in the register.

47.   Termination statement

(1)   A termination statement must specify—

    (a)   the commonhold association's proposals for the transfer of the commonhold land following acquisition of the freehold estate in accordance with section 49(3), and

    (b)   how the assets of the commonhold association will be distributed.

(2)   A commonhold community statement may make provision requiring any termination statement to make arrangements—

    (a)   of a specified kind, or

    (b)   determined in a specified manner, about the rights of unit-holders in the event of all the land to which the statement relates ceasing to be commonhold land.

(3)   A termination statement must comply with a provision made by the commonhold community statement in reliance on subsection (2).

(4)   Subsection (3) may be disapplied by an order of the court—

    (a)   generally,

    (b)   in respect of specified matters, or

    (c)   for a specified purpose.

(5)   An application for an order under subsection (4) may be made by any member of the commonhold association.

48.   The liquidator

(1)   This section applies where a termination application has been made in respect of particular commonhold land.

(2)   The liquidator shall notify the Registrar of his appointment.

(3)   In the case of a termination application made under section 44 the liquidator shall either—

(a)   notify the Registrar that the liquidator is content with the termination statement submitted with the termination application, or

(b)   apply to the court under section 112 of the Insolvency Act 1986 to determine the terms of the termination statement.

(4)   The liquidator shall send to the Registrar a copy of a determination made by virtue of subsection (3)(b).

(5)   Subsection (4) is in addition to any requirement under section 112(3) of the Insolvency Act 1986.

(6)   A duty imposed on the liquidator by this section is to be performed as soon as possible.

(7)   In this section a reference to the liquidator is a reference—

(a)   to the person who is appointed as liquidator under section 91 of the Insolvency Act 1986, or

(b)   in the case of a members' voluntary winding up which becomes a creditors' voluntary winding up by virtue of sections 95 and 96 of that Act, to the person acting as liquidator in accordance with section 100 of that Act.

49.   Termination

(1)   This section applies where a termination application is made under section 44 and—

(a)   a liquidator notifies the Registrar under section 48(3)(a) that he is content with a termination statement, or

(b)   a determination is made under section 112 of the Insolvency Act 1986 by virtue of section 48(3)(b).

(2)   This section also applies where a termination application is made under section 45.

(3)   The commonhold association shall by virtue of this subsection be entitled to be registered as the proprietor of the freehold estate in each commonhold unit.

(4)   The Registrar shall take such action as appears to him to be appropriate for the purpose of giving effect to the termination statement.

Termination: winding-up by court

50.   Introduction

(1)   Section 51 applies where a petition is presented under section 124 of the Insolvency Act 1986 for the winding up of a commonhold association by the court.

(2)   For the purposes of this Part—

(a)   an 'insolvent commonhold association' is one in relation to which a winding-up petition has been presented under section 124 of the Insolvency Act 1986,

(b)   a commonhold association is the 'successor commonhold association' to an insolvent commonhold association if the land specified for the purpose of section 34(1)(a) is the same for both associations, and

(c)   a 'winding-up order' is an order under section 125 of the Insolvency Act 1986 for the winding up of a commonhold association.

51.   Succession order

(1)   At the hearing of the winding-up petition an application may be made to the court for an order under this section (a 'succession order') in relation to the insolvent commonhold association.

(2)   An application under subsection (1) may be made only by—

(a)   the insolvent commonhold association,

(b)   one or more members of the insolvent commonhold association, or

(c)   a provisional liquidator for the insolvent commonhold association appointed under section 135 of the Insolvency Act 1986.

(3)   An application under subsection (1) must be accompanied by—

(a)   prescribed evidence of the formation of a successor commonhold association, and

(b)   a certificate given by the directors of the successor commonhold association that its articles of association comply with regulations under paragraph 2(1) of Schedule 3.

(4)   The court shall grant an application under subsection (1) unless it thinks that the circumstances of the insolvent commonhold association make a succession order inappropriate.

52.   Assets and liabilities

(1)   Where a succession order is made in relation to an insolvent commonhold association this section applies on the making of a winding-up order in respect of the association.

(2)   The successor commonhold association shall be entitled to be registered as the proprietor of the freehold estate in the common parts.

(3)   The insolvent commonhold association shall for all purposes cease to be treated as the proprietor of the freehold estate in the common parts.

(4)   The succession order —

    (a)   shall make provision as to the treatment of any charge over all or any part of the common parts;

    (b)   may require the Registrar to take action of a specified kind;

    (c)   may enable the liquidator to require the Registrar to take action of a specified kind;

    (d)   may make supplemental or incidental provision.

53.   Transfer of responsibility

(1)   Where a succession order is made in relation to an insolvent commonhold association this section applies on the making of a winding-up order in respect of the association.

(2)   The successor commonhold association shall be treated as the commonhold association for the commonhold in respect of any matter which relates to a time after the making of the winding-up order.

(3)   On the making of the winding-up order the court may make an order requiring the liquidator to make available to the successor commonhold association specified —

    (a)   records;

    (b)   copies of records;

    (c)   information.

(4)   An order under subsection (3) may include terms as to —

    (a)   timing;

    (b)   payment.

54.   Termination of commonhold

(1)   This section applies where the court —

    (a)   makes a winding-up order in respect of a commonhold association, and

    (b)   has not made a succession order in respect of the commonhold association.

(2)   The liquidator of a commonhold association shall as soon as possible notify the Registrar of —

    (a)   the fact that this section applies,

    (b)   any directions given under section 168 of the Insolvency Act 1986 (liquidator: supplementary powers),

    (c)   any notice given to the court and the registrar of companies in accordance with section 172(8) of that Act (liquidator vacating office after final meeting),

    (d)   any notice given to the Secretary of State under section 174(3) of that Act (completion of winding-up),

    (e)   any application made to the registrar of companies under section 202(2) of that Act (insufficient assets: early dissolution),

    (f)   any notice given to the registrar of companies under section 205(1)(b) of that Act (completion of winding-up), and

    (g)   any other matter which in the liquidator's opinion is relevant to the Registrar.

(3)   Notification under subsection (2)(b) to (f) must be accompanied by a copy of the directions, notice or application concerned.

(4)   The Registrar shall —

    (a)   make such arrangements as appear to him to be appropriate for ensuring that the freehold estate in land in respect of which a commonhold association exercises functions ceases to be registered as a freehold estate in commonhold land as soon as is reasonably practicable after he receives notification under subsection (2)(c) to (f), and

    (b)   take such action as appears to him to be appropriate for the purpose of giving effect to a determination made by the liquidator in the exercise of his functions.

SCHEDULES

SCHEDULE 1
APPLICATION FOR REGISTRATION: DOCUMENTS

Introduction

1.   This Schedule lists the documents which are required by section 2 to accompany an application for the registration of a freehold estate as a freehold estate in commonhold land.

Commonhold association documents

2.   The commonhold association's certificate of incorporation under section 15 of the Companies Act 2006.

3.   Any altered certificate of incorporation issued under section 80 of that Act (change of name).

4.   The articles of association of the commonhold association.

Commonhold community statement

5.   The commonhold community statement.

Consent

6.   (1) Where consent is required under or by virtue of section 3—
       (a)   the consent,
       (b)   an order of a court by virtue of section 3(2)(f) dispensing with the requirement for consent, or
       (c)   evidence of deemed consent by virtue of section 3(2)(e).
     (2) In the case of a conditional order under section 3(2)(f), the order must be accompanied by evidence that the condition has been complied with.

Certificate

7.   A certificate given by the directors of the commonhold association that—
       (a)   the articles of association submitted with the application comply with regulations under paragraph 2(1) of Schedule 3,
       (b)   the commonhold community statement submitted with the application satisfies the requirements of this Part,
       (c)   the application satisfies Schedule 2,
       (d)   the commonhold association has not traded, and
       (e)   the commonhold association has not incurred any liability which has not been discharged.

SCHEDULE 2
LAND WHICH MAY NOT BE COMMONHOLD LAND

"Flying freehold"

1.   (1) Subject to sub-paragraph (2), an application may not be made under section 2 wholly or partly in relation to land above ground level ('raised land') unless all the land between the ground and the raised land is the subject of the same application.
     (2) An application for the addition of land to a commonhold in accordance with section 41 may be made wholly or partly in relation to raised land if all the land between the ground and the raised land forms part of the commonhold to which the raised land is to be added.

Agricultural land

2.   An application may not be made under section 2 wholly or partly in relation to land if—
       (a)   it is agricultural land within the meaning of the Agriculture Act 1947,
       (b)   it is comprised in a tenancy of an agricultural holding within the meaning of the Agricultural Holdings Act 1986, or
       (c)   it is comprised in a farm business tenancy for the purposes of the Agricultural Tenancies Act 1995.

Contingent title

3.   (1) An application may not be made under section 2 if an estate in the whole or part of the land to which the application relates is a contingent estate.

(2)　An estate is contingent for the purposes of this paragraph if (and only if)—

    (a)　it is liable to revert to or vest in a person other than the present registered proprietor on the occurrence or non-occurrence of a particular event, and

    (b)　the reverter or vesting would occur by operation of law as a result of an enactment listed in sub-paragraph (3).

(3)　The enactments are—

    (a)　the School Sites Act 1841 (conveyance for use as school),

    (b)　the Lands Clauses Acts (compulsory purchase),

    (c)　the Literary and Scientific Institutions Act 1854 (sites for institutions), and

    (d)　the Places of Worship Sites Act 1873 (sites for places of worship).

(4)　Regulations may amend sub-paragraph (3) so as to—

(a)　add an enactment to the list, or

(b)　remove an enactment from the list.

SCHEDULE 3
COMMONHOLD ASSOCIATION

PART 1
ARTICLES OF ASSOCIATION

Introduction

1.　In this Schedule 'articles' means the articles of association of a commonhold association.

Form and content

2.　(1)　Regulations shall make provision about the form and content of the articles.

    (2)　A commonhold association may adopt provisions of the regulations for its articles.

    (3)　The regulations may include provision which is to have effect for a commonhold association whether or not it is adopted under sub-paragraph (2).

    (4)　A provision of the articles shall have no effect to the extent that it is inconsistent with the regulations.

    (5)　Regulations under this paragraph shall have effect in relation to articles—

        (a)　irrespective of the date of the articles, but

        (b)　subject to any transitional provision of the regulations.

    (6)　Section 20 of the Companies Act 2006 (default application of model articles) does not apply to a commonhold association.

Alteration

3.　(1)　Where a commonhold association alters its articles at a time when the land specified in its articles is commonhold land, the alteration shall have no effect until the altered version is registered in accordance with this paragraph.

    (2)　If the commonhold association makes an application under this sub-paragraph the Registrar shall arrange for altered articles to be kept in his custody, and referred to in the register, in place of the unaltered version.

    (3)　An application under sub-paragraph (2) must be accompanied by a certificate given by the directors of the commonhold association that the altered articles comply with regulations under paragraph 2(1).

    (4)　Where the Registrar amends the register on an application under sub-paragraph (2) he shall make any consequential amendments to the register which he thinks appropriate.

PART 2
MEMBERSHIP

Pre-commonhold period

5.　During the period beginning with incorporation of a commonhold association and ending when land specified in its articles becomes commonhold land, the subscribers (or subscriber) to the association's memorandum of association shall be the sole members (or member) of the association.

Transitional period

6.   (1)   This paragraph applies to a commonhold association during a transitional period.

    (2)   The subscribers (or subscriber) to the association's memorandum of association shall continue to be members (or the member) of the association.

    (3)   A person who for the time being is the developer in respect of all or part of the commonhold is entitled to be entered in the register of members of the association.

Unit-holders

7.   A person is entitled to be entered in the register of members of a commonhold association if he becomes the unit-holder of a commonhold unit in relation to which the association exercises functions—

    (a)   on the unit becoming commonhold land by registration with unit-holders under section 9, or

    (b)   on the transfer of the unit.

Joint unit-holders

8.   (1)   This paragraph applies where two or more persons become joint unit-holders of a commonhold unit—

        (a)   on the unit becoming commonhold land by registration with unit-holders under section 9, or

        (b)   on the transfer of the unit.

    (2)   If the joint unit-holders nominate one of themselves for the purpose of this sub-paragraph, he is entitled to be entered in the register of members of the commonhold association which exercises functions in relation to the unit.

    (3)   A nomination under sub-paragraph (2) must—

        (a)   be made in writing to the commonhold association, and

        (b)   be received by the association before the end of the prescribed period.

    (4)   If no nomination is received by the association before the end of the prescribed period the person whose name appears first in the proprietorship register is on the expiry of that period entitled to be entered in the register of members of the association.

    (5)   On the application of a joint unit-holder the court may order that a joint unit-holder is entitled to be entered in the register of members of a commonhold association in place of a person who is or would be entitled to be registered by virtue of sub-paragraph (4).

    (6)   If joint unit-holders nominate one of themselves for the purpose of this sub-paragraph, the nominated person is entitled to be entered in the register of members of the commonhold association in place of the person entered by virtue of—

        (a)   sub-paragraph (2),

        (b)   sub-paragraph (5), or

        (c)   this sub-paragraph.

Self-membership

9.   A commonhold association may not be a member of itself.

No other members

10.   A person may not become a member of a commonhold association otherwise than by virtue of a provision of this Schedule.

Effect of registration

11.   A person who is entitled to be entered in the register of members of a commonhold association becomes a member when the company registers him in pursuance of its duty under section 113 of the Companies Act 2006 (duty to maintain register of members).

Termination of membership

12.   Where a member of a commonhold association ceases to be a unit-holder or joint unit-holder of a commonhold unit in relation to which the association exercises functions—

        (a)   he shall cease to be a member of the commonhold association, but

        (b)   paragraph (a) does not affect any right or liability already acquired or incurred in respect of a matter relating to a time when he was a unit-holder or joint unit-holder.

13.   A member of a commonhold association may resign by notice in writing to the association if (and only if) he is a member by virtue of paragraph 5 or 6 of this Schedule (and not also by virtue of any other paragraph).

Register of members

14.   (1)   Regulations may make provision about the performance by a commonhold association of its duty under section 113 of the Companies Act 2006 (duty to maintain register of members) where a person—
        (a)   becomes entitled to be entered in the register by virtue of paragraphs 5 to 8, or
        (b)   ceases to be a member by virtue of paragraph 12 or on resignation.
       (2)   The regulations may in particular require entries in the register to be made within a specified period.
       (3)   A period specified under sub-paragraph (2) may be expressed to begin from—
        (a)   the date of a notification under section 15(3),
        (b)   the date on which the directors of the commonhold association first become aware of a specified matter, or
        (c)   some other time.
       (4)   A requirement by virtue of this paragraph shall be treated as a requirement of section 113 for the purposes of section 113(7) and (8) (offences).

Supplementary provisions

15.   (1)   Section 112(1) of the Companies Act 2006 (initial members of company) applies to a commonhold association subject to the provisions of this Schedule.
       (2)   The following provisions of that Act do not apply to a commonhold association—
       section 112(2) (new members);
       section 136 (membership of holding company).

CIVIL PARTNERSHIP ACT 2004
(2004, c. 33)

65. Contribution by civil partner to property improvement
       (1)   This section applies if—
        (a)   a civil partner contributes in money or money's worth to the improvement of real or personal property in which or in the proceeds of sale of which either or both of the civil partners has or have a beneficial interest, and
        (b)   the contribution is of a substantial nature.
       (2)   The contributing partner is to be treated as having acquired by virtue of the contribution a share or an enlarged share (as the case may be) in the beneficial interest of such an extent—
        (a)   as may have been then agreed, or
        (b)   in default of such agreement, as may seem in all the circumstances just to any court before which the question of the existence or extent of the beneficial interest of either of the civil partners arises (whether in proceedings between them or in any other proceedings).
       (3)   Subsection (2) is subject to any agreement (express or implied) between the civil partners to the contrary.

66. Disputes between civil partners about property
       (1)   In any question between the civil partners in a civil partnership as to title to or possession of property, either civil partner may apply to—
        (a)   the High Court, or
        (b)   the family court.
       (2)   On such an application, the court may make such order with respect to the property as it thinks fit (including an order for the sale of the property).

TRIBUNALS, COURTS AND ENFORCEMENT ACT 2007
(2007, c. 15)

CHAPTER 2
RENT ARREARS RECOVERY

Abolition of common law right

71. Abolition of common law right

The common law right to distrain for arrears of rent is abolished.

Commercial rent arrears recovery

72. Commercial rent arrears recovery (CRAR)

(1) A landlord under a lease of commercial premises may use the procedure in Schedule 12 (taking control of goods) to recover from the tenant rent payable under the lease.

(2) A landlord's power under subsection (1) is referred to as CRAR (commercial rent arrears recovery).

73. Landlord

(1) In this Chapter 'landlord', in relation to a lease, means the person for the time being entitled to the immediate reversion in the property comprised in the lease.

(2) That is subject to the following.

(3) In the case of a tenancy by estoppel, a person is 'entitled to the immediate reversion' if he is entitled to it as between himself and the tenant.

(4) If there are joint tenants of the immediate reversion, or if a number of persons are entitled to the immediate reversion as between themselves and the tenant—

    (a) 'landlord' means any one of them;

    (b) CRAR may be exercised to recover rent due to all of them.

(5) If the immediate reversion is mortgaged, 'landlord' means—

    (a) the mortgagee, if he has given notice of his intention to take possession or enter into receipt of rents and profits;

    (b) otherwise, the mortgagor.

(6) Subsection (5) applies whether the lease is made before or after the mortgage is created, but CRAR is not exercisable by a mortgagee in relation to a lease that does not bind him.

(7) Where a receiver is appointed by a court in relation to the immediate reversion, CRAR is exercisable by the receiver in the name of the landlord.

(8) Any authorisation of a person to exercise CRAR on another's behalf must be in writing and must comply with any prescribed requirements.

(9) This Chapter applies to any other person entitled to exercise CRAR as it applies to a landlord.

74. Lease

(1) 'Lease' means a tenancy in law or in equity, including a tenancy at will, but not including a tenancy at sufferance.

(2) A lease must be evidenced in writing.

(3) References to a lease are to a lease as varied from time to time (whether or not the variation is in writing).

(4) This section applies for the purposes of this Chapter.

75. Commercial premises

(1) A lease (A) is of commercial premises if none of the demised premises is—

    (a) let under lease A as a dwelling,

    (b) let under an inferior lease (B) as a dwelling, or

    (c) occupied as a dwelling.

(2) The 'demised premises' in this section include anything on them.

(3) 'Let as a dwelling' means let on terms permitting only occupation as a dwelling or other use combined with occupation as a dwelling.

(4) Premises are not within subsection (1)(b) if letting them as a dwelling is a breach of a lease superior to lease B.

(5)   Premises are not within subsection (1)(c) if occupying them as a dwelling is a breach of lease A or a lease superior to lease A.

(6)   This section applies for the purposes of this Chapter.

76.   Rent

(1)   'Rent' means the amount payable under a lease (in advance or in arrear) for possession and use of the demised premises, together with—

    (a)   any interest payable on that amount under the lease, and

    (b)   any value added tax chargeable on that amount or interest.

(2)   'Rent' does not include any sum in respect of rates, council tax, services, repairs, maintenance, insurance or other ancillary matters (whether or not called 'rent' in the lease).

(3)   The amount payable for possession and use of the demised premises, where it is not otherwise identifiable, is to be taken to be so much of the total amount payable under the lease as is reasonably attributable to possession and use.

(4)   Where a rent is payable under or by virtue of Part 2 of the Landlord and Tenant Act 1954, the amount payable under the lease for possession and use of those premises is to be taken to be that rent.

(5)   This section applies for the purposes of this Chapter except sections 71 and 85.

77.   The rent recoverable

(1)   CRAR is not exercisable except to recover rent that meets each of these conditions—

    (a)   it has become due and payable before notice of enforcement is given;

    (b)   it is certain, or capable of being calculated with certainty.

(2)   The amount of any rent recoverable by CRAR is reduced by any permitted deduction.

(3)   CRAR is exercisable only if the net unpaid rent is at least the minimum amount immediately before each of these—

    (a)   the time when notice of enforcement is given;

    (b)   the first time that goods are taken control of after that notice.

(4)   The minimum amount is to be calculated in accordance with regulations.

(5)   The net unpaid rent is the amount of rent that meets the conditions in subsection (1), less—

    (a)   any interest or value added tax included in that amount under section 76(1)(a) or (b), and

    (b)   any permitted deductions.

(6)   Regulations may provide for subsection (5)(a) not to apply in specified cases.

(7)   Permitted deductions, against any rent, are any deduction, recoupment or set-off that the tenant would be entitled to claim (in law or equity) in an action by the landlord for that rent.

78.   Intervention of the court

(1)   If notice of enforcement is given in exercise (or purported exercise) of CRAR the court may make either or both of these orders on the application of the tenant—

    (a)   an order setting aside the notice;

    (b)   an order that no further step may be taken under CRAR, without further order, in relation to the rent claimed.

(2)   Regulations may make provision about—

    (a)   the further orders that may be made for the purposes of subsection (1)(b);

    (b)   grounds of which the court must be satisfied before making an order or further order.

(3)   In this section 'the court' means the High Court or the county court, as rules of court may provide.

79.   Use of CRAR after end of lease

(1)   When the lease ends, CRAR ceases to be exercisable, with these exceptions.

(2)   CRAR continues to be exercisable in relation to goods taken control of under it—

    (a)   before the lease ended, or

    (b)   under subsection (3).

(3)   CRAR continues to be exercisable in relation to rent due and payable before the lease ended, if the conditions in subsection (4) are met.

(4)   These are the conditions—
   (a)   the lease did not end by forfeiture;
   (b)   not more than 6 months has passed since the day when it ended;
   (c)   the rent was due from the person who was the tenant at the end of the lease;
   (d)   that person remains in possession of any part of the demised premises;
   (e)   any new lease under which that person remains in possession is a lease of commercial premises;
   (f)   the person who was the landlord at the end of the lease remains entitled to the immediate reversion.

(5)   In deciding whether a person remains in possession under a new lease, section 74(2) (lease to be evidenced in writing) does not apply.

(6)   In the case of a tenancy by estoppel, the person who was the landlord remains 'entitled to the immediate reversion' if the estoppel with regard to the tenancy continues.

(7)   A lease ends when the tenant ceases to be entitled to possession of the demised premises under the lease together with any continuation of it by operation of an enactment or of a rule of law.

Right to rent from sub-tenant

81.   Right to rent from sub-tenant

(1)   This section applies where CRAR is exercisable by a landlord to recover rent due and payable from a tenant (the immediate tenant).

(2)   The landlord may serve a notice on any sub-tenant.

(3)   The notice must state the amount of rent that the landlord has the right to recover from the immediate tenant by CRAR (the 'notified amount').

(4)   When it takes effect the notice transfers to the landlord the right to recover, receive and give a discharge for any rent payable by the sub-tenant under the sub-lease, until—
   (a)   the notified amount has been paid (by payments under the notice or otherwise), or
   (b)   the notice is replaced or withdrawn.

(5)   A notice under this section takes effect at the end of a period to be determined by regulations.

(6)   Regulations may state—
   (a)   the form of a notice under this section;
   (b)   what it must contain;
   (c)   how it must be served;
   (d)   what must be done to withdraw it.

(7)   In determining for the purposes of this section whether CRAR is exercisable, section 77 applies with these modifications—
   (a)   if notice of enforcement has not been given, references to that notice are to be read as references to the notice under this section;
   (b)   if goods have not been taken control of, section 77(3)(b) does not apply.

(8)   In this section and sections 82 to 84—
   (a)   'sub-tenant' means a tenant (below the immediate tenant) of any of the premises comprised in the headlease (and 'sub-lease' is to be read accordingly);
   (b)   'headlease' means the lease between the landlord and the immediate tenant.

82.   Off-setting payments under a notice

(1)   For any amount that a sub-tenant pays under a notice under section 81, he may deduct an equal amount from the rent that would be due to his immediate landlord under the sub-lease.

(2)   If an amount is deducted under subsection (1) or this subsection from rent due to a superior sub-tenant, that sub-tenant may deduct an equal amount from any rent due from him under his sub-lease.

(3)   Subsection (1) applies even if the sub-tenant's payment or part of it is not due under the notice, if it is not due because—
   (a)   the notified amount has already been paid (wholly or partly otherwise than under the notice), or
   (b)   the notice has been replaced by a notice served on another sub-tenant.

(4)   That is subject to the following.

(5)　Subsection (1) does not apply if the landlord withdraws the notice before the payment is made.

(6)　Where the notified amount has already been paid (or will be exceeded by the payment), subsection (1) does not apply (or does not apply to the excess) if the sub-tenant has notice of that when making the payment.

(7)　Subsection (1) does not apply if, before the payment is made, payments under the notice at least equal the notified amount.

(8)　Subsection (1) does not apply to a part of the payment if, with the rest of the payment, payments under the notice at least equal the notified amount.

(9)　Where the notice has been replaced by one served on another sub-tenant, subsection (1) does not apply if the sub-tenant has notice of that when making the payment.

83.　Withdrawal and replacement of notices

(1)　A notice under section 81 is replaced if the landlord serves another notice on the same sub-tenant for a notified amount covering the same rent or part of that rent.

(2)　A notice under section 81 served on one sub-tenant is also replaced if—
　(a)　the landlord serves a notice on another sub-tenant for a notified amount covering the same rent or part of that rent, and
　(b)　in relation to any of the premises comprised in the first sub-tenant's sub-lease, the second sub-tenant is an inferior or superior sub-tenant.

(3)　The landlord must withdraw a notice under section 81 if any of these happens—
　(a)　the notice is replaced;
　(b)　the notified amount is paid, unless it is paid wholly by the sub-tenant.

84.　Recovery of sums due and overpayments

(1)　For the purposes of the recovery of sums payable by a sub-tenant under a notice under section 81 (including recovery by CRAR), the sub-tenant is to be treated as the immediate tenant of the landlord, and the sums are to be treated as rent accordingly.

(2)　But those sums (as opposed to rent due from the immediate tenant) are not recoverable by notice under section 81 served on an inferior sub-tenant.

(3)　Any payment received by the landlord that the sub-tenant purports to make under a notice under section 81, and that is not due under the notice for any reason, is to be treated as a payment of rent by the immediate tenant, for the purposes of the retention of the payment by the landlord and (if no rent is due) for the purposes of any claim by the immediate tenant to recover the payment.

(4)　But subsection (3) does not affect any claim by the sub-tenant against the immediate tenant.

Supplementary

85.　Contracts for similar rights to be void

(1)　A provision of a contract is void to the extent that it would do any of these—
　(a)　confer a right to seize or otherwise take control of goods to recover amounts within subsection (2);
　(b)　confer a right to sell goods to recover amounts within subsection (2);
　(c)　modify the effect of section 72(1), except in accordance with subsection (3).

(2)　The amounts are any amounts payable—
　(a)　as rent;
　(b)　under a lease (other than as rent);
　(c)　under an agreement collateral to a lease;
　(d)　under an instrument creating a rentcharge;
　(e)　in respect of breach of a covenant or condition in a lease, in an agreement collateral to a lease or in an instrument creating a rentcharge;
　(f)　under an indemnity in respect of a payment within paragraphs (a) to (e).

(3)　A provision of a contract is not void under subsection (1)(c) to the extent that it prevents or restricts the exercise of CRAR.

(4)　In this section—
　'lease' also includes a licence to occupy land;
　'rent' and 'rentcharge' have the meaning given by section 205(1) of the Law of Property Act 1925(c 20).

PERPETUITIES AND ACCUMULATIONS ACT 2009
(2009, c. 18)

Application of rule against perpetuities

1. **Application of the rule**
   (1)   The rule against perpetuities applies (and applies only) as provided by this section.
   (2)   If an instrument limits property in trust so as to create successive estates or interests the rule applies to each of the estates or interests.
   (3)   If an instrument limits property in trust so as to create an estate or interest which is subject to a condition precedent and which is not one of successive estates or interests, the rule applies to the estate or interest.
   (4)   If an instrument limits property in trust so as to create an estate or interest subject to a condition subsequent the rule applies to—
        (a)   any right of re-entry exercisable if the condition is broken, or
        (b)   any equivalent right exercisable in the case of property other than land if the condition is broken.
   (5)   If an instrument which is a will limits personal property so as to create successive interests under the doctrine of executory bequests, the rule applies to each of the interests.
   (6)   If an instrument creates a power of appointment the rule applies to the power.
   (7)   For the purposes of subsection (2) an estate or interest includes an estate or interest—
        (a)   which arises under a right of reverter on the determination of a determinable fee simple, or
        (b)   which arises under a resulting trust on the determination of a determinable interest.
   (8)   This section has effect subject to the exceptions made by section 2 and to any exceptions made under section 3.

2. **Exceptions to rule's application**
   (1)   This section contains exceptions to the application of the rule against perpetuities.
   (2)   The rule does not apply to an estate or interest created so as to vest in a charity on the occurrence of an event if immediately before the occurrence an estate or interest in the property concerned is vested in another charity.
   (3)   The rule does not apply to a right exercisable by a charity on the occurrence of an event if immediately before the occurrence an estate or interest in the property concerned is vested in another charity.
   (4)   The rule does not apply to an interest or right arising under a relevant pension scheme.
   (5)   The exception in subsection (4) does not apply if the interest or right arises under—
        (a)   an instrument nominating benefits under the scheme, or
        (b)   an instrument made in the exercise of a power of advancement arising under the scheme.

3. **Power to specify exceptions**
   (1)   The Lord Chancellor may by order provide that the rule against perpetuities is not to apply—
        (a)   in cases of a specified description, or
        (b)   if specified conditions are fulfilled.
   (2)   Different descriptions and conditions may be specified for different purposes.
   (3)   Any order under this section may include such supplementary, incidental, consequential or transitional provisions as appear to the Lord Chancellor to be necessary or expedient.
   (4)   In this section 'specified' means specified in the order.
   (5)   The power to make an order under this section is exercisable by statutory instrument.
   (6)   A statutory instrument containing an order under this section may not be made unless a draft of the instrument has been laid before and approved by a resolution of each House of Parliament.

Perpetuity period

5. **Perpetuity period**
   (1)   The perpetuity period is 125 years (and no other period).
   (2)   Subsection (1) applies whether or not the instrument referred to in section 1(2) to (6) specifies a perpetuity period; and a specification of a perpetuity period in that instrument is ineffective.

Perpetuities: miscellaneous

6.   Start of perpetuity period

(1)   The perpetuity period starts when the instrument referred to in section 1(2) to (6) takes effect; but this is subject to subsections (2) and (3).

(2)   If section 1(2), (3) or (4) applies and the instrument is made in the exercise of a special power of appointment the perpetuity period starts when the instrument creating the power takes effect; but this is subject to subsection (3).

(3)   If section 1(2), (3) or (4) applies and—
    (a)   the instrument nominates benefits under a relevant pension scheme, or
    (b)   the instrument is made in the exercise of a power of advancement arising under a relevant pension scheme,
    the perpetuity period starts when the member concerned became a member of the scheme.

(4)   The member concerned is the member in respect of whose interest in the scheme the instrument is made.

7.   Wait and see rule

(1)   Subsection (2) applies if (apart from this section and section 8) an estate or interest would be void on the ground that it might not become vested until too remote a time.

(2)   In such a case—
    (a)   until such time (if any) as it becomes established that the vesting must occur (if at all) after the end of the perpetuity period the estate or interest must be treated as if it were not subject to the rule against perpetuities, and
    (b)   if it becomes so established, that does not affect the validity of anything previously done (whether by way of advancement, application of intermediate income or otherwise) in relation to the estate or interest.

(3)   Subsection (4) applies if (apart from this section) any of the following would be void on the ground that it might be exercised at too remote a time—
    (a)   a right of re-entry exercisable if a condition subsequent is broken;
    (b)   an equivalent right exercisable in the case of property other than land if a condition subsequent is broken;
    (c)   a special power of appointment.

(4)   In such a case—
    (a)   the right or power must be treated as regards any exercise of it within the perpetuity period as if it were not subject to the rule against perpetuities, and
    (b)   the right or power must be treated as void for remoteness only if and so far as it is not fully exercised within the perpetuity period.

(5)   Subsection (6) applies if (apart from this section) a general power of appointment would be void on the ground that it might not become exercisable until too remote a time.

(6)   Until such time (if any) as it becomes established that the power will not be exercisable within the perpetuity period, it must be treated as if it were not subject to the rule against perpetuities.

8.   Exclusion of class members to avoid remoteness

(1)   This section applies if—
    (a)   it is apparent at the time an instrument takes effect or becomes apparent at a later time that (apart from this section) the inclusion of certain persons as members of a class would cause an estate or interest to be treated as void for remoteness, and
    (b)   those persons are potential members of the class or unborn persons who at birth would become members or potential members of the class.

(2)   From the time it is or becomes so apparent those persons must be treated for all the purposes of the instrument as excluded from the class unless their exclusion would exhaust the class.

(3)   If this section applies in relation to an estate or interest to which section 7 applies, this section does not affect the validity of anything previously done (whether by way of advancement, application of intermediate income or otherwise) in relation to the estate or interest.

(4)   For the purposes of this section—
    (a)   a person is a member of a class if in that person's case all the conditions identifying a member of the class are satisfied, and
    (b)   a person is a potential member of a class if in that person's case some only of those conditions are satisfied but there is a possibility that the remainder will in time be satisfied.

9.   Saving and acceleration of expectant interests

(1)   An estate or interest is not void for remoteness by reason only that it is ulterior to and dependent on an estate or interest which is so void.

(2)   The vesting of an estate or interest is not prevented from being accelerated on the failure of a prior estate or interest by reason only that the failure arises because of remoteness.

10.   Determinable interests becoming absolute

(1)   If an estate arising under a right of reverter on the determination of a determinable fee simple is void for remoteness the determinable fee simple becomes absolute.

(2)   If an interest arising under a resulting trust on the determination of a determinable interest is void for remoteness the determinable interest becomes absolute.

11.   Powers of appointment

(1)   Subsection (2) applies to a power of appointment exercisable otherwise than by will (whether or not it is also exercisable by will).

(2)   For the purposes of the rule against perpetuities the power is a special power unless—
    (a)   the instrument creating it expresses it to be exercisable by one person only, and
    (b)   at all times during its currency when that person is of full age and capacity it could be exercised by that person so as immediately to transfer to that person the whole of the interest governed by the power without the consent of any other person or compliance with any other condition (ignoring a formal condition relating only to the mode of exercise of the power).

(3)   Subsection (4) applies to a power of appointment exercisable by will (whether or not it is also exercisable otherwise than by will).

(4)   For the purposes of the rule against perpetuities the power is a special power unless—
    (a)   the instrument creating it expresses it to be exercisable by one person only, and
    (b)   that person could exercise it so as to transfer to that person's personal representatives the whole of the estate or interest to which it relates.

(5)   Subsection (6) applies to a power of appointment exercisable by will or otherwise.

(6)   If for the purposes of the rule against perpetuities the power would be a special power under one but not both of subsections (2) and (4), for the purposes of the rule it is a special power.

12.   Pre-commencement instruments: period difficult to ascertain

(1)   If—
    (a)   an instrument specifies for the purposes of property limited in trust a perpetuity period by reference to the lives of persons in being when the instrument takes effect,
    (b)   the trustees believe that it is difficult or not reasonably practicable for them to ascertain whether the lives have ended and therefore whether the perpetuity period has ended, and
    (c)   they execute a deed stating that they so believe and that subsection (2) is to apply to the instrument,
that subsection applies to the instrument.

(2)   If this subsection applies to an instrument —
    (a)   the instrument has effect as if it specified a perpetuity period of 100 years (and no other period);
    (b)   the rule against perpetuities has effect as if the only perpetuity period applicable to the instrument were 100 years;
    (c)   sections 6 to 11 of this Act are to be treated as if they applied (and always applied) in relation to the instrument;
    (d)   sections 1 to 12 of the Perpetuities and Accumulations Act 1964 (c 55) are to be treated as if they did not apply (and never applied) in relation to the instrument.

(3)   A deed executed under this section cannot be revoked.

Accumulations

14. Restriction on accumulation for charitable trusts

(1) This section applies to an instrument to the extent that it provides for property to be held on trust for charitable purposes.

(2) But it does not apply where the provision is made by a court or the Charity Commission for England and Wales.

(3) If the instrument imposes or confers on the trustees a duty or power to accumulate income, and apart from this section the duty or power would last beyond the end of the statutory period, it ceases to have effect at the end of that period unless subsection (5) applies.

(4) The statutory period is a period of 21 years starting with the first day when the income must or may be accumulated (as the case may be).

(5) This subsection applies if the instrument provides for the duty or power to cease to have effect—
   (a) on the death of the settlor, or
   (b) on the death of one of the settlors, determined by name or by the order of their deaths.

(6) If a duty or power ceases to have effect under this section the income to which the duty or power would have applied apart from this section must—
   (a) go to the person who would have been entitled to it if there had been no duty or power to accumulate, or
   (b) be applied for the purposes for which it would have had to be applied if there had been no such duty or power.

(7) This section applies whether or not the duty or power to accumulate extends to income produced by the investment of income previously accumulated.

Application of statutory provisions

15. Application of this Act

(1) Sections 1, 2, 4 to 11, 13 and 14 apply in relation to an instrument taking effect on or after the commencement day, except that—
   (a) those sections do not apply in relation to a will executed before that day, and
   (b) those sections apply in relation to an instrument made in the exercise of a special power of appointment only if the instrument creating the power takes effect on or after that day.

(2) Section 12 applies (except as provided by subsection (3)) in relation to—
   (a) a will executed before the commencement day (whether or not it takes effect before that day);
   (b) an instrument, other than a will, taking effect before that day.

(3) Section 12 does not apply if—
   (a) the terms of the trust were exhausted before the commencement day, or
   (b) before that day the property became held on trust for charitable purposes by way of a final disposition of the property.

(4) The commencement day is the day appointed under section 22(2).

17. The Crown

(1) This Act does not extend the application of the rule against perpetuities in relation to the Crown.

(2) Subject to that, this Act binds the Crown.

18. Rule as to duration not affected

This Act does not affect the rule of law which limits the duration of non-charitable purpose trusts.

19. Provision made otherwise than by instrument

If provision is made in relation to property otherwise than by an instrument, this Act applies as if the provision were contained in an instrument taking effect on the making of the provision.

20.   Interpretation

(1)   For the purposes of this Act this section contains provisions relating to the interpretation of these expressions—

(a)   power of appointment, general power of appointment and special power of appointment;

(b)   relevant pension scheme;

(c)   taking effect (in relation to a will);

(d)   will.

(2)   A power of appointment includes—

(a)   a discretionary power to create a beneficial interest in property without the provision of valuable consideration;

(b)   a discretionary power to transfer a beneficial interest in property without the provision of valuable consideration.

(3)   Section 11 applies to interpret references to a general or special power of appointment.

(4)   Each of these is a relevant pension scheme—

(a)   an occupational pension scheme;

(b)   a personal pension scheme;

(c)   a public service pension scheme.

(5)   The expressions in subsection (4)(a) to (c) have the meanings given by sections 1 and 181(1) of the Pension Schemes Act 1993.

(6)   An instrument which is a will takes effect at the testator's death.

(7)   A reference to a will includes a reference to a codicil.

EQUALITY ACT 2010
(2010, c. 15)

PART 15
FAMILY PROPERTY

198.   Abolition of husband's duty to maintain wife

The rule of common law that a husband must maintain his wife is abolished.

199.   Abolition of presumption of advancement

(1)   The presumption of advancement (by which, for example, a husband is presumed to be making a gift to his wife if he transfers property to her, or purchases property in her name) is abolished.

(2)   The abolition by subsection (1) of the presumption of advancement does not have effect in relation to—

(a)   anything done before the commencement of this section, or

(b)   anything done pursuant to any obligation incurred before the commencement of this section.

MORTGAGE REPOSSESSIONS (PROTECTION OF TENANTS ETC.) ACT 2010
(2010, c. 19)

1.   Power of court to postpone giving of possession

(1)   This section applies if—

(a)   the mortgagee under a mortgage of land which consists of or includes a dwelling-house brings an action (other than an action for foreclosure) in which the mortgagee claims possession of the mortgaged property, and

(b)   there is an unauthorised tenancy of all or part of the property.

(2)   When making an order for delivery of possession of the property, the court may, on the application of the tenant, postpone the date for delivery of possession for a period not exceeding two months.

(3) Subsection (4) applies where an order for delivery of possession of the property has been made but not executed.

(4) The court may, on the application of the tenant ('the applicant'), stay or suspend execution of the order for a period not exceeding two months if—

   (a) the court did not exercise its powers under subsection (2) when making the order or, if it did, the applicant was not the tenant when it exercised those powers,

   (b) the applicant has asked the mortgagee to give an undertaking in writing not to enforce the order for two months beginning with the date the undertaking is given, and

   (c) the mortgagee has not given such an undertaking.

(5) When considering whether to exercise its powers under this section, the court must have regard to—

   (a) the circumstances of the tenant, and

   (b) if there is an outstanding breach by the tenant of a term of the unauthorised tenancy—

      (i) the nature of that breach, and

      (ii) whether the tenant might reasonably be expected to have avoided breaching that term or to have remedied the breach.

(6) The court may make any postponement, stay or suspension under this section conditional on the making of payments to the mortgagee in respect of the occupation of the property (or part of the property) during the period of the postponement, stay or suspension.

(7) The making of any payment pursuant to—

   (a) a condition of an undertaking of a kind mentioned in subsection (4)(c), or

   (b) a condition imposed by virtue of subsection (6),

is not to be regarded as creating (or as evidence of the creation of) any tenancy or other right to occupy the property.

(8) For the purposes of this section there is an 'unauthorised tenancy' if—

   (a) an agreement has been made which, as between the parties to it (or their successors in title), is or gives rise to—

      (i) an assured tenancy (within the meaning of the Housing Act 1988), or

      (ii) a protected or statutory tenancy (within the meaning of the Rent Act 1977), and

   (b) the mortgagee's interest in the property is not subject to the tenancy.

(9) In this section 'the tenant', in relation to an unauthorised tenancy, means the person who is, as between the parties to the agreement in question (or their successors in title), the tenant under the unauthorised tenancy (or, if there is more than one tenant, any of them).

CHARITIES ACT 2011
(2011, c. 25)

PART 1
MEANING OF 'CHARITY' AND 'CHARITABLE PURPOSE'

1.   Meaning of 'charity'

(1) For the purposes of the law of England and Wales, 'charity' means an institution which—

   (a) is established for charitable purposes only, and

   (b) falls to be subject to the control of the High Court in the exercise of its jurisdiction with respect to charities.

(2) The definition of 'charity' in subsection (1) does not apply for the purposes of an enactment if a different definition of that term applies for those purposes by virtue of that or any other enactment.

2.   Meaning of 'charitable purpose'

(1) For the purposes of the law of England and Wales, a charitable purpose is a purpose which—

   (a) falls within section 3(1), and

   (b) is for the public benefit (see section 4).

(2)   Any reference in any enactment or document (in whatever terms)—
    (a)   to charitable purposes, or
    (b)   to institutions having purposes that are charitable under the law relating to charities in England and Wales,
    is to be read in accordance with subsection (1).
(3)   Subsection (2) does not apply where the context otherwise requires.
(4)   This section is subject to section 11 (which makes special provision for Chapter 2 of this Part onwards).

3.   Descriptions of purposes

(1)   A purpose falls within this subsection if it falls within any of the following descriptions of purposes—
    (a)   the prevention or relief of poverty;
    (b)   the advancement of education;
    (c)   the advancement of religion;
    (d)   the advancement of health or the saving of lives;
    (e)   the advancement of citizenship or community development;
    (f)   the advancement of the arts, culture, heritage or science;
    (g)   the advancement of amateur sport;
    (h)   the advancement of human rights, conflict resolution or reconciliation or the promotion of religious or racial harmony or equality and diversity;
    (i)   the advancement of environmental protection or improvement;
    (j)   the relief of those in need because of youth, age, ill-health, disability, financial hardship or other disadvantage;
    (k)   the advancement of animal welfare;
    (l)   the promotion of the efficiency of the armed forces of the Crown or of the efficiency of the police, fire and rescue services or ambulance services;
    (m)   any other purposes—
        (i)   that are not within paragraphs (a) to (l) but are recognised as charitable purposes by virtue of section 5 (recreational and similar trusts, etc.) or under the old law,
        (ii)   that may reasonably be regarded as analogous to, or within the spirit of, any purposes falling within any of paragraphs (a) to (l) or sub-paragraph (i), or
        (iii)   that may reasonably be regarded as analogous to, or within the spirit of, any purposes which have been recognised, under the law relating to charities in England and Wales, as falling within sub-paragraph (ii) or this sub-paragraph.
(2)   In subsection (1)—
    (a)   in paragraph (c), 'religion' includes—
        (i)   a religion which involves belief in more than one god, and
        (ii)   a religion which does not involve belief in a god,
    (b)   in paragraph (d), 'the advancement of health' includes the prevention or relief of sickness, disease or human suffering,
    (c)   paragraph (e) includes—
        (i)   rural or urban regeneration, and
        (ii)   the promotion of civic responsibility, volunteering, the voluntary sector or the effectiveness or efficiency of charities,
    (d)   in paragraph (g), 'sport' means sports or games which promote health by involving physical or mental skill or exertion,
    (e)   paragraph (j) includes relief given by the provision of accommodation or care to the persons mentioned in that paragraph, and
    (f)   in paragraph (l), 'fire and rescue services' means services provided by fire and rescue authorities under Part 2 of the Fire and Rescue Services Act 2004.
(3)   Where any of the terms used in any of paragraphs (a) to (l) of subsection (1), or in subsection (2), has a particular meaning under the law relating to charities in England and Wales, the term is to be taken as having the same meaning where it appears in that provision.
(4)   In subsection (1)(m)(i), 'the old law' means the law relating to charities in England and Wales as in force immediately before 1 April 2008.

4. The public benefit requirement

(1) In this Act 'the public benefit requirement' means the requirement in section 2(1)(b) that a purpose falling within section 3(1) must be for the public benefit if it is to be a charitable purpose.

(2) In determining whether the public benefit requirement is satisfied in relation to any purpose falling within section 3(1), it is not to be presumed that a purpose of a particular description is for the public benefit.

(3) In this Chapter any reference to the public benefit is a reference to the public benefit as that term is understood for the purposes of the law relating to charities in England and Wales.

(4) Subsection (3) is subject to subsection (2).

5. Recreational and similar trusts, etc.

(1) It is charitable (and is to be treated as always having been charitable) to provide, or assist in the provision of, facilities for—
   (a) recreation, or
   (b) other leisure-time occupation,
   if the facilities are provided in the interests of social welfare.

(2) The requirement that the facilities are provided in the interests of social welfare cannot be satisfied if the basic conditions are not met.

(3) The basic conditions are—
   (a) that the facilities are provided with the object of improving the conditions of life for the persons for whom the facilities are primarily intended, and
   (b) that—
      (i) those persons have need of the facilities because of their youth, age, infirmity or disability, poverty, or social and economic circumstances, or
      (ii) the facilities are to be available to members of the public at large or to male, or to female, members of the public at large.

(4) Subsection (1) applies in particular to—
   (a) the provision of facilities at village halls, community centres and women's institutes, and
   (b) the provision and maintenance of grounds and buildings to be used for purposes of recreation or leisure-time occupation,
   and extends to the provision of facilities for those purposes by the organising of any activity.
   But this is subject to the requirement that the facilities are provided in the interests of social welfare.

(5) Nothing in this section is to be treated as derogating from the public benefit requirement.

6. Registered sports clubs

(1) A registered sports club established for charitable purposes is to be treated as not being so established, and accordingly cannot be a charity.

(2) In subsection (1), 'registered sports club' means a registered club within the meaning of Chapter 9 of Part 13 of the Corporation Tax Act 2010 (community amateur sports clubs).

INDEX

Access to Neighbouring Land Act 1992
ss 1–6, 8   *203–208*

Administration of Estates Act 1925
ss 1–3, 5–9, 15, 17, 21–29,
31–55, Sch 1   *100–116*

Administration of Justice Act 1970
ss 36, 38A, 39   *145–146*

Administration of Justice Act 1973
s 8   *154*

Administration of Justice Act 1982
ss 20–22   *190–191*

Charities Act 2011
ss 1–6   *329–331*

Civil Partnership Act 2004 ss 65, 66   *319*

Commonhold and Leasehold
Reform Act 2002 ss 1–36, 43–54,
Schs 1–3   *302–319*

Contracts (Rights of Third Parties)
Act 1999 s 1   *246*

Criminal Law Act 1977 s 6   *175–176*

Equality Act 2010 ss 198, 199   *328*

Family Law Act 1996 ss 30–40,
54–56, Sch 4   *224–234*

Forfeiture Act 1982 ss 1–3, 5   *189–190*

Human Rights Act 1998 s 3, Sch 1   *244*

Inheritance (Provision for Family and
Dependants) Act 1975 ss 1–20,
23–25   *158–173*

Insolvency Act 1986 ss 335A–342,
423–425   *194–199*

Intestates' Estates Act 1952 s 5,
Sch 2   *120–122*

Land Charges Act 1972 ss 1–14, 17   *147–154*

Landlord and Tenant Act 1927
ss 18, 19   *116–118*

Landlord and Tenant Act 1954
ss 23–38A, 41A, 43, 43ZA, 64, 69   *122–137*

Landlord and Tenant Act 1985 ss 1,
4, 11, 13, 14, 17   *191–194*

Landlord and Tenant Act 1988
s 1–5   *199–201*

Landlord and Tenant (Covenants)
Act 1995 ss 1–13, 15–21,
23–26, 28   *208–221*

Land Registration Act 1925 s 70   *99–100*

Land Registration Act 2002 ss 1–93,
95–106, 108, 110–112, 115–121,
123–127, 129–132, 134, 135,
Schs 1–6, 8, 10, 12   *256–301*

Law of Property Act 1922 s 145,
Sch 15   *9–10*

Law of Property Act 1925 ss 1–10,
12–15, 20–22, 24, 27, 31, 33, 34,
36–39, 41–72, 74–75, 77–111,
113–116, 121, 122, 130–132,
134–161, 173–176, 184–190, 193,
195, 196, 198–202, 205, 207,
208, Sch 1   *30–99*

Law of Property Act 1969 ss 23–25   *143–145*

Law of Property (Joint Tenants)
Act 1964 ss 1–3   *142*

Law of Property (Miscellaneous
Provisions) Act 1989 ss 1–3   *201–203*

Leasehold Property (Repairs) Act
1938 ss 1, 3, 7   *118–119*

Limitation Act 1980 ss 15–23, 26–32,
38, Sch 1   *176–185*

Matrimonial Causes Act 1973 ss
24–25, 37   *155–158*

Matrimonial Proceedings and
Property Act 1970 s 37   *146*

Mortgage Repossessions (Protection of
Tenants etc.) Act 2010 s 1   *328–329*

Perpetuities and Accumulations Act
1964 ss 1–15   *138–142*

Perpetuities and Accumulations Act
2009 ss 1–3, 5–12, 14, 15,
17–20   *324–328*

Powers of Attorney Act 1971 ss 5–7   *146–147*

Prescription Act 1832 ss 1–8A   *1–3*

Protection from Eviction Act 1977
ss 1–3, 5   *173–175*

Senior Courts Act 1981 ss 49, 50,
112–114, 116–127   *185–189*

Treasure Act 1996 ss 1–10   *221–223*

Tribunals, Courts and Enforcement
Act 2007 ss 71–79, 81–85   *320–323*

Trustee Act 1925 ss 12–20, 22, 24–28,
31–55, 57–64, 66–70   *11–30*

Trustee Act 2000 ss 1–33, 35,
36, 39   *247–256*

Trustee Delegation Act 1999 ss 1, 2, 7, 10, 11   *245–246*

Trusts of Land and Appointment of Trustees Act 1996 ss 1–23, Sch 1   *235–244*

Variation of Trusts Act 1958 s 1   *137–138*

Wills Act 1837 ss 1, 3, 7, 9, 10, 11, 13–18C, 20–31, 33, 33A   *3–9*

Wills Act 1968 s 1   *143*

Wills (Soldiers and Sailors) Act 1918 ss 1–5   *9*